THE PEYOTE CULT

This is the classic work on peyotism, originating in Weston La Barre's studies of the use of peyote in the rituals of fifteen Native American tribes in the 1930s.

It has been revised many times. This is the latest edition (the fifth, enlarged edition).

The Peyote Cult is still quite generally considered to be the one outstanding work on peyote… La Barre follows the search for the 'mystic experience' through use of chemical substances – a new fashion albeit as old as history – in an unusually objective manner.

Richard Evans Schultes, *Psychedelic Review*

WESTON LA BARRE

Weston La Barre (1911-1996) is best known for his work in anthropology and ethnography, in which he drew on the theories of psychoanalysis and psychiatry. Born in Uniontown, PA, La Barre studied at Princeton and Yale, and later taught at Rutgers, Northwestern, Wisconsin and Duke universities. La Barre conducted field work across North and South America, and later through India, China, Africa and Europe. He studied the Plains Indians and their peyote cult with Richard Evans Schultes (which resulted in the 1938 book *The Peyote Cult*).

Weston La Barre's masterwork is *The Ghost Dance: The Origin of Religion* (1970), which draws together his explorations of shamanism, world religion, Native American culture, altered states of consciousness and the use of drugs in belief systems. His other books include *The Human Animal* (1954), *They Shall Take Up Serpents* (1962), *Culture In Context* (1990), and *Muelos* (1985).

BOOKS BY WESTON LA BARRE

The Peyote Cult
The Aymara Indians of the Lake Titicaca Plateau
The Human Animal
Materia Medica of the Aymara
*They Shall Take up Serpents: Psychology of the Southern
   Snake-handling Cult*
*Shadow of Childhood: Neoteny and the Biology of
   Religion*
The Ghost Dance: The Origins of Religion
Culture in Context, Selected Writings of Weston La Barre
Muelos: A Stone Age Superstition about Sexuality

The Ghost Dance is now available from Crescent Moon

Peyote drummer (above).
Peyote altar with osage rattle (opposite).
Both late 19th century.

THE PEYOTE CULT

Weston La Barre

CRESCENT MOON

Crescent Moon Publishing
P.O. Box 1312, Maidstone, Kent, ME14 5XU, England.

First published 1938. This edition 2011. Reprint 2020.
© Weston La Barre, 1938, 1959, 1964, 1975, 1989, 2011, 2020.

British Library Cataloguing in Publication data available for this title.

ISBN-13 9781861713032 (PBK)
ISBN-13 9781861717849 (PBK)
ISBN-13 9781861717856 (HBK)

For George Devereux,
friend of three decades
at the Menninger Clinic,
Parachute School, China,
et in partibus infidelium

CONTENTS

PREFACE TO THE FIFTH EDITION

vii

The peyote religion, under the Native American Church, is now fairly well grown into another religious denomination. Surprisingly few changes in doctrine or ritual format from the standard Kiowa-Comanche meeting have occurred in the last fifty years—a situation to which the exact recording in the present volume has perhaps contributed. The repeated and unanimous defenses of peyotism by American anthropologists have also well settled in law the Constitutional rights of practitioners of this native religion. At the same time, dissident White groups have failed to achieve influence or legitimacy for such synthetic sects as the "Neo-American Church," which sought to borrow the prestige, legitimacy, and privilege of the authentic Indian tradition.

The texts of the earlier editions have been left entirely unchanged in this one. The only small modifications of the original discussions are embodied in the successive historical supplementary appendices: (1) archeology has established the unexpectedly greater antiquity of peyotism, although deer-hunting symbolism and the parched corn of the peyote breakfast, for example, were long considered to be undoubtedly very old in Mexico; (2) earlier acquisition has been shown in some tribes than the well-remembered dates of informants in the text; and (3) there is increasing evidence that northeastern Mexico and southwestern Texas have been more important in diffusion than tribes in the Southwest. None of this revises the descriptions of aboriginal doctrine or ritual.

The present edition represents the thirteenth printing by the fifth publisher, if the Spanish translation into *El culto del peyote* be counted, testifying to a continued interest among Indians and others in the history and spread of this very old Indian religion.

PREFACE TO THE SECOND EDITION

Every era must write its own ethical Baedekers. But to know only one's own tribe is to be a primitive, and to know only one's own generation is mentally to remain always a child. We all need perspective in historic time and in ethnic space in order to assess, indeed even to sense, the naïve quiddity of our own day. Imprisonment in the contemporary is the worst of all intellectual tyrannies.

Even the last three quickly successive youth generations offer some parallax of change for this social triangulation so basic to any intellectual sophistication. The early Beatniks (with some notable exceptions such as Allen Ginsberg and Lawrence Ferlinghetti) were fundamentally anti-intellectual or, perhaps more fairly, non-intellectual in their wish to experience directly the uncluttered basic values of living and feeling. Even their few writers, like Kerouac, conveyed more of a mood and way of life than a program; or, like Burroughs, a retching nausea at the hollowness of life and the self-deceiving, self-victimizing lies of fat-cat squares. The Beats were dropouts from meaningless middle-class life. The Beats' alienation from the socio-economic milieu included jettisoning most of the cultural and intellectual past as well. If the Organization Man in a grey flannel suit symbolized what they contemned, the Beats were the automatic obverse: studiously unwashed where he was groomed to the teeth, negligently hairy where he was assiduously shaven and shorn, effortlessly alive where he was hung up on ambitious striving for an empty future. The Beat ethic was alienation, uninvolved cool, simplification of life and the stubborn disconformity of Thoreau. Beats relished the cryptic and wry anti-rationality of Zen Buddhism, but they progressed intellectually barely to the pseudo-profundities of Kahlil Gibran. Beat idiom was that of urban underworld deviance and the white Negro.

The Hippies inherited the momentum of the conspicuous, intransigent and journalist-dramatized Beat generation. Hippie idiom was that of the hipsters, the in-the-know argot of demimonde jazzmen and ghetto Negroes seeking identity and self-defined belonging—to which college hipsters added the arcane jargon of reference to Frodo and the Middle Earth. After the pilgrimage to India of Allen Ginsberg and Alan Watts (and with some influence from older Vedantist mystics like Aldous Huxley), the reigning cult changed from Zen Buddhism to Hindu mysticism, and beads and bells were added to sandals and beards. Even Beatles and movie stars took on *gurus* for a while, and Hindu *ragas* joined folk music and jazz. Must reading changed from Salinger and Golding to Tolkien. Mailer was a more sophisticated and articulate writer than Kerouac, if no less exhibitionist and raucous. But the high point of social critique was the post-Céline black humor of Lenny Bruce. Some knowledgeable social historian must one day correlate the music, the dances, the movies, the poetry, novels and entertainments of these various eras.

The naïve compulsion to wear the outward badge of inner belief meant succeeding styles of clothing as well. Whereas Beats were satisfied to signalize their alienation by wearing Army-Navy store castoffs, frayed faded jeans, and cheap chino work clothes, by contrast the Hippies sought greater and greater variety in bizarre and *outré* exotic clothing that ranged from African and Amerindian to Hinduist; and some Yippies have moved on to a crisp and eclectic, extravagant but urbane tailoring of their own, featuring the unfussy and comfortable soft turtleneck, discreetly belled bottoms and sleek Nehru jacket, often graceful with young faces and body line, and no longer aggressively ugly like Beat garb. Although beads came in with Beats, and bold male jewelry with Hippies, "unisex" dress is still a bit limited by fear that the male is the "uni" and the female the sexy in this drag.

Whereas the Beats were loudly and disgustedly non-political, the Yippies became thoroughly politicized, and Yippies were a major force in the candidacy of McCarthy, and in the upsurge of anti-war feeling that ended in the abdication of the hated L.B.J. As effective *hommes engagés*, witty and committed Yippies even got their message across to perceptive adults. Any thinking (and moral) man must perforce be alienated from the outrage going on in Viet-Nam and feel frustrated that even the most articulate moral discernment seems powerless to stop from headlong disaster and shame the blind bullying forces that rule us still. In this moral sump, intellectuals and the newly intellectual young remain the only American hope. Masters of the put-on, Yippies ran a pig for president, and their sharp irony managed both to baffle and to infuriate uncomprehending adult squares. Hobbit, Frodo and Middle Earth fantasy were succeeded by the more subtle *double entendre* of the chronicles of Narnia, and by the more *engagé Steppenwolf* and *Tin Drum*. Demonstration moved back from Washington onto the college campus, from Columbia and California to the most obscure of regional seminaries. The seizure of power, or at least the flat confrontation of power structures, was the order of the day. After the assassinations of Kennedy and King, young people increasingly read Malcolm X and *Soul on Ice*. The Negro, the young and the Viet-Nam conscript perceived they had common cause against unheeding adult establishments, and they aimed beyond passive picketing to change the situation, if necessary with violence. Concerning the racial problem, parental liberals had long mouthed smug slogans of social decency—and were frightened and scandalized when young people took these injunctions with literal immediacy, seeking to smash hypocritical old social and sexual taboos and to refashion a racially more decent society. For themselves at least, many young people solved the racial "problem" simply by serious integrity in their own behavior. The wave of the future is here inevitably and irresistibly on the side of liberals and the young, and bigots might as well become accommodated to this fact. Likewise, the Pill is only part of the sexual revolution. The Graduate now views *Hair*, Marat nude in a scenario by de Sade, John Lennon on the record sleeve, and *The Boys in the Band*—besides making more than one Harrad experiment.

This minimally sketched social history is necessary as a backdrop against which to view the rise of psychedelicism and the rediscovery of ancient American Indian psychotropic plant substances. Whereas Beats had used mainly pot or grass (*Cannabis* spp.), with occasional pan-peyotl or synthetic mescaline, the Hips searched out a whole pharmacopeia of psychedelic stuffs—the psilocybin-containing *teonanacatl* mushroom (the lost Aztec narcotic rediscovered by Roger Wasson in living Mazatec use in Mexico), morning-glory seeds (the Aztec *ololiuhqui*), creeping myrtle and nutmeg, as well as barbiturates and amphetamines like speed, and such outrageous put-on jobs as inner banana-skin scurf, rotten green peppers and chlorinated lettuce. Allen Ginsberg led a movement to legalize pot, but the high priest of exploration of inner space was Timothy Leary, who extolled the very powerful, very dangerous and destructive LSD, lysergic acid diethylamide. But whereas largely ex-college Beats had included such older mentors as Henry Miller and others, Hippies now attracted successively younger Teenyboppers, and the use of pot and LSD spread downward to the high-school level, to the great alarm of their parents. The young seemed to be seeking delusion before they had properly lost their illusions.

It is not often that a doctoral dissertation is published, much less in successively enlarged editions of which the present paperback is the fifth. This was the first ethnographic monograph to be written on the Indian peyote religion, and it was consciously modeled on Leslie Spier's classic study of the Plains Indian Sun Dance. This striving to emulate the meticulous scholarship of my dissertation advisor at Yale has not been wholly wasted: the present study has been so far accepted as authoritative by Indians themselves that when new tribes acquire the peyote cult, I am told, they consult the book you hold in your hand for the proper ritual details. I am not entirely comfortable with this situation. It means that, perhaps unfortunately, the peyote rite has changed in the last thirty years almost not at all—added to which an awesome responsibility for theological accuracy rests on the shoulders of a youthful graduate student who never in his most grandiose moments had calculated being the author in a religion of the book.

But let no one suppose a doctoral candidate is ever a free man. The Boasian tradition, of which Spier was a distinguished exemplar, considered that the search for meaning was dubious enough, but scientific generalization in anthropology was close to original sin. Spier, further, was highly suspicious of all psychology and especially of the new culture-and-personality anthropology then being born at Yale in the seminars of Edward Sapir. Hence the reader is presented here only with strictly verified and verifiable facts—save for a few surreptitious footnotes and a paragraph or two in which, almost guiltily, I venture a summarizing opinion. For omitting, under such surveillance, even immediately relevant psychology, the book was taken seriously to task by a perceptive reviewer, the late Géza Róheim, from whom, in other contexts, I later learned much.[1]

In any case, for better or worse, my moral stand on Indian peyotism has not budged in a third of a century. From the first deposition against a Senate anti-peyote bill, made with Boas, Kroeber and others[2] in 1937, and the "Statement on Peyote" in *Science* made with McAllester, Slotkin, Omer Stewart and Sol Tax[3] in 1951, up to the Texas Civil Liberties Union case won last spring (1968) by Sam Houston Clinton, Jr., I have wholeheartedly, consistently and unequivocally defended the Native American Church as being, in culture-historical terms, a *bona fide* faith entitled to full Constitutional guarantee of religious freedom, whether we share its native theology or not. As to firsthand knowledge of the Church, I have repeatedly eaten peyote with Indians during two field trips in 1935 and 1936, so that I know what it is like, though, except for one time in New Haven to study physiological effects, have had none in thirty years. But I have neither joined the Native American Church as did, fatuously I think, Dr. James Slotkin, nor have I sponsored or espoused either the Phanerothyme Center in Cambridge or the Student Society for the Study of Hallucinogens at

[1] Géza Róheim, review of "The Peyote Cult," *Psychoanalytic Quarterly*, 8 (1939) 248-249. The knowledgeable reader of *The Human Animal* (Chicago and London, 8th printing, 1968) will recognize the intellectual debt I owe to Róheim, *The Origin and Function of Culture* (New York: Johnson Reprint Corporation, 1968). Once again, perhaps justifiably, the Americanist Åke Hultkrantz has criticized the present book for what he regards as its lack of elaboration of peyotist theology (*Current Anthropology*, 1 [January 1960] p. 57). Carlos Castaneda, *The Teachings of Don Juan: A Yaqui Way of Knowledge* (Berkeley: University of California Press, 1968, and New York: Ballantine Books, 1969), has to some degree remedied this.

[2] *Documents on Peyote, 1937*. Statements by F. Boas, A. L. Kroeber, A. Hrdlička, J. P. and M. R. Harrington, W. La Barre, V. Petrullo, R. E. Schultes, Elna Smith, and Chief Fred Lookout (Osage) against U.S. Senate Bill 1399 (Feb. 8) Seventy-fifth Congress, first session. Mimeographed. 137817. Washington, D.C.: Government Printing Office.

[3] "Statement on Peyote" by W. La Barre, D. P. McAllester, J. S. Slotkin, O. C. Stewart, and Sol Tax, *Science*, 114 (1951) 582-583.

Beloit. British eaters from Havelock Ellis down to Aldous Huxley, as well as the pseudo-peyotists among the Lawrencites around Mabel Dodge Luhan, have all seemed to me ethnologically spurious, meretricious and foolish poseurs.

Given the claim to authority and knowledge, despite my firm but apparently ambiguous behavior, I may perhaps be permitted, now at long last, to express my opinions on the use of peyote. I remain convinced that there is no grave danger or evil in the Indian use of natural pan-peyotl in religious ceremonies, and so long as I have a voice in the matter I propose that Indians continue to practice their faith unhindered. The alkaloids in the whole plant are not synergistic but antagonistic; in the strict sense the alkaloids are only mildly toxic and have little or no untoward effect in the amounts used; the amount of mescaline is small and barely minimal pharmacodynamically; and peyote, I am certain, is in no sense addictive. Thus I defend the Native American Church among Amerindian aborigines; but I deplore the "Neo-American Church" among Caucasoid Americans who pretend to follow their "religion" through the use of mescaline as a "sacrament." Ethnographically the latter is a wholly synthetic, disingenuous and bogus cult, whose hypocrisy (one would suppose) honest young people would discern and despise; indeed, to it could properly be applied the old missionary cliché against peyotism as the "use of drugs under religious guise." Since the rationale in both Native and "Neo-American" Church is ideological, the discussion can fairly be ideological too. To achieve this we need a step backward into Amerindian ethnological history, in order to contrast Indian with psychedelist epistemology.

Botanists expert in New World hallucinogens, most notably Schultes at Harvard, have repeatedly[4] wondered how it could be that, given the wide range of plant genera in the Old and New Worlds, and given the fact that hallucinogens occur as alkaloids, glycosides, resins, essential oils and others in seeds, sap, stem, leaves, bark and other parts of plants—and also given the fact that in land area the Old World is larger than the New, and

[4] Richard Evans Schultes, "Botanical Sources of the New World Narcotics," *Psychedelic Review*, 1 (1963) 145-166; "Hallucinogenic Plants of the New World," *Harvard Review*, 1 (1963) 18-32; "Native Narcotics of the New World," *Texas Journal of Pharmacology*, 2 (1961) 141-167; "The Search for New Natural Hallucinogens," *Lloydia*, 26 (1966) 293-308; "Ein halbes Jahrhundert Ethnobotanik amerikanischer Hallucinogene," *Planta Medica*, 13 (1965) 125-157; "The Place of Ethnobotany in the Ethnopharmacologic Search for Psychotomimetic Drugs," in D. Efron (ed.), *Ethnopharmacologic Search for Psychoactive Drugs* (Washington, D.C.: Public Health Service Publication No. 1645 [1967]) 33-57; and "Native Narcotics of the New World," *The Pharmaceutical Sciences*, 3rd Lecture Series 1960 (Pt. V, Pharmacognosy), pp. 138-185. For a biochemical summary, see also Norman A. Farnsworth, "Hallucinogenic Plants," *Science*, vol. 162, no. 3858 (6 December 1968) 1086-1092.

that inquisitive man has existed for a much longer period in the Old World than in the New—nevertheless the American Indians knew some forty local species of hallucinogens, whereas all the inhabitants of the rest of the world had scarcely half a dozen. I have described earlier the "narcotic complex" of the New World,[5] and have attempted elsewhere an ethnological answer to the statistical question,[6] which need therefore only be summarized here.

By no means have "neo-American" psychedelists learned of all the psychotropic plants that palaeo-Americans knew. Besides *Lophophora williamsii* (peyotl) and *Basidiomycete* spp. (teonanacatl), *Erythroxylon coca* (cocaine) and *Nicotiana Tabacum*, these include *Ilex* spp. both in North and South America, the *Virola* snuffs and *Piptadenia peregrina*, the red bean *Sophora secundiflora*, various mints, *Daturas*, morning-glories, *Theobroma cacao*, the "death vine" *Banisteriopsis caapi*, *Paullinia cupana* or "pasta guarana," *Haemadictyon amazonicum* (yahé), as well as many native American alcoholic drinks.[7] In all instances, the principle was the same; the mind-moving effect of the plant was proof enough to them that it contained supernatural mana or "power." The epistemological touchstone for truth for American Indians from the most ancient times was just this experience of "medicine power"—sought in some regions by all young men in the "vision quest" and everywhere at least by shamans or "medicinemen"—and some substances in use, such as *Amanita* mushrooms, go back as far as the mesolithic palaeo-Siberians. That is to say, American Indian religion is based on direct psychodynamic and pharmacological experience of the supernatural *mysterium tremendum et fascinosum*, in their various languages *manitou, wakan, orenda* and the like.

With this historic ideological background, it is evident that American Indians were *motivated to explore* a plant world that afforded such impressive *subjective* experiences, and this cultural disposition may account for the surprising array of substances they did in fact discover. By contrast, European epistemology from Heraclitus and the pre-Socratic nature philosophers onward found the authority for belief in the common *koiné* world of intersubjective experience, and upon this world of group-validated experience Europeans have built their science and technology. Thus, epistemological techniques among Amerindians and among Europeans are

[5] Weston La Barre, "The Narcotic Complex of the New World," *Diogenes*, 48 (1964) 125-138; "Le complexe narcotique de l'Amérique autochtone," *Diogène*, 48 (1964) 120-134; and "El complejo narcótico de la America autóctona," *Diógenes*, 48 (1964) 102-112; and "I Narcotici del Nuovo Mondo Autoctono," *Etnoiatria*, 2 (1969) [in press].

[6] "Old and New World Narcotics: A Statistical Question and an Ethnological Reply," *Economic Botany*, in press, 1969.

[7] Weston La Barre, "Native American Beers," *American Anthropologist*, 40 (1938) 224-234.

xiv

diametrically opposed; the two groups have quite different cognitive maps. Indians still actively seek in peyote the supernatural visionary experience; but Europeans strenuously pursue the sophisticated critique that seeks assiduously to rid experience of idiosyncratic subjective elements.

"Consciousness expanding" is a normal and necessary activity of young people in seeking and finding their identity. The question is only that of the nature and validity of the consciousness. Allen Ginsberg perhaps may be granted the poet's franchise to experiment aesthetically with psychedelics because he brings back articulate writing of his experience; and Peter Orlovsky has an impeccable patent to cry "Stop the world, I want to get off!" because he is making a moral, not a scientific statement. It may be legitimate, too, for a citizen to take a civil rights stand, as many anthropologists have, in favor of authentic religionists like the Indian peyotist, whose epistemological premises they do not share. It is the shaky claim to a secular and scientific posture of others like Aldous Huxley and Timothy Leary that makes us queasy—in addition to our profoundly differing view that, like science, effective social criticism requires as clear a head and articulate a tongue as possible, rather than a drugged mind seeking private feeling or the semantically ineffable. We do not question the right of the religionist or the artist to their chosen pursuits, but only point out that the self-defined scientist must take the most meticulous precautions against self-deception; and if messianic mystics and poseur "scientists" like Koestler and Leary ask to be judged as scientists, then so they must be. Meanwhile, the really "cool" mind will greet the claims of such LSD advocates with the same skepticism accorded any cultist convert; and on properly scientific grounds these Utopiates are sadly vulnerable.[8]

The designation "consciousness expanding" for psychedelic drugs is itself question-begging. It rests on the Bergsonian philosophic notion that the normal consciousness is selective of sensory input. This may indeed be the case. Symbols, languages, cognitive maps may all perhaps constitute such filters of experience—and indeed it is the nature of all organisms to be selective of the elements in their environment. But it is a giant step to the psychedelists' rationale: certain drugs supposedly inhibit metabolically this normal brain process—that is, they destroy the "restraint" of symbols, languages and cognitive maps enculturated into men by each tribal "establishment" and *beneficially* free us for "total experience" (incidentally, a rather paranoid concept, that). But does an insensate hostility to all categories really "free" us intellectually? Or, rather, does it not make all intellectual activity and communication impossible? Of course all categories of meaning are "artificial"—but is communication possible without agreed-

<hr>

[8] Richard Blum and Associates, *Utopiates: The Use and Users of LSD-25* (Behavioral Science Series: A Publication of the Institute for the Study of Human Problems, Stanford University, New York: Atherton Press, 1964).

upon categories? And can we be sure that "heightened" perception of ineffable truth is not lowered critical faculty as in drunkenness and dreams?

Moreover, it is not immediately evident that an abnormal toxic functioning of an adaptive organ, the brain, is necessarily a supernormal functioning epistemologically, or that destruction of our modalities for handling experience necessarily increases our fund of experience; or that, even if this were so, the destruction of the categorizing function allows us to deal either usefully or critically with that "total experience." It would seem that *sapiens* is logically doomed to have even a psychedelic *hypothesis*, and that isn't cricket. Meanwhile, the empirical fact that psychedelic drugs often release "primary process" id material that the person cannot handle, so that he becomes clinically psychotic for varying periods, or even suffers permanent impairment of the central nervous system, should give us pause, at least long enough to entertain alternative hypotheses—for this "establishment" that is threatened is the organically evolved brain itself, in which we must insist the scientist has a vested interest.

We may even, alas, be forced to a dour and puritanical Freudian hypothesis that experience itself necessarily conditions and structures our apperception of further experience; or that human experience is also always and necessarily contaminated by traditional cognitive maps, of which it is useful to become aware—like discovering grammar in our speech, without in the process giving up language. Likewise, if we can be sure that parents and all previous human beings have been so perfectly mistaken in all their categories and judgments, we ought at least have the moral wit to suspect that we too might conceivably, in some small part, be mistaken—and hence not really justified in destroying our genes and thus the rights of future beings to be human.

Institutionalized modes of self-deception—advertising and mass "entertainment" which cozen us and confirm rather than edify and help us face our predicament—are already Establishment enough for us not to need further pharmacological escape from growing up for the young. For in this they merely ape their elders' escapist follies more efficiently; and this is to waste the great potential of properly rebellious young people as useful critics of the past. The Utopiates mistake the enemy; it is the escapist within themselves. Not satisfied to be merely zombies of the idiot box, they hunger to embrace more delusion and more. Besides, too much one-way consumption of non-reality on the boob tube robs one of developing sophistications to cope reactively with real human two-way situations, and leaves one the passive puppet of others' manipulations. One might even make the shocking discovery that this is an imperfect world—and has been such for quite some time before we came along—but that a self-destructive psychedelic tantrum is a better way to change oneself for the worse than reality for the better. History is what you can't cop out from.

As for currently available "psychedelics," each year $200 million are devoted to associate youthfulness, health, beauty, acceptance, sex and success with the consumption of alcohol; a similar amount is spent to convince us that tobacco smoking brings virility, a mindless look on a cowboy face, freedom, contentment, and the blonde in the new-model car. The Nirvana-mongers make the wrong pitch, since these positive things are what most Americans want who lack them. Besides, since the successful and ongoing adventure of the Peace Corps (probably the greatest social invention of this century, as division of political power was of the eighteenth), Yippies and their successors are gradually coming to realize that the world desperately needs them, and will be irretrievably lost without their social perception and earnestness. Psychedelicist propaganda is losing hold, and nothing is at once so quaint and so damned as to be dated and old hat. One impressario says, "It is ironic that, starting with behavioral science postulates, we came closer and closer to the wisdom of the religious mystics." It is certainly something; but I am not sure that the proper word is "ironic." That word should be saved for the predicament of "scientists" who would pull the rug out from under all scientific ratiocination, their own included.

1975

PREFACE TO THE FIRST EDITION

The field work which is a partial basis of this study was begun in the summer of 1935, when the writer was a member of the Laboratory of Anthropology at Santa Fé ethnological group which worked with the Kiowa under Dr. Alexander Lesser of Columbia University. The field work was continued alone in the summer of 1936 with funds granted by Yale University and the American Museum of Natural History. Field data were gathered with varying completeness from fifteen tribes: Kiowa, Comanche, Shawnee, Kickapoo, Osage, Quapaw, Seminole, Delaware, Pawnee, Cheyenne, Caddo, Oto, Ponca, Kiowa Apache and Wichita; in the case of the Kiowa, Oto, and Wichita two peyote meetings each were attended.

The debt to my almost constant field companion, Charles Apekaum (Kiowa), game warden, ex-Navy man, graduate of Chilocco, Haskell, and Carlisle, and my chief interpreter, is such that I may say my work could not have been carried out with such comparative facility and speed without his aid. His knowledge of people and places was invaluable to me. Special appreciation is expressed to Mr. Alfred Wilson (Cheyenne) of Thomas, Oklahoma, several times state president of the Native American Church, for lending me numerous letters and other documents from the official files of the organization, and to Jim Waldo (Kiowa) and Kiowa Charley for similar documents, including the articles of incorporation and state charter. To Jim Pettit (Oto) of Red Rock, local president of the Native American Church, and Charles Tyner (Quapaw) of Miami, the added debt of personal hospitality was incurred. The following informants were of particular help in gathering data: Cecil and Henry Murdock (Kickapoo); Sly Picard, George May and Henry Hunt (Wichita); Jim Aton, Belo Kozad and Homer Buffalo (Kiowa); Howard White Wolf (Comanche); Carl Pettit, Murray Little-crow, and Mrs. George Pipestem (Oto); Albert Stamp (Seminole); Tom and Collins Panther (Shawnee); Tennyson Berry (Kiowa Apache); Robert Little-dance and Louis MacDonald (Ponca); Mack Haag (Cheyenne); Elijah Reynolds (Delaware); and Sun Chief and James Sun-eagle (Pawnee). To Jonathan Koshiway (Oto), founder of the Church of the First-born, I wish to express appreciation for his painstaking efforts at completeness of information made on my behalf.

In a study of this scope one necessarily incurs considerable debts to colleagues for aid generously given and gratefully received. The notes of James Mooney on Kiowa, Comanche, and Tarahumari peyote, deposited in the Bureau of American Ethnology, as well as manuscripts by Frances Densmore on Winnebago, and Dr. Truman Michelson on Sauk and Fox peyote, were made available through the generosity of Dr. Matthew Stirling, to whom I express particular thanks. Mrs. Elna Smith very kindly lent further Bureau of American Ethnology material which had been in her care. Mr. D. F. Murphy of the Indian Office amplified my Osage notes, and Mr. John Collier, Commissioner of Indian Affairs, has been generous with information of legal and administrative nature. To Donald Collier, student at the University of Chicago, and Ing. Luis Híjar y Haro of Mexico City, I express appreciation for bibliographic items, as well as to Dr. Ralph Beals of the University of California at Los Angeles. Richard Schultes, student at Harvard University, who was with me for an ethnobotanical study during several weeks of my second summer of work, has also been generous in giving help on bibliographic as well as botanical and pharmaceutical matters. Dr. E. A. Hoebel of New York University made available his notes on Northern Cheyenne and Comanche peyote. Dr. Ruth Benedict of Columbia University and Dr. M. E. Opler of the University of Chicago have aided with Mescalero Apache notes, and the latter has very generously lent valuable manuscript notes on Tonkawa, Carrizo and Lipan peyotism. Dr. Frank Speck of the University of Pennsylvania was fertile with suggestions during the second period of field work, and since its completion has contributed important Delaware material. Mrs. Erminie Voegelin, student at Yale University, kindly lent her voluminous notes on Shawnee peyote, as did Mrs. Anne Cooke for the Ute, and John Noon, student at the University of Pennsylvania, for the Kickapoo. Dr. A. H. Gayton kindly lent an interesting paper on datura. While the present paper was still in proof form, Dr. Leslie A. White of the University of Michigan and Dr. Fred Eggan of the University of Chicago generously lent material on Taos and Northern Cheyenne peyotism respectively.

To Dr. Edward Sapir of Yale University, to the Laboratory of Anthropology at Santa Fé, and to Dr. Clark Wissler of the American Museum of Natural History, I wish to express my thanks for making available the funds on which field work was undertaken. To Dr. Sapir and to Dr. John Dollard of the Institute of Human Relations at Yale University I owe the warm personal debt of founding a knowledge and an interest in matters of psychological import herein treated. And to Dr. Leslie Spier, my dissertation adviser, I express gratitude for his constant stimulating interest, valuable bibliographic help, and leads of considerable ethnographic significance.

ILLUSTRATIONS

PLATES

TEXT FIGURES

MAP

The Peyote Cult

INTRODUCTION

PEYOTE (Nahuatl, peyotl) or *Lophophora williamsii* Lemaire, is a small, spineless, carrot-shaped cactus growing in the Rio Grande Valley and southward. It contains nine narcotic alkaloids of the isoquiniline series, some of them strychnine-like in physiological action, the rest morphine-like. In pre-Columbian times the Aztec, Huichol, and other Mexican Indians ate the plant ceremonially either in the dried or green state. This produces profound sensory and psychic derangements lasting twenty-four hours, a property which led the natives to value and use it religiously. Peyote is not, however, the same as teo-nanacatl, as Safford believed; the latter is a narcotic mushroom which likewise had a Mexican distribution. The term "peyotl" is also used in Mexico to designate other cacti and non-cacti, some of which, like peyote, are reputed to have aphrodisiac and other properties.

Physiologically, the salient characteristic of peyote is its production of visual hallucinations or color visions, as well as kinaesthetic, olfactory and auditory derangements. Psychiatrists have used it (experimentally) with unsatisfactory results in producing temporary psychosis, and therapeutically its use has been similarly disappointing because of the uncertainty of action of the antagonistic alkaloids of pan-peyotl. First, exhilaration is produced by the strychnine-like alkaloids, followed by profound depression, nausea and wakefulness, and finally, under the influence of the morphine-like alkaloids, brilliant color visions are produced, which last for several hours. There are no ill after-effects, and peyote is not known to be habit-forming. These properties have led to a number of non-ritual uses by natives for prophesying, clairvoyance, finding lost objects and the like, as well as empirically for the cure of all manner of illnesses.

In Mexico peyote was used seasonally in an agricultural-hunting religious festival, preceded by a ritual pilgrimage for the plant. Participants danced all night around a fire to the rasp-music of the shaman, as they ate the drug in this tribal celebration. Since about 1870 the cult has spread to the United States, particularly in the Plains, where nearly all groups use it. In the Southwest transitional region peyote became deeply involved in shamanistic rivalries and witchcraft, and in the Plains with war. A pre-peyote narcotic, the "mescal bean" (*Sophora secundiflora*) had there prepared the way for its introduction. The Plains cult is like the warriors' societies of earlier times in some respects. The Kiowa, Comanche and Caddo were the chief agents of the spread of the cult throughout the entire Plains region to southern Canada and parts of the Great Basin. The standard ritual is an all-night meeting in a tipi around a crescent-shaped earthen mound and a ceremonially-built fire; here a special drum, gourd rattle and carved staff are passed around after smoking and purifying ceremonies, as each person sings four "peyote songs." Various water-bringing ceremonies occur at midnight and dawn, when there is a "baptism" or curing rite, followed by a special ritual breakfast of parched corn, fruit, and boneless meat.

The Caddo-Delaware John Wilson had peyote visions that led him to modify the altar and ceremony; this new form has spread to the Caddo, Delaware, Quapaw, Osage and others. Wilson was one of a long line of Indian prophet-messiahs, and his "moon" has been somewhat exploited economically. The Oto teacher, Jonathan Koshiway, founded a Christianized version of peyotism which spread to the Omaha, Winnebago and others. An organization of confederated tribes known as "The Native American Church" grew out of Koshiway's "Church of the First-born" (which latter spread to Negro groups also). The cult has had considerable legal difficulties.

Praying and doctoring in meetings, and occasionally public confession of sins, are the major means for the liquidation of life-anxieties of this profoundly functional cult's many present-day communicants. In the following pages we shall attempt to delineate the history of the study of the cult, the various botanical questions surrounding peyote, its physiological action and the various ethnological, psychological and historical questions involved in its diffusion.

First of modern students to describe the peyote rite was James Mooney, who visited the Kiowa, Comanche, Tarahumari, and "a number of other tribes, among them the Mexican tribes of the Sierra Madre, and as far south as the City of Mexico."[1] But at his death he had published no further study of peyote; ethnographers of the period were in general concerned with preserving complete records of older native cultures, and ignored or paid scant attention to the modern cult of peyote. Mooney himself gave little notice to the rite in his monographs on the Cheyenne and the Kiowa,[2] although at the time he was undoubtedly the authority on the subject.

Wissler, for example, barely mentions the peyote cult.[3] Indeed, in its role of modern destroyer or supplanter of older native religions, peyote was even a matter of concern[4] and annoyance to some ethnographers. Lumholtz, with wonted thoroughness, published considerable data on Huichol and Tarahumari peyote in 1898 and later, and Kroeber in 1902 wrote a chapter on Arapaho peyote which has remained a model for later investigators.[5]

It remained for Paul Radin, however, in his studies of Winnebago peyote,[6] to point out to ethnographers an engrossingly interesting, but widely ignored, religious cult which was growing and spreading before their very eyes. Since the appearance of his papers in

---

[1] Mooney, *A Kiowa Mescal Rattle*, 64–65; *Mescal Plant and Ceremony* (from which dates the medical and pharmaceutical interest in peyote); statement in *Peyote, as Used in Religious Worship*, 58.

[2] *The Cheyenne*, 418; *Calendar History*, 237–39.

[3] *The American Indian*, 376.

[4] Skinner, *Material Culture*, 42–43; *Societies of the Iowa*, 693–94, 724.

[5] Lumholtz, *Tarahumari Dances; Huichol Indians; Explorations en Mexique; Symbolism of the Huichol; Unknown Mexico;* Kroeber, *The Arapaho*, 398–410.

[6] Radin, *Sketch of the Peyote Cult; The Winnebago Tribe*, 388–426; *Crashing Thunder*.

the years following 1914, the ethnographic literature on peyote has grown considerably, due importantly to the impetus Radin gave such studies. Lowie devoted a chapter partly to peyote in his book *Primitive Religion*; Rouhier paid some attention to ethnographic questions in his pharmacological monograph on peyote; and Wagner wrote a short comparative paper based largely on the Comanche and Huichol cults. Petrullo's *Diabolic Root* was devoted entirely to Delaware peyotism.[7]

No comparative treatment of the peyote cult of the order of Mooney's on the Ghost Dance, Lowie's on Plains societies, or Spier's on the Sun Dance had ever been made when Dr. Maurice Smith of the University of Oklahoma began his studies. The unfortunate death of this investigator, however, prevented the finishing of his work, of which only a short paper[8] has seen publication. But studies of the peyote cult in individual tribes, both published and in manuscript, have multiplied to such an extent since the time of Kroeber's and Radin's studies that the time appears ripe to attempt an integrated comparative treatment of the religon.

[7] Lowie, *Primitive Religion*, 200–204; Rouhier, *Monographie du Peyotl*; Wagner, *Entwicklung und Verbreitung*; Petrullo, *The Diabolic Root*.

[8] Smith, Mrs. Maurice G., *A Negro Peyote Cult*.

BOTANICAL AND PHYSIOLOGICAL ASPECTS OF PEYOTE

BOTANY

Numerous errors involved in the study of peyote, many of them still widely current, make it advisable to identify our subject-matter clearly at the very outset of our study. The plant peyote was first described by Sahagun in 1560 as a narcotic cactus used ritually by the Chichimeca, the root peiotl.[1] Jacinto de la Serna[2] in 1626 mentioned peyote, which he distinguished from other intoxicants. The first properly botanical description was made in 1638 by Hernandez,[3] the naturalist of Philip II of Spain, under the rubric De Peyotl Zacatensi, seu radice molli et lanuginosa. Ortega,[4] again, in 1754, mentioned peyote as used in a Cora dance.

Since 1845 peyote has had numerous modern botanical classifications, being listed variously as *Echinocactus williamsii* Lem., *Anhalonium williamsii* Lem., *Mammillaria williamsii* Coulter, *Echinocactus lewinii* Hennings, *Mammillaria lewinii* Karsten, *Lophophora lewinii* Thompson, etc. The commonest designation in the older ethnological literature is *Anhalonium lewinii* or *A. williamsii*. For a considerable period it was thought that these last were two species—a point argued both on botanical and ethnographic grounds—but the present classification of peyote is as a single species, the unique member of its genus, *Lophophora williamsii*.[5]

[1] "They [the Chichimeca] have a considerable knowledge of plants and roots, their qualities and their virtues. They were the first to discover and use the root called peiotl, which enters among their comestibles in the place of wine" (Sahagún, *Histoire générale*, 10: 661–62). Again, "There is another herb, like tunas of the earth [tunas is the Spanish name for the fruit of the prickly pear, *Opuntia opuntia*]; it is called peiotl; it is white; it is produced in the north country; those who eat or drink it see visions either frightful or laughable; this intoxication lasts two or three days and then ceases" (Sahagún, *Historia general*, 3: 241; in Safford, *An Aztec Narcotic*, 294–95).

Translations from the Spanish have been made with the aid of Mr. H. W. Tessen of the Yale Graduate School.

[2] "Teonanacatl [has] . . . the same properties as *ololiuhqui* or *peyote*, since when eaten or drunk, they intoxicate those who partake of them, depriving them of their senses, and making them believe a thousand absurdities" (*Manual de Ministros*; in Safford, *An Aztec Narcotic*, 309–10).

[3] "Peyote of Zacatecas, or soft and lanuginous root. The root is of nearly medium size, sending forth no branches nor leaves above ground, but with a certain wooliness adhering to it, on which account it could not be aptly figured by me" (*De Historia Plantarum*, 3: 70; in Safford, *An Aztec Narcotic*, 295. See also Rouhier, *Monographie du Peyotl*, 43–44).

[4] "Nearby [the leader] was placed a tray filled with peyote, which is a diabolical root [raíz diabolica] that is ground up and drunk by them so that they may not become weakened by the exhausting efforts of so long a function" (Ortega, *Historia del Nayarit;* in Safford, *An Aztec Narcotic*, 295).

[5] Those interested in the taxonomic problem should consult the numerous botanical references in the bibliography. Britton and Rose, in their four volume work on the Cactaceae classify peyote as *Lophophora williamsii*, which will be followed in the present study.

The peyote plant is a curious and unique little cactus. It has no spines whatsoever, and ranges from the carrot-like to the turnip-like in shape and size, without, however, any branches or leaves. The rounded top surface, which alone appears above the soil (and which, cut off and dried, becomes the peyote "button"), is divided radially by straight, or slightly spiral, or sinuous furrows that in some specimens become so complex as to lose the appearance of ribs altogether. These ribs bear little tufts or pencils of matted grayish-white hair, not unlike artists' fine camel's-hair brushes. It is from these that the cactus takes both its modern botanical designation, *Lophophora* ("I bear crests") and its Aztec name *peyotl* (from the resemblance to cocoon-silk). In the center of the top there is a little spot of closely matted fuzz, from which the ribs derive and grow; the flower, borne on a stalk, grows from here too, the pinkish-whitish blossom growing into a rapidly maturing club-shaped pinkish-reddish fruit.[6]

ETHNOBOTANY

Several matters regarding the botany of peyote should be discussed, for their having given rise to legends about the plant. After discussing the nefarious uses to which the Chichimeca put peyote, Hernandez writes that

on this account the root scarcely issues forth, but conceals itself in the ground, as if it did not wish to harm those who discover and eat it.[7]

Dr. Parsons[8] recounts a Taos origin legend in which peyote acts even more spectacularly. A warrior on the war-path heard a singing, and when he approached,

the plant would go open and shut like this [the narrator moves his finger-tips close together and then opens them] . . . Then the plant told the Indian to come inside. But the opening was so small. Then it got bigger; it got to be a big hole in the ground, a square hole. The Indian went down the hole. There was a big hollow place down there in the ground, round like a kiva.

And the story continues, telling of how the Indian learned the peyote rite from the man in the kiva. On scrutiny this appears to be the Kiowa origin legend for peyote, modified by the addition of familiar Pueblo folk-tale motifs. The Kiowa themselves say,

you must look closely at peyote, because it is like a mole when it comes on top of the ground—if you don't look closely it is gone again.

[6] The most succinct and complete description of the plant is found in Britton and Rose, *The Cactaceae*, 83–84.

Peyote's range is comprehended within an irregularly-shaped lozenge from Deming, New Mexico, to Corpus Christi, Texas, to Puebla, Sombrerete, Zacatecas, and back to Deming. That is, the valley of the Rio Grande (north), Tamaulipecan Mountains (east), the watershed of the affluents of the right bank of the Rio Grande de Santiago and Rio de Mezquital (south), and the foothills of the Sierra Madre, the Sierra de Durango and the Sierra del Nayarit (west). It prefers the calcareous and argillaceous soils of the Cretaceous formation in the north of this region.

[7] In Safford, *Aztec Narcotic*, 295; see also *Narcotic Plants*, 401.

[8] Parsons, *Taos Pueblo*, 63.

These curious legends, however, are not without some histological[9] and ecological reality. In this semi-desert region the subterranean funnel-formed tap-root of the plant is covered with woody scales which form a rigid shell. Rouhier writes:[10]

All this chlorophyll-region [the portion above the ground] is tumid, plump and fleshy, firm and elastic to the touch, when, after the season of heavy rains, the plant is replete and vigorous. During the hot season it droops and shrivels, becomes soft, and has a dull rumpled look. It retracts then into the rigid cylinder formed by the desiccated corky desquammated part of the stem; the plant literally gives the impression of pulling its head into its neck. (M. Diguet has told us that the plant, at this time, buries itself in the soil, as though drawn, by a powerful force of traction of its adventive radicles, at the base of the funnel which its taproot has bored.)

Another matter of ethnobotanical interest concerns the supposed existence of two varieties of peyote.[11] In discussing Peyotl Zacatensis Hernandez[12] writes that "they say they are male and female." The Huichol likewise distinguish two kinds of Peyote, one, the more active and bitter in taste and presenting smaller and more numerous mammillations on the surface, called Tzinouritehua-hicouri, "Peyotl of the Gods," the other, whose physiological effect is less pronounced, called Rhaïtoumuanitarihua-hicouri, "Peyotl of the Goddesses." In the opinion of Rouhier,[13] "The Peyotl of the Goddesses . . . is the young form of *Echinocactus williamsii* [= *Lophophora williamsii*], and the Peyotl of the Gods is its adult form."

Nor is this the end of the matter. It is well known that sex is attributed to plants in the Plains, but there is also a well-defined pattern regarding the sex[14] specifically of peyote

[9] The best histological account is in Rouhier, *Monographie*, 34–42; the work of Dr. Helia Bravo, *Nota acerca de la Histologia*, is more recent. Richard Schultes at Harvard has also pursued histological studies. It is noteworthy that the Indians ordinarily take only the upper portion of the plant, which contains a larger proportion of the alkaloids according to Rouhier.

[10] Rouhier, *op. cit.*, 25. I am persuaded that many such insights would be afforded us in ethnography if we had a less cavalier attitude toward native science and history: for after all even our own science grows from criticism of traditional notions.

[11] From the middle of the last century there has raged an acrimonious debate as to whether there are two varieties of peyote corresponding to *Anhalonium williamsii* and *A. lewinii*. The former, it was contended, had seven or eight straight ribs and lacked most of the alkaloids of the latter, which had more numerous (twelve or more) sinuous ribs. This long, somewhat nationalistic debate may be regarded as ended since Rouhier (*Monographie*, 67) in 1926 figured a bicephalous plant on the same root, one head being a true *williamsii*, the other a perfect *lewinii*. It is apparent that the *lewinii* "variety" is merely an older plant, which often takes the *williamsi* aspect in its younger stages of growth; the more numerous alkaloids of the former more mature plant is likewise purely a growth-phenomenon, as are the rib-configurations and mammillations, though environmental and seasonal conditions may be involved as well.

[12] Hernandez, *De Historia Plantarum*, 204, "Se dice que hay macho y hembra." Inaccurately translated by Safford, *Aztec Narcotic*, 295, and Rouhier, *Monographie*, 43. The simplest and most obvious translation is the most satisfactory. According to the Lipan (Opler, *Use of Peyote*, 279) male peyotes bloom red, female peyotes white.

[13] Diguet, *Le Peyote*, 25; Rouhier, *Monographie*, 133.

[14] *Handbook of the American Indians*. 1: 604b. Spier informs me this is also Navaho and perhaps Pueblo as

throughout Mexico and the Plains. The Huichol have a tutelary goddess for peyote called Hatzimouika; the peyote deity of the Tarahumari, on the other hand, is male, and great reverence is paid by them to the hikuli walúla sälíami, or "hikuli great authority," literally, who is surrounded by smaller plants, his "servants," and who, not satisfied with mere sheep and goats, demands the sacrifice of oxen.

Being persons, peyote plants naturally talk and sing on occasion. Lumholtz[15] writes of the Tarahumari belief that

in the fields in which it grows, it sings beautifully, that the Tarahumare may find it. It says, "I want to go to your country, that you may sing your songs to me." . . . It also sings in the bag while it is being carried home. One man, who wanted to use his bag as a pillow, could not sleep, he said, because the plants made so much noise.

Bennett and Zingg[16] mention the Tarahumari belief that the singing one hears as the bakánawa moves about in the night near the sleeper may be made clearer by chewing a bit of the plant. Indeed, Mooney[17] says the Tarahumari find the peyote by hearing its song, Híkurówa, which it sings day and night. Peyote speaks to the Tarahumari shaman during the night of dancing and curing, and encourages him with words and by singing to him. The fetish-plant in the ceremony proper is placed on the altar under a half-gourd resonator; the rasping of the shaman, thus amplified, is very pleasing to peyote, who manifests his strength by the amount of noise produced with his aid.

In the Plains, however, when pleased with the singing, the peyote goddess actually joins in with it.[18] The Kiowa call her sę¹mąyi, literally, "Peyote Woman." Mooney describes a Kiowa peyote rattle on which she is represented, and at her feet the Morning Star, which heralds her approach. A Taos origin legend for peyote tells of a warrior aban-

---

well. As indicated elsewhere, peyote, teo-nanacatl and associated plants have repeatedly been thought to be aphrodisiacs. The supposed sex of the plants may have some reference to this belief; cf. the Huichol belief that "Maize is a little girl whom one sometimes can hear weeping in the fields; she is afraid of the wild beasts, the coyote and others that eat corn" (Lumholtz, *Unknown Mexico*, 2: 279). Different colors of corn belong to different deities also; it is interesting to note that the Huichol attribute different colors symbolically to peyote which have no effective reality (Rouhier, *op. cit.*, 133). In 1935, in a non-peyote context, Apekaum told me that cotton plants in a field we were passing were male and female; some trees were male, too, and others female, he thought. No botanical realities were involved in any of these cases. The Jivaro also attribute sex to plants (Karsten, *Civilization*, 301, 304–06, 314–15, 323) as do the Aymará and others.

[15] Lumholtz, *Unknown Mexico*, 1: 362.

[16] Bennett and Zingg, *The Tarahumara*, 295.

[17] Mooney, *Tarumari-Guayachic;* Lumholtz, *Unknown Mexico*, 1: 365; Bennett and Zingg, *The Tarahumara*, 293.

[18] This auditory hallucination of hearing voices in peyote intoxication is most striking. Several explanations may be offered: the cultural (the belief is common in Mexico and the Plains that peyote talks and sings), the physiological (white observers, many in obvious ignorance of the ethnographic facts, have reported aural hallucinations), or the physical (the peculiarly resonant vibrations of the water-drum echoing from the taut, cone-shaped canvas of the tipi). A physiological constant for Indians and whites (culturally modified) seems indicated. See Mooney, *A Kiowa Mescal Rattle*, 65; Parsons, *Taos Pueblo*, 63.

doned by his companions, who heard a singing and rattling near where he lay, and finally discovered it coming from the blossom in the center of the top of the plant.

The Shawnee[19] say that if you listen carefully you can "catch songs" from Peyote Woman. The Kickapoo likewise have the concept of the peyote "goddess" who sometimes sings in meetings when pleased; one informant further said that "the spirit of a woman who had been faithful to peyote sings after she has passed away. Sometimes we put pieces of food near the fire for spirits of a dead man or woman or child. Sometimes you hear a man's voice too." The Lipan say they hear "Changing Woman's" voice in peyote meetings. The Wichita believe it is kicuʻídie, "the woman who stays in the water," and her little son, wiʻkɪdiwɪdá, "the boy who rolls along the banks of the water," who are mentioned in prayer, and who give power in meetings. The "peyote-woman" belief is attenuated elsewhere in the Plains.[20]

NAMES FOR PEYOTE

Native terms for peyote differ somewhat in denotation and connotation. For clarity sake we shall list only those terms referring specifically to *Lophophora williamsii*. Native classifications of cacti, as well as extensions of the term "peyotl," will be discussed in an appendix, as involving special problems.

The Huichol of Jalisco call peyote hícuri, hicori, xicori or hicouri (in the notation of speakers of different European languages); sometimes they refer to it metaphorically as foutouri, "flower." The Cora of the Tepic mountains term peyote huatari, houtari or watara; the Tepehuane of Durango, kamaba. The Tarahumari of Chihuahua call it híkuli or hikori, sometimes adding, according to Lumholtz, the epithet wanamé (or houanamé), "superior," to designate the peyote par excellence; the same meaning appears to be indicated in the reduplication híkurí-íkuríwa.[21]

The Opata[22] call it pejori, the Otomi beyo. The Pima of the Gila River region use the name peyori. The Comecrudo or Carrizo of Tamaulipas call peyote kóp, and Gatschet recorded the term kúampamát for "bailar el peyote" ("many are dancing [the peyote dance]"). The Lipan name is xʷucdjiyahi, "pricker one eats." The Tonkawa of south-

---

[19] Statements without references are understood to be made from my own field work.

[20] The Cora peyote goddess appears to be "Mother Hūrimoa" (Preuss, *Die Nayarit-Expedition*, 103). Tarahumari dancers sometimes imitate hikuli's talk with a sound which reminded Lumholtz of the crow of a cock (*Tarahumari Dances*, 455). The Lipan information is from Opler (*The Use of Peyote*).

[21] Diguet, *Le peyote et son usage*, 21, 25; Rouhier, *Monographie*, 4; Safford, *An Aztec Narcotic*, 297; Lumholtz, *Unknown Mexico*, 1: 357, 2: *passim;* Preuss, *Die Nayarit-Expedition*, 103; Bennett and Zingg, *Tarahumara*, 135; Mooney, *Tarumari-Guayachic*.

[22] Rudo Ensayo (1760) in Mooney, *Tarumari-Guayachic*. A note by F. W. H[odge] indicates a purely medicinal use of peyote for the Opata. Otomi: Leon, *fide* Mooney; Mooney doubts this, somewhat unwarrantedly I think. Pima: Alegre, in Mooney, *Tarumari-Guayachic*. Comecrudo: *Handbook of the American Indians*, 1: 209a; Mooney, *Tarumari-Guayachic*, whose source is probably Gatschet. Lipan: Opler, *The Use of Peyote*. Tonkawa: Mooney, *op. cit*. Taos: Parsons, *Taos Pueblo*, 114, note 115. Mescalero Apache: Rouhier, *Monographie*, 4 (Opler records this as xuc); Safford, *An Aztec Narcotic*, 297; Mooney, *op. cit*. Comanche: Mooney, *Miscellaneous Notes;* the present writer recorded wɔ'kwe[PI] and pua'kɪt (= "medicine").

14

ern Texas call peyote nonč-gá[i]ɛn; the Taos name is walena, the generic term for "medicine." Mescalero Apache call it ho or hos; the Wichita nesac'. The Comanche wokwi or wokowi is said by Mooney to be the generic name for cacti.[23] The Arapaho call peyote hahaayā^{n}x. Most of the Oklahoma tribes have their own version of the term peyotl, such as the Kickapoo pi·yot, or, like them, they may use some older native term for "medicine" such as natá[i]noni. John Wilson (Caddo-Delaware), curiously, called peyote "sugar" or "bee-sugar"; and some Anadarko Delaware call peyote-eating "ear-eating."

Whites have used numerous confusing and erroneous non-botanical terms for *Lophophora williamsii*. Of these usages the commonest, "mescal," "mescal beans" or "mescal buttons" are the most confusing. Mescal (from the Nahuatl mexcalli, "metl [maguey] liquor") in northern Mexico, properly refers to the *Agave americana* or *Agave* spp. baked in earth ovens and widely eaten in the Southwest, and from which the Mescalero Apache take their name. By extension the term is applied to the intoxicant distilled from the native beer, pulque, also made from *Agave* spp. A more precise designation of this native brandy (as opposed to the native beer) is tesvino and its variants, from the Nahuatl tehuinti or teyuinti, "intoxicating."[24]

"Mescal bean" as used to designate *Lophophora williamsii* is quite indefensible, being wrong on two counts: the "mescal" bean proper is *Sophora secundiflora* (= *Broussonetia secundiflora*) or, incorrectly, *Erythrina flabelliformis*. The former is a red bean which was used in a pre-peyote narcotic cult of the southern Plains, to be discussed later. The adjectival use of "mescal" in the designations "mescal beans" or "mescal buttons" no doubt comes from the known intoxicating properties of the distilled liquor mescal, as extended in meaning to other unfamiliar new intoxicants, *Sophora secundiflora* (bean), and *Lophophora williamsii* (cactus); the term "dry whisky" bears this out. Lumholtz,[25] indeed, wrote that the Texas Rangers, during the Civil War, when taken prisoner and deprived of all other stimulating drinks, soaked peyote (which they called "white mule") in water and became intoxicated on the liquid. Further confusion of peyote with mescal has arisen from the north Mexican habit of mixing the two in a drink. Dealers call peyote the "turnip

[23] Mooney (*Peyote Notebook*, 21) likewise says the Kiowa term for peyote sɛ[i] means "prickly" or "prickly fruit" and is generic for all cacti. But peyote, it will be remembered, is conspicuous for its lack of spines; perhaps this was an older term for the prickly pear, *Opuntia opuntia*, transferred to the more recently known plant. In any case it occurs nowadays in many compounds: sɛ[i]mąyi, "peyote woman," sɛ[i]pi[i], "peyote meeting," etc., and in the phrase behábe sɛ[i]ɔki, "smoke, peyote power." (Compare the Comanche hos mäbä'mho'i.) See also Mooney, *Calendar History*, 239; Rouhier, *Monographie*, 4; Kroeber, *The Arapaho*, 399; Speck, *Notes on the Life of John Wilson*, 552.

[24] See *Handbook of the American Indians*, 2: 845, 846 (the Yuma, Mohave, Ute, Apache, etc., use it). The Mescalero Apache do not derive their name from the use of the peyote, "mescal," as Mooney stated, being so designated long before they knew or used peyote. In the second etymology see Siméon, *Dictionnaire*, 436; also Safford, *An Aztec Narcotic*, 293. See also La Barre, *Native American Beers*, 225.

[25] Lumholtz, *Unknown Mexico*, 1: 358. For "dry whiskey" see the *New Century Dictionary*, Supplement: "Mescal Buttons." For the other names see Rouhier, *op. cit.*, 4; Britton and Rose, *The Cactaceae*, 3: 84 (the spelling pellote of Velasco, from Mooney, is a Castillianization of the Nahuatl); *Peyotes, datos para su estudia*, 209. The spelling pezote in Alarcón, *Tratato de las Supersticiones*, 131, is obviously a copyist's error.

cactus" or "dumpling cactus" from its shape, to which also refers the local Mexican term biznagas, "carrot." A local name in Starr County, Texas, where the plant grows abundantly, is challote, but the usual dealers' name is "peyote buttons," from their flat shape when dried.

ETYMOLOGY OF PEYOTE

A precise understanding of the meaning of this term is essential, for it gives a linguistic clue of primary importance in botanical identification. Molina[26] in 1571 recorded the Nahuatl term peyutl, whose elastic and unprecise sense designates something white, shining, silky or woolly, and which applies to the moth-cocoon, a spider-web, a fine tissue, or, indeed, from its appearance (familiar enough to the Aztecs) even to the pericardium or covering of the heart. Rémi Siméon, in his Nahuatl dictionary of 1885, lists "Peyotl or Peyutl—A plant whose root served to make a drink that took the place of wine (Sahagun); silkworm cocoon; pericardium, envelope of the heart."[27]

This etymology, the oldest as well as the most authoritative, is accepted by Rouhier.[28] The present writer, having been informed of its linguistic impeccability, further finds it explanatory of otherwise curious extensions of the term "peyotl" in Hernandez,[29] as well as later Mexican usages. Various plants in Mexico besides *Lophophora williamsii*, some of them not even belonging to the Cactus Family, have been called "peyote." In each case, however, there has been some part of the plant to which the meanings of flocculence or cocoon-like woolly pubescence descriptively can legitimately apply. An appendix is devoted to the clearing up of this terminological confusion.

[26] de Molina, *Vocabulario*, 80, "Peyutl—capullo de feda, o de gufano." The Spanish o and u constitute a single phoneme in Nahuatl, according to Mr. Benjamin Whorf, so the vowel is purely a matter of recording. On the other hand, Reko's etymology in *Was bedeutet das Wort Teo-Nanacatl?* (lent through the courtesy of R. E. Schultes) is inadmissable. He writes: "Pe-yotl, Old-Aztec Pi-yautli, is quite clear in its etymology: Pi is the significative (or affix) for 'little.' . . . Yau-tli is always something narcotic or strong narcotic-smelling substance. Yau- is the root, -tli the post-positive article (substantive significative) . . . A pi-yautli (pe-yotl) is therefore the mildly intoxicating poison, in contrast with Hua-yautli (today Guayule, sap of the Gum-tree, which smells very strong) which means extremely intoxicating." This is an ad hoc forcing of an etymology on a word, according to Whorf: in the first instance "old Aztec" pi-yautli appears to be an assumed rather than a quoted form; but even so, -yautli should not give -yotl or -iotl of Sahagun's recording, but an unchanged -yautli. If the rules for Nahuatl sound-change are to be observed, peyotl must come from an uncontracted stem of two syllables, plus the absolutive suffix, this stem being pe-yo; -yautli, on the other hand, must come from a contracted stem, originally of two syllables, ya-wi (the -i standing for a variable or unknown vowel), plus the absolutive suffix, having the form -tl when preceded by a vowel, -tli when preceded by a consonant, i.e., a contracted stem. As for the first syllable, pi- and pe- are absolutely distinct phonemically in Aztec. The etymology, therefore, is neither phonetically nor phonemically correct, and assumes random and unexplained sound changes. The writer is grateful to Mr. Whorf for the preceding information. P. Augustin Hunt y Cortes (in Rouhier, 7) derives peyotl from the active verb pepeyoni, pepeyon, "to move, to stir, to set into motion, to excite, to activate." Other offerings are "child" and a derivation from peyonanic, "stimulate, goad, prick, incite." These are untenable for the same reasons that Reko's is.

[27] Siméon, *Dictionnaire* 412, 436.

[28] Rouhier, *Monographie* 7.

[29] *De Historia Plantarum*, 3: 70 (Peyotl Xochimilcensi). Peyote, because of its abundance in certain localities, figures frequently in place names.

16

We have now touched upon the etymological connotation of "peyotl," and its extended denotation in Mexican usage. But one further matter remains to be pointed out, viz., incorrect identification and misusages involving peyote. Safford[30] in 1915 adequately indicated the identity of the modern peyote of the Plains with the peiotl of Sahagun and other earlier Spanish writers. Not content, however, with proving this somewhat obvious point, he went beyond and even contrary to his evidence and attempted to prove the identity of peyote with a further narcotic mentioned in Spanish sources, a yellow thin-stemmed mushroom, called teo-nanacatl by the Aztec. This confusing and wholly erroneous identification is discussed at length in an appendix, inasmuch as it has unfortunately won wide acceptance.

A more widespread error is the application of the terms "mescal," "mescal bean" or "mescal button" to the cactus *Lophophora williamsii* or peyote. These misusages are common in the literature on peyote, and arise from confusion with a pre-peyote narcotic of the southern Plains and Texas, the red bean of *Sophora secundiflora*, a true member of the Bean Family. The word "mescal" as applied either to the cactus or the bean is erroneous and misleading, and should properly be applied only to the "Indian cabbage" (*Agave* spp.) of the Southwest, or the brandy distilled from Agave-beer or pulque.[31] The true "mescal bean" is discussed elsewhere.

PHYSIOLOGY OF PEYOTE INTOXICATION

The present section of our study proposes to deal with the physiology of peyote intoxication only insofar as it may be supposed to have influenced the form of native culture-patterns and rites surrounding its use. The efficacy of native doctoring with peyote, however, must be decided on the basis of properly controlled medical experiments, of a sort discussed in Appendix 6, and is not at issue here.

So far as the brute effect of the drugs is concerned, the first stage is one of physical and mental exhilaration. To this physiological fact no doubt is due the Mexican use of peyote in foot-races, in war and for allaying hunger and thirst when on fasting pilgrimages for the plant. Expression of this exhilaration by dancing is common in Mexico, and is found likewise among the Tonkawa, the Lipan and sporadically in the Plains.[32]

[30] Safford, *An Aztec Narcotic*; see also other items by this author in the bibliography.

[31] See the *New Century Dictionary*, "Pulque," 4841, a word conjectured to be of Carib (Haiti or Cuba) or Spanish origin. Agave and maguey are the American aloe, sometimes called "century plant" (cf. "maguey," 3578, "agave," 108). "Mescal" proper, therefore, = Agave americana = maguey = American aloe = "century plant."

[32] White Wolf (Comanche) tells of Kuaheta, at the time acting as fireman in Comanche Jack's meeting, that he once failed to return after having asked to leave the tipi. Commissioned to investigate, White Wolf found him outside "jumping like a deer" from deep peyote intoxication. Hoebel relates a similar experience in a Northern Cheyenne meeting. Tonakat, the well-known Kiowa "witch," once forced a man to get up and dance in a meeting (*Autobiography of a Kiowa Indian*, recorded by the writer, 1936). Jonathan Koshiway (Oto) laughingly told me of a meeting in Kansas where the singer's jaw became locked; the whole meeting was upset while they shook and fanned him with cedar incense until his jaw "came back." This may have been an effect of the strych-

Gross attitudinal behavior may be exhibited in extreme cases. Lumholtz[33] says of the Huichol that

in a few cases a man may consume so much that he is attacked with a fit of madness, rushing backward and forward, trying to kill people, and tearing his clothes to pieces. People then seize upon him, and tie him hand and foot, leaving him thus until he regains his senses. Such occasions are thought to be due to infringements of the law of abstinence imposed upon them before and during the feast.

This semi-psychotic state is no doubt as much conditioned culturally as the Malay "running amok"; in Mexico early Spanish writers repeatedly describe native visions as sometimes horribly frightening as well as sometimes laughable. Indeed, in Mexico, among the Mescalero, and the early Plains users, aggressions welling up under peyote intoxication commonly took the form of witchcraft fear and counter-witchcraft. Typically in the Plains, however, the attitude repeatedly emphasized is that of inter-tribal brotherhood and an individual feeling of friendliness and well-being. Nevertheless some fifty native visions collected indicate great variability in the psychic state. A Taos instance records euphoria to the point of laughter,[34] but Crashing Thunder (Winnebago)[35] experienced a state of deep depression and intense *fear*:

The next morning [he writes] I tried to sleep. I suffered a great deal. I lay down in a very comfortable position. After a while a fear arose in me. I could not remain in that place, so I went out into the prairie, but here again I was seized with this fear. Finally I returned to a lodge near the one in which the peyote meeting was being held, and there I lay down alone. I feared that I might do something foolish to myself if I remained there alone, and I hoped that someone would come and talk to me. Then someone did come and talk to me, but I did not feel any better. I went inside the lodge where the meeting was taking place. "I am going inside," I told him. I went in and sat down. It was very hot and I felt as though I was going to die. I was very thirsty, but I feared to ask for water. I thought that I was surely going to die. I began to totter over. I died and my body was moved by another life. I began to move about and make signs. It was not myself doing it and I could not see it. At last it stood up. The eagle feathers and the gourds, these it said, were holy. They also had a large book there. What was contained in the book my body saw. It was the Bible. . . . Not I, but my body standing there, had done the talking [this schizoid quality of consciousness in peyote intoxication has been frequently noted by white observers]. After a while I returned to my normal condition. Some of the people present had been frightened thinking I had gone crazy. Others, on the other hand, liked it. It was discussed a great deal; they called it the "shaking state."

The vision experiences of John Wilson (Caddo-Delaware) and Enoch Hoag (Caddo) are typical results of physiologically-induced hallucinations in individuals whose culture-background highly values vision-experiences.[36] The Enoch Hoag "moon" had its origin

---

nine-like alkaloids in peyote, as in the case of Tom Panther (Shawnee) who became unable to talk or sing once in George Fry's meeting: "it took me four or five minutes to say the word 'study'," he said.

[33] Lumholtz, *Huichol Indians*, 9.

[34] Parsons, *Taos Pueblo*, 63.

[35] Radin, *Crashing Thunder*, 198-99.

[36] Fernberger (*Further Observations*, 368), citing Petrullo, writes: "The best reporters of this group of

apparently in a (tetanic?) trance, wherein he saw himself as dead, with many people around him weeping and his arms composed on his chest as with a corpse. His companions tried to give him water with a spoon, but his jaws were stiff—a common symptom of strychnine poisoning.[37]

The stimulating effect of peyote may partly account for the holding of meetings at night, for there is no desire or ability to sleep for ten or twelve hours after eating peyote; however, all-night meetings for various purposes are not unknown in the Plains, and the older culture pattern merely exploits the physiological fact as a limiting condition probably. Some observers report that, although there is heightened reflex-activity (including those of the skin), peyote induces a partial skin anaesthesis. A Zacatecas ceremony reported by Arlegui,[38] on the occasion of the birth of the first male child, appears to utilize this virtue of the plant:

The relatives gather and invite other Indians to a horrible ceremony of which the father is the object. They give him to drink a brew concocted of a root called peyot and which not only has the property of intoxicating him who drinks it, but also renders him insensible and drugs the flesh and paralyzes the whole body. This drink is administered to the patient after twenty-four hours of fasting. Then he is seated on a staghorn in a place specially chosen for this. The Indians come with sharpened bones and teeth of different animals. Then with different ridiculous ceremonies, they approach the unfortunate victim one by one; each one makes a wound on him, without pity, making a great deal of blood flow out; and as those present are numerous, the wounds are many and the unfortunate person is so maltreated that, from head to foot, he offers a lamentable spectacle. . . . According to how the miserable victim has borne this, they augur the valor which the son of a father who has suffered so much will possess.

The stages of peyote intoxication have been noted by natives. Writing of the Kiowa and Comanche, Mooney[39] maintained that "in the peyote ceremonies, the songs of those

---

Indians [Delaware] insist that visions may occur under peyote intoxication but that it has become socially admirable to suppress these visions and that, after some practice, this may be successfully accomplished." But after establishing ordinarily friendly relations with informants I found no such reticence about visions; these, indeed, were publicly discussed in the Sunday forenoons after meetings (usually spent lounging under "shades" quietly exchanging peyote experiences). Many, like Spotted Horse (Kiowa), Tom Panther (Shawnee) and Sly Picard (Wichita) distinguished the ordinary effects of peyote from full-blown "visions"; and some corrective modesty is occasionally exhibited for the familiar Plains assertiveness and individualism, for, in fact, through peyote visions individuals push themselves to positions of leadership and influence. Fernberger continues: "The informants also state that they are able to control visions when they occur, that is, to change the vision to that of any particular known object or to hold a vision that occurs in consciousness for a considerable time. Both of these statements are totally at variance with the descriptions of all previous observers of the visual manifestations." We disagree with this dictum; many informants would paraphrase the statement of Tom Panther (Shawnee) that in peyote intoxication, "I wasn't boss of myself." White observers too have remarked on the dualism of consciousness exhibited by Crashing Thunder. One might even go so far as to say that this is a reason natives think of peyote as an *external* "power" working its influence on them.

[37] Is the peculiar mode of wearing a blanket in meetings due to the necessity of supporting the back in strychnine-opisthotonus (from lophophorine and anhalonine)?

[38] Arlegui, *Crónica*, 144; Rouhier, *Monographie*, 331.

[39] Mooney, in Rouhier, *op. cit.*, 344.

present are more vigorous after midnight," and informants frequently indicate their awareness of this.[40] Kroeber says of this period late in the intoxication that[41]

the physiological discomforts have usually worn off, and the pleasurable effects are now at their
height. It appears that new songs, inspired perhaps by the visions of the night, are often composed
during this day.

Many well known songs composed by such leaders as Quanah Parker (Comanche), Enoch
Hoag (Caddo) and John Wilson (Caddo-Delaware, called Nishkúntu or "Moonhead") are
said to have arisen from the auditory hallucinations of peyote intoxication. The popular
song "Heyowiniho" came to John Wilson in a synaesthetic auditory hallucination in which
he heard the sound of the sun's rising. Crashing Thunder[42] said of the beating of a drum
that "the sound almost raised me in the air so pleasurably loud did it sound to me." Other
kinaesthetic derangements have been reported in visions.

The dilation of the pupils of the eyes possibly explains the Huichol[43] belief that the
squirrel- and skunk-fetishes of their ceremony can see better than ordinary people, guiding
and guarding the hikuli-seekers on their way. Visual phenomena, indeed, are perhaps the
most conspicuous effects of peyote eating. The colors red and yellow, usually with reference to birds and feathers, are common in both Mexican and Plains peyote symbolism.[44]
The widespread Plains belief that peyote makes one see better may derive from pupil-
dilation; white observers have reported acuter vision in peyote intoxication from this cause.
Indians frequently manifest a marked "photophobia" even in the mild morning sunlight
after meetings, and many younger men affect colored glasses at this time.

The peyote alkaloids cause increased salivation, and there is a constant noise in meetings
of spitting as the users eat peyote; in some meetings attended individual tin-can spittoons
were provided. The increased flow of saliva probably accounts for the thirst-allaying
effect of the plant encountered in the origin legends and elsewhere, but this and the
diuretic[45] action of the drugs cause thirst to reappear more strongly later. A regular feature,

[40] "We're pulling for daylight now—that's the time those boys sang a little faster" (Voegelin, *Shawnee Field Notes*). "I wish you could see Quanah's songs—they just like beautiful race horses—go fast" (Mooney, *Peyote Notebook*, 12).

[41] Kroeber, *The Arapaho*, 404–405. Maillefert (*La Marihuana*, 6) says that marihuana habitués in Mexico have special songs that they sing together; a marked feature of the Mexican use of drugs, of which this may be a case, is the pattern of group-narcosis.

[42] Radin, *Crashing Thunder*, 178.

[43] Lumholtz, *Unknown Mexico*, 2: 272.

[44] This is obviously heavily culture-conditioned, but Klüver (*Mescal*, 41) records the predominance of red and green early in peyote intoxication, and yellow and blue in later stages, with possible reference to the Ladd-Franklin phylogenetic theory of color vision.

[45] Maillefert (*loc. cit.*) says marihuana habitués believe water decreases the effect of the drug, and therefore they do not use it when smoking. Although the peyote leader must otherwise be present all through the meeting (to prevent rival witching among the Apache), a fixed part of the Plains ritual is his exit alone at midnight to whistle at the four points of the compass, an opportunity which is no doubt exploited. Again, spitholes are a part of Tarahumari altars (Lumholtz, *Unknown Mexico*, 1: 365).

therefore, of the typical Plains ritual is the bringing in of water at midnight and in the morning, which is passed around clockwise.[46] The widespread taboo on the use of salt in connection with peyote may have some reference to this action of the plant.[47] On the other hand, the use of sweet[48] foods is a necessary part of the ritual; these are stereotyped both in the Plains and Mexico to include parched corn in sugar-water, sweet fruit, and sweetened meat either dried and powdered or cut into chunks, and candy is a regular feature in some meetings. Sugar may in effect relieve the stage of depression in peyote intoxication somewhat.[49]

The classification of plants into male and female on the basis of their physiological action has, as we have seen, a botanical basis. We are convinced on the other hand, however, that peyote has no effect whatsoever in the curbing of an appetite for liquor. Both native and white apologists[50] for peyote advance this argument in extenuation and defence. Natives are perfectly sincere in their belief that the antagonism of peyote and alcohol is physiological (even in the face of conspicuous contrary evidence),[51] and Plains Indians are annoyed and hurt at the widespread association of drinking and peyote-eating through the confusion of the term "mescal." Yet the stubborn ethnographic fact remains that in Mexico peyote is commonly drunk *with* tesvino or mescal.

Various other physiological effects noted by whites find native parallels. Many of the visions recorded for natives deal with synaesthesias of sight and hearing and smell, and

[46] The Caddo, however, make a point of not drinking water at night, as though looking upon the meeting as a vision-ordeal; this aberrance is given point by the fact that they do no doctoring in peyote meetings either, and must make four rounds of the drum before quitting, no matter if it takes until noon of the next day.

[47] The Comanche exclude the eating of pork also, but whether this is because pork is commonly a salt meat or because it is oily like the flesh of another tabooed food animal, the bear, I do not know.

[48] Maillefert (*op. cit.*, 6–7) says marihuana smokers believe that sugar augments the effect of the "grifos" ("reefers" in Harlem parlance), so they eat sweets while smoking them. Compare the consuming of honey with teo-nanacatl in Mexico.

[49] The Arapaho (Kroeber, 407) use a more magical means to this end: they tie four bunches of yellow-hammer or other feathers at the northeast, southeast, southwest and northwest poles of the tipi to brush the bodies of worshippers who become tired.

[50] E.g., Skinner, *Societies of the Iowa*, 694.

[51] For mescal (the agave-drink distilled from pulque) and peyote are mixed and *used together* in northern Mexico. Yet Mooney often and at length produced this argument with regard to alcohol; Skinner said it destroyed the desire of tobacco as well (see appendix on the Native American Church). But peyote, physiologically and culturally, is only one more means of achieving the culturally valued state of psychic derangement, and such fundamentally deep-rooted patterns as this one is in native America do not change over-night. Even so, is the cure any better than the disease? The writer was a little startled when a Kiowa friend, an ardent peyote user, suggested that we go to a neighboring town one mid-week to drink. When I sought to discover his attitude on this he soon made it clear that it was no matter of moral sentimentality but purely one of physiology: there wasn't another peyote meeting until Saturday, so what was the harm? One can eat lobsters one day and ice-cream the next, but one ought not eat them the same day. This informant conceived of the antagonism as a fight between liquor- and peyote-power, a matter-of-fact attitude probably not universal, and by no means as cynical as it seems.

there occur cases of taste- and smell-hallucinations as well as the more common auditory and visual ones. Kinaesthetic derangements are also not unknown.[52]

One final question is less of physiological than psychological and ethnographic import. Along with teo-nanacatl, marihuana (*Cannabis* spp.) and the Peyotl Xochimilcensis (*Cacalia cordifolia*), peyote has been said to have an aphrodisiac action. This association suggests that a matter of Spanish-White or Mexican-Indian ethnography is involved.[53] But love-magic was not unknown either in Mexico or the Plains, and it is conceivable that this new medicine (particularly since it was used for "witching") because of its other spectacular effects, might have been valued for this purpose also.

We have now discussed the bearing of physiological reactions on the peyote ritual and other native behavior: the *exhilarating* first effect of the drug (in the allaying of hunger and thirst on the march, to give courage in war, and strength in dancing and racing) and the second stage of *depression* and *visions* ("running amok," witchcraft-suspicion, psychic fear-states, euphoria and feeling of brotherhood, partial anaesthesia, the "suffering to learn something" characteristic of the Plains vision quest, synaesthesias, auditory hallucinations, and "catching songs," visual hallucinations, and "learning" of painting- and bead-designs, symbolical birds and feathers, etc.).

We found, too, behavior definitely related to the pupil-dilating power of peyote as well as its sialogogue and diuretic action; the injunction against salt and the use of sweet foods, however, may involve culture-historical matters. We have been skeptical of the alleged anti-alcoholic virtue of peyote, and have likewise doubted that *physiologically* peyote is either aphrodisiac or anaphrodisiac, despite heated claims on both sides. The efficacy of native doctoring with peyote is a special problem treated elsewhere along with the therapeutic and psychiatric experiments of Whites.

The following ethnographic part of our study deals first with the non-ritual uses of peyote, arising from its special properties, and secondly with the ritualization of its use.

[52] Rouhier (*Monographie*, 320) however suggests that the illusions of phonation (the distance, strangeness and hollowness of the voice) may not be entirely sensory, i.e. auditory, but may also be a matter of voice-production; he cites Ellis, Putt, and Eshner.

[53] Note the ritual necessity that a woman bring the morning water into a meeting formerly restricted to men, and the mythological significance of the "Peyote Woman." Opler (*The Influence of Aboriginal Pattern*) says that Mescalero saw women in visions and wanted them, believing that if one began with visions of women they would stay with him. Crashing Thunder (Radin, 177) confessed that at one time he attended meetings chiefly to find "a woman whom I cared to marry permanently. Before long," he says, "that was the only thing that I would think of when I attended the meetings." We have on the other hand, however, the healthy skepticism of an Oto who said, "You can see dead people in meetings, but peyote won't get you a woman you desire though. *She* makes up her mind." But may not other explanations than the physiologically-aphrodisiac be involved? Might there not be an association with promiscuity of the ritual mingling of the sexes (for in the older Sun Dance just this was implied when the main lodge-pole was brought in) in a region where sexual segregation ritually was usual? Compare the injunction of one Ghost Dance prophet to the people not to think of women, but to join hands with them on either side and dance the Ghost Dance. Would he have made the explicit statement if it had not been implicitly considered reasonable to expect natural sexual arousement or preoccupation in a rite in which men and women are not separated? Indeed, there is evidence among the Shawnee at least that sexual opportunities afforded through the Ghost Dance were not left unexploited.

THE ETHNOLOGY OF PEYOTISM

NON-RITUAL USES OF PEYOTE

An Oto in all seriousness informed the writer that "peyote doesn't work outside meetings, because I have tried it"—a belief understandable in a group whose sole acquaintance with the plant is through a recent ritual.[1] Nevertheless, owing to its marked physiological properties peyote is widely used both in Mexico and the Plains non-ritually, a fact which forms an interesting ethnological background to the rite proper.

One of the most important and striking of these uses is in prophecy and divination. We find the Spanish missionaries in Mexico early protesting against this abomination. The confessional of Padre Nicolás de León[2] contains the following questions for the priest to ask the penitent:

Art thou a sooth-sayer? Dost thou foretell events by reading omens, interpreting dreams, or by tracing circles and figures on water? Dost thou garnish with flower garlands the places where idols are kept? Dost thou suck the blood of others? Dost thou wander about at night, calling upon demons to help thee? Hast thou drunk peyotl, or given it to others to drink, in order to discover secrets, or to discover where stolen or lost articles were?

This last was no idle matter, as appears from other evidence; Hernandez[3] says that

[the Peyotl Zacatensis] causes those [Chichimeca] devouring it to be able to foresee and to predict things; such, for instance, as whether on the following day the enemy will make an attack upon them; or whether the weather will continue favorable; or to discern who has stolen from them some utensil or anything else; and other things of like nature which the Chichimeca really believe they have found out.

Padre Arlegui,[4] after mentioning the therapeutic uses to which the Zacatecans put peyote, complains that

this would not be so bad if they did not abuse its virtues, for, in order to have a knowledge of the future and find out how their battles will turn out, they drink it brewed in water, and, as it is very strong, it intoxicates them with a paroxysm of madness, and all the fantastic hallucinations that come over them with this horrible drink they seize upon as omens of the future, imagining that the root has revealed to them their future.

---

[1] Rouhier (*Monographie*, 91, n. 1) argues immense antiquity for peyotism, *circa* 300 years B.C., among the Chichimeca on quasi-historical grounds. Our knowledge of peyote from Spanish documents goes back to the sixteenth century in Mexico. A manuscript in the Library of Congress reports the trial of a Taos Indian, February 3–8, 1719, for having "taken peyote and disturbed the town" (cf. Twitchell, *Spanish Archives*, 2: 188). See Bandelier, *Manuscript;* Mooney, *Tarumari-Guayachic.*

[2] Adapted from Lewin, *Phantastica*, 96, and Nicolas de León in Brinton, *Nagualism*, 6.

[3] Hernandez, *De Historia Plantarum*, 3: 70.

[4] Arlegui, *Crónica*, 2: 154–55 in Urbina, *El Peyote y el Ololiuhqui*, 26.

Prieto[5] says of a Tamaulipecan group that

often in these orgies was wont to impose silence, at the height of their drunkeness, the voice of some ancient, who, assuming a magisterial tone, prognosticated to them future events, usually depicting them as sad and unhappy, and in spite of the lugubriousness of his predictions, he usually ended his harangue by exhorting them to enjoy in the dance the interval between the present and the next unhappiness.

Alarcón[6] adds other functions and relates of other drinks similarly used:[7]

If the consultation is about a lost or stolen article or concerning a woman who has absented herself from her husband, or some similar thing, here enters the gift of false prophecy, and the divining that has been pointed out in the preceding treatises; the divination is made in one of two ways, either by means of a trance or by drinking peyote or ololiuhqui or tobacco to attain this end, or commanding that another drink it, and ordering him to remain under its spell; and in all this goes implicitly hand in hand the pact with the devil who by means of said drinks appears to them and speaks to them, giving them to understand that he who speaks to them is the ololiuhqui or the peyote or whatever beverage that they had drunk for the said end; and the sorry part of it is that many put faith in [the drink] as in the very lying cheats themselves, [indeed] even more than in the evangelical predicators.

As we move farther north in Mexico the use of peyote in prophesying becomes valuable in warning of the approach of the enemy.[8] For the Tarahumari Lumholtz[9] says that the

[5] Prieto, *Historia y Estadistica*, 123-24, in Mooney, *Peyote Notebook*.

[6] Alarcón, *Tratado de los supersticiones*, 195.

[7] Lindquist, *The Red Man*, 70-71, is in error in stating that the Zuñi use peyote for religious purposes; moreover the document of 1720 cited refers to Taos, not Zuñi. Mr. An-che Li assures me that the Zuñi lack peyote even today. Lindquist has evidently confused peyote with datura; see for example Safford, *Narcotic Plants*, 405, 406. Still other plants, e.g., datura, cohoba snuff, coca, yahé, aya-huasca, etc., were used in Middle America as prophetic aids; see for example Safford, *op. cit.*, 393; Gayton, *Narcotic Plant Datura*.

[8] Bennett and Zingg (*The Tarahumara*, 135) write that "in a culture where animals are thought to talk and cattle are supposed to warn their masters of impending drought or plague, it is not surprising that plants also are imbued with personality and harmful or helpful attributes. The small ball of cacti is especially revered by the Tarahumara." Some *Mammillaria* spp. have a striking resemblance to a head of hair; one figured in Higgins with flowing white "hair" is called "Old Man Cactus"; again, natives have an intense fear of even touching these plants—an attitude recalling the Pima belief that even one drop of Apache blood falling on a person would make him ill (Hrdlička, *Physiological and Medical Observations*, 243). In this connection it is interesting to note that Spier has collected evidence bearing on the magical use of enemies' scalps. The magical malevolence of the enemy or his scalp is cited (*Warfare*) for the Maricopa, Yuman and Piman groups, Navaho, Jicarilla, and Pueblo. The Yumans and Pimans required stringent purification from contact with the enemy or his scalp; the Pimans, again, along with the Navaho and Pueblos turned this power to account in curing and rain-bringing. Spier states that for the Pima-Papago the scalp is turned into an ally against the enemy, and made a specific prophylactic against such enemy-engendered dangers as paralysis, swooning at the sight of blood or a violent death; the Maricopa, indeed, convert a scalp into one of themselves, much as a captive is ceremonially converted and purified. Further still, according to Spier, the Maricopa and Yumans received prophetic foreknowledge of the enemy from these scalps, which therefore they carried with them to war. Still more strikingly, scalps are thought to laugh and cry and babble incessantly, much as the noisily talkative peyote plant is supposed to do.

[9] Lumholtz, *Tarahumari Dances*, 452; also *Unknown Mexico*, 1: 372-74.

various kinds of hikori were particularly good "to drive off wizards, robbers, and Apaches, and to ward off disease." Of *Anhalonium fissuratum* he says "robbers are powerless against it, for Sunami calls soldiers to its aid," while the variety Rosapara "is particularly effective in frightening off Apaches and robbers."

In the Comanche version of the usual Plains origin tale of peyote, the leader of a group on the warpath goes up alone to an Apache camp where a peyote ceremony is in progress. Though an enemy, he is invited in, the leader telling him that peyote had predicted his coming in a vision.[10] One Comanche informant said eating peyote enables one to *hear* an enemy coming, though still far away; peyote likewise predicted the success of one of the last Comanche horse-raids, and aided in its prosecution.

From these uses of peyote in war it is no jump to its fetishistic use as a protector in war[11] and in ordinary witchcraft. Sahagun[12] writes that peyote

[10] Spier (*Warfare*) writes that "Clairvoyance on the part of the shaman who accompanied a war party is noted for Maricopa, Yuma, Pima, and Papago [as well as] in the Plains and Plateau." Zuñi war chiefs, he adds, sought sound-omens on the eve of setting out on the warpath. In this last connection the detailed similarities in attitude and conduct of war-expeditions, peyote-pilgrimages, and salt-gathering expeditions in Mexico and the Southwest should not be overlooked. (The Huichol shooting of the peyote plant, however, is a hunting rather than a war symbolism, that of hunting the hikuli-deer of the peyote origin legend.) Information on the Comanche horse-raid is from E. A. Hoebel; unfortunately the Government took most of these peyote-given horses back again.

In the 1850's the only Kiowa who ate peyote was Big Horse. When he wished to know the whereabouts of an absent war party he would take a drum and a rattle into a tipi, saying "g^{y}ägüɲbonta" (I am going to look for medicine), eating peyote and afterward telling what he had seen; sometimes he made the sound of an eagle, the bird that flies high above the earth and sees afar.

C. W., president of the Kickapoo Native American Church, often has prophetic peyote visions; Kishkaton says they are of "Judgment Day" when the "new world" will come, and makes them a proselytizing argument for peyote. The debt to earlier Kickapoo prophets is obvious. A specific Caddo prophecy among the visions collected would have prevented a serious industrial accident if it had been properly interpreted.

[11] In the Plains the "father peyote" is often carried as a fetish. Kroeber (*Arapaho*, 406) cites a typical case: "The pouches used to contain the peyote plant have room for only one of the disks, which is usually carried more or less as a personal amulet, in addition to being the center of worship during ceremonies. A circular area of bead-work covering the front of the pouch itself, is said to represent the appearance of a peyote-plant while being worshipped. In the center a cross of red beads represents the morning star. Around the edge of this circular bead-work are eight small triangular figures, which denote the vomitings deposited by the ring of worshippers around the inside of the tent in the course of the night. The yellow fringe around the pouch represents the sun's rays."

War Eagle, Delaware (Speck, *Delaware Peyote Symbolism*) told of a man gassed in the World War whom peyote cured after his case had been pronounced hopeless. Quanah Parker, the famous Comanche chief, used to carry a peyote on his chest as protection in battle. A Ponca story tells of J. W. and his wife returning home as a cyclone was coming up; when they finally arrived the house was destroyed, but in an undisturbed drawer they found four articles still intact: a "peyote chief," a bag of peyotes, a Bible, and a peyote drum-stick.

[12] Sahagún, *Historia general*, 3: 241; *Histoire générale*, 737. Lumholtz (*Unknown Mexico*, 2: 354) adds marihuana to the list of plants which protect against witchcraft injury: the doctor comes on a Tuesday, Thursday or Friday, reverses the ill person's sandals, shirt and drawers, recites the credo backwards to summon the owl, and burns a heap of marihuana and old rags in the house. Many persons also carry marihuana in their girdles as a protection against sorcery. The Cocopa and Yuma uses of an unidentified plant (awimimedje) to offset fatigue and give luck suggests peyote (Gifford, *Cocopa*, 268).

is a common food of the Chichimecas, for it stimulates them and gives them sufficient spirit to
fight and have neither fear, thirst, nor hunger, and they say it guards them from all danger.

De la Serna[13] said that ololiuhqui and peyote were carried by persons "forsaken of God"
as charms against all injuries, and Arlegui deplored the custom of parents to "hang little
bags on their children, and inside of them in place of the four Evangels that they place
around the necks of children in Spain, [to] place peyot or some other herb." Arias described
a surreptitious worship of the fetish: the natives hung the herb in the choirs "as a special
creation of the malignant spirit which they designate with the name of Naycuric," and
they communicated with the numen by drinking an infusion of peyote instead of wine.[14]

Peyote is also a powerful protection against witchcraft in ritual foot-races. Rivals are
liable to throw bones and herbs on the track and cause the Tarahumari runner to be be-
witched and lose the race, which is run at night. For this contingency, however, "hikuli
and the dried head of an eagle or a crow may be worn under the girdle as a protection."[15]
Peyote is a great protection too when traveling, both in war and on peyote-pilgrimages.[16]

The Comanche commonly wore peyotes in buckskin bags attached to beaded bandoliers,
recalling the mescal bean bandolier which the Kiowa and others commonly wore in battle.
Indeed, peyote was even a part of the Θawikila and Kispoko war bundles of the Shawnee,
long before they knew the generalized peyote ritual—a custom similar to the Iowa use of
mescal beans in their war bundles.[17]

[13] De la Serna, in Safford, *An Aztec Narcotic*, 390; Arlegui in Urbina, *El Peyote y el Ololiuhqui*, 26; Arias,
in Urbina, *loc. cit.*

[14] See the modern Tepecano votive bowl altar used with peyote or marihuana (Lumholtz, *Unknown
Mexico*, 2: 124–25).

[15] Lumholtz, *op. cit.*, 1: 284–85. The Wichita use the "mescal bean" in racing, and the Kiowa as a prophylactic against stepping on menstrual blood. Peyote is associated with racing in Mexico by the Huichol, Tamauli-
pecans, and Tarahumari (Lumholtz, *Unknown Mexico*, 2: 49–50; Prieto, *Historia y Estadistica*, 123–24; Lumholtz,
op. cit., 1: 372; Bennett and Zingg, *Tarahumara*, 136–37, 295, 338).

[16] A Wichita leader envisioned a flag three months before being drafted into the army; the fetish-peyote
he carried over-seas miraculously escaped confiscation during an inspection and disinfection of clothing, and
because of it he was only slightly wounded in battle. One meeting I attended was in performance of a vow if
the Bonus legislation then pending would pass. This same leader prophetically dreamt of how peyote would
protect him on a pilgrimage to Mexico and aid him through the customs with a supply of plants, and all happened
as predicted.

The Tarahumari dare not touch the dekúba (datura) plant lest they go crazy or die; this presents a problem
since the plants are common in their winter caves. The peyote shaman, however, armed with the more powerful
plant uproots the datura with impunity. Peyote is the only cure for the otherwise fatal disease which comes from
touching dekúba (Bennett and Zingg, *op. cit.*, 138, 294).

[17] Hoebel, *Comanche Field Notes;* Voegelin, *Shawnee Field Notes*. The Iowa Red Bean medicine bundle
was used for war, horse stealing, hunting and horse racing (Skinner, *Ethnology of the Ioway Indians*, 245–47,
Societies of the Iowa, 718–19). A similar mescal war bundle and cult was present among the neighboring and
related Oto. The Red Medicine bundles of the Pawnee contained mescal beans likewise; indeed the Pawnee are
thought to be the origin of the Iowa bundle and associated war-dance. The Pawnee "kill" the beans by breaking
and stirring them in a large kettle, drinking the concoction toward morning until they vomit, to "clean out"
the body. There is an unmistakable similarity to the "black drink" ritual vomiting here (see Appendix 4).

But in Mexico and the Southwest war and witching are closely connected ideologically. As a matter of fact, peyote itself as well as the peyote shaman's rasp, is employed in Tarahumari witchcraft.[18] Among the Mescalero Apache,[19] however, witching *within* the tribe by rival peyote shamans was an ever-present anxiety, their feuds being conceived in terms of battles and war, with the "shooting" of arrows and struggles to see who had the more powerful and compelling songs. The Mescalero peyote leader was merely a shaman *primus inter pares*, whose major function was to prevent witching in meetings. The purpose of the Tonkawa peyote songs, it is said, was to ward off the enemies' witching. Witching with peyote is less in evidence in the Plains, save among the Kiowa, Comanche, and Cheyenne who early received it, but as late as the time when the Caddo-Delaware messiah John Wilson took peyote and the Ghost Dance to the Quapaw there was witching by "shooting" objects. The Northern Cheyenne feared the "trickiness" of peyote itself; and the Lipan fireman was chosen for his braveness because "he has to go out at night to get wood and it is a frightening job sometimes, especially when one is under the influence of peyote; peyote is sure a joker!"

Besides this fetishistic use in war, peyote was also used somewhat more "technologically" to cure wounds. Alegre writes that the Sonoran

manner of curing the wounds is with peyote, that they call peyori after it has been made into a

[18] Mulato, sunami, and rosapara cacti, however, protect against Apache machinations; Mooney (*Tarumari-Guayachic*) cites a Chalája arroyo near Conaguchi (from chärä or chälä, "squirrel," the epithet of witches) where witches were formerly burned; cf. the use of the squirrel-fetish in the Tarahumari peyote ritual. In Tamaulipas intertribal peace was so precarious that peyote mitotes were commonly held in remote and inaccessible intermediate mountain regions; the recital of war deeds was sometimes part of the rite (Prieto, in Mooney, *Tarumari-Guayachic*). De la Serna (in Safford, *An Aztec Narcotic*, 310) describes the use of teo-nanacatl in witching. For Tarahumari witching with hikuli see Lumholtz, *Unknown Mexico*, 1: 314, 323–24, 371–72.

[19] A favorite diversion of witches to weaken the leader was to make his assistants vomit (Opler, *The Influence of Aboriginal Pattern*). My Kiowa companion vomited in a Ponca meeting, the first he had ever attended in that tribe. He attributed it to their unfriendly feeling and felt considerably relieved when we visited next morning a meeting held by old friends among the Oto; but he himself had once witched a Comanche in a meeting (*Autobiography of a Kiowa Indian*). Tonkawa data is from Opler, *Autobiography of a Chiricahua Apache*. The exploits of the Kiowa witch Tonakat have already been mentioned. The Comanche "used it in the old times, but not rightly; the medicine men used it for sorcery, so people got scared and stopped using it" (Hoebel, *Comanche Field Notes*). Among the Cheyenne, Flacco and Cloud Chief strongly opposed the introduction of peyote; the former said "it was used to witch people and make them crazy." The Northern Cheyenne (Hoebel, *Field Notes*) and Lipan (Opler, *The Use of Peyote*) and Winnebago "fear states" may have a physiological basis.

Mrs. Voegelin (*Shawnee Field Notes*) quotes an informant: "Wilson showed them how to swallow mescal beads . . . N. S. didn't go; she was afraid of them. The Delaware had it too; she never wanted to go look. John Wilson also taught them how to shoot a person with red beads two inches long; the person would fall down, hard; then John Wilson doctored on them with medicine. [Several Shawnee] crept up in the grass when the Quapaws were holding a Ghost Dance once, at night. S's wife got shot. . . . Finally some one spoke to John Wilson, "You men, you abuse the women." An old Peoria woman who went all the time, and swallowed those red beads—she was kind of crazy—told Wilson that. The agent finally stopped it . . . When they were shot, John Wilson used peyote to bring them back."

powder, with which they fill the cut, cleaning it and renewing it three times every two days, or with a species of balm composed of [maguey].

Prieto says that, in Tamaulipecan war, among the provisions carried by the women in the rear were

gourds full of peyote and water . . . and in addition to all these provisions they carry some plants, which, chosen and prepared beforehand serve to stop hemorrhages from the wounds, and to aid in their curing.

The Opata used pejori for arrow-wounds, cleaning them out with cotton squills on sticks dipped in the powder; the Lipan put peyote on wounds of all kinds.[20]

The other therapeutic uses of peyote are various. At Taos it was used for snake-bite. The Caxcanes of Teocaltiche employed peyote for cramps and fainting spells, the Chichimeca for relieving painful joints. The Tarahumari apply peyote externally for bruises, snake-bites and rheumatism. The Huichol use few remedies except hikuli, unlike the Tepecano who use many, but it is good for anything from a minor ache to a major wound. Medicinal uses are also recorded for the Tepecano, Yaqui, Opata, Pima, Papago, Cora and Lipan.[21]

In the Plains a Wichita case of blindness of fifteen years' standing was cured by the sole application of peyote-infusion.[22] Radin cites a similar Winnebago case. The Kiowa use peyote as a panacea: uses are recorded for tooth-ache, hemorrhages, head-ache, consumption, fever, breast pains, skin disease, hiccough, rheumatism, childbirth, diabetes, colds and pulmonary diseases in general. Mooney records the further use as a "tonic aperitif." The Shawnee chew peyote into poultices for sores and snake-bites and eat it for colds, pneumonia, rheumatism, aches and pains.[23]

The remaining non-ritual uses of peyote are quite varied. The Acaxee employed it in some manner in their ball games, probably eating it in small doses, according to Beals. In Tlaxcala peyote was used by "the auxiliary forces of the conquistadores, in order not to feel fatigue on their marches"—a widespread use in Mexico; in the Plains the typical

---

[20] Alegre, *Historia de la Compañía*, 2: 219-20; Prieto, *Historia y Estadistica*, 131. It is not proven that peyote applied externally has an anaesthetic or anodyne action (the Zacatecan use in the child-birth ceremony is internal); but natives recognize the ability of peyote to induce a stuporous state. The Aztec (Gerste, *Notes sur le médicine*, 51) used peyote to stupify sacrificial victims. But peyote does not cause sleepiness, and the following Maratine Indian battle song (in Prieto, *op. cit.*, 119-20; Mooney, *Peyote Notebook*) should perhaps be translated "become stuporous:" "The women and ourselves shouting with pleasure, Shall drink peyote and shall fall asleep." For Opata data see Ensayo, in Mooney, *Tarumari-Guayachic;* for Lipan see Opler, *The Use of Peyote.*

[21] Parsons, *Taos Pueblo*, 59; Flores, in Urbina, *El Peyote y el Ololiuhqui*, 26; Rouhier (*Monographie*, 96) adds the Caxcane use "for swellings and spasms"; Hernandez, *De Historia Plantarum*, 3: 70; Safford, *An Aztec Narcotic*, 295; Bennett and Zingg, *The Tarahumara*, 294; Hrdlička, *Physiological* and *Medical Observations*, 173, 242, 244, 250, 251; Lumholtz, *The Huichol*, 9; *Unknown Mexico*, 2: 241-42.

[22] Would pupil-dilation from peyote cause temporary "cures" satisfying the uncritical?

[23] Radin, *Crashing Thunder*, 183, 196; Mooney, *The Mescal Plant*, 9. Lumholtz (*Unknown Mexico*, 2: 157) himself confidently prescribed peyote for a scorpion-sting.

origin legend tells of peyote aiding a seriously wounded warrior or a woman and child left behind by their companions without food or drink. The legend is not unlike the common Plains stories of receiving power from animals in a stress-situation; Old Man Horse (Kiowa) said "peyote is the only plant from which one can get power," obviously thinking in terms of the old vision quest. Peyote in fact gave power to perform shamanistic tricks in the old days.[24]

The Tarahumari, among other things, left a hikuli plant with the corpse, the motive for which is unstated.[25] A Wichita, captured in war and imprisoned, was aided in escaping unseen from the enemy camp by his fetish-plant; the lobbying power of peyote in influencing Federal bonus legislation has already been mentioned. Indeed, peyote has had a record of unbroken success in preventing Federal anti-peyote legislation.[26]

RITUAL USES OF PEYOTE

Despite the unsatisfactory state of the literature, it is clear that the ceremonial use of peyote in Mexico differs widely from that in the Plains. First we shall characterize the Mexican type by summarizing the Huichol and Tarahumari rites, and later adding comparative Mexican data.

[24] Beals, *Comparative Ethnology*, 131 (Acaxee); Rouhier, *Monographie*, 12, fn. 3 (Tlaxcala). The Kiowa witch Tonakat fixed a fireplace in the form of a turtle, the source of his power, and used a meeting once for shamanistic display, being shot with a cartridge and remaining unharmed, etc. A Caddo-Delaware tells of a famous Kiowa doctor who used similar tricks in doctoring a woman. He held a black handkerchief over her to see the location of the disease, dipped a feather in water, cut the skin and removed two $1\frac{1}{2}''$ bugs, the wound healing immediately. Both popped when thrown into the fire, thus prognosticating her recovery from a twenty years' illness. Wild Horse (Caddo-Delaware) said doctors did "wizard sleight-of-hand tricks" in meetings; "some Indians can make you believe you see things." Some Tonkawa who visited the Kiowa about 1890 performed tricks in meeting like eating fire (Mooney, *Peyote Notebook*).

[25] Lumholtz, *Unknown Mexico*, 2: 241–42.

[26] The suppression of peyote was sought under an act of Jan. 30, 1897 (29 Stat. 506), Sect. 6 of the Food and Drugs Act of June 30, 1906 (34 Stat. 768–72), Sect. 11 of the same act, and Service and Regulatory Announcement No. 13, Dept. of Agriculture, Bureau of Chemistry (issued May 3, 1915)—all without success. Specific Federal anti-peyote bills were next attempted: Senate 1862 (65th Congress 1st Sess. Apr. 17, 1917), House of Representatives 10669 (64th Congress 1st Sess.), House of Representatives 4999 (65th Congress 1st Sess. June 12, 1917), House of Representatives 2614 (65th Congress 2nd Sess. May 13, 1918–Oct. 7, 1918). These all failed of passing. An anti-peyote proviso attached as a rider to Appropriations bill House of Representatives 8696 of March 28, 1918 was deleted before passage, under pressure from a powerful and alert Indian lobby. Later bills were House of Representatives 398 (66th Congress 1st Sess.), House of Representatives 2071 (about March 29, 1924), House of Representatives 5057 (not passed by Senate, but amended as:) House of Representatives 5078 (about Jan. 24, 1924, 68th Congress 1st Sess.)—all defeated. The Senate bill 1399 of Feb. 8, 1937 is pending at the present writing.

State laws against peyote have been more successful. The Oklahoma law of March 11, 1899 was automatically repealed by omission in the codification of the state laws; the Darnell bill of 1927 was defeated April 13, 1927. The following states have anti-peyote laws: Colorado (before 1923), Idaho, Iowa, Kansas, Montana (by 1925), Nebraska, Nevada (by 1918), New Mexico, North Dakota (before 1923), South Dakota, Utah (before 1918), and Wyoming (1929). The Native American Church is incorporated in Oklahoma and Montana, however, under state charters.

Though the most important of their fiestas, Huichol peyotism is a seasonal matter, the hikuli seldom being eaten outside the ceremonial period in January. In October a preliminary trip lasting fifteen days each way is made to Real Catorce (San Luis Potosí) to obtain the plants. The eight or twelve pilgrims bathe and sleep in the temple with their wives the night before leaving, not washing again until the feast some four months later. After receiving new names for the trip, the next morning they pray around a fire, wearing squirrel tails tied to their hats, and sacrifice five tortillas[27] to the fire. Then, after sprinkling their heads with a deer-tail dipped in water steeped with certain herbs, all weep as each man puts his right hand on his wife's left shoulder and bids her farewell.[28]

Their route is full of religious associations, since formerly the gods went out to seek peyote and now are met with in the shape of mountains, stones and springs; their dreams en route are also important in deciding religious arrangements for the coming year (who is to sacrifice cattle for rain, who is to be fire-maker, etc.). The pilgrims carry sacred hour-glass shaped gourds and the leader also carries the yákwai, a ball of native-grown tobacco called macuchi, which is solemnly distributed after they pass Puerta de Cerda. In the afternoon they place ceremonial arrows toward the four corners of the world, and sit around a fire until midnight. Tobacco belongs to the personified fire; after much praying the leader touches the tobacco-ball with his plumes and wraps small portions in corn husks[29] "so that they look like diminutive tamales," and each man puts one in a special tobacco-gourd tied to his quiver. This act symbolizes the birth of tobacco and henceforth they must preserve ritual order on the march, and only cease to be the "prisoner" of Grandfather Fire when the sacred bundles are given back to him, i.e., burned.

On the fourth afternoon the women at home gather to confess their sins to Grandfather Fire; they knot palm-leaves lest they forget the name of even a single lover and the men consequently find no hikuli. After this public confession each woman throws her leaf into the fire and becomes ritually clean. The men make a similar confession "to the five winds" a little beyond Zacatecas and burn their tallies in the fire. The hikuli-seekers are henceforth gods and the leaders fast (save for eating stray plants) until they reach the peyote country.[30]

Arrived, they line up, each man with an arrow on his bow-string which he points successively to the six regions of the world without letting it fly. As they march toward the mesa-"altar" where the leader has seen hikuli as a "deer," each man shoots two arrows

[27] The trip is made after the rainy season and the corn harvest (Lumholtz, *Unknown Mexico*, 2: 127); the roasting of corn is of equal ritual importance with the hikuli-harvest and the deer-hunt: the three, indeed, deer, corn and peyote are symbolically the same (Lumholtz *op. cit.*, 2: 156, 279).

[28] Lumholtz, *Unknown Mexico*, 2: 82, 126–27, 141, 157, 271, 272; *Handbook of the American Indians*, 1: 576–77; Klineberg, *Notes on the Huichol*, 449. For the gourd-symbolism see also Lumholtz, *op. cit.*, 2: 57–58, 129, 220; for the arrows, *Handbook of the American Indians*, 2: 663.

[29] Cf. the universal corn shuck cigarette of Plains peyotism (a region of deep-rooted pipe ceremonialism), a remarkable case of culture-continuity.

[30] Lumholtz, *Unknown Mexico*, 2: 129–35.

each over five hikuli plants, crossing over their tops that they may be taken "alive." They make a ceremonial circuit of the mesa, but the "deer" assumes the form of a whirlwind and disappears, leaving two hikuli in his tracks; there they sacrifice votive bowls, arrows, paper flowers, beads, etc., and pray. After this they return to get their five hikuli, and eat and gather others. The whole ceremony is of hunting deer, and after five days they reverse the logs of their fireplace and return home with gourds of holy water, wood for the shaman's rasp, sotol for the "godseats," yellow paint material and the hikuli they have gathered. Their tobacco-gourds and faces are painted yellow, the color of the God of Fire. The face-painting represents the faces or masks of the gods, and expresses prayers for rain, luck in deer-hunting and good crops, symbolized as corn field, cloud, ear of corn, "rain-serpent," squash-vine and -flower designs.[31]

Approaching home, they must hunt deer until they have enough for the feast, before being freed from the ritual restrictions of continence, fasting, and non-use of salt, meanwhile being sustained by slices of green hikuli eaten from time to time. The deer meat is cooked and then cut into small cubes which are strung (precisely as peyote is) on cords.[32] The deer-killing is to obtain rain for the next growing season.[33] The hunting period over, men and women bathe for the first time since the beginning of the hikuli-pilgrimage.

For the hikuli feast the men deck their hats lavishly with brilliant macao and hawk feathers, and wear supernumerary girdle-pouches; the women wear strings of yellow and red plumes across the back. A temple fire, another at the east of the patio to "guard" the dancers, and a third at the north for visitors from the underworld are built in a special fashion: the shaman carefully brings an eighteen-inch billet of green wood, offers it to five directions and finally to the sixth by placing it on the ground, after which others place sticks pointing east and west on this molitáli or "pillow" of Grandfather Fire.[34]

Then the shaman and hikuli-seekers ceremonially circle the freshly white-plastered "god-house of the Sun," enter, pray aloud and give a long account of their journey until late at night. The temple fire place (áro) is a circular clay basin in the center with a slightly raised rim; the poker is the "arrow" of the God of Fire. The niches at the west of the temple behind the shaman are filled with god-images; the others sit on either side of him in a semi-circle on sotol or century-plant stools. Their wives, flower-garlanded and painted, sit farther back in the temple, while the pilgrims smoke and sing all night about Great-grandfather Deer-Tail, the Morning Star and all the other gods who, long ago, went out to seek hikuli. The next morning all wash their faces, heads and hands in water from the hikuli-country, and salute the rising sun with a bowl of burning incense, sprinkling water

[31] Lumholtz, *The Huichol*, 8; *Unknown Mexico*, 2: 129–32, 141, 277–78; for the use of the water see 2: 57–58, 220.

[32] Cf. the Plains mode of preparing the meat, though the memory of the meaning of this feature (like the corn shuck cigarette and ritual parched corn) is long since gone.

[33] Lumholtz, *Unknown Mexico*, 2: 132–35, 153, 156, 189, 271. The triple corn-deer-peyote symbolism is completed when the women grind peyote on a metate.

[34] Lumholtz, *Unknown Mexico*, 2: 54, 272, 273–74. Cf. the Plains "fire-stick" and fire-arrangement.

to the four corners of the world with a flower and praying for life and for luck in hunting deer.[35]

Meanwhile the patio has been prepared for dancing. Beside the fire are jars of holy water and tesvino, a stuffed fetish-skunk tied to a stick, and a stuffed grey squirrel decorated with dark green beetle wing-covers, small clay birds, feathers and a crucifix.[36] The shaman, sitting west of the main fire (behind the usual ceremonial arrows, plumes, tamales, and a pot of hikuli-liquor) sacrifices water to the six regions with a stick; then, with assistants on either side who take turns helping him, the shaman sings the mythological songs, unaccompanied by a drum, and the long dance begins.[37] Both sexes take part in the dance, "a quick, jumping walk with frequent jerky turns of the body," in a circle counter-clockwise around the shaman and the fire—though the circle tends to an ellipse as they approach the fetish-animals at the northwest.[38]

At sunrise of the third and last day comes the corn-roasting ceremony which gives its name to the entire festival, Rarikira (from raki, "toasted corn").[39] The shaman fastens a plume with a ribbon in the hair of the woman who is to do the toasting and gives her a coarse straw whisk to stir the corn on her comal, supported on three stones over the fire. The hikuli-seekers appear with large varicolored ears of corn in their pouches, and after ceremonial circuits they shell it, sacrificing five grains to the fire. The woman then prepares the esquite, and all eat this, together with deer meat and broth, thus ending the festivities.[40]

The Huichol ritual paraphernalia is heavily symbolized. With his eagle and hawk plumes the singing shaman can see and hear everything anywhere, cure the sick, transform the dead, and even call down the sun; they symbolize the antlers of deer, and deer-antlers in turn symbolize peyote and the "chair" of Grandfather Fire. Peyote itself symbolizes both corn and deer, while the flames of the greatest shaman of all, Grandfather Fire, are his plumes (the brilliantly-colored macao is his particular bird). Deer-antlers, furthermore, for the Huichol symbolize arrows,[41] arrows being the symbol *par excellence* of prayer. Again, arrows symbolize a bird flying with outstretched neck, the feathered portion representing the

---

[35] Lumholtz, *Unknown Mexico*, 2: 29–31, 142–44, 149–50.

[36] Spanish friars came in after 1722, but Huichol peyotism is almost wholly free of Christian beliefs (*Handbook of the American Indians*, 1: 576–77). Even the "baptism" rite is probably native.

[37] Klineberg (*Notes on the Huichol*, 449) mentions special dances led by "angels" the next day—a boy and a girl dressed in their finest. It is not clear if this refers to the dance leaders or to the ceremonial "race for life" with the eating of cake-animals and spraying of the runners by the elders. But elsewhere Lumholtz describes a dance with carved bamboo serpent-sticks, deer-tails on short sticks, and whiskbroom "combs" (*Unknown Mexico* 2: 49–50).

[38] Lumholtz, *Unknown Mexico*, 2: 272, 274–75.

[39] But the whole peyote ritual might be divided into (1) the trip for hikuli, (2) the deer hunt, and (3) the roasting of corn, though peyote-deer-corn are symbolically identical.

[40] Lumholtz, *Unknown Mexico*, 2: 279. Tamaulipecan peyotism is similarly a hunting and first-fruits ceremony.

[41] "The idea of the antlers being arrows readily occurred to the Huichol, since they are the animal's weapon of attack and defence" (Lumholtz, *Symbolism of the Huichol*, 69).

heart. The peyote plant, finally, is considered the drinking-bowl of the god of fire and wind.[42]

This intricate symbolic complex (corn = peyòte = drinking-bowl of Grandfather Fire = god of wind = whirlwind = deer = deer-tracks = peyote = deer-antlers = shaman's plumes = deer antlers = chair of Grandfather Fire = flames of fire = brilliant bird [macao] plumes = flying bird = arrow = prayer for rain, corn and deer-hunting, etc.) is deeply rooted in Huichol religion, and each one of the symbolic equations has a ritual reflex.[43]

TARAHUMARI

Tarahumari peyotism is on the decline in Samachique, Quírara and Guadalupe, though still remaining around Narárachic; in Guadalupe the bakánawa cactus is valued instead. From two or three to a dozen men make the month-long trip to the region around the mouth of the Rio Conchos at any time of the year, though usually not in the rainy season. They first purify themselves with copal incense; on the way anything may be eaten, but in the hikuli country they eat only piñole, and speech is forbidden. Arrived, they erect a cross near the first plants found, in order to find an abundance of others, and carefully cut off the tops with wooden sticks to leave the roots uninjured. They sing and eat green peyote while gathering it and in the evening they dance the dutubúri around the cross and a fire. The harvesting lasts several days, some taking turns dancing while the others sleep. Each variety of hikuli is put in a separate bag, for they would fight if mixed.[44]

The plants are left on a blanket in the mountains near home, and the blood of a slaughtered sheep or goat is sprinkled on them to "feed" them, with a special song. After drying they are placed in covered ollas away from the house. The hikuli-seekers are met on their

[42] Lumholtz, *Unknown Mexico*, 2: 7-8, 56, 172-73, 201-203; *Handbook of the American Indians*, 1: 663b; *Symbolism of the Huichol*, 42, 66, 71, 174; *The Huichol*, 10.

[43] Bits of deer meat, corn-tamales and strung peyote-plants are treated with exactly equivalent ritual. In the peyote dance serpent-sticks are thrust into the air (like prayer sticks, praying for rain?), and small whisks made of materials brought from the hikuli-country represent deer-tails. In the origin legend, peyote first arose in the tracks of a gigantic deer; indeed, when the gods first used peyote they ground deer-antlers on a metate with water to make an intoxicant, just as peyote is ground to make "tea" and corn to make tesvino. The fire is built in a special way suggesting deer-antlers or the god-chairs. Arrows as definitely symbolize prayer as the prayer sticks of the Southwest. The poker or fire-arrow of Grandfather Fire is smeared with blood and decorated with plumes; it is his "pillow" and the rest of the sticks are his "chair." (One "appearance" of the god is a heart, modelled of the paste of the sacred wáve seed toasted and ground like corn, and renewed in the god-house every five years.) Facial paintings of the Huichol are called úra, "spark," being made of a yellow root dug in the peyote country when the hikuli is gathered; yellow particularly symbolizes the fire gods, of whom there are two. Tatévali, "Grandfather Fire," is the god of prophesying and curing shamans whose birds are the macao, royal eagle, cardinal bird, etc. The other, Tatótsi Mára Kwári, "Greatgrandfather Deer-tail," is the god of singing-shamans, whose bird is the white-tailed hawk. Their relationship is peculiar: Greatgrandfather Deer-tail, the symbol of fertility, is the son of Grandfather Fire, from whose plumes he sprang. Lumholtz (*Symbolism of the Huichol*, 10-11) explains the difficulty by indicating that the former represents a spark, the latter a fire fed by wood.

[44] Bennett and Zingg, *The Tarahumara*, ix, 136, 291-92; Mooney, *Tarumari-Guayachic*; Lumholtz, *Tarahumari Dances*, 453; *Unknown Mexico*, 1: 362.

33

return with singing, and a fiesta is held with the sacrificial sheep or goat. The dutubúri and the hikuli-dance are then danced all night around a large open-air fire, much green peyote and tesvino being consumed. This ceremony is to "cure" the pilgrims: the shaman's necklace of *Coix lachryma-Jobi* seeds is dipped into a bowl of agua-miel, sotoli, or mescal, each one receiving a spoonful, while the shaman sings of hikuli standing on a Job's Tears seed as big as a mountain.[45]

Tarahumari hikuli-feasts are held at other times also. The women grind the plants with water on a metate into a thickish brown liquid. The dancing-patio is carefully swept with a straw broom and several crosses are planted, and near one of these the peyote is piled with jars of "tea" and tesvino, baskets of unsalted tamales and bowls of meat and "medicine." A large fire is built with logs in an east-west position and hikuli and yumari are danced all night.[46]

Near the shaman and his assistants who sit west of the fire is a leaf-covered hole into which they carefully spit; the olla-cuspidor of the men to one side and the women to the other is passed around and emptied here also. With a drinking-gourd rim the shaman makes a circle on the ground and in it the right-angled cross of the world-symbol. Then he inverts a gourd over a hikuli placed on the cross, as a resonator for his rasp; hikuli enjoys this music and manifests his strength by the noise produced.[47] The shaman's headdress is of bird-plumes, which prevent the wind from entering and causing illness; through them the birds impart to him all their wisdom. The assistants, of both sexes, carry incense bowls of copal, kneeling and crossing themselves at the cross, and then pass out the peyote.[48]

At times the shaman dances, at times his assistants, and women may dance either separately or simultaneously with the other men participants. The bare-footed men are wrapped to the chin in white blankets; the women wear clean skirts and tunics. The clockwise dancing (with a turn of the body at the shaman's place) consists in a "peculiar quick, jumping march, with short steps, the dancers moving forward one after another, on their toes, and making sharp, jerky movements, without, however, turning around." The men have deer-hoof sonajas, and the rasping and singing are continuous save when the shaman politely excuses himself to the fetish hikuli; others must also ask permission to

[45] Bennett and Zingg, *op. cit.*, 292; Lumholtz, *Unknown Mexico*, 1: 363. The rasp is not used in the fiesta on returning from the trip, but in later ones.

[46] Lumholtz, *Unknown Mexico*, 1: 171-72, 343-44, 363-64. The shaman's women assistants are called rokoro, "stamens"; he is the pistil—a botanically erroneous symbolism, however.

[47] The Tarahumari rasp is definitely associated with peyotism, indicating (Bennett and Zingg, *The Tarahumara*, 71) a Huichol provenience; but they list rasps for the Cora, Mayo, Pima ("rain sticks"), Hopi (in the kachina dance) and N. Paiute (to charm antelope into a corral). The rasp is not exclusively Uto-Aztecan however; it occurs for the Wichita, Hidatsa, Salinan, and archaeologically in Illinois. Tarahumari Brazil-wood rasps are brought from the hikuli-country.

[48] Lumholtz, *Unknown Mexico*, 1: 313, 363-66; Bennett and Zingg, *op. cit.*, 293; Mooney, *Tarumari-Guayachic.*

leave the patio. In the intermittent dancing they beat their mouths with the palm imitating hikuli's talk, or cry "Hikuli vava! (Hikuli over yonder!)" in shrill falsetto.[49]

At dawn the dancing stops at three raps on the shaman's rasp. All rise and gather at the east cross. Then the shaman, followed by a boy with a gourd of palo hediondo medicine (ohnoa roots steeped in water), "cures" each one with his rasp wetted in the medicine, as they cry, "Thank you!" The shaman makes three long raspings with his stick on the man's head; its dust is so potent in curing that it is carefully gathered from around the resonator and preserved in buckskin bags. A spoonful of other medicines is sometimes swallowed as the shaman blows and makes passes; sometimes tesvino exclusively is used. Blankets are also smoked with copal now. Then, facing the rising sun, the shaman makes three raspings at arms' length, waving home hikuli who had come from the east early in the morning, riding on green doves, to prevent sorcery in the meeting; now he turns into a ball and returns, accompanied by the owl. Doctoring of the sick as well as "curing" may now occur. Then all wash carefully, and after the shaman sacrifices tortillas and tesvino as they stand in a line facing east, they all participate in a feast.[50]

Comparison of Mexican Peyote Rituals

Huichol peyotism is more intricate and important than Tarahumari, though it is seasonal only and the latter venerated several varieties of cactus. The state of the literature advises caution, but a far better case could be made for the Huichol as a center of diffusion: the neighboring Cora, for example, had a vigorous peyote rite, while the Tubar, who share tesvino and the yohe dance with the Tarahumari and otherwise resemble them culturally, lack it.[51] Beals, however, points out that since the Cora-Huichol do not live within the region of growth of peyote, they must have borrowed it; our sole knowledge of Huichol peyotism is modern, unfortunately, but the Cora rite is known from 1754. On the whole, the gaps in our knowledge are too great to discuss possible centers of diffusion of Mexican peyotism; they may, indeed, lie in the little known area to the northeast.[52]

---

[49] Lumholtz, *Unknown Mexico*, 1: 367–69, 371; Bennett and Zingg, *The Tarahumara*, 293. Near Eagle Pass a folk-Catholic saint is El Santo Niño de Jesús Peyotes, whose attributes are a staff, gourd, feathered hat and basket similar to but distinct from El Santo Niño de Atoche. In Mexican legend he is a little boy; his statue is in the cathedral or cathedral square at Rosales, Mexico. Another attribute is said to be the crescent moon.

[50] Lumholtz, *Unknown Mexico*, 1: 292–93, 314, 344, 347–48, 371–72, 384; Bennett and Zingg, *The Tarahumara*, 294. The ceremony is called napítshi nawlíruga, "moving (dancing) around the fire" (Lumholtz, *Unknown Mexico*, 1: 364). In the dry season the Tarahumari dance the yumari almost nightly to the Morning Star, and sacrifice tesvino to the sun; a man is often deputed to do the dance alone while the others work in the fields, to bring rain (Lumholtz, *op. cit.*, 1: 352). The Morning Star is important in the Cora rite too (Lumholtz, *op. cit.*, 1: 344; Preuss, *Nayarit-Expedition, passim*) as well as figuring in Plains peyotism, though somewhat vaguely.

[51] Lumholtz, *Unknown Mexico*, 1: 357–58, 444; Bennett and Zingg, *The Tarahumara*, 360, 366–67, 379, 383.

[52] Beals, *Comparative Ethnology*, 131. He adds, though, that "This [use] may also be aboriginal, and very probably dates back to the separation of the Huichol from their peyote-using relatives, the Guachachiles." He cites Thomas and Swanton (*Indian Languages*, 22) but evidence is meagre. For the Cora we have Ortega (in

A relatively full account of the Tamaulipecan rite is extant:[53]

One of the Tamaulipecan tribes would usually hold feasts for only those of its own community, or it would invite some of those that were neighbors and friends. They took place generally by night. Devoting two or three previous days to the preparation of a sufficient quantity of peyote, and the gathering of fruits of the season, and in allotting certain fruits of the chase, which, broiled on the hearth that illuminated the feast, were served at a common banquet. The feast always had an object among these peoples. With feasts they celebrated the beginning of summer, which was the season least rigorous for these nude people, or the abundant harvests of corn, or of forest fruits, or their victory in some attack on their enemies. When these feasts were held for one tribe alone they took place commonly in the rancherías where they lived permanently. But when one who was promoting the feast invited some of his neighbors, then he chose an intermediate point between the two places that they inhabited, and that was picked out generally in the most inaccessible or hidden places in the mountains. As soon as everything was prepared for the banquet and the guests had collected, a great bonfire was lighted. They placed around it the fruits of the hunt prepared before hand. Those that took part in the dance immediately formed a circle around the fire, and to the measured beats of the drum (the drum was made of an aro of wood over which they attached the parchment of a deer or a coyote) which, united with the voices, composed the music. They took part in the dance alternately raising one foot and then the other, or the whole circle started circling around the fire. During the dance dancers and spectators broke out in discordant howls, each one reciting in his own strophes, alluding to the cause that was motivating the feast. Of this versification I have already previously given you an idea: relative to the celebration of some triumph gained in their skirmishes; and in the same way they directed their phrases to the sun, to the moon, and to the clouds, when they were enjoying good weather; to the earth and to the rain when they had an abundance of fruit; and finally to their strength and bravery when they recalled their hunts in the mountains or their wars. The poetic enthusiasm of the guests became more animated with the first fumes of the peyote, which, placed on a counter that was improvised on the trunk of a tree, was served to them by young Indian girls and the old men, and in the same gourds, jars, or rude baked clay vases. This class of feast always used to end with the complete drunkenness of all the guests, who, exhausted moreover by the dance, fell asleep around the almost burnt-out fire. [As previously noted, prophecy was a feature of these rites]. In addition to these feasts that are called mitotes, they also have other games and recreation during the hours of the day, such as ball, fighting, and foot-racing; and these games are often that which gives the motive for their mutual discontent, and sometimes precipitates formal wars among them.

Safford, *An Aztec Narcotic*, 295, and *Narcotic Plants*, 402): "Close to the musician was seated the leader of the singing whose business it was to mark the time. Each of these had his assistants to take his place when he should become fatigued. . . . They began forming as large a circle as could occupy the space of ground that had been swept off for this purpose. One after the other went dancing in a ring or marking time with their feet, keeping in the middle the musician and the choirmaster whom they invited, and singing in the same unmusical tone that he set them. They would dance all night from five o'clock in the evening to seven o'clock in the morning, without stopping or leaving the circle. When the dance was ended all stood who could hold themselves on their feet; for the majority from the peyote and the wine which they drank were unable to utilize their legs or hold themselves upright."

[53] Prieto, *Historia y Estadistica*, 123-24.

We note in this account the connection of peyote with corn harvests, deer hunting and war; and dancing, racing and a morning ceremony are also mentioned. Regarding the ball-game:[54]

Among the Acaxee [peyote] was reported to have been placed on one side of a ball ground during a game; its further use here is unknown, but it is likely that it was taken in small doses by the players during the game, as is done in the kicking race of the Tarahumare in modern times.

Chichimecan peyote-eating appears to be connected with war:

Those that eat it or drink it see frightening and laughable visions. This spree lasts two or three days and then stops. It is a common food of the Chichimecas, for it stimulates them and it gives them sufficient spirit to fight and have neither fear, thirst, nor hunger, and they say it guards them from all danger.

The Zacatecan use of peyote seems likewise to pertain to war, since they eat it to learn the outcome of battles. The drugging and ceremonial wounding of the father of a new-born male child, further, is to augur its valor in war. The Caxcane used peyote cere-monially, with associations unknown to us, but the Tlaxcaltecan use points again, though uncertainly, to war. Preuss writes that "the god of the Morning-Star has a close relation-ship to this cactus, among the Huichol," and the Morning Star has definite war asso-ciations.[55]

Dancing is commonly associated with peyotism in the Mexican area, being recorded for the Comecrudo, Chichimeca, Cora, Huichol, Tamaulipecan, Tarahumari and Lipan.[56] Use in ritual racing is known for the Tarahumari, Huichol and Tamaulipecan tribes; and the Acaxee tied strips of deer-hide or -hooves (the word used means either) on the instep as an aid in climbing hills—a custom recalling the carrying of hikuli-deer in racing and the Wichita use of mescal beans. The ritualized journey for peyote is recorded for the Cora, Huichol, Tarahumari, Tepecano and somewhat doubtfully for the Tlaxcaltecan.[57]

The ceremonial fire has no definitive association with peyotism in Mexico,[58] though it

[54] Beals, *Comparative Ethnology*, 131.

[55] Sahagún, *Historia general*, 3: 241 (Chichimeca); Prieto, *Historia y Estadistica*, 119–20, cites a Maratine Indian (Tamaulipecan) peyote song referring to war. Arlegui, in Urbina, *El Peyote y el Ololiuhqui*, 26; see also Rouhier, *op. cit.*, 12, note 3, 96, 331, note 3; Alegre, in Urbina, *op. cit.*, 26; Preuss, *Die Nayarit-Expedition*, 39. The Morning Star is the principal Cora god (Lumholtz, *Unknown Mexico*, 1: 511, see also *Handbook of the American Indians*, 1: 348a). Elder Brother among the Huichol is the god of wind and hikuli (Lumholtz, *Symbolism of the Huichol*, 42). The Tarahumari dance yumari for the Morning Star (Lumholtz, *Unknown Mexico*, 1: 344). In the Plains the drum-lacing signifies the Morning Star. Spier (*Yuman Tribes*, 165) writes: "[The battle leader's] song first described the morning star, 'big star,' which in some unidentified way is connected with war. Just what was his function in battle was not ascertained." He also dreamed he saw cacti fighting like men.

[56] Mooney, *Tarumari-Guayachic*; Sahagún, *Historia general*, 3: 118; Ortega, *Historia del Nayarit*, 22–23; Lumholtz, *Unknown Mexico*, 1: 367–68, 2: 274–75; Prieto, *Historia y Estadistica*, 123–24.

[57] Racing (Tarahumari, Huichol, Tamaulipas, Acaxee): Lumholtz, *Unknown Mexico*, 1: 284–85, 2: 49–50; Prieto, *Historia y Estadistica*, 123–24; Beals, *The Acaxee*, 8.

[58] Beals (*Comparative Ethnology*, 127, 141, 211–12) lists it for Southern Mexico, Jalisco-Tepic, Southwest.

is a prerequisite of the Plains rite even on the hottest summer nights; nor has the copal incense of the Huichol and Tarahumari any relation to the Plains use of sage and cedar.[59] The corn shuck cigarette among the Huichol and Tarahumari is, furthermore, in a somewhat different context, though Plains ceremonial cigarettes are certainly Mexico-Southwest in origin.[60] The gourd rattle is Mayo, Tarahumari, Gila River Pima, Walapai, Havasupai, Pueblo, Mescalero, Lipan, Karankawa, Wichita, Seri, Chitimacha, Cherokee, Creek, Koasati and Yuchi (i.e., southern Mexico, the Southwest, peripheral Plains and Southeast) and therefore has no special association with peyote, though again, it may be the origin of the gourd rattle in the central and northern Plains.[61] Though the staff is a constant feature in the Plains ceremony, in Mexico[62] this is decidedly not the case. The shaman's rasp among peyote-using tribes is noted only for the Cora, Huichol and Tarahumari—and has a far wider distribution among non-users of peyote, while being absent in the Plains rite.[63] The Tamaulipecan aro with drum-head of coyote- or deer-skin is unlike the peyote drum of the north, and further, the use of the drum is untypical in the Mexican rite.[64]

On the other hand, the use of parched corn is more clearly a part of Mexican peyotism, as is also deer-hunting.[65] "Plant-worship" is most evident perhaps for the Tarahumari, who

[59] Lumholtz, *Unknown Mexico*, 1: 362, 2: 54; Bennett and Zingg, *The Tarahumara*, 295. See also Wissler *The American Indian*, 213; *Handbook of the American Indians*, 1: 604b. In the Plains some tribes differentiated twigs and leaves as male and female.

[60] The Tarahumari feast for the moon involves smoking to make clouds (Lumholtz, *Unknown Mexico*, 2: 130; *Tarahumari Dances*, 441). The Huichol carry "tamale-" cigarettes in their gourds and offer them to Grandfather Fire.

[61] Bennett and Zingg, *The Tarahumara*, 67; Beals, *Aboriginal Survivals*, 32; Russell, *The Pima*, 168; Spier, *Havasupai Ethnography*, 272; Lumholtz, *Unknown Mexico*, 1: 313; Opler, *The Influence of Aboriginal Pattern, The Use of Peyote;* Sayles, *An Archaeological Survey*, Table 2; Oliver, in Gatschet, *The Karankawa Indians*, 18; Gatschet, in Swadesh, *Chitamacha Texts;* Kroeber, *The Seri*, 14, 42; Roberts, *Musical Areas*, 21; Paz, *Koasati Field Notes*; Bartram, *Travels*, 502; Speck, *Yuchi*, 61.

[62] Tarahumari officials are called igúsuame, "stick-bearers" (Bennett and Zingg, *op. cit.*, 375–76) but this may be an Hispanicism. However, Aztec merchants (Sahagun) carried staffs. But so far as the peyote ritual is concerned, the staff is not mentioned for the Cora-Huichol or Tarahumari; and the various names for the peyote staff in the Plains suggests either an indigenous or a Southwestern, not a Mexican, origin.

[63] Bennett and Zingg, *The Tarahumari*, 71, 293–94; Lumholtz, *Unknown Mexico*, 1: 366–67. The Tarahumari hunter used a notched deer-bone rasp. The Cora, Mayo, and Pima, Hopi and Northern Paiute suggest a general Uto-Aztecan occurrence of the trait, but the rasp, is also Wichita, Hidatsa.

[64] Prieto, *Historia y Estadistica*, 123–24. See the Plains section for discussion of drums.

[65] A little white flower, tōtó, of the wet corn-producing season symbolizes corn for the Huichol and is a prayer for it, being plastered on women's cheeks, woven in girdles, etc. (Lumholtz, *Unknown Mexico*, 229–30). The Tamaulipecan rite celebrates the harvest and deer-hunting as well as war; the Tepehuane all-night rite with a mimicry of deer-hunting ends with a feast on the first "toasted corn" of the season (Lumholtz, 1: 479). Acaxee corn toasted on the ear was the usual food on war-parties (Beals, 10). Concerning the standardized parched-corn in sugar-water of the Plains, note that the Aztec made offerings of toasted corn (sometimes with honey), and to the culture-hero Opuchtli offered mumuchtli "a sort of corn which when toasted opens up and shows the white marrow [popcorn] forming a very white flower. They said this represented hail, which is attributed to the water gods." (Sahagún, *A History of Ancient Mexico*, 1: 36, 40, 87.)

revere hikuli, bakanawa, mulato, rosapara, sunami, ocoyomi and dekuba; the Tepecano sometimes substitute marihuana or rosa maria (*Cannabis sativa*) for peyote in their worship,
and elsewhere other plants are involved.[66] Birds are a recognizable feature in Mexican
peyotism: the Huichol macao, humming-bird and swift are noted, and the Tarahumari
humming-bird, green dove and owl.[67]

Bennett and Zingg on the Tarahumari would as well apply to all Mexican peyotism:[68]

. . . the use of peyote resembles an elaborate curing ceremony rather than a cult. There is nothing
to suggest a society centered around peyote-eating . . . . The group of peyote-eaters does not involve
any exclusiveness, requirements, or ritual pertaining to individuals. The peyote ceremonies are
not given for the pleasure of eating the plant, but to cure some disease.

Properly speaking, then, Mexican peyotism is a tribal affair, centering around the shaman,
on whose shoulders rests the whole tribal welfare as involved in abundant corn harvests,
successful deer-hunting, and success in war (which he may prognosticate).[69] Shamanistic
curing is conspicuous in both Huichol and Tarahumari peyotism. Beals,[70] writing of northern Mexico says that

the degree of shamanistic influence apparent at present is greater than at some time in the past . . .
Possibly the use of peyote also had some influence in extending and reviving shamanistic concepts.
. . . Visionary experiences reach their highest development ordinarily in religions of the shaman-
istic type.

[66] Bennett and Zingg, *The Tarahumara*, 138, 295; Lumholtz, *Unknown Mexico*, 1: 357-58 (wherein all
but the last named are cacti), 2: 124-25 (Tepecano). The accepted etymology of teonanacatl, "divine mushroom,"
suggests the same attitude; in the Antilles "among the most prominent of the plants worshipped . . . [are]
mushrooms, pines, opuntias, zapos, and zeybas." (Rafinesque, cited in Bourke, *Scatological Rites*, 91; but
Rafinesque is an undependable authority). The Cherokee called casine yapon (the "black drink") "the beloved tree" (Bartram, *Travels*, 357). It is also said that in Virginia toadstools were an object of worship because
of their mysterious growth (Bourke, *ibid.*). In Peru coca was looked on with veneration and suppliants must
approach priests only with some in their mouths. Compare the use and attitudes toward tobacco, mescal beans,
datura, guarana paste, cohoba, chocolate (*Theobroma cacao*), ayahuasca, yahé, etc.

[67] Lumholtz, *Unknown Mexico*, 2: 172-73, 207, 263 ff. The Huichol had hikuli-shields; curiously, Crow-Neck
(Kiowa) about 1860 made a peyote shield according to a vision he had at Mescalero, but he threw it away when
he was captured on his first fight in Mexico. The Kiowa, however, had heraldic shield-societies before peyote,
of which this is probably an aberrant example. (For the bird and arrow equation see Spier, *Yuman Tribes*, 331,
Lumholtz, *op. cit.*, 2: 201-202.) See also Lumholtz, *op. cit.*, 1: 313, 323-24, 371-72; *Tarahumari Dances*, 452.

[68] Bennett and Zingg, *The Tarahumari*, 294.

[69] Lumholtz, *Unknown Mexico*, 1: 311, writes: "Without his shaman the Tarahumare would feel lost, both
in this life and after death. The shaman is his priest and physician. He performs all the ceremonies and conducts
all the dances and feasts by which the gods are propitiated and evil is averted, doing all the singing, praying,
and sacrificing. By this means, and by instructing the people what to do to make it rain, and secure other benefits,
he maintains good terms for them with their deities, who are jealous of man and bear him ill-will. He is also on
the alert to keep those under his care from sorcery, illness, and other evil that may befall them . . . the Tarahumare . . . keeps his doctor busy curing him, not only to make his body strong to resist illness, but chiefly to
ward off sorcery, the main source of trouble in the Indian's life."

[70] Beals, *Comparative Ethnology*, 128.

These remarks go far toward explaining the differential diffusion of peyotism. Peyote never penetrated the Yuman Southwest, perhaps because the *dream* performed the psychological function of the peyote vision (which, moreover, was not very significant in Mexico). Again, the ritual use of peyote failed to penetrate the Pueblo Southwest or the Aztec, both strongholds of priestly religion; perhaps the stereotyped institutional rituals of these regions stifled such orgiastic individual emotional experiences as peyote is' calculated to induce. On the other hand, peyotism entered the shamanistic Southwest (the Mescalero) and one Pueblo, Taos, where the kachina cult was weak, and once it reached the individualistic vision-valuing Plains, it fairly ran riot.

Mescalero Apache and Transitional Forms of Ritual

Peyote came to the Mescalero[71] about 1870, in the same "general movement which resulted in its adoption by a large number of the tribes of the United States."[72] Like other Apache ceremonies its origin was attributed to an individual's encounter with a power, but the tribe involved was the Tonkawa, Lipan or "Yaqui." Like the Plains groups, the Mescalero made a trip south to get peyote,[73] which was kept by the shaman for ceremonial use only, lest private individual users who did not "know" and have the right to use the power go mad. The primary purpose of meetings was for doctoring,[74] though "occasionally a peyote meeting was called for some other purpose—for peyote, like other sources of supernatural power, was believed to be efficacious for locating the enemy, finding lost objects, foretelling the results of a venture, etc."

The news that a peyote shaman is conducting a meeting for a sick person spreads rapidly, and all who are to attend bathe at noon of the appointed day.[75] At nightfall they

[71] This entire section is summarized from data collected by M. E. Opler. I gratefully acknowledge the courtesy and generosity of his lending me the article *The Influence of Aboriginal Pattern* before publication, as well as *The Autobiography of a Chiricahua Apache*, and unpublished notes on Lipan, Tonkawa and Carrizo peyotism; it would be difficult to establish Mexican-Plains continuities without these invaluable data and the warm coöperation of Dr. Opler.

[72] The Mescalero are listed neither in Shonle (*Peyote: The Giver of Visions*, 53–75) nor in Newberne and Burke, *Peyote*. Mescalero peyotism, like Tarahumari, is on the decline.

[73] The Lipan make a smoke and pray when the first plant is found; they are hard to find unless one eats one, then "a noise like the wind" comes, and one by one the plants appear "just like stars." Only the tops are cut off.

[74] Though this was general in Mescalero ceremonialism, they also controlled the weather thus, found lost objects, located the enemy, etc.; a Chiricahua prayed for health, in the name of Yusn and Child of the Water. The Lipan formerly did not use it for doctoring apparently. The Tonkawa, according to Mooney, performed shamanistic tricks in peyote meetings; and a Carrizo chief, for example, filled the tipi once with down-feathers blown from his mouth, then sucked them all in save one which he gave to a Lipan visitor. Others made a bear, turtle, and buffalo, etc., appear.

[75] The Lipan wash themselves with yucca or soapweed and perfume themselves with mint, and use the same kind of sage in meetings as they wear in their hats against lightning. The Tonkawa wore G-string, leggings and blanket, and preferably long hair and face paint; native perfumes were proper but white men's were forbidden. The Carrizo entered barefoot, wearing only a G-string. Some Lipan fasted the day before.

enter the tipi, where the peyote chief is sitting west of the fire facing the door, with a gourd rattle in one hand and an incised wooden staff in the other.[76] The staff is his protection against witchcraft, and he "sings to it"; he exchanges the gourd for the drum of his assistant, but retains the staff in his left hand. In front of him on an eagle feather or piece of buckskin lies the large talismanic "chief peyote" or "Old Man Peyote."[77]

He is assisted by a door-keeper and a fire-tender, who builds a crescent mound of earth around the fire-pit with the horns east, and keeps the fire going all night.[78] Once having entered, one is not supposed to leave the tipi until morning save briefly, taking one of the eagle feathers lying on either side of the door, and replacing it as soon as possible. The peyote,[79] in a sack or on a woven tray, is first eaten by the peyote chief, who then administers their first buttons to novices, using two eagle-tail feathers as a spoon, with three ritual feints, after which these "fly" into their mouths. Then after smoking[80] the peyote is passed around by the assistants as the leader prays. Beginning at the southeast the drum is passed clockwise as each person sings four songs, his own ceremonial songs or songs received in visions, while the leader or his assistants shakes the rattle. The leader sings most of the songs.

There was a mild bias against women[81] among the Mescalero; they received medicine power, but could not become a peyote chief, because the responsibilities of the office were too great—for a leader must prevent anything happening between even the greatest of rival

[76] The Lipan leader "is supposed to stop all arguments in there; he has to watch all the men." Unlike the Mescalero, the Lipan staff and gourd were passed around clockwise (both preceding the drum); the retention of these by the leader is probably an aspect of his special authority among the Mescalero, since the Lipan lacked the rasp, retained by the leader, which might have been transmitted from Mexico. The Tonkawa sometimes used a lard-can drum covered with buckskin, and passed the rattle (aberrantly) after it; the leader never drummed.

[77] Some shamans trace a cross of pollen on the chief peyote. The Tonkawa use the largest one they can find, put some red paint on the top, and surround it with smaller buttons on a fine buckskin; they claimed to be able to see far off with the aid of peyote and to detect witchcraft. Some Lipan like the Mescalero put peyote buttons in a circle around the fire pit and the chief peyote (cf. the Comanche placing of them in a sage horseshoe west of the altar).

[78] The Lipan fire-tender, like the Carrizo and some Mexican groups, made simply a fire-pit, with no crescent altar; this form originated with the Mescalero or in northwestern Mexico, not around the lower Rio Grande. The Carrizo, like the Tamaulipecan, held the ceremony in the open.

[79] The Lipan used peyote green or dry or pounded up in a wooden bowl, which was passed like the drum from the southeast. The Carrizo made a peyote "tea" (compare the neighboring Karankawa "black drink"). The Tonkawa used a flat basket. Among the Mescalero (also Lipan and Kiowa), "Care was taken to keep the 'fuzz' from the top of the peyote button from coming in contact with the eye, for it was thought to cause blindness."

[80] Not all Mescalero leaders do this; oak-leaf cigarettes are usually used but one leader has a red stone Sioux pipe, which is passed clockwise. The Lipan smoke oak-leaf or corn husk cigarettes at the beginning and at the end. Their eagle wing-bone whistle in peyote is recent, and not all Mescalero leaders use it.

[81] The Carrizo on each side of the door had a woman wearing a red blanket; the one at the south had hers fastened with a red flicker feather, the other with a woodpecker. This non-exclusion of women is Mexican. But the Lipan allow no women around; they may not even erect the peyote-tipi. The Tonkawa originally allowed no women in peyote meetings; but doctoring gradually broke down this restriction.

shamans in meetings.[82] In this he was aided by the chief peyote which "he frequently consulted . . . to ascertain whether anything were amiss; any evil thoughts or efforts at witchcraft were said to 'show' on this 'chief peyote'." A favorite device of witches to weaken the leader was to make his assistants vomit the peyote.

Peyotism was readily accepted by the Mescalero, in whose older culture were patterns of receiving supernatural power from animals, etc. Indeed, Opler calls the Mescalero

a tribe of shamans, active or potentially active [and peyote became another among many sources of power for them]. It will be readily grasped, however, that since peyote leadership and the conduct of peyote rites were open to any one who claimed a supernatural experience with the plant, since, in other words, an individualistic, shamanistic premise underlay the utilization of peyote for religious purposes, centralized leadership and definite organization could not be achieved. The Mescalero use of peyote never developed into a cult or society with a regular membership and place of meeting, with officers and principals selected or agreeable to the entire body of devotees . . . [even with the] emphasis on curative rites. . . .

This, in Mexico, made the rite tend to be tribal in character, the shaman quasi-priest. Mescalero peyotism, therefore, is truly transitional between the Mexican all-inclusive rite of *tribal* cure and the individualistic Plains *societal* ceremony; no equilibrium was permanently reached between the two, and Opler adduces abundant evidence of the *rival* nature of peyotism among competing shamans.[83] The concept was that everyone was to get in rapport with his power(s) via peyote, with the peyote shaman, however, remaining the figurehead leader—a multiple "working together" of powers, peyote being the power *par excellence* that worked with other powers. The Mescalero, then, attempted to force the physiologically somewhat refractory individual peyote experience into the shamanistic mold. The leader remained the arbiter and mediator, and held special symbols of authority, the staff and the rattle, to compensate for his real loss of status as cynosure, when participants in the curing rite were enlarged beyond the patient and his relatives.

Notable is the lack of Christian elements in Mescalero peyotism, in contrast with some Plains groups; indeed, "far from becoming a weakened and Christianized version of native beliefs, the Mescalero Apache acceptance of peyote resulted instead in an intensification of the aboriginal religious values at many points."[84] On the other hand, when we recalled the

[82] "The virulence of these rivalries and attempts to harm others at peyote meetings led to the development of a number of protective measures and safeguards." For these see Opler, *The Influence of Aboriginal Pattern.*

[83] In the old shamanistic curing, the shaman was the performer and the others merely onlookers, but in peyotism the inevitable physiological effects of the drug made all present potential receivers of power, and shamanistic display and rivalry was correspondingly increased. This had not wholly disappeared even in early Plains peyote-using groups: the Tonkawa, Lipan, and Kiowa had shamanistic displays of power in peyote meetings, and we have recorded considerable witchcraft anxiety in early Kiowa, Comanche, Caddo, and Tonkawa meetings.

[84] The reasons for this are several: a nomadic people presents few opportunities for the establishing of missions; the Apache were one of the American Indian groups last subjugated; they are notoriously suspicious and unfriendly toward innovation, and recognized the alien origin even of peyotism; and further, the rite they

history of their relations with Whites and such psychologically similar cults as the Ghost Dance of the Plateau, Great Basin and Plains, it is somewhat surprising that a warlike and predatory group like the Mescalero did not associate peyote and anti-White feeling. Opler has recorded a Tonkawa peyote ceremony with clear anti-White features; but the Mescalero had an aboriginal ceremony before peyote whose function was the consternation and defeat of enemies, and this, directed toward the whites, usurped the function of ritual opposition through peyote.[85]

KIOWA-COMANCHE TYPE RITE

Aside from the John Wilson, John Rave, and Church of the First-born variants, the basic Plains ceremony is remarkably. homogeneous in various tribes. Since the Kiowa and the Comanche, historically considered, were the center of this diffusion,[86] in the interests of economy we choose their ceremony to detail as the "Plains type-rite." In the following account care is taken that every statement be specifically true of the Kiowa and at the same time representative of the Plains; minor Comanche differences are shown in footnotes.

Living beyond the habitat of peyote, all Plains tribes have to make pilgrimages for it or buy it. The journey is not ritualized, but there is a modest ceremony at the site: on finding the first plant, a Kiowa pilgrim sits west of it, rolls a cornshuck cigarette and prays, "I have found you, now open up, show me where the rest of you are;[87] I want to use you to pray for the health of my people." He sings and eats green plants while harvesting them; only the tops are taken, that the root may regenerate buds, a fine large one being saved as a "father peyote" for meetings later.[88]

Many groups, like the Kiowa, "vow" meetings as in the Sun Dance. They may be held in gratitude for recovery from illness, on a child's first four birthdays, for doctoring the sick, to pray for the successful delivery of a child, or for the health of the participants in general. Present too is the possibility of instruction and power through a peyote vision; in the Plains this is the primary motive, with doctoring second. In the last twenty years "holiday meetings" have been introduced.[89]

---

received from Mexico had few or no Christian elements in it. It might be suggested that the "baptism" ceremonies in the morning or the ritual breakfast are Christian in origin; but this is thoroughly doubtful, since it occurs in pre-White peyotism (e.g., Lipan).

[85] In the Plains, peyotism largely followed the Ghost Dance frustration of anti-White sentiment and preached conciliation instead; such Christian elements as were added had a largely propagandist function in this direction.

[86] Wagner, *Entwicklung und Verbreitung*, 74; Shonle, *Peyote: Giver of Visions*, 55.

[87] As told, this seemed to have reference to the miraculous proliferation of the Biblical loaves and fishes, but it is sufficiently similar to aboriginal hunting beliefs.

[88] The Comanche and others usually had a meeting on the spot, eating green peyote.

[89] The Kiowa now have five Easter meetings, six on New Year's Day, four to six on Thanksgiving, and two or three on Armistice Day (by World War soldiers and sailors). Bert Crow-lance vowed to eat a hundred if all the Kiowa boys returned safely from the War (but this is an enormous quantity actually to have eaten). The Kiowa differ from other groups in having no funeral meetings; mourners commonly abstain for several months from meetings. Meetings have been held for heyoka-like display. The Comanche formerly held meetings before a war journey to invoke peyote's protection from the enemy, and to prophesy the outcome of the battle.

43

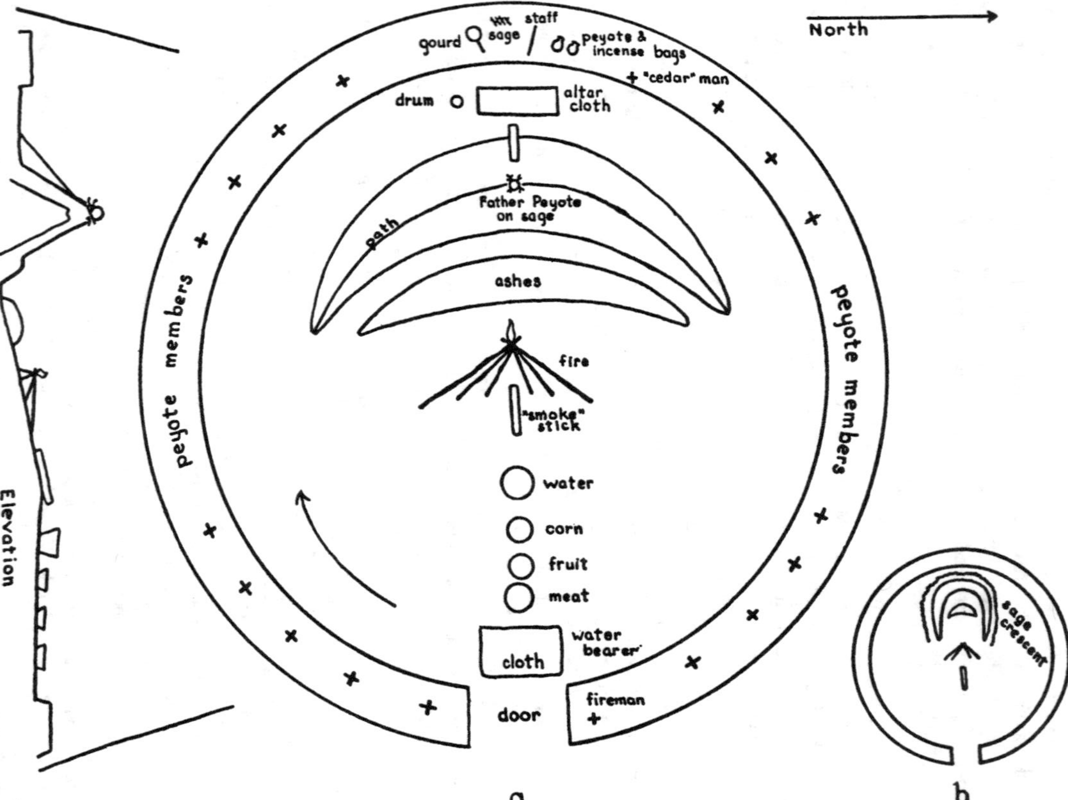

Fig. 1. Arrangement of interior of tipi for peyote meeting. a, Kiowa "standard" peyote meeting; b, Comanche horseshoe moon variant.

44

In preparation, the Kiowa commonly take a sweatbath.[90] In the old days buckskin dress was prescribed, but nowadays a "blanket" or folded sheet for men and a shawl for women satisfies this requirement; buckskin moccasins are more comfortable than stiff-soled shoes during a night spent sitting cross-legged. Older men still paint for meetings; one leader for example had a yellow hair-part with a short red forehead line perpendicular to this, vertical red lines in front of the ears, and yellow around the eyes.[91]

The sponsor selects his leader (ᴅωλk̆i) or himself acts as one; a leader usually has his own drummer (o'ᴅ'asodek̆i) and fireman (ɢ'iɢ'uk̆i), and some a "cedar man" also. The sponsor's womenfolk erect the tipi, prepare and bring the food and water the next morning. The floor is carefully cleaned and plumes of sagebrush are spread around the inside of the tipi, as in a sweat-lodge, for a seat. The sponsor stands the cost of the meeting (from twenty-five to fifty dollars), or others may help in paying; he also supplies the peyote or pays the leader for it, but communicants often bring their own buttons also.

The leader supplies the paraphernalia: the staff (ᴅo'ᴅę̈ä, "brace-to hold-stick") of bois d'arc, the gourd rattle, eagle wing-bone whistle, cedar incense, altar cloth, drum, and perhaps his personal "feathers" for doctoring. The drum (ᴅωä'ᴅω or ʙώλkωᴅωä`ᴅω) is a No. 6 cast-iron three-legged trade-kettle with the bail-ears filed off. The buckskin head is well soaked and tied over the kettle, a third- or half-filled with water into which ten or a dozen live coals (and sometimes herb-perfumes) have been dropped; the Kiowa say the drum represents thunder, the water in it rain, and the coals lightning. Seven marbles are put under the buckskin around the outside kettle rim to serve as bosses for the thong wound once-and-a-half times round them; the same thong is passed through each loop and laced criss-cross seven times under the kettle, unknotted, to tighten the head and form on the bottom the seven-pointed "Morning Star." The single drumstick (ʙωλkωtωn) is straight, carved, beaded, and embellished with a buckskin tassel or fringe on the handle end. The gourd-handle is also beaded and fringed, and tufted with red horse-hair (ɢuλks'ǫgʸä) at the top end passing through the gourd, the neck of which is plugged with half a spool; the gourd

---

[90] "A sweatbath was always undergone by warriors preparing for war . . . and perhaps generally, before any serious or hazardous undertaking . . . . Sweating was important in medical practice for the cure of disease . . . . Sometimes the friends and relatives of the sick person . . . assembled in the sweathouse, sang and prayed for the patient's recovery" (*Handbook of the American Indians*, 2: 661b). The peyote meeting and sweating present many such analogies.

[91] Painting is commonly dictated in visions: a Kiowa saw a red-bird after a meeting once as a red-blanketed man who told him to use red paint thereafter. Comanche formerly went in wearing only breech-clout and "blanket," being painted white or yellow all over the body. One Comanche had an all-over body yellow with blue zigzags up the arm and down the side and leg, with a red zigzag paralleling this (on the outside of the arm and therefore on the inside of the leg); on each cheek a small blue-bordered red spot, and a large three-inch red spot on the breast under the throat. The Tonkawa painted the top of the fetish-plant red also. Leaders often wear otter skin braid-coverings, and at certain points in the ritual fur headdresses. Mescal beans as necklaces or on moccasin- and gourd-fringes are common (the Kiowa wear them on their moccasins as protection against stepping on menstrual blood). The "blanket," or sheet (in the summer), is invariable.

itself may be covered with texts or symbolical drawings.[92] Participants are free after midnight to use the cult drumstick and gourd or their individual ones as they choose. Formerly
"only the leader brought in the medicine fan with him, but now many young men bring
them in who have no special business to." These have a beaded and fringed cylindrical
handle, with feathers loosely supported in individual buckskin sockets sewed around the
shafts; often they are notched, tipped with horse-hair, or down feathers are added at the
base—as individual "visions" dictate. The leader also supplies the fetish "father peyote,"
but no Bible is used in the Kiowa or usual Plains ceremony.[93] Formerly only old men and
warriors attended meetings, but now women and girls over thirteen come in, when not
menstruating, though they may not sing the songs or use the paraphernalia.[94]

The tipi is entered any time after nightfall, with a preliminary clockwise circuit outside as in the sweatbath (all circuits inside must be clockwise also). Sometimes several
line up behind the leader, who prays briefly: "I am going into my place of worship. Be with
us tonight." Entrance however is often informal and made one by one, before the leader
comes in with his rattle and staff in one hand, and his paraphernalia-satchel[95] in the other;
he sits west of the fire, which has been started by the fireman, north of the door, who comes
in first of all. His drummer is south of him, to his right, his cedar-man (if there is one) north
and left. Others enter and informally take places, but after he is seated they kneel on the
right knee at the door for a moment, looking to him for permission to enter and be assigned
a place; the sponsor meanwhile may call out, "Come in! So-and-so," to these, informally
welcoming them. A tipi some twenty-five feet in diameter seats thirty people comfortably.
In summer the sides are raised to allow a breeze to blow through.

At the west center, horns to the east, is the crescent altar[96] (piétɒω) with a groove or
"path" (ɢ'ωmhon̩) along it from horn to horn, interrupted by a flat space in the center
where the "father peyote" is later to rest on sprigs of sage. The "path" symbolizes man's

[92] Mooney (*A Kiowa Mescal Rattle*, 64–65) describes a Kiowa gourd with the Peyote Woman, peyote,
moon, ash crescent, and Morning-Star under her feet heralding her morning approach with water.

[93] The basic rite is practically free from Christian symbolism. Some call the sage under the fetish a "cross";
some leaders make a cross under the water-bucket or in the water with feathers at midnight. Mooney wrote that
"many of the mescal eaters wear crucifixes . . . the cross representing the cross of scented leaves . . . while
Christ is the mescal goddess." But all crosses are not necessarily Christian. See Appendix 8.

[94] Older men carry real "feathers," but younger ones often bring small, ribbed, commercial, folding ladies'
fans—an interesting compromise. The Comanche nácihɪta "resting-stick, to walk," was formerly a bow, according to Hoebel, on war-party meetings, while the drum was formerly of wood. The Lipan formerly used a
bow, hit with a stick.

[95] Following a suggestion of Dr. Wissler, I made a special note of this and found that the ubiquitous satchel
is as much a "trait" of the peyote leader's paraphernalia as his staff or gourd or feathers.

[96] The Kiowa moon is crescent-shaped, the Comanche horseshoe-shaped—a significant point in tracing
provenience of altars in other tribes. Some Comanche garland the entire west side of the altar with sage, in which
the fetish rests. In war the Comanche used a shield as an altar. A cement moon made by a Choctaw adopted by
the Kiowa was an innovation much in disfavor, as was a Seminole altar made among the Caddo; the symbolical
interior of the latter was removed to make a simple crescent. Indeed, many Caddo are moving away from the
John Wilson symbolic cement moon.

path from birth (southern tip) to the crest of maturity and knowledge (at the place of the peyote) and thence downward again to the ground through old age to death (northern tip). The crescent, carefully shaped beforehand by the fireman out of clayey earth, also represents the mountain range of the origin story where sęmąyi or "Peyote Woman" first discovered the plant. East of it in a shelving depression is a fire, constantly mended by the "fire-chief" during the night to keep it in a worm-fence arrangement, the closest approximation to the ritual crescent-shape possible with straight sticks. The accumulating ashes are shaped with great care into another crescent between fire and altar. A "smokestick"[97] is kept smoldering in an east-west position close to the fire to light all cigarettes.

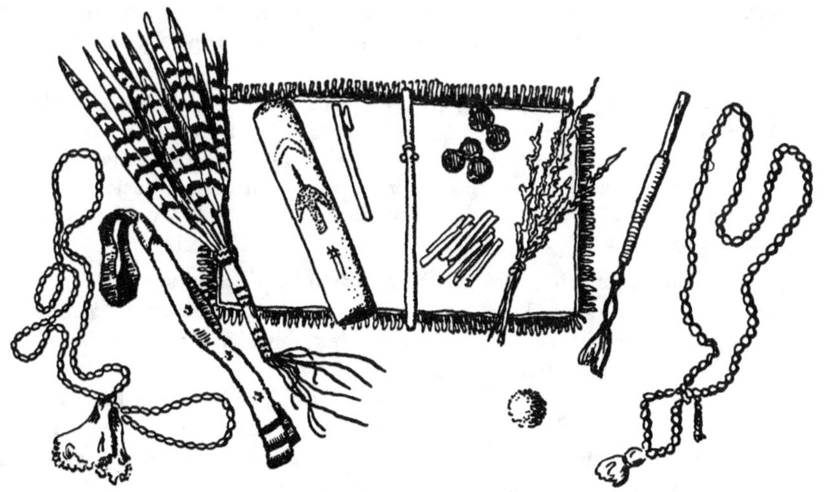

Fig. 2. Peyote paraphernalia. *Left to right*, Mescal bean necklace; "peyote" necktie from a strip of trade-blanket with selvage stripes, and beadwork representing peyote buttons; beaded and fringed pheasant feather fan; black velvet, gold-fringed altar cloth; smokestick carved with water bird, etc., eagle bone whistle; drum-stick; peyote buttons; corn husk cigarette "papers"; bundle of sage plumes; pile of powdered cedar incense; a beaded, fringed, and carved drumstick; mescal bean necklace.

All seated, the leader places the father peyote on the sage sprigs, orienting it by the thorn or mark made when he cut it.[98] After this the ceremony is considered begun, all

[97] Cf. the Huichol "pillow" for Grandfather Fire.

[98] Belo Kozad's (Kiowa) father peyote had been Quanah Parker's (Comanche) and was handed around after the meeting almost as an heirloom. Mumsika (Comanche) still preserves a famous peyote button of Kutubi's (Hoebel). Howard White Wolf (Comanche) has a peyote he addresses as "older brother" since it had cured him as a baby. Clyde Koko (Kiowa) quit peyote one Christmas night and gave Charley two father peyotes to take back to Laredo and plant with smoke and prayer; uncertain, the latter brought them back to find Koko had completely changed his mind: "I never made such a mistake in my life. If you'd done that it sure would have ruined me. I've learned a lesson!"

informal talking and joking ceases, and others entering are late-comers. Everyone begins to stare at the fetish peyote and the flickering fire.[99] Then the leader leans his eagle-humerus whistle against the west outside of the moon, mouth end up, takes out his cedar incense bag, gourd, tobacco, etc., and arranges them conveniently near him.

The first ceremony is smoking or praying together. The leader makes himself a cigarette of Bull Durham with corn husk "papers" dried and cut to shape, and passes the makings clockwise to the rest, including women.[100] His own made, the fireman presents the smoke-stick to the leader (who may first offer it courteously to his drummer) and this too is passed to the left. While all smoke, the leader prays: "beha′be sɛ̨i′ɒɔki (smoke, peyote power). Be with us when we pray tonight. Tell your father to look at us and listen to our prayers." He holds his cigarette mouth end toward the peyote and motions upward that it may smoke as he prays:

We are just beginning our prayer meeting. We want you to be with us tonight and help us. We want no one to be sick at this meeting from eating peyote. I will pause again at midmight to pray to you. I will pause again in the morning to pray to you. [Then he prays for the person who is sick or whose birthday the meeting celebrates or for relatives and participants.] If there are any rules connected with you, peyote, that we don't know of, forgive us if we should break them, as we are ignorant.

All pray silently to ɒómɒɔki, "earth-creator" or "earth-lord," and older men may add their prayers aloud after the leader. Then, following the leader, all snuff their cigarettes in the ground and place them on the west curve of the altar, outside, or at either horn; the fire-man may gather those of women, old people or visitors.

The incense-blessing ceremony immediately follows. The leader (or his "cedar-man") sprinkles some dried and rubbed cedar on the fire; then he makes four clockwise motions of the peyote bag toward the fire, takes out four buttons and passes the bag. Kneeling on both knees, he reaches down beneath the hides or blankets of the seat, and bruises a tuft of sage between his palms, and smelling it with deep inhalations, rubs his hands over and

[99] "The neophyte is constantly exhorted not to allow his eyes to wander, but to keep them fixed upon the sacred mescal in the center of the circle." (Mooney, *The Mescal Plant*, 11). Changing the cross-legged position too often, leaning backward on one elbow or the like to rest is considered frivolous, indicating lack of seriousness. One may leave the meeting at any time with permission, but it is best to try to wait till after midnight, unless there is the emergency of nausea from peyote. In leaving and entering the leader is always consulted to see if the path to ones seat is "clear," i.e., that no one is eating peyote or smoking; as smoking or eating peyote is concep-tually praying, it is extremely bad manners to pass between a person doing either and the altar fire, hence the need for instruction from the leader. This is old Plains etiquette (*Handbook of the American Indians*, 1: 442b). Thus, to avoid his having to pass before smokers, the brand might be passed backwards to the fireman; his move-ments in tending the fire never entail passing before anyone, and the feather given him by the leader symbolizes delegation of power to enter or leave as necessary for wood. But no one may pass between him and his seat while tending the fire.

[100] Corn shucks are standard, but Comanche and Shawnee sometimes use black-jack oak-leaves (just so the materials are native). Interestingly, the elbow pipe is never used in the Plains, but at Mescalero a pipe was used instead of the usual Southwestern cigarette—a case of reverse or reciprocal borrowing.

down his head, breast, shoulders and arms, with outward downward movements, ending with the thighs. Though the peyote may not yet have reached them, the others follow suit, reaching out their palms to absorb the blessing of the incense and rubbing themselves.

This done, all eat[101] their peyote, to the accompaniment of much spitting out of the woolly center of the buttons; hereafter during the night in the intermissions of singing, anyone can call for the peyote bag (the incense burning may or may not be repeated). Then more cedar is sprinkled on the fire and the leader makes four motions with the staff in his left hand and the rattle in his right toward the rising incense smoke.[102] The drummer motions similarly with the drumstick, pulling smoke from the fire to the drum. The leader takes a bunch of sagebrush from between the tipi-cover and pole behind him (previously prepared by the fireman), holds it with his staff and the singing begins.[103] The drummer shifts his

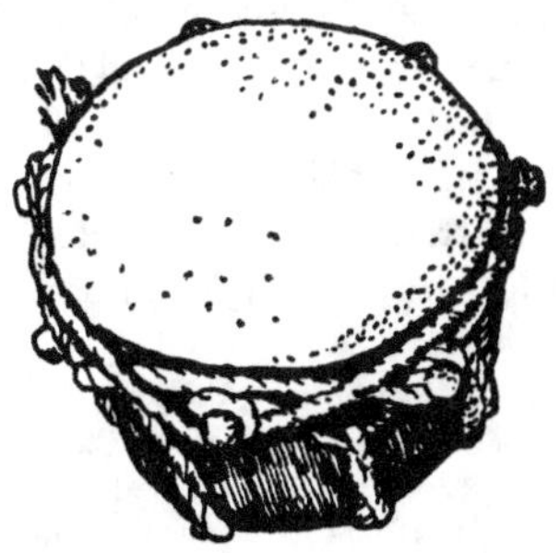

Fig. 3. Peyote drum with lashing around bosses.

left thumb over the drumhead or sloshes the water inside on it or blows on it to get the proper tension and tone, then the leader holds his staff and sage at arm's length between himself and the fire and rattles for the Hayätinayo or Opening Song.[104] The leader exchanges

[101] There are many individualized modes of eating peyote. Hoebel describes a Comanche way: chew into a ball, spit into palm of hand, rub in clockwise circle, swallow bolus. On the war-path one spits in his hands again and rubs his head and ears, the better to hear. Belo said he once ate a button when each person sang. Kiowa often make several clockwise motions of buttons toward the fire before eating, to prevent nausea, or hold the palms out toward it and rub themselves. One may request another to chew peyote for him if he has bad teeth or is sick, and swallow the bolus so prepared. The number of buttons eaten ranges from four to about thirty.

[102] Mooney (*Miscellaneous Notes*) mentions an odorous root from New Mexico, but is unclear about its use; cedar incense was universal in the writer's experience. The sage may be passed around also; some chew, eat it.

[103] Cf. the whisk of sage used in sweat-bathing; in view of other parallels, this otherwise functionless item in the peyote meeting should not be overlooked.

[104] This is the first of four sets of four songs each, sung at stated times in the ritual; the others are: Yáhiyano (midnight water song), Wakahó (daylight song for morning water) and Gayatina (Closing Song). All are Esikwita (Mescalero); all end with a fast unrhythmical shaking of the gourd. The two Kiowa groups seįhoṇ (Peyote Road) and Goihoṇ (Kiowa Road) differ in that in the former only the initial song of each group is set, in the latter all songs of all four groups are set.

his staff and rattle for the drum the latter always passing *under* the staff,[105] and the drummer sings four songs of his own choosing. The paraphernalia, staff preceding drum, are then passed to the left; each man sings to the drumming of the man on his right, and then himself drums for the man on his left.[106] This singing, rattling, and drumming forms the bulk of the ceremony during the night. At intervals older men pray aloud, with affecting sincerity, often with tears running down their cheeks, their voices choked with emotion, and their bodies swaying with earnestness as they gesture and stretch out their arms to invoke the aid of Peyote. The tone is of a poor and pitiful person humbly asking the aid and pity of a great power, and absolutely no shame whatever is felt by anyone when a grown man breaks down into loud sobbing during his prayer.[107]

About midnight the leader announces that he is going to put incense on the fire after the next four songs, and when he does, everyone blesses himself in the smoke. The announcement gives the fireman time to mend the fire and build up the ash moon[108] and sweep the cigarette butts into the fire. If the paraphernalia are north of the door they are passed backwards to the leader drum first, if at the south (i.e. past the door) clockwise and staff first as usual. Smoking stops, and the leader, to the drumming of his assistant, sings the Midnight Song.[109] When the first of the four is finished, the fireman (sometimes given a

[105] There are specific and detailed rules about passing the paraphernalia. Ordinarily, save in the case of the leader and his assistant at the opening song, etc., the paraphernalia (here the staff) never move counter-clockwise. The drum always passes inside the staff, i.e., proximally, the staff at arm's length in the left hand, the drum being passed under it with the right, when for any reason this occurs. The symbolism of this is perhaps obvious. A man may not be the singer more than once in a round, but he may be successively drummer, singer and drummer. (Though the staff may not go backward, the drum may, and in this case A receiving the staff, passes the drum with his right hand under his outstretched left, from the man on his right to the man on his left, B. A then sings to B's drumming; the staff is then passed forward from A to B, and the drum exchanged or passed backward from B to A, this time A drumming and B singing. Still going clockwise, the staff may be passed from B to C, and the drum from A to B, C singing this time and B drumming a second time.)

[106] At the east door the drum may be passed as stated to the second man so that the first man south of the door gets a chance to sing (because the fireman is too far away to drum for him) then an exchange and normal passing again, staff first. If a person right of the singer is old, sick, a woman or a visitor, he may request a friend to drum for him of the leader; the friend moves clockwise and sits by him temporarily. Women neither drum nor rattle nor sing (but like other participants they tend to sing softly favorite songs or the universally known set songs). Men try to make their four songs different from those previously sung, but favorites may be repeated.

[107] Kutubi (Comanche) in a war-party peyote meeting once visioned that they would be killed, and wept and upbraided peyote for doing this. H.H. (Wichita) during a meeting wept with total unrestraint for his brother and nephew, who had been hurt in an auto accident.

[108] The Kiowa sometimes make a hummingbird of the ashes (a prominent Kiowa family is called Hummingbird); cf. the Comanche, Oto, Shawnee, Yuchi and (?) Ute ash-birds.

[109] Peyote Road cultists: one fixed song, three optional; Kiowa Road: four fixed songs. The words of the standard song are unintelligible. Many tribes use their own language for these set songs (e.g., one Winnebago group). The schism in the Kiowa, if such it may be called, is excessively minor and communicants of one are freely welcomed in the other; though it purports (probably wrongly) to be the original and more pure rite, the Kiowa Road (led by Atape) is felt to be an uncalled-for variant.

feather for this errand by the leader) leaves, gets a bucket of water, returns, sets it in front of the fire and unfolds a blanket on which he sits in line with it facing west. The leader, finishing the second song, blows four increasingly loud blasts on the eagle wing-bone whistle (to imitate the water bird) then replaces it by the peyote and sings the last two songs. While his assistant holds the staff and gourd, he spreads an altar cloth just west of the fetish, and places on this the staff, gourd, sage and his fan, together with the "feathers" of communicants passed to him for this purpose; the drum is to the south of this, the drumstick, etc., on the cloth.

After cedar-incensing, the fireman makes a smoke, puffs four times and prays, thanking those responsible for the honor of being chosen fire-chief, and praying for the leader and his family, the sick and the absent. Next the leader prays, then the drummer, using the same cigarette, and to complete the figure of a cross, the man to the north or "cedar-man" prays. When the butt is placed by the altar, the fireman makes a circuit of the altar and passes the bucket to the man south of the door. Quiet conversation is permitted in the somewhat informal drinking period.[110] When the fireman has drunk, the leader passes back the fans and the paraphernalia to where the singing had been interrupted, and leaves the tipi. He goes about thirty feet east of the tipi, whistles four times and prays, repeating this at the south, west and north.[111] When four songs are completed, he returns, blessing himself in the incense smoke which the drummer throws on the fire.[112] Now is the preferred time to leave the tipi and stretch cramped legs. Singing continues as before until dawn.

As the first grey light appears, the leader tells the fireman to waken or notify the woman who is to bring the water (she has no special seat, if she has attended the meeting). The fireman always brings the midnight water, a woman that at dawn.[113] The leader whistles four times, even in the middle of a song, when the fireman tells him she has arrived outside. When the singer finishes his four songs, the leader calls for the paraphernalia and sings the

[110] Mooney (*The Mescal Plant*, 8) writes: "At midnight a vessel of water is passed around, and each takes a drink and sprinkles a few drops upon his head." We believe Mooney has slipped into error here, for this "baptismal" ceremony comes in the morning when the contents of the drum, not the bucket, are used. Non-Kiowa data likewise agree on this point. According to Mooney, the leader drinks first among the Comanche. The Caddo drink no water at this time: "One must suffer to peyote." Such abstemiousness with a thirst-producing substance like peyote suggests the psychological flavor of the vision quest. Note that Anhalonium means "without salt." "If there is suffering, this is the time. That's the reason I took a good rest so I could stand it. Many a time I have fallen over at this time. The hour of the Crucifixion. Everyone is suffering now . . . the dark hour" (Simmons, in *Peyote Road*).

[111] "The four whistles at midnight by the leader outside the tipi are to notify all things in all directions that they were having a meeting there at the center of the cross . . . calling the great power to be with us while we were drinking so that it could hear our prayers and bless us" (Hoebel, *Comanche Field Notes*).

[112] Others may be incensed when they reënter too, and everyone holds out his fan for the blessing. If a communicant is smoking when another reënters, it is good manners to place the cigarette on the ground temporarily that he may pass in front of him.

[113] There is a suggestion that this woman, usually the wife of the sponsor, symbolizes sẹimạyi or "Peyote Woman"; the Morning Star heralds her approach (see Mooney, *A Kiowa Mescal Rattle*).

four Morning Songs; after the first of these the woman enters, arranges a blanket and sits as did the fireman. Finishing the three remaining songs, the leader calls for feathers and spreads them with the paraphernalia on the altar cloth, as at midnight. A smoke is made for the woman, who thereupon prays, after which the leader and his assistants smoke it. Doctoring[114] is best done at this time; the leader may do this, or he may ask an older man to fan the patient with consecrated feathers from the altar cloth.

Then the fireman spills a little water before the fire, the woman drinks, and the bucket moves clockwise as before from south of the door. The woman makes a circuit of the altar, picks up her blanket and takes the bucket out. The feathers are passed out again, and the paraphernalia returned to the place of the next singers in the circle (because of such ritual interruptions, praying, passing of peyote, etc., a complete round of the drum requires two or three hours).

While waiting for the ritual breakfast, the meeting is again somewhat informal. Several women may leave to help the water-woman prepare the food, and younger men may go outside for a stroll and a secular smoke. Old men often lecture younger members on behavior at this time, "preaching" directly to a relative, and more indirectly to others.[115] When he has finished another old man may exhort: "You must do as that old man has said. He's had

[114] Doctoring is second only to the vision for individual knowledge and power in the Plains. Kiowa peyote doctors have special prestige among other tribes. In 1936 I sponsored a Kiowa meeting near Stecker, Oklahoma, for Belo Kozad to doctor Ernest Kokome who was suffering from tuberculosis. (Ernest had given me his trade-blanket beaded peyote-necktie in 1935 on the morning after a meeting at which I had admired it.) After midnight, Belo chewed four peyote and gave them to Ernest, fanning him with feathers and cedar incense; then he made a cross in front of the patient with a glowing coal, and, putting it in his mouth, blew all over the face and chest of the sick young man, who unbuttoned his shirt for the purpose. Next Belo fanned or batted him with his feathers, the patient holding up his palms to absorb the medicine virtue. Finally he took a mouthful of water and blew it on Ernest's head, praying and beseeching in the name of Jesus Christ for him to get well. Peyote gave Belo the power to doctor thus and not be burned by the coal.

Peyote was brought to the Creek, indeed, for doctoring by Jim Aton (a famous Kiowa peyote doctor). Much in demand, he has doctored in peyote meetings of the Yuchi, Shawnee, Kickapoo, Creek, Caddo, Osage, Comanche, Kiowa Apache, Kiowa, Mescalero Apache and Quapaw; also whites and Mexicans. His methods of doctoring have been described previously. The well-known Comanche peyote doctor, Jim Post-oak, "hollers like a bear in doctoring." (People often imitate the animal-sources of their power in the morning, in the midst of others' singing, either from peyote-"euphoria" or in praise of particularly good singing.) Peyote doctoring by Old Man Horse (Kiowa) influenced the Oto rite of the Church of the First-born too. Peyote can perform cures unassisted outside meetings also, as shown by the case of Tommy Cat who ate peyote over the protests of his nurse in a hospital and was cured.

[115] Polonian obviousness is usually the note in these harangues (sit up straight and keep awake in meetings, wear clean clothes and bathe before coming, wear a blanket, keep your mind on good things in the ceremony, don't look around the tipi, don't drink whiskey, don't lie to your wife or show off, but pray for your wife and children, respect old people, humble yourself, go home again if you come to a crowded meeting)—but occasionally specific admonitions are made. A Kiowa jokester, J. S., had had trouble with his wife, and was plainly talked to in meeting. Quanah Parker used to lecture young people in the morning. Long prayers are another means of making psychological transactions. Some tribes make individual public confessions at this time.

experience. What he's telling you is good." At this time too visitors are given opportunity to express gratitude for the hospitality of their host, who in turn thanks them for coming.

When the food arrives outside, the fireman notifies the leader, who calls for the para-phernalia and sings four songs, the last of which is the Quitting Song. The food meanwhile is passed in and placed in line with the father-peyote and fire, west-to-east thus: water, parched corn in syrup, fruit and meat.[116] No one sits east of it as in the water ceremonies. The four songs completed, the leader tells the drummer to unlace the drum, and all the paraphernalia are passed around (between the food and the fire at the east) for everyone to handle,[117] as an older woman ("because food is their life-work") or a Ten-Medicine keeper, who typically functions at such Kiowa group-prayers, asks a blessing. The leader then removes the father peyote from the altar, and when he puts it in his satchel with the rest of the paraphernalia the meeting is ended.

Complete social informality now reigns as the food is passed to the man south of the door and thence clockwise. Much joking[118] goes on during this meal, which has none of the seriousness of the Christian partaking of the Host. When the fireman has finished eating, at the leader's instruction, he leads the line out of the tipi.[119] The tipi may be taken down immediately, or moved bodily a little, but the older men drift back into its shade and lie around talking and exchanging peyote experiences.[120] As meetings are ordinarily held on Saturday nights, Sunday forenoon is free for such visiting, talking and dozing under arbors. Nearly everyone stays for a secular dinner at noon, and they take home what they cannot eat; sometimes other guests come who have not attended the meeting.

[116] Mooney, *The Mescal Plant*, 8.

[117] Some rattle the marbles of the drum, put them in the mouth and spit them into the palm. Members commonly "baptize" themselves with the drum-water, using the drumstick to moisten the palm and rubbing the hair, face, chest, arms and thighs as in blessing with cedar incense; some paint themselves with the charcoal in the drum. The remaining water in the drum is poured along the moon. The sage under the peyote may be passed to the patient, if there is one, or it may be requested for absent ailing relatives.

[118] Sometimes the stories have a moral point; the following was told by O. W. (Comanche) to E. R. (Dela-ware): the leader of a Wichita Easter meeting had a fine watch, costing from $150 to $200. At daylight, before water time, wanting to display it, he put it down by the feathers. A man to the north was singing and making vigorous punches toward the peyote. When he looked at his watch later, "it was just a mess of works in there loose, and the hands dropped off," though nobody had touched it. "It don't pay to go in there and then try to show off."

[119] "The first shall be last and the last shall be first." Hoebel says the Comanche fire-chief takes one step out-side, turns completely around once, and continues his way, the others exiting in a straight fashion. Cf. the Huichol turns.

[120] A Comanche told me a Kiowa ate a lot of peyote once and tried to sing a Comanche song. He sang the wrong words, which meant "Mentula exposita est, Mentula exposita est!" (Cf. the Oto jokes about songs.) A typical experience of Belo Kozad involves the hearing of a new peyote song, psychological anxiety, a moral, and an explanation about power-getting: A peyote song, without words, once came to him in a vision. He seemed to be in the south, in soft grass. In the distance he saw a man, whom he followed. He did not know it, but this man represented Temptation. Belo followed the man, who was leading him off somewhere. Suddenly the man kicked backwards with his foot [a familiar folkloristic element] and went on. When Belo approached he

Having now characterized the Huichol-Tarahumari type-rite for Mexico, the Lipan-Mescalero for the transitional nomad Southwest, and the Kiowa-Comanche as the historical prototype for the Plains, we may attempt a comparison and contrasting of them.

In Mexico as a whole "curing" is perhaps the most salient characteristic, while both curing and doctoring are conspicuous in Mescalero. In the Plains, while doctoring is an important feature it is by no means indispensable.[121] Peyotism in Mexico, therefore, has a *tribal* character, while in Mescalero the ceremony is a *forum for rival shamans*—a trait not altogether absent in early Plains rites—and in the Plains peyotism has a *societal* nature. These facts have an important bearing on the cultural manifestations of the physiological action of peyote. In Mexico visions are turned to the uses of prophecy;[122] in Mescalero they enable a shaman to detect rival witchcraft; while in the Plains, visions are a source of individual power. These categories should not be made too rigid, however, for clairvoyance, if not prophecy, as well as witchcraft anxiety are known for early Plains peyotism, and on the other hand, peyote medicine-power is a source of Mescalero shamanistic rivalry. Yet as indications of relative emphasis these statements might be allowed to stand.

The Mexican symbolisms point to an association with hunting, agriculture and gathering activities, and the typical anxiety expressed in the religion is the desire for rain. In Mescalero, peyote is the focal point for the warfare of antagonistic powers, and expresses the mutal suspicion of formerly small local groups; the intense and ever-present anxiety is the fear of aggression and reprisal by witchcraft. In the early Plains peyote ceremonies, associations with warfare were prominent (influenced no doubt by a forerunner of peyotism there, the mescal bean ceremonialism), though in later times this element had become so nearly absent that Mooney could point quite properly to the "international" character of the cult in his time.[123]

---

found apples there; he refused to take one. Further on the man kicked back with his other foot. This time Belo found dollar bills and playing cards; these he refused too. A third time he found pictures of beautiful girls in various poses, but he withstood temptation. Finally he came to the top of a hill, over the brow of which the man had disappeared ahead of him. Then he heard the man talk to him from behind: "The apples, the cards, and the pictures all meant temptation. You have withstood them all. Upon the top of this hill you will find good fortune if you take this peyote." Belo went up and saw there a terrible chasm, crossed by a bridge of a single tipi pole. The man said that the pole had to be crossed with four steps; if he did this he would have great curing power. The man danced forward and backward across the pole to show Belo, singing this song the while. But Belo was afraid to cross the chasm and turned back thus not acquiring the curing power.

[121] Indeed, among some groups like the Caddo, doctoring is expressly absent.

[122] In Mescalero, too, "prophecy and advice were no small part of the performance. It was rarely that his power did not vouchsafe the shaman some reassuring information concerning the longevity of his patient, the number of grandchildren with which he would be blessed, and the future state of his fortunes." They also controlled the weather thus, found lost objects, located the enemy, etc., but doctoring was the main feature of Mescalero peyote meetings.

[123] Shonle (*Peyote: Giver of Visions*, 57) notes that peyote was latterly a reservation phenomenon, when tribal enmities were gone. The Ghost Dance had been anti-White; peyotism was a compromise, and the friendly inter-tribal contacts growing out of the Ghost Dance could now be exploited.

Areal contrasts in minor points are no less striking. Dancing was conspicuous in Mexico, less important transitionally, and on the whole lacking in the Plains. Painting of a symbolic nature was ritually significant in Mexico; in the Plains individual styles were dictated by peyote visions. Peyotism in Mexico is a seasonal matter, but in the Plains the rite occurs the year around (in the south the trip for peyote may have been associated more with the ritual salt pilgrimage, in the north with the ritualized war journeys; parallels are also suggested in the Maricopa ritualized mountain-sheep hunting and Navaho deer hunting).

In Mexico peyote was a tribal affair and women participated on equal terms with the men in dancing, etc. In Mescalero, women were excluded from meetings, as in the Plains also originally. The rite was held principally outdoors in Mexico, and in a tipi transitionally and in the Plains—a patio arrangement in Mexico, and an altar centering around the "moon" in the Plains. Ritual racing and ball games[124] are part of Mexican peyotism, but not elsewhere. Smoking is inconspicuous in Mexico, but in the Plains it has been important enough to involve church schisms.[125] Huichol peyote had no drum, though elsewhere in Mexico a wooden drum was used, while in the Plains the water-drum (intrusive from the Southwest) is universal. The rasp is Mexican, but the Plains rite has the gourd rattle and eagle wing-bone whistle in addition to the drum. The "staff" is a special problem in the Plains.

The Huichol and Tarahumari have a squirrel fetish in addition to the fetish plant; the Plains have only the latter. Ceremonial drunkenness with tesvino, etc., is an integral part of Mexican "curing"; in the Plains peyote and alcohol are so far mutually exclusive that the familiar propaganda calls the first a specific against the second. The alleged aphrodisiac virtue of peyote is a Mexican belief; but curiously enough in Mexico, where many "peyotes" were said by natives to be aphrodisiac, Lumholtz pronounced *Lophophora williamsii* definitely anaphrodisiac; while in the Plains, where the natives most strenuously deny this virtue for peyote, enemies of the cult most consistently claim that it produces aphrodisiac orgies.[126]

In Mexico the shaman alone sings, though his assistants may "spell" him; in the Plains all male participants drum and rattle. In Mescalero, though the drum circles the tipi, the staff and gourd remain with the leader. Finally, Mexican and Mescalero peyotism are almost wholly free of Christian elements; so too were the early Plains rites diffusing from the Kiowa-Comanche, though in the John Wilson rite, the Oto Church of the First-born

---

[124] Cf. Tamaulipecan rites and the black-drink ball-game of the Southeast. (The black drink was as nearby as the Karankawa.) The Southwest-Southeast connections are more than superficial; Beals (*Comparative Ethnology*, 142) believes there is a probable connection of Southwest-Mexican alcoholic drinks with the Southeastern black drink.

[125] Curiously the cigarette of the region farther west is universal in the intrusive Plains peyote rite, while at Mescalero the stone elbow pipe is passed around in the calumet fashion of the Plains in one leader's ceremony.

[126] Is this a culture-environmental problem?—for the same substance which was spectacularly aphrodisiac in Lame Deer, Montana, was stubbornly anaphrodisiac in Philadelphia. Unfortunately for the accusing school of thought, Bennett and Zingg's trait-distribution tables indicate a negative association of sexual promiscuity and the ritual use of peyote in Mexico.

(and its successor, the Native American Church) and the Winnebago Rave-Hensley variant, Christian symbolism and interpretations are frequent.

Common elements are numerous: the ceremonial trip for peyote (more elaborate in
Mexico, to be sure), the meeting held at night, the fetish peyote, the use of feathers and
the abundance of symbolisms connected with birds, the ritual circuit, ceremonial fire and
incensing, water ceremonies, the "Peyote Woman," morning "baptism" or "curing" rites,
"talking" peyote, abstinence from salt, ritual breakfast, singing, tobacco ceremonials, public
confession of sins, Morning Star symbolisms, and (for nothern Mexico) the crescent moon[127]
altar. The fear of being blinded by the peyote-fuzz is Mescalero, Lipan and Plains, and the
water-drum is shared by both non-peyote Southwestern groups and those of the Plains who
have the peyote rite. The use of parched corn in sugar water, boneless, sweetened meat and
fruit for the "peyote breakfast" may be regarded as universal for peyotism, wherever found.

[127] Opler says that "in no other Mescalero ceremony is a mound of earth in the shape of a crescent found.
On the other hand, crude earth tracings did grace a Mescelero rite occasionally, and the moon was much in
evidence in ritual song and design. The staff of the peyote shaman seems an innovation at first thought; yet it has
a counterpart in the 'old age stick' held by the singer in the girl's puberty rite." The gourd in Mescalero has
exclusively peyote associations. On the whole, the standard Plains ceremony appears to have taken shape among
the Lipan-Mescalero. But Curtis (*North American Indian* 19: 199–200) says that the White Mountain Apache
were the first United States users and that "the ritual [in the United States] is obviously copied from the
Wichita ceremonial form."

COMPARATIVE STUDY OF PLAINS PEYOTISM

We have now compared the basic Plains rite with that of Mexico and the transitional Lipan-Mescalero. Yet an independent development of this basic rite in the Plains and a multiform flowering of the cult there, influenced by older cultural concepts of a different nature, necessitates a discussion of more minute variants within the region. In other words, we have determined in the previous section the major variations of the peyote ceremony as aboriginally constituted, and now trace the fate of the cult as it invaded a different cultural terrain and came under the influence of other culture patterns, including the Christian.[1]

Trip for Peyote. A typical nine-day trip was made by the Cheyenne in 1914 from Watonga, Oklahoma, to Laredo, Texas. Ten "peyote boys" contributed the total cost of $61.85, and several suitcases full of buttons were brought back (about 1,400 each); these were bought from a White dealer in Laredo.[2] Another time a Southern Cheyenne, then President of the Native American Church, brought back a special trailer full of peyote from Romer, Texas. The northern Plains tribes make infrequent pilgrimages for the plant, depending largely upon supplies shipped from Texas or bought from Indians nearer the source. One Wichita leader sold 40 acres of land to buy a car in which to make a trip to Mousquis, his fourth or fifth such trip in about ten years. An early Comanche party going for peyote in the Apache region had much the character of a war journey; as described by Hoebel it involved a clairvoyant discovery of the enemy, prophecy of the outcome, and a horse-raid. Typically, however, the Kickapoo "chip in" money for peyote pilgrimages, and precede this with prayers for the safe-keeping of the travellers.

Rite at Site. The Lipan[3] say that

peyote is pretty hard to find when you are looking for it . . . a person who is not used to it doesn't recognize it though he is in the middle of a whole clump of peyote. Once he sees one, another appears and so on until they all come out just like stars. If you are having a hard time finding them you do this: when you find just one by itself you eat it. When it takes effect, when you get a little dizzy, you will hear a noise like the wind from a certain direction. Go over there . . . from the place where the noise is coming you will get many peyote plants.

Mrs. Voegelin[4] reports an interesting Shawnee concept:

You can get power by visiting the peyote patch in Texas, and telling it at evening that you want help to cure people and get medicine. You sprinkle tobacco there. The next morning, when the

---

[1] For convenience of reference I have followed with all possible care the sequence of the development and appearance of elements laid down in the Kiowa-Comanche type-rite (above), of which the following paragraphs are largely comparative discussions.

[2] Mooney, *Miscellaneous Notes*, 40.

[3] Opler, *Lipan Apache Field Notes*.

[4] Erminie Voegelin, *Shawnee Field Notes*.

Morning Star comes up, the person goes to the patch where he put the tobacco and when he comes close he hears a rattler rattling. If he has nerve enough to go over there, likely he does not find a snake there, but just something to scare him. If he does find a snake there, he grabs the rattlesnake (which is coiled up on top of the medicine) and takes it off and then he picks one peyote button from that place. Then he goes to another bunch and picks another button . . . . Perhaps at the fourth spot where he picks his fourth button, the snake is there again and he must remove it. . . . Jim Clark related this defying of a rattlesnake to the obtaining of another very powerful herb in the old days.[5]

The typical Plains gathering ceremony has been described to the writer for the Kiowa, Wichita, and Kickapoo: one sits west of the first peyote found and makes a smoke-prayer before orienting the plant with a thorn or mark that it may be properly used as a "father peyote" later; this first plant shows the gatherer where to find more.

Vowing of Meetings. Spier has traced the pattern of "vowing" the Sun Dance in the Plains and it is interesting to note the persistence of this trait in the peyote ceremony. It is particularly a pattern of the Algonquian-speaking peoples; but we have recorded it for the Kiowa and Wichita as well as the Shawnee, Kickapoo, and Northern Cheyenne.[6]

Time of Meetings. Peyote meetings are generally held Saturday nights so that the fore-noon of the following Sunday may be spent relaxing and talking under a "shade"; but the Comanche and Seminole sometimes set theirs for Sunday night, following the White pattern for religious meetings.[7] The Caddo, Tonkawa and Lipan often had four meetings on suc-cessive nights, particularly for sick persons; the Caddo sometimes mark four birthdays with meetings a year apart. Holiday meetings on Easter, New Year's, Thanksgiving and Christmas are common; an Arapaho meeting was once held with a Christmas tree. Many tribes like the Northern Cheyenne drink tea outside meetings, when practising songs or "to sharpen one's mind" when solving some particularly knotty personal problem, but some groups maintain that it is forbidden to use peyote outside meetings, for it would be useless then, even for doctoring. The frequency of meetings throughout the year would be difficult to ascertain, though there is no seasonal restriction as in Mexico; perhaps one or two meetings a month in each tribe might be an average number when the whole year is considered.

Purpose. Doctoring of the sick is the commonest reason given for calling a meeting; but though infrequently expressed as an official motive, the vision-producing physiological effect of peyote is probably the major reason. However, so various are the stated purposes of meetings, that one is led to conclude that when a man wishes to have one, he ordinarily finds little difficulty in discovering a reason for it. A Lipan Apache said,

[5] Ritual gathering of plants is not unknown elsewhere; see Mooney, *The Sacred Formulas.*

[6] See G. A. Dorsey in *Handbook of the American Indians,* 2: 650a (Sun Dance), as well as Spier's *The Sun Dance of the Plains Indians.*

[7] Hoebel says the Comanche formerly did not have all night meetings because of the danger of attack while under the influence of the drug.

In the early days they just had a good time for one night. It was not used as a curing ceremony then . . . . At first they wanted to have good visions, that's what they were after. But then, recently, they began to use it as a medicine for sick people.[8]

The Kickapoo and Caddo do not doctor in meetings; the latter pray for the sick, however, and commonly have four meetings in close succession for this purpose, as well as on the first four anniversaries of a child's birth or a man's death.

The primary reason for Northern Cheyenne meetings is social, with doctoring second; they knew of meetings held for rain, but despite prolonged droughts in their region never made them themselves. Comanche formerly held meetings to exercise clairvoyance about the enemies' position, to obtain protection from them[9] and to ascertain by prophecy the outcome of battle; like the Mescalero they also held meetings to divine and combat sorcery, and one meeting was held to celebrate the surveying of their lands. Delaware meetings were for the welfare of the community in general, to show hospitality to visiting friends and to mark the first four anniversaries of a death.[10] Kickapoo hold meetings to obtain rain, in consolation for a death, to name a child[11] and for a dead person.[12]

Mescalero ate peyote to locate the enemy, to find lost objects and to foretell the future as well as for curing.[13] The Osage have funeral meetings, and meetings to "see the face of Jesus" or the faces of their dead relatives;[14] the Oto say they can see the deceased in meetings too. In the Oto Church of the First-born, Jonathan Koshiway baptized, married, and conducted funerals; the Pawnee have no funeral meetings but celebrate birthdays, New Year's Eve, Christmas and Easter.[15]

A typical Ponca meeting attended at White Eagle was to doctor a sick child with peyote tea. Another, a Shawnee meeting at McCloud, had been vowed if the soldiers' bonus legislation passed Congress. One Shawnee held meetings for his eldest daughter yearly for thirteen years; sometimes they hold purely social meetings and for health and doctoring, but not for rain. Wichita, on the other hand, set up meetings to pray for rain and good crops, on anniversaries, and for doctoring; and a Wichita "bonus" meeting was held in 1936. Prophecy has been present in Wichita meetings also. The Winnebago[16] have death-consolation

---

[8] Opler's data suggest that even the vision-seeking motive is recent among the Lipan.

[9] The Lipan prayed for protection from their enemies as well as for health and long life.

[10] Petrullo, 48. The mourning council meeting was not unfamiliar in pre-peyote times. One such council was held for Tarhe, chief priest of the Wyandot, at Upper Sandusky, in the old days, attended by all the tribes of Ohio, the Indiana Delaware and the Seneca of New York (*Handbook of the American Indians*, 2: 294).

[11] Four older men pray and the child is passed clockwise around the tipi as every one present calls out its name.

[12] Meetings are held *for* the corpse, which is present "facing east" (head west) in the meeting; at the funeral next day he faces west. The writer omitted to attend an Osage meeting at Hominy because it was a funeral meeting.

[13] Cf. the uses of datura.

[14] La Flesche, *Peyote as Used in Religious Worship*, 21.

[15] A favorite Indian holiday in Oklahoma is Memorial Day, when graves are lavishly decorated.

[16] Densmore, *The Peyote Cult.*

meetings, death-anniversary meetings and meetings to doctor the sick. At Taos[17] meetings are for curing, or simply when "someone thinks they ought to have a peyote meeting."

Participants. The Carrizo had two women by the door to bring water into the meeting, but the Lipan permitted no women to be present or even erect the tipi. In the early days the Kiowa, Comanche, Tonkawa, Sauk, and Oto prohibited women from attending, and only old men used peyote, but forty or fifty years ago women started coming in to be doctored and gradually came in for other reasons, though they could not use the ritual paraphernalia; under no circumstances may a menstruant woman enter.[18] The restriction against women appears to apply only to groups who early had peyote, when it still had much of the flavor of a warriors' society about it; for example, the Arapaho, Cheyenne, Ponca, Kickapoo, Mescalero, Shawnee, Taos and Wichita apparently always allowed women to attend.[19] In the Iowa meeting the women formed the outer of two concentric circles, the men the inner, and the former were allowed only two buttons.[20] Women never use eagle feather fans.

Some tribes, like the Caddo, still have a strong objection to the presence of White men in meetings, but other groups do not object to White men as such.[21] A number of tribes have a bias against the attendance of Negroes, but this is not the case at least with the Kiowa, Wichita, and Kickapoo.[22]

Visiting. All Indians, however, of whatever tribe, are welcome in the meetings of all other tribes.[23] For example, at a Shawnee leader's meeting at McCloud there were 12 Kickapoo, 6 Shawnee, 3 Caddo, 2 Kiowa, 2 Whites, a Wichita, a Seminole, a Sauk-and-Fox, an Oto, a Potawatomi and a Negro—a not untypical aggregate.[24] Individual users visit around a great deal in trying to "learn about peyote"; an old Kickapoo user had been in meetings of the Arapaho, Cheyenne, Caddo, Delaware, Wichita, Apache, Kiowa, Osage, Yuchi, Sauk-and-Fox, Oto, Iowa, Shawnee, Comanche, Pawnee and Ponca. Indeed, the very origin legend of peyote indicates a period of beginning inter-tribal contacts, and peyotism

[17] Parsons, *Taos Pueblo*, 12 ff.

[18] Only two cases are known of women who fully participated in meetings: Dog-woman (deceased), wife of John Red-turtle (Cheyenne) sang and beat the drum; a woman at Taos, Apekaum says, sings in meetings like men.

[19] Kroeber, *The Arapaho*, 398–99; Opler, *The Influence of Aboriginal Pattern*; Parsons, *Taos Pueblo*; the rest field investigation.

[20] Skinner, *Societies of the Iowa*, 725.

[21] One William Richard Nebuchadnezzar West ate peyote with the Kiowa for years. Petrullo mentions one Pat Noonigan who ate with the Delaware, and the Shawnee had a white participant for some twenty years. Early white familiarity with peyote in Texas must be postulated to account for its use by Texas Rangers in the Civil War (Lumholtz, 1: 358).

[22] A Negro brought by the Kiowa drummed and sang along with the rest in a Shawnee meeting; the former existence of a Negro "peyote" church near Tulsa argues for a considerable amount of such contact.

[23] Again accepting the Caddo, who are over-suspicious for reasons discussed later.

[24] The most homogeneous meeting I attended was a special tribal Wichita one which, nevertheless, was attended by three Kiowa, four Comanche, and two Whites, beside fourteen Wichita.

in later days became the specific vehicle of inter-tribal friendships, when mutual warfare disappeared.

Place of Meeting. The typical place of meeting for the Plains, as well as Taos, Mescalero, and Lipan, is the tipi. The Arapaho-Winnebago peyote tipi has twelve poles, symbolizing the earth.[25] The Pawnee have special painted tipis for peyote, as in the Ghost Dance; and, like the Pawnee, the Wichita and Winnebago dismantle the tipi immediately at the end of a meeting.[26] The Osage, Quapaw, Omaha, Northern Winnebago and others[27] have special peyote churches, or "round houses" (really polygonal), and many, like the Taos, hold winter meetings in the home of some member.

But meetings were held elsewhere too in the past. The Carrizo had meetings in the open within a circle of sticks. The first Kiowa meetings took place within a circle of upright poles with canvas stretched around it, open to the sky; Comanche also used simple wind-breaks as do even now the Northern Cheyenne, who sometimes also hold the ceremony on a hill-top in the open.[28] The Caddo have held meetings in a canvas-covered subconical "stick house" holding over forty people in two rows; and the Bannock of Idaho, on account of opposition to peyotism, have held meetings in backwoods log-houses—in short, the holding of the meeting in a tipi, while common and typical, is not ritually required.

Bathing. The Lipan customarily washed their hair in yucca suds before a meeting, and perfumed themselves with mint. In the Plains and at Mescalero they take a sweatbath or a bath with water; the Arapaho[29] plunge once against the current and once with it, then rub themselves with teaxuwine^n or waxuwahan and other scented plants. The Osage build a sweat lodge as an integral part of their church, in a direct line east of it. A man in Hominy specializes in giving Osage old-style sweat baths, but some of them somewhat ostentatiously travel to Claremore, a hundred miles away, to take "radium baths" before meetings.

Painting. Face and body painting is recorded for the Arapaho, Comanche, Delaware, Kiowa, Oto, Shawnee, Tonkawa, Wichita and Winnebago, yellow being the commonest color used by the Arapaho and Comanche.[30] A Kiowa story tells of the acquiring of

[25] Radin, *The Winnebago Tribe*, 415.

[26] Murie, *Pawnee Indian Societies*, 638; Densmore, *The Peyote Cult*.

[27] Radin, *A Sketch of the Peyote Cult*, 2; *The Winnebago Tribe*, 388.

[28] Hoebel, *Northern Cheyenne Field Notes*.

[29] Kroeber, *The Arapaho*, 399; Smith (Mrs. Maurice G.), *A Negro Peyote Cult*, 452, note 10; see also *Handbook of the American Indians*, 2: 661.

[30] Kroeber, *The Arapaho*, 404–405; see also Petrullo, *The Diabolic Root*, 101. Shawnee sometimes paint their temples; Oto use red bars below side burns. Delaware examples from Speck: red hair-part, red-blue-red-blue-red horizontal lines over the bridge of the nose and cheeks (Wilson's Big Moon meetings); red and blue lines below and at corners of eyes ("crying for repentance"); green zigzags in yellow cheek spots, two red and one blue line at corner of eyes; all red chin bounded by a blue semilunar arc on the upper lip and up the cheeks (representing the altar "moon"); and blue red-bordered dots on each cheek-bone and forehead representing peyote-buttons (a woman's design).

an individual paint design in a vision of a red bird which turned into a man. The Tonkawa even painted the fuzz on the top of the fetish peyote red, according to Opler. Painted stripes symbolize for the Wichita the extent of one's experience with peyote: a beginner paints the part of the hair yellow and puts one blue line on his face, adding up to four finally: "He's supposed to know something then." Both men and women painted for Winnebago meetings.[31]

Clothing and Headdress. Formerly native dress was prescribed for Plains peyote meetings, and even now a blanket (in summer a folded sheet) among male communicants and a shawl among female is common—to symbolize affiliation with "blanket Indians." Younger men, otherwise in ordinary White dress, often wear a "peyote-necktie" made of an old-fashioned trade blanket, beaded, and with the selvage-stripes as a design; soft neckerchiefs drawn through rings with "water-bird" and "Morning-Star" designs are also common. The Arapaho[32] water-woman wears a symbolically painted buckskin dress; men wear special wrist-bands and headdresses of yellow hammer and woodpecker feathers. Carrizo men wore only a loincloth in meetings, not even moccasins; the women attendants wore red blankets, the one to the north with woodpecker feathers and the one to the south with a red flicker feather.[33] Iowa wear Kiowa-Comanche style leggings, the thongs of which are knotted with "red medicine" or mescal beans.[34]

A turban or head-scarf has been observed among the Delaware, Shawnee, Kickapoo, Wichita and Winnebago,[35] but the otterskin cap of the Kiowa and Winnebago is optional. At Taos the variant dress of the "peyote boys" has become a symbol of the strife of the old and the new. The young men who use peyote cut out the seats of their trousers, thus converting them into a G-string and leggings and necessitating a blanket, and let their hair grow in Plains fashion.[36] Among older Osage men the "roached" style of scalp lock was formerly still in vogue, but the younger men who have adopted the peyote religion wear their hair long, parted and braided on each side with ribbons and yarn.[37] Among the Winnebago, on the other hand, the progressivism of the peyote cult demands that long hair be cut, and Crashing Thunder discovered that it was a "shame to wear long hair."[38]

Ritual Restrictions. Salt may not be eaten on the day that peyote is consumed among the Huichol, Tarahumari, Arapaho, Comanche, Kickapoo, Wichita, etc.; the distributional gaps are more likely gaps in our information than lack of the taboo, which is probably

[31] Radin, *Crashing Thunder,* 182.

[32] Kroeber, *The Arapaho,* 403, 405.

[33] Opler, *Lipan Apache Field Notes.*

[34] Skinner, *Ethnology of the Ioway Indians,* 261.

[35] Densmore, *Winnebago Songs of the Peyote Ceremony.*

[36] Parsons, *Taos Pueblo,* 119.

[37] Speck, *Notes on the Ethnology of the Osage,* 163.

[38] Radin, *Crashing Thunder* 186-87.

universal at least among the early Plains users of peyote.[39] It is also considered hygenically if not ethically unwise to use peyote in connection with alcoholic drinks; indeed, many insist that the former cures addiction to the latter. The Arapaho[40] did not bring sharp instruments into a peyote meeting, a taboo elsewhere unreported.

Officials. The "road chief" is the most important individual in a meeting. Kroeber writes of the Arapaho leader in a manner which might apply to any Plains leader:[41]

The leader of each ceremony is sole director of it. He may . . . base [his ceremony] partly on visions during previous ceremonies. In other cases, he follows ceremonies that he has participated in, changing or adding details to suit his personal ideas. No two ceremonies conducted by different individuals are therefore exactly alike; but the general course of all is quite similar.

We do not agree with Petrullo that the leader is a mere "figurehead." Indeed, as we shall see later, the variation in ceremonies is a function of leadership far more than of tribal affiliation. The leader has full authority to change the ceremony in any way he wishes, and his permission must be asked and secured even in such little matters as leaving the tipi temporarily; even the fireman, his chief assistant, constantly consults with him and receives directions.[42]

In fact, peyote leadership is a matter bringing much prestige, and in these days is a major means of advancement among one's fellows. John Rave, Albert Hensley, Jonathan Koshiway, Quanah Parker and John Wilson find parallels to a less degree in all peyote leaders, and rare is the man who does not seize the apportunity presented by his authority to introduce some change, however trifling, into the ceremony.[43] Each tribe has a limited number of recognized peyote leaders which can be named. The Shawnee, for example, have nine only and the Pawnee have only eight recognized leaders in a population of eight hundred. In the case of the Osage the number of leaders is further limited by the number

[39] Anhalonium means "without salt." The salt-taboo is a common Southwestern one, unconnected with peyotism there (e.g., Kroeber, *The Seri*, 45) but associated in Plains peyotism with such borrowed Southwestern traits as the water-drum.

[40] Kroeber, *The Arapaho*, 400.

[41] *Idem*, 398. "The slight variations in pattern," writes Opler of the Mescalero, ". . . undoubtedly owe their existence to the fact that there are a number of peyote shamans, each eager to assert his own individuality and 'way' by some minor departure or 'rule'."

[42] The peyote shaman in Mexico was certainly no figurehead, and the peyote leaders of the Carrizo, Tonkawa, Lipan and Mescalero were important in preventing rivalry.

[43] The authority of the leader finds ritual reflection throughout the John Wilson "moon": e.g., only the leader might smoke and pray, and others calling for smokes were frowned upon as presumptuous. Further, John Wilson's "moon" contains his "grave" alongside that of Jesus Christ, and his initials W. (Wilson) or M. (Moonhead). The altar, indeed, represented Moonhead's face; he even prescribed face-painting styles with his initials in them. A man equated with Jesus Christ is scarcely a negligible person. Koshiway (Oto) performed marriages and baptisms and conducted funerals in the Church of the First-born. The point is just as well demonstrated by the negative cases of those who aspired to peyote leadership and failed. Even the local Pawnee President of the Native American Church, James Sun-eagle, does not lead meetings.

of permanent "churches" available; Murphy lists eighteen "East Moons" on the reservation and three "West Moons."

Originally the officials in a peyote meeting appear to have been limited to the "road-chief," drummer, and "fire-chief."[44] The "cedar-chief" is a later development. Among the Winnebago the leader, drummer and cedar-man symbolize respectively the Father, the Son and the Holy Ghost, and the leader gives the drummer his staff even as God delegated authority to Jesus.[45] In the Quapaw "Big Moon" the officials number eight: three firemen north of the door (required since every person must be fanned with feathers every time he reënters the tipi), the leader, drummer and cedar-man west of the altar, and in addition "one good man" at each arm of the altar-crucifix cross-piece.

Economics. On the basis of 13,300 peyote users in 1922 (and the number has since substantially increased) in the United States alone, it is clear that the cult is of economic significance in a number of ways. The price of peyote from dealers in Laredo, who supply most of the northern Plains and Great Basin users, is from $2.50 to $5.00 a thousand buttons; it is said that "the inhabitants of the small town of Nuevo Laredo, on the Mexican side of the Rio Grande, derive their livelihood almost exclusively from the peyote trade." Schultes estimates $20,000 as the annual commercial transactions involved north of the Rio Grande.[46]

The Tarahumari used to combine their peyote journeys with trading and other commercial transactions, but the trip was otherwise profitable since peyote itself commanded a good price; Lumholtz says one plant cost a sheep at one time in Tarahumariland, and he himself was asked $10 for a dozen plants.[47] The Huichol sold part of their harvest sometimes to non-pilgrims.[48]

In the Plains the sponsor usually meets the expense of a meeting himself, but some groups like the Oto pass around a vessel in the morning for a "free-will offering." At Taos the peyote chief bears the expense, though others may make contributions to help defray the cost. The chief expense at Tarahumari, as elsewhere, is the sacrificial beef. The total cost of a meeting varies considerably, according to the number of persons fed at the secular meal the next day. Meetings that Mooney attended in 1918 cost $15, $58 (including a beef

[44] Delaware meetings appear to have had only road-man and fire-guard (Harrington, *Religion and Ceremonies*, 188) but this may be an error of omission. The Kiowa, Pawnee, Cheyenne, Iowa, and Taos all have the "cedar-man" in addition.

[45] Radin, *A Sketch of the Peyote Cult*, 3; *The Winnebago Tribe*, 388. Densmore (*Winnebago Songs of the Peyote Ceremony*), lists only three leaders but may not be counting the fireman. See Skinner, *Societies of the Ioway*, 724; Parsons, *Taos Pueblo*, 62 ff.

[46] Schultes, *Peyote and Plants Used*, 129–31.

[47] Excessive prices for peyote have been reported elsewhere. Mooney says (*Miscellaneous Notes*, 30) an Oklahoma White dealer once charged 25 cents a button, though they cost him only $5.00 a thousand. Hoebel says a Comanche once traded a fine horse for five hundred buttons. See Bennett and Zingg, *The Tarahumara*, 291–92; Lumholtz, *Tarahumari Dances*, 453–55.

[48] Diguet, *Le Peyote et son usage*, 28.

costing $35), and $80 respectively, but these amounts seem excessive. The writer has sponsored an average meeting costing only about $15, and Hoebel has supplied "groceries" for meetings at from $6 to $10 only.[49]

Considering their importance and authority, it is not surprising that the peyote chiefs come in for some financial recompense. The Tarahumari peyotero was given a quarter of the slaughtered beef, and one peyote doctor at Narárachic made his entire living by peyote cures. Several Kiowa doctors nearly or completely match this. A Sioux doctor at Taos was given a silk dress of the patient's wife, a belt and $5 cash. Indeed, one of the complaints against Wilson, the Caddo-Delaware peyote messiah, was that he over-exploited the financial opportunities afforded by peyote leadership.[50] Victor Griffin (Quapaw) claims to be the only man authorized by Wilson to make Big Moons, and for the building of a small Quapaw "round house" near Miami, Oklahoma, he and his assistant, Charles Tyner (Quapaw) received $750. There was and is considerable exchanging of gifts in connection with peyote meetings and inter-tribal visiting; feathers, drum sticks, etc. are common gifts, as well as "father peyotes" which have become heirlooms.[51]

Amount of Peyote Eaten. The minimum number of buttons eaten by each participant is usually four. Several persons claim to have eaten 75 to 100 or more, but the average is nearer a third or a fourth of this.[52] Personal observations tend to confirm Mooney's esti-

[49] Parsons, *Taos Pueblo*, 60; Bennett and Zingg, *The Tarahumara*, 293, xiv; Mooney, *Miscellaneous Notes,* 60 ff.

[50] Big Moon leaders apparently required fees; Speck (Peyote MSS.) says the Seneca were too poor to pay more than the leader's carfare when the cult was brought to them. Wilson himself met his death when some horses given him by the Quapaw and tied to the back of his wagon pulled backward at a crossing as a locomotive approached, and some of his enemies assert that this was in punishment for his avariciousness and economic exploitation of peyotism. He even charged money for sweatbaths he prepared in connection with meetings.

[51] Cf. Kroeber, *The Arapaho*, 410. A Shawnee gave the meeting-tipi to two old men the next morning, and the writer has exchanged gifts with several tribes, notably the Oto and the Kiowa.

[52] Koshiway said he ate 100 once: "I was like a Ford, all broken down, connecting rods loose. The next day I was overhauled and hitting on all four, and went to work." Belo Kozad, well-known Kiowa leader, said he ate 100 green peyote once but had a "hard time keeping it down." Big Bow (Kiowa) claims to have eaten 75 at the time of his prophetic vision of the World War. One Oto sometimes eats 40 to 50 at which a man comes and instructs him. Alfred Wilson (Cheyenne) for eight years President of the Oklahoma N.A.C. said he ate 84 green ones once. Densmore (*Winnebago Songs of the Peyote Ceremony*) says Winnebago ate 40 to 100, and many of them ate 60; elsewhere (*The Peyote Cult*) she states a Winnebago usually ate 15, but some ate up to 40. Lipan (Opler, *Lipan Apache Field Notes*) ate 12 to 50. A Tonkawa leader (Opler, *Chiricahua Apache*) ate 40. Users at Taos (Parsons, *Taos Pueblo*, 66) ate as many as 60, but usually about 20 or 30. Mescalero (Opler, *The Influence of Aboriginal Pattern*) ate from 4 to 40, with 12 as a "generous amount." Iowa (Skinner, *Societies of the Iowa*, 724–25) considered 16 a good amount, women being restricted to 2. Huichol (Lumholtz, *The Huichol Indians*, 9) rarely ate more than 4 or 5 daily, but at times consumed up to 20. An Arapaho stated under oath (*Peyote as Used in Religious Worship*, 49) he had eaten 12–30 peyote at different times, agreeing with Kroeber's average of 12, with amounts of more than 30 eaten sometimes. A White observer in a Comanche meeting said he had seen them eat 30 or 40 apiece (Simmons, *The Peyote Road*). An Osage, on the other hand, stated before an official group that 5 was the upper limit for women and 7 for men (*Peyote as Used in Religious Worship*, 31), a statement open to doubt.

mate of 12 to 20 as a night's average consumption; he said that 90 was the most any Kiowa had ever eaten, and he believed this was possible since the individual was powerfully built —although that number would amount to about a pound and a half. This may be so, but one is skeptical of alleged consumptions of more than 30 or 40 average-sized buttons in the dry form. For the green form we should set the maximum at considerably fewer, perhaps 15 or 20 good-sized plants, which even so is a liberal estimate. About 300 each was the average for two Winnebago meetings, and assuming an ordinary group of 20 communi-cants this amounts to only 15 buttons apiece. We should call this a fair estimate of the average for beginners and old users combined in a meeting; before accepting larger esti-mates it should be recalled that there is a certain prestige in eating and retaining large amounts of peyote, a fact which may color statements somewhat. Peyote is also consumed as tea, especially by the old and the sick; in one case 24 discs made 15 cups of tea, and in another 30 made 2 quarts of the infusion. A pneumonia patient drank the latter, one cupful every two hours, to induce perspiration deemed necessary for his cure.

Peyote Paraphernalia in General. Typical Plains peyote paraphernalia includes minimally the leader's satchel, gourd rattle, water drum, drum stick, staff, feathers, eagle wing-bone whistle, corn shucks and loose tobacco, bags for peyote and cedar incense, altar cloth, sage, water bucket and ritual-breakfast containers. The rasp is not used by the Lipan or Mes-calero or in the Plains, and the whistle is recent for the two former. The Lipan previously used a bow struck with a stick in place of the later one-sided tambourine drum; the kettle drum, from Mexico, is still more recent.[53] Mescalero shamans sometimes added the use of pollen, which they used to trace a cross on the father peyote, and like the Tonkawa, occa-sionally served the peyote on woven trays instead of in bags. Taos paraphernalia is standard Plains in type. A common color for Arapaho peyote objects is yellow; Skinner thought the beadwork on Iowa gourds and magpie feather fans indicated a Kiowa or Kiowa-Apache provenience. Among the Delaware and others each devotee has his own gourd rattle, but this (like personal drum sticks and feathers) may not be used until after midnight.[54]

Staff. From ancient times, and possibly before Columbus, the cane or staff was a symbol of authority in Mexico,[55] and for this reason we should hesitate before labeling this feature of peyote an Hispanicism. Again, Opler equates the staff of the Mescalero shaman (which

[53] Opler, *Lipan Apache Field Notes.*

[54] Opler, *The Influence of Aboriginal Pattern; Chiracahua Apache;* Parsons, *Taos Pueblo,* 3; Kroeber, *The Arapaho,* 402, 405; Skinner, *Ethnology of the Ioway,* 249 (but the Christian symbolism here is Plains); Harrington, *Religion and Ceremonies,* 187–88; Petrullo, *The Diabolic Root,* 53.

[55] The cane was the symbol of the Aztec merchant, and his friends did this utlatl or otate great reverence at a feast on the return from his travels; it symbolized Yiacatecutli, the god of merchants. Slaves were also sacrified at a temple rite involving the canes (Sahagún, *A History of Ancient Mexico,* 1: 41–42). Among the Huichol the staff of the judges in the native courts are accorded "a superstitious reverence" as symbols of authority (Lumholtz *Unknown Mexico,* 2: 250). And although Governor Valdes had visited most of the pueblos to appoint native governors and captains by the year 1642, in Tarahumari the native term for leaders is igúsuame, "stick-bearers" or selígame, "lance-bearers" (Bennett and Zingg, *The Tarahumara,* 375–76).

he holds throughout the ceremony, not passing it around with the drum) with the "old age stick" held by the singer in the aboriginal girl's puberty rite.

Similar syncretism with older patterns seems to have occurred also in the Plains. The Comanche used a bow for a staff when holding peyote meetings on the war path, but the term naci-hɩta means literally "resting stick-to walk," according to White Wolf. In the Iowa Red Bean war bundle ceremony, the rattle was held in the left hand [sic] while the bow and arrow were waved in the right as the person sang. The Delaware call the leader's staff "arrow," and so also do the Osage, Quapaw and Oto; the Ponca, on the other hand, call it a "bow." The Kiowa suggest that a bow was formerly used, but the term DO'Dę'ä means "brace-to hold-stick"; it must be of bois d'arc (*Maclura pomifera* C. K. Schneider), however, and some are nocked at the top and bottom like a bow. The Lipan "cane" was called ilkibenatsi'e or "ram-rod."[56]

The Shawnee, according to Mrs. Voegelin, called the peyote staff the walking stick of the old, but the red tassel at the top symbolized the head-dress worn with a single feather at the war dance. The t'owayennemö of Taos was held in the left hand "for the strength of life," and the red and white horsehair tufts encircling the top (so Dr. White was told) were there "because the White man is above the Indian." A Delaware staff which Dr. Speck saw contained designs representing a tipi, water, the door of the lodge, the blue sky and fire, symbolized by the colors of the bead-work.

Reinterpretations of the meaning of the staff are common. A Wichita called it the "staff of life." The Iowa staff represents the staff of the Saviour, while the Winnebago variously interpret it as a shepherd's crook and the rod with which Moses smote the rock (in obvious reference to the leader's calling for water in the ceremony). Differences in the staff have even come to symbolize a schism in the Winnebago church: that used by Rave was decorated, as elsewhere in the Plains, but Clay used a simple undecorated staff, lacking even feathers, calling attention to the fact that Moses staff was undecorated.[57]

Gourd Rattles. Rattles made of gourds (*Lagenaria* spp.) have become universal in the Plains since the spread of peyotism; but the Iowa had a small gourd rattle with beaded handle in their Red Bean war bundle dance, and the peripheral-Plains distribution of this trait in pre-peyote times has been traced elsewhere. Some groups (Delaware, Osage, Ute, etc.) have individual rattles for each participant.[58] A large one seen at Apache, Oklahoma, made by Spotted Crow (Cheyenne) had drawn on it a moon with a fire and a Morning Star in negative, together with the following "Jesus talk:"[59]

[56] Skinner, *Societies of the Iowa*, 718; Harrington, *Religion and Ceremonies*, 187–88; Opler, *Lipan Apache Field Notes.*

[57] Parsons, *Taos Pueblo*, 65; Skinner, *Societies of the Iowa*, 725; Radin, *A Sketch of the Peyote Cult*, 4, 21; Densmore, *The Peyote Cult* (but there is no biblical authority for this in Exodus 7. 19, 20. or concerning Aaron's rod in Exodus 8 or 10.13).

[58] Skinner, *Societies of the Iowa*, 724; Cooke, *Ute Field Notes.*

[59] Winnebago gourds often have on them pictures of Christ, the cross and "crown" of thorns, the shepherd's crook and other Christian symbols (White Buffalo, in Blair, *The Indian Tribes*, 282; see also Harrington,

Help me O Lord
My God O save me
According to thy Mercy
O God my heart is
fixed. I will sing
And give praise
Even with my glory.

A Wichita gourd was said by one informant to represent the world or sun; the beads are
"people talking" and the bead-work in general is "things on the earth," while the horse-
hair tuft dyed red on the top represents the rays of the rising sun. A Delaware gourd of
Dr. Speck's has bead-work on its handle symbolizing morning (blue), fire (red) and a row of
X X X's (the songs sun).[60]

Drum. The standard peyote drum, already described for the Kiowa, made of a small
iron kettle with seven bosses in the lacing, is found also among the Arapaho, Comanche,
Iowa, Cheyenne, Lipan, Pawnee, Ute, Shawnee, Kickapoo, etc.[61] The Kickapoo say the
seven marbles represent the days of the week, just as the twelve eagle feathers of the fan
symbolize the twelve months of the year; the four coals which are dropped into the
water of the drum are lightning, the water rain and the drumming itself thunder.[62]

In drumming, the vessel is given an occasional shake to wet the head with the contained
water, and the left thumb is used to test the tone and tighten the head: sometimes too the
head is sucked or blown upon, so that the water is forced to ooze through the skin. The
Ponca, however, do not permit the drum head to be touched—"peyote makes the sound,
not the hand,"[63] they say—and hence make a handle of the lacing-rope twisted upon itself.

Religion and Ceremonies, 188; *Handbook of the American Indians*, 2: 355b; Kroeber, *The Arapaho*, 400, 405;
Radin, *Crashing Thunder*, 20).

[60] The best gourds are relatively small, not more than 3″ in diameter, somewhat flattened on the top rather
than spherical, and elongated toward the handle. A hole is made through the gourd opposite the neck, cut off
an inch or so from the round part; a stick is thrust through these, the neck hole being reinforced and made smaller
by whittling down half a spool and glueing it in. There is no peg transversely through the portion emerging
through the top, but both this and the handle part are usually covered with tightly-sewn buckskin to which
bead-work is attached; some handles are carved or left plain. A tuft of red-dyed horsehair is often put on the
top and a buckskin fringe at the bottom; shot or pebbles make the sound.

[61] Kroeber, *The Arapaho*, 400; Skinner, *Ethnology of the Ioway*, 249; *Societies of the Iowa*, 724; Hoebel,
Voegelin, Opler, and Cooke, *Field Notes;* Mooney (*Miscellaneous Notes*) says Comanche drums had eight marbles
sometimes, as had also the Shawnee, according to Mrs. Voegelin.

[62] The Kickapoo once tried a four-legged brass kettle instead of the regulation three-legged iron one, but
soon discarded it, having decided that the tone was not right (this probably rationalizes some criticism of their
ostentation). The Caddo had a 10-marbled crock drum with a deer skin head; the Oto, who have the kettle drum,
sometimes use a crock, as do the Omaha (Gilmore, *The Mescal Society*, 166; *Uses of Plants*). The Delaware sometimes used otter skin instead of deer skin, with four bosses tightened with a sharp stick or deer-horn (Harrington, *Religion and Ceremony*, 188; Petrullo, *The Diabolic Root*, 50).

[63] Cf. the Mexican belief about the peyote under the gourd-resonator. Such taboos in regard to drums are
also Iroquoian I believe, and possibly Southeastern.

Old Man Sack (Caddo) also forbade blowing on the drum, "even when it cups up and sounds like a tin can," a Kiowa peyote-boy said; in the stricter Caddo moons no water is drunk until the drum has made four rounds, with the result that some of their meetings consequently last well into the forenoon of the next day—a genuine ordeal according to informants. Among the Iowa, and possibly also in some Caddo Delaware "Big Moons" the drum chief accompanies the drum around the circle, drumming for each singer. The Jesse Clay style of drumming among the Winnebago, described by Densmore, is common among the southern tribes: a rapid unaccented beating before the beginning of the singing, gradually slackening to match the speed of the voice. Another mannerism may be noted at the end of each song, when the rattle is shaken unrhythmically as fast as possible during the last few bars of the song, then suddenly stopped with the last drum beat.[64] The water drum is typically Southeastern in distribution, but its presence in the Plains peyote cult must be accounted another Southwestern feature, inasmuch as it was standardized and diffused over the Plains before Southeastern groups in Oklahoma received peyote and hence could have introduced the trait into it.[65]

Feathers. Feathers are important in peyote symbolism. In the original Comanche rite only the leader brought in a medicine fan with him; "now many young men bring them who have no special business to." Skinner wrote that eagle feathers were "badges of the society" among peyote-using Iowa; women were never allowed to use eagle feathers in

[64] Skinner, *Societies of the Iowa*, 726; Densmore, *Winnebago Songs of Peyote Ceremonies.*

[65] The Chickasaw beat on a wet deer skin tied over the mouth of a large clay pot (Adair, *History*, 140). The Choctaw beat with one drumstick on a deer skin stretched over an earthen pot or kettle (Swanton, *Social and Religious Beliefs*, 222); they used the goat skin covered cypress knee drum as well (Bushnell, *Choctaw*, 22), and also bear skin and deer skin (Swanton, *op. cit.*, 224). The Koasati older drum was deer skin over a cypress knee, and later the small iron kettle (Paz, *Field Notes*). The Taskigi Creek used a hollow vessel partly filled with water (Speck, *The Creek Indians*, 137). The Yuchi, besides the log drum, had the pot drum, containing water, about 18″ high; the hide was usually decorated with a wheel-like design and the privilege of beating the drum was invested in a certain individual (Speck, *Yuchi*, 61, cf. the Caddo, in some respects a peripheral Southeastern group and who have the "crock" drum). The Catawba and Quapaw also had the pot-drum (Speck, *Catawba Texts; Handbook of the American Indian*, 2: 335b). It is not known if the Tonkawa water-drum is pre-peyote, but the Lipan pottery drum is late according to Opler. The water-drum of the Southeast is continuous through the Antilles into South America (Wissler, *The American Indian*, 154).

Wissler makes no mention of Mexican or Southwestern occurrences of the kettle-drum or water-drum, but the trait is common in these regions. The Aztec had the kettle-drum (Sahagun, *A History of Ancient Mexico*, 1: 87, 91). Beals (*Comparative Ethnology*, 112, 188, Table 71) lists the atabale or kettle-drum in Tehueco, Culiacan, Tepic (Zentispac), Tarasco, and Mexico. The pottery drum is Lacandone, Natchez and Chitimacha also (Swanton, *Aboriginal Culture*, 708, in Beals, 188). Stevenson (*The Zuñi*, 39) mentions a Tepehan pottery drum struck loudly at certain ceremonies to insure the presence of beings who would keep the singing of songs correct. The Western Apache have "male" and "female" water drums (Henry, J., *Cult of Silas John Edwards*). The Huichol use no drum in the peyote ceremony; the Tamaulipecan peyote-drum is the wooden type, as is also the Tarahumari drum (Bennett and Zingg, *The Tarahumara*, 67–68) and the Huichol drum, which is "alive" (Lumholtz, *Unknown Mexico*, 2: 32–34). The Taos is the standard peyote drum; but the pottery drum is found among non-users of peyote: e.g., Navaho, Chiricahua, W. Apache, Jicarilla, Yavapai and Pueblo in general (Spier, information).

meetings, however. Younger Oto men carry modern ribbed folding-fans, older ones commonly an entire wing. The individual fans of the Northern Cheyenne, as elsewhere, are not produced until the full effects of the peyote come on, some time after midnight. The eagle feather fans of the Winnebago represent the wings of birds mentioned in Revelations, while the Kickapoo state that the twelve feathers of the eagle fan symbolize the twelve months of the year; twelve is a common Delaware ritual number also.[66]

The Arapaho hang bunches of feathers on the northeast, northwest, southeast and southwest tipi poles to brush off the bodies of tired worshippers. The Mescalero use eagle feathers as a spoon to feed their first peyote to neophytes. The Winnebago, like other tribes, pass a feather around with the staff in its circuit. The Kiowa, Ponca and others use feathers in the water rites: the former make a cross in the midnight water with the feathers of all present, held in a bunch, while the latter place a single feather across the top of the bucket and whistle along the feather. The use of feathers among the Ponca, where cedar incensing is not a strong trait, is especially conspicuous: a feather is passed to the fireman as a symbol of authority, allowing him to leave the tipi without express permission each time from the "road-man," and there is a "baptism" with feathers in the water ceremonies too. The vanes of Ponca feathers are often notched. The red blankets of the two Carrizo women helpers were fastened with a woodpecker and a flicker feather respectively.[67]

Feathers are common in visions too. A Kiowa envisaged his barred hawk-feathers as a ladder rising through the smoke hole of the tipi to heaven, like a Jacob's Ladder, and another time as rippling water. Feathers are commonly arranged and cut, colored and tufted, etc., in accordance with visions seen during meetings.[68] Jonathan Koshiway (Oto) had assembled a favorite fan from individual gift feathers, each of which had a different history —one from an old Osage woman who wished for him her long life, two from Hunting-horse (Kiowa), and the like. An interesting development in the Big Moon ceremony is the ritual necessity for each person to be fanned at the fire by the fireman or others every time he re-enters the tipi. This trait is Delaware, Caddo, Osage and Quapaw[69] in distribution, the latter having two special "guards" at the north and south arms of the altar cross who are charged with fanning each entrant; ordinary incensing with cedar has been reported even among the Ute and is probably universal in peyotism. Perhaps with the same purpose in mind, protection from dangerous influences, the Mescalero takes an eagle feather from either side of the door as he makes his exit, returning as soon as possible.[70]

[66] Hoebel, *Comanche Field Notes*; Skinner, *Societies of the Iowa*, 724, 758; Densmore, *The Peyote Cult*; Parsons, *Taos Pueblo* ,65; Speck, *A Study of the Delaware*, passim.

[67] Kroeber, *The Arapaho*, 405–409; Opler, *The Influence of Aboriginal Pattern*; Radin, *Crashing Thunder*, 176; Opler, *Carrizo Field Notes*. The feather as a symbol of delegated authority is also found in the Ghost Dance.

[68] Cf. Boas, *Anthropology*, 91, " . . . the feathers of the Dakota Indians . . . by the way they are cut and painted, express warlike exploits."

[69] Hills, *Eating Medicine with the Quapaws*.

[70] Harrington, *Religion and Ceremonies*, 188; Opler, *The Influence of Aboriginal Pattern. Handbook of the*

Birds. We have already noted the importance of birds in Huichol and Tarahumari peyote symbolism, and are to discover that they are equally significant in the Plains. Here the "water-bird" somewhat ambiguously suggests a bird that lives in the water or the bird involved with the whistling for the midnight water. Arapaho songs refer to peyote and the birds which are its messengers, and sparrow hawk, yellow hammer and other woodpecker feathers are common in their meetings. When the fireman goes to get the water he carries an eagle wing, and the whistling which he makes is said to imitate the cry of a bird in search of water (the end of the eagle wing-bone whistle is finally dipped into the water bucket, as though it were the bird drinking).[71]

The Comanche peyote bird is the "sun-eagle," said to be just under the rising morning sun; "Comanches always mention that bird in their meeting." This bird, the kʷina-óhap (literally, "eagle-yellow"), which is represented in the shaped ashes west of the peyote fire, "flashes like the sun; . . . water bird feathers are used just because they are pretty." In this connection it is interesting to recall the Tarahumari place name Couwápigóchi, "place of the wapigóri," from the name of a fishing bird, "a cross between an eagle and a hawk, with feet like an eagle," which the Mexicans call aquillala, and the brilliantly colored macao and other birds belonging to the Huichol "Grandfather Fire."[72]

The Kiowa represent their "water-bird" on peyote tie-slides as a long-necked bird like a kingfisher or crane; these have been traded all over the Plains. If a Kiowa peyote-user sees an eagle in a vision, he thereafter carries his eagle-feather fan in his left hand as a sign of this.[73] The peyote bird is prominent in symbolic Kiowa paintings also. Jonathan Koshiway, the Oto peyote teacher, said:

The peyote spirit is like a little humming bird. When you are quiet and nothing is disturbing it, it will come to a flower and get the sweet flavor. But if it is disturbed, it goes quick.

Hence the admonitions to sit quietly in meetings and "study" to see if you can "maybe learn something." Tom Panther, a Shawnee leader, called the ash-bird

a holy bird; it drinks as well as we do of the holy water [i.e. some of the ritual water is poured on the ash-figure in the morning] and it gets alive a little when people drink, and from then on is lively until morning.

The martin is said to be the Shawnee peyote bird, as indicated perhaps in the "scissors-tail" shape of some ashes. A Mexican who had long lived with the Wichita had an inter-

---

American Indians, 1: 455–56, "The downy feather was to the mind of the Indian a kind of bridge between the spirit world and ours." Note the Ponca whistling along the water bucket feather.

[71] Kroeber, *The Arapaho,* 403, 405, 407.

[72] The Oto and Arapaho wear tufts of down feathers on their hair in meetings; cf. the Tarahumari shaman's feather headdress which tells him all the bird knew and protects him by preventing air from entering his head and making him ill (Lumholtz, *Unknown Mexico,* 1: 313).

[73] Mooney, *Peyote Notebook,* 18. Crashing Thunder visioned an eagle with outspread wings in a meeting once (Radin, 188–89).

esting vision during the water-ceremonies of an Arapaho meeting, when he saw a white feather of the leader "turn into Christ and boss the bald-eagle feather of the fireman around." The association of birds with peyotism, therefore, appears to be universal in the Plains and Mexico alike.

Fetish Peyote. Peyote is the only plant toward which the Kiowa and other typical non-agricultural Plains tribes have a religious attitude and from which they can get "power." Yet the fetishistic attitude as a psychological phenomenon is not unknown in the Plains of pre-peyote times; the Kiowa taime or Sun Dance image and the "Ten-Medicine" bundles have widespread parallels in the Plains—the Cheyenne fetish-arrows and sacred heart, the Iowa red bean war-bundles, and the ubiquitous medicine-bundles of which the Blackfoot are a type.[74] The Arapaho wore the fetish-plant in an amulet pouch covered with beads, and when placed on the altar a head-plume was sometimes put nearby. The Cheyenne also carry exceptionally large specimens in beaded buckskin cases,[75]

the beadwork being in the form of a star to represent the sun [?] and the case being suspended from his neck by four strands of beads "to represent the four thoughts that lead to peyote."

A Wichita informant carried a peyote button with him to France in the late War, and the fetish miraculously escaped detection during the sterilizing of uniforms; it protected him until he could return to collect his soldier's bonus in 1936, when a special meeting was held to thank peyote for these boons.

Some Shawnee call the hogimá or "peyote chief" the messenger between humans and God; others call it the "interpreter" or the Holy Ghost. Crashing Thunder addressed the most holy peyote medicine as "grandfather," but the usual designation of the fetish is "peyote chief" or "father peyote." While Wolf (Comanche) called it "elder brother" because as a child one specific plant had protected him during an illness.

The Winnebago are evidently influenced by an older tribal pattern in their use of two sacred peyotes, one "male" and the other "female." John Wilson in an early Caddo meeting near Fort Cobb, Oklahoma, "before the country opened," placed three peyote buttons on the moon (symbolizing the Trinity of leaders?); his drummer saw one of these turn into a person he had known in life. The Lipan usually had only one hucdjiya'isia, or "big peyote lying," but sometimes put buttons in a circle around the fire pit, somewhat like the Comanche who placed them in the sage crescent west of the fire.[76]

The Osage, with their usual flair for ostentation, place the "chief peyote" "within the marked outline of a heart and set upon a beaded cylinder support," according to Dr. Speck.

---

[74] Huichol peyote fetishes include the squirrel, skunk, birds and the shaman's fetish plant; the Tarahumari have the squirrel, birds and peyote plant; the southern Plains birds and the peyote plant; and the northern Plains the plant only—an interesting degeneration in complexity of symbolism, a sort of diffusionist law of inverse squares.

[75] Kroeber, *The Arapaho*, 401, 406; letter of L. L. Meeker to Mooney.

[76] Radin, *Crashing Thunder*, 181-82; *A Sketch of the Peyote Cult*, 21; *The Winnebago Tribe*, 389, "They are regarded by a number of people, certainly by Rave, with undisguised veneration [i.e., the peyote "chiefs"]."

Iowa father peyotes are notable for their size. The Tonkawa sometimes painted the fuzz on the plant red, as though it were a person. The Taos addressed the peyote chief as "Father Ear," probably carrying over to peyote a common Pueblo fetishistic attitude toward corn. Lipan and Mescalero father peyotes were an active ally of the shaman leading the meeting, as any attempt at witchcraft would "show" on it and inform him of something amiss.[77]

Some individuals particularly cherish and prize their "father peyotes." A well-known Wichita leader showed the writer his private collection of them one forenoon after a meeting.[78] Some famous "peyote chiefs" are almost heirlooms. Belo Kozad, a prominent Kiowa peyote leader, has one which once belonged to the famous Comanche chieftain, Quanah Parker. This was passed around at the end of the meeting and handled with the utmost reverence.[79]

Bible. Peyote-users have also taken over the typical Protestant fetishism of the Bible, but this Christian element in peyote meetings is confined exclusively to Siouan-speaking groups. Radin states categorically that "the use of the Bible is an entirely new element introduced by the Winnebago," but there is good reason to believe that Hensley borrowed this trait from more southerly Oklahoma groups which he visited in the early days of Winnebago peyotism. The Omaha placing of an open Bible near the father peyote may indeed have been influenced by the Winnebago (who put the peyote directly on the open book), and so too the Iowa, but the Oto use of the Bible in the Church of the First-born probably preceded it in Oklahoma, where, indeed, John Wilson's Big Moon cult embodied Christian elements. Further, the reading of the Bible is a feature of the Rave rite only, not of the Clay version, a more aboriginal form.[80]

The Winnebago use the New Testament, especially Revelations. Hensley used to have the singing stop at intervals, so that the younger educated men might translate and

[77] Skinner, *Societies of the Iowa,* 724; Opler, *Chiricahua Apache; The Influence of Aboriginal Pattern; Lipan Apache Field Notes;* Parsons, *Taos Pueblo,* 64–65. Cf. the Anadarko Delaware phrase "ear-eating" for peyote-eating (Speck, *Notes on the Life of John Wilson,* 552).

[78] An especially handsome and regular one, oriented with a thorn on its "north" side, had fifteen full radial lines of hair-tufts. Of three others, one was kept in a woman's small mirrored vanity-case, a pomade jar, and a silk handkerchief, all carefully wrapped up. Another very old one was given his brother-in-law, Yellow Bird, by a Comanche. A cracked one was kept in a beaded buckskin pouch along with a Catholic medallion dated 1890; it had been given him by an Apache. He has also preserved one given his wife by Mexicans at El Rio on their first peyote trip in 1926, and tied up with the mother's he keeps two little ones which helped his little girl. And finally, there were seven which he laid behind the whistle one New Year's meeting to represent the seven days of the week; his daughter drank the water in which they were soaked and became well in seven days. She is a grown woman now and he still keeps these peyotes which have so well demonstrated their power.

[79] The Comanche leader Mumsika still preserves a famous peyote button formerly belonging to Kutubi which performed prophecies on an historical war party into Texas (Hoebel, *Comanche Field Notes*). The anxiety of Clyde Koko (Kiowa) when he thought he had lost his "father peyotes" after changing his mind about sending them back to their original country, well demonstrates the psychological reality of these fetishisms.

[80] Radin, *Crashing Thunder,* 169, note; Gilmore, *The Mescal Society,* 165–66; Speck (manuscript); Skinner, *Societies of the Iowa,* 724; Densmore, *The Peyote Cult; Winnebago Songs of the Peyote Ceremony.*

interpret portions for non-reading members. For some individuals at least, the Bible was the touchstone of behavior:

Then we went home [says Crashing Thunder] and they showed me a passage in the Bible where it said that it was a shame for any man to wear long hair. I looked at the passage. I was not a man learned in books, but I wanted to give them the impression that I knew how to read so I told them to cut my hair. I was still wearing it long at the time. After my hair was cut I took out a lot of medicines, many small bundles of them. These and my shorn hair I gave to my brother-in-law. Then I cried and my brother-in-law also cried. He thanked me, told me that I understood and that I had done well.

Another time, in a peyote vision, his body deserted Crashing Thunder and turned the leaves of the Bible until it came to Matthew 16 and read[81] that "Peter did not give himself up"; this meant that the peyote was troubling him because he was stubborn and would not acquiesce to its power.[82]

The Bible was also used to support rationalizations after the fact:[83]

At first our meetings were started without following any rule laid down by the Bible, but afterwards we found a very good reason for holding our meetings at night. We searched the Bible and asked many ministers for any evidence of Christ's ever having held any meetings in the day-time but we could find nothing to that effect. We did, however, find evidence that he had been out all night in prayer. As it is our desire to follow as closely as we can in the footsteps of Christ, we hold our meetings at night.

The Bible is said to mention peyote in several places:

And they shall eat the flesh in that night, roast with fire, and unleavened bread; and with bitter herbs they shall eat it (Exodus 12.8).

And this day shall be unto you for a memorial; and ye shall keep it as a feast by an ordinance forever (Exodus 12.14).

Mrs. Voegelin cites a Shawnee belief in a Bible reference to peyote, but it is somewhat ambiguous and obscure.[84]

Altars or "Moons." Peyote altars range in complexity from the simple war-shield of a Comanche war-party leader on which the peyote was laid, to the elaborate permanent symbolic concrete altars in the Big Moon round-house churches. All the Plains variants are built on the standard crescent altar, grooved from tip to tip by the "peyote road"

[81] Radin, *Crashing Thunder*, 200. This is indeed a miracle if he read it in Matthew 16.

[82] Radin, *Crashing Thunder*, 186–87; *Sketch of the Peyote Cult*, 5; *The Winnebago Tribe*, 394–95.

[83] Radin, *Sketch of the Peyote Cult*, 6; *The Winnebago Tribe*, 395–96. The reference to John 1.4 indicates nothing of relevance.

[84] Romans 11.16–18. No native with whom the writer is acquainted has to date noted the obvious Shakespearean reference to peyote, in the speech of Banquo as the three witches vanish incorporeally into thin air (Macbeth I, iii): "Were such things here as we do speak about, or have we eaten on the insane root that takes the reason prisoner?"

which devotees must follow to a knowledge of peyote.[85] Interpretations of the moon symbolism are almost as numerous as individual users; for, given the physiological effects of peyote and the acceptance in Plains culture of the individual vision "authority," standardized meanings are not to be expected. One Shawnee, for instance, said the mound represented the mountain of the origin story where "Peyote Woman" first found peyote; another that the place of the peyote on the moon represented the space between Jesus Christ's eyes, just over the brain, and the arms of the crescent his arms as he lay face downward on the cross: "If we eat the peyote which is on his brain, maybe it will make us think too."

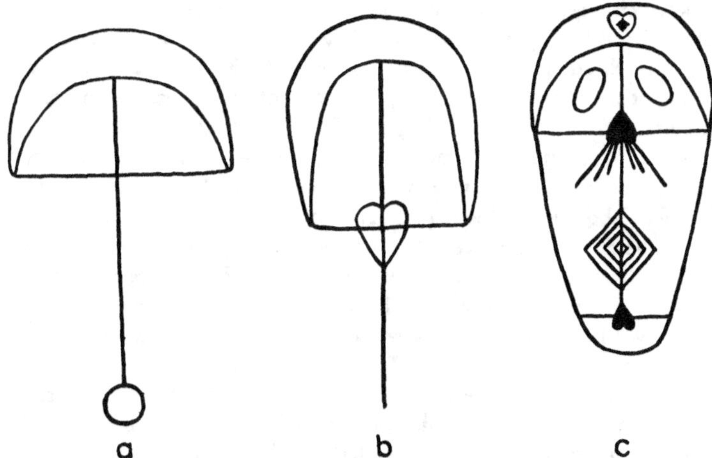

Fig. 4. Peyote altars or moons. a, Basic Caddo-Delaware moon with a mound at the east of the cross; b, the Caddo Big Moon altar; c, Enoch Hoag (Caddo) moon, as drawn by Elijah Reynolds (probably the same as Petrullo, Plate 5 B).

Again, given these factors and the nature of peyote leadership, it is not surprising to find variations run riot; sometimes even the same leader does not conduct two meetings exactly alike, or construct the moon precisely the same (changing the ashes, etc.) Three Osage leaders, for example, change the tribal altar by simply turning everything through 180° to make a "West Moon." John Elcare (Delaware) is said to have a unique "fish moon," north of the fire and facing east, which he feeds and gives to drink. The Omaha[86] dug a heart-shaped fireplace eight to twelve inches deep to represent the heart of Jesus. We were unable to discover the exact nature of Leonard Taylor's (Cheyenne) "Heart Moon," no longer conducted, but it appears rather to resemble a Winnebago altar figured by Dens-

[85] The Carrizo-Lipan had no crescent mound, which is probably of Mescalero origin.
[86] Gilmore, *The Mescal Society*, 165–66.

more: a heart superimposed on a cross in the fireplace, under the fire, with a small mound to the east representing the earth.

This mound opposite and to the east of the crescent appears to be of Caddoan origin.[87] Jimmy Hunter's moon shows this in perhaps its earliest, and certainly its simplest form: a line joining the mound and the center of the crescent, with another crossing this from horn to horn of the crescent. Bob Dunlap's moon has a further minor addition, a heart at the juncture of the crossed lines. The moon of Ernest Spybuck, pictured in Harrington, is Shawnee rather than Delaware-Caddo, but shows definite Big Moon influence; it is intermediate in complexity, perhaps, between the Caddoan small moons and the elaborately symbolic John Wilson Big Moon. The Enoch Hoag moon[88] (a favorite among the Caddo nowadays) shows features parallel with the Wilson moon: it has a star and a heart at the hair-parting or forehead of the altar "face," ash mounds simulating eyes, an inverted heart at the crossing of the altar-lines as a nose, four concentric lozenges for an oracular mouth, and another heart east of this resembling a cleft chin; the moon itself is the figure's hair. Moonhead's (i.e. John Wilson's) altar similarly represents a man's head, and contains the leader's initials or "foot-prints" and his "grave" alongside that of Jesus. The Black Wolf moon is another elaboration of the Big Moon type.

It must not be thought, however, that the bold innovations begun by John Wilson and others have resulted in a complete chaos of individualism. It requires considerable prestige and force of personality to vision a moon impressively enough to gain an adequate following. In recent years leaders in the Native American Church have expressed themselves unfavorably on the growing variety and profusion of rival moons, and have urged a return to the standardized simplicity of the older more deeply entrenched forms. Perhaps for this reason, and personality factors as well, several new "moons" have been considerably less than complete successes. A case in point is that of Albert Stamp (Seminole). His design is not strikingly original or different from the moons of the Caddo among whom he lives: he has six concentric lozenges to Hoag's four and has added three concentric triangles. That is all. But his moon has not found acceptance, and he has dismantled his cement altar, removing the entire central symbolic portion, leaving only the crescent and simple polygonal apron.[89]

This is only a single instance of a general movement back to more "pure" original forms,

---

[87] Cf. *Handbook of the American Indians*, 2: 2b, 661: "Formerly among the southern Plains tribes a buffalo skull was placed on a small mound in front of the sweat house, the mound being formed of earth excavated from the fireplace." The original Comanche and Caddo moons appear to have been more horseshoe- than crescent-shaped, and the apron of the Caddoan Big Moons obviously developed from an elongation of the horns. The introduction of the heart is apparently Caddoan also, influenced probably by the Catholic "Sacred Heart" of Jesus.

[88] Enoch Hoag was at one time John Wilson's assistant or drummer.

[89] A Comanche told Hoebel of a "moon" with the entire tipi-floor of cement; if this is identical with one I was told about, it has been subsequently destroyed. The rationalization given was that the cement floor distorted the sound of the drum, and a return to an earthen floor was made.

stimulated perhaps by the standardizing influence of the Native American Church. This sentiment has had its effect even upon followers of the Wilson Big Moon rite, which is apparently dying out among the Caddo-Delaware (though still strong among the Osage and Quapaw), in favor of the "more Caddo" Hoag moon. If a generalization might be made about the influence of the three tribes most important in the diffusion of Plains peyotism— the Kiowa, the Comanche and the Caddo (who because of their southerly position first received the new religion)[90]—we might call the Kiowa the original standardizers and teachers, who have departed only in the most minute ways from earlier forms; the Comanche the proselytizers and missionaries of the new religion; and the Caddo[91] the innovators.

Fire. Nowhere is the kind of wood for the fire ritually prescribed. Mulberry, slippery elm, cottonwood and black jack are said not to be good because they pop and give off sparks, tending to scatter the carefully piled-up ashes. Red bud, which gives off much light and little heat, is a favorite for summer use, while box alder is considered good for winter. But "Grandfather Fire" (as the Delaware, Winnebago, Kickapoo and Shawnee address it) is built in a ritually prescribed way, like the angle of a worm-fence with the apex to the west. The Shawnee say the first four sticks represent tipi poles. The ritual number of peyotism, seven, appears in the number of sticks prescribed for the Northern Cheyenne and Taos.[92]

The fire stick at a Kickapoo-Shawnee meeting attended near McCloud, Oklahoma, was elaborately carved with a crescent, a bird, a father peyote on a rosette, the word "Christ" and crossed sticks.[93] The Caddo say this fire stick is the "heart," while the twelve interlacing sticks of the fire are the "ribs" and the two ash mounds the "lungs" of Jesus; in some Caddo moons two fireman put sticks on alternately.[94] The Wilson moon of the Quapaw

[90] The Kiowa and Caddo are therefore at opposite extremes; the Kiowa were the leading spirits in the institutionalizing of peyotism in the Native American Church, which gathered to itself even the earlier Church of the First-born. In this respect they are the "Catholics" of the movement, and, tired of the warring rival Protestantisms let loose by Caddo visionaries, many groups are undergoing an "Oxford Movement" back to the simplest earlier native forms, sans Bible and sans elaborate altars, which after all have been the vehicles for prestige and wealth of ambitious individualism.

[91] Several of Petrullo's examples (Hoag, Black Wolf, etc.) are Caddo rather than Delaware. His Hoag moon (*The Diabolic Root*, pl. 5, B, p. 181) was given to the writer with a half-ellipse joining the moon-tips to form the lower part of the "face," and the ash-mounds in position as "eyes," and the two eastern hearts reversed.

[92] Hoebel, *Northern Cheyenne Field Notes*; Parsons, *Taos Pueblo*, 64.

[93] This specimen is figured in Schultes, *Peyote and Plants Used*, 7. Is this a reflex of an older Kickapoo pattern? The prophet Kanakuk furnished his followers with a chart showing a path through fire and water, and gave them prayer sticks graven with religious symbols. See *Handbook of the American Indians*, 1: 650b, "Kanakuk."

[94] Petrullo, *Diabolic Root*, 50, 101, 113. The symbolism of twelve of the Caddo here is clearly a Delaware borrowing; cf. the twelve panels in the Big Moon altars, the twelve eagle feathers, and the twelve sticks of the fire. See Speck, *Delaware Big House*, for the symbolism of twelve (twelve "heavens" etc.; cf. the twelve steps in the altar apron of the Wilson moon). Petrullo says the twelve sticks represent the months of the year or the tail-feathers of the eagle.

and Delaware has three firemen who sit by the door to fan entrants. The Arapaho[95] leader chooses his hictänäⁿtcä or "fire chief" by silently pointing an eagle wing-feather at him, which the latter uses as a fan during the ceremony; the feather of the Ponca fireman is a symbol of authority. The ceremonial fire as a trait is Mexican, Southwestern, Southeastern and southern Plains (e.g., Caddo and Hasinai), but as involved in peyotism it is a Mexican-Southwestern borrowing rather than Southeastern.[96]

Ashes. An interesting feature, remotely suggesting the Southwest, is the building up of the ashes of the peyote fire into a figure. The commonest form is a crescent, smaller than and parallel to the crescent of the earthen moon, which is nearly universal in the Plains. At an early date the Comanche began making the ashes into the shape of a "sun eagle" and the Kiowa into a "hummingbird." The Shawnee and Kickapoo call it a "water bird"; one Shawnee leader occasionally makes buffalo heads. A Pawnee leader, Good Sun, makes an "eagle" in the ashes. Jonathan Koshiway (Oto) says the bird is "the holy spirit when Jesus was baptized; it's got good eyes like an eagle—you can't fool it."[97]

The separation of the ashes into two piles in the Big Moon rite comes in for similarly varying interpretations. A Delaware informant said that on one's journey in life toward the peyote "if you're the right kind of fellow you can pass the fire and everything opens up" like the Red Sea. Some say the two ash piles are the lungs of Jesus; others that one is the grave of John Wilson and the other the grave of Jesus Christ. Some Osage say the whole interior of the altar represents a grave.

Smoking. Most of the variations in this ceremony are rather minor. In some groups like the Kiowa only the leader or an older man prays; in others like the Oto all pray aloud at the same time with individual prayers. The Kickapoo ask permission of the leader to make a smoke prayer. The Caddo stop the singing while a prayer is going on, but this is not universal elsewhere. The rule not to pass a smoker or a person chewing peyote appears everywhere, save in the Wilson rite; in this only the leader smoked, and "show-offs" who made requests for tobacco were frowned upon. This descriptive fact is minuscule in importance, save in pointing out the authority of the leader and personality traits of Wilson himself. The original ceremony, as indicated by the Lipan, was a communal smoke at the beginning. The Osage are said to smoke cigars in their peyote meetings, but the usual in-

[95] Kroeber, *The Arapaho*, 401. See also Speck, *A Study of the Delaware Big House*, 47, 51. Cf. the Arapaho, Sitting Bull, the Ghost Dance prophet giving feathers to his assistants.

[96] The ceremonial fire we have seen is Huichol and Tarahumari (cf. the "pillow of Grandfather Fire" of the Huichol with the "heart" of the Caddo-Delaware peyote fire: both are used as a "smoke stick"). The Caddo ceremonial fire, however, was pre-peyote (*Handbook of the American Indians*, 2: 2b; Swanton, *Aboriginal Culture*, 701). Beals (*Comparative Ethnology*, 127) lists the ceremonial fire for the Tarahumari, Caddo, Hasinai, Chitimacha, Houma, Natchez, Tunica, Taënsa, Jalisco (Cutzalán), Mexico, and Maya (Lacadone); it is lacking in Tepic-Culiacan, Old Sinaloa, Old Sonora, Southern Sierra and Tamaulipas (whence a southern Plains provenience for the ceremonial fire in peyotism is implausible). See also Beal's map 26, 209; table 121, 211-12.

[97] It is believed that the Yuchi example figured by Petrullo in Plate 2 is erroneous in the placing of the ash eagle and in the presence of the redundant ash crescent.

sistence is on native materials, the corn shuck or, occasionally, the oak leaf cigarette.[98]

In view of the nearly universal ritual use of tobacco in the Americas, the negative cases which occur are interesting. This is traceable to the influence of White Protestantism of the "Russellite" sect in Kansas upon the founder of the Church of the First-born, Jonathan Koshiway. Persuaded by the Kiowa, however, Koshiway and the Oto later abandoned this prohibition, but meanwhile it had spread to other groups. The Iowa[99] "threw away" smoking along with liquor, and did not smoke in peyote meetings. The conjectured Oto origin of Winnebago peyotism is seemingly confirmed by their rejection of smoking in the Jesse Clay meetings:[100]

My elder brother [says Crashing Thunder upon conversion to peyote] hereafter I shall only regard Earthmaker as holy. I will make no more offerings of tobacco. I will not use any more tobacco. I will not smoke, nor will I chew tobacco. I have no further interest in these things.

The non-use of tobacco in peyote meetings appears to be Pawnee[101] as well. Nowadays, as though in compensation for his earlier defection from the pure native rite, Koshiway uses extraordinarily long six-inch corn shucks.

Sage. Sagebrush is used in several ways in peyote meetings: around the periphery of the tipi as a seat, in a cross or rosette under the father peyote on the altar, and in the perfuming ceremony before eating peyote, when it is rubbed between the palms, smelled and rubbed over the head and arms, body and legs.[102] Sometimes a bunch of sage tied together is passed around with the singing-staff also.[103] Dr. Parsons says that at Taos[104] the perfuming is done "to keep the smell of it [on us] so we won't feel weak or dizzy"; and as a similar protective function of sage is reported by Opler for the Lipan and the "Sun Dance weed" by Mrs. Cooke for the Ute, it is evidently wide-spread. The Ute sometimes place a willow rope around the tipi, about four feet in from its circumference.

Passing of Objects. The standard clockwise circuit of tobacco, sage, peyote, paraphernalia, water, food and persons has already been described. This trivial ritual has nevertheless been made the vehicle of expression of the leader's authority to change it. Sometimes the circuit begins at the door (Lipan), sometimes at the leader or cedar chief (Iowa), and elsewhere smokes may begin at the leader but food and water at the southeast.[105] In

---

[98] Interestingly, though the bulk of modern peyotists are Siouan, Caddoan and Algonquian groups, none used the elbow pipe in the ceremony—only Taos. See Wissler, *The American Indian*, 26, fig. 6.

[99] Skinner thought peyote destroyed the appetite for tobacco (*Societies of the Iowa*, 694, 726).

[100] Radin, *Crashing Thunder*. See Kroeber, *The Arapaho*, 401; Parsons, *Taos Pueblo*, 64, for standard form.

[101] Murie, *Pawnee Indian Societies*, 640–41.

[102] The importance of taking a comparative viewpoint is indicated by the statement of Gilmore, *The Mescal Society*, 165, " . . . the Omaha, of Nebraska, have interjected the use of wild sage, *Artemesia gnaphalodes*, in connection with mescal ceremonies, that plant having been an immemorial symbol of sacredness among the Omaha." But see Kroeber, *The Arapaho*, 399, 401; Radin, *The Winnebago Tribe*, 415 and others.

[103] In view of other peyote parallels, note the sweat bath sage-whip.

[104] Parsons, *Taos Pueblo*, 65. The Arapaho (Kroeber, 402), Kiowa, and others chew bits of sage.

[105] Skinner, *Societies of the Iowa*, 722.

the morning after the untying of the drum the ritual paraphernalia and the father peyote are commonly passed around for participants to handle (Kickapoo, Kiowa, Ponca, etc.) The Ponca make a point of passing the water between the fire and the paraphernalia at the altar-cloth in the midnight ceremony.

The obsessive, involutional quality of ritualism is nowhere better illustrated than in the minutiae of these rules for passing. We have particularized for the Kiowa the standard modes of passing paraphernalia,[106] but even experienced "peyote boys" are in need of instruction concerning the "way" of an unfamiliar leader when they visit other tribes. The Northern Cheyenne, for example, may not pass the drum in his clockwise circuit to leave the tipi, save in grave emergencies when permission is asked of the leader through the fireman. One may not pass a person praying or smoking or eating peyote, and must again consult the leader to see if the way out is clear; there is still another obstacle in the fireman, for no one may exit between him and his seat while he is fixing the fire (the smoker may temporarily put his smoke on the ground before him, or the fireman temporarily take his seat in these cases).

The Clay rite of the Winnebago has a unique method of passing objects: clockwise along the north from the leader to the fireman at the east, then counter-clockwise back to the leader and around along the south to the door, and again clockwise to the leader. The Caddo meticulously observe another rule in entering and leaving the tipi, as though the interior were divided into north and south sides: those on the south enter clockwise and exit counter-clockwise, while those on the north enter counter-clockwise and exit clockwise.

These sometimes complicated "rules" are not the least part of "learning about peyote," and the ordering of them by the leader reflects similarly complex psychological transactions among individuals. For instance, the simple matter of leaving the tipi at recesses is involved in schism among the Caddo. Translating the terms, they cite the full-blood Caddo, Enoch Hoag's, as the "systematic way," or "pure tribal way," to which they are currently returning (because the leader must be consulted before leaving); the half-Caddo, John Wilson's, is "any kind of way" (because he is said to have abrogated some of these rules). The Seminole, Stamp, attempted a compromise, allowing persons to exit without permission if they observed the rules about not passing in front of a smoker or eater of peyote; "I'm right in the middle," he said. But Elijah Reynolds says, "The older men were skeptical. He just made it up to gain influence among others. It's a kind of racial feeling there."

Praying. Minor variations occur in this procedure too. The Cheyenne are said to pray at great length—"an hour or more sometimes," a Comanche told me. The Oto use cedar incense instead of tobacco when they pray. The Ponca pray in unison and audibly before the meeting, seated. The Winnebago stand up together to pray, and the leader stands up to

---

[106] Harrington (*Religion and Ceremonies*, 189) may be in error in stating that the staff is passed to the drummer's *right*; the native painting contradicts this; cf. Kroeber, *The Arapaho*, 402, for the standard method; concerning passing persons, see Parsons, *Taos Pueblo*, 65.

pray with a confessant west of the altar. The Shawnee pray on getting the dirt for the "moon," getting the sage, making the moon, putting a cross on it, cutting the corn shucks, when the food is brought in, etc. The door-man in Pawnee meetings makes a special prayer of dismissal. Often, as with the Kiowa and Oto, the "tribal priest" or curator of the tribal palladium is asked to make an official prayer at some time in the meeting. At Taos the chief prays before the line of worshippers enters inside, and all pray inside. Murie says all the Pawnee pray after the closing song, when the sun's first rays strike the altar through the opened door.[107]

Mrs. Voegelin gives a typical Shawnee prayer:

My prayer is that of a pitiful man. And also these people here, visitors, I wish my creator to answer my prayer to take pity on those visitors. They came to my daughter's meeting for some good reason to learn something about my daughter's meeting. So each of us give blessing, and bless the water that was brought in this morning. So let our friendship purify it, that we might drink this water, to give us long life, and a better life; and I ask our father to bless all my children, and my wife, and all of us who are in this meeting tonight. I am glad my friends came here to help me with my prayer tonight, my daughter's birthday meeting, and we thank thee for this food she brought in, that our friends who are going to eat this food, that they might feel better from now on in everyday life. We ask in the name of Jesus, Amen. (He then cried ceremonially at the finish of the prayer; a few tears ran down his cheeks.)

Praying in peyote meetings appears to have much of the psychological flavor of the old vision quest. The speaker's voice becomes louder as he proceeds, earnest and quavering as he sways with the fullness of his emotion and stretches out his hands toward the peyote and the fire. Sometimes his speech is wholly interrupted by uninhibited broken sobbing as he cries out for the pity of the supernaturals. John Rave, the Winnebago teacher, said that "only if you weep and repent will you be able to attain knowledge." Several of the Delaware face-paintings collected by Dr. Speck represent "crying for repentance."

Incense. Cedar incense is invariably placed on the fire at the beginning of the ceremony to purify the paraphernalia and to "bless" the participants before they eat peyote. A patient or one sick from eating peyote is incensed and fanned with an eagle wing, and incense is burnt for the fireman at midnight when he returns with the water, for the leader on returning from the whistling ceremony outside, and for the water woman in the morning. Others extend the incensing and fanning to every person who re-enters the tipi after a recess, and the Wilson rite[108] has special officials to perform this duty. Many leaders about

[107] Radin, *Crashing Thunder*, 171, 175–77, 185–87; cf. *The Winnebago Tribe*, 394–95; Parsons, *Taos Pueblo*, 64. Murie, *Pawnee Indian Societies*, 637.

[108] Cedar was used to purify the Delaware Big House (Speck, *A Study of the Delaware*, 171), which may account for the special cedar-man in the Delaware rite of Wilson. But the pattern may have been reinforced by the censer of the Catholics, by whom Wilson is known to have been influenced. The Mescalero ascribe sickness after eating peyote to witching by rival shamans. Mooney mentions an odorous root from New Mexico used protectively perhaps, in Kiowa or Comanche meetings. See Kroeber, *The Arapaho*, 402–403; Parsons, *Taos Pueblo*, 65, 105; Densmore, *The Peyote Cult; Winnebago Songs of the Peyote Ceremony.*

midnight provide for the cedar smoking of personally-owned feathers, drum sticks, gourds, etc., and permit individuals to use their own after midnight until morning in place of the equipment provided by the leader.

Method of Eating. Peyote is most commonly eaten in the raw dried state as "buttons," but when obtainable, in the green form also, which is said to be more potent in action. Sometimes both are provided in the same ceremony, as well as peyote "tea," a dark-brown infusion made of soaked and boiled buttons. For the old and sick the buttons may be soaked and softened in water, or pounded dry in mortars and molded into small moist balls; the latter form is reported for the Arapaho, Caddo, Delaware, Lipan, Osage and Winnebago. In chewing the dry buttons the Kiowa, Mescalero and others take care to pick off the fuzz on the top lest it cause sore eyes and blindness.[109]

Singing. The leader always sings the four sets of Esikwita or Mescalero Apache songs as his assistant drums: Hayätinayo (Opening Song), Yahiyano (Midnight Song), Wakaho (Daylight Song) and Gayatina (Closing Song). All the other songs, sung by the participants during the rounds of the drum, are entirely optional. But the standard set songs are not everywhere used: those of the Ponca are said to be Comanche. The ritual songs of the Pawnee are in the Pawnee language, and those of the John Rave rite are in Winnebago (though the followers of Jesse Clay still use the Apache songs.) The circumstances of the origin of some famous songs by Quanah Parker, John Wilson (e.g., Heyowiniho) and Enoch Hoag (e.g., Yanahiano) are widely known.[110]

Many show Christian influence. The Iowa, for example, sing the following songs with Indian vocables, but in a high-pitched style which makes the English words nearly unrecognizable:

   i. Jesus' way is the only way.
   ii. Saviour Jesus is the only Saviour.
   iii. Oh, Lord, Lord, Lord! It is not everyone who says that who shall be saved.
   iv. I know Jesus now.
   v. You must be born again.

The closing song of the Winnebago varies; Yellowbank gave this one:

[109] Opler, *The Influence of Aboriginal Pattern;* cf. Parsons, *Taos Pueblo,* 63, 65.

[110] Mooney, *Miscellaneous Notes,* 8; *Peyote Notebook,* 12, 14. Dr. Maurice G. Smith collected a number of peyote songs near Anadarko in 1930 (see Densmore, *Winnebago Songs of the Peyote Ceremony*) as did Richardson in 1935 (Kiowa largely); see also Klineberg, *Notes on the Huichol,* 458. Radin (*A Sketch of the Peyote Cult,* 3; *The Winnebago Tribe,* 388) implies that the paraphernalia circulate only among the four leaders and others sing only occasionally. Songs are best in the morning when the unpleasant effects of the peyote have worn off (cf. Mooney, *The Mescal Plant;* Kroeber *The Arapaho,* 404–405; Rouhier, *Monographie,* 344). Koshiway (Oto) told a joke in the morning about a partially deaf man's misunderstanding the song "Jesus in the glory now, he ya na ha we," and singing "Jesus in Missouri now." Jack said, laughing, "He must be getting close, He's just over the river now!" Opler's informant said the Lipan can sing songs of a personal ceremony such as bear songs in peyote meetings, but not masked dancer songs.

This is the road that Jesus showed us to walk in.

The followers of Rave close with the Lord's prayer and a song about wings:

There are many wings [repeated five times]
It is God's will that there should be many wings.

The first of these is said to have come from the Arapaho, the second from Isaiah 6. 2, although a New Testament explanation is offered.[111] The last song of the Pawnee meeting refers to Christ.[112]

Other Winnebago songs (with repetitions omitted) are as follows:
God, I thank you for all you have done for me through Jesus' name.

(This is an opening song, according to Yellowbank. Another opening song:)

God's Son says, "Get up and follow Me." Jesus said, "You shall enter into the kindgdom of God."

The following are two morning songs:

Jesus said, "Whoever asks Me for water, I will give him the water of life.
If I give him water he will never thirst again.

The sun is coming up now. God made that light for us.
We are living now. God made us. To God is the glory.

Other peyote songs are not sung at ritually-set times:

Jesus, how do we know, Jesus, how do we know [him]?
We think about Jesus wherever we are.

How did I know, How did I know Jesus?

When I die I will be at the door of heaven and Jesus will take me in.

God said in the beginning, "Let there be light,"
He meant it for you.

Son of God, have pity on us [repeat]
Son of God, when you come again,
Where your people (the angels) are, let us be.

This is God's way [repeat]

[111] Skinner, *Societies of the Iowa*, 728. Densmore, *The Peyote Cult:* "The greatness (power) of God is made manifest through seven beasts, as prophesied. One beast is in power now, as seen by the troubles of the present time, all of which are according to prophecy. There is some spirit [the seraphim] praising God constantly, which signifies that we also should do that in order to inherit eternal life."

[112] Murie, *Pawnee Indian Societies*, 637.

Whosoever believeth in Him will have everlasting life.
This is God's way.

We are living humbly on this earth [five times]
Our Heavenly Father, we want everlasting life through Jesus Christ.
We are living humbly on this earth.

He is the only way, Christ is the Way of Life,
He is the only way.[113]

Radin[114] adds the following Winnebago songs:

Ask God for life and he will give it to us.

God created us, so pray to him.

To the home of Jesus we are going, pray to him.

Come ye to the road of the son of God; come ye to the road.

Midnight Ceremonies. The whistling outside the tipi at the four quarters is variously rationalized. The Kickapoo say the leader's circuit follows that of the singing inside, the Shawnee that he whistles at the cardinal points "on account of the four different winds." The Northern Cheyenne, according to Hoebel, say they are following the instructions of their culture-hero Sweet Medicine in this, while the Comanche say the whistling is to "notify all things in all directions that we are having a meeting here in the center of the cross, and calling the great power to be with us while we drink so that it could hear our prayers." The Winnebago "flute" blown at this time is to "announce the birth of Christ to all the world"; it also represents the trumpet of the Day of Judgment, and the leader's otter skin hat symbolizes Christ's crown of glory. Other Winnebago[115] say the whistling symbolizes the song of praise of the birds in heaven whom God created. The Arapaho say the whistling is an eagle's cry when it is searching for water, and imitates its coming from a great distance until it dips its beak into the water.[116]

The midnight songs of the Pawnee are said to be for the protection of the man who fetches the water. Old-time Comanche used a paunch for the water, but a bucket is everywhere now used; Comanche and Iowa drinking begin at the cedar chief, rather than south of the door as is usual. The Ponca leader dips a feather in the water and sprinkles patients and those nearby with it; and Shawnee sacrifice a cupful to the earth before drinking. The Kickapoo and others drink directly from the bucket when the fireman brings the midnight

[113] Densmore, *The Peyote Cult; Winnebago Songs of the Peyote Ceremony.*
[114] Radin, *A Sketch of the Peyote Cult,* 5; *The Winnebago Tribe,* 395.
[115] Densmore, *The Peyote Cult;* Radin, *The Winnebago Tribe,* 416–17.
[116] Kroeber, *The Arapaho,* 403. A more concrete physiological reason for the leader's exit was suggested in the preceding section.

water, but use a cup when the woman brings the morning water, in graceful symbolism. Some say the woman represents "Peyote Woman"; others, like the Wichita, identify her with older native powers.[117]

The Lipan have no midnight water ceremony. The Hoag (Caddo) rite has no water ceremonies until the drum has made four rounds of the tipi, but water is brought in for visitors who might call for it or provided outside to be drunk at recesses.[118] In Moonhead's meeting the fireman gets a feather from the leader on leaving and touches the peyote on his return as he is fanned and incensed with cedar.

Recess. After the midnight water ceremony anyone can leave on permission of the leader when he has returned from the whistling ritual outside and been incensed with cedar smoke. People usually leave in twos and threes, as the meeting continues, but they return promptly since others may wish to go out. The Pawnee are apparently unique in their midnight recess: after the water ceremony all leave for a ten to twenty-five minute period, the paraphernalia meanwhile resting on the altar cloth.

Doctoring. Doctoring in peyote meetings (save those of the Kickapoo, Caddo and possibly the Osage)[119] is of prime importance, and in a majority of cases is the expressed purpose of calling a meeting. The supposed therapeutic virtues of peyote, or in the less technological view, its "power," have been important in the history of the cult. Quanah Parker, the great Comanche proselytizer of peyote, at first opposed to it, was cured of a stomach ailment in 1884 and became one of the most enthusiastic proponents of the herb. Peyote doctoring has been the occasion many times of the spread of peyotism from tribe to tribe (e.g., the Kiowa bringing it to the Creek). Kiowa doctoring was also probably influential in modifying the Church of the First-born on Koshiway's visit in their country, and in bringing it into the fold of the Native American Church.

The motives for the spread of peyotism in the Plains could perhaps be equally divided between doctoring and power-seeking, but the dichotomy is somewhat artificial in terms of native ideologies: indeed, the chief "power" one gets in meetings is for doctoring.[120] Winnebago attitudes recorded by Radin[121] find parallels elsewhere:

---

[117] Skinner, *Societies of the Iowa*, 725, 727. Murie (*Pawnee Indian Societies*, 637) misplaced emphasis in stating that midnight ceremonies as such are peculiar to the Pawnee, yet he was correct, I believe, in implying that their special midnight recess was unique.

[118] Cf. Petrullo, *The Diabolic Root*, 116. Spybuck follows this Caddo-Delaware custom (Voegelin, *Shawnee Field Notes.*) Cf. the painting in Harrington (*Religion and Ceremonies*, pl. 9); but Spybuck is Shawnee not Delaware.

[119] The Osage case is offered thus tentatively as it was in answer to a leading question in a public hearing. See Office of Indian Affairs, *Discussion Concerning Peyote*, 44.

[120] Certainly doctoring was the most important element in the Southwest; cf. Bennett and Zingg, *The Tarahumara*, 294: "The use of peyote resembles an elaborate curing ceremony [among the Tarahumari] rather than a cult." Opler (*The Influence of Aboriginal Pattern*) writes that "Apache ceremonialism had for its primary object the curing of disease," and peyotism came within this framework.

[121] Radin, *A Sketch of the Peyote Cult*, 12–13; *The Winnebago Tribe*, 423.

The first and foremost virtue predicated by Rave for the peyote was its curative power. He gives a number of instances in which hopeless venereal diseases and consumption were cured by its use; and this to the present day is the first thing one hears about it. In the early days of the peyote cult it appears that Rave relied principally for new converts upon the knowledge of this great curative virtue of the peyote . . . . Along this line lay unquestionably its appeal for the first converts. Its spread was due to a large number of interacting factors. One informant claims that there was little religion connected with it at first, and that people drank the peyote on account of its peculiar effects.

Densmore[122] says that prayer during Winnebago peyote doctoring "are petitions to God for the recovery of the sick person, not affirmations of his recovery."

Opler quotes a Lipan informant on doctoring:[123]

In the early days they just had a good time for one night. It was not used as a curing ceremony then . . . . At first they wanted to have good visions, that's what they were after. But then, recently, they began to use it as a medicine for sick people . . . . If a sick person comes in the tipi, they see what is the matter with him. Perhaps a witch has shot something into him, a bone or something like that. It is seen. Then the sick one rolls a cigarette and gives it to someone there who he thinks can cure him. Perhaps some man says, "I think I can take that out with the help of peyote and these other men." So he does his ceremonial work in there and extracts what is bothering the patient . . . . He sucks it out usually with his own lips, not with a tube. It is nasty work right there. It might be dirty and full of pus. But the medicine man doesn't think of it in that way. To them it is just as if they were sucking nice juice out of something. Yet it will look terrible to others . . . All the bad things have to go into the fire and burn down to ashes . . . . Sometimes they suck out things like insects which have been shot into people and these things pop. Sometimes when they throw the evil object in the fire it blazes up blue but does not pop.

Northern Cheyenne and Shawnee patients sit in special places in the peyote tipi, as in the sweat lodge, suggesting that older patterns of doctoring are involved; as we have seen, the sweat lodge is an integral part of the Osage peyote round-house plan. That associations of curing by peyote and curing in the sweat lodge lie close to the surface finds affirmation in an interesting Arapaho case:[124]

One of the recent modifications of the peyote ceremonial was devised by a firm devotee, to cure a sick person. The originator of this new form of the worship believes himself to have been cured by the drug. In this ceremonial, which was repeated four times, the tent seems to have represented a sweat house, and a path led from the entrance to a fire outside, as before a sweat lodge. The ritual, while remaining a peyote ceremony, conformed more or less to the ordinary processes of doctoring a sick person.

[122] Densmore, *Winnebago Songs of the Peyote Ceremony*, 3.

[123] To be sure, diagnosis of illness by clairvoyance, etc., is resorted to, but this is to be expected when witchcraft is the main cause of sickness. (Cf. the combination of doctoring and divination with cohoba snuff in Haiti. Safford, *Narcotic Plants*, 393.) Obsessive elements of interest to psychiatry are found both in the witchcraft fear and in the methods chosen to cure the ill.

[124] Kroeber, *The Arapaho*, 405.

One could easily over-emphasize the novelty of such a procedure, considering the widespread use of peyote in doctoring, yet even the Caddo, who do not doctor with peyote, often have four meetings to pray for the recovery of the sick person; certainly cures by peyote do not rest entirely on the "technological" procedure of the patient's eating and drinking peyote, but others present "help" by eating in the name of the sufferer and praying. This is not at all unlike the presence of relatives and others in the sweat bath praying for the patient's recovery; the various uses of sage, the fire pits in some altars, and the ritual necessity for a fire even on the hottest summer nights further suggest sweat bath parallels.[125]

Peyote is a panacea in doctoring. A Cheyenne woman was cured of a cancer of the liver which had been pronounced hopeless at a White hospital. Such invidious distinctions between White and peyote doctoring are common; for the former represents merely human skill, and is not the unmodified herb the direct creation of God? Belo Kozad, himself a well-known Kiowa peyote doctor, spoke as follows:

When my sick wife was in there I chewed peyote for her. Her skin got like wood bark—the hair come out. The doctors couldn't make it. We give it up, can't do anything. [It was] diabetes, and we shoot him every time she eats. That spoils the people; they lose the mind and the skin gets bad. That morphine for Howard [Sankadote, who was ill the night of the meeting and could not be present] make him talk funny. It just ruin the people in the mind. *Come* to peyote! God knows more than any people!

Perhaps Belo had every "pragmatic" right to talk thus: had he not himself cured a boy's hemorrhage by eating one hundred green peyotes for him? Peyote indeed is a famous cure for tuberculosis and respiratory diseases.

John Bearskin (Winnebago) knew of two cures by "Sister Etta" in meetings: one a woman with goitre, the other a boy who had previously been dumb.[126] Pneumonia also readily yields to peyote, producing beneficial perspiration when thirty buttons are drunk over a period of hours in two quarts of water. The writer has seen doctoring with peyote for a crushed thigh, tuberculosis, and malnutrition (?) in a two-year-old child; this last cried fretfully in the early part of the meeting, but was fed "tea" until it was blue and quiet in strychnine tetanus by morning. The wife of our Quapaw host had also been "operated on in church."

A Sioux doctor, who had gotten his power from a vision in which peyote turned into a man, doctored at Taos; but an acquaintance of Dr. Parsons imputed his trachoma to witchcraft on the part of "foreigners" who came to large meetings. He found that peyote water prevented the inflammation of his eyes. Another boy's leg was "all gone, rotten," and the boy himself emaciated. Peyote men prayed over him for a month, whereupon he

[125] Kiowa and Comanche parallels with older doctoring methods have been collected also. One of the latter involves a 2 foot mound in the tipi with a cedar sprig on it, a fire, a woman assistant, smoking of tobacco, and blowing on the patient.

[126] Densmore, *The Peyote Cult; Winnebago Songs of the Peyote Ceremony.*

became well and fat, though his leg remained drawn up because he had taken too much White man's medicine. The wife of a peyote man, herself cured of neck sores by the plant, asserted that witch sickness is lacking nowadays in Taos because of the power of peyote in exorcizing witchcraft; a peyote chief, however, holding a button in his hand, had had to remove a porcupine quill which some witch had shot into her nose. At Taos even anti-peyotists consider it good for cures, and Dr. Parsons, no doubt with some reason, makes the query: "Will peyote find its character of witch prophylaxis an introduction to the southern pueblos?"[127]

Peyote is equally successful in treating mental cases. An Oto informant told of four successive meetings held for a man who had "gone crazy" when his wife left him. Formerly under observation at Norman, he was afraid people were coming for him during the meeting; he could hardly talk, wanted to run out and people had to wrestle with him. Old Man White Horn gave him a peyote and told him it would protect him; finally, in the third successive meeting the man "came to" and asked what had been happening. Another Oto patient chopped wood incessantly, rolled and unrolled strings, etc., and used to have "meetings" by himself, drumming, singing and eating peyote all alone. An Oto told me of a Taos boy who had "gone crazy"; some said it was peyote that was doing this. But a doctor from west of Albuquerque came and pulled a snake and a dead water dog out of him; these had been his medicines, taught him by his father, and it was decided that he had clearly broken some taboo surrounding his father's medicine.

"*Preaching.*" An interesting feature of peyotism, probably deriving from earlier patterns, is the moral lecture in the morning. In one Caddo "moon" the leader "talks to the boys, teaches them, just like a preacher, telling them to do the right thing through life, and the consequences if they didn't do the right things." White Wolf (Comanche) says Quanah Parker lectured younger people in the morning; so too did Kickapoo, Carrizo, Shawnee and Wichita leaders.

After passing peyote, the Delaware leader "addresses the peyote and the fire, prays, and often delivers a regular sermon or moral lecture." In the Iowa meeting:[128]

The peyote chief . . . leads in the preaching and Bible reading . . . . The leader (or, as the writer understands it) perhaps some visiting preacher of the faith, gets up and delivers a sermon, while the cedar chief casts some more incense on the fire. [He commonly exhorts them to confession.] The leader then calls on other preachers to talk, and then asks the fire chief [to pass the peyote again] . . . . Meanwhile he continues to read the Bible and exhort all sinners to repent. He points out that all the old ways have been given up, and with them their "idols," such as the great drum of the religious dance.

John Wilson ordinarily began his meetings with a talk by himself; the Oto are commonly addressed in meetings by their "tribal priest." The estrangement of the lively J. S. (Kiowa)

[127] Parsons, *Taos Pueblo*, 60, 67–68.
[128] Harrington, *Religion and Ceremonies*, 189; Skinner, *Societies of the Iowa*, 725.

and his young wife was composed through moral homilies delivered by older relatives in a peyote meeting—a typical occurrence.

At the end of the Pawnee meeting[129]

the members . . . sit in their places and talk over their experiences . . . . The leader closes the meeting at noon with a lecture, or sermon, on ethical matters, speaking especially against the use of alcohol.

Possibly Osage "testimony" may have some relation to this.[130] The Winnebago[131]

ceremony is opened by a prayer by the founder and leader, this being followed by an introductory speech . . . . During the early hours . . . speeches by people in the audience [are made], and the reading and explanation of part of the Bible.

The midnight sermon, after the midnight water, also occurs:[132]

Then the leader asks anyone he desires to make a speech. This may emphasize any point in regard to peyote.

The moral harangue is no doubt derived from earlier Plains patterns, though it is a South-western feature as well, among the Rio Grande Pueblos and elsewhere.[133]

Prophecy. The gift of prophecy has often been claimed by individuals in native America. The first well-known such was Popé of the Pueblo Revolt in 1680, but his successors were many: Wabokieshiek, or "White Cloud," the Winnebago-Sauk prophet of the Black Hawk War; the Delaware prophet of Pontiac's Conspiracy (1762); Tenskwatawa, twin brother of Tecumseh, and the well-known "Shawnee Prophet" (1805); Kanakuk, the Kickapoo[134] reformer (1827); Smohalla, the Sokulk dreamer of the Columbia (1870–1885); Tavibo, the Paiute; Nakaidoklini, the Apache (1881); Wovoka, or Jack Wilson, the Paiute prophet of the Ghost Dance of 1889 and later; Skaniadariio, or "Handsome Lake," the Seneca teacher, etc.[135]

[129] Murie, *Pawnee Indian Societies*, 637.
[130] "[At] 5 o'clock in the morning, when suddenly the singing ceased, the drum and the ceremonial staff were put away, and the leader, beginning at the door, asked each person, 'What did you see?'" (La Flesche, in *Peyote as Used in Religious Worship*, 33).
[131] Radin, *A Sketch of the Peyote Cult*, 3; *The Winnebago Tribe*, 388.
[132] Radin, *Crashing Thunder*, 176; Densmore, *The Peyote Cult*.
[133] Wissler, *The American Indian*, 189: "One prominent feature of Nahua life was the elaboration of the moral lecture. In the Pueblo region of the Rio Grande the chiefs and head men were given to daily moral lectures. . . . Perhaps we are again dealing with a general characteristic of New World society." Cf. the Tamaulipecan harangue (Prieto, *Historia y Estadistica*, 123–24).
[134] The prophecies and predictions of C. W. (Kickapoo president of the Native American Church) on the basis of his visions have an old-time flavor, though colored by Christianity and proselytizing for peyote: he prophesied the "Judgment Day" and the "new world" to come; "it will be too late to go in [the peyote tipi] when the time comes—you've got to start now," Kishkaton reports him as saying.
[135] *Handbook of the American Indians*, 1: 65a, 309–10, 401–402, 650; 2: 371a, 587a, 885–86. Cf. the elaborate Quichua and Aztec Messiah legends.

Save for the revelations of the Caddo-Delaware John Wilson, and the teachings of
John Rave and Jonathan Koshiway, this tradition has become much attenuated as regards
peyotism. Large-scale prophecies can no longer be made to skeptical and disillusioned audi-
ences, but prophecy in minor matters still occurs via peyote (e.g., the Delaware case in
which a serious industrial accident might have been avoided if he had only been able to
interpret correctly a warning peyote gave him). Old-time Comanche could hear the enemy
while still away off when they ate peyote, and in making raids could discover the whereabouts of horses, etc. White Wolf, again, visioned Charley Seminole's face all bloody at a
peyote meeting, but was unable to interpret the prophecy; somewhat later, sure enough,
the Seminole accidentally shot himself under the eye.

In the origin story of peyote, when the Kiowa or Comanche were on the war-path,
the Apache leader knew of their leader's approach to the tipi where they were having a
meeting, and told his fireman to invite him in, whence the visitor brought peyote back to
his tribe; this story is known all over the southern Plains. Around 1870 the only Kiowa
who ate peyote was Pabo, or Big Horse. When he wished to find the whereabouts of an
absent party he would go into a tipi and say "gʸähgūṇboṇta" (I am going to look for medicine), and would drum and rattle and eat peyote, and tell the results of his inquiry afterward. Pabo's power was from the eagle, but Kiowa owl-doctors had clairvoyant powers
in pre-peyote times. Another Kiowa user miraculously predicted the coming of telegraph
lines and the railroad to Anadarko, having previously never seen either, and a Wichita
predicted the World War.

"Baptism" and Other Morning Ceremonies. The "curing" ceremonies of Mexico and the
Southwest still find a reflex in the Plains "baptism" in the morning ceremonies. The leader
in the tipi whistles for the water as in the midnight ceremony, and a smoke is made for the
bearer, the only difference being that this time it is a woman, often symbolically costumed,[136]
who some say represents Peyote Woman of the legend. Many groups, however, have a
ritual "baptism" in this morning ceremony, which is lacking at midnight.[137] The Arapaho,[138]
for example, untie the drum and pass it around the circles; each man wrings out the wet
drum head, makes a loop of the lacing-rope and throws it lasso-fashion over his foot to
symbolize the roping of horses, presses the seven marbles of the drum to various parts of his
body, and drinks a little of the drum water. The worshippers then wash the paint from
their faces, and comb their hair, a towel, a mirror, a comb and water making the round of
the tipi; then finally the drinking water is passed around.

The Delaware file out behind the fireman to greet the rising sun with prayer, and,
standing in the same relative positions they occupied in the tipi, wash their faces with the
water which the fireman pours on their hands; those who fall down at this time are said

<hr>

[136] Kroeber, *The Arapaho*, 403–404; Densmore, *The Peyote Cult.*
[137] Mooney (*The Mescal Plant*, 8) errs, we believe, in citing a Kiowa midnight baptism.
[138] Kroeber, *The Arapaho*, 404.

to be visiting heaven. The rest re-enter for the ritual breakfast. The Caddo similarly file out to wash and comb their hair, and preserve the same order even at the secular meal at noon. The Iowa wash with soap and water as they sit in the tipi; "the peyote chief himself carries the water to show his humility, because of Biblical references to the washing of feet." The Shawnee are marshalled outside in two lines at sun-up to wash their faces and "do arm exercises." The Kickapoo, Wichita, Oto, Northern Cheyenne and others pass the drum and sometimes all the ritual paraphernalia around to be handled; some lick the drum stick dipped in the water and touch it to various part of their bodies. The Ponca leader, using a feather, shakes water on participants both at midnight and in the morning, and as in some other groups, waters the drum also.[139]

The ritual "quitting songs" are sung by the Pawnee just at dawn, as the first rays of the sun strike the altar through the opened door; the last song is sung five times, and each member then prays in turn to God. The "baptism" ceremony of the Winnebago John Rave cultists (derived from the Oto) is more Christian in tone than that of the Jesse Clay rite (of Arapaho origin). Rave dipped his fingers in a peyote infusion, and passed them over the forehead of a new member saying, "God, His holiness," (or, as some say, "God, the Son, and the Holy Ghost").[140] A little water is also poured on the ground as a sacrifice. The well-nigh universal mode of disposing of the remaining water in the drum is to pour it along the earthen "moon."

Peyote Breakfast. The foods in the ritual breakfast in the tipi are so standardized as scarcely to allow comparative treatment. They are merely minor variations on the theme: water, parched corn in sweetened water, fruit and dried sweetened meat.[141] From the Lipan (roasted corn, yucca fruit, wild fruit and meat, according to Opler) to the Ute (canned corn, canned peaches and corned beef, as reported by Mrs. Cooke) the uniformity is striking. These foods are eaten from a common set of four vessels,[142] which are passed around with a single spoon in each. Sometimes ground hominy or parched corn mush is substituted, and Hoebel reports the Northern Cheyenne use of Cracker Jack for the parched corn. Beef is the usual meat, in boneless chunks or dried, pounded and sweetened, but pork (tabooed

[139] Petrullo, *The Diabolic Root*, 93; Harrington, *Religion and Ceremonies*, 190; Skinner, *Societies of the Iowa*, 727; Voegelin, *Shawnee Field Notes*; Hoebel, *Northern Cheyenne Field Notes*. "Baptism" is Lipan also.

[140] Murie, *Pawnee Indian Societies*, 637; Radin, *A Sketch of the Peyote Cult*, 3, 5; *The Winnebago Tribe*, 389; Densmore, *The Peyote Cult*. It is said that "the peyote-eaters wanted to get baptized and unite with the church in Winnebago, but the clergyman in charge would not permit them, so they went and did their own baptizing through their leader John Rave."

[141] Some add cookies and candy. The use of sweet foods and the sweetening of others recalls the eating of teo-nanacatl with honey, and the eating of sweet-meats while smoking "grifos" or marihuana. See Maillefert, *La Marihuana*, 6–7.

[142] Mopope (Kiowa) painted a special set of white enamel-ware vessels for Kozad's meetings: water-bucket (tipi and "water-bird"), parched-corn pan (ear of corn and four-direction feathers), fruit-pan (thunderbird, fruit within a crescent design) and meat-dish (cooking fire, buffalo horns and sun design).

for the Comanche) is reported for the Ponca and Northern Cheyenne.[143] Wild fruits are somewhat preferred to canned varieties, but are not always obtainable. Although the original meanings and connections with agricultural, gathering and hunting ceremonies have long since been lost sight of, the feeling for the proper foods in a peyote breakfast is still quite strong in the Plains, a remarkable instance of culture continuity.

[143] A recurrence of an old custom ascribed to Sweet Medicine appears in the Northern Cheyenne peyote breakfast, when an individual takes five pieces of meat across the lodge to a visitor (Hoebel, *Northern Cheyenne Field Notes*).

PSYCHOLOGICAL ASPECTS OF PEYOTISM

A descriptive account of a ritual pattern, however meticulously detailed it be, must always fall short of reality unless supplemented by further information regarding its functioning in terms of individuals. The older descriptive ethnography and the newer interest in the dynamics of culture are as necessary to each other as anatomy and physiology, of which, indeed, they are the anthropological parallels. We accordingly embark upon the somewhat anecdotal filling in of the pattern sketched in the preceding section.

Every student of peyote has been met with a sometimes odd mixture of suspiciousness and candor, an ambivalence in attitude derived primarily from the native attitudes toward peyotism itself. Most of the younger adherents of the cult have had White schooling of a sort, but though the express intent of this schooling has been the deculturation of the Indian, on returning to their tribes old loyalties are characteristically reestablished and old ways of thinking fallen into; the total effect of Christian teaching on peyotism, therefore, has not been particularly profound.

But all peyote adherents are aware of the efforts, both religious and secular, to suppress the movement, and most of them are familiar with the arguments advanced against peyote as an allegedly harmful drug. They have commonly met this with the counter-propaganda that peyote is a specific cure for alcoholism, but nevertheless this attitude on the part of bearers of the powerful and prestige-full White culture has not left them unimpressed, and there is a consequent lack of psychological security in their belief and practice of peyotism. Though the cult is a compromise solution between Christianity and older native religions, there is still a large number of persons whose attitude toward peyote is thoroughly precarious—as evidenced by the vacillations, defections and rationalizations we are about to list.

Save for the Caddo (and there are perhaps historical reasons for this) ordinary sincerity and interest are met by the Plains practitioners with corresponding candor and friendliness toward the ethnographer. There is no very great difficulty in a sympathetic White man's attending a peyote meeting nowadays. Indeed, some groups, out of naïve faith in the plant's power, seem even to invite attendance in the hope of producing a propagandist for the cult to counteract the unfriendliness which they feel, and not unrightly, has arisen from ignorance and prejudice. An instance of this good faith and even naïveté occurs in an Osage petition to Congress that in the event of a law being passed to regulate the use of peyote, an exception be made for the "Indian lodges using it as a sacrament," and they promised to use it only under the supervision of reservation superintendents![1] And a sincerity not open to doubt was evidenced by a Cheyenne, one time president of the Native American Church, who sent 200 peyote buttons on his own initiative through his agency-

[1] *Peyote as Used in Religious Worship*, 11, lent through the courtesy of Alfred Wilson (Cheyenne).

superintendent to a chemist at Stanford University, requesting a thorough and disinterested scientific analysis, and offering his further services if necessary.[2]

Another factor making for insecurity of belief and practice has been the intense opposition on the part of some leaders of older cults in the tribe itself. We will recur to this subject in discussing the history of peyote in specific groups, but cite here the rather accentuated example of hostility at Taos.[3] Dr. Parsons tells of a lawsuit between a "peyote boy" and one of the Mexican Penitentes which was resolved by both paying the costs, to prevent the betrayal of native customs. Thereafter the chiefs said:

[Peyote] does not belong to us. It is not the work given to us. It will stop the rain. Something will happen.

But as desire for rain is the typical anxiety reflected in native ritual in the agricultural Southwest, the peyote boys retorted in the same vein. In the drought of 1922 they said:

"Now it is so dry this summer because the peyote boys can't have their meetings; they used to bring so much rain." [Indeed, nowadays,] the townspeople are given to referring all their inclination to feud to the peyote situation.

But there is ample evidence that this tendency existed before peyote ever came to Taos. On the other hand, the wife of one peyote-user asserted that there was no more "witch sickness" in the town because of the peyote people, who were able to exorcize witches; nevertheless, one man attributed his trachoma to witching by "foreigners" in peyote meetings.

Such intense seriousness is in marked contrast to the situation in some Plains tribes, where peyote jokes are told at times in the forenoons after meetings, when sufficient rapport has been established. A Comanche story tells of a leader who took his expensive watch into a meeting and laid it on the altar cloth near the father peyote to "show off." A man shaking the gourd vigorously on the north side was making motions toward the father peyote, and miraculously the watch became broken up; "it was just a mess of works there loose, and the hands dropped off." The informant was highly amused at this story. An Oto told the tale of a man whose jaw became stiff as he was singing, a contretemps which upset the whole meeting. Though this effect was apparently due to peyote, the story was greeted with much laughter. People laugh at the incorrect singing of peyote songs too. We have already mentioned the one involving the alarming proximity of the Messiah just

---

[2] Letter of Mack Haag (Cheyenne), Calumet, Oklahoma, to Dr. R. W. Miles, San Francisco, California, Sept. 16, 1925, and reply Oct. 2, 1925. What unfriendliness the writer met was largely the projection of individual suspiciousness, e.g., that of a Caddo who concocted a preposterous story out of his own imagination. When I returned to Anadarko in 1936 with a White companion who remained for several weeks, this man circulated the story that James Mooney's son and the son of the Commissioner of Indian Affairs had arrived to make a thorough check-up on peyote, that to obtain an "absolute lowdown" we had a man stationed on every corner in the town to check up on every Indian who took a drink of beer in a saloon, picked up a woman, or was overheard swearing—in any of a dozen Indian languages!

[3] Parsons, *Taos Pueblo*, 66–68.

across the river in Missouri. Another story is told of a visiting Kiowa who attempted to sing a Comanche song in meeting. He mispronounced the words and sang, "*Mentula exposita est! Mentula exposita est!*" All the auditors of this story laughed at this further proof that the Comanche have "no shame."

The attitudes surrounding the plant itself are interesting. Perhaps the Tarahumari[4] attitudes are most accentuated:

Those who have never eaten peyote fear it most. Should they touch the plant, they believe they would go crazy or die. Those who have once eaten it at a fiesta need have no fear of it, providing they treat it properly.

At Tarahumari feasts of the dead peyote protects the living from the ghost of the deceased, quite as eating it prevents bears from attacking the hunter or deer from running away from him; it confers invulnerability from the Apaches and warns of their approach, and likewise foils the machinations of sorcerers and robbers. In short, "hikuli is a powerful protector of its people under all circumstances."

The Lipan well represent the attitude of early users in the United States:

If a fellow is not scared, is not afraid of it, he will surely have a good time. A fellow who is afraid of it just gets dizzy and frightened. He sees things that frighten him. What he sees is not true, but is just playing a joke on him . . . . When a fellow is honest and good natured it is easy for him. But when a fellow is rough and ill tempered he will have a hard time learning from peyote. It will scare him and make it hard for him . . . . The chief peyote is pretty tough. It watches what is going on. It keeps everything straight. It is a plant, but it can see and understand better than a man. If someone has wrong thoughts, he had better look out or he will go crazy. . . .

When they first start eating peyote they put their thoughts on something good, something they want, for they say that whatever you are thinking about when you start is what you will see all during the night in your vision . . . . Sometimes a man sees a vision and it scares him and he goes out running. But he is all right the next day. The thing that frightened him won't happen unless he thinks about it all the time and it frightens him continually. Then he begins to be afraid of it and thinks it will happen. But if he holds it off—holds off the bad thoughts that frighten him— nothing will occur . . . . Sometimes it makes you dream something pleasant, sometimes it makes you dream something dangerous . . . . In the morning, just after the meeting is over, you can tell others what you saw.

Hoebel writes that

the trickiness of peyote is emphasized by the Cheyenne. They constantly reiterate that a man must keep hold of himself and also that he must live straight or peyote will shame him.

---

[4] Datura or Jimsonweed was also greatly feared; it killed or drove crazy anyone who touched it. Only shamans armed with the more powerful peyote dared uproot it. Bakanori was used by runners to rub on their legs or to carry in the girdle to counteract witchcraft in the ritual races; but if kept too long this plant also would drive a man crazy or kill him. See Bennett and Zingg, *The Tarahumara*, 136–38, 292, 338, 347; Lumholtz, *Unknown Mexico*, 1: 359–60, 372–74; also Mooney, *Tarumari-Guayachic*.

A Delaware rationalized the unpredictable effect of peyote somewhat differently:[5]

I had the feeling once that it was going to make me foolish, but that happens to everybody, and is a test of one's faith in peyote.

Vomiting of peyote is a punishment for one's sins, but it cleanses the body of its impurities in the process and purifies the blood. Part of the symbolism in the bead-work on an Arapaho fetish-pouch is the "vomitings" deposited in a ring around the inside of the tipi.[6]

It would be naive to suppose that peyote tastes any less unpleasant to natives than it does to Whites. But we should remember that peyote is eaten by Indians influenced by strong motives and deep belief, and the consequent physiological state is easily and adequately rationalized. It is not surprising that a man addicted to alcohol and shamed by it before both Indians and Whites believes that "whiskey and peyote fight in a man, and usually peyote wins and brings it out." No doubt such a cure *ad nauseam* is as good as any, and more effective than some. The depressing effect of peyote is also well recognized and measures are taken to overcome it. The Arapaho have feathers at four corners of the tipi to brush persons who tire during the meeting, and the "smoke" at Taos is made to overcome the depression of the early stages of eating, as sage is similarly used in the Plains.[7]

But suffering is counted even a positive virtue among people who had the "vision quest" in the old days. A crippled Indian at Miami told me that "to get power from peyote a man must suffer to it." The four rounds of the drum without water among the Caddo suggests an intention of making the meeting an ordeal, and Mrs. Voegelin's Shawnee informant emphasized that the Spybuck moon modelled on the Caddo was "hard." Most informants would consider the Osage, who have "beds" in their meeting-houses sometimes, not merely ostentatious but also "soft"; one old man said that sage under the blankets of the seat as a cushion indicated a decadent generation, for did not they sit on the bare ground in the old days? A Kickapoo informant said Quanah Parker used to warn them that the taste of peyote wasn't good, though "it would keep you on the right path." About 2:10 in the morning a Comanche informant of Simmons said:

If there is suffering, this is the time. That's the reason I took a good rest: so I could stand it. Many a time I have fallen over at this time. It's getting on to what they call the dark hour, the hour of the Crucifixion. Everyone here is suffering now.

The Winnebago[8] elaborated into a dogma the physiological effect of peyote in producing occasional vomiting:

[5] Opler, *The Use of Peyote; Lipan Apache Field Notes;* Hoebel, *Northern Cheyenne Field Notes;* Petrullo, *The Diabolic Root,* 71.

[6] Can this be a reflex of an older pattern? Spier (*The Sun Dance,* 473) lists as a part of the Sun Dance of the Arapaho, Kiowa and Southern Cheyenne a prepared drink and the induction of vomiting. Kozad (Kiowa) believed peyote had a good effect whether vomited or not—the virtue being in the quantity eaten. Cf. the emetic rites in connection with the "black drink."

[7] Kroeber, *The Arapaho,* 406–407; Parsons, *Taos Pueblo,* 65.

[8] Radin, *A Sketch of the Peyote Cult,* 5–6, 19–20; *The Winnebago Tribe,* 395.

If a person who is truly repentant eats peyote for the first time, he does not suffer at all from its effects. But if an individual is bull-headed, does not believe in its virtue, he is likely to suffer a great deal. . . . If a person eats peyote and does not repent openly, he has a guilty conscience, which leaves him as soon as the public repentance has been made. . . . If a peyote-user relapses into his old way of living, then the peyote causes him great suffering. . . . The disagreeable effects of the peyote varied directly with a man's disbelief in it. This explanation [Rave] persistently drummed into the ears of beginners, who otherwise become terrified and give up too soon.

We have already noted the Huichol-Tarahumari belief that peyote sees and punishes evil deeds. Similarly, when as an old man Kutubi (Comanche) became sick he gave his father peyote to Mumsika, reasoning that he had "probably eaten something peyote didn't allow"; this is probably the same father peyote which years before had predicted a bad fate for a war party. The leader had wept and strenuously upbraided peyote for this and may later have felt some guilt for his presumptuousness. In any case he held peyote responsible both times for his bad fortune.

But if peyote is blamed for bad fortune, it is also accredited with the liquidation of manifold anxieties. Fear of death is perhaps the most conspicuous anxiety in Plains culture. It is not surprising, therefore, that doctoring plays a major part in the cult. But the power and authority of peyote are relied upon in other ways too. In a number of tribes peyote or peyote tea is used whenever the individual finds himself confronted with any important personal problem. To be sure, it is the individual's *total wishes* which ultimately find expression in the course of action followed, but the consultation with peyote composes conflicts and gives an authority to the decision which the "unaided" individual might not have been able to summon.[9]

The protective function of the father peyote is most highly patterned, perhaps, among the Mescalero Apache.[10] In this culture the aggressions arising from the particular socio-economic system of marriage find expression in intense witchcraft activity. But for the typical aggressions which a culture engenders, a culture often has a patterned solution to offer. For though the means used were magical, the aggressions and counter-aggressions were *real* in the psychological sense, and peyote had a real function in witch-prophylaxis. Shamanistic rivalry was most virulent and witchcraft-anxiety was correspondingly as intense as the projected hatreds. One never knew what dangerous and powerful supernatural possessions

[9] E.g., Charles Lonewolf (Kiowa) in *Peyote as Used in Religious Worship*, 53; Hoebel, *Comanche Field Notes*. Again, all the prestige of the culture itself was behind Old Man White Horn's pronouncement to the psychotic Oto, R. E., that peyote would protect him. This individual suffered apparently from an obsessional neurosis (stereotyped actions, collecting string, rolling and unrolling balls of it, persecutory fears, avoidance of people, fear of being pursued etc.). If his difficulties had originally arisen from real or supposed aggressions upon him of members of his group, the therapeutic value of the assertion that the fetish would protect him is obvious. For the belief that it would protect him was shared by all the others present, and he had the support of the enormous impetus a deep-seated culture-pattern possesses. The importance of the fetish plant as a psychic "authority" should likewise not be minimized.

[10] Opler, *The Influence of Aboriginal Pattern, passim.*

a hated rival possessed, hence a number of protective devices were developed in Mescalero peyotism.[11] Yet characteristically in this uncomfortable culture, the power of peyote was itself dangerous, and elaborate care had to be exercised in removing the fuzz from the top of the buttons before eating. Should it touch the eyes, it would cause blindness!

In the Plains the fear is often expressed, not without justification, that the white man is ever about to take away the peyote religion from the Indian, as he has taken almost everything else material and immaterial. But the frequency of this asserveration, sometimes in contexts which the writer thought were unrealistic, indicates that Indians view peyote in a sense as a protector from the Whites. Peyote is rather confidently thought to be able to take care of itself—which accounts for the comparative ease with which a white man can obtain entrance to a meeting, where he will be exposed to "proof" of peyote's power. We need not emphasize this function of peyote beyond its true proportions, but it may be recalled that peyote enabled a native to escape from a white man's jail; that it aided peyote pilgrims to bring plants undeterred through the white man's customs; that it is the sovereign remedy for the evil of the white man's whiskey; that peyote has so far protected itself against the white man's attempted sumptuary legislation; that it miraculously escaped detection and confiscation in a white man's war, through which it protected its bearer; and, not least in psychological importance, that peyote characteristically succeeds (because it is of God, not man) in cures which the white doctor has long since given up as hopeless.

This function of peyote as protector is rooted in earlier history: it sees from afar the approach of the enemy, predicts the results of battle and protects one in battle from the hazards of war. Peyote would have prevented a gun accident, and an accident with a mechanical saw, in instances collected, if the persons involved had only been able to understand its warning. And in another case, when a serious automobile accident had already happened, peyote quelled the anxiety of worrying relatives in assuring an ultimate cure. Again, Mary Buffalo, White Wolf's mother and Belo Kozad's wife had all lost many children, until they took their sons into peyote meetings and prayed to the power that they be spared; in each case the son grew to manhood. Peyote is the comforter in the event of death also; a funeral meeting is often held as the last rite of respect to the deceased, and some groups hold anniversary meetings for four years after the death.

But peyote punishes as well. An inconstant result of its physiological action is the production at times of an intense fear-state. Rave, for example, (Winnebago)[12] in a period of mental stress experienced his fear:

Suddenly I saw a big snake. I was very much frightened. Then another one came crawling over

<hr>

[11] For one matter, the shaman's staff never left his hand to be passed around as in the Plains; and each individual had some prophylactic fetish in his hand which he never dared relinquish throughout the meeting. Note, too, the fetish peyote on the altar: on this the leader could detect evil thoughts and acts, such as the magic intrusive "shooting" of water-beetles and feathers by rival shamans into each other.

[12] Radin, *Crashing Thunder*, 180, see also 193–94, 198–99; *A Sketch of the Peyote Cult*, 8–9; Densmore, *Winnebago Songs of the Peyote Ceremony*.

me. "My God! Where are these snakes coming from?" There at my back there seemed to be something also. So I looked around and saw a snake about ready to swallow me entirely. It had arms and legs and a long tail. The end of its tail was like a spear. "Oh God! I am surely going to die now," I thought. Then I turned in another direction and I saw a man with horns and long claws and with a spear in his hand. He jumped for me and I threw myself on the ground. He missed me. Then I looked back. This time he started back but it seemed to me that he was directing his spear at me. Again I threw myself on the ground and he missed me. There seemed to be no escape for me.

A similar experience of Crashing Thunder (Winnebago) is noted elsewhere; and in a story told of Bear Track (Cheyenne) and his Osage wife on their visit to the Holy Land, the parents seem to have communicated some of their anxiety and fear surrounding mysterious experiences there to their small daughter, who awoke screaming one night at a presence she saw in the room.

The peyote meeting of many groups has incorporated in it a powerful mechanism for the liquidation of individual anxieties in the practice of public confession of sins. It is difficult to over-estimate the importance of this feature.[13] On the exhortation of the leader, many members rise and accuse themselves publicly of misdemeanors or offenses, asking pardon of persons who might have been injured by them. How large a part peyote has in the production of such states is an open question (for the pattern of public confession is wide-spread aboriginally in the New World); but that confession to the father-peyote and his authority, and repentance before the group is of profound significance cannot be doubted. More than ritual tears stream down the confessant's cheeks as he acknowledges his faults and asks aid to keep his promise to mend his ways.

Peyote often figures in matters of personal adjustment. The story of John Rave is too well known to require more than mention here. The somewhat similar history of Jonathan Koshiway (Oto) is likewise interesting in showing how a compromise was struck between the older pagan culture and Christianity, to whose influence this individual had been exposed. The personal solution in Koshiway's case seems to have been a perfectly satisfactory one: in the Church of the First-born he doctored and "hollered" like the source of his power in good old Indian fashion, and on the other hand baptized, conducted funerals and married couples just as in white churches. The statements of Crashing Thunder's father[14] indicate a somewhat less happy and inclusive solution, which involved the sacrifice of the old customs:

[13] Skinner, *Societies of the Iowa*, 725; Radin, *Crashing Thunder*, 177; *A Sketch of the Peyote Cult*, 5–6, 19–20; *The Winnebago Tribe*, 395; Densmore, *The Peyote Cult; Winnebago Songs of the Peyote Ceremony*. Confession is present in Iowa, Oto, and Winnebago peyotism. But I have noted non-peyote instances of public confession among Aztecs, Aurohuaca, Carrier, Chichimeca, Crow, Dogrib, Eskimo, Guatemaltecans, Huichol, Ijca, Inca, Iroquois, Maya, Nicarao, Plains Cree, Plains Ojibwa, Salteaux, Shawnee, Slave, Tahltan, Western Apache, Yellowknife, and Yucatecans. Related practices are reported for the Arikara, Blackfoot, Southern Cheyenne, Oglala, and Sarsi.

[14] Radin, *Crashing Thunder*, 171, 186–87; Petrullo, *The Diabolic Root*, 111.

The peyote people are rather foolish for they cry when they feel happy about anything. They throw away all the medicines that they possess and whose virtues they know. They give up all the blessings they received while fasting, give up all the spirits who blessed them. They stop giving feasts and making offering of tobacco. They burn up all their holy things, destroy the war-bundles. They stop smoking and chewing tobacco. They are bad people. They burn up their medicine pouches, give up the Medicine Dance and even cut up their otter-skin bags.

Crashing Thunder, as we have seen, was himself persuaded by peyote cultists that it was disgraceful to have his hair long, and he gave his shorn hair with his medicine bundles to his brother-in-law, as both wept and as he received the thanks of his relatives. Clothing and headdress are also symbols of conflict between the old and the new for Taos and Osage.

A dramatic solution of a life-long problem was offered Crashing Thunder in peyotism. He had lied about having gotten power from a vision-experience in connection with the the older native religion: so important for personal prestige was this experience that he was betrayed into fabrication to obtain it. But he never lied to himself. All his life he was aware of the deception, and being a man of marked fundamental honesty, he keenly felt the fraud. Finally at the age of forty-five he did achieve through peyote the experience which he had missed in his youth. His conversion to the peyote religion was consequently most profound: "It is the only holy thing that I have become aware of in all my life," he said simply, after this experience.

Jack Thomas (Delaware) solved a problem of major importance to himself through peyote. He had been appointed a Government policeman, and found considerable conflict between his duty and his sympathies. Finally he became gravely ill, and a meeting was put on by his brother and another relative to pray for his recovery. In this meeting the answer came to him:

The others in the tipi did not like me. Peyote told me this. I had been a man-catcher. That was the reason. The two persons that loved me prayed for me and I got well. I did not go back to my job of man-catcher. Peyote showed me that it is wrong.

The mechanisms for social control afforded by the public and communal nature of the cult (as opposed to the individualism of the older religions in the Plains) are on the whole very effective. The speeches of the leaders and old men give ample opportunity for the expression of opinions concerning the conduct of younger members in peyote meetings and out. We have already noted the case in which a Kiowa marriage was saved from destruction by timely advice and reprimand addressed to the husband in a peyote meeting. The prayers, too, which almost any individual may make by calling for a smoke, are further vehicles for quite various psychological transactions.

Peyote leadership carries with it much prestige, and the great road-chiefs like Quanah Parker, Belo Kozad, Old Man Horse, White Horn, John Rave and Jonathan Koshiway are spoken of with considerable respect. In the case of John Wilson peyote was further made the vehicle of economic success. But the negative instances are just as interesting. We have already mentioned A. S., a Seminole who lived and married among the Caddo. He built a moon of the general John Wilson-Enoch Hoag type, which differed from these in only minor details. His bid for personal prestige, however, received so little support on the part of his group that he removed the inner symbolic part of his altar to the woods nearby, and left only the crescent and apron of a "small moon."

Another case is that of H. B., a Kiowa. This group has been unimpressed by any major changes in the rite, and success in leadership lies along rather conventional lines since they regard themselves as the repositors of the original native rite. H. B. aspired to be a peyote leader and to increase his prestige through the cult. His wife's brother was the leader of the minutely variant "Kiowa Road," his mother's brother, further, was one of the two original users of peyote among the Kiowa and his step-father was an owner of one the "Ten Medicine" bundles. All in all his chances might have seemed good in the beginning. But a train of bad luck befell him: his wife died, his step-son fell sick, and his mother's brother died, all within a year. His mother quarreled with the rather well-to-do wife of her nephew, C. A., who among the middle-aged men is perhaps the most promising and widely accepted peyote leader (though he still modestly confines himself to the job of "fire chief"). Then, as C. A. said—and he was not above sabotaging his rival H. B.'s chances—"he couldn't quite make the grade, because people wondered why all these things had happened to him; some fellows are like that."

There is much therefore that is psychologically precarious in peyotism. Personal histories and happenings to the individual determine his attitude toward the cult, and the attitude may change as new anxieties arise and old ones are solved. A typical conversion perhaps is that of John Bearskin (Winnebago), described by Densmore:[15]

The parents of John Bearskin belonged to the medicine lodge and he belonged to that organization until 1912. The mother of John Bearskin became sick in 1905 and told him that she was near to death. He was so distressed that he went to town and became drunk. The next morning they wakened him and said that his mother was dead. His father died in 1909. At that time he had a little girl two years old and his sister had a little girl five years of age. Both children died a week after his father's death. Bearskin's father left him a farm with house, stock and implements. He disposed of these, spent part of the proceeds and with the remainder brought a house in Winnebago [Nebraska] but later sold that and spent the money. He was drifting from place to place and working as he had opportunity when a cousin wrote him about peyote, advising him to return and use it. He went back and on January 19, 1912, he and his two daughters joined the peyote organization, being baptized by John Rave. His wife joined later, during an illness. Since that time he has not wavered in his attachment to the peyote cult, neither has he gambled nor used liquor nor tobacco.

But there are skeptics who do not join. Michelson[16] quotes a Sauk informant, who first belonged and later quit the cult:

[15] Densmore, *Winnebago Songs of the Peyote Ceremony.*
[16] Michelson, *Sauk and Fox Myths.*

I do not believe in it because it gives you the same effect as whisky when you are drunk four or five days; only peyote will affect you when you eat it once. I have eaten so there *is* nothing in it. I quit five years ago. And another reason why I do not believe in it is because the man did not know who the manitou was who did the talking [in the Peyote origin legend]; because the men pitied by manitous, among us Sauks, knew who they were, such as Wolf, Wisake, Turtle, or such as that.

An Oto informant was skeptical at first about the power of peyote, and experimented with it: for two days he drank tea to test its virtues, and then went to a meeting. There he was converted or "saved" when he realized that he was "pitiful like a stick."

Delos Lonewolf (Kiowa) quit peyote and became a preacher again, though he had been an important peyote leader and one-time president of the Oklahoma Native American Church; he had had "family troubles" and was apparently persuaded thereto by his wife. Cecil Horse and Albert Cat (Kiowa) have also recently quit peyote. When Kiowa Jim lost his son, he gave his staff, gourd and feathers to Baptiste Derond (Oto), a brother-in-law of Jonathan Koshiway. Derond was later killed in an automobile accident. His younger brother Frank now has the paraphernalia, but according to Koshiway, "they are afraid of them, and want to return them," since they are associated with misfortune.[17]

Sometimes Christianity itself is invoked in defence of peyote. Old Man Green (Oto) used arguments from the Bible to confound a Protestant minister who had been unfriendly to the native religion. He quoted from Genesis 1.12 an opinion from God Himself upon His completing the creation of green herbs: "and God saw that it was good." Said Green, "Peyote was there then. If you condemn peyote, you condemn God's work." On the whole, however, peyotism and Christianity are mutually exclusive in the southern Plains at least, so far as membership in the one or the other is concerned. This is partly due to the usual time peyote meetings are held (i.e., Saturday night and Sunday forenoon), but partly also to the intransigeance and stubbornness to native overtures on the part of white Protestant ministers.

Bert Crow-lance (Kiowa) is an interesting case of a man who has tried both the old religion and peyote, and found both unsatisfactory. In 1935 he attempted the vision quest, fasting and praying on a hill west of Anadarko. A hernia had partially incapacitated him for work, and he was seeking means to support his large family. He went out to fast and pray in the hope (so he told the writer) of finding gold and diamonds in Oklahoma through a vision, and failing that, oil, which would make him rich. But before he had completed the required four days, his deceased mother appeared to him in a vision and told him that there were snakes around which endangered him, and that he must return later with a pipe, which he had forgotten. But the second attempt was no more successful than the first.

[17] A Wichita told an anecdote which he thought evidenced his own very good fortune. During a storm he was trying to get to a meeting at Red Rock in his old car, which failed him. A tragedy occurred in this meeting: Riley Fawfaw (Oto) was killed by lightning. A supporting wire had been put on the tipi and along this the lightning apparently traveled, for money in his pocket was melted, his neighbors made unconscious and others thrown about the tipi by the force of the bolt. Unfortunately it seemed inexpedient to inquire more deeply into detailed attitudes about this incident.

Crow-lance had gone to a number of peyote meetings. In one of them he prayed that his sick daughter be made well. She later died. Crow-lance in disgust threw his peyote feathers into the Washita River. A friend who heard of this was horrified:

Only when a Kiowa *dies* do you throw things in the river. Your children and grandchildren are living. That's a mistake, and he must right it now. We're getting after him now—he threw away all his good feathers!

The articles were recovered in part, and selections of gourds and feathers were made by other peyote-users. Another anecdote we have already recounted of a father peyote which was almost returned to the place where it had been gathered. Again, Timbo (Comanche) formerly had many cattle and horses. He has lost all of them now, and this he blames on the displeasure of peyote. In short, all manner of happenings are attributed to the approval or ill favor of peyote, and rare is the event which may not be rationalized on this basis.

From these data, then, it may be well seen that peyotism functions in all ways as a living religion: peyote christens the new-born and protects their early years, teaches the young, marries young men and women, rewards and punishes the behavior of adult years, and buries the dead—offering throughout consolation for troubles, chastening for bad deeds or thoughts, and serving as the focus for tribal and intertribal life. Peyotism is without question the living religion of the majority of Plains Indians today. Perhaps the statement of a Delaware may make this clear:[18]

The old Delaware religion is too heavy for us who are becoming few and weak. It is too difficult; Peyote is easy in comparison. Therefore we who are weak take up this new Indian religion. This is the very objection raised by the old men, taking it up. But Peyote knows that the Indian's burden of becoming educated and at the same time keeping up the old religion is too heavy, for he said that to the old woman who was the first to discover our new religion. Peyote is to be the Indians' new religion. It is to be for all the Indian people and only for them.

The intent of the present section was to give the reader some sense of the emotional immediacy of peyotism to the present-day Plains Indian. Such a study might properly be termed "functional," and in biological analogy corresponds to the physiology or dynamic aspect of the anatomy or descriptive morphology attempted in our preceding discussion of cultural traits and patterns. But we must at once abandon our analogy, lest like some others we extrapolate illegitimately terms which have meaning in one universe of discourse into another where they serve only to produce confusion. In biology and medicine, anatomy may perhaps be understood wholly divorced from palaeontological and physical-anthropological (i.e., historical) considerations, but this is peculiarly not the case with any attempt to discuss a culture-pattern functionally or psychologically. Here the immediacy and the momentum of past history, that is the functioning of culture-patterns in terms of individuals, is precisely the point at issue. And here the aggregation of traits into a complex is less the result of organismic-biological factors than of "historical accident" (e.g.,

<hr>

[18] Petrullo, *The Diabolic Root*, 76.

the use of parched corn in the Plains ritual breakfast—its function in the religious pattern of an agricultural economy having long since been in abeyance). The traits of a complex do not gain their relatedness or their adhesiveness from any biological-organismic "function"; culture-traits are not chromosome-linked genes, and change of one trait of a pattern need not organically change the rest. Indeed, if we can speak of "the peyote cult" at all, it is only after demonstrating its historical continuity as such.

For Bert Crow-lance and Homer Buffalo, we maintain, judged from the vantage-point of any other culture than their own, would remain enigmas or examples of inexplicably bizarre behavior if we did not fall back on history—on the decadent pattern of the vision-quest, and on patterns now almost vanished of prestige and power-seeking, etc. But the problem of the ethnologist as we see it is not the reporting of the outlandish and the picturesque; it is the discovery of plausible motivations in terms of native meanings, the discovery of the essentially humane in its to us often disguised manifestations. In practice, then, *we can never know enough history* either biographical or cultural, in explaining a present culture as it functions in individuals acting in such and such a (historically-conditioned) way. We feel the more free, therefore, to trace in the next section the history of a pre-peyote Plains narcotic used ritually, inasmuch as it affords an insight into the historical problem.

HISTORICAL INTERPRETATIONS

THE PRE-PEYOTE MESCAL BEAN CULT

As we have noted in the section on the botany of peyote, the use of the term "mescal" is surrounded with considerable confusion, and is persistently used in the older literature to designate *Lophophora williamsii* or peyote. The true mescal is the *Agave* spp. whose cabbage-like center is baked by the tribes of the Southwest and northern Mexico as a food; "mescal" also refers to the brandy distilled from mescal beer or pulque. No doubt it is due to their intoxicating properties that two other distinct plants, *Sophora secundiflora* and *Lophophora williamsii*, have been called, respectively, "mescal bean" and "mescal button." A further confusion of these last has been contributed to by the fact that both have been involved in Plains cult uses.

Sophophora secundiflora is an evergreen shrub bearing two or three tough-shelled red seeds in a bean-like pod. Known in Mexico as "toleselo" and elsewhere as mescal-bean, coral-bean,[1] frijolito, frijolillo and mountain laurel,[2] it contains the extremely toxic narcotic alkaloid sophorine or cytisine,[3] the physiological action of which accounts for its ceremonial use by natives. This is a powerful poison causing nausea, convulsions and finally death by asphyxiation; it is said[4] to resemble nicotine closely in physiological action. A more complete botanical and physiological account appears in an appendix, and we are here concerned only with its ethnographic aspects.

Havard says that the Indians near San Antonio

formerly used the seed as an intoxicant, half of a seed producing a delirious exhilaration followed by a deep sleep lasting two or three days.

Opler tells a Chiricahua Apache coyote story in which the trickster pounded up a number of the beans and gave them to the people to eat:

So while the people were out of their minds, Coyote cut out their hair in patches the way Indians cut their hair. So there they were, crazy.

Lumholtz says that the Tarahumari added the root (?) of the frijolillo to their maguey wine "as a ferment," and Bennett and Zingg report an archaeological occurrence at a Rio Fuerte site in Chihuahua on a Basket-Maker horizon:

Containers found here and in another site held nothing but a few seeds of the poisonous wild "bean," which may have ceremonial significance.

---

[1] "These beans are often confused with those of a certain species of *Erythrina*, which are sometimes sold in their place in the markets of Mexico, but which are not at all narcotic" (Safford, *Narcotic Plants*, 397).

[2] Not to be confused with the "mountain laurel" *Kalmia latifolia*.

[3] Henry, *The Plant Alkaloids*, 395, 398.

[4] Henry, *op. cit.*, 397; cf. Safford, *Narcotic Plants*, 397.

This inference is not implausible when we recall the Mexican mode of keeping peyote.[5]

The use of peyote in racing and in ball games is noted for the Tarahumari and Tamauli-pecan groups, and in this connection it is interesting to learn that the Wichita used to eat mescal beans before they ran a race. A Cheyenne informant said that his tribe used the "red-berry" as an eye-wash long before they knew of peyote, though he never heard of their eating it; "it's poison," he said. The Comanche used to get mescal beans from near Fort Stanton, apparently for ornamental purposes only.[6] Like most of the Plains tribes, the Kickapoo used mescal beans chiefly as beads, but in common with the Cheyenne they used them medicinally: for earache they boiled, mashed and strained the beans through a cloth.

The Kiowa use the kɔnkoλ or mescal beans typically, as beads in peyote meetings, much as they formerly wore bandoliers of them on the warpath. One Kiowa is said to have chewed the inside of a mescal bean before breaking a bad wild horse bareback. A Kiowa peyote chief had several of the beans on his moccasin heel-fringe, to protect from the dangers of inadvertently stepping on menstrual blood, and another Kiowa "peyote boy" had a mescal bean attached to the thong of his gourd rattle. Mescal beans are clearly thought to possess great medicine-power.

The Iowa had leggings which Skinner thought might have been of a modified Kiowa-Comanche type, with a perforated scarlet mescal bean (Iowa, maka shutze, "red medicine") knotted on each thong of the fringe. The Omaha used as beads and good luck charms bright red beans which Gilmore thought were *Erythrina*, and which they called maka^n-zhide or "red medicine" likewise. In adopting the use of chinaberries (*Melia azerdache* L.) as beads, they likened them to mescal beans and called them, curiously, maka^n-zhide sabe, "black red-medicine."[7] Pawnee informants said that long ago they used bat or mescal beans for medicine "to strengthen the body," but now use them only for decoration. The Oto used to eat "liar(?) berries" or mescal beans in one of their lodges; they had the inter-esting superstition that they breed (recalling the sex attributed to peyote):

Tie two or three in a bundle, leave it a year or so, and when you open it again you'll have a dozen.

The inference that the Pawnee and Oto used the mescal bean ritually is borne out by the Iowa, who had a full-fledged ceremony called the "Red Bean Dance:"[8]

This is an ancient rite (ma^{n}kácutzi waci) far antedating the modern peyote eating practice but on the same principle. The society was founded by a faster who dreamed that he received it from

<hr>

[5] Bellanger, in Havard (Bulletin 519: 6); Opler, *The Autobiography*; Lumholtz, *Unknown Mexico*, 1: 256; Bennett and Zingg, *The Tarahumara*, 358. The use of frijolillo in maguey liquor (which equates with mescal) probably accounts for the usage "mescal bean." Since the text was written further Apache material has ap-peared (Castetter and Opler, *Ethnobiology of the Chiricahua and Mescalero Apache*, 54-55).

[6] Mooney, *Miscellaneous Notes*, 6. Schultes figures a Kiowa necklace of true mescal beans (*Sophora secundiflora* Ortega, Lag. ex DC.) strung on buckskin, with a piece of red ribbon, beaver fur and a child's ring enclosing a bundle of dried beaver-testis "medicine" in a lace handkerchief, as trinkets or amulets.

[7] Skinner, *Ethnology of the Ioway*, 261; Gilmore, *Uses of Plants*, 99.

[8] Skinner, *Societies of the Iowa*, 718-19.

the deer, for red beans (mescal) are sometimes found in deer's stomachs.[9] There are four assistant leaders, besides the leader, and it is their duty to strike the drum and sing during ceremonies.

In this society members were obliged to purchase admission from some one of the four assistant leaders. This was done in the regular ceremonial way. A candidate brought gifts and heaped them on the ground before the assistant leader and begged for the songs, etc., which he taught them and was then a leader. There was no initiation ceremony. During performances the members painted themselves white and wore a bunch of split owl-feathers on their heads. Small gourd rattles were used and the members while singing held a bow and arrow in the right hand which they waved back and forth in front of the body while they manipulated the rattle with the left.

This ceremony was held in the spring when the sunflowers were in blossom on the prairie, for then nearly all the vegetable foods given by wakanda were ripe. The leader, who was the owner of a medicine and war bundle called maⁿkácutzi warúhawe connected with this society, had his men prepare by "killing" the beans[10] by placing them before the fire until they turned yellow. Then they are taken and pounded up fine[11] and made into a medicine brew. The members then danced all night, and just past midnight they commenced to drink the red bean decoction. They kept this up until about dawn when it began to work upon them so that they vomited[12] and prayed repeatedly, and were thus cleansed ceremonially, the evil having been driven from their bodies. Then a feast of the new vegetable foods[13] was given them and a prayer of thanks was made to wakanda for vegetable foods and tobacco.

The connection of the maⁿkácutzi warúhawe, or red bean war bundle with the society is not altogether clear to me, save that it was a sacred object possessed by the society which brought success in war, hunting, especially for the buffalo, and in horse-racing.[14] Members of this society tied red beans around their belts when they went to war, deeming them a protection against injury.[15] Cedar berries and sagebrush were also used with this medicine.[16] Sage was boiled and used to medicate sweat baths on the war trail.

Further information is afforded by Harrington,[17] who collected a typical red bean bundle figured by Skinner, indicating a Pawnee parallel to the Iowa cult:

In addition to the two varieties of Ioway war bundles before described, a third sort was found, Maⁿkaⁿshudje oyu, or Red Medicine Bundles.... This was not discussed with the others, for the reason that the Ioways claim that it did not originate with them, but was derived from the Pawnee, who, in return for many presents, gave them authority to use it, and instructed them

[9] Cf. the origin of peyote in deer's foot-prints or hooves.

[10] "The maⁿkácutzi beans were supposed to be alive. Those I have seen in the possession of various Iowa were kept in a buckskin wrapper which was carefully perforated that they might see out." Cf. the ability of the father peyote to see.

[11] Cf. the preparation of peyote by grinding on metates like corn.

[12] Cf. the black drink ceremony to the east, and the Plains Sun Dance.

[13] Early peyotism was likewise an agricultural "first-fruits" rite.

[14] The Wichita used mescal beans in horse-racing too. Cf. the use of peyote in racing and deer-hunting, and the use of datura in deer-hunting.

[15] Cf. the fetishistic use of the father peyote in war.

[16] Cedar and sage are likewise involved in peyotism.

[17] Harrington, quoted by Skinner, *Ethnology of the Ioway,* 245-47.

in its preparation and ritual. The legend of its origin among the Pawnee was not known to my informants.

The bundle, says Chief Tohee, belonged to a society, whose annual meeting was held about the time corn is ripe.[18] There was but one main bundle, but each member had a "flute" or whistle, and a small package of medicine. When the time approached for the meeting, the member who was to give the feast sent a crier or "waiter" around to the different members, calling them to meet at a certain night in his bark house or tipi, whichever he was using at the time. All painted themselves and fixed themselves up in their best style for the occasion. Music was furnished by a number of singers, who kept time to the sound of drumming upon a tight bow-string,[19] and the sound of small gourd rattles. During the ceremonies the singers seated themselves in four different places at the side of the lodge, corresponding to the four directions, and sang in each one the verses pre-scribed by tradition, the order being: east, south, west, and north.[20] The dance is said to have con-sisted of peculiar jumping movements.

Now, the "Red Medicine" which forms the basis of the bundle, is the sacred red Mescal bean (*Erythrina flabelliformis*) which seems to have narcotic or perhaps intoxicating properties when taken internally.[21] Formerly widely used by the Indians of the Southern Plains[22] to produce dreams or visions at certain ceremonies, it has now been supplanted by the more powerful "button" cut from the Peyote cactus, which is sometimes wrongly also called "mescal," thus taking the name of its predecessor.

When morning put an end to the dances of the ceremony under discussion, a large number of the red beans were broken up, or "killed" as the Indians say (regarding the beans as alive) and stirred up with water in a large kettle, together with certain herbs which are said to make the decoction milder in action. Then all the participants drank a cup or two of the mixture. The only description of the action of the drug was that everything looks red to the drinker for a while, when he vomits, and evacuates the bowels, which the Indians say, cleans out the system, and benefits the health, even in the case of children. The medicine drinking, and the stupor and purg-ing consequent upon it end the ceremony.

It is said that the bundle has been handed down for a number of generations, since it was obtained from the Pawnee, all in one family, which must have benefited considerably, one would think, from the valuable presents necessary to join the society.... The [bundle's] taboo was very strict, forbidding its owners to break the bones[23] of any animal under any circumstances. They must never allow the bundle to touch the ground either....

When not in use, it was kept carefully wrapped in hides or canvas so as to exclude the weather, hanging on a pole standing just east of the owner's lodge, in front of the doorway. In addressing the bundle, they called it "Grandfather," and made offerings to it by throwing tobacco on the ground near the pole where it hung. On festal occasions the sweet smoke of burning cedar twigs was wafted upon it as an offering.

In time of war, a special man was appointed to carry it, as was the case with most war bundles.

[18] Compare note 13.

[19] The Delaware, Osage, Quapaw and Oto call the leader's peyote staff an "arrow," the Ponca a "bow."

[20] Cf. peyotism's four ritual songs, and the whistling outside at midnight at the four points of the compass.

[21] But *Erythrina flabelliformis* contains no toxic alkaloids; see Appendix 2.

[22] Did that truculent and little-known group, the Caddo, have the mescal cult?

[23] Has this taboo any reference to the boneless meat of the peyote ritual breakfast?

Like them, too, it was opened when the enemy was sighted, when its enclosed amulets were put on by the warriors. Tooting their war-whistles, they rushed gaily into battle, confident of the Red Medicine's protection.

Mrs. Voegelin[24] quotes an informant on a Shawnee use of mescal in a war connection:

Čalikwa's grandfather gave him one of these mescal beans (manitowimskočii'Oa). This old man knew prayers about these beans . . . . He had four grandsons. He made a prayer to give each of these boys a bean—one apiece . . . . He made a prayer about how the Creator made these beans and how they're used, using tobacco . . . out in the woods; he built a fire, where he offered prayer. This old man wanted his grandsons to be warriors. So he told the first grandson to swallow one of those beans.

When the first boy swallowed the bean, the bean came out. He told the boy, "You can never be a powerful man or anything; there's something in the way, that that bean didn't want to stay (inside you)." This happened to three of the boys. The last grandson to take the bean was Čalikwa; when he took it, the bean didn't come out. So when he saw his grandson keeping that bean, the old man was thankful. He told him, "Now you have a power; any time you see a battle you'll be the leader." [And so he was in 1865, when the Shawnee almost wiped out the Tonkawa in battle.]

HISTORY OF THE DIFFUSION OF PEYOTISM

Far too little is known—or probably ever will be known—about peyotism in Mexico to attempt to reconstruct its history; but our earliest Spanish sources indicate its pre-Columbian presence among the Aztec, and probably also the Cora-Huichol.[25] But the latter do not live in the region of growth of the plant, whence Beals argues that they must certainly have borrowed the cult. Rouhier claims immense antiquity for Huichol peyotism, but unconvincingly. If, indeed, as Beals with great plausibility argues, peyote is historically associated with shamanism, then it may have been involved in a late re-invigoration of shamanistic elements, at the expense of the priestly-saceradotal elements of an older, impoverished culture stratum. Evidence is even less conclusive for other Mexican groups, but on the whole it appears that the ritualization of the use of peyote was already vigorous in many parts of Mexico at the time of the first Spanish contact.

The approximate age of the peyote cult among the Tarahumari is likewise unknown to us. It is not so integrated into their culture as in the case of the Huichol, and in nearly all respects the southern cult is more complex than the northern. Furthermore, Tarahumari peyotism has for some time been in decline, indicating perhaps a borrowing which was not

---

[24] Voegelin, *Shawnee Field Notes.*

[25] The Huichol, for whatever such evidence is worth, in the mythological songs of their shamans, recite how the world began and how they were taught to hunt deer, to seek hikuli and to raise corn (Lumholtz, *Unknown Mexico*, 2: 8). The route they take in gathering peyote is from beginning to end full of religious and mythological associations, and they meet their deities on the way in the shape of mountains, stones, springs, etc. (*idem*, 2: 132). According to their traditions, they originated in the south, but got lost under the earth as they wandered northward, reappearing in the country of the hikuli (*idem*, 2: 23). Such deep-rooted symbolisms as theirs argues age.

sufficiently rooted—the neighboring Tubar, for example, did not use hikuli, though their customs otherwise much resembled the Tarahumari. Both Lumholtz and Bennett and Zingg consider Tarahumari peyotism a diffusion from the Cora-Huichol; certainly the Tarahumari themselves show very little indication of being a center of diffusion in Mexico in their lack of characteristic traits.[26]

Despite our comparative ignorance of the region, a much better case could be made for northeastern Mexico as a center of diffusion, for the region immediately south of the Rio Grande is one of the abundant growth of peyote. The oldest use in the United States is in this region, rather than in the Southwest as represented by the Mescalero. Tonkawan peyotism, for example, may be quite old: Velasco wrote in 1716 that many of the Indians of Texas drank "pellote" in connection with their dances. The Lipan got peyote from the Carrizo before white contact, according to Opler's informants. The Lipan used to go to a place called Biɣagulgai, which was "wide grass country beyond the Pecos in Texas," where the Mescalero came sometimes to meet them. Wagner says the Mescalero got peyote from the Lipan about 1880, but later Plains history of the cult as evidenced by the Kiowa leads us to accept the date 1870 set by Opler, as more plausible. Opler has well accounted for the ready acceptance by the Mescalero of this shamanistically-colored complex, and its integration into their pattern of aggression by witchcraft; he believes that peyotism was brought to their door by the same movement which brought it to the Plains, though Mescalero peyotism is appreciably older.[27]

From Dr. Parsons' careful account, it is clear that Taos practises the classical Plains rite. Contact with the Arapaho-Cheyenne version dates at least as far back as 1907, and tentative beginnings of this sort continued in later years.[28] Interestingly, Cozio recorded in 1720 the prosecution of a Taos Indian who had taken peyote and disturbed the town.[29] In any case the history of peyote at Taos has been a stormy one.[30] About 1918 the hierarchy

[26] Bennett and Zingg, *The Tarahumara*, 360, 366–67, 379, 383, 386; Lumholtz, *Unknown Mexico*, 1: 357–358, 444 (but see 1: 378).

[27] Velasco, *Dictamen Fiscal*, 194; Opler, *The Autobiography; Lipan Field Notes; The Influence of Aboriginal Pattern;* Wagner, *Entwicklung und Verbreitung.* Opler says that peyote was introduced within the memory of the oldest living Mescalero; after 1910 it was in decided decline.

[28] Parsons, *Taos Pueblo*, 62–63. The origin legend is Kiowa. Mooney received a letter dated July 18, 1921 from the Taos Indian, Star Road, relative to trials of "peyote boys."

[29] Cozio, *Proceso.*

[30] In 1921 on the orders of the Governor, Manuel Cordova, a peyote meeting was raided and the blankets and shawls of all participants somewhat highhandedly confiscated. Prominent medicine-men refused to doctor "peyote boys" because the new religion was prejudicial to their vested interests. In 1923 two adherents of the cult were whipped, one twenty-five lashes, by the Lieutenant-Governor. Three men were fined $700, $800 and $1000, and the case ultimately reached the American court; the judge decided that the Governor had no right to impose such heavy fines, reversed the judgment and ordered the return of the property. This done, the officers resigned from office, and for a time there were no secular officers at Taos because no one wanted to take up the controversy. In 1931 the confiscated property taken ten years before had still not been returned, the Council refusing even to consider a $10 fine in compensation; $25 was demanded for the return of each shawl and blanket.

became bitterly opposed to peyote, and turned three men out of their kiva membership in an attempt to rout it out. Dr. Parsons[31] believes that the weakness of the kachina cult at Taos accounts perhaps for peyote getting any foothold there at all. It is no coincidence that the Water Kiva, which has to do with the main elements of the kachina cult, the pilgrimage, is the one most outstandingly opposed to peyote. Considerable political activity has erupted over the issue, and Dr. Parsons surmises that the protective influence of a recently deceased political figure in the pueblo was also of significance. It may well be that recent Federal legislation will so strengthen the hand of the civil authorities at Taos that the suppression of peyote can be accomplished; in 1923 the number of "peyote boys" was only 52 in a population of 635.

In the Plains the most important tribes in the diffusion of the peyote cult were the Kiowa, the Comanche, and to a lesser degree perhaps, the Caddo. Most Kiowa agree that they got peyote and the accompanying ritual from the Mescalero Apache. The usual story is that a raiding party came to the Apache country, and that during an Apache peyote meeting being held at the time, the leader by clairvoyant means was made aware of the approach of the war-party leader. He told his fireman to invite the man in, enemy though he was. In this manner the man learned the ceremony, and at the end he was presented with peyote and ritual paraphernalia to take back to his tribe.[32]

Pabo, or Big Horse, was the only user among the Kiowa about 1868 or 1870, and Mooney began to notice Kiowa peyote only around 1886, so the vigorous activity of a cult proper may be said to date from about this time (though friendly contacts with the Mescalero in his opinion dated as far back as 1850 or before).[33] But the introduction of peyote was not exclusively the doing of one tribe, any more in the case of the Kiowa than of other groups. Tribal contacts have been multiple since the cessation of intertribal warfare, and one is not at all inclined to discount the vague information from Kiowas that they knew of peyote from the Cáyeso, the Zé·bakiɛni or "Long Arrows," the Yæk'i (a loose designation for various north Mexican tribes) and the Kωɔnhɛɢo. These last so-called "bare-footed" people are probably the Carrizo, who ranged within the region of growth of peyote. The Tonkawa[34] also made visits to the Kiowa around 1890 and performed shamanistic tricks in peyote meetings. We therefore set the date of Kiowa peyotism somewhat earlier than Shonle's[35] "before 1891" (her data were based on official Government sources which might not have become cognizant of the cult until late in its history), for Kiowa were holding meetings by 1880 or before. The Kiowa probably contributed little or nothing

[31] Parsons, *Taos Pueblo*, 80, note 64; 99, note 166; 118; John Collier, in *Peyote as Used in Religious Worship*.

[32] This widespread origin legend of the Plains is also Mescalero and Lipan, and from certain indications I suspect that it is Tamaulipecan also.

[33] Mooney, in *Handbook of the American Indians*, 1: 701, "Kiowa Apache."

[34] Mooney, *Peyote Notebook*, 14.

[35] Shonle, *Peyote; The Giver of Visions*, 54. Jack Sankadote, for example, was carried into a meeting as a baby by his father, and he is in his fifties.

definitive to the general shape of the ceremony, most of whose features were already standardized among the Lipan and the Mescalero.[36]

At one time, however, there was intense opposition to peyote on the part of some
Kiowa. In the winter of 1887–88 Bąįgᵛä had a revelation on the strength of which he claimed
to be the successor to Pate'te or "Buffalo-Bull-Coming-Out" (the "Buffalo Prophet" of
1881–82 who had promised to bring back the buffalo if his followers joined him in resisting
the Whites and returning to the old customs). He organized a group of about thirty into an
order called Baiyui or "Sons of the Sun," with a special costume, singing of guedωgᵛä, or
old "going-to-war" songs, smoking ceremony and dance. These he commanded to resume
the old costume, weapons and customs, and distributed to them a sacred new fire made with
a drill to take the place of fires kindled with flint-and-steel or matches. The Sons of the Sun
were bitterly opposed to peyote on the ground that it was in conflict with the Ten Medicine Bundles, though since its introduction some years before there had been no special
opposition to peyote. One of their rules was to drink always from an individual cup or
bucket, in pointed contrast to the peyote custom.

Bąįgᵛä predicted that a great whirlwind would come in the spring, followed by a four-
day prairie-fire in which the Whites and all their works would be destroyed and the buffalo
and the old Indian life restored. He ordered all the Kiowa to gather at Elk Creek, where
they would be safe when the catastrophe came. He claimed that his followers would be
invulnerable to the white soldiers' bullets, and that he himself could kill the latter with the
glance of his eye as far as he could see them. As the time grew near there was intense excit-
ment and the whole tribe, save for a few skeptical chiefs and medicine men, assembled at
the appointed spot. When the holocaust failed to materialize the people lost faith in him.
He held his original group together until the coming of the Ghost Dance in the fall of 1890.
Shortly before this his son had died, and when the Ghost Dance came he claimed to have
seen the fresh tracks of this son on his grave, resurrected, and through this revelation attempted to identify his group with the Ghost Dance, without, however, any success. His
disciples continued to ride around together in a group, and maintained their bitter hostility
to peyote, but were not taken seriously. Finally, indeed, Lone Bear and other Sons of the
Sun, became staunch peyote-users themselves and opposition vanished.

The first Comanche user of peyote was Buigᵛat, who married an Apache woman and
is said to have learned it from the Mescalero. Other early users were Dešode ("Smart
Man") and Tašipa, but by far the most important peyote leader among the Comanche was

[36] Several older Kiowa patterns parallel peyote usages (e.g. the smoking ceremony of the Old Women
Society: leader west of central fire, lieutenants on either side of the door, five dishes of food from the fire eastward; the Buffalo Medicine Men's Society bundle-repair meeting with a sage "stage," etc.), and the Kiowa-
Comanche had the all night singing and beating on a rolled-up hide on the eve of departure on the war-path.
But such parallels from the tribes one knows best lead to often naive particularistic explanations and should be
guarded against. As a matter of fact it is the wide distribution of sweat bath doctoring and society meeting
which accounts for the ease with which peyotism made its way in the Plains. The following two paragraphs are
partly based on data gathered by Donald Collier, a colleague of the Laboratory of Anthropology Kiowa trip.

Quanah Parker. Previously opposed to it, he later changed his mind when peyote cured an illness of his. One of the earliest Comanche meetings was held east of Fort Sill in 1873 or 1874, about the time Kicking Bird was imprisoned there. Quanah subsequently visited the Cheyenne, Arapaho, Ponca, Oto, Pawnee and Osage among others[37] and conducted meetings among them in the early 1890's. The Comanche origin legend is similar to that of the Kiowa, except that the White Mountain Apache were involved

Regardless of priority, the prestige of both these tribes as teachers of peyote is considerable.[38] Due to their influence, peyote spread rapidly in Oklahoma until it assumed the proportions of an "international" religion such as the Ghost Dance had been. Distinctly a reservation phenomenon in the days following the cessation of inter-tribal warfare, peyotism was able to exploit the friendly contacts growing out of the Ghost Dance. As Opler writes, "The spread and increased prominence of peyote ceremonies coincided suggestively with the final triumph of white civilization over the tribes of our western plains, those very groups upon whom peyote obtained so strong a hold."

The express intention of Indian policy of the period was the deculturation of the natives, to be obtained by sending the children to white schools, away from the influence of tribal life.[39] But this policy prepared the way for peyotism in several ways: it weakened the tradition of the older tribal religions without basically altering typical Plains religious attitudes, and multiplied friendly contacts between members of different tribes. Friendships made as school-boys account for considerable visiting and revisiting from tribe to tribe, and nearly ideal conditions for the diffusion of the cult were established. When Eagle Flying Above (Pawnee) got peyote from White Eyes (Arapaho) the sign language was the vehicle used, but in modern times the use of English as a lingua Franca is an enabling factor of great importance in the diffusion of the cult. Thus, ironically, the intended modes of deculturizing the Indian have contributed preëminently to the reinvigoration of a basically aboriginal religion.

Among the groups of considerable secondary importance in this diffusion, the Caddo are perhaps outstanding. The variations which the Caddo-Delaware messiah John Wilson began, and taught to the Quapaw, Osage and other "Big Moon" worshippers, is a somewhat special historical development and is treated in an appendix. The significance of the Oto in the development of the Christianized version among the Omaha, Winnebago and other Siouan groups is shown in another appendix on the history of the Church of the First-born and other peyote churches.

[37] In judging the relative importance of the Kiowa and the Comanche in the diffusion of peyotism, one should recall that Comanche was historically the lingua Franca of the southern Plains. Quanah took peyote to the Caddo and Wichita it is said, though he was not the first to do so; he led meetings among the Cheyenne and the Arapaho in 1884. Petrullo (*The Diabolic Root*, 129) says he learned peyote about 1868 in Arizona, New Mexico and Old Mexico.

[38] "It is desirable to eat with the Comanche or the Kiowa because they are reputed to have learned of Peyote many years before the others." (Petrullo *op. cit.*, 33.)

[39] *Handbook of the American Indians*, 2: 870b; cf. Mooney, in *Peyote as Used in Religious Worship*, 13–14, 15; Rouhier, *Monographie*, 102.

In the diffusion of the standard rite the Arapaho and the Cheyenne perhaps come next after the Kiowa and the Comanche. Jock Bullbear was one of the earliest Arapaho users, learning it from the Comanche when he returned from Carlisle[40] in 1884, and by 1891 Arapaho peyotism came to the attention of Mooney. A Cheyenne and Arapaho custom in connection with peyote meetings is the giving of presents to friends and visitors the next morning after a meeting.[41] The sweat lodge doctoring modification of Arapaho peyotism has been described previously.

The Bannock of Idaho have used peyote since 1906–1911, apparently against consider-able opposition. They formerly met in log-houses in the backwoods, and did not use the plant openly until the Oklahoma Native American Church was organized. The Cheyenne are believed by the writer to be the source of their cult.

The Blackfoot in 1913 were said to lack[42] the peyote religion, but Wissler states that he heard them singing peyote songs within a hundred yards of the very agent who denied the existence of the cult among them. Alfred Wilson (Cheyenne), who as president of the Native American Church has occasion to know, says that the Blackfoot have peyote, though they were officially[43] listed as non-users in 1922.

The Five Civilized Tribes received peyote at a very late date. Wagner[44] in 1932 said that the Creek, Choctaw and Chickasaw do not eat peyote; this agrees with the state-ments of Jim Aton (Kiowa) who said the Cherokee did not have it when he himself took peyote to the Creek in 1931. The Seminole have also taken it up recently, but some ac-quaintance with the plant must be postulated as early as 1922, since Newberne and Burke[45] list 40 users among the 101,506 population of the combined Five Tribes. The influence involved here is probably the Yuchi, who in turn got it from the Cheyenne.[46]

The Cheyenne are currently a source for peyote among the Blood in Canada, who were being organized in the summer of 1936. The Canadian Cree and Chippewa are very recent partial converts too; the latter received it from the Chippewa of Minnesota.[47]

The Cheyenne in Oklahoma used peyote before 1885, the date of the first Government census. The Government scout Flacco was violently against it and said that it was used "to witch people and make them crazy." Cloud Chief, of the Snake Clan, also opposed the coming of peyote, as he had previously opposed the Ghost Dance. But Leonard Tylor

[40] Jock Bullbear's and Mooney's testimonies in *Peyote as Used in Religious Worship*, 40, 48, 57.

[41] Kroeber, *The Arapaho*, 410. The practice apparently is also Kiowa and Oto.

[42] Wissler, *Societies and Dance Associations*, 436; the statement was made in conversation.

[43] Newberne and Burke, *Peyote: An Abridged Compilation*, table.

[44] Wagner, *Entwicklung und Verbreitung*, 84, footnote.

[45] Newberne and Burke, *op. cit.*, 33 ff.

[46] Petrullo, *The Diabolic Root*, 71–72.

[47] Wilson said that one Smith had been in Oklahoma from a group on the Yukon River in southern Alaska; they were said to have used it for fifteen years. Jenness (letter to Schultes) reported a rumor that a little peyote had filtered into Salishan groups of British Columbia but Gunther (letter to Schultes) reported its absence among the Flathead and Kutenai.

and John Turtle went to the Kiowa country in 1884–85 and learned the ceremony. A little later, in 1889–90, Henry White Antelope and Standing Bird visited the Comanche and learned Quanah Parker's "way." Tylor later got a "heart moon" of his own (Caddo influence?) some time after the allotment of lands.

Northern Cheyenne peyotism is largely parallel in its history to that of the Southern Cheyenne. It began among them around 1900 or before, some of them having learned it at Haskell; recently they have become affiliated with the Native American Church. Hoebel writes:[48]

There has been a limited amount of friction between the religious conservatives and the Peyote worshippers, and a distinction is drawn between a Peyote leader and a medicine man. For example, a ranking Peyote leader volunteered to give me much esoteric information on old cultural ways, explaining that he could talk to me about sacred things because he is not a medicine man. The Peyote people have taken over the entire leadership of tribal life. All members of the tribal council are Peyote worshippers and probably 80 per cent of the adults in the tribe are affiliated with the Peyote cult. Only the very old men abstained from Peyote and held to the old medicine beliefs. Among the Northern Cheyenne, Issiwin or the Sacred Hat is still revered and is under the care of an old medicine man. The Peyote leaders took a sacred button to the hat keeper and asked him to put it in the ancient bundle with the old hat but they claim not to know whether the keeper had done so or not. My guess is that they did know but did not care to tell.

There is a tendency to separatism between the sections on the reservation, but nothing suggesting a schism in Northern Cheyenne peyotism; there is interparticipation in meetings of the various groups, though there is a mild rivalry between the Muddy Creek and the other territorially-defined groups.

The Delaware got peyote from the Kiowa and Comanche about 1886, the earliest users including Chief Charles Elkhair, Joe Washington, James C. Webber, George T. and John Anderson, Benjamin Hill, Reed and Frank Wilson, Mrs. Allie Anderson, Mrs. Ora Spybuck and Mrs. Little Tethlies. Washington's family still has the original articles given them by the Comanche.[49]

Iowa peyote[50] was in full swing in 1914, but is said to have died out since 1922. In this tribe the introduction of peyote

has driven out of existence almost all the other societies and ancient customs of the tribe; almost all of the Iowa in Oklahoma are ardent peyote disciples, and only . . . a few . . . still follow the older customs.

Peyotism has relaxed the rules of secrecy about the older medicine ceremonies also, and may perhaps be ultimately responsible for the final deculturation of the Iowa.

[48] Hoebel, *Northern Cheyenne Field Notes.*
[49] Letter from Fred Washington to Dr. F. G. Speck, April 21, 1932. Petrullo (*The Diabolic Root,* 165) says the Delaware got peyote from the Kiowa; there is obvious Caddo influence too, via John Wilson.
[50] Skinner, *Societies of the Iowa,* 693–94, 724; *Medicine Ceremony of the Menomini; Ethnology of the Ioway,* 190, 217, 248–49.

Kansa[51] peyotism came from the Ponca about 1907. It was very strong among them by 1915, "having apparently superseded all of the old Kansa beliefs."

Henry Murdock (Kickapoo) brought the new religion from Quanah Parker and the Comanche in 1906; but he had personally known of peyote before, having gone to Mexico in 1864. Quanah had known Murdock before the peyote religion began spreading and invited his friend by letter to visit him. He put on a meeting in his honor, taught him the ceremony and presented him with peyote paraphernalia. The set songs in the Kickapoo rite are Comanche, and the custom of making the ashes into a bird likewise indicates a Comanche provenience for the ceremony. The Kickapoo were originally much against peyote.[52]

Peyote began to have a limited adherence among the Menomini a little before 1914, owing largely to marital ties with Winnebago and Potawatomi users.[53] The ritual has the Christian character of the Winnebagos' and membership in the peyote society not only precludes any in all the other societies, but also demands the abandonment of all ancient practices and destruction of their paraphernalia. Skinner believed that

its success will mean the death-blow to all the ancient customs of the tribe, already decadent, without the compensation of any advantageous or progressive substitute.

The spread of the cult has been met with determined opposition among the Menomini, and some peyote users later sought and received reinstatement in the older tribal rites.

One Modoc in Oklahoma, Sam Ball, married a Quapaw woman and took up peyote as a result. At present he is the only one,[54] but such marital ties have often before been the source of the spread of peyote.

Peyote was introduced to the Omaha[55]

in the winter of 1906–07 by an Omaha returning from the Oto in Oklahoma. He had been much addicted to alcoholics, and was told by an Oto that the plant and the religious cult practiced therewith would be a cure. On his return he sought the advice and help of the leader of the Mescal Society of the Winnebago, next door neighbors tribe of the Omaha. He and a few other Omaha, who also suffered from alcoholism, formed a society which has since increased in numbers and influence against much opposition, till it includes about half the tribe.

The medicine-men were particularly opposed to the use of peyote; one native Omaha,

[51] Skinner, *Societies of the Iowa*, 758.

[52] "We the undersigned members of the Kickapoo Tribe of Indians in Kansas most earnestly petition you to help us keep out the pellote, or mescal, from our people. We realize that it is bad for us Indians to indulge in that stuff. It makes them indolent, keeps them from working on their farms, and taking care of their stock. It makes men and women neglect their families. We think it will be a great calamity for our people to begin to use the stuff . . . . We most urgently petition you that immediate action must be taken before the stuff gets hold of our people" (Seymour, *Peyote Worship*, 183).

[53] Skinner, *Medicine Ceremony of the Menomini*, 24, 42–43, 97.

[54] Speck, *Delaware Peyote Symbolism*.

[55] Gilmore, *The Mescal Society*, 163–67; *The Uses of Plants*, 104–106; Mooney, *Tarumari-Guayachic*; Speck, *Delaware Peyote Symbolism*; testimony of Sloan in *Peyote as Used in Religious Worship*, 35. Murie, *Pawnee Indian Societies*, 637.

Thomas L. Sloan, prepared a bill against peyote and presented it to the Nebraska State Legislature, but later suffered a change of heart.

The Osage are a typical example of the multiple origins for peyotism in one tribe. Chief Lookout testified[56] that the Osage had peyote about 1896, and in a petition to Congress signed by him and Eves Tallchief, Edgar McCarthy and Arthur Bonnecastle, it was stated that Chief Black Dog and Chief Clermont established lodges among them in 1898. The source was Caddo, and nearly all the 800 full-bloods were ultimately peyote users; the Quapaw ceremony may also have had an influence upon them. The Caddo-Delaware messiah, John Wilson, came to the Osage in 1902, after most of them around Hominy and elsewhere had known of it.[57] The younger Osage who embraced the new religion could be distinguished from the conservatives in their wearing of braids decorated with ribbons and colored yarn, in place of the older roached style of headdress. In the last year or so an Osage named Morell has invited the Caddos Alfred Taylor and Ben Carter to bring the "Enoch" (Caddo) moon to his home; he already had a Wilson moon on his place, but his sons wanted to have the more basic Caddoan moon.[58]

The Tonkawa first brought peyote to the Oto very long ago; Koshiway places this as far back as 1876 (which is not implausible in view of the earliest Kiowa and Comanche contacts with the plant). This must not be regarded, however, as the date of the vigorous functioning of the cult, but it is well to recall here the Oto mescal bean cult which may have facilitated the borrowing of the later narcotic.[59]

We have elaborated in an appendix the origin of the Christian elements in Oto peyotism, which spread to other Siouan groups (Omaha and Winnebago). The Church of the First-born embodied Russellite doctrines familiar to the Oto teacher Koshiway.[60] It was

[56] *Peyote as Used in Religious Worship*, 10-11, 30-31, 43, 44-45. This booklet was compiled after 1911, giving for "twenty years [ago]" a maximally early date of 1891; but other internal evidence indicates a publication date of 1916, giving the date 1896 as quoted.

[57] Speck, *Notes on the Ethnology*, 171.

[58] No doubt with the memory of the fate of Albert Stamp's attempted "moon" among the Caddo, Taylor exhibited considerable modesty when this flattering offer was made. "I appreciate that offer," he said, "but I'm just Alfred Taylor, that's all I am, and I never did run a meeting, and I would rather you'd get somebody else from down home who runs meetings to do it for you." Several weeks later my informant said he didn't think Taylor would accept, though he might drum or build the fire "like a servant"—"He's afraid the Caddos will think he is pushing himself ahead too much, but he has even drummed for Enoch Hoag; he just don't like to jump ahead of everybody too much away from home." This abnegation is all the greater when it is understood that the Osage are accustomed to make handsome money gifts on such occasions.

[59] Koshiway compared the smoke-meeting before the war path to peyote: "They have a meeting and smoke the pipe together and leave the next day. This clears up the enemies, and you can prophesy then. Peyote is similar to this—all night." Another older pattern interestingly survives among the Oto: in the informal morning period in the tipi, joking relationship seems to function.

[60] One wonders if the Russellite eschatology was not made more acceptable historically among the Oto because of an approximation to certain Ghost Dance notions. In any case, the curious prohibition on smoking may have symbolized, on the one hand, the rejection of older patterns of religious smoking, reinforced by the prohibition of secular smoking too.

incorporated in 1914, though its roots may have gone back as far as 1896, apparently with some consultation with the Shawnee,[61] and the consent of White Horn (Oto) leader of the older and already established native peyote ceremony. Its influence on the Native American Church and the Negro Church of the First-born is elsewhere discussed, as are also the specific Christian elements in peyotism as a whole. The famous meeting 14 miles east of Red Rock at which the Kiowa leaders Belo Kozad and Jack Sandkadote and an Apache named Star visited the Oto, was responsible for the amalgamation of the Church of the First-born and the Native American Church. Dugan Black, leader of the first Oto meeting attended, is stated to have gotten his "road" from Little Henry (Kiowa) and uses Kiowa songs; another Oto leader uses Conklin Hummingbird's fireplace.

The Ponca are said by Shonle[62] to have gotten peyote from the Southern Cheyenne in 1902–04, but native information indicates that there were Comanche sources too (Ponca songs, e.g., are frequently Comanche). The Cheyenne, White Horse, brought them the cult in September, 1904, but when they heard that it was recent among this group, they went to Quanah Parker among the Comanche "to get to the bottom of it." The late Robert Buffalo-head was the earliest leader of the Cheyenne rite. A suggestion of Caddo influence appears again in the rules surrounding the drum; the typical Ponca peyote drum has a handle made of the twisted rope-end of the lacing. "The old people are strict, and you're not allowed to put your hand on the drum [head]," we were told.

Eagle Flying Above, who later became oil-wealthy, was the first Pawnee user of peyote, obtaining it from White Eyes, an Arapaho friend, about 1890 or a little later. Several months later Sun Chief, the writer's informant, took it up. At the death of Eagle Flying Above, Sun Chief was the only Pawnee leader, and all the others learned the rite from him; he has eaten peyote since 1892–94, but only later became a leader. A still earlier source appears to be the Quapaw,[63] whom two Pawnee youths visited in 1890, but the cult became vigorous only after further instruction from the visiting Arapaho. There was some opposition to peyote among the Pawnee in the early days: "they didn't understand it." The leaders of the opposition were Sky Chief, head of the Kuyau or "Doctor Dancers," and Good Buffalo, leader of the Buffalo Dance ceremonialists; later, however, both joined the peyote-users. The cult is found chiefly among the Pítahauírata, where the form originated, but found a later following among the Chauí, then the Kítkaháxki and a few Skidi.

It is interesting to note that, as with the Shawnee and others, Pawnee peyote was early involved in the Ghost Dance excitement. The leader claimed from peyote the same sort of revelations acquired in the Ghost Dance trance, and taught that while under the in-

[61] Mooney, *Tarumari-Guayachic*, 38.

[62] Shonle, *Peyote: The Giver of Visions*, 55.

[63] Murie, *Pawnee Indian Societies*, 636–37. Wagner (*Entwicklung und Verbreitung*, 75) disputes Shonle's statement that they got it from the Quapaw, on the ground of the greater complexity of the Quapaw rite. His argument is unimpressive and a priori: John Wilson was the source of that complexity. Cf. Opler, *The Autobiography*.

fluence of peyote one could learn the rituals belonging to bundles and societies; in this manner he himself amassed considerable star lore. One unusual Pawnee feature was the use of a special Ghost Dance form of painted tipi for peyote meetings; minor changes were made in the type of drum and rattle also.[64]

The Potawatomi first had peyote sometime between 1908 and 1914, but little else is known about it there. Quapaw peyotism derives from the Caddo-Delaware. The Ree[65] [Arikara] were strongly against the cult, and it apparently died out among them by 1924. Ed Butler brought Sauk[66] peyote directly from the Tonkawa:

In the early days women were not allowed to be members, and the manitou who gave the man this medicine made it a rule that it should be used [only] in war-time . . . It is only a war-bundle among other tribes.

But the Sauk have been tenacious of their older religion and its fetishes,[67] though peyotism is now strong among them; indeed, about 1923, attempted affiliation with the Native American Church failed because five rival chiefs ran different meetings.[68]

The Seminole have started the religion only recently, about the same time as the Chero-kee; they have learned it through the Yuchi, Caddo and Kiowa. George Anderson (Dela-ware) brought the Wilson moon to the Seneca in 1907, when eighteen men and women be-came members. One of the Seneca had a Quapaw wife, who gave him the idea of obtaining the moon; they were too poor to pay Anderson's usual fee, and merely gave him car-fare home.[69]

The Shawnee Jim Clark received peyote from the Comanche in the late 1890's. Infor-mants say the Shawnee have had peyote as a plant for a long time, using it to keep from getting tired on the march, for moistening the mouth when dry-camping and to relieve hunger. The first Absentee Shawnee meeting was held by the Scotts in 1900, under the tutelage of the Kickapoo. John Wilson was among the Shawnee about 1894, and George

[64] There may be Doctor Dance parallels in peyotism (e.g., an earthen altar, a fire in a round hole in the center of the tipi, doctoring at night with coals, fan or sucking horn, presence of the relatives of the patient in the meeting, etc.); another older Pawnee pattern in peyote may be the special morning prayer-maker south of the door.

[65] "PEYOTE FAILS. It is a good thing that peyote is stopped for it was doing more harm than good. Our young men of the reservation were just beginning to start in eating the devil's root . . . Peyote fails because it has no mouth so can not speak to its followers of their origin and destiny, nor as to sin, repentance, forgive-ness, salvation nor of anything else. It has no ears, so can not hear prayer; it has no eyes, so it can not see a per-son's needs; no hands so can not help; no mind, so can not think. It is therefore unable to ask God for the thing which its worshipers need, and which they plead with it to implore God for. Our boys tried to make others be-lieve that peyote is a God and a religion, but if one wants to believe in mysterious things it must be Christ or peyote." (Sam Newman, Ree[Arikara], in *The Indian Leader*.)

[66] Michelson, *Sauk and Fox Myths*.

[67] Skinner, *Observations on the Ethnology*, 10, 85.

[68] Native American Church, President's Report, 1925.

[69] Speck, *Delaware Peyote Symbolism*.

Fourleaf (Delaware) brought peyote to White Oak from Mexico about 1898. Ernest Spy-buck got his moon from the Delaware near Dewey, while the Panthers are said to use the Yuchi manner. The majority of the Shawnee, however, use the standard Kiowa-Arapaho moon. Some Shawnee liken the leader's staff to the staff in the Green Corn Dance, and there is a legend of getting power from peyote which some say was not peyote but another plant which preceded it.[70]

A Sioux introduced peyote to the Uintah and Ouray Agency.[71] The Ute around Fort Duchesne have used peyote "on the sly" since before 1916; the cult was vigorous around Randlette, Utah, by the spring of 1916. Mrs. Cooke attended a Ute meeting in 1937 about ten miles from Whiterocks; an informant told her that

sometimes they have a half moon instead of a crescent—depending on the size of the moon in the sky at that time. . . . They had twice had a moon which had eyes and a mouth made in it—this is "God peeping."

This last suggests a Caddoan "Big Moon" influence, but the motif of the changing moon must be Ute, as it is not encountered elsewhere. The Gosiute near the Salt Lake Desert began about 1921, as did the Paiute west of Salt Lake City. Little is known of these groups, but possibly Cheyenne teaching is responsible; Southern Ute visited Oklahoma peyote groups as early as 1910 according to information of Dr. Parsons.[72]

The Wichita, like the Shawnee, claim to have had peyote long before they learned to eat it in meetings. In one of their rain ceremonies they used a medicine bundle containing four objects: feathers, a little buckskin doll, a piece of flint and peyote. The ceremony was called hä·ctiaš, "fire-people-around," and they sang all night for four nights to bring rain. The coming of the peyote ritual, therefore, aroused no hostility:

No Wichita was ever against it [Sly Picard says]; they couldn't be, as all our medicine men and women had peyote in their medicine—the whole tribe.

Yellow Bird (Wichita-Kichai) may have eaten peyote as early as 1889, before the Washita bridge between Anadarko and Gracemont was built, and Sly's father used it in 1892, learning it from the Caddo. But they were dissatisfied with the Caddo moon, and invited Frank Moitah (Comanche) and Salo (Kiowa) to teach them. Old Man Horse (Kiowa) is usually credited, however, with bringing peyote to the Wichita about 1902.

In 1893 and 1894 the Winnebago John Rave visited peyote eaters in Oklahoma (though he had eaten it as early as 1889,) and again in 1901. On the return from his second trip he tried to introduce the religion, but without success save among a few of his own relatives.

[70] Voegelin, *Shawnee Field Notes.*

[71] *Peyote, An Insidious Evil,* 3–4; Office of Indian Affairs, *Discussion Concerning Peyote,* 13.

[72] Much of this information is from Alfred Wilson, a Southern Cheyenne. His presidential report for 1925 (Sixth Annual Convention of the Native American Church) cites "locals" for the Caddo, Wichita, Pawnee, Arapaho, Yuchi, Kiowa, Oto, Shawnee, Ponca, Sauk and Fox, Cheyenne, and Omaha. Parsons, *Taos Pueblo,* 61; Willard Park informed me in 1936 that the Paviotso lacked peyote.

In 1903 or 1904 Rave went to South Dakota, Minnesota and Wisconsin to preach the new religion; he had been visiting the Kiowa and Comanche, as well as the Oto. Somewhat later Jesse Clay was taught the rite at Winnebago by a visitor called Arapaho Bull, and Dick Griffin learned another version from the Osage at Pawhuska, at a time when John Wilson was there. Yellowbank said that the Winnebago of Nebraska got peyote from the Arapaho, and thence it came to the Winnebago of Wisconsin. Thunder Cloud was among those opposing it, but by 1914 nearly half the tribe were adherents.[73]

The Yankton of South Dakota by 1916 had a peyote cult strong enough to warrant the sending to Congress of a petition to pass an anti-peyote bill signed with ninety-two names. The Yuchi affiliated with the Creek around Sapulpa and Kellyville, received peyote from the Cheyenne. Shonle cites three additional groups we have not yet included. These are the Shoshoni, who received peyote in 1919, the Sioux (1909–10) and the Crow (1912). Comparisons of the present list with Shonle's gives on the whole earlier dates, yet this need not be considered in any sense a discrepancy. Shonle's data were based on government sources, and should stand as indicating the dates when the various cults became virile enough to attract official notice. Our own data, based on native sources, give on the other hand what are probably the earliest contacts and introductions of the rite, without reference to the number or percentage of adherents in any tribe. It is evident from them too that tentative starts and multiple origins are the rule rather than the exception, and Shonle's information and our own should be regarded as supplementary rather than contradictory.[74]

Although peyotism is gone or decadent among the Tarahumari and the Mescalero, it is still vigorously spreading in the United States and southern Canada. Conceivably it could spread until it embraced all Plains, Basin and Woodlands groups whose earlier culture is sufficiently consonant with its concepts, and it may have some slender chance of spreading in the southern and eastern Pueblos and Plateau, but scarcely elsewhere, for both geographical and cultural reasons. The cult may be expected to spread for some time in the future, but when its inevitable decadence and probable ultimate disappearance will have been accomplished, we may have witnessed in it the last of the great intertribal religious movements of the American Indian.

The present section sums up the external history of the diffusion of peyotism so far as it can be known from our Mexican sources, and in the Plains, where it appears that the pre-peyote mescal bean cult prepared the way somewhat for the use of the narcotic cactus.

The Plains rites are basically derived from the Kiowa, Comanche and Caddo peyote ceremonies, which in turn derive from the Mescalero Apache (whence the diffusion traces back to the Lipan and Tonkawa through the Carrizo perhaps to Tamaulipecan groups). The Kiowa and the Comanche led in the diffusion of the standard aboriginal ceremony,

[73] Radin, A Sketch of the Peyote Cult, 4–5, 7; The Winnebago Tribe, 394, 400, 415, 423; Crashing Thunder, 169–70, 179, 185; Lowie, Notes Concerning New Collections, 289; Densmore, The Peyote Cult; Winnebago Songs of the Peyote Ceremony; Speck, Delaware Peyote Symbolism.
[74] Seymour, Peyote Worship, 184; Petrullo, The Diabolic Root, 71–72; Shonle, Peyote; The Giver of Visions, 55.

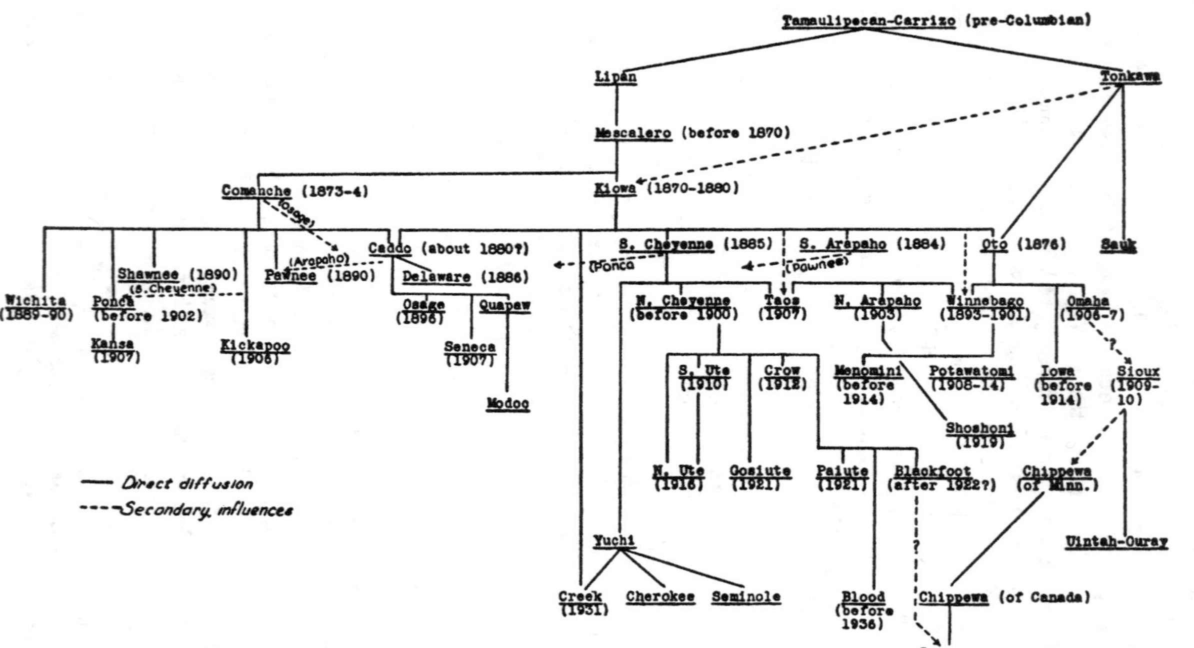

Fig. 5. Chronological outline of the diffusion of peyotism.

122

but the Caddo variant was powerfully influenced by the individual, John Wilson, and diffused to the Osage, Quapaw, Delaware and others in a somewhat modified form. This is the subject of a special appendix.

The Oto are probably the crucial group in the diffusion of the later Christianized version of peyotism among such Siouan groups as the Winnebago and Omaha. Here again an individual gave a new turn to the ceremony by summing up in himself two streams of culture, the aboriginal and the Christian. Jonathan Koshiway is discussed in an appendix on the Native American Church, and a special appendix is devoted to the matter of Christian elements in the cult. The diagram on the opposite page sums up the external history of peyotism succinctly.

APPENDIX 1: PEYOTE IN MEXICO

The connotative etymological implications of the term "peyotl" become valuable when an understanding of its wider denotative applications is sought. In Hernandez' original description, *Lophophora williamsii* is called "Peyotl Zacatensi, seu radice molli et lanuginosa"[1]—that is to say, the whitish flocculence which gains the plant both its Aztec and modern botanical names, is again pointed out in Hernandez' Latin synonym, "soft and lanuginous root."

But Hernandez distinguished two peyotes, "Peyotl Zacatensi" and "Peyotl Xochimilcensi,"[2] the latter not even one of the Cactaceae, and one wonders at the classification until the plant is botanically described:

This peyote, a rather excellent medicine, has a heavy round root covered with woolly rootlets, in addition to other roots which resemble acorns, because of their form and size, growing out in every direction . . . . It has few stems . . . with yellow flowers at their extremities.

From even this brief characterization it is clear that the term "peyotl" was extended to this non-cactus (later identified as *Cacalia diversifolia* or *C. cordifolia*)[3] because of its balanoid lanuginous roots. The latter species is sold in the drug markets around Guadalajara, Jalisco, as "peyote"; specimens from Alvarez, San Luis Potosí, locally known as "cachan," are valued as an aphrodisiac and remedy for sterility, the rhizic-orchic pubescence of the plant being evidently viewed in terms of sympathetic magic.

Dr. Alfonso[4] applies the term peyote or piote further to *Cacalia sinuata*, La Llave, and *Etchevarria coespitosa* Dec., the former Compositae, the latter one of the Crassulaceae. One of the Compositae, *Senecio* spp., ranging from Cerro del Pino to the Valley of Mexico is thus described:

The tap-root is tuberous-ovoid, size of a small hen's egg, a little curved above, carrying almost all [its bulk] in the heavy extremity . . . . All the surface is covered with a nap formed of long matted hairs of the color of cannel, and a number of long roots.

[1] Hernandez, in Safford, *Aztec Narcotic*, 295; *Peyotes, Datos para Estudia*, 204.

[2] In simpler Mexican cultures, peyote was in the hands of shamans; this other peyote appears to derive its name from the priests of a certain class in the higher Aztec culture: "According to some authorities, the highest grade of these native hierophants bore among the Nahuas the symbolic name of 'flower weavers,' Xochimilca, probably from the skill they had to deceive the senses by strange and pleasant visions (Xochimilca, que asi llamavan á los mui sabios encantadores)" (Torquemada, in Brinton, *Nagualism*, 298).

[3] A specimen in Mooney, *Peyote Notebook*, 56, was so identified. Schultes viewed this and identified it as *C. cordifolia* which in addition has cocoon-shaped pods. Cf. the use of *Lophophora* as an aphrodisiac.

[4] Alfonso, in Rouhier, *Monographie*, 3; Santoscoy, *Nayarit*, 32. Schultes (*Peyote and Plants Used*, 135) lists *Cotyledon caespitosa* Haw. as a Crassulaceous "peyote."

The "Peyote of Tepic"[5] (*Senecio hartwegii*) is smaller and more globular than the above, and contains no alkaloid, the gluey, sticky sap having no effect on the dove or the rat. The "Peyote of Querétaro" (*Echinocactus turbinatus* Henning), said to be distinguished from *Anhalonium* only by the spiral disposition of the hair-pencils, is a common form of *Lophophora williamsii*.

In the case of all these non-cacti to which the term peyote has been applied, the plants have exhibited descriptively either a lanuginous or pubescent surface-nap, or balanoid, orchitic, or nut-like root-nodules, and in some cases both; in one case there was a cocoon-shaped pod in addition. But Schultes[6] lists other "peyotes" which may not fit this explanation: Compositae: *Senecio calophyllus* Hemsl., *S. Hartwegii* Benth., *S. ovatiformis* Sch. Bip., *S. Petasitus* DC and *Cacalia* spp. (e.g., *C. cordifolia* HBK); Leguminosae: *Rhynchosia longe-racemosa* Mart. & Gal.; and even one of the Solanaceae, *Datura meteloides* DC.

All the above are non-cacti, but many Cactaceae have also been called "peyote." These include: *Anhalonium Englemannii* Lem., *A. prismaticum* Lem., *A. furfuraceum* Wats., *A. pulvilligerum* Lem., *A. areolosum* Lem., *Lophophora williamsii* Lem., *Ariocarpus fissuratus* (Englm.) K. Schum., *Astrophytum myriostigma* Lem., *A. asterias* (Zucc.) Lem., *Pelecyphora aselliformis* Ehrenb., and *Strombocactus disciformis* DC. The diminutive "peyotillo" has been applied to *Dolichothele longimamma* Britton and Rose, and *Solisia pectinata* Britton and Rose.[7]

---

[5] *Peyotes, Datos para Estudia*, 111, 206, 208. This non-cactus "peyote" of Tepic may have been the false clue leading Rouhier to believe an earlier range of peyote into Tepic.

[6] Schultes, *Peyotes and Plants Used*, 135. The Reko etymology preferred by Schultes (p. 136) so far as botanical evidence goes derives peyotl from Aztec pi- (small) and -yautli or -yolli (herb with narcotic odor or action), making "peyotillo" a double diminutive. Schultes has accepted, at the instance of the present writer, the thesis that *Cacalia* spp. might well enough fit the "velvety, cocoon-like" etymology, but argues nevertheless that "this etymology does not seem to explain the application of the same name to the great array of plants which possess no soft or silky parts whatsoever." Schultes is undoubtedly right on this point in terms of descriptive botany; yet may not some items be included in our lists illegitimately? *Anhalonium prismaticum* Lem., for example, is called hikuli, not peyote, and is only partly its terminological equivalent. And does the "little narcotic" etymology explain all these instances?

[7] Urbina, in Harms, *Über das Narkotikum*, 31; Schultes, *op. cit.*, 135.

APPENDIX 2: PEYOTE AND THE MESCAL BEAN

Far the commonest designation for peyote in the older literature is "mescal bean," a curiously persistent misusage, since either in the dried or the green state *Lophophora williamsii* resembles a bean even less than a mushroom, Safford's teo-nanacatl. On probing more deeply into this confusion, a wide-spread pre-peyote narcotic cult of the southern Plains was discovered. The ethnographic results of this study are presented in the text, but a brief characterization of the "mescal bean" proper is essential as well.

Collected specimens of the old Plains "red bean" (=mescal bean proper) have been identified by authorities at the Harvard Botanical Museum as *Sophora secundiflora* (Ortega) Lag. ex DC.[1] Variously known as "mescal bean" (southern Plains), "colorín" (Coahuila, Nuevo León, Texas), "frijolillo" (Nuevo León, Texas), "frijolito" (Texas), "evergreen coral-bean," "coral-bean" and "mountain laurel" (southern New Mexico), this plant grows from Coahuila to San Luis Potosí, western Texas and southern New Mexico, being specially characteristic of the dry limestone hills. It is not, however, the "mountain laurel" *Kalmia latifolia*, being a true member of the Fabaceae or Bean Family; the term "coral-bean" is likewise applied to two other legumes of Texas, both, however, *Erythrina* spp., not *Sophora*.[2]

Sophora secundiflora contains the highly toxic narcotic alkaloid sophorine, $C_{11}H_{14}ON_2$, which is identical with cytisine (=ulexine, =baptitoxine). Resembling nicotine closely in physiological action, the contents of one bean are said to be able to produce nausea, convulsions and even death by asphyxiation in man.[3] *Sophora secundiflora* (=*Broussonetia*

[1] There is no problem of identifying the old Plains "red bean" with the "mescal bean"; both Schultes and I obtained Kiowa specimens in the field. The problem is the correct botanical classification of the specimens, and the wide-spread misusage of their name for peyote.

[2] Standley, *Trees and Shrubs*, 435; Dayton, *Important Western Browse Plants*, 87; Boughton and Hardy, *Mescalbean*, 5; Opler, *Autobiography*. The Chiricahua "Mountain laurel" is *S. secundiflora*.

[3] Henry (T. A.), *The Plant Alkaloids*, 395; Dayton, *op. cit.*, 89. Havard (*Report on the Flora*, 500) says the alkaloid sophoria [sic] was isolated by Dr. H. C. Wood in 1877 as a whitish, amorphous substance producing convulsions, temporary loss of voluntary movement, and distressing vomiting; again (*Drink Plants*, 39) he says sophorine [sic] is an irritant-narcotic. Another alkaloid, matrine, is found in *Sophora* spp. (Nagai, Plugge, Kondo *et al.* in Henry (T. A.), *The Plant Alkaloids*, 398). Havard, citing one Bellanger, says the Indians near San Antonio formerly used the seed as an intoxicant, half of one producing a delirious exhilaration followed by a deep sleep lasting two or three days; a whole bean, according to Dr. Rothrock's informant, would kill a man. Dayton, 89, says children have been known to die from the effects of eating seeds of *S. secundiflora*; in any case, a rupture of the hard, leathery coat of the bean would be required for the release of the alkaloid in the bean-flesh.

Cattle and sheep appear to be more affected by the leaves of the plant, which also contain the alkaloid, than by the beans. The effect on them is marked: sheep fed about one percent body weight of the leaves were paralyzed in the legs for days and calves fed as little as .25% of body weight of fresh leaves died in 45 hours; one fed 1.0% died in 1¾ hours. Recovery in sheep sometimes required 12 days, in calves up to 16 days (Boughton and Hardy).

secundiflora) itself is a handsome evergreen shrub or small tree, eight to thirty-five feet high, bearing thick, leathery, dark glossy green leaves. The violet-blue bunches of flowers appearing in the spring give off a strong rank fragrance, and from these develop, in the sum-mer, woody pods, satiny outside, two to four inches long, and containing one to four hard-shelled bright red beans.[4]

Safford[5] states that "these beans are often confused with those of certain species of *Erythrina*, which are sometimes sold in their place in the markets of Mexico, but which are not at all narcotic." It is therefore possible, and indeed probable, that the beans used as necklaces and bandoliers in the Plains were both *Sophora* spp. and *Erythrina* spp.; Mooney[6] for example had specimens of red bean necklaces identified as *S. secundiflora* and *E. fruticisa*. The confusion of the two closely related groups is understandable when the beans alone are available for diagnosis; the bean of *Sophora secundiflora* differs from that of *Erythrina flabelliformis*, for example, in little more than the shape of the hilum, or scar of attachment, that of the former being rounded and of the latter more linear, while the beans of *E. corraloides* are more elongate than those of *Sophora*. Gilmore's[7] identification of the Omaha "red-medicine" with *Erythrina* spp. may possibly be wholly correct since he mentions only decorative and magic uses for the beans; but in view of the chemical composition of the two, any ritual narcotic use must *a fortiori* refer to *Sophora secundiflora*, the "mescal bean" proper.

[4] Condensed and synthesized from Boughton and Hardy; Havard, *Report on the Flora*, 458, 500; *Drink Plants*, 39–40; Standley, 435; Dayton, 87–89.

[5] Safford, *Narcotic Plants*, 398.

[6] Mooney, *Tarumari-Guayachic* (quoting Safford?).

[7] Gilmore, *Uses of Plants*, 99 writes: "The Omaha traveling into Oklahoma have found them [chinaberry] there, and have taken up their use. They already had employed for beads as well as for a good-luck charm the bright red seed of a species of *Erythrina*. They say it grows somewhere to the southwest, toward or in Mexio. They call it 'red medicine,' maka[n] zhide (maka[n], medicine; zhide, red). When the seeds of Melia (azerdache L.) [chinaberry] were adopted for use as beads, they likened them to maka[n] zhide, and so call them maka[n]-zhide sabe, 'black red-medicine'."

APPENDIX 3: PEYOTE AND TEO-NANACATL

The already sufficiently intricate ethnobotanical problem of peyote has been further
complicated by an erroneous identification of a narcotic mushroom used by the Aztecs
with the cactus peyotl. Safford[1] identifies the two by a somewhat casual use of his evidence,
and mystifies himself with the consistent contradiction offered by all the early Spanish
writers to his assumption. He composes the contradiction by assuming that the Aztecs did
not recognize the dried discoidal button as the same plant as the green cactus; despite
overwhelming etymological evidence he supposes they called the former teo-nanacatl and
the latter peyotl. Only a complete review of the evidence can clear up this misapprehen-
sion.

The Spanish writers consistently describe the two separately, with detailed circumstantial distinctions which leave no room for misunderstanding. Sahagun,[2] says

[The Chichimeca] had a great knowledge of herbs and roots and knew their qualities and their
virtues. They themselves discovered and first used the root that they call peiotl and those that
used to gather and eat them used them in place of wine, and they did the same with those that they
call nanacatl, which are toadstools [hongos malos] that also make one drunk like wine.

Again, in a special chapter on intoxicating plants, Sahagun distinguishes the two:

There is another herb like tunas of the earth [the Spanish name for the fruit of the prickly pear,
Opuntia opuntia] which is called peiotl. It is white. It grows in the northern part. Those that eat it
see frightening and laughable visions. This intoxication lasts two or three days and then stops ...[3]

There are some little mushrooms in their land that they call teonanacatl. They grow under the
grass of the fields or pastures. They are round. They have a sort of high stem [pie], thin and round.
They are eaten with great relish, but they harm the throat and make one drunk.[4]

---

[1] Safford, *An Aztec Narcotic* 294; *Identification of Teonanacatl, Narcotic Plants; Peyote,* 1278–79.

[2] Sahagún, *Historia general,* Lib. 10, cap. xxix: " . . . ellos mismos discubrieron, y usaron primero la raíz
que llaman peiotl, y los que comian y tomaban la usaban en lugar de vino, y lo mismo hacian de los que llaman
nanacatl que son los hongos malos que emborrachan tambien como el vino." The authoritative edition of Jourdanet and Simeon, 661–62 translates nanacatl as "champignon vénéneux."

[3] Sahagún, *Historia general,* 3: 241–42: "Hay otra yerba como tunas de tierra, se llama peiotl, es blanca,
hacese ácia la parte del norte, los que la comen ó beben vén visiones espantosas ó irrisibles." (Lib. 11, cap. vii, pt.
i, "De ciertas yerbas que emborrachen.") Jourdanet and Simeon, 737, unfortunately describe tunas as "une . . .
plante qui rapelle la truffe," which *is* a mushroom. Sahagun's work is virtual dictation from Aztec informants,
later translated with painstaking care into Spanish. It is difficult to assume, as did Safford, that such able herba-
lists did not know the difference between a cactus and a fungus.

[4] "Hay unos honguillos en esta tierra que se llaman teonanacatl, críanse debajo del heno en los campos ó
páramos; son redondos, tienen el pie altillo, delgado y redondo, comidos son de mal sabor, dañan la garganta y
emborrachan." (*Idem,* 3: 241–42.) To be sure our own best scientific knowledge must always be the touch-stone
for the data of the various folk-sciences; yet one is not entitled to a lofty and comprehensive *á priori* distrust of
native knowledge, particularly when detailed with such clarity as this.

Still further to emphasize the point, Sahagun in the next section of this chapter[5] goes on to speak of edible mushrooms:

The cone-shaped mushrooms (mushrooms or nanacatl) *genus campos agrorum* in the mountains are good to eat. They are cooked because of this, and if they are raw or badly cooked, they produce vomiting or diarrhea, and they kill one,

and he continues to list and describe a number of other edibles.

The naturalist Hernandez[6] is even more explicit. He describes teo-nanacatl under the heading "De nanacatl seu Fungorum genere"; and from the harmless white mushrooms, iztacnanacame, the red mushrooms, tlapalnanacame, and the yellow-orbicular mushrooms, chimalnanacame, he distinguishes teonanacatl as "teyhuinti," that is, "intoxicating." Simeon's Nahuatl dictionary even uses nanacatl as an illustration:[7]

Teonanacatl, espece de petit champignon qui a mauvais gout, enivre et cause des hallucinations; il est medicinal contre les fievres et la goutte . . . . Teyuinti, qui enivre quelqu'un, enivrant; teyhuinti nanacatl, champignon enivrant.

Safford quotes this evidence himself!

Padre Jacinto de la Serna[8] records for us another compound of the Nahuatl word for mushroom, and describes the fungus while likewise specifically distinguishing it from peyote and ololiuhqui:

To this meeting had come an Indian . . . who had brought some of the mushrooms that are gathered in the monte, and with these he had performed a great idolatry. But before proceeding with my story I wish to explain the nature of the said mushrooms, which in the Mexican language are called Quahtlananacatl, "wild mushrooms." . . . These mushrooms were small and yellow and . . . were collected by priests and old men, appointed as ministers for these impostures, who would proceed to the place where they grow and remain almost the whole night in prayer and in superstitious conjuring; and at dawn, when a certain little breeze known to them would begin to blow, then they would gather the narcotic,[9] attributing to it deity, with the same properties as ololiuhqui or peyote, since when eaten or drunk, they intoxicate those who partake of them, depriving them of their senses, and making them believe a thousand absurdities.

In Safford it appears that de la Serna distinguished these from Picietl, tobacco, also. There

[5] "Las setas (hongos ó nanacatl) hacen genus campos agrorum en los montes, son buenas de comer . . . " (Sahagún, *Historia general*, 3: 243).

[6] Hernandez, in Safford, *Aztec Narcotic*, 293. The very word itself means "mushroom!" Reko's etymology for teo-nanacatl, "divine nourishment," is unsound according to Whorf; and indeed, there is nothing of the edible *par excellence* about fungi (see Schultes, *Peyote and Plants Used*, 136–37).

[7] Simeon, in Safford, *Identification of Teonanacatl*, 400, 412.

[8] de la Serna, *Manual de Ministros*, 261.

[9] Cf. the Huichol peyote-gathering ritual and the wind which arises.

is an implied confusion, to be sure, in Alarcón, but he supplies confirmation of this last point, along with interesting ethnographic details:[10]

One should notice that in almost every case that they are moved to offer a sacrifice to their imagined gods, there comes to take charge of it and preside over it some quack, medicine-man, seer or diviner from among other Indians, the majority of them falling back on their crazy ceremonies, or on whatever whim arises when they are deranged from the drinking of what they call ololiuhqui or pezote [sic] or tobacco, whatever it might be called in particular localities.

The Franciscan Fray Toribio de Benvento mentions teo-nanacatl, to which he gives an erroneous etymology:[11]

They had another kind of drunkenness . . . which was with small fungi or mushrooms [hongos ó setas pequeñas] . . . which are eaten raw, and, on account of being bitter, they drink after them or eat with them a little honey of bees, and shortly after that they see a thousand visions, especially snakes. They went raving mad, running about the streets in a wild state [bestial embriaguez]. They called these fungi "teo-na-m-catl," a word meaning "bread of the gods."

Tezozomoc,[12] again, related that at the coronation of Montezuma the Mexicans gave wild mushrooms [hongos montesinos] to the strangers to eat; that the strangers became drunk, and thereupon began to dance. Diego Duran[13] gives further particulars of the coronation of Montezuma II; he says that after the usual human sacrifices had been offered, all went to eat raw mushrooms (hongos crudos), which caused them to lose their senses, more than if they had drunk much wine. In their ecstasy many of them killed themselves with their own hands, and by virtue of the mushrooms had visions and revelations of the future.

The conclusion from all this evidence is obvious: the peyote of the Plains, *Lophophora williamsii*, is identical with the peiotl, peyotl, pellote, peyote, pejori, peyori or bejo of the Aztec and other Mexican tribes, but this cactus is wholly distinct from the little yellow thin-stemmed fungus teo-nanacatl, and Safford's identification of the two is erroneous.

[10] Safford, *Aztec Narcotic*, 291. Indeed in this short sub-chapter, Sahagun distinguishes and describes coatlxoxouhqui = ololiuhqui [its seeds] peyotl, tlapatl, tzintzintlapatl, mixitl, teonanacatl, tochtetepo, atlepatli, aquiztli, tenxoxoli and quimichpatli! Alarcón, *Tratado*, 131; also in Urbina, *El Peyote y el Ololhiuqui*, 27.

[11] *Ritos Antiquos;* in Kingsborough, 9: 17. Jourdenet and Simeon, translators of Sahagún, *Histoire général*, 738, have: "[Teonanacatl] c'est-à-dire: champignon dangereux. Le terme générique est nanacatl qui se met en composition avec d'autres mots pour désigner les diverses espèces de champignons."

[12] *Crónica Mexicana;* in Kingsborough, 9: 153. The fact that *raw* mushrooms are mentioned disposes of Safford's supposition that *dried* peyote buttons are meant.

[13] Duran, *Historia de las Indias*, 564, quoted from Kingsborough's *Mexican Antiquities* by Bourke, *Scatological Rites*, 90.

APPENDIX 4: "PLANT WORSHIP" IN MEXICO AND THE UNITED STATES

Peyote is only one of several narcotics in the southern United States and Mexico which because of their physiological action find ritual and other uses. Since, in many of these, uses are related, there arises the problem of their possible historical relationship. In any case, it is illuminating to study the general background of attitudes out of which peyotism grew.

CACTI

The Tarahumari of northwestern Mexico, though their hikuli cult is less elaborate than that of the Huichol, have a complex of "worship" and use of several varieties of cacti. Besides hikuli wanamé (*Lophophora williamsii*) Lumholtz[1] lists the following:

Mulato (a *Mammilaria*), believed to make the eyes large and clear to see sorcerers, to prolong life, and to give speed to runners who eat it.[2]

Rosapara (a more advanced vegetative form of the same, but with many spines) which has very keen eyes for Tarahumari wrong-doing; it punishes by driving the offender mad, or throwing him down a precipice; "it is therefore very effective in frightening off bad people, especially robbers and Apaches.[3]

Sunami (*Mammilaria fissurata*),[4] rare, but even more powerful than wanamé, for it calls soldiers to its aid. The drink produced from it is strongly intoxicating. Deer cannot run away from you, nor bears harm you when carrying this cactus.[5]

[1] Lumholtz, *Unknown Mexico*, 1: 372–74. These short paragraphs are summaries, not direct quotations.

[2] Cf. the physiological action of peyote-alkaloids, discussed elsewhere (dilation of the pupil, increased reflex excitability). The use of narcotics in this area in connection with racing appears again with peyote in northern Mexico, and with the "mescal bean" (*Sophora secundiflora*) among the Wichita. The Acaxee used peyote in their ball play, much as the "black drink" (*Ilex cassine*) was used in the Southeast. Cf. Mooney's (*Tarumari-Guayachic*) "Muráto," apparently identical with Lumholtz' Mulato, that "is used mostly in races, not ground up, but tied whole around waist, at back."

[3] Lumholtz, *Unknown Mexico*, 1: 373. In this region narcotics in general are much employed in connection with war, and the magical "witching" of the enemy—whose power is not merely physical but magically malevolent too. "Mescal beans" were part of the war-bundle in some southern Plains tribes, and both peyote and datura were used clairvoyantly and prophetically in war connections. The attitude that the enemy is a witch, Dr. Spier informs me, is widespread among both the Yumans and Athapascans of the Southwest. Cf. also peyote and captured scalps (e.g., Maricopa) talking, and being danger-ridden.

[4] This is an instance where it is rewarding conscientiously to respect native categories and ethnobotanical statements for hordenine (=anhaline, one of the alkaloids of Lophophora) was discovered in *Anhalonium fissuratum* in 1894 by Heffter (see Appendix 5, fn. 5).

[5] Mooney, *Tarumari-Guayachic*, says sunami is very much respected, and is used only by doctors. Women doctors grind them on metates, placing the plant upright and crushing it with one blow (cf. the "killing" of mescal beans in the Plains). Doctors assemble for this feast, which requires the sacrifice of a beef. Special rites attend its gathering, and it must be gathered in a black blanket and bleeds red blood. It must be kept in a double basket in a cave, lest it hear quarreling in the house. It dislikes fire, and after ten or twenty years it loses its

Hikuli walúla sälfami, "hikuli great authority," is the greatest of all; it is extremely rare, and Lumholtz never saw a specimen, though it was described to him as "growing in clusters of from eight to twelve inches in diameter, resembling wanamé with many young ones around it."[6]

Ocoyome, unlike the preceding hikuli which are good, is used only for evil purposes. It has long white spines or "claws," and comes from the Devil. If accidentally touched with the foot, it would break one's leg; it also throws offenders over precipices.[7] Lumholtz says it was very rarely used, and Mooney says the Tarahumari used it not at all—though the "Apaches" did—since it was "poison." Mooney describes the plant as having a reddish down, root and surface, which may account for the Apaches' tying it around their waists to make them brave, in their battles.[8]

Bennett and Zingg are perhaps referring to the same plant under the name "peyote cimar-ron," which is "small, red, and ineffective; it is not used or even touched, since the abuser might die." "Peyote christiano" (híkuli dewéame), a larger, green variety, apparently Lophophora, is considered the "most efficacious."[9]

Bennett and Zingg give two other kinds of cactus used by the Tarahumari:[10]

Witculíki (Mex. *biznaga, Mammillaria hyderi*), a ball cactus of the gorges, is roasted about four minutes in ashes, after being split and divested of its spines; the soft center is squeezed into the ear in case of ear-ache or deafness. (This curiously echoes of the talking peyote stories.)

Bakánawa or bakánori, a small ball cactus, is used by the Indians of the barrancas. Shamans, not peyoteros, carry small bits of the root in their bags; it can be kept only three years, after which it must be sold or hidden, lest the owner go crazy. The shaman chews and anoints the patient with it. So powerful is it that runners use it three days before racing; one man died of fear after having of-fended this plant.

NON-CACTI

Of the ritually used narcotics of this area we have already discussed the "mescal bean," or *Sophora secundiflora*, and teo-nanacatl, the sacred mushroom of the Aztec and Chichi-

---

virtue and must be replanted with copal incensing where originally found. Doctors rub tizwin-and-sunami over the heart and rest of the body, for it makes one win races. *Anhalonium fissuratum* has a striking resemblance to deer-hooves; it is likely the hikuli referred to in this and other Tarahumari-Huichol tales—but it should be re-called that peyotism in Mexico is also connected with deer-hunting.

[6] Lumholtz, *Unknown Mexico*, 1: 373–74; Mooney, *Tarumari-Guayachic*, says this variety is as big as a man's hat. The description probably refers to an occasional polycephalous specimen of *Lophophora williamsii* (hikuli wanamé).

[7] Lumholtz, *Unknown Mexico* 1: 374; *Tarahumari Dances*, 253, 452–54; cf. Mooney's (*Tarumari-Guayachic*) kókoyómi. Mooney thought Lumholtz' "walulasahane" was Tepecano, not Tarahumari.

[8] The resemblance of some *Mammillaria* spp. to a head or scalp of hair is quite striking; Higgins, in fact, figures an "Old Man Cactus" with long flowing white "hair."

[9] Bennett and Zingg, *The Tarahumara*, 290.

[10] Bennett and Zingg, *op. cit.*, 137, 295. The users of bakánawa believe it to be even more powerful than peyote. One can more easily believe that the ataxic gait of a peyote-intoxicated person would "throw" him over a cliff or break a leg, than that it would result in any conspicuously superior racing ability.

meca.[11] The use of marihuana (*Cannabis* spp.) in counteracting sorcery, and other beliefs surrounding its employment are also elsewhere discussed.[12] The use of the mescal-bean of the southern Plains and the various alcoholic drinks[13] of Mexico and the Southwest are perhaps related to the "black drink" made of the leaves and twigs of the "beloved tree" (*Ilex cassine*), which is distributed continuously from the Carolinas to the Rio Grande, with a continuation of the trait across the Antilles into northeastern and central South America.[14]

But the narcotic exhibiting perhaps the most numerous parallels in usage with peyote

[11] Dorman, in Bourke, *Scatalogical Rites*, 91, says mushrooms were "worshipped" in the Antilles, in Virginia, and possibly also in California. The Siberian use of *Amanita* spp. is well-known, but no doubt these sporadic uses are all independent of each other.

[12] Lumholtz, *Unknown Mexico*, 2: 354; see also notes 41, 45, 48 in Appendix 6.

[13] The writer has published elsewhere on the subject of the numerous native American beers (see *Native American Beers*). So far as a cactus-source of these is concerned, the following groups make use of *Cereus giganteus* Englm. and *C. Thurberi* Englm. for their sahuaro drink: Huichol (?), Pima, Maricopa, Yuma, Papago, Halchidoma (?), and San Carlos Apache.

[14] The ilex "black drink" is Catawba (*Handbook of the American Indians*, 1: 150a, 2: 1000–1001); Alibamu (Forster, *Bossu*, 254, 261, 294, 354–55); Creek (Swanton, *Social Organization and Social Usages*, 307, 445; Adair, in Swanton, *Social and Religious Reliefs*, 265; Speck, *The Creek Indians*, 110, 117–18, 134; Bartram, *Travels*, 449, 507), both Taskigi and Mikasuki; Cherokee (Bartram, *Travels*, 357); Chickasaw (Swanton, *Social and Religious Beliefs*, 240); Koasati (Paz, *Koasati Field Notes*); Yuchi (Speck, *Ethnology of the Yuchi*, 122–24, 135); Natchez (Charlevoix, *Histoire de l'Isle*, 166; du Pratz, *Histoire*, 2: 46, 3: 13); Atakapa (Forster, *Bossu*, 1: 354–55), Chitamacha (Gatschet, in Swadesh, *Chitamacha Texts*) and Karankawa (Oliver, in Gatschet, *The Karankawa Indians*, 18–19). Also in Florida (de Laudoniére, in Lewin, *Phantastica*, 279; Safford, *Narcotic Plants*, 417; Romans, *A Concise Natural History*, 94), and also possibly in Virginia (Beverly, *History of Virginia*, 175–80; Ribault [1666], Dominique de Gourages [1567], McCullough, Le Moyne—all in Havard, *Drink Plants*, 41–42; Lawson, *History of Carolina*, 380–82 [1860 ed.]; Adair, *The History of the American Indian*, 108). A similar emetic rite is also found among the "Cutalchich" of Texas (Cabeza de Vaca, in Safford, *Narcotic Plants*, 416–17), the Tainan or Greater Antilles Arawak (Gower, *The Northern and Southern Affiliations*, 39–40), the Lesser Antilles Carib and Guiana (Dixon [R. B.], *Some Aspects*, 1–12), the Amazon Basin (Wissler, *The American Indian*, 213), Jivaro and Canelo of Ecuado (Karsten, in Lewin, *Phantastica*, 279–81; Safford, *Narcotic Plants*, 413, 416); Guarani of Northern Bolivia (Safford, *op. cit.*, 413; Spruce, *Notes of a Botanist*, 2: 419–20). See also Thurnwald, *Economics*, 65; Harrington, *Cuba Before Columbus*, 295, 388–89; Spier, *Yuman Tribes*, 181; *Handbook of the American Indians*, 2: 32a, 145–46; Sapir, *Kaibab-Paiute*. An interestingly parallel distribution (which may have historical relevance) is that of fish and arrow poisons. Fish poisons are reported for northeastern South America, the Orinoco valley, the upper Amazon, the Antillean Carib; the Tarahumari, Acaxee, Opata and in California; the Catawba, Taskigi Creek, Cherokee, Koasati, Yuchi and Iroquois (cf. the blow-gun of the Creek, Cherokee, Choctaw, Iroquois, Yuchi, central Carib, Florida Key-dwellers, natives of Hispaniola and of northeastern South America). Arrow poisons are found in Sonora, Central America, the Guianas, the Antilles (Carib), Florida Arawak (?) and, in historic times, the Tarahumari, as well as in South America. The Opata, curiously, used yerba de fleche to poison deer at water-holes. Beals (*Comparative Ethnology*, 115, 193) also lists poison arrows for the Southern Diegueño, Chumash, Cahuilla, Yavapai, Havasupai, Navaho, Western Apache, Lipan, Natchez (?), Seri, Mixtec and in Sinaloa and Culiacan. Spier adds the Blackfoot and perhaps other Plains groups to this list. The group with poison arrows south of the Great Lakes (*Jesuit Relations*, 8: 302, in Gower, 21) one would guess is Iroquois.

is datura.[15] Gayton lists as datura-users in the Southwest[16] the Pima, Zuñi, Navaho, Hopi, Havasupai, Walapai, Mohave, Yuma and Cocopa, and in California the Akwa'ala, Southern Diegueño, Pass Cahuilla, Gabrielino, Luiseño, Serrano, Chumash, Salinan, Miwok, Eastern and Western Mono, and the Foothill and Southern Valley Yokuts. This distribution is continuous with that in northwestern Mexico among the Opata, Tepehuane, Cora, Tepecano and Aztec.[17]

The parallel uses of peyote, cohoba snuff and datura in prophecy and divination have been summarized elsewhere,[18] but there are further interesting uses of datura. The Aztec of Mexico[19] had special officials who took ololiuhqui (the seeds of datura) to discover cures for illnesses, to find lost or stolen property, to ascertain the origin of long sickness due to witchcraft, etc., receiving pay for their services. Sometimes they prescribed the drug for their patients; datura was also used empirically as an anodyne in setting fractures, and it may have been one of the drugs employed to stupefy sacrificial victims, though peyote is the only one identified. Ololiuhqui was also mixed with tobacco and the ashes of venemous insects to make the sacred ointment of the priesthood; set on altars it was called Divine Meat.[20] The Cora[21] refer to daturas in their songs and myths, but their use of it is not known.

In northern Mexico, the Tepehuane used toloache [datura] in place of peyote.[22] Tepecano prayers refer to datura as the husband of Corn Daughter and the son-in-law of Father Sun; having taken two mistresses, he was punished for this by being stuck head downward in the ground and commanded to give mortals whatever they begged of him. They believe him to have great riches, which they pray for and "borrow." Datura is one of the five narcotics whose flowers decorate a love charm.[23]

[15] We ignore for our purposes the South American area of the use of datura, though it is surely connected with the Mexican culturally and historically, as well as the South American use of coca, tobacco, cohoba snuff (*Piptadenia peregrina*), guarana (*Paullinia cupana* or *P. sorbilis*), chocolatl (*Theobroma cacao*), aya-huasca (*Banisteria caapi*) and yajé (*Haemadictyon Amazonicum* Spruce). Many of the uses of these plants in war, prophesying, divination, ordeals, and doctoring are strikingly similar to the Mexican uses of marihuana, datura, teo-nanacatl and peyote.

[16] The sources for these are cited in Gayton, *The Narcotic Plant Datura*, a manuscript to which I am much indebted.

[17] Note the parallel uses of datura in South America found among the Inca, Matacuna, Chancay, Sipibo, Cocoma, Omagua, Jivaro, Canelo, Quijo, Zaparo, Guanes (Guanuco?), Chibcha and in Darien (after Gayton), The "wysoccan" used by the Pamunky (Beverly, *History of Virginia*, 2: 24) is said to be a datura (Safford, *Daturas*, 557-58); the sporadic use as a medicament in Jamaica (Beckwith, *Notes on Jamaica*, 9, note 5, 28) may not be aboriginal.

[18] The writer hopes in due time to publish further data on New World narcotics.

[19] De la Serna, in Safford, *Daturas*, 551, Arlegui, *Crónica*, 144; Rouhier, *Monographie*, 331.

[20] Gerste, *Notes sur la médicine*, 51. This may be the source of Reko's erroneous teo-nanacatl etymology.

[21] Preuss, *Nayarit-Expedition*, 1: 231.

[22] Diguet, *Le Peyote et son Usage*, 21, note 1.

[23] Mason, *Tepecano Prayers*, 138, 139, 142, 143. Cf. the supposed aphrodisiac effects of peyote, teo-nanacatl, and marihuana.

In the Southwest, the Pima had a jimsonweed song which brought success in deer-hunting[24] and cured vomiting and dizziness. The White Mountain Apache[25] mixed the root of *D. meteloides* with their corn beer to make it more intoxicating. The Apache of Bourke[26] credited datura with the power of making men crazy, but denied using it medicinally or ceremonially. The Havasupai[27] eat datura leaves occasionally apparently for purely secular pleasure, and also use the drug in their arrow poison. At Zuñi[28] datura was one of the medicines formerly belonging to the gods, and only the rain priests and directors of the Little Fire and Cimex fraternities could use it; the rain priests propitiated birds with the powdered root, or a man ate it to bring rain. They also administered it to clients who had been robbed, to discover the thief, and to patients with broken bones; the pulverized root and flower were also used with corn meal for all types of wounds. In myth the daturas were once brother and sister who walked the earth and saw who committed thefts, but the Divine Ones said they knew too much and caused them to disappear into the earth forever; perhaps for this reason it is also used to communicate with the dead. The Navaho[29] eat the root of *D. meteloides*, and sometimes "the Indians under its influence, like the Malays run amuck and try to kill everybody they meet." There is a record of Hopi doctoring with datura.[30]

Nearly all the tribes of southern California used datura. The Akwa'ala, Yuma, Mohave and Eastern Mono took it to acquire gambling luck; the Central Miwok did not eat it, but considered that a dream about datura aided one's gambling fortune.[31] Of the remaining tribes of the region who used it ceremonially, some features were held in common: (1) it was not taken before puberty,[32] (2) it was usually administered to a group,[33] and (3) a supernatural helper, sometimes an animal, was sought.[34]

In southwestern California the use of datura is strongly ritualized in the Chungichnich cult of the Luiseño, and Northern and Southern Diegueño. According to Kroeber the ritual is comparatively recent and overlies an older, simpler use of the plant over a wider area.

[24] Russell, *The Pima*, 299–300. Cf. sunami of the Tarahumari for deer hunting, and the mescal bean for buffalo hunting.

[25] Hrdlička, *Physiological and Medical Observations*, 28; cf. *Handbook of the American Indians*, 2: 837b.

[26] Bourke, *The Medicine-Men*, 455.

[27] Spier, *Havasupai*, 249, 269.

[28] Stevenson, *Ethnobotany of the Zuñi*, 46, 47, 88; *The Zuñi Indians*, 385; Parsons, A *Zuñi Detective*, 168–70. Every single instance in this paragraph finds parallels in the uses of peyote: the powdering of the root, rain-getting, discovery of robbers, as an anodyne, for wounds, etc., differentiation in sex and communication with the dead. Note also in connection with rain-making the "water-bird" of peyotism.

[29] Lumholtz, *Unknown Mexico*, 1:4; *The American Cave-Dwellers*, 389; cf. the running amuck with peyote.

[30] Robbins *et alii*, *Ethnobotany of the Tewa*, 55, note 1.

[31] References from Gayton, *The Narcotic Plant Datura*.

[32] Cf. the use of peyote formerly only by adult warriors.

[33] Cf. the group use of marihuana, teo-nanacatl and peyote in Mexico.

[34] Again compare peyote, particularly in the Plains.

In the Chungichnich ceremony datura is given to boys as a preliminary ritual in puberty observance; its use is not seasonal, nor do women ever partake of it.[35]

The Mountain Cahuilla[36] are typical of groups who had the simpler datura rite in puberty ceremonials before the addition of Chungichnich ritualism.

Manet (datura) was given to boys of 18–20 in a ceremony lasting 3 to 6 days in which other younger boys of 6–10 years were taught clan and "enemy" songs by their fathers. The paha or leader prepared strings of reed, eagle and flicker feathers which were worn by the dancers, who practiced away from the village. The drinking ceremony or kiksawel took place inside the ceremonial dance house, and women and children were warned away by the manet-dancer's bull-roarer.[37] Each boy was given a drink of a decoction of datura pounded in a mortar by the clan chief. The men in the enclosure took each boy by the waist, and they all danced around the fire, led by the manet-dancer. The boys remained unconscious in the house all night when the effect of the drug became manifest, and were removed the following afternoon to a secluded cañon where for a week they were taught songs and dances nightly. The last afternoon a sand-painting was made and its symbolism explained. After an ant-ordeal and a fire-dance they were regarded as men and full-fledged members of the clan.

A second group of tribes in the San Joaquin basin and Sierra Nevada foothills had a datura-drinking ceremonial every spring for both sexes shortly after the age of puberty.[38]

The participant's social status was not changed and the rite alone constituted a ceremonial unit, the tananhibina or tanabi-drinking of the Western Mono. Dancing to clappers took place until the children fell unconscious, whereupon they were carried away to special camps by relatives. If a person appeared to be covered with blood or maggots and vermin (the causes of sickness), they were brushed off with an eagle-feather brush.[39] In discovering the sickness the seer used an eagle-bone whistle which enabled him to "hear" the sickness; if a man had poison, one could see where it was. One could also see things at very great distances, as well as discover what medicine-man had caused the death of people by witchcraft. The seer could likewise find lost articles and discover wealth by means of datura. The drinkers were guarded during this time lest they harm themselves or be harmed. Some men did not have any datura-visions; this was because some medicine-man feared his bad deeds would be discovered, and hence rendered the drink harmless by magic and "covered up" those persons. If a medicine-man wanted to become very powerful, he took tanabi on ten successive seasons. Datura leaves were placed on the forehead of a dead person to drive out the spirit,[40] and people boiled tanabi leaves so the steam filled their house that the spirit of the dead man would not return to them in dreams.

In view of these repeated parallels in the attitudes and usages surrounding both peyote and datura, it is certainly not without significance that their distribution, while contiguous,

[35] Kroeber (*Handbook* 462, 589, 593, 609, 613–14) lists tribes who may lack it. See also Kroeber, *Anthropology*, 309–311.

[36] Summarized from Gayton, citing W. D. Strong, *Aboriginal Society*.

[37] Cf. the preparation of peyote in Mexico.

[38] Summarized from Gayton.

[39] Cf. this and the following elements with peyote usages.

[40] Cf. the Mexican use of peyote.

is mutually exclusive in northern Mexico and the southwestern United States: peyote is generally central and northeastern in Mexico, whence it spread northward and eastward into the Plains, while datura is northwestern in Mexico and extends through the Pueblo and nomadic Southwest to southern California. And if the "black drink," native American beers in Mexico and the Southwest, and the mescal bean be all counted with peyote and datura as part of one general distribution, we have a large continuous area or "narcotic complex" across the whole southern United States and northern Mexico. Such large general distributions are not unknown (e.g., bear ceremonialism), and datura (via Central America), ilex drinks (via the Antilles) and aboriginal alcoholic liquors (continuous from the Southwest through Mexico and Central America to include the entire northern three-quarters of South America) are surely connected ultimately with the same traits in South America—more particularly since not alone are the plants involved the same, but also detailed "superorganic" attitudes and ritual manifestations.

APPENDIX 5: CHEMISTRY OF PEYOTE

Alkaloids are found in a number of cacti: *Cereus peruvianus, C. pecten aboriginum, Pilocereus sargentianus* Orcutt, *Phyllocactus ackermanii, P. russelianus, Echinocereus mamillosus, Mammillaria cirrhifera, M. uberiformis, M. centricirrha, Anhalonium prismaticum, A. fissuratum,*[1] and *Lophophora williamsii. Lophophora* in its mature state, however, is notable for the number of alkaloids which it contains, nine being known at present.

The long and hotly-disputed botanical question of *Anhalonium williamsii* versus *A. lewinii,* beyond its ethnographic significance in accounting the plants "male" and "female," has a chemical aspect for a time obscuring their botanical identity. *A. williamsii* (young specimens of *Lophophora*) contains only the alkaloid Pellotine,[2] while *A. lewinii* (the mature *Lophophora*) contains at least nine, as follows:[3] Anhaline ($C_{10}H_{15}ON$), Anhalamine ($C_{11}H_{15}O_3N$), Mescaline ($C_{11}H_{17}O_3N$), Anhalonidine ($C_{12}H_{17}O_3N$), Anhalonine ($C_{12}H_{15}O_3N$), Lophophorine ($C_{13}H_{17}O_3N$), Pellotine ($C_{13}H_{19}O_3N$), Anhalinine and Anhalidine. Lophophorine is an oily colorless liquid; mescaline crystallizes only in the presence of atmospheric CO_2; and anhalonidine crystallizes imperfectly; the rest are crystalline. Their physiological activity appears to increase with their chemical complexity.[4]

Hordenine was first isolated from *A. fissuratum* by Heffter in 1894 and shown to be identical with Späth's anhaline from *Lophophora* in 1920; Heffter isolated pellotine in 1894, mescaline, anhalonidine, anhalonine and lophophorine in 1896, Kauder adding anhalamine is 1899. Capellman collaborated with Heffter on mescaline in 1905. If Heffter first isolated the *Lophophora* alkaloids, Späth is to be largely credited with establishing their chemical constitution and synthesizing them: mescaline in 1920, anhalamine in 1921, and anhalonidine and pellotine in 1922. Röder in 1922 and Gangl in 1923 collaborated in establishing the chemical constitution of others of the alkaloids.[5]

[1] Tschirsch, *Handbuch*, 680.

[2] Henry (T. A.), *The Plant Aklaloids*, 194; Moureu, *Review*, 519; Heffter, *Ueber zwei Cacteenalkaloïde*, 2977; *Ueber Pellote*, 309 ff.; Späth, *Über die Anhalonium; I, Anhalin und Mezcalin*, 129; Kunkel, *Handbuch*, 836; Schumann, *Über giftige Kakteen*, 106.

[3] Henry (T. A.), *loc. cit.* The more recently discovered anhalinine and anhalidine are cited from Schultes, *Peyote and Plants Used*, 134.

[4] Rouhier, *Monographie*, 196, 201, 205, 212.

[5] Henry (T. A.), *The Plant Alkaloids*, 194–95; Moureu, *Review*, 520; Heffter, *Ueber zwei Cacteenalkaloïde*, 2976; *Ueber Pellote*, 69–73; Späth, *Ueber die Anhalonium: I, Anhalin und Mezcalin*, 129, 138–39; II, *Die Konstitution*, 97, 263. Anhalonine has been found in *A. jourdanianum* (Henry, *op. cit.*, 194; Heffter, *Ueber Pellote*, 427) which is identical with *Lophophora*. See Heffter, *Ueber zwei Cacteenalkaloïde*, 2976–77, also vols. 29: 216, 223–25, 227; 34: 3005, 3008, 3013; Heffter and Capellman, *Versuch zur Synthese*, 38: 3634–40; Kauder, *Über Alkaloide*, 190–98. Späth, with Gangl and Röder, *Über de Anhalonium*, IV, VI; Kunkel, *Handbuch*, 836.

APPENDIX 6: PHYSIOLOGY OF PEYOTE

ACTION OF THE INDIVIDUAL ALKALOIDS OF LOPHOPHORA WILLIAMSII

Since the alkaloids of peyote fall into two classes with regard to physiological action, the strychnine-like (increased reflex-irritability to the point of tetanus) and the morphine-like (sedative-soporific) and since there are important ethnographic considerations concern-the supposed "sex" of peyote, we discuss the action of each alkaloid before characterizing pan-peyotl physiologically. The two groups are somewhat antagonistic in action; ethno-graphic indications seem to point to the earlier action of the strychnine-like alkaloids, and a delayed reaction of the morphine-like. However, the size of the dose and the continued ingestion of buttons during the night cause variations in the length of the different periods of intoxication.

The peyote-alkaloids might be arranged in a scale, with mescaline at the morphine-like extreme and lophophorine at the other: (morphine-like) mescaline, peyotline, anhaline, anhalamine, anhalonidine, anhalonine, lophophorine (strychnine-like). Peyotline, however, has a variable effect on different individuals, while anhalonine has been accounted of the the morphine-like group by Rouhier.[1] The color-visions so conspicuous in peyote-intoxica-tion are chiefly produced by mescaline.[2] Lophophorine is the most toxic.[3] Physiologically the effects of the individual alkaloids are:[4]

Mescaline: slowing of pulse, slight headache, sensation of heaviness in the limbs lasting one to several hours; heavier doses, feeling of discomfort and fullness of stomach (even when injected intravenously) in addition to the above symptoms; still heavier doses, accentuation of symptoms and appearance of color-visions.

Peyotline: in about an hour reduces the pulse approximately one-quarter the normal number of beats; two hours after ingestion, heaviness of eyelids, sensation of fatigue, aversion to all physical or mental effort; has no marked analgesic action but is a fairly good sedative and has a very apprecia-ble hypnotic and anodyne action.

Anhaline [= hordenine]:[5] exercises a paralyzing effect on the central nervous system.

Anhalamine: this has not been adequately studied physiologically. Nor have *Anhalinine* and *Anhalidine*.

[1] Rouhier, *Monographie*, 231.

[2] Kobert, *Lehrbuch*, 1008–1009; Rouhier, *op. cit.*, 227; Henry (T. A.), *The Plant Alkaloids*, 199: Dixon (W. E.), *The Physiological Action*, 71. Rouhier (*op. cit.*, 228, 231) places peyotline in the strychnine group; it has a narcotic and tetanic effect on animals, to be sure, but in man, according to Jolly, it causes slight hypnosis, but no anaesthesia. Schmiedeberg puts it in the morphine group, which we have followed (cf. Kobert, *Lehrbuch*, 1009).

[3] Henry (T. A.), *The Plant Alkaloids*, 199; Rouhier, *op. cit.*, 238; Dixon (W. E.), *The Physiological Action*, 71.

[4] Condensed from Rouhier, *op. cit.*, 227–32. Note "pellotine" is the same as "peyotline."

[5] Henry, *loc. cit.* Staub and Grassmann (*Über die Wirkungsgrenze*, 336) state, in dogs, increased heartbeat and pressure.

Anhalonidine: only slight sleepiness and dull sensation in head; pulse not affected.

Anhalonine: produces no sensible effect, except perhaps a slight sleepiness.

Lophophorine: the most toxic, has no narcotic action; a quarter-hour after ingestion an accentuated sickening feeling in the back of the head, with hotness and blushing of face, slight pulse diminution; symptoms disappear after 40 minutes.

"In short," says Rouhier,[6] "save for anhalonidine which, in strong doses, provokes in the frog paralysis of the motor nerve-ends (which is not observed otherwise in mammals), the alkaloids of peyote act on the central nervous system. . . . [Mescaline] acts on the brain, which it paralyzes. [Lophophorine] is antagonistic in action to this, augmenting the irritability of the spinal cord and its elongations. . . . Peyotline, anhalonine and anhalonidine hold a middle place between the two preceding. They produce in the frog a soporific effect (due to the paralysis of the brain or central nervous system), followed by an effect of tetanus. Anhalonidine and anhalonine have identical physiological effects. The paralyzing effect of the former is of long duration. That of the second is much reduced and is lacking in warm-blooded animals."

ACTION OF PAN-PEYOTL

The native use of peyote, however, involves of course the whole series of alkaloids, and we must discuss the physiological effect of pan-peyotl preparations. Since antagonistic alkaloids are at work, it is not surprising to find several stages of physiological action with the whole plant. Dixon writes:[7]

The action may be divided into a preliminary stage and a stage of intoxication. In the former there is excitement, a feeling of exhilaration, and diminished kinaesthetic sensations, performances involving effort being hardly noticed; the face is flushed, and the pupils dilated; there is a tendency to talkativeness, which may become wandering later, when the patient begins to feel "lightheaded."

This stage quickly passes away, and is followed by one of intoxication, in which there is a great inclination to lie down, although there is never any tendency to sleep. The pupils are now widely dilated, but act sluggishly to light. On attempting to walk, the gait closely resembles that in alcoholic intoxication, and in all bodily movements requiring precision, the incoördination is evident. The body is generally in a tremulous condition, the tremors showing well when the attention is fixed on anything held in the hand. Reflexes over the whole body are much increased, including the skin reflexes, although there is considerable blunting of painful and tactile sensation. Twitching of muscles occurs in various parts of the body, especially noticeable in the face, and there is a curious feeling as if the face, lips, tongue, etc., were much swollen.

[6] Rouhier, *op. cit.*, 231. I have modified and added to Rouhier's classifications. Ellis (*Mescal: A New Artificial Paradise*) describes the effects on the central nervous system as "acute cerebrasthenia." The lethal dose of anhalonine hydrochloride for rabbits is 0.16 to 0.2 grams per kilogram of body weight; lophophorine kills frogs by a dose of only 0.011 grams per kilogram of body weight. (Henry, *op. cit.*, 199).

[7] Dixon (W. E.), *The Physiological Action*, 79–81. Rouhier (*op. cit.*, 268–69): "Intoxication by peyote in man comprises two very distinct phases, one, general superexcitement, contentment; euphoria, the other of nervous sedation, of more or less accentuated physical indolence, and of hypocerebrality; this last phase is almost entirely filled with the production of color-visions." Henry (*op. cit.*, 199) likens this preliminary stage to alcoholic intoxication.

As in *cannabis indica*, time is over-estimated, possibly as a result of the rapid flow of ideas[8] and the inability to fix the attention. Perception of space is also modified,[9] on one occasion giving the impression that the ground sloped away in all directions.

Perception may be considerably delayed; for example, one may look at a person one knows well, and it is only after scanning his features for what appears to the experimenter a considerable time, that recognition occurs;[10] it is possible, however, that this may be explained by the increased time-relation. The attention cannot be fixed, as the least stimulus is sufficient to alter the train of thought; thus it was found impossible to fix the attention on a book, and a subsequent examination of notes attempted during intoxication showed incoördination both as regards language and writing.

On two occasions when deeply under the influence of the drug, there was an indescribable feeling of dual existence; thus after sitting with closed eyes subjectively examining the color visions, on suddenly opening them for a brief space one seems to be a different self, as on waking from a dream we pass into a different world from that in which we have been. This may be to some extent comparable to the rhythmical rise and fall of the "physical waves" in Indian hemp intoxication.[11]

But by far the most remarkable of these subjective phenomena are the sensory hallucinations,[12]

[8] Fernberger (*Observations*, 270) mentions "a very clear but rapidly changing focus of attention"; see also his *Further Observations*, 367. Crichtly (*Some Forms*, 102) notes the "rapidity of change," though visions "lasted many hours." It is in this that the "indescribability" of the visions lies (Ellis, *Mescal: A New Artificial Paradise*).

[9] Fernberger (*Observations*, 269) notes "distortion of time and space"; and (*Further Observations*, 367) a "grave upsetting of space and time . . . space was extremely extended and time extremely slowed." Maggendorfer (*Intoxikationspsychosen*, 355–56) notes for mescaline a time and space derangement, similar to those in other "intoxikationpsychosen." Crichtly (*op. cit.*, 105) describes micropsia and megalopsia, or gravely deranged perception of size.

[10] In these careful statements by Dixon (on a subject not notable for the accuracy of all observers) many physiological bases for ethnographic observations I have made may be found, e.g., the mistaking in a Kiowa meeting of the medicine-man Tonakat by an informant for a hideous alligator-like monster; he believed then he had seen this witch "for what he was."

[11] The writer testifies to the accuracy of Dixon's somewhat amazing statement. So marked have been the physical effects of the first stage of intoxication, that when these pass off to give rise to the feeling of physiological normality (introspectively), one almost has a distrust of the existence of these spectacular mental displays particularly if the observer is of a markedly non-"psychic" or skeptical cast of mind. The visions arise in the midst of a psychological state I can only describe as one of perfectly *plausible* "epistemological orientation," sometimes acutely felt in alcoholic intoxication. The feeling of dissociation with this unfamiliar and spectacular side of ones peyote-intoxication experience has suggested to some observers incipient schizoid psychoses. Small wonder natives often exhibit curiously ambivalent attitudes toward their visions, and sometimes explicitly reject and disclaim them as "bad," the result of trickery by the peyote power ("he's testing me") or by some human witch present. Hoebel in conversation has insisted on the Northern Cheyenne attitude of suspicion of peyote's "trickiness." But I wholly disagree with Havelock Ellis and others who have argued for the "ineffability" of visions, and even less do I see in peyote-intoxication any approach to the mystical state of the epistemological *convincingness* of the *visions*. It is this *concomitant* state of seeming objectiveness and reality-orientation which accounts for the marked feeling of duality. On this point, cf. Drs. Monakow and Morgue: "[Peyote produces] a particular state of dreaming, without losing, relatively, the idea of orientation, accompanied by pseudo-hallucinatory phenomena."

[12] Ellis (*Mescal: A Study of a Divine Plant*, 60) reports a "vague olfactory hallucination"; Fernberger (*Observations*, 269) and the writer have noticed kinaesthetic derangements which have parallels in native visions.

especially visual. These arise gradually, and are at first only seen with closed eyes .... The visions rapidly become more marked, until on closing the eyes a regular kaleidoscopic play of colours can be seen with either eye, precisely the same; hence the condition must be central.

These colours may assume all kinds of fantastic shapes; they are never still, but constantly in motion, sometimes in a circular or to-and-fro manner, but more generally there is a kind of pulsation somewhat similar to that in the cinematograph.[13]

Both native visions and white observations testify abundantly to the phenomena of synaesthesis, or the perception of the data of one sense in terms of another. Rouhier figures a painting made by an experimenter in which the sound of a bell is seen as a surréaliste aggregate of flowing, pulsating lines; and a subject of Havelock Ellis had a "curious sensation of tasting colors." Crichtly mentions a color-taste synaesthesia also.[14] All these phenomena are physiological constants, as indicated by comparison of native visions with white experimenters' observations.

After visual hallucinations far the commonest are auditory ones. The writer, with a number of other observers, has noted the preternatural resonance, hollowness, discreteness and far-away quality of one's own voice; if vocal disfunction were involved one would expect a raising of pitch here, hence it is probably auditory. On this point Dixon bears critical evidence:[15]

The whole effect of the sound of the piano was most curious and delightful, the whole air being filled with music, each note of which seemed to arrange itself around a medley of other notes which appeared to me to be surrounded by a halo of colour pulsating to the music. Nasal hyperaesthesia was also present, though less evident than either the visual or auditory phenomena.

The more strictly physiological effects may be summed up as follows:[16]

Skin: no local irritation on injection of pan-peyotl; one observer reports partial skin anaesthesia, but this does not affect cutaneous reflex-excitability, which is much increased.

Respiration: moderate amounts in Rana esculens produce no effect, but in toxic doses respiration becomes quicker and shallower, death ultimately occurring from paralysis of the respiratory center. In man respiration is ordinarily not affected, but some observers report shallower and more rapid breathing with "occasional long-drawn and deep sighs, and a painful feeling of suffocation." Still another observer states that "respiration slows immediately after injection but is not influenced in a durable manner."[17]

Hearing is very acute (Fernberger, *ibid.; Further Observations*, 371), but subject to hallucination and synaesthetic derangement.

[13] Some fifty native peyote "visions" were collected in the original dissertation from which this paper is derived.

[14] Rouhier, *op. cit.*, 315, fig. 44; Ellis, *Mescal; A Study*, 68; Crichtly, *Some Forms*, 106.

[15] Dixon (W. E.), *The Physiological Action*, 81.

[16] Based largely on Dixon and Rouhier, with additional data from Jaensch, Wiley, Crichtly, Prentiss and Morgan, Ellis, Fernberger, Wertham and Bleuler, Lewin, Maggendorfer, Staub and Grassmann.

[17] Rouhier, *op. cit.*, 232. But Dixon writes, "In man the nervous effects are extremely interesting, but on account of the respiratory depression which is liable to occur it is not desirable to experiment too freely; it is necessary to remember that this substance, like Indian hemp, varies considerably in its effects on different individuals, and that the element of idiosyncrasy is marked."

Circulation: in the frog a marked effect on heart-beat: diminished rapidity, but increased duration; in the dog a small dose causes a slight rise in pressure, stronger doses considerable depression on the heart and vasodilation; in the cat mescaline causes initial lower pressure, slowly rising, and with a larger dose a greater initial fall, more marked slowing in beat, with variable promptness in recovery. In man .05 gr. of lophophorine causes marked slowing of beat but a rise in pressure and force. An ordinary dose of four "buttons" produces a 15-25% fall in the number of beats, with a slow recovery from a sharp drop unless more are eaten. But death in guinea pigs and frogs comes through paralysis of respiration, not of the heart, since in Wiley's experiments it would beat 15-20 minutes after the death of the animal. "All this evidence points to the conclusion that the main effect of these alkaloids is a direct one on cardiac muscle . . . [since] very large doses, quite non-therapeutic in amount, are . . . required before the colour visions . . . are observed.

Salivation: increased in the cat, whether administered by mouth or subcutaneously; the alkaloids are secreted in the saliva (one cc. of cat saliva produces the same symptoms in a frog); in man salivation is somewhat increased.

Digestive system: in small doses pan-peyotl is constipating, according to some. In the cat large doses produce diarrhea and blood in the feces. In man and the quadrupeds all sensations of hunger are suppressed or absent during the period of intoxication, but the appetite returns somewhat increased after recovery; on first injection or ingestion there is a marked nausea and feeling of fullness in the stomach which passes off, without, however, hunger arising.

Blood, secretions, etc.: no increase in the coagulability of the blood; pancreatic and biliary secretions unaffected.

Kidneys: peyote alkaloids chiefly excreted by the kidneys; experiments show increased renal blood supply, and pan-peyotl is markedly diuretic.

Eyes: in the later stages of intoxication the pupils are widely dilated, accompanied by lack of accommodation and consequent photophobia.

Nervous system: sizeable doses produce their most marked effect on the nervous system: wakefulness (despite cardiac and muscular depression), exaggeration of all reflexes (due to selective action on the spinal cord). A frog injected with pan-peyotl became "exceedingly susceptible to stimuli, until even the slightest touch or even a breath of cold air is sufficient to give rise to a little nervous explosion, with the resulting contraction of several muscles"; the frog became rigid in tetanus as the reflexes degenerated. Convulsions are produced in the dog with 1/5 cc. of pan-peyotl, sometimes light, sometimes as violent as those of strychnine; death in convulsions with 1 cc. per kilogram of body weight. Pan-peyotl immediately kills a rabbit with a dose of 2 cc. per kilogram of body weight, injected intravenously; 2 cc. injected in the lymphatic sac paralyzes a frog. An injected cat shows "ataxic gait, with jerky and stiff movements"—a staccato effect in an animal notable for the legato quality of its movements—with "irregular twitchings of muscles over the whole body." The same effects, less marked because of relatively smaller doses, appear in man as in other mammals. Extraordinary doses cause qualitatively and quantitatively the same reactions: the writer has seen a child, quite ill and suffering from malnutrition, brought very fretful into a peyote meeting and fed peyote "tea" until rigid in strychnine-like tetanic opisthotonos.

Psychic state: exceedingly variable, varying culturally, with the stages of intoxication, and in the individual himself at different times. Mexican visions sometimes have a frightening tone, sometimes one of hilarity. The writer had marked confirmation of this while still ignorant of this ethnographic fact: in an Oto meeting in 1936 visions were of monstrous animals so ridiculous and hilariously funny that proper self-restraint in meeting was difficult; yet, in a control experiment comfortably conducted in New Haven, the psychic state developed into one of stark, galloping, psychotic terror, quite inexplicable on realistic grounds (later, parallels were found in Winnebago material and in white observations). Curiously enough Dixon noted in a cat photophobia, dilated pupils and a fixed "stare . . . [and] most of the physical elements of 'terror.' . . . The ears were drawn back, the hair over the body, especially the tail, becomes erected, there is twitching of the superficial muscles, the respiration being shallow and hurried, and the heart weak and irregular." One experimenter's subject became possessed of the fixed idea that he was being poisoned, when the intoxication had thoroughly developed. This experience, once felt, is so strikingly physiological that one is tempted to wonder if there is any hypersecretion of adrenalin, perhaps in adjustmental reaction to the effect of the alkaloids on the heart. Dixon thought *Lophophora* differed from *Cannabis indica* in never provoking merriment; yet Wertham and Bleuler had one subject who achieved a state of to him quite meaningless hilarity. Fear states are present among native users also, to judge from the content of some visions recorded; conceivably these might be the psychic end-results of the intensified reflex-excitability induced by the strychnine-like alkaloids. However, one should bear in mind throughout the antagonistic effect of the alkaloids, which together with individual, cultural and other differences (physiological state, amount eaten, the form in which the drug is taken—infusion or solid, dry or green—the continued eating of it in late stages of intoxication, etc.) contribute to widely variable reactions. The experiments of Wertham and Bleuler are impressive in this connection.[18] This variability for the same subject at different times, Indians explain, is conditioned by what one starts thinking about when the intoxication begins.[19]

PEYOTE AS APHRODISIAC AND ANAPHRODISIAC

We have previously noted the use in Mexico of teo-nanacatl, *Cacalia* spp. and *Cannabis* spp. for their supposed aphrodisiac virtues. Peyote too has become involved in this use, but it has been as warmly defended as attacked, some indeed maintaining that it is a specific anaphrodisiac. It can hardly be both. The present writer, as a matter of fact, considers this less a problem of physiology than one of ethnology, psychology or even psychiatry, and is persuaded that in the pharmacological-physiological sense there exist neither aphrodisiacs nor their opposite, anaphrodisiacs.

The matter is not to be settled off-handedly by resort to experiments on white subjects; it is a more intricate question of culture and personality. If white subjects argue heatedly for peyote's aphrodisiac and anaphrodisiac virtues, this proves nothing physiological. It merely indicates the long notorious fact that given the somewhat anti-sexual tradition of

[18] Wertham and Bleuler, *Inconstancy of the Formal Structure of the Personality*, The general thesis of these experimenters was that personality types might be studied as they were exteriorized in mescaline intoxication via the Rorschach test. One of the observers described two personalities in a normal subject in two periods of intoxication, not knowing that it was the same person. They conclude, interestingly: "It is suggested that these observations indicate that the form of a personality is not a constant, but that it may be influenced by outer circumstances, and that the usual psychologic "type" of a person does not necessarily exhaust the description of the formal structure of his personality."

[19] "What an excellent use for a medical congress," Sir Francis Galton dryly wrote Havelock Ellis (*Mescal: A Study*, 71, note), "to put one half of their members under mescal, and to make the other half observe them."

west European culture, the typical anxiety of its culture-bearers is sexual. This is scarcely the case with the Plains Indians I have observed. As expressed in ritual, symbolism and prayer, the typical anxiety of these natives is that about life itself—and the culture-historical background out of which this has grown will be readily recalled by students of Plains ethnography (constant warfare, prestige symbolisms, the coming of the Whites with new diseases, superior weapons, etc.).

We shall merely cite here, therefore, instances showing up the order of "proof" so far adduced to support these contrary stands about peyote. Lumholtz leads the anaphrodisiac school:

Another marked effect of the plant is to take away temporarily all sexual desire. This fact, no doubt, is the reason why the Indians, by a curious aboriginal mode of reasoning, impose abstinence from sexual intercourse as a necessary part of the hikuli cult.[20]

Wertham and Bleuler also write of subjects that[21] "efforts to conjure up an erotic scene were unsuccessful." Fernberger,[22] however, exhibits a still more naïve sense of evidence:

[An ethnographer] reports that in the Peyote Cults investigated there is no actual, implied or even symbolic eroticism[23] which marks these ceremonies off from practically every other known American Indian ceremony of any tribe or group [!]. In order to test the validity of some of these reports, nine mature members of the faculty . . . submitted together to extreme peyote intoxication.[24] [The experiment was performed in a group *because* it] gave the opportunity for suggestion of one observer upon another [and permitted a ceremony complete with rattles and drum. Consequently[25]] one unexpected and unforeseen result of this investigation is the evident strongly anti-aphrodisiac[26] effect of the drug. This would again explain, for social psychology and for anthro-

[20] Lumholtz, *Unknown Mexico*, 1: 359; cf. *Explorations in Mexique*, 181–82. It is a curious west-European mode of reasoning that leads one to *expect* in all psychic upsetments such as this the emergence of the sexual anxiety—more particularly in the case of peyote intoxication, which provokes marked fall of heart-beat, physical and mental depression at one stage, uncomfortable "stomach fullness" and acute nausea!

[21] Wertham and Bleuler, 60. The presence of prior suggestion is blatantly obvious. Cf. Karwoski, 212: "To the sexologist an easy way of obliterating temporarily the genital response is offered since mescal is a powerful an-aphrodisiac . . . . My own experience confirms the an-aphrodisiac properties of mescal, but the fact that under its influence I found my imagination turning to erotic situations, although temporarily impotent, is an illustration of the persistence of conditioning that offers an interesting suggestion with reference to the extirpation experiments reported in the controversy over the James-Lange theory of emotions." Unfortunately, *culture* cannot be extirpated.

[22] Fernberger, *Further Observations*, 368. But Fernberger misunderstood his informant, Petrullo, who (*The Diabolic Root*, 8, note) of course disclaims this statement from "which" on.

[23] Field workers protest privately, but not often enough explicitly, against the projection of these culturally- and personally-subjective values into other cultures. The envisaging of primitive cultures as unspoiled Arcadias where one's frustrated dreams for one's own culture come true, is at least as old as Tacitus' "Germania," and is still going on, not alone among laymen.

[24] We repeat that results *either positive or negative* for white observers have no bearing on the problem as regards natives, as this problem is cultural.

[25] Fernberger, *Further Observations*, 377.

[26] All but one vomited.

pology, the purely and totally unerotic character[27] of the ceremonies of the Peyote Cults so unusual to American Indian ceremonies.[28]

It seems alike profitless to enter into a discussion of those who argue the aphrodisiac properties of peyote.[29] These have often enough been missionaries and administrators whose use of the argument in bitter attacks on the Native American Church shows them to be scarcely disinterested. Certainly from the evidence so far at hand we can only heartily endorse the opinion of Klüver[30] that "the drug apparently does not influence the sexual sphere in any specific way."

THERAPEUTIC USES OF PEYOTE

From the physiological relation of the peyote alkaloids to strychnine and morphine, considerable enthusiasm was early shown about their pharmacodynamics and possible therapeutic uses. Jolly[31] in 1896 experimented on pellotine [= peyotline] as a hypnotic and soporific, for when used in small doses in man the fall of the pulse initially is accompanied by sleepiness. Heffter[32] likewise reports a marked heaviness of limbs and eyelids. Loaeza,[33] apparently using pan-peyotl preparations, maintained that peyote and *Cereus serpentinus* (organillo) had value as tonics or cardiac regulators, but variable action and individual idiosyncrasy is marked. Henry[34] says the therapeutic dose of pellotine is one-third to two-thirds of a grain, but that it is only "slightly narcotic." The high toxicity of lophophorine discourages its therapeutic use. Rouhier[35] wrote in 1926 that "properly speaking, therapeusis by peyote does not yet exist. Although the drug was introduced in the American

[27] It is scarcely surprising that one does not find in Indian ceremonies what is not there.

[28] Had Fernberger investigated such of his predecessors as Lumholtz, the novelty of his results would have impressed him less. And had his experiments been more critical he would not be superfluously supplied with an "explanation" to a problem where no data to be explained exist (compare the a-priorism of the "parapsychologists"). But Fernberger continues: "For every one of the observers the anti-aphrodisiac effect of the drug was marked and continued, in most cases, for at least 24 hours after the period of intoxication. Efforts at erotic stimulation proved ineffective. In several cases physical automanipulation of the genitals failed to produce the usual physiological effect. The calling up of erotic images—visual and verbal—were equally ineffective."

[29] An able and sincere field worker has told the writer of an experience at a meeting which ended for him in orgasm. But he would agree that detailing of similar White "aphrodisiac" experiences is edifying more as regards individuals than the drug. This paper aims to deal with the *native* peyote cult.

[30] Klüver, *Mescal, the Divine Plant*, 101; but peyote is a complex of physiologically antagonistic drugs of quite variable reaction.

[31] Jolly, *Über die schlafmachende; Über Pellotine*, 375–76. This effect is all the more remarkable since Heffter in similar experiments noted that pellotine produced in the frog excitability and reflex tetanus.

[32] Heffter, *Über Pellotin*, 327–28.

[33] Loaeza, in del Campo, *Peyote*, 145. Koang-Hobschette (*Les Cactacées*, 41) says cactine, the active element of *Cereus grandiflorus* Mill. is used like digitalis as a cardio-tonic, strengthening the systole and diminishing the diastole like strychnine.

[34] Henry (T. A.), *The Plant Alkaloids*, 199.

[35] Rouhier *Monograhie*, 340.

146

pharmaceutical market[36] for twenty years, from which it has since disappeared, it is still unknown to the great medical public." On the whole, however, the therapeutic possibilities of *Lophophora* seem unimpressive.[37]

USES IN PSYCHIATRY

Because peyote produces what has been described as a "mescal psychosis," it has been suggested that it might be a useful approach for the psychiatrist in the study of schizophrenia. The production of "horrible depressions" in a subject of Prentiss and Morgan and "fear that his life was leaving him," as well as the unaccountable hilarity of Wertham and Bleuler's subject, suggests a similar value, if any, in the study of manic-depressive psychoses too. No doubt psychoses may be exteriorized with increased facility in peyote intoxication, but this strikes one as a crude method and subject to the introduction of extraneous factors over which there is no control.[38]

Hutchings used pellotine as a hypnotic on psychotic patients in the St. Lawrence State Hospital. Pilcz likewise reports this use of peyote as a sedative for the insane, but Warburg states that these experiments have met with little success, on account of the by-effects of the alkaloids. Dr. Goodall of the Carmarthen Asylum, according to Havelock Ellis, tried peyote on melancholic and stuporous patients, but "beyond dilation of pupils and rapidity [!] of heart action, the results were nil." Martindale and Westcott report that formerly peyote was used in neurasthenia, hysteria and asthma; it is hard to see in some cases where the cure is any superior to the disease, however. Briau employed peyote in "anxiety states," but the extremely variable emotional states under peyote intoxication

[36] Parke Davis and Co. formerly manufactured the drug. See their *Newer Pharmacology*.

[37] But not to all persons! The typical over-enthusiasm with which new materia medica are received is itself an interesting ethnographic commentary. Prentiss and Morgan (*Therapeutic Uses*, 4–5) prescribed it variously for "cramps, griping and colic . . . [and] nervous headache" as well as "tickling in the throat." They also report (*The Alkaloids of Anhalonium*, 123–37) uses by other doctors. Two brothers, doctors, prescribed peyote for their brother who was suffering from "softening of the brain." He died a few months later, uncured. Nevertheless, they prescribed peyote for their sister, who was "very low and out of her head;" she later recovered. Richardson (D. A.), (*A Report*, 194–95) reports still more spectacular sequelae. He administered peyote to a man with "frontal cephalalgia." "Expecially would I remark," he says, "on the clearing of the skin of pimples over the chest and back, and a marked softening of the hair, which before the exhibition of the anhalonium was dry, with a tendency to break easily." It nevertheless also decreased the abnormal oiliness of the skin. Further, he thought it was a solvent for uric acid, likely to be of value for stones in the bladder. Lastly, "In my opinion, anhalonium is a superior cardiac tonic, and, like nitroglycerine, its effects are prolonged after the administration of the drug is withdrawn."

The efficacy of peyote in native doctoring seems as little established also. Reasons of ethnographic nature have already been cited for doubting the anti-alcoholic virtue of peyote. Indeed, the leader of one meeting I attended I visited in jail later in the week; he had been arrested for drunken street-fighting. I could uncharitably cite half-a-dozen similar cases, but it seems amply enough demonstrated that there is no relation of exclusiveness between peyotism and alcoholism.

[38] Klüver, *Mescal, The "Divine" Plant*, 97, 108. Prentiss and Morgan, *Anhalonium Lewinii*, 581; Wertham and Bleuler, *Inconstancy in the Formal Structure*, 52, 60.

147

make even tentative conclusions precarious.[39] Indeed, peyote would be calculated to aggravate asthma and anxiety states under some circumstances!

Bensheim found different mescal reactions in cycloids and schizoids, but Wertham and Bleuler somewhat surprisingly discovered both reactions in a single person, and argued for the inconstancy of the formal structure of the "personality." Probably, however, peyote had no definitive importance in either case though the former used only mescaline and the latter pan-peyotl. Zucker induced mescaline intoxication in the hallucinated insane, but far too many variables appear to be involved here. Zador conducted experiments on the blind and patients with disordered vision, using mescaline, the chief hallucination-producing alkaloid of peyote. Klüver discussed color predominance in reported visions (red-green in the initial phases, blue-yellow later). This suggests selective action of the alkaloids on various regions of the retina, evidence bearing on the Ladd-Franklin phylogenetic theory of color vision. Possibly, too, colors predominant in peyote-symbolisms of natives may have a physiological meaning. Klüver's "form-constants" in peyote-intoxication may have similar significance, but he dealt largely with White visions only.[40]

PEYOTE AS A DRUG

Of more concern, however, to those who interest themselves in the welfare of Indians is the possible ill effect or habit-forming nature of the drug. On this point we quote the opinions of those better qualified than the writer to speak.

Briau,[41] in his psychiatric study, emphasized

the innocuousness of peyote. . . . No signs of grave intolerance were ever exhibited, nor any accident more disagreeable than vomiting, all too frequent at the beginning of a treatment with opiates. There was no notable organic upsetment produced during the time of action of the medicament. The effects on the circulation, respiration, digestive system and excretory functions have not appeared noxious. We have frequently examined urine for the existence of abnormal constituents revealing some derangement of the liver or the kidneys. In short, never during our researches have distressing secondary phenomena been manifested (headache, obnubilation, confusion, psychic and physical depression, or gastro-intestinal disturbances). . . . No brutality in the action [of pan-peyotl] can be remarked.

Briau believes the drug non-habit forming. Rouhier expresses himself more guardedly: That peyote-mania can sometimes exist, we will not dispute. We merely remark, to explain our

[39] Hutchings, in Heffter, *Ueber Pellote*, 409; Pilcz, *Ueber Pellotin*, 1121–22; Warburg, in Bennett and Zingg, *The Tarahumara*, 136; Ellis, *Mescal: A Study*, 71; Martindale and Wescott, *The Extra Pharmacopoeia*, 1: 836; Briau, in Koang-Hobschette, *Les Cactacées.* Karwoski (*Psychophysics*, 212) suggests that peyote might heighten rapport in psychoanalysis; cf. Deschamps.

[40] Bensheim, *Typenunterschiede*, 121; Wertham and Bleuler, *Inconstancy in the Formal Structure*, 70; Zucker, *Versuche*, 107; Zador, *Meskalinwirkung bei Störung*, 30; *Meskalinwirkung;* Klüver, *Mescal, The "Divine" Plant*, 36–39, 41; Ladd-Franklin, *Colour and Colour-Theories, passim.*

[41] Briau, in Koang-Hobschette, *Les Cactacées*, 73–74; Rouhier, *Le Peyotl*, 337; Ellis, *Mescal: A New Artificial Paradise*, 141.

optimism on the subject, that the drug does not seem to provoke that irresistible physiological appetite, nor that "state of need," purveyors of the great toxicomanias which opium, cocaine, heroine or alcohol create.

Havelock Ellis expresses himself as follows:

The few observations recorded in America and my own experiments in England do not enable us to say anything regarding the habitual consumption of mescal in large amounts. That such consumption would be gravely injurious I cannot doubt. Its safeguard seems to lie in the fact that a certain degree of robust health is required to obtain any real enjoyment from its visionary gifts.

The last statement is somewhat gratuitous, if not erroneous.[42]

Hrdlička[43] writes as follows:

My views . . . are that any substance which is capable of producing such effects on the brain and nervous system if abused is bound to produce harm. Fortunately peyotl is rather scarce, is used on special occasions only—in a large majority of cases—and thus it is probably quite free from any permanent injury.[44] The drug can perhaps be likened to nicotine, and like the latter will doubtless

[42] An editorial *Paradise or Inferno?* (Editorial, 390) sharply rebuked Ellis for the attractiveness which he had ascribed to mescal intoxication, basing the criticism on grounds of medical ethics.

[43] Letter to Schultes, Feb. 21, 1936. My own experience leads me fully to endorse Hrdlička's careful statement. Elsewhere in the text are cited numerous cases of natives who, in good faith I believe, gave up the use of peyote entirely upon the rising of special or acute anxieties. My informants, on the other hand, quite as frankly admitted that there were some individuals who showed signs of addiction, in the sense that they consumed the plant often and abundantly, but these are not clear uncomplicated instances of drug-addiction; I trust such native candor implicitly. Besides, peyote is not wholly pleasant ("You must suffer to peyote").

[44] The issue of the native religious use of the drug is indeed a complex one. But whatever else may be said, it is only fair to the Indians to state that the bitterest and most unmeasured condemnations of the drug have issued from quarters which are scarcely disinterested. Whatever the merits of the case, those persons are concerned with the deculturation of the Indian, and see in the peyote religion a formidable obstacle to their progress in inducting the native into modern life. The doubtless good intentions of such persons have on occasion, however, led them into errors of judgment when, for instance, they would argue that peyotism is merely out-and-out drug addiction in religious guise (e.g. Daiker, Hughes, Newberne and Burke, Seymour, Watermulder, and the writers in the Indian Rights Association and Literary Digest articles;) Lindquist, for example, feels free to commit numerous errors of fact yet still pontificate on the "false gods" of "the cult of Death" which is "nothing but an evil" (*The Red Man*, 72, 73, 75). For, given the Plains religious and ideological background, the peyote cult is entirely plausible as a religion, and the issue is properly one of religious freedom.

The intellectual "authority" in west European culture is, of course, the empirical and pragmatic (or putatively), while that of the Indian in this religion, as elsewhere, can correctly be termed mystical, if we understand by this a super-normal knowledge-technique transcending ordinary epistemological considerations. For there can be no shadow of a doubt concerning the deep and humble sincerity of the worship and belief—and sincerity perhaps, even in the absence of other ingredients, is the chief component of a living religion. And if the chief function of a religion is the liquidation of the anxieties and the solution of the fears and troubles of its adherents, then surely the peyote religion eminently qualifies as such.

The issue then balances somewhat delicately on the point of "authority," which is really at bottom a matter of comparative ethnography. If, as we believe, the scientific is truly the most mature knowledge-technique man has yet perfected, then facile and off-hand condemnation of peyotism on its basis is even less possible. Aside from the probable ultimate disappearance of the Native American Church, a generous and libertarian philosophy

not affect different individuals to the same degree. Also, as with nicotine, it may be quite impossible with our present means to detect the harm it has done. Besides which it is quite possible that the system may build up some resistance or safeguard against it and thus prevent any substantial injury. I should by no means join myself to those who see in it any *great* danger.

---

would condemn present attacks on it as often misguided and even oftener uninformed. The chief human difficulty in the world today is the adjustment of one culture to another, of one absolutistic ideology and Weltanschauung to another. But the scientific spirit itself would protest against the dictatorship of any one ideology, of whatever sort; there is too much chance that any self-contained scheme be dangerously wrong, when unchecked by modifying differing beliefs. Science, indeed, has been lifted above the level of folklore precisely because the spectacle of variously conditioned culture-historical outlooks has necessitated self-criticism and an objective comparative survey of beliefs. A fetishistic attitude toward science and its tentative pronouncements, therefore, is itself folkloristic in tone. This however, is not to suggest any distrust in the ability of the scientific method to obtain such sound results as have been so far achieved; but it is intended to point out the real limitations in our information.

Although the best modern scientific knowledge would indicate that the alkaloids in peyote do not perform the manifold therapeutic miracles which natives ascribe to it, one might still well wonder whether harsh sumptuary laws would not work more positive hardship and harm than the drug itself. If not the injustice then certainly the inexpedience of such exercise of civil authority has been amply demonstrated in the Eighteenth Amendment and its sorry consequences. We may not presume therefore to judge what should be the administrative fate of the peyote cult. The emotional and ideological side of the religion is not open to judgement; and on the properly scientific and physiological side of the question the simple fact is that we actually don't know enough about it.

APPENDIX 7: JOHN WILSON, THE REVEALER OF PEYOTE

The life and career of a remarkable individual were successively involved in the several traditions of the Ghost Dance, mescalism, old Algonquian shamanistic "shooting" ceremonies and finally peyotism. Both for its intrinsic interest and its historical significance we give here in some detail the life of this man. Wilson appears first as a leader in the Ghost Dance movement of the 1890's. Mooney[1] writes:

> The principal leader of the Ghost dance among the Caddo is Nĭshkûntŭ, "Moon Head," known to the whites as John Wilson. Although considered a Caddo, and speaking only that language,[2] he is very much of a mixture, being half Delaware, one-fourth Caddo, and one-fourth French. One of his grandfathers was a Frenchman. As the Caddo lived originally in Louisiana, there is a considerable mixture of French blood among them, which manifests itself in his case in a fairly heavy beard. He is about 50 years of age [in 1892–93], rather tall and well built, and wears his hair at full length flowing loosely over his shoulders. With a good head and strong, intelligent features, he presents the appearance of a natural leader . . . . He was one of the first Caddo to go into a trance, the occasion being the great Ghost dance held by the Arapaho and Cheyenne near Darlington agency, at which Sitting Bull presided, in the fall of 1890. On his return to consciousness he had wonderful things to tell of his experiences in the spirit world, composed a new song, and from that time became the high priest of the Caddo dance. Since then his trances have been frequent, both in and out of the Ghost dance, and in addition to his leadership in this connection he assumes the occult powers and authority of a great medicine-man, all the powers claimed by him being freely conceded by his people.

Captain Scott, who visited the Caddo in 1890–91 during the period of their greatest excitement about the Ghost Dance, also met Wilson, of whom he writes:[3]

> John Wilson, a Caddo man of much prominence, was especially affected [by the Ghost Dance], performing a series of gyrations that were most remarkable. At all hours of the day and night his cry could be heard all over camp, and when found he would be dancing in the ring, possibly upon

[1] Mooney, *The Ghost Dance*, 903–905.

[2] Capt. Hugh L. Scott, in Mooney, *The Ghost Dance*, 904.

[3] We have elsewhere expressed the opinion that the Caddo had an historical significance in the spread of peyotism second only to that of the Kiowa-Comanche, and that Wilson represents this Caddoan influence predominantly. Though he had Delaware blood, this numerically small group could scarcely have wielded the influence or exercised the prestige necessary to account for the spread of his "moon;" the Caddo, on the other hand, who early had peyote, did have this prestige. We therefore believe Petrullo in error in claiming Wilson as a Delaware. Speck (*Notes on the Life*, 540) writes that "His associations with the Comanche and Caddo, to whom he was related by blood, were close." Petrullo himself, indeed (*The Diabolic Root*, 44) indicates Caddoan influences on Wilson: "John Wilson, the originator of the Big Moon, was living among the Caddo. He was one of the first Delaware to eat peyote. He belonged to the Black Beaver band . . . held by the Government at the Wichita and Caddo reservations. It was there that Wilson was born and raised." Petrullo also says Wilson made visits to Arizona and New Mexico before returning to make his moon on the Caddo reservation.

one foot, with his eyes closed and the forefinger of his right hand pointed upward, or in some other ridiculous posture. Upon being asked his reasons for assuming these attitudes he replied that he could not help it; that it came over him just like cramps.

Wilson soon became a well-known doctor in this connection. Scott continues:

John Wilson had progressed finely, and was now a full-fledged doctor, a healer of diseases, and a finder of stolen property through supernatural means. One day, while we were in the tent, a Wichita woman entered, led by the spirit. It was explained to us that she did not even know who lived there, but some force she could not account for brought her. Having stated her case to John, he went off into a fit of the jerks, in which his spirit went up and saw "his father" (i.e., God), and who directed him how to cure this woman. When he came to, he explained the cure to her, and sent her away rejoicing. Soon afterwards a Keechei man came in, who was blind of one eye, and who desired to have the vision restored. John again consulted his father, who informed him that nothing could be done for that eye because that man held aloof from the dance.

When Mooney visited the Caddo on Sugar Creek late in 1895,

John Wilson came down from his own camp to explain his part in the Ghost dance. He wore a wide-brim hat, with his hair flowing down to his shoulders, and on his breast, suspended from a cord, about his neck, was a curious amulet consisting of the polished end of a buffalo horn, surrounded by a circlet of downy red feathers, within another circle of badger and owl claws. He explained that this was the source of his prophetic and clairvoyant inspiration. The buffalo horn was "God's heart," the red feathers contained his own heart,[4] and the circle of claws represented the world. When he prayed for help, his heart communed with "God's heart," and he learned what he wished to know. He had much to say also of the moon. Sometimes in his trances he went to the moon and the moon taught him secrets . . . He claimed an intimate acquaintance with the other world and asserted positively that he could tell me "just what heaven is like." Another man who accompanied him had a yellow sun with green rays painted on his forehead, with an elaborate rayed crescent in green, red, and yellow on his chin, and wore a necklace from which depended a crucifix and a brass clockwheel, the latter, as he stated, representing the sun.

On entering the room where I sat awaiting him, Nĭshkûntŭ approached and performed mystic passes in front of my face with his hands, after the manner of the hypnotist priests in the Ghost dance, blowing upon me the while, as he afterward explained to blow evil things away from me before beginning to talk on religious subjects. . . .[5] Laying one hand on my head, and grasping my own hand with the other, he prayed silently for some time with bowed head, and then lifting his hand from my head, he passed it over my face, down my shoulder and arm to the hand, which he grasped and pressed slightly, and then released the fingers with a graceful upward sweep.[6]

A curious mixture of Caddoan (?) mescalism, Ghost Dance, Delaware "shooting"

[4] Note the prominence of hearts in the altar elaborated by Wilson. According to Petrullo (*The Diabolic Root*, 45) "John Wilson . . . had received some Catholic instruction." These probably derive, therefore, from the Catholic "Sacred Heart." (The heart is present in Huichol religion, but even if not wholly aboriginal [Aztecan influence?] and Catholic-influenced there too, it is quite independent of the Wilson heart motifs.)

[5] Cf. the prominence in Wilson's moon of brushing each person entering with feathers.

[6] Cf. the Winnebago leader's similar praying with confessants in peyote meetings.

ceremonies and early peyotism occurred among the Shawnee when Wilson came to them about 1889. The Quapaw were being taught the Ghost Dance, in which a small water drum was used to accompany the circling of the dancers, alternately men and women. Wilson showed them how to swallow mescal beans, and also how to "shoot" them into a person so that he or she would fall down. Then he doctored the person with peyote to bring him back to consciousness. A number of tribes were involved in these doings, according to Mrs. Voegelin, the Shawnee, Delaware, Mohawk, Peoria, Caddo (?), Quapaw, Iowa and Oto. Gradually, however, Wilson turned from the Ghost Dance to peyote. Already in Mooney's time he was "prominent in the mescal [i.e., peyote] rite, which has recently come to his tribe [the Caddo] from the Kiowa and Comanche."[7]

Both mescalism and the Ghost Dance, in his person, have traceable influence upon peyotism. This syncretism of cultures in one personality is of considerable interest.

Before Wilson had quite reached the age of forty, he had lived the life of an ordinary Indian of Oklahoma. He was addicted to moderate drinking. He frequented the social dances and gambling gatherings usual among reservation groups of his type. He had participated likewise in the contemporary religious ceremonies performed by the Delaware. . . . As a vagrant, not however in the condemning sense of the term, he had wandered as most Oklahoma Indians do, from tribe to tribe and inevitably also among the whites experiencing the wide range of personal and social contacts which might be inferred from the statement. Anderson states, in short, that his uncle had lived a sinful life but adds in effect that he had not been guilty of any major offences. He was married to a woman of Delaware and Caddo descent and had an adopted son, Black Wolf, reputed to be also part Delaware part Caddo, and who is still living (1932) and carrying out Wilson's teachings and ministrations.

About this time he attended a Comanche dance, where a Comanche man presented him with a peyote button and told him to give it a trial—which he did in an unusually thorough manner. Speck continues:

Before long he concluded to adopt the advice given and to retire from worldly companionship, to make the trial and to study its outcome. With this objective in mind he informed his wife, secured provisions for a few weeks stay in camp and together they drove away in a wagon to a little creek where an abundant supply of fresh drinkable water might be had. The place he selected was a secluded "clean and open place" where they would be alone free from intrusion and worldly distractions. Anderson thinks that Wilson remained there about two or three weeks but he does not remember hearing him say how long. When all was ready he began his innovation to the mysteries of Peyote the first night by eating 8 or 9 "buttons." We learn that during the period of self exposure to the power of Peyote he took the medicine at frequent intervals during the day or night as the impulse prompted him using about the same quantity each time it was taken. As soon as he began, using the words of the informant, *"Peyote took pity on him"* for his humble mien and sincere desire to learn its power. During the whole period he allowed nothing to distract him, giving his entire thought and wish to learn what Peyote might teach him. The outcome was the revelation

[7] Speck, *Notes on the Life,* 540–42; cf. also Petrullo, *The Diabolic Root,* 80.

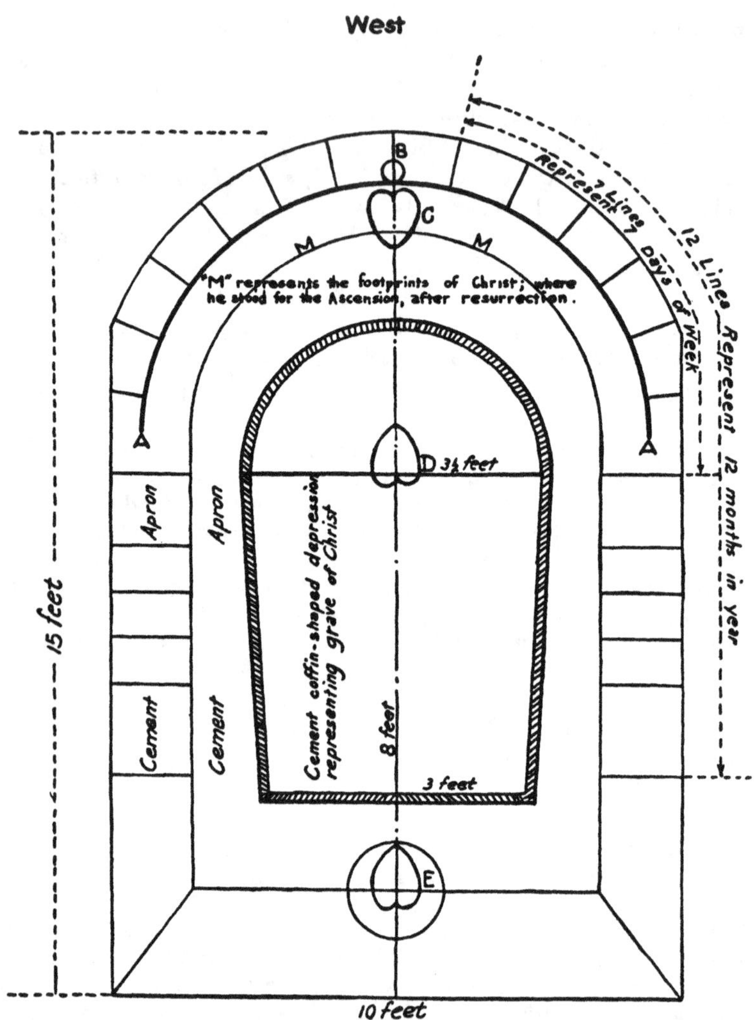

Fig. 6. An Osage altar of the John Wilson Big Moon type. A, "Peyote path," or Moon-Head (Wilson's name); B, hole for "arrow" when not in use; C, "Heart of Goodness" where father peyote is placed; D, Heart of the World above which the ritual fire is built; E, the Sun, giver of life. The east-west line is the "straight road" the way to heaven, or "thinking straight"; the north-south line represents "the road across the world"; together they form a cross symbolic of the crucifixion.

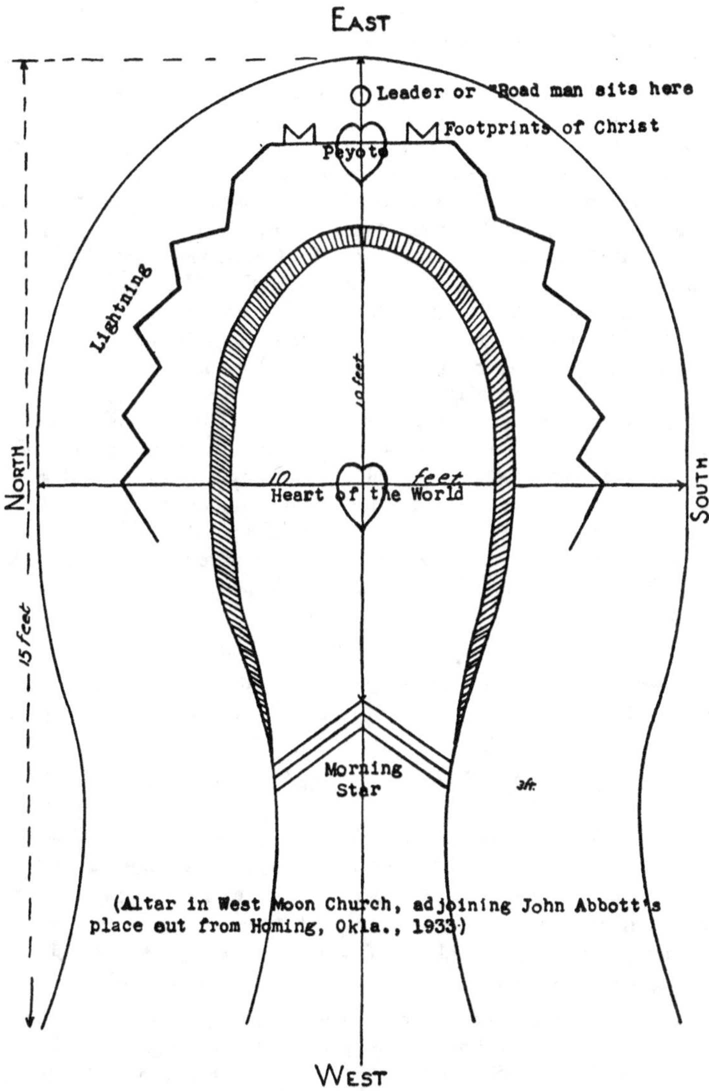

Fig. 7. A variant Osage moon of somewhat esoteric symbolism. This and the Osage moon in Figure 6 are reproduced through the courtesy of Mr. D. F. Murphy.

that motivated him for the rest of his life and made him a teacher of the Peyote doctrines, which he himself exclusively evolved through the revelations given him at this time.

During the time of his sojourn, Wilson did not fast or undergo other abnegations but lived normally. . . . Each time Wilson took peyote during those days and nights of seclusion he ate about fifteen peyote "buttons." . . . During the two weeks or so of his experimental seclusion, Wilson was continually translated in spirit to the sky realm where he was conducted by Peyote. In this estate he was shown the figures in the sky and the celestial landmarks which represented the events in the life of Christ, and also the relative positions of the Spiritual Forces, the Moon, Sun, Fire, which had long been known to the Delawares, through native traditional teachings, as Grandfather and Elder Brothers. Here, too, he was shown the grave of Christ, now empty, "where Christ had rolled away the rocks at the door of the grave and risen to the sky." He was shown, always under the guidance of Peyote, the "Road" which led from the grave of Christ to the Moon in the Sky which Christ had taken in his ascent. He was told by Peyote to walk in this path or "Road" for the rest of his life, advancing step by step as his knowledge would increase through the use of peyote, remaining faithful to its teachings . . . [and if he did] he would finally, just before his death, bring him into the actual presence of Christ and of Peyote . . . . The details of construction of the earth works to form the "Moon" which he was to construct in the Peyote tent were all revealed to him with their meanings as Peyote continued his instructions to Wilson during his visits to the sky. . . . Also came revelations as to how the face should be painted, the hair dressed. Of major importance, however, was the complete course of instruction given to Wilson by Peyote in the singing and syllabization of the numerous Peyote songs which were to form the principal parts of the ceremony of worship. Anderson felt certain that Wilson possessed and used no less than two hundred of these songs.[8]

Wilson's original moon, however, passed through an evolution, for Anderson's drawing in Speck is considerably simpler in design than those depicted for the Osage by Murphy, or photographed by the author for the Quapaw. An early version, apparently, is one collected from Henry Hunt (Wichita) near Anadarko. In this the crescent or "moon" is elongated to imitate the parted hair of an Indian, whose eyes are the two mounds of ashes between its horns; a line runs from the father-peyote to the east, terminating in a mound with five circles concentrically zoning it like a globe-map, with another line at right angles to this drawn from tip to tip of the crescent, making a cross, at the intersection of which is drawn a heart resembling a man's nose. There is also a heart at the "parting" of the hair, on which the fetish peyote rests, and a third one on the top of the zoned mound at the east. This altar is said to symbolize Moonhead's face, and indeed it much resembles one when seen from the eastern door. Speck says in confirmation of our conjecture that

at first, he said, he made a small "Moon," increasing its size day by day symbolical of his progress in spiritual knowledge. By the end of his sojourn amid spiritual environment, he came to make the so-called large "Moon," the Wilson "Moon" which has become typical of his followers.[9]

[8] "In response to the question as to whether Wilson ever spoke of the Peyote songs as symbolizing the singing of birds, Anderson asserted that he had heard of this among other Peyote sects but had never heard Wilson express it." (Speck, op. cit., 542 note.)

[9] Some of Wilson's Caddoan teachings were sufficiently unlike those of the Delaware to antagonize them.

But Wilson, no doubt, made still later additions, for these early moons entirely lack the elaborate apron symbolism of the Osage and Quapaw altars.

A Delaware informant said Wilson's moon was first used north of Lookeba, Oklahoma. Black Wolf and George Caddo were early converts to his version—which, indeed may initially have been not so different from the older Caddo moon with a cross and mound east of the crescent (the Wilson division of the tipi into north and south side, for example, is an old one in Caddoan ceremonial organization).[10] The symbolism of the Wilson "Big Moon" receives varied interpretations nowadays. The Osage call the three hearts of the altar the "Heart of Goodness," the "Heart of the World," and the "Heart of Jesus;" others interpret the "world" as the "sun." The ashes are the graves of Christ and Wilson for some, the dividing of the Red Sea for others. Some say the whole firepit is the grave of Christ, and the ash mounds his lungs, as the figure under the fire is his heart. The twelve lines of the altar apron are variously the twelve steps to heaven, the twelve heavens of Delaware mythology, the twelve months of the year, the twelve feathers of the eagle's tail, etc. The symbolism of seven for the "days of the week" is possibly Southwestern in origin (cf. the seven bosses of the drum). Diamond-shaped figures close to the sun-mound represent Christ's foot-prints, according to Petrullo,[11] while the "WW" or "MM" at the west of the altar are said to mean this for the Quapaw ("Moonhead" or "Wilson" depending on one's position while reading the initials). The cross of the altar, of course, is symbolical of the Crucifixion. The cigarette of corn husk is known as the "Pipe of Jesus" among the Delaware.[12]

Peyote taught Wilson many variations in the ceremony as well. He used a crock instead of a kettle for the peyote drum. At one period in the development of the ritual only the firemen did the drumming besides the leader and his assistant (i.e., four men, three firemen and the leader's assistant, proceeded clockwise around the tipi with the drum, drumming for each singer in turn, instead of the standard method of passing the drum for all to use); Wilson did not require the drum to make four rounds, for this might occasionally have interfered with the morning rite of filing out of the tipi "to meet the sun" with raised arms and prayer. In his rite only the leader made the initial prayer-smoke, though older men might ask for smokes later in the night if they so desired. Cigarettes could be made only at one of four places, one informant stated: at the leader's place, at the north or south at the ends of the cross, and at the fireman's place, and the leader had to smoke all of them first. Upon reentering after a recess, each person was incensed and fanned by the firemen

---

A Delaware informant of Petrullo (*The Diabolic Root*, 66) said, "It [peyote] should be eaten in order to get well, not to have visions." (Benedict's study indicated, one recalls, that in the Woodlands only puberty-visions occurred, while in the Plains adults too may obtain them.) Again (p. 68) "Wilson was wrong. Peyote is good, but it is good and powerful medicine, not a religion like the Big House. [For instance] four boiled Peyote placed on top of the head will help in cases of insanity."

[10] Cf. the Pawnee (Murie, *Pawnee Indian Societies*, 642).

[11] Petrullo, *The Diabolic Root*, 172.

[12] Petrullo, *op. cit.*, 56–59, 67, 96, note 29.

and others to blow away whatever evil influences might cling to him from the outside night. In time Wilson added special functionaries at the cross-bars of the crucifix to perform this fanning, making eight officials: two fanners, three firemen-drummers and three leaders (road man, drummer and cedar man) symbolizing the Father, Son and Holy Ghost of the Christian Trinity. In the Wilson rite there was much touching of the father peyote as communicants made their circuit of the altar on reentering. It is said that water could be asked for at any time, and permission to leave was not necessary if the rules about passing in front of an eater or smoker were observed.

Wilson himself took his "moon" to the tribes of northeastern Oklahoma. The Shawnee were influenced impermanently, and today only Ernest Spybuck has a modified Big Moon. The Seneca were influenced through the Quapaw, whom Wilson first succeeded in deeply influencing. The Quapaw leader, Victor Griffin, made a moon at Devil's Promenade which was modified around 1906 or 1907 from Wilson's moon.[13] The Delaware around Dewey were much influenced by Wilson from 1890–92 on.[14] But the Osage were the most important converts. By 1902 "most of the Indians at the Hominy camp and elsewhere in the Nation [had] taken it up and become devoted to it."[15] Black Dog, one of the first Osage converts, introduced the "West Moon" in which the door is at the west and the altar similarly reversed; most of the Osage moons today, however, are the standard Clermont east moons. The Potawatomi may have been influenced by the teachings of Wilson somewhat also.[16] Wilson's nephew, Anderson, brought the Seneca peyote in 1907 on the request of a Seneca married to a Quapaw woman.[17]

The economic motive seems evident in much of Wilson's behavior. Speck tells of the introduction of peyote among the Osage as follows:[18]

[About 1891] John Wilson was on his way from Anadarko to conduct meetings among the Delawares around Copan. While passing through the Osage nation he visited Tall Chief, a Quapaw married to an Osage woman. While here Wilson was stopped by an Osage who had previously attended Peyote meetings among the Delawares and requested to meet a group of Osage and tell them about his revelations and his convictions and instruct them in its rules. He consented and complied with their wishes. The Osage in attendance at his meeting were convinced and converted. He accordingly stayed on with them about three weeks. Black Dog was at the time Chief of the Osage. His tribe was won over in force to the Wilson sect of Peyote worshippers. . . . J. Wilson

[13] Petrullo (*The Diabolic Root*, 103). He claims to be Wilson's authorized successor and has revised his moon. Petrullo (*op. cit.*, 4) says John Quapaw is Wilson's real successor.

[14] Harrington (*Religion and Ceremonies*, 156) says Wilson brought the Lenape peyote from the Washita River Caddo as well as the Ghost Dance in 1890–92, which died out with him among the Delaware (*idem*, 190–91).

[15] Speck, *Notes on the Ethnology*, 171.

[16] On the mere score of Christian elements we do not agree, however, that Wilson's influence necessarily extended to the Wichita, Winnebago, Kickapoo, and Omaha (Petrullo, *The Diabolic Root*, 79). See following appendices.

[17] Speck, *Notes on the Life*, 554.

[18] *Idem*, 553.

then returned to Anadarko, leaving behind him among the Osage two young Delawares who stayed back attracted by the prospects of fortune offered by the wealthy Osage. Wilson had received presents from the tribe of new converts amounting to considerable value, a wagon, a carriage, a buggy and teams of good horses and harness for each and other horses, fourteen in all, not to mention blankets, goods and money.

His death occurred after a similar mission to the Quapaw. He had been among them to conduct a meeting and was returning to Anadarko in a buggy with a Quapaw woman and another woman. Wilson's wife was still living at the time, and he was either offered the Quapaw woman or demanded her while among the tribe. Speck quotes his nephew:[19] Anderson said he did not like to think this but that the Quapaw were not all good people and had possibly been actuated by a desire to establish a home for Wilson in order to keep him and his ministry in their midst.

In any event, Wilson had been given a number of horses, which were tied to the back of his buggy. While crossing a railroad track, these horses pulled back and prevented their crossing just as a locomotive bore down upon them. Wilson was instantly killed. His detractors maintain that this was just punishment for his failure to live up to his own teachings. Since this period many communicants have fallen away from his "moon," for his own[20] moral instructions . . . referred to abstinence from liquor, to restraint [in] sexual matters and fidelity to matrimony.

Though influenced by Catholic teachings, Wilson had a peculiar and specific attitude toward the Bible.[21] According to Speck,[22] he instructed the Indians to seek knowledge by direct communion and to avoid consulting the Bible or the Gospels for the purpose of moral instructions. He insisted that the Bible was intended for the white man who had been guilty of the crucifixion of Christ and that the Indian who had not been a party to the deed was exempt from guilt on this score and that therefore, the Indian was to receive his religious influences directly and in person from God through the Peyote Spirit, whereas Christ was sent for this mission to the white man.

He nevertheless embodied in his person many of the messianic characteristics of his several native prophet predecessors; a Delaware informant said "John Wilson used to perform miracles" in meetings, such as divining what was in a man's mind, and telling him who the persons were that he saw in a vision. The Osage, at least formerly, had a marked reverence for Wilson. Speck wrote in 1907 that[23]

[19] *Idem,* 544.

[20] *Idem,* 546.

[21] For this reason we doubt the soundness of Petrullo's inference that the Omaha, Winnebago, etc., were influenced by Wilson. These groups actually used the Bible in meetings and read from it. This influence, we believe, traces to another teacher, the Oto Jonathan Koshiway.

[22] Speck, *Notes on the Life,* 547.

[23] Speck, *Notes on the Ethnology,* 171.

pictures of Wilson are in demand among the devotees, who kiss them on sight. The man has been deified since his death.

There is much variation of opinion about Wilson among Indians of various tribes, but perhaps the statements of his nephew, George Anderson, are authoritative if not entirely disinterested. Speck says:[24]

An idea seems to have become current, either through the rumors of designing persons who opposed him or through exaggeration among his followers, that Wilson is responsible for having told his associates that he would return to life again after death and also that they should pray to him in the Peyote meetings . . . . Anderson denies that Wilson made either assertion. He had heard Wilson tell in his meetings that at times the worshippers when taking peyote might see him, as some are said since to have done, his face appearing to their vision over the fire. [With reference to the second statement Wilson on the contrary warned them not to pray to him, but through peyote to God.] . . . . This warning has not, however, prevented the practice of praying directly to and through John Wilson from becoming frequent among some of the Osages . . . and probably among the Quapaw.

In both the latter groups [Anderson] has seen Wilson's portrait placed on the "moon" in the Peyote lodge near the peyote "button" and the crucifix. Some who do this, he is convinced, actually concentrate thought upon Wilson instead of Peyote. And Anderson regards both practices as contrary to the teachings of Wilson. A custom has also spread among the Osage to wear a portrait button of John Wilson on the coat or, when in native dress, upon one of the fur or feather ornaments . . . Anderson's testimony [was] that John Wilson told his followers that *he was not sent by God to fulfill a mission*, but that he was *shown* by Peyote how to conduct religious worship in the Peyote meetings in order to cure disease, heal injury, purge the body from the effects of sin[25] and to lead the Indians to reach the regions "above" *hukweyun* in Delaware, or heaven, where they would *see Peyote and the Creator*.

The Caddo and Delaware, nevertheless, display considerable "touchiness" on the subject of John Wilson even today, since other tribes have ridiculed his real or supposed claims to divinity. Native criticism is not lacking either on the score of his economic exploitation of peyote leadership.[26] Petrullo[27] writes that

[24] Speck, *Notes on the Life*, 549.

[25] Wilson taught that the number of peyote required to be eaten varies according to the amount of impurity in the "heart" and stomach of the individual, "which impurity resulting from sins committed he likened to 'dirt'" (Speck, *Notes on the Life*, 545). The more frequently the communicant attended peyote meetings, the less dirt, obviously, there could accumulate. The degree of nausea, Wilson taught, is the punishment meted out for sin (cf. John Rave's teaching).

[26] To be sure the pattern of gift-giving is deep-rooted in the Plains, yet it is a curious coincidence at least that Wilson should have taken peyote to the Quapaw, who own the largest lead and zinc mining fields in the world, and the Osage, made notoriously wealthy through oil. Anderson told Speck that the Osage had given Wilson $200 for building them a moon, and Charles Tyner (Quapaw) told me that he and Victor Griffin (Quapaw) had received $500 for an altar in one sum and some hundreds of dollars in money gifts later. The Osage once gave Anderson $20 and his wife $10 because his uncle, John Wilson, had built their moon (Speck, *op. cit.*, 551). Wilson even used to charge $1 per person for the sweatbaths he gave before meetings.

[27] Petrullo, *The Diabolic Root*, 82; cf. 45, 95.

his enemies claim that in the course of his life he professed to have had fresh visions which always were interpreted to his personal gain. . . .

However, his followers staunchly deny these allegations. Perhaps in answer to the accusation of being mercenary, Wilson, with one of his followers named Wolf, themselves set up a meeting once, at which they showed their generosity by giving away all their clothes with other gifts until they were clad only in breechclouts.[28] Yet even so the belief is widespread that his death was due to his exploitation of the gift-giving pattern to the extreme of demanding a Quapaw woman for his wife.[29]

The Wilson sect is still strong among the Osage and the Quapaw, but elsewhere, even among the Delaware and Caddo, it is waning considerably. The Caddo show a disposition to return to the Enoch Hoag "moon," which is considered more "pure" and aboriginal.[30] But antagonisms to new elements Wilson sought to introduce date as far back as 1885. About this time Elk Hair was hunting in Comanche territory and learned a ritual he has since kept without change:[31]

Elk Hair preferred the Comanche way because it was the pure Indian way . . . . We brought back to our people the pure Peyote rite and we have used Peyote in the right way ever since.

Elk Hair, according to Petrullo,[32] "has barely managed to keep a following among the Delawares of Dewey," but this region is the stronghold of the Anderson family and if defection of the Anadarko groups to the Hoag moon is any indication, we may expect a reinvigoration of the Elk Hair rite. Indeed, War Eagle wrote from Dewey in 1932 that[33]

Bacon Rind [whose recent death is mentioned in the letter] was one of the last of the old people who beli[e]ved in [the] Wilson cult; these first followers of peyote are about all gone. [The] small moon now prevales in the Osage. It will be a blessing to the world when all the Quapaws and what few Delawares [are left practicing it] will change [to the standard peyote rite].

[28] Petrullo, *op. cit.*, 45; cf. 104.

[29] His followers, in any case, betray their expectancy of financial reward. It was remarked, for example, that the impecunious Seneca gave Anderson only his trainfare when he brought peyote to them. Griffin, more business-like, always arranges beforehand the amount of compensation he is to receive.

[30] Cf. the case of the Caddo Alfred Taylor whom the Osage invited to introduce the basic Caddo moon—even the Osage are turning from the Wilson rite.

[31] Petrullo, *op. cit.*, 43.

[32] *Idem*, 31–32.

[33] War Eagle, letter to Speck from Dewey, Oklahoma April 1, 1932. We believe Petrullo, as shown by this letter, has over-emphasized the decadence of the basic rite at Dewey. The Wilson-Elk Hair antagonism is shown in even trivial ways. The latter use the feathers of swift-flying birds to "hurry up" the medicine cure, the faster the singing of songs, the quicker the cure. The Wilson cultists, who sing slowly, accuse the little moon followers of "putting too much vigor and speed into their healing and praying meetings as is typified by their inclination to decorate their Peyote paraphernalia with Hummingbird feathers, symbolical of the acme of speed." (Speck, *Notes on the Life*, 551; thanks are due to the University of Pennsylvania Committee of Faculty Research, for Grant No. 93 on which his work was done.)

APPENDIX 8: CHRISTIAN ELEMENTS IN THE PEYOTE CULT

Very few ascertainably Christian elements are discoverable in Mexican peyotism. Some such as "curing" with rosaries of Job's-tears beads dipped in tesvino, eating bits of the idol's body and the like, may be largely aboriginal.[1] "El Santo Niño de Peyote" of Santa Rosalia is apparently a local variation of El Santo Niño de Atoche; the mission of El Santo Nombre de Jesus Peyotes is so-called merely from the a bundance of the plant there-abouts. The overlay of Mexican Catholicism is elsewhere thin and localized also. The Hui-chol[2] see the saints in their color visions as pictures or giant men and women walking about; sometimes they press the saints into service in their rain-making ceremonies. The cross[3] in tesvino-curing and those on the Huichol peyote patio may really derive from an old native four-point symbolism. The Tarahumari[4] call the large green hikuli "peyote christiano," in contrast to a small, red, ineffective one called "peyote cimarrón," and Chris-tian Tarahumari lift their hats to the plant and make the sign of the cross, but the essential ritual was unmodified by Christian ideas. None of these Christian features is common to Mexican peyotism.

The rite as it came to the United States, then, was aboriginal in character, as far as we can ascertain. Opler writes that[5]

there is no hint of the influence of Christianity in the Mescalero use of peyote. The growth of the cult among these people has been maintained entirely within the traditional bounds of Apache ceremonialism. Indeed, far from becoming a weakened and Christianized version of native beliefs, the Mescalero Apache acceptance of peyote resulted instead in an intensification of the aboriginal religious values and concepts at many points.

This characterization would equally well fit the basic Kiowa-Comanche rite of the Plains, in which Christian elements are quite absent. These elements in the Plains are distinctly a secondary development, stemming from the Oto Koshiway and such Oto-influenced

---

[1] "[De la Serna] adds that . . . they delighted in caricaturing the Eucharist, dividing among their congre-gation a narcotic yellow mushroom for the bread, and the inebriating pulque for the wine. Sometimes they adroitly concealed in the pyx, alongside the holy water, some little idol of their own, so that they really followed their own superstitions while seemingly adoring the Host. They assigned a purely pagan sense to the sacred formula, 'Father, Son, and Holy Ghost,' understanding it to be, 'Fire, Earth, and Water,' or the like" (Brinton, *Nagualism*, 28); Bennett and Zingg, *The Tarahumara*, 369, 385. *Coix Lachryma Jobi* was an early Spanish in-troduction, but may have replaced some native seed (e.g., mescal) used as beads. Serna's mushroom is probably teo-nanacatl.

[2] Klineberg, *Notes on the Huichol*, 449; Lumholtz, *Unknown Mexico*, 1: 314; 2: 170, 189.

[3] Lumholtz, *op. cit.*, 2: 171–72, 272; Bennett and Zingg, *The Tarahumara*, 294.

[4] Bennett and Zingg, *op. cit.*, 290; Lumholtz, *Unknown Mexico*, 1: 360–61. On Tarahumari Christianity see *Handbook of the American Indians*, 2: 692b; the ease of acceptance suggests congruence with aboriginal forms.

[5] Opler, *The Influence of Aboriginal Pattern*.

groups as the Omaha, Iowa and Winnebago[6] and the groups taught by John Wilson, such as the Delaware, Quapaw and Osage.

Arapaho-Winnebago officials and ritual food are given Christian symbolism:[7]

During the evening the leader represents the first created man, the woman dressed up is the New Jerusalem, the bride waiting for the bridegroom. The cup used by the leader and the woman is supposed to symbolize the fact that they are to become one; the water represents the God's gift, His Holiness. The corn represents the feast to be partaken of on the Day of Judgment and the fruit represents the fruit of the tree of life. The meat represents the message of Christ and those who accept it will be saved.

The Winnebago, Quapaw and Osage peyote officials represent the Father (the leader), the Son (the drummer) and the Holy Ghost (the cedar-man); the trinity of hearts in the Big Moon may represent much the same idea in the Osage-Quapaw rite.

Koshiway said that the bird into which the Oto ashes are shaped is

the Spirit descending when Jesus was baptized: the Holy Spirit, like an eagle, with good eyes; you can't fool it. [The ashes themselves represent] a prayer for the white hair of old age, and the fire is like the fire through which God spoke to Moses. Peyote is like a "telescope" through which you can see God.

The Delaware twin piles of ashes symbolize Christ's lungs; Mary Buffalo says one pile is the grave of Christ, the other of John Wilson, among the Osage; the Quapaw say the whole coffin-shaped fire-pit is Christ's grave. The Ponca, according to Brabant, believed the body of the Saviour would emerge from the altar and become visible to those who had eaten enough of the sacred plant. Among the Caddo,

the first stick in the fire represents the heart. There are twelve other sticks which represent the ribs [of Christ, as the ashes his lungs].[8]

The paraphernalia of the ceremony are also given Christian interpretations. The Delaware followers of Wilson call the corn husk cigarette the "pipe of Jesus." And of an unspecified group Mooney writes that

many of the mescal eaters wear crucifixes, which they regard as sacred emblems of the rite, the cross representing the cross of scented leaves upon which the consecrated mescal rests during the ceremony, while the Christ is the mescal goddess.

Some Kiowa leaders make a cross under the water bucket, and cross the feathers in the water before drinking[9] and the peyote staff, like that of the Delaware, often has an incon-

<hr>

[6] The Winnebago did not introduce the first Christian elements, as Radin believed. A Taos Indian (Plains-influenced?) once visioned Christ (Parsons, *Taos Pueblo*, 66).

[7] Radin, *The Winnebago Tribe*, 418; Densmore, *The Peyote Cult*.

[8] Petrullo, *The Diabolic Root*, 101, 113; Brabant, in Seymour, *Peyote Worship*, 182. Cf. Gilmore's Omaha (*The Mescal Society*, 165–66) whose fireplace is the heart of Jesus.

[9] But there seemed to be a certain quality of propaganda for the ethnographer's benefit in one Kiowa doctoring meeting, when the name of Jesus was mentioned in prayers with unwonted frequency.

spicuous cross near the top. The twelve feathers of the Omaha leader's fan represent the twelve apostles of Christ. The Winnebago fans differ for the John Rave and the Jesse Clay rites, but both sects use eagle feathers which represent the wings of the birds mentioned in Revelations. John Rave's staff is symbolic of the "shepherd's crook," and the mound of earth in the altar is "Mt. Sinai." White Buffalo said that gourd rattles among the Nebraska Winnebago commonly bore drawings of Christ, his cross and crown, etc., and Radin says they often bear drawings of scenes from the Bible as well as peyote visions. A Cheyenne gourd seen at Apache and made by Spotted Crow had the following "Jesus talk" on it:

Help me O Lord My God O save me According to thy Mercy O God my heart is fixed. I will sing And give praise Even with my Glory.

The Winnebago explain that the exchange of gourd and drum between the leader and his assistant when singing the set songs means that "God gives power to Christ, in Heaven and earth," just as the leader delegates his authority. The blowing of the leader's "flute" at the four points of the compass is to announce the birth of Christ to the world, and later it symbolizes the trumpet of the Day of Judgment, when Christ will appear wearing the crown of glory (symbolized by the leader's otter skin hat, worn at this time).[10]

The Bible as an additional piece of peyote paraphernalia probably stems from the Christianism of the Oto, who used it in their meetings, being mentioned also for the Iowa, Omaha and Winnebago. The New Testament, and particularly Revelations, is a favorite among the Rave cultists (Jesse Clay's followers do not use the Bible)—Crashing Thunder finding in it authority for a hair-cut, and others discovering reasons after the fact for holding their meetings at night. Three Old Testament texts are widely known also:

And they shall eat the flesh in that night, roast with fire, and unleavened bread; and with bitter herbs they shall eat it. (Exodus 12.8.)
And this day shall be unto you for a memorial; and ye shall keep it as a feast by an ordinance forever. (Exodus 12.14.)
For if the firstfruit be holy, the lump is also holy: and if the root be holy, so are the branches. . . . Boast not against the branches. But if thou boast, thou bearest not the root, but the root thee. (Romans 11.16 and 18.)

Various other Biblical references appear in the ceremony. Among the Iowa the leader carries the water himself in the morning to show his humility, and because of Christ's washing of feet mentioned in the Gospels. The Winnebago equate the physiological action of peyote with Christ's casting out devils. A Comanche said suffering is caused by one's sins and lack of faith in peyote, and that point in the night when nausea is commonly

---

[10] Petrullo, *The Diabolic Root*, 96, cf. 56–59, 67, 96, note 9; Mooney, *A Kiowa Mescal Rattle*, 65; Harrington, *Religion and Ceremonies*, 186–88; Gilmore, *The Mescal Society*, 165–66; *Uses of Plants*, 106; Densmore, *The Peyote Cult*; Radin, *A Sketch of the Peyote Cult*, 4, 12; *The Winnebago Tribe*, 416–17; White Buffalo in Blair, *The Indian Tribes*, 282 (letter of April 15, 1909).

severest is called the "Dark Hour, the hour of the Crucifixion." A Kickapoo leader often cast his prophecies in Biblical language. A Kiowa, again, appeared to have a belief about the first peyote found which parallels the miraculous proliferation of the loaves and the fishes in the Bible. Koshiway compared the Indians to the fishermen on the Sea of Galilee, when Christ said "Peace, be still!" to the angry waves, just as peyote says it to the storm-tossed Indians in this latter-day world. And for the man who lives a good life, the ashes of the fire will open up like the waters of the Red Sea, and he can pass through the fire to the father peyote along the "Peyote Road" on the moon.[11]

Some two dozen songs, previously reported in the text, show Christian influence. The closing song of the Negro Church of the First-born was the Christian hymn, "Till We Meet Again," but the majority of peyote songs have native words. The Rave rite, derived from the Oto and the Quapaw (influenced by the Christianity of Jonathan Koshiway and John Wilson, respectively), contained more Christian elements in symbolism and song than the Jesse Clay cult. This was the more aboriginal, yet he back-handedly quoted the Scriptures to justify the plain staff ("like Moses' ") of his ceremony as against the decorated staff of Rave. Occasional peyote visions show Christian influence: some of Crashing Thunder's were of this sort, and a Kiowa had visions of a mitred priest who nodded smilingly and approvingly at the father peyote on the altar, but in the visions collected Christian elements are uncommon.[12]

Mexican peyotism and the Wilson rite were influenced by Catholicism, but the Church of the First-born and the Native American Church by Protestantism (the Russellites, the Mormons, etc.). At the first Oto meeting attended a vessel was passed around in the morning for a "free-will offering," as in Protestant churches, and the Pawnee, Kiowa and others have "Ladies' Auxiliaries" to the local Native American Church. These women have quilting parties, can fruit, make up box lunches to raise church money and visit the sick, much as their White sisters do. Other White elements appear in the meetings themselves. The Iowa leader and fireman, for instance, shake hands with everyone in the tipi after the ritual feast, in token of friendship and good will. The Osage and Quapaw "round-houses," too, are in obvious imitation of White peoples' churches, but the Osage are criticized for ostentation along White "leisure class" lines. More conservative groups make disparaging remarks about the "beds" in their meetings, their electric lights in the round house, and their cigars—some Osage churches are even provided with spittoons!

Yet when all these features have been summed up, it is still clear that the layer of Christianity on peyotism is very thin and superficial indeed. Furthermore, the Christian-

<hr>

[11] Skinner, *Societies of the Iowa*, 724, 727; Gilmore, *The Mescal Society*, 165–66; *The Uses of Plants;* Densmore, *Winnebago Songs of the Peyote Ceremony; The Peyote Cult;* Radin, *A Sketch of the Peyote Cult,* 5–6; *The Winnebago Tribe,* 394–95; *Crashing Thunder,* 186–87, 200; Simmons, in Mooney, *Miscellaneous Notes.*

[12] Skinner, *Societies of the Iowa,* 727–28; Murie, *Pawnee Indian Societies,* 637; Densmore, *The Peyote Cult; Winnebago Songs of the Peyote Ceremony;* Radin, *A Sketch of the Peyote Cult,* 5; *The Winnebago Tribe,* 395; *Crashing Thunder,* 193–94; Smith [Mrs. M. G.], *A Negro Peyote Cult.*

ized Wilson and Rave rites among the Caddo and Winnebago are currently losing followers to the more conservative Hoag and Jesse Clay moons—and there are frequent expostulations against the mixing of the native religion with the White.[13] Some groups feel no inconsistency in belonging to both the peyote church and some White Protestant sect as well, but the unfriendliness of the functionaries of the latter groups toward peyotism and their lack of reciprocal tolerance has driven many borderline cases openly into the peyote church. The Indians feel, perhaps rightly, that peyotism is their last strong link with the aboriginal past, which others are trying to destroy. Hence it has contributed greatly to the sense of community and morale of the Indian groups in Oklahoma.

Of course apologists sometimes use Christian arguments to confound the enemies of the cult, as when peyote and the water are equated to the Catholic use of bread and wine in Communion,[14] or when Old Man Green (Oto) told a minister that he was condemning God's work in attacking peyote. But these do not proceed from any profound faith in Christianity. A Shawnee comment is most typical:

Christ was born only several hundred years ago, not when the world was created, like peyote.

Prayers are still addressed to the older tribal deities in peyote meetings: the Winnebago to Earthmaker, the Oto to Wakan, the Cheyenne to Mayan, etc. A Kickapoo summed up the religious history of his tribe as follows:

We had medicine bags before Jesus was born over in Bethlehem, in the old country. The old generation worshipped idols. When God's son was going to be born, they were trying to make the people believe God. And after Jesus was born, they commenced this [peyote].

Nevertheless, it should be reiterated that on the whole, despite the apparent and superficial syncretism with Christianity, peyotism is an essentially aboriginal American religion, operating in terms of fundamental Indian concepts about powers, visions and native modes of doctoring. The Christianity of many native Christians is precarious at best—as we have seen from various case histories—when it comes into any very serious conflict with native culture. Perhaps most peyote-users would echo the words of the famous Comanche chief, Quanah Parker, with reference to the superiority of peyotism over Christianity:

The white man [he said] goes into his church house and talks *about* Jesus, but the Indian goes into his tipi and talks *to* Jesus.[15]

<hr>

[13] The turmoil among the Caddo seems to grow out of the attempt to mix Christian with native motives and John Wilson is nowadays by no means universally revered. "There have been some Delawares living with the Caddo who have from time to time tried to introduce the Catholic faith in the Peyote meeting. Often they used the crucifix on the Peyote on the moon. All these attempts have met with opposition from most of the Delawares" (Petrullo, *The Diabolic Root*, 77).

[14] Petition of 62 Osage to the Senate Committee on Indian Affairs, in *Peyote, as Used in Religious Worship*, 64–67.

[15] Simmons, *The Peyote Road*.

APPENDIX 9: THE NATIVE AMERICAN CHURCH AND OTHER
PEYOTE CHURCHES

The many attempted anti-peyote legal measures, and the frank hostility of some persons[1] to peyotism early stimulated the cultists to seek some sort of legally-guaranteed security for their worship. The first of several incorporated peyote churches, the Oto Church of the First-born, has heretofore been little known. Peyote came to the Oto under the late White Horn's leadership from the Tonkawa some time before 1896. The original rite is said to have been "just like the Apache," which is to say, the standard pre-John Wilson Plains type. But the Oto, like other tribes, began to have "government trouble" about their worship shortly before the World War. A group of younger men, Frank Eagle, George Pipestem, Charles MacDonald and Charles W. Dailey, who had been away to school and were considerably influenced by White Protestantism, sought, at this juncture, to use the White man's weapons in their own defence. But by far the most important figure in this movement was Jonathan Koshiway.

Although enrolled as a Sauk-and-Fox, Koshiway's mother was an Oto. He had formerly lived in northeastern Kansas, and had been an Indian evangelist for the Church of Latter-Day Saints.[2] As an individual Koshiway was considerably influenced by Middle Western Protestantism, and solved for himself the adjustmental problem of double culture-bearers by discovering that the old native religion of his childhood was the *same* as the White Christianity of his maturity, with merely different phrasing and vocabulary. Did not God speak to Moses through a burning bush, like the Indians' peyote fire? When God viewed his creation, does not the Bible say that "God saw that it was good," and was not the little peyote plant one of the herbs of the field thus created? Did not Christians also make use of wafers and sacramental wine just as the Indians used the flat buttons of the sacred herb and peyote "tea"? Did not Christianity even embody the Plains ritual number in the "Four Foundations" of Love, Faith, Hope, and Charity?

Jack was a "Bible student" in Kansas City at one time, and is notably fluent in these

[1] The cult use of peyote has been persecuted not alone by legislatures and religious groups. The following broadside, obtained from Alfred Wilson(Cheyenne) through Enoch Smokey(Kiowa) was posted at Harry Ehoda's home in Mountain View, Oklahoma: "To all Indians addicted to the use of peyota and other forms of heathen or pagan forms of worsihip. You are herby warned to sease form such degrading practices. Our Government has spent and is spending thousands of dollars each month to educate and life up the Indians and the Ku Kluck Klan of this state have determined that no Indian who has been educated by the Government shall come back home and debouch his people. Take Due Warning. The Clan in Your Community Will Look After You and Other Ku Kluck Klan of Okla."

[2] Cf. Harry Rave (brother of John), quoting another Indian, in Seymour, *Peyote Worship*, 182: "'My friend we must organize a church and have it run like the Mormon Church'." Could this have been Koshiway? Mormon interest in peyotism is indicated in letters to C. Warden (Arapaho) of Gary, Oklahoma, from the Latter Day Saints, which I have seen. See the *Book of Mormon*, I Nephig: 2–28.

syncretic interpretations, being called upon frequently to speak in peyote meetings, especially when visitors are present to whom explanations are in order. Another important influence upon Koshiway—as well as upon George Deroin (Iowa) of Perkins, who may once have been his associate—was that of the Russellites, a somewhat desiccated Protestant cult of the Middle West, who did not believe in any "earthly" government. This dogma naturally suited a group in difficulties with temporal government. Koshiway explained to me that the name finally chosen for the organization is a "heavenly name" and that the church proper is "up there"; yet practical peace must be made with Caesar on earth, and this Koshiway set about with care to do.

First of all he consulted White Horn, leader of the native peyote rite, and gained his support. Koshiway generously states that White Horn was the co-founder of the Church of the First-born, but the fact appears to be that the latter's role consisted in giving the official approval of the older established peyote cult. Koshiway also visited many white ministers to get their advice on organization. There appears to have been some friction about this, and even Koshiway ended up by insisting that the peyote church should not be "under" any white Protestant church, but independent. Then, despite the fact that the Russellites preach non-cooperation with the Government and the ultimate break-up of all temporal governments, Koshiway went to a lawyer in Perry, Oklahoma, H. F. Johnson, and sought legal advice. On December 8, 1914, the "First-born Church of Christ" was incorporated under the laws of Oklahoma and received a charter for an organization located at Red Rock, Oklahoma, signed by Benjamin F. Harrison, the Secretary of State.[3] The articles of incorporation were signed by Jonathan Koshiway and four hundred and ten other names.

Koshiway wanted an "authorized" preacher to come and baptize the newly constituted church's adherents, but this never became a regular practice, if, indeed, it ever actually occurred at all. A reluctance to come half-way was manifested by the Protestant groups concerned, and in time Jack himself took up all the usual functions of a minister, marrying, conducting funerals and in addition doctoring in meetings and "hollering" the way his source of medicine power does. Secondary Shawnee influences occurred in this later period, but the chief ritual difference between the usual peyote rite of the Plains and that of the Oto Church of the First-born is directly traceable to the influence of the Russellites.

This difference was over the question of smoking in meetings. As Koshiway reconstituted the Church, the preliminary smoking of corn shuck cigarettes was abolished—a remarkable innovation when one recalls the deeply entrenched ceremonial use of tobacco in the Plains, but when a narcotic was sacrificed in the ritual, tobacco went, not peyote. Koshiway took peyote to a group of Oto in Kansas under Charley Rubido, and by this time the work of syncretism which had been accomplished became evident, for,

when we examined the literature [says Koshiway] we found that [the native Russellites under Rubido and the Koshiway peyotists] were just alike.

[3] Data on this charter from a note in Mooney, *Peyote Notebook*, 38.

168

In both groups smoking was omitted, and cedar leaves were burned in place of this at intervals of prayer. When the leader called upon an individual to pray, he was given cedar to burn to produce smoke and bear away the prayer. The Bible was a conspicuous part of the meeting also.[4]

The later history of the Church of the First-born was influenced by the interaction of Koshiway and the later-founded Native American Church. At Cheyenne, a little town northwest of Calumet, Oklahoma, a group of Oto, Kiowa and Arapaho had an intertribal conference to decide upon measures of defence for peyotism. Jack took the Oto charter to this conference and explained his solution of the problem. James Mooney at this, or a later conference, was influential in persuading the assembly to adopt this method of organization, but many of the group apparently objected to the element of White religion implied in the title "First-born Church of Christ" and rejected the name. The title ultimately chosen was the "Native American Church," which emphasized the intertribal solidarity of the cult, as well as its aboriginality.

Koshiway's behavior at this point is interesting. He had not succeeded in making himself the head of the church of his naming as extended in a state-wide organization. As he himself puts it he "began to deny" the First-born Church of Christ, and "joined" the Native American Church, where, though he was less important as an individual, he nevertheless was a member of a larger and more official in-group. He is much amused in his attitude toward the remnants of the Oto church; says he,

They were so religious [about smoking]—I converted them, and then they turned around and said I wasn't right; that's how peculiar us Indians are!

As a matter of fact, however, Koshiway seems to have believed that the true belief about peyote was *a fortiori* what he, the founder of the church, successively believed. When later he re-introduced the smoking of tobacco into the ceremony, he actually was himself backsliding into the older native custom and retreating from the Russellite-influenced no-smoking rule. The real Puritans, obviously, were the Kansas group who retained the rule. A curious and amusing compensation is evident in the most modern reconstitution of the Oto smoking ceremony: the "shucks" in meetings attended were fully twice as long as those normally used in the Plains rite!

The present Oto church in Oklahoma, under the presidency of James Pettit, considers itself a local branch of the Native American Church, but the Kansas group still carries on the Russellite no-smoking rule. The return to the older standard pattern came about in this way.[5] The well-known Kiowa leader, Belo Kozad, came to the Oto with Jack Sankadote (one of the two original Kiowa users) and an Apache named Star. The meeting was held

---

[4] This element introduced by Albert Hensley into Winnebago peyotism, was probably influenced by the Oto church, when Hensley made his visits in Oklahoma.

[5] With this native "Oxford Movement" cf. the parallel cases of the Caddo defection from the Wilson rite to the Enoch Hoag "moon" and the Hensley separatists to the Rave and Jesse Clay groups, the latter in each case representing a more aboriginal phrasing of the ceremony.

fourteen miles east of Red Rock, and Koshiway's attendance at this was a turning-point. Belo prayed to peyote—a practice itself rejected by Koshiway—that Jack take up his "road." Jack maintained his disapproval of smoking, but for some time had apparently come to prefer being an accepted member of the larger group to being an important outsider. Somewhat later, he revisited the Kiowa and his friend Albert Cat, attending several meetings there. At one of these Belo offered Koshiway a prayer-smoke, and finally after some hesitation he took it—a very small act objectively, to be sure, but symbolizing the healing of a schism in the native peyote religion. On this trip south Koshiway had been given money gifts, and a sick woman the Oto had brought with them had been doctored by Old Man Horse (Kiowa); these factors perhaps weighed somewhat in favor of his embracing the state-wide cult. In the ideology of Belo (and most Kiowa as well) there was no theoretical objection to Christian churches, but the usual attitude was that peyotism and Christianity were mutually exclusive *alternatives*.[6] Still later Belo Kozad again visited the Oto and led a meeting, and this time Koshiway was his assistant or drummer, and Koshiway now had his place in the classic rite. His adaptability and good humor have given him a position of considerable importance in Oto peyotism, though he is by no means the oldest user—more important perhaps even than that of Sam Bassett, the "tribal priest."

Several other fore-runners of the Native American Church should be mentioned. In 1897 the Oto brought the new religion to the Omaha and Winnebago of Nebraska and by 1909 there was an organization called the Union Church of mescal-eaters at Winnebago, Nebraska, which made use of the Bible.[7] The Omaha formed a similar organization called the American Indian Church Brother Association, whose elaborate symbolic crest is figured in Wagner. The Kiowa United American Church mentioned by Mrs. Voegelin may also have been a fore-runner of the Native American Church.

This organization was formed by an intertribal group which met at El Reno and included Mack Haag (Cheyenne) of Calumet, Sidney White Crane of Kingfisher, Charles W. Dailey (Oto), George Pipestem (Oto), and Charles E. Moore (Oto), all of Red Rock, Frank Eagle (Ponca) of Ponca City, Wilbur Peawa (Comanche) of Fletcher, Mam Sookwat (Comanche) of Baird, and Apache Ben of Apache, Oklahoma.[8] A certificate of incorporation was granted to "The Native American Church" at Oklahoma City under the Great Seal and the signature of the Secretary of State, dated October 10, 1918, and signed by

---

[6] Which is of course mere theory; actually there is considerable unconscious syncretism, and Belo himself frequently refers to Jesus in his prayers.

[7] *Report on the case*, in Safford, *Aztec Narcotic*, 306. "Twelve years ago the Otoes brought the new religion to the Winnebagoes and Omahas of Nebraska .... In talking with Albert Hensley, one of the prominent leaders, he said, 'The mescal was formerly used improperly, but since it has been used in connection with the Bible it is proving a great benefit to the Indians. Now we call our church the Union Church instead of Mescaleaters'" (Letter, April 15, 1909 in Blair, *The Indian Tribes*, 282.)

[8] From articles of incorporation kindly lent me by James Waldo (Kiowa). The original paper was lost by Mooney in Washington; Kiowa Charley's copy gives the date Oct. 29, 1919—probably a duplicate reissue. Other data from Murdock and Wilson.

Alfred Wilson (Cheyenne), Louis McDonald (Ponca), Delos Lonewolf (Kiowa) Herman McCarthy (Osage) and Tennequah (Comanche). The strongly intertribal nature[9] of the organization is indicated by the various tribal affiliations of the men elected to the offices of the Native American Church. The constitution under which the charter was obtained was changed at Washington in the administration of Ned Brace, and several amendments were made in 1935. Frank Cayou (Omaha) of Hominy has for some time been seeking a national charter from Congress, through Secretary Ickes and Commissioner Collier, so far with no success.

Formerly there was an annual tax of two dollars for each individual member of the state organization, one half kept by the local group and the other half sent to the state head-quarters, but later this was changed to a ten dollar tax per tribe. In Oklahoma there are now (1936) twenty-four tribes organized in the church, and these send two delegates from each local church (if there are several locals there may be as many as six delegates from one tribe). The yearly convention is held the last Friday in November, formerly always in El Reno, though in 1936 it was held in Hominy. El Reno is the site of "The Wigwam," a young Indian men's fraternal organization which once maintained a museum-meeting room convenient for these conventions, hence the Native American Church was incorporated as of this place. Because of the many native languages represented, English is the lingua Franca of negotiations at conventions. The chief function of the state organization so far has been the mobilizing of political power and application of pressure on legislative groups, in the preservation of what the Indians regard as their constitutionally guaranteed right of religious freedom.

The Winnebago and Omaha of Nebraska, and also the Indians of South Dakota, Wisconsin and Kansas have patterned their constitutions after that of the original Oklahoma Native American Church. The Native American Church is now also incorporated in Montana and Nebraska;[10] in the latter state Jesse Clay was the first president[11] of an actively evangelistic group which sends "missionaries" into new regions, ambitious of making peyote the universal Indian religion. In Oklahoma there are local tribal organizations within the Native American Church. For example, among the Kickapoo there is a "men's club" which meets after every peyote meeting and a "women's club" which meets on the second Thursday of every month. The Ponca also have a "Ladies' Auxiliary," as do

[9] From 1918 to 1936 the officials have been (president, vice-president and treasurer, respectively): Frank Eagle (Ponca), Mack Haag (Cheyenne), Calumet, Louis MacDonald (Ponca), Ponca City; Mack Haag, Delos Lonewolf (Kiowa), Carnegie, James Waldo (Kiowa), Verden; Delos Lonewolf, Alfred Wilson (Cheyenne), Thomas, James Waldo; Alfred Wilson, Ned Brace (Kiowa) Mountain View, Oscar Whyel (Kickapoo); Alfred Wilson, Ned Brace, Louis Toyebo (Kiowa); Ned Brace, Frank Cayou (Omaha), Edgar McCarthy (Osage); Frank Cayou, Alfred Wilson, Edgar McCarthy. George Pipestem (Oto) of Red Rock was the secretary of the Native American Church from its founding until his death in 1936.

[10] Letter of C. C. Guinn of Guinn & Maddox, Attorneys, to Mack Haag, President of the Native American Church, dated Hardin, Montana, Feb. 16, 1926; Densmore, *The Peyote Cult*.

[11] Elections of officials are held yearly in Nebraska instead of every two years as in Oklahoma.

also the Pawnee. These data are of course incomplete, but it is believed that they are representative.

Of particular interest, however, is the Negro Church of the First-born, formerly existing near Tulsa, Oklahoma.[12] The founder was John Jamison who was born in Lincoln Co., Oklahoma. His parents for some reason were given allotments, and he grew up among the Iowa, speaking Iowa, Pawnee and Comanche. When he sought to take up the peyote cult, the younger men were less friendly than the older ones; they resented a Negro's taking the "old Indian religion." The rite which he conducted was the typical Indian one, but involved more use of the Bible than was general; the elements of the drum, gourd dishes for sacred food, medicine feathers, cane, sage, cedar, canvas tipi and chief peyote button were all present. Jamison sometimes dressed in a chief's bonnet, blanket and moccasins. He conducted meetings as far back as 1920 which Indians sometimes attended, and occasionally he was sent for to conduct Indian meetings. In 1926 Jamison died of a brain concussion after he had been attacked by a half-crazed Negro. The cult did not survive his death; it had never been popular outside a small group, though some persons were attracted by the healing he attempted to do. But even the devoted became suspicious when they learned of Government hostility to their practices. As Mrs. Smith writes,

This attitude on the part of the negroes is doubly interesting in view of the rebellious attitude which the Indians displayed under the same circumstances.

Jamison's rite differed in a number of respects from the standard Plains ceremony: the peyote on the moon was eaten by the leader at midnight; the leader sat at the west with four "sisters" to his right and four "brothers" to his left (including his drum and cedar man); the fireman north of the door was usually the same man in every meeting. Participants sat "goat fashion," i.e., kneeled and sat on their heels, when singing or eating peyote. The leader sang Indian songs or hymns indifferently. After an opening prayer the leader, or a male assistant, read a passage from Scripture, and toward morning a member talked on the passage. During the midnight song, the ashes of the ritual fire were made "heart-shaped," then this was deliberately destroyed by the leader[13] and the ashes swept to the side. This "burning the heart of the fire" signified the "end of the day." There was a recess at midnight and the drummer beat to signify the close of this period, after which the communicants reentered and ate peyote and sang until daylight.

As the sun rose, they threw open the door and, all standing, sang the closing song, "Till We Meet Again." The sun is supposed to hit the center of the fire "heart." Then the "sis-

[12] Condensed from Mrs. M. G. Smith's article, *A Negro Peyote Cult*. Mrs. Smith does not mention any possible Oto influence, which, in view of the near-identity of the name appears probable.

[13] This occurs in no Indian peyote ceremony known to the writer. This deliberate destructive act suggests a symbolic aggression. The psychic mechanisms underlying this behavior have been shown with fine perception in John Dollard's penetrating book *Caste and Class in a Southern Town*.

ters" leave and serve a sweetened meal which must contain no salt. There is no ceremonial smoking[14] as in the Indian ceremony, and cedar smoking is used only once toward the beginning. The food served is parched corn soaked and sweetened, beef prepared the "Indian way" (roasted, ground and sweetened; or dried, soaked, stewed, ground and sweetened), fruit, cereal or mush and finally water. The presence of parched corn is an interesting object lesson in the stability of a culture trait; centuries later and hundreds of miles away from the Mexican corn-harvesting ritual we find members of another race still practising the now meaningless pattern. The mere accident of historical association of parched corn and peyote has imposed a cultural compulsion!

Jamison always took Epsom salts[15] Friday night before the meeting, usually held on Saturday nights, and a hot bath before going to the meeting. If he ate salt or otherwise failed to follow these rules, he would see "spooks" and "crazy things." Further syncretism with Christian elements is evidenced in the following confession of faith, a copy of which was possessed by all the faithful and framed:

David Walker
Director
Our Motto: "The World for Christ"
Christ, the Good Shepherd
[picture of group sitting goat fashion, paraphernalia]
Church Covenant
of the Church of the Firstborn
"Hebrews 12th Chapter, 23rd verse"

We, the undersigned believers in Jesus Christ, do by virtue of Scriptural Faith submit ourselves to the cause of Christ and the Gospel; to live therein; to walk therein; to teach therein; to sing therein; to pray therein; to preach therein; to baptize therein; to observe all the ordinances of Him who has called us to peace, that God may have all the glory thereof. In testimony whereof we the undersigned hereunto set our hands, by virtue of our own free will.

John C. Jamison
Conductor in Charge

Mrs. Lucinda Walker	Mrs. J. L. Ramsey
Mother of the Household of the Faith	Assistant
Katie Hoggins	Mrs. Polly Marshall
Secretary of the Household of the Faith	Assistant.

The quotation from Hebrews 12.23 is the source of the name of the church:

[But ye are come] to the general assembly and church of the firstborn, which are written in heaven, and to God the Judge of all, and to the spirits of just men made perfect.

[14] This again suggests Oto influence.
[15] Cf. the related emetic rites!

173

Unlike the Oto group, Jamison never succeeded in getting his "moon" incorporated, although there are suggestions[16] that Negro groups in South Dakota may have been influenced by peyotism.

[16] Reko, *Ein Kaktus die Gespenster*, 431: "Die Christian Peyotl Church in South Dakota benutzt diese Dinger an Stelle der Hostie und verabreicht sie bei der Kommunion and die Glaübigen. Daneber haben sie jenseits der Grenze noch eine nicht unbedeutende Kunschaft in der nordamerikanischen Indianer und den Schwarzen die die Mescalbottons [sic] freilich keineswegs zum Kommunizieren benützen."

BIBLIOGRAPHY TO THE 1938 EDITION

ADAIR, JAMES. *The History of the American Indians* (London, 1775).

DE ALARCÓN, HERNANDO RUIS. *Tratado de las supersticiones y costumbres gentilicas, 1629* (Anales del Museo Nacional de Mexico, vol. 6, 1898).

ALBERTS, ——. *Einwirkung des Meskalins auf komplizierte psychische Vorgänge* (Dissertation. Heidelberg, 1920).

ALEGRE, F. J. Historia de la Compañía de Jesus en Nueva-España (3 vols. Mexico, 1841–42).

ALTIMIRANO, FERNANDO. *Anhalonium Lewinii: Cacteas* (Gaceta Médica de Mexico, vol. 36: 59–64, 1900).

DE ALVA, BARTOLOMEO. *Confessionario mayor y menor en lengua mexicana . . . y pláticas contra las supersticiones de idolatría* (Mexico, 1634).

AMERICAN PHARMACEUTICAL ASSOCIATION. *Yearbook* (vol. 8, 1919; vol. 10, 1921; vol. 13, 1924). *Proceedings* (vol. 36: 378, 1888; vol. 46: 844, 1898; vol. 47: 744, 1899; vol. 48: 636, 1900).

ANGIER, R. P. *Letter to Robert Hall* (Hearings Senate Indian Affairs Committee; Indian Appropriation Bill. Washington, D. C., 1919).

DE ARLEGUI, P. J. *Crónica de la provincia de Zacatecas* (2nd ed. 1851).

ARMENDARIZ, ——, ED. *Alcaloide del Peyote* (Informes Sec. 3 A, Anales del Instituto Médico Nacional de Mexico, vol. 5; 1903).

BACKEBERG, CURT. *Kakteenjagd zwischen Texas und Patagonien* (Berlin, 1930). *Neue Kakteen; Jagden, Arten, Kultur* (Berlin, 1931).

DE BALSALOBRE, GONÇALO. *Relación autentica de las idolatrías, supersticiones de los Indios del Obispado de Oaxaca* (Reprint. Museo Nacional, Mexico, 1892).

Baltimore Cactus Journal, vol. 2: 247, 1896.

BANCROFT, H. H. *The Native Races of the Pacific States of America* (5 vols. London, 1875–76).

BANDELIER, A. F. *Manuscript* (in Report Madrid Exposition, in Harvard Peabody Museum, 1893).

BARTRAM, WILLIAM. *Travels through North and South Carolina, Georgia, East and West Florida, the Cherokee County . . . with Observations on the Manners of the Indians* (Philadelphia, 1791).

BASAURI, CARLOS. *Monografía de los Tarahumaras* (Mexico, 1929).

BEALS, RALPH L. Aboriginal Survivals in Mayo Culture (American Anthropologist, vol. 34: 28–39, 1932). *The Acaxee, a Mountain Tribe of Durango and Sinaloa* (Ibero-Americana, No. 6, 1933). *The Comparative Ethnology of Northern Mexico before 1750* (Ibero-Americana, No. 2, 1932).

BECKWITH, MARTHA WARREN. *Notes on Jamaica Ethnobotany* (Publications, Vassar Folklore Foundation, No. 8: 1–47. Poughkeepsie, N. Y., 1927).

BENEDICT, RUTH FULTON. *The Vision in Plains Culture* (American Anthropologist, vol. 24: 1–23, 1922).

BENNETT, WENDELL C., AND ROBERT M. ZINGG. *The Tarahumara* (Chicago, 1935).

BENSHEIM, H. *Typenunterschiede bei mescalin versuchen* (Zeitschrift für die gesamte Neurologie und Psychiatrie, vol. 121: 531–43, 1929).

BERINGER, K. *Experimentelle Psychosen durch Meskalin* (Zeitschrift für die gesamte Neurologie und Psychiatrie, vol. 24, 1920).
Experimentelle Psychosen durch Meskalin (Vortrag auf der südwestdeutschen Psychiater-Versammlung in Erlangen, 1922).
Intoxication due to Alkaloid from Mescaline: Resulting Mental and Physical Phenomena (Archivo Argentino de Neurologia, vol. 2: 145–54, 1928).
Der Meskalinrausch, Seine Geschichte und Erscheinungsweise (Monographien aus dem Gesamtegebiete der Neurologie und Psychiatrie, vol. 49: 35–89, 119–315, 1927).

BEVERLY, ROBERT. *History of Virginia, by a Native and Inhabitant of the Place* (2nd ed. London, 1722).

BLAIR, E. H. *The Indian Tribes of the Upper Mississippi Valley and Region of the Great Lakes* (Cleveland, 1912).

BOAS, FRANZ. *Anthropology* (Encyclopedia of the Social Sciences, vol. 2: 73–110. New York, 1930).

BOLITHO, WILLIAM. *Article* (The New York World, January 3, 1929).

Boston Herald [article] (April 14, 1927).

BOUGHTON, I. B., AND W. T. HARDY. *Mescalbean (Sophoro Secundiflora) Poisonous for Livestock* (Texas Agricultural Experiment Station, Bulletin No. 519, 1935).

BOURKE, JOHN G. *The Medicine-Men of the Apaches* (Annual Report, Bureau of American Ethnology, 9: 443–603, 1892).

    On the Border with Crooke (New York, 1891).

    Scatalogical Rites of All Nations (Washington, 1891).

BOYER, JACQUES. *Visual Hallucinations from Peyote* (Nature, vol. 55, whole number 2760: 403–06, 1927).

BRAVO, HELIA H. *Las Cactaceas de Mexico* (Mexico, 1937).

    Nota acerca de la Histología del Peyote, Lophophora williamsii, Lemaire (Anales del Instituto de Biologia, 1931).

BRESLER, J. *Anhalonium Lewinii* (Psychiatrische-Neurologische Wochenschrift, vol. 7: 249–55, 1905–06).

BRIAU, R. *Du Peyotl dans les Etats anxieux* (Thesis. Université de Paris, 1928).

BRINTON, DANIEL G. *Nagualism* (American Philosophical Society, Proceedings, vol. 33, 1894).

    Notes on the Floridian Peninsula, Its Literary History, Indian Tribes and Antiquities (Philadelphia, 1859).

    Religions of Primitive People (New York, 1897).

BRITTON, N. L., AND J. N. ROSE. *The Cactaceae* (4 vols. Washington, D.C., 1922).

BUCHANAN, D. N. *Meskalinrausch* (British Journal of Medical Psychology, vol. 9; 67–88, 1929).

BUHLER, K. *Handbuch der Psychologie*, Vol. 1, *Die Strucktur der Wahrnehmungen;* Part 1, *Ersehungsweisen der Farben* (1922).

BUSCHMANN, J. C. *Die Spuren der aztekischen Sprache im nördlichen Mexico und höheren amerikanischen Norden* (Abhandlungen der Königlichen Akademie der Wissenschaft zu Berlin für 1854: 106–07, 1859).

BUSHNELL, DAVID I. *The Choctaw* (Bulletin, Bureau of American Ethnology, 48. Washington, 1909).

CAIRNS, H. *Divine Intoxicant* (Atlantic Monthly. vol. 144, no. 5: 638–45, 1929).

DEL CAMPO, JUAN MARTINEZ. *Peyote* (Anales del Instituto Médico Nacional de México, vol. 6: 142–43, 1904).

DE CARDENAS, JUAN. *Primera Parte de los problemas y secretos maravillosos de las Indias* (2nd ed. Museo Nacional de Arqueología, Historia y Etnología, no. 17: 145–208, 1913).

CASTETTER; E. F., AND M. E. OPLER. *The Ethnobiology of the Chiricahua and Mescalero Apache* (Bulletin, University of New Mexico, Ethnobiological series, vol. 4, no. 5, 1936).

CASTETTER, E. F. AND RUTH M. UNDERHILL. *Ethnobiology of the Papago Indians* (University of New Mexico Bulletin, Biological Series, vol. 4, no. 3, whole no. 275. Albuquerque, 1935).

CERONI, LUIGI. *L'intossicazione mescalinica (Autoespierienze)* (Rivista Sperimentale de Freniatria, vol. 56, 1932).

DE CHARLEVOIX, P. F. D. *Histoire de l'Isle Espangnole ou de St. Dominique* (Amsterdam, 1733).

CHOTZEN, ——. *Article* (Psychiatrisch-Neurologische Wochenschrift, 1909).

COBO, BERNABÉ. *Historia del Nuevo Mundo* (4 vols. Sevilla, 1890–93).

COLLIER, DONALD. *Peyote: A General Study of the Plant, the Cult and the Drug* (in Survey of Conditions of Indians in United States, vol. 34. Washington, 1937).

CONKLIN, EDMUND S. *Photographed Lilliputian Hallucinations* (Journal of Nervous and Mental Diseases, vol. 62: 133–40, 1925).

COOKE, ANNE M. *Northern Ute Field Notes* (Manuscript).

CORLETT, WILLIAM T. *The Medicine-man of the American Indian* (Baltimore, 1935).

CORONA, ROSENDO. *Los Huicholes del Pueblo de Santa Caterina* (1888).

COULTER, JOHN M. *Preliminary Revision of the North American Species of Cactus, Anhalonium and Lophophora* (U. S. National Herbarium, Contributions, vol. 3: 91–132. Washington, 1894).

COZIO, ANTONIO VALVERDE. *Proceso contra un Indio de Taos que había tomado peyote y alborotado el pueblo* (1720).

CRICHTLY, M. *Some Forms of Drug Addiction: Mescalism* (British Journal of Inebriety, vol. 28, no. 3: 99–108, 1931).

CURTIS, E. S. *The North American Indian* (20 vols. Cambridge, 1907–1930).

Curtis' Botanical Magazine, vol. 73, fig. 4296, 1847.

DAIKER, F. H. *Liquor and Peyote, a Menace to the Indian* (Report, Thirty-Second Annual Lake Mohonk Conference: 62–68. Albany, 1914).

DAUL, A. *Illustriertes Handbuch der Kakteenkunde* (Stuttgart, 1890).

DAYTON, W. A. *Important Western Browse Plants* (U. S. Department of Agriculture, Miscellaneous Publication, No. 101. Washington, 1931).

DENSMORE, FRANCES. *The Peyote Cult and Treatment of the Sick among the Winnebago Indians* (Bureau of American Ethnology, Manuscript 3205, 1931).

    Winnebago Songs (Bureau of American Ethnology, Manuscript 1971, n.d.).

    Winnebago Songs of the Peyote Ceremony (Bureau of American Ethnology, Manuscript 3261, 1932).

DEPARTMENT OF AGRICULTURE, BUREAU OF CHEMISTRY. *Service and Regulatory Announcement, No. 13* (Washington, 1915).

DESCHAMPS, ANDRÉ. *Ether, Cocaine, Hachich, Peyotl et Démence précoce* (Paris, 1932).

Diccionario Universal. Appendice, Vol. 1 (Mexico, 1856).

DIGUET, LEON. *Les Cacteceas utiles du mexique* (Paris, 1928).

    Le Peyote (Paris, 1929).

    Le Peyote et son usage ritual chez les Indiens du Nayarit (Journal de la Société des Americanistes de Paris, n.s. vol. 4, no. 1: 21–29, 1907).

    La Sierre du Nayarit (Nouvelles Archives des Univers Scientifiques. Paris, 1928).

DIXON, R. B. *Some Aspects of the American Shaman* (Journal of American Folk-Lore, vol. 21: 1–12, 1908).

DIXON, W. E. *The Physiological Action of the Alkaloids Derived from Anhalonium Lewinii* (Journal of Physiology, vol. 25: 69–86, 1899–1900).

DIXON, W. E., AND EDMUND WHITE. *A Preliminary Note on the Pharmacology of the Alkaloids Derived from the Mescal Plant* (British Medical Journal, vol. 2: 1060–61, 1898).

Documentos inéditos ó muy raros para la historia de Méjico (35 vols. Mexico, 1905—).

Documentos para la Historia de Mexico (20 vols. Mexico, 1853–57).

DOLLARD, JOHN. *Caste and Class in a Southern Town* (New Haven, 1937).

DORMAN, RUSHTON M. *The Origin of Primitive Superstitions* (Philadelphia, 1881).

DRAGENDORFF, GEORG. *Die Heilpflanzen der verschiedenen Völker und Zeiten* (Stuttgart, 1898).

DURÁN, DIEGO. *Historia de las Indias de Nueve-España y Islas de Tierra Firme* (2 vols, Mexico, 1867, 1880).

EDITORIAL. *Paradise or Inferno?* (British Medical Journal, vol. 1: 390, 1898).

EDITORIAL. *Peyote* (Outlook, vol. 115: 645–46, 1917).

ELLIS, HAVELOCK. *Mescal: A New Artificial Paradise* (Contemporary Review, vol. 73: 130–41, 1898).

    Mescal: A Study of a Divine Plant (Popular Science Monthly, vol. 61: 52–71, 1902).

    A Note on the Phenomena of Mescal Intoxication (Lancet, vol. 1, whole no. 3849: 1540–42, 1897).

ENGELMANN, GEORGE. *Cactaceae of the Boundary* (Report on the United States and Mexican Boundary Survey, vol. 2: 1–78. Washington, 1859).

    Synopsis of the Cactaceae of the Territory of the United States and Adjacent Regions (American Academy of Arts and Sciences, Proceedings, vol. 3: 259–314, 345–46, 1852–57).

ENSAYO, RUDO (EUSEBIO GUITERAS, TR.). *Rudo Ensayo* (Records, American Historical Society of Philadelphia, vol. 5, Philadelphia, 1894).

EWELL, ERVIN E. *The Chemistry of the Cactaceae* (Journal of the American Chemical Society, vol. 18: 624–43, 1896).

EWERS, HANNS HEINZ. *Die Besessenen: Seltsame Geschichten* (Munich, 1922).

Farmacopia Méxicana. (4th ed. Mexico, 1904).

FERÍAS, PEDRO. *Idolatrías de Chiapas, 1585* (Anales del Museo Nacional de México, vol. 6, 1892).

FERNBERGER, SAMUEL W. *Further Observations on Peyote Intoxication* (Journal of Abnormal and Social Psychology vol. 26: 367–78, 1932).

    Observations on Taking Peyote (American Journal of Psychology, vol. 34: 267–70, 616, 1923).

FIGG, HERBERT B. *Mescal* (Pharmaceutical Journal and Pharmacist, vol. 127: 240–41, 1931).

FLORES, ANDRÉS ESTRADA. *Relación y mapa del partido de San Pedro Teo-caltiche* (Manuscript, 1659).

FOERSTER, C. F. *Handbuch der Kacteenkunde in ihrem ganzen Umfange* (Leipzig, 1846; 2nd ed. 1885).

FÖRSTER, E. *Selbst-experiment im Mescalinrausch* (Zeitschrift für die gesamte Neurologie und Psychiatrie, vol. 127: 1–14, 1930).

FORSTER, J. R., TR. *Bossu: Travels through that Part of North America Formerly Called Louisiana* (2 vols. London, 1771).

FORTUNE, R. F. *Omaha Secret Societies* (Columbia University Contributions to Anthropology, vol. 14. New York, 1932).

FOURNIER, P. *Les Cactées et les plantes grasses* (Paris, 1935).

FRANK, PAUL. *Field Notes on the Peyote Cult of the Mescalero* (Manuscript, 1931).

GARCÍA, BARTHOLOMÉ. *Manual para administrar los Santos Sacramentos* (Mexico, 1760).

GATSCHET, ALBERT S. *The Karankawa Indians* (Archaeological and Ethnological Papers, Peabody Museum, Harvard University, vol. 1: 69–167, 1891).

GAYTON, A. H. *The Narcotic Plant Datura in Aboriginal American Culture* (Thesis. University of California Library, 1928).

GELB, ADHÉMAR. *Über den Wegfall der Wahrnehmung von "Oberflächenfarben"* (Zeitschrift für Psychologie, vol. 84: 193–257, 1920).

GERSTE, A. *Notes sur la médicine et la botanique des anciens Mexicains* (Rome, 1909).

GIFFORD, W. E. *The Cocopa* (University of California Publications in American Archaeology and Ethnology, vol. 31: 259–334, 1933).

GILMORE, MELVIN R. *The Mescal Society among the Omaha Indians* (Publications, Nebraska State Historical Society, vol. 19: 163–67, 1919).

    Uses of Plants by the Indians of the Missouri River Region (Annual Report, Bureau of American Ethnology, 33: 43–154, 1911–12 [1919]).

GOWER, CHARLOTTE D. *The Northern and Southern Affiliations of Antillean Culture* (American Anthropological Association, Memoir 35, 1927).

GRACE, G. S. *The Action of Mescaline and Some Related Compounds* (Journal of Pharmacological and Experimental Therapeutics, vol. 50: 359–72, 1934).

GRIFFITHS, DAVID. *Cacti* (U. S. Department of Agriculture, Circular No. 66. Washington, 1929).

GUTTMAN, A. *Bericht: Die Spaltung der Persönlichkeit durch ein Medikament* (Frankfort-am-Main, n.d.).

    Experimentelle Halluzinationen durch Anhalonium Lewinii (Bericht über den VI Kongress für experimentelle Psychologie. Göttingen, 1914).

    Halluzinationen und andere Folgeerscheinungen nach experimenteller Vergiftung mit Anhalonium Lewinii (Mescal) (Zeitschrift für die gesamte Neurologie und Psychiatrie, vol. 24: 50–53, 1921).

    Medikamentöse Persönlichkeitsspaltung (Monatsschrift für Psychiatrie und Neurologie, vol. 56: 161–87, 1924).

HALE, E. M. *Ilex Cassine, the Aboriginal North American Tea* (U. S. Department of Agriculture, Bulletin 14 Washington, 1891).

HALL, ROBERT D. *Affadavit on Peyote* (Bulletin, Office of Indian Affairs, 21 Washington, 1923).

HAMET, RAYMOND. *Sur l'action physiologique de la mezcaline, alcaloïde principal du Peyotl* (Bulletin de l'Academie de Médicine, vol. 105: 46–54, 1931.

HAMMOND, G. P., ED., AND A. REY, TR. *Balthasar de Obregon: History of Sixteenth Century Explorations* (Los Angeles, 1928).

Handbook of the American Indians (Bulletin, Bureau of American Ethnology, 30. 2 parts. Washington, 1907, 1910).

HARMS, H. *Über das Narkotikum Peyotel der alten Mexicaner* (Monatsschrift für Kakteenkunde, vol. 31: 90–92, 1921).

HARRINGTON, M. R. *Cuba Before Columbus* (Indian Notes and Monographs, No. 17, 2 vols. New York, 1921).
— *New Kiowa Collection* (Masterkey, vol. 11: 132, 1937).
— *Religion and Ceremonies of the Lenape* (Indian Notes and Monographs, vol. 19, 1921).

HARTWICH, CARL. *Die Menschlichen Genussmittel* (Leipzig, 1911).

HAVARD, V. *Drink Plants of the North American Indians* (Torrey Botanical Club, Bulletin, vol. 23: 33–46, 1896).
— *Report on the Flora of Western and Southern Texas* (Proceedings, U. S. National Museum, vol. 8: 449–533, 1886).

HEFFTER, A. *Articles* (Journal de chimie et de pharmacie, vol. 1, 1895; vol. 8, 1898).
— *Über Pellotin* (Therapeutische Monatshefte, vol. 10: 327–28, 1896).
— *Ueber Cacteenalkaloïde* (Berichte der Deutschen chemischen Gesellschaft, vol. 20, pt. 1: 216–27, 1896; vol. 31, pt. 1: 1193–99, 1898; vol. 34, pt. 2: 3004–3015, 1901).
— *Ueber Pellote* (Archiv für Experimentelle Pathologie und Pharmakologie, vol. 34: 65–86, 1894; vol. 40: 385–429, 1898).
— *Ueber zwei Cacteenalkaloïde* (Berichte der Deutschen chemischen Gesellschaft, vol. 27, pt. 3: 2975–79, 1894).

HEFFTER, A., AND R. CAPELLMAN. *Versuch zur Synthese des Mezcalins* (Berichte der Deutschen chemischen Gesellschaft, vol. 38, pt. 3: 3634–40, 1905).

HENNINGS, PAUL. *Eine Giftige Kaktee, Anhalonium Lewinii, N. Sp.* (Gartenflora, vol. 37: 410–11, fig. 92; Berichte des Botanischen Vereins der Provinz Brandenburg in Berlin, Feb. 10, 1888).

HENRY, JULES. *The Cult of Silas John Edwards* (Manuscript).

HENRY, THOMAS ANDERSON. *The Plant Alkaloids* (2nd ed. London, 1924).

HERNANDEZ, FRANCISCO. *De Historia Plantarum Novae Hispaniae* (Anales del Instituto Médico Nacional, vol. 4, no. 11: 204, 1900).

HERNANDEZ, TOPETE DIEGO. *Ceremonias que celebran a la fecha los Huicholes* (El Indio, vol. 1: 45, 1924).

HERRERA, ALFONSO. *Sinonimia vulgar y científica de algunas plantas silvestras y de varias de las que se cultivan en México* (La Naturaleza, vol. 6, no. 8, 1883).

HERRERA, A. L. *Farmacopia Latino-Americana* (Mexico, 1921).

HIGGINS, E. B. *Our Native Cacti* (New York, 1931).

HIJAR Y HARO, ING. LUIS. *El Peyote a través de los siglos* (Revista Mexicana de Ingeniería y Arquitectura, vol. 15, no. 9: 543–63; no. 11: 665–92, 1937).

HILL, A. F. *Economic Botany* (New York and London, 1937).

HILL, J. R. *Note on Mescal Buttons* (Pharmaceutical Journal, vol. 64, 4th series, vol. 10: 191, 1900).

HILLS, F. D. *Eating Medicine with the Quapaws* (Manuscript).

HIRSCHT, K. *Bericht über die Jahressammlung* (Monatsschrift für Kakteenkunde, vol. 5, 1895).

HOEBEL, E. ADAMSON. *Comanche Field Notes* (Manuscript).
— *Northern Cheyenne Field Notes* (Manuscript).
— *The Wonderful Herb: An Indian Cult Vision Experience* (Manuscript).

HRDLIČKA, ALEŠ. *Physiological and Medical Observations among the Indians of the Southwestern United States and Northern Mexico* (Bulletin, Bureau of American Ethnology, 34 Washington, 1908).

HUGHS, W. *Perils of Peyote* (Commonweal, vol. 9: 719, 1929).

HUTCHINGS ——. *Report on the Use of Pellotine as a Sedative and Hypnotic* ([St. Lawrence] State Hospital, Bulletin, 1897).

Index Kewensis. Fasc. I, 136; II, 813, 1893; III, 156, 1894. First Supplement: 29, 253, 263, 1901–04. Second Supplement: 1905).

Indian Helper. Vol. 14: 26, April 21, 1899.

Indian Leader. Vol. 27: 26, March 21, 1924.

IXTLILXOCHITL, F. D'ALVA. *Histoire des Chichiméques* (Paris, 1840).

JACOD, GUILLARMOT. *La Pellotine chez les Alienés* (Thesis. Lausanne, 1897).

JAENSCH, E. R. *Über den Aufbau des Bewusstseins* (Zeitschrift für Psychologie und Sinnesorgane, Abt. I, Ergänzungsband 16: 305–07, 1930).

JAENSCH, WALTER. *Pharmakologische Versuche über Beziehungen optischer Konstitutionsstigmen zu den Halluzinationen* (Zentralblatt für die gesamte Neurologie und Psychiatrie, vol. 23, 1920).

JAHRREISS, W. *Störungen des Bewusstseins* (Handbuch der Geistekranken, vol. 1: 640–41, 1928).

JAMES, HENRY, Ed. *Familiar Letters of William James* (Atlantic Monthly, vol. 126: 1–15, 163–75, 305–317, 1920).

JANOT, M., AND M. BERNIER. *Article* (Bulletin des Sciences Pharmacologiques, vol. 40: 145–53, 1933).

JIMENEZ, —. *De la naturaleza y virtudes de las plantas de Neuva España.*

JOLLY, F. *Über die schlafmachende Wirkung des Pellotinum muriaticum* (Therapeutische Monatshefte, vol. 10: 328–29, 1896).

    Über Pellotine als Schlafmittel (Deutsche Medicinische Wochenschrift, vol. 22: 375–76, 1896).

JONES, C. C. *Historical Sketch of Tomo-Chi-Chi, Mico of the Yamacraws* (Albany, 1868).

JOURDANET, D., and RÉMI SIMÉON. *Histoire générale des choses de la nouvelle Espagne* (Paris, 1880).

Journal de Pharmacie et de Chemie (6me series, vol. 8: 519–23, 1898).

KALISCHER, S. *Über giftige Kakteen* (Monatsschrift für Kakteenkunde, vol. 5: 59–60, 1895).

KARSTEN, R. *The Civilization of the South American Indian* (New York, 1926).

KARSTEN, G., AND H. SCHENCK. *Vegetationsbilder, Heft. 8: Mexikanische Kakteen-, Agaven-, und Bromeliaceen-Vegetation* (Jena, 1904).

KARWOSKI, THEODORE. *Psychophysics and Mescal Intoxication* (Journal of General Psychology, vol. 15: 212–20, 1936).

KAUDER, ——. *Über Alkaloide aus Anhalonium Lewinii* (Archiv der Pharmazie vol. 237: 190–98, 1899).

    Über Alkaloide aus Mescal-buttons (Chemische Central-Blatt, vol. 1: 1244, 1899).

KELLY, E. L. *Individual Differences in the Effects of Mescal* (Journal of General Psychology, vol. 9: 462–72, 1933).

KING, EDWARD (Lord Kingsborough). *Antiquities of Mexico* (London, 1831).

KINNEY, B. *A Drug Peril under Religious Guise* (Native American, Jan. 1, 1921).

KLINEBERG, OTTO. *Notes on the Huichol* (American Anthropologist, vol. 36: 446–60, 1934).

KLÜVER, HEINRICH. *Mescal, The "Divine" Plant and Its Psychological Effects* (London, 1928).

    Mescal Visions and Eidetic Visions (American Journal of Psychology, vol. 37: 502–15, 1926).

KNAUER, ALWYN. *Psychologische Untersuchungen über den Meskalinrausch* (Zeitschrift für die gesamte Neurologie und Psychiatrie, vol. 4: 37–39, 1912).

KNAUER, A., AND W. J. M. A. MALONEY. *Psychic Action of Mescaline* (Journal of Nervous and Mental Diseases, vol. 40: 425–38, 1913).

KOANG-HOBSCHETTE, A. *Les Cactacées, leur utilisation général et thérapeutique* (Thesis. Université de Nancy. Paris, 1929).

KOBERT, RUDOLF. *Lehrbuch der Intoxikationen* (2 vols. Stuttgart, 1902–1906).

KRAEMER, HENRY. *Applied and Economic Botany* (2nd ed. New York, 1914).

KROEBER, A. L. *Anthropology* (New York, 1923).

    The Arapaho (Bulletin, American Museum of Natural History, vol. 18, 1907).

    Handbook of the Indians of California (Bulletin, Bureau of American Ethnology, 78. Washington, 1925).

    The Seri (Southwest Museum Papers, vol. 6. Los Angeles, 1931).

KUNKEL, A. J. *Handbuch der Toxikologie* (2 vols. Jena, 1901).

KUPPER, H. *Kakteen.*

La Barre, W. *The Autobiography of a Kiowa Indian* (Manuscript).

    Native American Beers (American Anthropologist, vol. 40, no. 2: 224–34, 1938).

Labouret, J. *Monographie de la Famille des Cactées* (Paris, 1858).

Ladd-Franklin, Christine. *Colour and Colour Theories* (New York, 1929).

de Landa, Diego. (B. de Bourbourg, Tr.). *Relation des choses de Yucatan* (Paris, 1864).

Landry, S. F. *Notes on Anhalonium Lewinii, Embelia Ribes, and Cocillaña* (Therapeutic Gazette, vol. 13, 3rd series, vol. 5: 1, 1889).

Langstein, ———. *Pellotin als Schlafmittel* (Prager Medicinische Wochenschrift, vol. 21: 446, 1896).

Lawson, John. *History of Carolina* (London, 1714; *reprint*, Raleigh, 1860).

Lemaire, C. A. *Article* (Berliner Allegemeine Gartenzeitung, vol. 3: 385, 1845).

    Cactearum aliquot novarum ac insuetarum in horto monvilliano cultarum accurata descriptio, Fasc. I. (Lutetiae Parisiorum, 1838).

de León, Alonzo. *Historia de Nuevo León* (in Documentos Inéditos ó muy raros para la historia de Méjico, vol. 25, 1909. Mexico, 1905–).

de León, Nicolas. *Camino del Cielo* (Mexico, 1611).

de Leon y Gama, Antonio. *Descripcion Histórica y Cronológia de las Dos Piedras* (2nd ed. Mexico, 1832).

Le Page du Pratz, Antoine S. *Histoire de la Louisiane* (3 vols. Paris, 1758; London, 1763, 1764).

Leroy, R. *Les états affectifs dans les hallucinations liliputiennes* (Journal de Psychologie normale et pathologique, 1928).

Leuba, J. H. *The Psychology of Religious Mysticism* (New York, 1929).

Lewin, Louis. *Anhalonium Lewinii* (Therapeutic Gazette, vol. 12, 3rd series, vol. 4: 231–37, 1888).

    Article (Berichte der Deutschen botanischen Gesellschaft, vol. 12: 9, 289, 1894).

    Les Paradis Artificiels (1928).

    Phantastica; Narcotic and Stimulating Drugs (New York, 1931).

    Ueber Anhalonium Lewinii (Pharmazeutische Zeitung, vol. 40: 343, 1895).

    Über Anhalonium Lewinii (Archiv für experimentelle Pathologie und Pharmakologie, vol. 24: 401–11, 1887–88).

    Über Anhalonium Lewinii und andere Cacteen (Archiv für experimentelle Pathologie und Pharmakologie, vol. 34: 374, 1894).

Lindquist, G. E. E. *The Red Man in the United States* (New York, 1923).

Lowie, R. H. *Notes Concerning New Collections* (Anthropological Papers, American Museum of Natural History, vol. 4: 274–329, 1910).

    Primitive Religion (New York, 1924).

Lumholtz, Carl. *The American Cave Dwellers* (Bulletin, American Geographical Society, vol. 26: 299–325, 1894).

    Explorations en Mexique de 1894 a 1897 (Journal, Société des Americanistes de Paris, vol. 7: 181–82, 1899).

    The Huichol Indians of Mexico (Bulletin, American Museum of Natural History, vol. 10: 1–14, 1898).

    Report of Explorations in Northern Mexico (Bulletin, American Geographical Society, vol. 23: 386–402, 1891).

    Symbolism of the Huichol Indians (Memoirs, American Museum of Natural History, vol. 3, pt. 1: 1–228, 1900).

    Tarahumari Dances and Plant Worship (Scribner's Magazine, vol. 16: 451–56, 1894).

    Tarahumari Life and Customs (Scribner's Magazine, vol. 16: 305–11, 1894).

    Unknown Mexico (2 vols. New York, 1902).

Macleod, William C. *The American Indian Frontier* (Philadelphia, 1924).

Maggendorfer, F. *Intoxikationspsychosen* (Handbuch der Geisteskranken, vol. 7: 159, 162, 355–56, 1928).

Maillefert, E. M. G. *La Marihuana* (Ethnos, vol. 1: 5–7, 1920 [Mexico City]).

MANAKOW, ——, ET —— MOURGUE. *Introduction biologique à l'etude de la neurologie et de la psychologie* (Paris, 1928).

MARTINDALE, WILLIAM, AND W. W. WESTCOTT. *The Extra Pharmacopoeia* (20th ed. 1932).

MARTINEZ, MAXIMINO. *Catalogo alfabetica de nombres vulgares y científicas de plantas que existen en México* (Mexico, 1923).

 Las plantas medicinales de México (Mexico, 1933).

 Plantas narcóticas de México (Dirección de estudias biológicas, Boletin, vol. 4: 1, 1925).

 Plantas útiles de México (Mexico, 1928).

MASON, J. ALDEN. *Tepecano Prayers* (International Journal of American Linguistics, vol. 1: 91–153, 1918).

MAYER, H. W. *Der Cocainismus* (Leipzig, 1926).

MAYER-GROSS, W., AND J. STEIN. *Pathologie der Wahrnehmung I, II* (Handbuch der Geistekranken, vol. 1, 1928).

 Über einige Abänderungen der Sinnestätigkeit im Mescalinrausch (Zeitschrift für die gesamte Neurologie und Psychologie, vol. 101, 1926).

MENDIETA, JERÓNIMO. *Historica Eclesiástica Indiana* (1596).

MERCK, E. *Berichte der chemischen Fabrik E. Merck* (Darmstadt, 1899).

 Merck's Index (4th ed. New York, 1930).

 Nicht offizielle Alkaloide (Wissenschaftliche Abhandlungen der Chemischen Fabrik E. Merck, vol. 22: 384–86. Darmstadt 1918).

MICHAELIS, PAUL. *Beiträge zur vergleichenden Anatomie der Gattungen Echinocactus, Mamillaria und Anhalonium* (Thesis Erlangen, 1896).

MICHELSON, TRUMAN. *Sauk and Fox Myths* (Bureau of American Ethnology. Manuscript 2736 Washington, n.d.).

MITCHELL, S. W. *The Effects of the Fluid Extract of A. Lewinii* (American Neurological Association, Transactions, vol. 22, 1896).

 Remarks on the Effects of Anhalonium Lewinii (the Mescal Button) (British Medical Journal, vol. 2: 1625–29 1896).

MOGILEWA, AFFANASIA. *Ueber die Wirkung einiger Kakteenalkaloide auf das Froschherz* (Archiv für experimentelle Pathologie und Pharmakologie, vol. 49: 137–56, 1903).

DE MOLINA, A. *Vocabulario de la Lengua Mexicana* (Leipzig, 1880).

Monatsschrift für Kakteenkunde. *Articles* (vol. 1: 93–94, 1891; vol. 4: 36–39, 1894; vol. 5: 14, 59, 94, 1895; vol. 7: 94, 1897; vol. 8: 110–11, 116, 127, 164, 1898; vol. 10: 161, 1900; vol. 21: 47–48, 183, 1911; vol. 31, 1921).

MOONEY, JAMES. *Calendar History of the Kiowa Indians* (Annual Report, Bureau of American Ethnology 17, pt. 1: 129–444. Washington, 1898).

 The Cheyenne Indians (Memoir, American Anthropological Association, vol. 1, no. 6, 1907).

 The Ghost Dance Religion (Annual Report, Bureau of American Ethnology 14, pt. 2: 641–1110. Washington, 1892 [1893].

 A Kiowa Mescal Rattle (American Anthropologist, o.s. vol. 5: 64–65, 1892).

 The Kiowa Peyote Rite (Der Urquell, Bd 1. Leyden, 1897).

 The Mescal Plant and Ceremony (Therapeutic Gazette, 3rd series, vol. 12: 7–11, 1896).

 Miscellaneous Notes on Peyote (Bureau of American Ethnology. Manuscript 1887. Washington, n.d.).

 Peyote Notebook (Bureau of American Ethnology. Manuscript 1930. Washington, n.d.).

 The Sacred Formulas of the Cherokee (Annual Report, Bureau of American Ethnology 7: 303–97. Washington, 1891).

 Tarumari-Guayachic, January 21, 1898 (Bureau of American Ethnology. Manuscript 2537. Washington, n.d.).

DE LA MOTA PADILLA, MATIAS ANGEL. *Historia de la Conquista de la Provincia de la Nueva-Galicia* (Mexico, 1870).

MOUREU, CHARLES. *Review* (Journal de Pharmacie et de Chemie, 6me séries, vol. 8: 519–23, 1898).

MURIE, JAMES R. *Pawnee Indian Societies* (Anthropological Papers, American Museum of Natural History, vol. 11: 543–644, 1914).

MURPHY, D. F. *Notes on Osage Peyote* (Manuscript).

NEWBERNE, R. E. L., AND C. H. BURKE. *Peyote: An Abridged Compilation from the Files of the Bureau of Indian Affairs* (Washington, 1922).

The New Century Dictionary (New York, 1914).

New Mescal Religion (Independent, vol. 66: 430, 1909).

NOON, JOHN A. *Notes on Kickapoo Peyotism* (Manuscript).

NORIEGA, JUAN MANUAL. *Curso de Historia de Drogas* (Mexico, 1902).

OCHOTERENA, ISAAC. *Nota acerca la identificación botanica de algunas de las plantas conocidas vulgarmente con el nombre de Peyotl* (Revista Mexicana de Biología, vol. 6: 95, 1926).

OFFICE OF INDIAN AFFAIRS. *Discussion Concerning Peyote, April, 1935.*

    Documents on Peyote, Part 1, May 18, 1937.

    Peyote (Office of Indian Affairs, Bulletin 21, 1923).

Old Coyote Protests (Commonweal, vol. 9: 585, 1929).

OLIVA, LEONARDO. *Lecciones de Farmacología* (vol. 2: 392. 1926).

OPLER, MORRIS E. *The Autobiography of a Chiricahua Apache* (Manuscript).

    Chiricahua Apache (Manuscript).

    The Influence of Aboriginal Pattern and White Contact on a Recently Introduced Ceremony, the Mescalero Peyote Rite (Journal of American Folk-Lore, vol. 49: 143–66, 1936 [1937]).

    Lipan Apache Field Notes (Manuscript).

    The Use of Peyote by the Carrizo and Lipan Apache Tribes (American Anthropologist, vol. 40, no. 2: 271–85, 1938).

OROZCO Y BERRA, MANUEL. *Geográfica de las lenguas y carta etnográfica de México* (Mexico, 1864).

ORTEGA, J. *Historia del Nayarit, Sonora, Sinaloa, y ambas Californias* (1887).

PARSONS, ELSIE CLEWS. *Taos Pueblo* (General Series in Anthropology, No. 2. Menasha, Wis., 1936).

    A Zuñi Detective (Man, vol. 16, no. 99: 168–70, 1916).

PAZ, LYDA. *Koasati Field Notes* (Manuscript).

PEREZ, BOLDE JESUS. *Dos observations hechas en el hombre sano, relativos a la acción del peyote* (Anales del Institut Médico Nacional, vol. 7, 1905).

PEREZ DE RIBAS, ANDRÉS. *Historia de los Triumphos de Nuestra Santa Fee en los Misiones de la Provincia de Nueva España* (Madrid, 1645).

PETRULLO, VINCENZO. *The Diabolic Root* (Philadelphia, 1934).

Peyote Cult Gaining among Indian Tribes (New York Times, November 12, 1936).

Peyote: Hearing before a sub-committee of the Committee on Indian Affairs of the House of Representatives, on H.R. 2614, 1918.

Peyote: An Insidious Evil (Indian Rights Association, No. 114, 1918).

Peyote: A Pernicious Indian Religion (Literary Digest, vol. 68: 34, 1921).

Peyote as Used in Religious Worship by the Indians (Compilation from Public Records and Congressional Hearings [no date, no author, Edgar McCarthy probable publisher]).

Peyotes, Datos para su Estudia (Anales del Instituto Médico Nacional de Mexico, vol. 4: 11, 203–14, 1899).

PFEIFFER, —— AND —— OTTO. *Abbildung und Beschreibung bluehender Cacteen* (Cassel, 1843).

PIERSON, D. L. *American Indian Peyote Worship* (Missionary Review of the World, vol. 28: 201, 1915).

PILCZ, ALEXANDER. *Ueber Pellotin* (Wiener klinische Wochenschrift, vol. 9: 1121–22, 1896).

PINCUSSOHN, L. *Zur Kenntnis des Pellotins* (Berliner klinische Wochenschrift, vol. 2: 44–47, 1907).

PONCE, PEDRO. *Breve relación de los dioses y ritos de la gentilidad* (Anales del Museo Nacional de Mexico, vol. 6, 1892).

Ponte, Dino. Il Peyotl (Giornale de Farmacie di Chimica et di Scienza Affini, vol. 82: 245-56, 1933).

Prentiss, D. W., and F. F. Morgan. The Alkaloids of A. Lewinii (National Medical Review, vol. 6: 147-51, 1896-97).

The Alkaloids of Anhalonium Lewinii (Mescal Buttons) with Notes upon Therapeutic Uses (Medical Society of the District of Columbia, Transactions for 1896: 123-27, 1897).

Anhalonium Lewinii (Mescal Buttons) a Study of a Drug with Especial Reference to its Physiological Action upon Man (Therapeutic Gazette, vol. 19, 3rd series, vol 11: 577-85, 1895).

Mescal Buttons: A. Lewinii, Henning (Lophophora Williamsii Lewinii, Coulter) (Medical Record: 258-66, 1896).

Therapeutic Uses of Mescal Buttons (Therapeutic Gazette, vol. 20, 3rd series, vol. 12: 4-7, 1896).

Preuss, Konrad T. Die Nayarit-Expedition, Erster Band: Die Religion der Cora-Indianer (Leipzig, 1912).

Prieto, Alejandro. Historia y Estadistica del Estado de Tamaulipas (Mexico, 1873).

Prinzhorn, Hans. Entrückung durch Rauschgift (Zeitschrift für Parapsychologie, January, 1918).

The Problem of Peyote (Review of Reviews, vol. 65: 437-38, 1922).

Putt, E. B. Mescal (Hearing Senate Indian Affairs Committee, Indian Appropriation Bill. Washington, 1919).

Mescal (Office of Indian Affairs, Bulletin 21: 7-12, Washington, 1923).

Quercy, Pierre. Hallucinations visuelles peyotliques (Congres de Blois, 1927).

Etudes sur l'hallucination (Etude clinique, vol. 1, Paris, 1930).

Radin, Paul. Crashing Thunder: The Autobiography of a Winnebago Indian (New York, 1926).

A Sketch of the Peyote Cult of the Winnebago: A Study in Borrowing (Journal of Religious Psychology, vol. 7: 1-22, 1914).

The Winnebago Tribe (Annual Report, Bureau of American Ethnology, 37. Washington, 1915-16).

Raffour, ———. La Médicine chez les Mexicains precolombiens (Thesis, Paris, 1900).

Ramírez, J. El Peyote (Estudias de Historia Natural 140. Mexico, 1904).

El Peyote (Anales del Instituto Médico Nacional de México, vol. 4, 1909).

Reko, B. P. Star-names of the Chilam Balam of Chuymayel (El México Antiguo, vol. 4: 124-25, 1937).

Reko, V. A. Botánica médica méxicana (Mexico, 1929-36).

La Flora Diabólica de México (Mexico, 1928).

Gespenster in Mexico (Mexico, 1925).

Ein Kaktus die Gespenster Ruft (Atlantis, vol. 7: 428-34, 1932).

Magische Gifte in Mexico (Deutsche Zeitung von Mexico, May 1924).

Der Peyotl-kaktus (Die Bruecke, vol. 2: 9-10, n.d.).

Rausch- und Betäubungsmittel der neuen Welt (Stuttgart, 1936).

Der Unheimliche Gast (Reichspost, Vienna, May, 1932).

Was bedeutet das Wort Teo-Nanacatl? (Manuscript).

Was ist Peyote? (Zeitschrift für Parapsychologie, 4: 7, July, 1929).

Report of the Secretary of the Interior on the Senate Bill 1399 Dealing with the Interstate Shipment of Peyote (Washington, 1937).

Report on the Case of the United States Versus Nah-qua-tah-tuck, alias Mitchell Neck. (Manuscript. Archives of the Bureau of Chemistry, Washington, 1914).

Richardson, D. A. A Report on the Action of Anhalonium Lewinii (Mescale Buttons) (New York Medical Journal, vol. 64: 194-95, 1896).

Richardson, Jane. Kiowa Peyote Songs (Manuscript).

Richet, C. Les Poisons de l'Intelligence (Paris, 1922).

Robbins, W. W., J. P. Harrington, and Barbara Freire-Marreco. Ethnobotany of the Tewa Indians (Bulletin, Bureau of American Ethnology 55. Washington, 1916).

Roberts, Helen H. Musical Areas in North America (Yale University Publications in Anthropology, No. 12. New Haven, 1936).

ROBLES, CLEMENTE, AND JOSÉ GOMEZ ROBLEDA. *Trabajo Inicial acerca de la Acción Fisiológica de Clorhidrata de Peyotina* (Anales del Instituto Biología, 1931).

ROMANS, BERNARD. *A Concise Natural History of East and West Florida* (New York, 1775).

ROUHIER, ALEXANDRE. *Monographie du Peyotl* (Thesis, Paris, 1926).

    Phénomenes de metagnomie experimentale observés au course d'une experience fait avec le peyotl (Revue metapsychique, 144–54, 1925).

    La Plante qui fait les yeux émerveillés- Le Peyotl (Paris, 1927).

    Les Plantes divinatoires (Paris, 1927).

RUSBY, H. H. *A. Lewinii* (Bulletin of Pharmacy, vol. 2: 126, 1888).

    Mescal Buttons (Bulletin of Pharmacy, vol. 8: 306, 1894).

    Mescal Buttons (Reference Handbook of the Medical Sciences, vol. 6: 456, 1903).

RUSSELL, FRANK. *The Pima Indians* (Annual Report, Bureau of American Ethnology, 26: 3–389, 1908).

SAFFORD, W. E. *An Aztec Narcotic* (Journal of Heredity, vol. 6: 291–311, 1915).

    Cactaceae of Northeastern and Central Mexico (Washington, 1909).

    Daturas of the Old World and the New (Annual Report, Smithsonian Institution, 1922: 536–67 [1923]).

    Identification of Teonanacatl of the Aztecs with the Narcotic Cactus L. Williamsii (Botanical Society of Washington, D. C., 1915).

    Narcotic Plants and Stimulants of the Ancient Americans (Annual Report, Smithsonian Institution, 1916: 387–424 [1917]).

    Peyote, The Narcotic Mescal Button of the Indians (Journal, American Medical Association, vol. 77: 1278–79, 1921).

DE SAHAGÚN, BERNADINO. *A History of Ancient Mexico by Fray Bernardino de Sahagún*, Vol. I. (Fanny R. Bandelier, Tr.) (Nashville, 1932).

    Histoire générale des choses de la Nouvelle-Espagne (D. Jourdanet and Rémi Siméon, Tr. and Ed.) (Paris, 1880).

    Historia general de las cosas de Nueva España (C. M. de Bustamente, Ed.) (3 vols. Mexico, 1829–30).

SALM-DYCK, OTTO. *Article* (Cact. hort. 34, 69).

    Article (Botanical Magazine, t. 4295).

SALM-DYCK, OTTO, AND —— DIETRICH. *Article* (Berliner Allegemeine Gartenzeitung, vol. 13: 385, 1845).

SANTOSCOY, ALBERTO. *Nayarit* (Collección de Documentos inéditos, historicos y etnográficos. Guadalajara, 1899).

    Notas etnograficas del Ing. oficial del Estado de Jalisco (Collección Documentos. Mexico).

SAPIR, EDWARD. *Kaibab Paiute Field Notes* (Manuscript).

SAUER, CARL O. *The Distribution of Aboriginal Tribes and Languages in Northwestern Mexico* (Ibero-Americana, No. 5, Berkeley, 1934).

SAVILLE, MARSHALL H., Ed. *Notes on the Superstitions of the Indians of Yucatan* (Indian Notes and Monographs, vol. 9: 202–08, 1921).

SAYLES, E. B. *An Archaeological Survey of Texas* (Medallion Papers, No. 17. Globe, 1935).

SCHEIDEWEILER, M. J. *Descriptio diagnostica nonnullarum Cactearum* (Bulletin de l'Academie Royale des Sciences de Bruxelles, vol. 5: 492, 1838).

Schmeideberg's Archiv für experimentelle Pathologie und Pharmakologie (vol. 24: 401–411. Leipzig, 1873).

SCHOOLCRAFT, H. R. *Historical and Statistical Information Respecting the History, Condition and Prospects of the Indian Tribes of the United States* (6 vols. Philadelphia, 1851–1857).

SCHULTES, RICHARD EVANS. *Peyote and Plants Used in the Peyote Ceremony* (Harvard Botanical Museum Leaflets, vol. 4, no. 7, 1937).

    Peyote Cult (Literary Digest, Nov. 13, 1937).

    Peyote Intoxication, A Review of the Literature on the Chemistry, Physiological and Psychological Effects of Peyotl (Thesis, Harvard University, 1936).

Peyote (Lophophora Williamsii) and Plants Confined with It (Harvard Botanical Museum Leaflets, vol. 5, no. 5, 1937).

SCHUMANN, KARL. *Articles* (Monatsschrift für Kakteenkunde, vol. 4: 36–37, 86, 1894; vol. 5: 77, 1895; vol. 6: 177–80, 1896).

Blühende Kakteen (Iconographia Cactacearum) (3 vols. Neudamm, 1913).

Cactaceae, Die Natürlichen Pflanzenfamilien (Leipzig, 1894).

Gesamtbeschreibung der Cacteen (Monographia Cactacearum, II) (Neudamm, 1903).

Über giftige Kakteen (Berichten der Pharmaceutische Gesellschaft; 103–10, 1895).

Science News Letter, September 20, 1930.

SERKO, A. *Im Mescalinrausch* (Jahrbücher für Psychiatrie und Neurologie, vol. 34: 355, 1913).

DE LA SERNA, JACINTO. *Manual de ministros de Indios para el Conocimiento de sus Idolatrías y Extirpación de Ellas* (Documentos inéditos, 104: 165. Madrid, 1892).

SEYMOUR, GERTRUDE. *Peyote Worship: An Indian Cult and a Powerful Drug* (Survey, vol. 36: 181–84, 1916).

SHELL, C. E. *Experience of Charles E. Shell while under the Influence of Pellote (Peyote) on June 21, 1909* (Office of Indian Affairs, Bulletin 21: 27–29, 1923).

SHONLE RUTH. *Peyote: The Giver of Visions* (American Anthropologist, vol. 27: 53–75, 1925).

SIMÉON, RÉMI. *Dictionnaire de la langue Nahuatl ou Mexicaine* (Paris, 1885).

SIMMONS, C. S. *The Peyote Road* (Manuscript).

SKINNER, ALANSON. *Associations and Ceremonies of the Menomini* (Anthropological Papers, American Museum of Natural History, vol. 13: 167–215, 1915).

Ethnology of the Ioway Indians (Bulletin, Public Museum of the City of Milwaukee, 5: 181–354, 1926).

Kansa Organizations (Anthropological Papers, American Museum of Natural History, vol. 11: 741–45, 1915).

Material Culture of the Menomini (Indian Notes and Monographs no. 20, 1921).

Medicine Ceremony of the Menomini, Iowa, and Wahpetan Dakota (Indian Notes and Monographs, vol. 4, 1921).

Observations on the Ethnology of the Sauk Indians (Bulletin, Public Museum of the City of Milwaukee, 5: 1–57, 1923; 59–95, 119–80, 1925).

Societies of the Iowa, Kansa, and Ponca Indians (Anthropological Papers, American Museum of Natural History, vol. 11: 679–740, 1915).

SLOSSEN, E. E. *Peyote Paradise* (Collier's, vol. 84: 44, 1929).

SMITH, B. *A Note on the Action of Mescal* (British Medical Journal, vol. 2 for 1913, p. 21).

SMITH, MAURICE G. *Peyote* (Oklahoma Daily, December 8, 1929).

SMITH, MRS. MAURICE G. *A Negro Peyote Cult* (Journal, Washington Academy of Sciences, vol. 24: 448–53, 1934).

SPÄTH, E. *Über die Anhalonium-Alkaloide. I. Anhalin und Mezcalin* (Monatshefte für Chemie, vol. 40: 129–52. Wien, 1920); II. *Die Konstitution des Pellotins, des Anhalonidins, und des Anhalamins* (idem, 42: 97–115, 1924); III. *Konstitution des Anhalins* (idem, vol. 42: 263–66, 1924); V. *Die Synthese des Anhalonidins und des Pellotins* (idem, vol. 43: 477–84, 1924).

SPÄTH, E., AND J. GANGL. *Über die Anhalonium-Alkaloide. VI, Anhalonin und Lophophorin* (Monatshefte für Chemie, vol. 44: 103–113, 1924).

SPÄTH, E., AND H. RÖDER. *Über die Anhalonium-Alkaloide. IV, Die Synthese des Anhalamins* (Monatshefte für Chemie, vol. 43: 93–111, 1924).

SPECK, FRANK G. *Catawba Field Notes* (Manuscript).

The Creek Indians of Taskigi Town (Memoir American Anthropological Association 2, no. 2, 1907).

Delaware Peyote Symbolism (Manuscript).

Ethnology of the Yuchi Indians (University of Pennsylvania, Anthropological Publications of the University Museum, vol. 1, no. 1. Philadelphia, 1909).

Notes on the Ethnology of the Osage Indians (Transactions, University of Pennsylvania, Department of Archaeology vol. 2: 159–71, 1907).

Notes on the Life of John Wilson, the Revealer of Peyote, as Recalled by his Nephew, George Anderson (General Magazine and Historical Chronicle, vol. 35: 539–56, 1933).

A Study of the Delaware Big House Ceremony (Publications, Pennsylvania Historical Commission No. 2. Harrisburg, 1931).

SPIER, LESLIE. *Havasupai Ethnography* (Anthropological Papers, American Museum of Natural History, vol. 29, pt. 3, 1928).

The Sun Dance of the Plains Indians (Anthropological Papers, American Museum of Natural History, vol. 14, 451–527, 1921).

Yuman Comparative Study: Warfare (Manuscript).

Yuman Tribes of the Gila River (Chicago, 1933).

SPINDEN, H. J. *Ancient Civilizations of Mexico and Central America* (Handbook 3, American Museum of Natural History, 3rd edition, 1928).

SPRUCE, RICHARD. *Notes of a Botanist on the Amazon and the Andes* (London, 1908).

STANDLEY, PAUL C. *Trees and Shrubs of Mexico* (Contributions, U. S. National Herbarium, vol. 23, pts, 1, 2, 3. Washington, 1920–23).

STAUB, H., AND W. GRASSMANN. *Über die Wirkungsgrenze einiger Gifte am isolierten Sängerherzen* (Archiv für experimentelle Pathologie und Pharmakologie, vol. 154: 317–41, 1930).

STEVENSON, M. C. *Ethnobotany of the Zuñi Indian* (Annual Report, Bureau of American Ethnology, 30: 31–102. Washington, 1915).

The Religious Life of the Zuñi Child (Annual Report, Bureau of American Ethnology, 5: 537–55. Washington, 1887).

The Zuñi Indians (Annual Report, Bureau of American Ethnology, 23. Washington, 1904).

SWADESH, MORRIS. *Chitamacha Texts* (Manuscript).

SWANTON, JOHN R. *Aboriginal Culture of the Southeast* (Annual Report, Bureau of American Ethnology, 42: 673–726. Washington, 1928).

Religious Beliefs and Medical Practices of the Creek Indians (Annual Report, Bureau of American Ethnology, 42: 473–672. Washington, 1928).

Social Organization and Social Usages of the Indians of the Creek Confederacy (Annual Report, Bureau of American Ethnology, 42: 23–472. Washington, 1928).

Social and Religious Beliefs and Usages of the Chickasaw (Annual Report, Bureau of American Ethnology, 44: 169–273. Washington, 1928).

THOMAS, CYRUS, AND JOHN R. SWANTON. *Indian Languages of Mexico and Central America and their Geographical Distribution*. Bulletin, Bureau of American Ethnology, 44. Washington, 1911).

THOMPSON, W. *The Species of Cacti Commonly Cultivated under the Generic Name Anhalonium* (Annual Report, Missouri Botanical Gardens, vol. 9: 127–35, 1898).

THURNWALD, RICHARD. *Economics in Primitive Communities* (Oxford, 1932).

THWAITES, R. G., Ed. *Jesuit Relations* (73 vols. Cleveland, 1896–1901).

TORO, ALFONSO. *Las plantas sagradas de los Aztecos y su influencia sobre el arte precortesiano* (Proceedings, Twenty-third International Congress of Americanists: 101–21, 1930).

TRIEDE, GEORG. *Die Alkaloide: Eine Monographie der natürlichen Basen* (2 vols. Leipzig, 1909).

TSCHIRSCH, A. *Handbuch der Pharmakognosie* (3 vols. Leipzig, 1909).

TWITCHELL, R. E. *Spanish Archives of New Mexico* (vol. 2: 188. 1914).

UNDERHILL, RUTH. *The Autobiography of a Papago Woman* (Memoir, American Anthropological Association, 46, 1936).

URBINA, MANUEL. *Article* (La Naturaleza, vol. 3, 1912).

El Peyote y el Ololuihqui (Anales del Museo Nacional de Mexico, vol. 7, 1900).

VASCHIDE, N. *Une Plante Divine: Le Mescal* (La Quinzaine, vol. 46: 112, 1905).

VELASCO, ——. *Dictamen Fiscal, Nov. 30, 1716* (Memoria de Nueva España, 27: 194).

VOEGELIN, ERMINIE. *Shawnee Field Notes* (Manuscript).

WAGNER, G. *Entwicklung und Verbreitung des Peyote Cultes* (Baessler-Archiv, vol. 15: 59–141, 1932).

WALTER, ——. *Les Excitants artificiales dans le travail intellectuel* (Paris, 1905).

WATERMULDER, G. A. *Mescal* (Report, Thirty-second Annual Lake Mohonk Conference: 68–76. Albany, 1914).

WERTHAM, FREDERIC, AND MANFRED BLEULER. *Inconstancy of the Formal Structure of the Personality: Experimental Study of the Influence of Mescaline on the Rorschach Test* (Archives of Neurology and Psychiatry, vol. 28, July, 1932).

WHITE, EDMUND. *Article* (Journal of Physiology, vol. 25: 69, 1899–1900).

WILEY, H. W. *Statement* (Office of Indian Affairs, Bulletin 21: 15–19, 1923).

WILLIAMS, P. WATSON. *Les Boutons de Mescal en Amerique* (Journal de Pharmacie de Belgique, vol. 3: 619–20, 1921).

WISSLER, CLARK. *The American Indian* (2nd edition, New York, 1922).

 Societies and Dance Associations of the Blackfoot Indians (Anthropological Papers, American Museum of Natural History, vol. 11: 359–460, 1916).

YOUNGKEN, H. W. *Drugs of North American Indians* (American Journal of Pharmacy, vol. 96: 489, 1924).

ZADOR, JULIUS. *Meskalinwirkung auf das Phantomglied* (Monatsschrift für Psychiatrie und Neurologie, vol. 77, 1930).

 Meskalinwirkung bei Störung des optischen System (Zeitschrift für die gesamte Neurologie und Psychiatrie, 127: 30, 1930).

ZADOR, JULIUS, AND K. ZUCKER. *Meskalinwirkung am Halluzinanten* (Zeitschrift für die gesamte Neurologie und Psychiatrie, vol. 227: 15–29, 1930).

ZEMAN, H. *Verbreitung und Grad der Eidetischen Anlage* (Zeitschrift für Psychologie, vol. 96: 208, 1925).

ZUCKER, K. *Versuche mit Meskalin am Halluzinanten* (Zeitschrift für die gesamte Neurologie und Psychiatrie, vol. 127: 107, 1930).

ZUCKER, K., AND ZADOR, J. *Zur Analyse der Meskalinwirkung am Normalen* (Zeitschrift für die gesamte Neurologie und Psychiatrie, vol. 127: 1–2, 1930).

PLATES

EXPLANATION OF PLATES

Plate 1. Peyote leaders. *Upper left*, Charley Apekaum (Kiowa) and Jonathan Koshiway (Oto); *upper right*, Alfred Wilson (Cheyenne) twice president of the Native American Church; *lower left and right*, Packing-Stone (Kiowa) a "Ten-Medicine" keeper and peyote leader in typical leaders' costume of blanket and buckskin clothes; the headdress is old Kiowa.

Plate 2. Altar and ash-birds. *Upper left*, Quapaw permanent cement altar of the John Wilson Big Moon rite. The ash mounds are the "graves" of John Wilson and Jesus Christ; the W's or M's on each side of the heart signify "Moon-Head" or "Wilson." The nearest heart of the mound is the Heart of the World, that under the fire the Sacred Heart of Christ, that on the moon the Heart of Goodness on which the father peyote rests. Seven lines around the apron represent week days, the twelve lines the months of the year. The ashes mean the parting of the Red Sea, or mean to some the sheep and the goats. This altar was made by the authorized builder, Victor Griffin, and his assistant, Charley Tyner. *Upper right*, Symbolic peyote painting by Mopope (Kiowa) showing sacred staff, seven-marbled drum, drumstick, gourd rattle, doctoring feathers, and altar or moon with ash crescent. The water bird intermediary is carrying a prayer from the father peyote on the altar across the ritual fire to the great spirit indicated by the seven rays of feathers of the rising sun. The lightning lines from the god-head result from the artist's visits to the Southwestern pueblos. *Center*, A fine example of the scissors-tail ash bird made at an Oto meeting near Red Rock, Oklahoma. *Lower*, An unusually fine example of the water bird ash bird made at a Shawnee meeting near McCloud. The burnt sticks finish out the scissors-tail of the bird. The smokestick in the foreground is carved with native and Christian symbols (now in Peabody Museum, Harvard University). (It is believed that the Yuchi altar of Petrullo, Plate 2, is erroneously figured and is of the order of those shown here.)

PEYOTE LEADERS

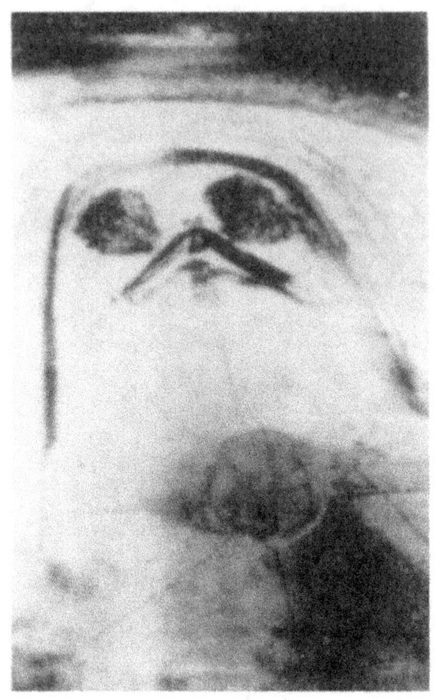
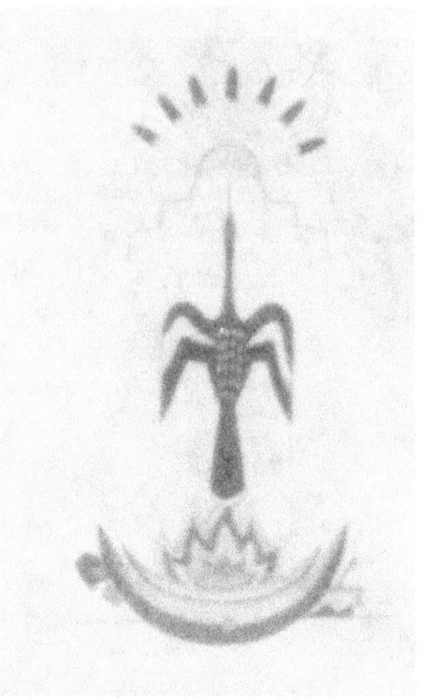

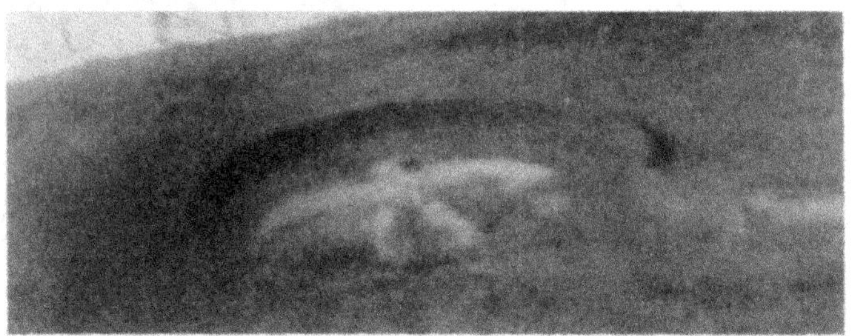

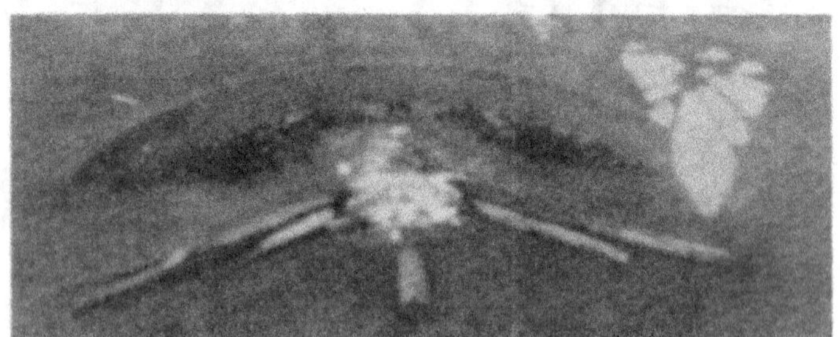

ALTAR AND ASH BIRDS

PEYOTE STUDIES, 1941–1960

PEYOTE (from the Aztec *peyotl*) is a small, spineless, carrot-shaped cactus, *Lophophora williamsii* Lemaire, which grows wild in the Rio Grande Valley and southward. It is mostly subterranean, and only the grayish-green pincushion-like top appears above ground, with spiral radial grooves dividing the puffy prominences which bear linearly-spaced tufts of fine gray-white flocculence, somewhat like artists' camels-hair paintbrushes. Cut off horizontally about ground level, and dried into a hard woody disc, this top becomes the so-called "peyote button"—often called "mescal button," confusingly since it does not come from the non-cactus succulent, the mescal proper, from whose fermented sap, pulque, the brandy mescal is distilled; also, erroneously, called "mescal bean" which is the Red Bean, *Sophora secundiflora* (ortega) Lag. ex DC; and, further, once quite mistakenly identified with the Aztec narcotic mushroom *teonanacatl*, a Basidiomycete, a true member of the Fungi. Nine psychotropic alkaloids, an unusual number even for a cactus, are contained in natural pan-peyotl; some of these are strychnine-like pharmacodynamically, others (notably mescaline) hallucinogenic. For this reason the psychotomimetic mescaline has been experimentally investigated in recent psychiatric research, along with its fellow-indoles such as lysergic acid; and for this reason, its hallucinogenic qualities, American Indians have used pan-peyotl in native "doctoring,"

This bibliographical essay was first published in *Current Anthropology*, vol. 1 (1960), no. 1. Submitted on September 11, 1958, it was the first to receive CA☆ treatment. It was sent to 13 scholars. Substantive comments were returned by David F. Aberle, Donald Collier, Åke Hultkrantz, Wilhelm Koppers, Marvin K. Opler, Louise Spindler, George Spindler, and Anthony F. C. Wallace. Those contributions that were incorporated by the author into text or notes are indicated by a star (☆).

witchcraft, and religious rituals. As a religious cult, peyotism is pre-Columbian in Mexico. Toward the end of the nineteenth century, peyotism spread, via Texan tribes and Athapaskans of the Southwest, to the Indians of the United States, mostly following the subsidence of the Ghost Dance, for which it largely substituted, now as a peaceful intertribal nativistic religion, in places somewhat acculturated to Christianity. It is now the major religious cult of most Indians of the United States between the Rocky Mountains and the Mississippi (including the remnants of eastern Algonkin tribes and the Siouan Winnebago), and additionally in parts of southern Canada, the Great Basin, and east-central California. The appeal of peyote is based upon the visions it induces, *viz.* its "medicine power," and its availability therefore in native doctoring is culturally based upon the aboriginal vision quest and the religious and ideological premises of this quest. Peyote is generally agreed by experts to be non-habit-forming; it is non-soporific and not, therefore, technically a "narcotic."

Some twenty years ago the present writer sought to summarize all that was then known about peyote (*Lophophora williamsii*)—its botany, ethnology and history, chemistry, psychology and physiology—as well as about the "mescal" bean (*Sophora secundiflora*) and the narcotic mushroom *teonanacatl*, both of which had been confused with peyote. This summary (La Barre 1938) was based upon the extensive published literature on peyote and peyotism, on the generous loan of current and unpublished field notes by many persons, and on the writer's own field trips during several years to fifteen peyote-using American Indian tribes.

In the subsequent two decades, peyotism has remained a lively subject of Americanist research. Despite the standardization of the rite, a number of new substantive details have been added to our knowledge. Peyotism has spread to several new tribes. Medico-psychiatric research on mescaline, the principal hallucinogenic alkaloid of the nine in natural panpeyotl, has progressed considerably beyond its status in 1938. Certain problems concerning the origin and diffusion of peyote have been argued and perhaps clarified. And, finally, important new problem-oriented and methodological studies have been made on the basis of peyote

data, which studies, not the least being the new and valuable materials on peyote music, are of wider general interest. It would probably be useful at the present time to summarize these studies for the general ethnologist and to attempt a perspective on the past as well as a prospect for future studies.

GENERAL WORKS

Of general works, the first to be mentioned is Gusinde's "Der Peyote-Kult" (1939), judiciously reviewed by Marvin Opler (1940b). Opler was critical of some *Kulturkreis* aspects of Gusinde's work and contrasted it methodologically with the Yale study. Despite the different approaches, Opler pointed out that, "Gusinde adds confirmation to La Barre's Yale University publication with substantial, though undeclared, agreement on most essential points" (p. 667). The most important of these, perhaps, concerns the early origins of peyotism in the United States, since Gusinde and La Barre worked entirely independently of one another and were ignorant of one another's researches. Opler states (p. 669) that, for Gusinde, the

Carrizo, Tonkawa, Lipan, and Mescalero are on the direct line of diffusion from northeastern Mexico. The Mescalero are seen as the link to the Kiowa and Comanche, and the latter provide the connection to the Caddo, Delaware, southern Cheyenne and Arapaho, and finally to the Ute and Shoshoni.

It is, in fact, to the later published field work of both the brothers Opler that we owe the clarification of early diffusion of peyote to Texas and the eastern Southwest,

a point on which Gusinde, La Barre, the Oplers, and most other students except Slotkin are in agreement. The major new contributions to our knowledge have been made at the other end of history, in respect of the modern diffusion of peyote to the Menomini, Navaho, Ute, and Washo. Slotkin has introduced alternative views concerning the diffusion of peyotism through the Hopi, Taos, and the Caddo, but specialists on these areas have questioned both his data and his conclusions, and his must be regarded as a minority viewpoint.

Slotkin's major work on peyote, *The Peyote Religion* (1956a), is extremely valuable for its summary of the present legal status of peyotism in state and federal laws (pp. 54–56), for its discussion of the local organizations and officers of the Native American Church (pp. 57–64), and for its excellent "Bibliography on Peyotism North of the Rio Grande, 1850–1955" (pp. 143–87). This bibliography of more than 550 items contains only 55 already cited by La Barre, and over 300 before and 77 since 1937 not in La Barre, so that the bibliographies largely supplement one another and together account for over a thousand items. As will be noted later, Slotkin was also responsible for the publication of a number of colonial documents, though some of these have been disputed as referring to peyote. In addition, he published a number of documents on the Native American Church, known to but only summarized in La Barre. Slotkin's *The Peyote Religion* must be regarded as the major source on the Native American Church, of which Slotkin was an officer. The real value of Slotkin's original contributions and documentations can scarcely be disputed, though his manner of presentation has been

194

criticized (La Barre 1957b) and also some of his conclusions (Beaver 1952).

The other extended works on peyotism include works by Aberle and Stewart on Navaho and Ute peyotism, Stewart on Washo-Northern Paiute, Slotkin and McAllester on Menomini, McAllester on peyote music, and the Spindlers on the place of peyotism in Menomini acculturation. These studies will be discussed below. Another general work is "La Magia del Peyotl" (Aguirre Beltrán 1952), an excellent though brief study, containing new material on the uses of peyote in colonial Mexico. "El Peyote al Traves de los Siglos" (Hijar y Haro 1937) is interesting for its somewhat standard bibliography placed in chronological order. Leonard (1942) has published documents indicating that in 1620 the Inquisition prohibited the use of peyote in Mexico, where it had been used for detecting thefts and for divination and prognostication. The distinguished botanist Schultes believes, on the basis of information recorded by Sahagun, that *Lophophora williamsii* has been used as a religious sacrament since 300 B.C., hence has been an item in economic botany for over two thousand years, and, on the basis of information in B. P. Reko, that it has been used as far south as Yucatan (Schultes 1938b). Schultes points out also that peyote was a problem to missionaries in Texas in 1760, and thinks that peyote came to the Kiowa Reservation earlier than is now assumed, though he has not demonstrated that the Kiowa were in that position at that date. Underhill has written a good summary, "Peyote" (1952), based on standard sources. She has also sharpened our awareness that the slight ritualization of the "peyote journey" of Plains tribes may have been influenced by the more developed ritual journeys in Mexico and the Southwest (1954: 649):

A trait of Huichol and Tarahumara which did not reach the north until later times is the use of peyote. Connected with it is the ceremonial journey, with restrictions and special language. A similar journey is found among the Papago, where the object is not peyote but salt. Perhaps the salt journeys of both Hopi and Zuni may be faint echoes of it, as also the Taos camp at Blue Lake. The warpath behavior of the Chiricahua Apache with its restrictions and its special language . . . may be another echo, perhaps learned from the Papago who were neighbors and enemies.

However, we believe that such an influence on the ritualization of the peyote journey must have come through Apache groups in the Southwest and Texas, rather than through the Pueblo groups, though this adds an interesting sidenote to the standard theory of the diffusion of peyote.

LEGAL STATUS OF PEYOTISM

As earlier noted, Slotkin's work is the standard one on the legal status of peyotism and the Native American Church. Stewart added some interesting new data in his spirited argument against a Colorado state anti-peyote law (1956a). He notes that the Native American Church of Saskatchewan was chartered on November 3, 1954, and that a new group appeared legally in North Dakota on January 9, 1954. Twelve states have now issued charters to the Native American Church. The Twelfth Annual Meeting of the Church was held at Scottsbluff, Nebraska, from June 28 to July 1, 1956.

The use of peyote has been a burning legal issue especially among the Navaho. In a newspaper article datelined from Window Rock, Arizona (*New York Times* 1954), it was stated that thirteen members of the Native American Church had been jailed by the Navaho tribal leaders, and that Texas, Arizona, and New Mexico now prohibit the transportation and sale of peyote; nevertheless, the buttons, which cost ten to eleven dollars per thousand in Texas, were commonly available on the Navaho Reservation at five to ten cents each.

Missionaries have continued their determined hostility toward peyotism.[1] Niedhammer, in a "Statement on Peyote" (n.d.) prepared for his ecclesiastical superiors at the Saint Labre Indian Mission to the Cheyenne of Tongue River Reservation, condemned the use of peyote by Indians. Based on this document was an article (Scully 1941) which ended in the promulgation of the dictum that there is a complete incompatibility between peyotism and the Catholic religion. Curiously, an American Medical Association committee urged in its report of November 25, 1948, to the U.S. Secretary of the Interior, that the use of peyote be nationally outlawed as a habit-forming drug (Associated Press 1948; see also Braasch, Branton, and Chesley 1949). We can only conclude that these doctors did not base their opinion on adequate medical evidence. Certainly ethnologists who have used peyote repeatedly and have observed in circumstantial detail its use among Indians, in both cases without such assumed effects, quite uniformly agree that peyote is not habit-forming. This was asserted in a "Statement on Peyote" signed by La Barre, McAllester, Slotkin, Stewart, and Tax (La Barre *et al.* 1951). This document is in essential agreement with an earlier series of standard statements by Boas, Kroeber, Hrdlička, J. P. and M. R. Harrington, La Barre, Petrullo, Schultes, Elna Smith, and Osage Chief Fred Lookout against the (Chavez) Senate Bill 1399 of February 8, 1937. Although the final opinion must necessarily be a medical one, informed anthropologists are firmly united in their judgment and will doubtless continue to protest the neglect of medical evidence in the formulation of medical opinion (*Documents on Peyote* 1937).

PSYCHIATRIC RESEARCH

Psychiatric research on mescaline has continued to increase in recent decades. Claude and Ey (1934) reported on mescaline as an hallucinogenic substance; and Freedman, Aghajanian, Ornitz, and Rosner (1958), on the patterns of tolerance of lysergic acid and mescaline in rats. Denber and Merlis (1956a) studied the action of mescaline on brain-wave patterns in schizophrenics before and after administering Electric Shock Therapy, the antagonism between mescaline and Chlorpromazine (1956b), and also wrote on the therapeutic implications of mescaline-induced states (1954). Merlis and Hunter (1954) published on the effects of administration of mescaline to schizophrenics after Electric Shock Therapy; and Denber (1955), on its action in epileptics. Guttmann (1936), writing on artificial psychoses produced by mescaline, emphasized the paranoid states that occasionally accompany mescaline intoxication which have been observed among both Indian (Radin 1926) and White subjects. The same authority was co-author of a study of mescaline and depersonalization (Guttmann and Maclay 1936) that reported research at Maudsley Hospital, London, and that stated that, "Mescalin [sic] depersonalization is identical with this symptom in morbid states, and therefore can be used as a model for therapeutic experiments" (p. 203). Himwich gives the formulas of various neurohormones, psychotomimetic agents, and tranquilizing drugs, including mescaline, in his research on drugs (1958), and had earlier shown that mescaline is psychotomimetic and that azacyclonol could suppress its effects (Himwich in Cholden 1956). Hoch (1952) and Kant (1931) also worked on the experimental induction of psychoses by mescaline. Abram Hoffer had experimented with mescaline for over three years by 1954, in his research on schizophrenia at the University of Saskatchewan—work supported, like Guttmann and Maclay's, by a grant from the Rockefeller Foundation. Lindemann and Malamud (1933) have made experimental analyses of the psychopathological effects of intoxicating drugs, including mescaline. De Ropp's book, *Drugs and the Mind* (1957), has a chapter on "The Mind and Mescaline" (pp. 27–60); he uses mostly European sources of earlier date, but cites the Statement, earlier mentioned, by American ethnologists in *Science*. Slotta and Szyszka (1933), working in São Paulo, Brazil, have reported new discoveries concerning mescaline. Wallace (1959) considers that response to mescaline intoxication depends very considerably on the cultural and situational milieu, as well as on individual personality. Wertham has twice published on mescaline and pain (1952a, 1952b). Wikler (1957) has summarized recent psychiatric and pharmacological work on mescaline.[2] This selection of psychiatric researches on mescaline does not pretend to be exhaustive of the relevant copious modern studies on psychopharmacology, but it is believed that it constitutes a representative sampling.

SPECIAL PROBLEMS

Basing his argument exclusively on textual evidence from colonial documents, the present writer early argued against Safford's facile identification of peyote and the Aztec narcotic *teonanacatl*, since the latter was always specifically identified as a narcotic mushroom (La Barre 1938, Appendix 3: "Peyote and Teo-Nanacatl," pp. 128–30). The final solution of the problem could, of course, rest only on properly botanical evidence. Subsequently the botanist Schultes rediscovered a narcotic *Basidiomycete* in Mexico, which he identified with the Aztec mushroom *teonanacatl*, reporting first in a botanical publication (Schultes 1939) and later in an anthropological journal (Schultes 1940b). The provocative, lavishly expensive ($125.00), and somewhat inaccessible work on mushrooms, including *teonanacatl*, by a wealthy amateur and J. P. Morgan partner (Wasson and Wasson 1957; Wasson 1956), is a rediscovery of the Aztec narcotic mushroom. Although in agreement on the botany and the ethnology of *teonanacatl*, these authors disagree upon the etymology of the word. La Barre had questioned Benvento's etymol-ogy, "bread of the gods," which was accepted by Safford and others, but Schultes (1940b) cites Simeón and V. A. Reko (as later did Wasson) to support the earlier etymology. The present writer, although now a minority of one, still retains his skepticism regarding this point in Safford also, and further points out that this question will ultimately be settled only by linguistic specialists. It is gratifying, incidentally, that among professional anthropologists the misleading term "mescal bean" as applied to *Lophophora williamsii* has been dropped, though still retained by British literary writers; there is no such listing in the latest *General Index* of the American Anthropological Association publications ([1951] 53: 37). Schultes has also written interestingly on the aboriginal therapeutic uses of *Lophophora williamsii* (Schultes 1940a).

Another disagreement, this time between ethnologists, has occurred over the relationship of peyotism to "mescalism," the former cult dealing with *Lophophora williamsii* (a cactus) and the latter with the "red bean" (*Sophora secundiflora*, a true member of the FABACEAE or Bean Family). The earlier Red Bean Cult was found among the Apache, Comanche, Delaware, Iowa, Kansa, Omaha, Osage, Oto, Pawnee, Ponca, Tonkawa, and Wichita, according to Howard (1957). This evidence was contained in La Barre's original dissertation, now on deposit in the Sterling Library at Yale University, but was condensed in the final published account (1938) which merely distinguished peyote and the "mescal bean" botanically and suggested a "Red Bean Cult" that may have preceded peyotism in Texas and the Plains. On the basis of "mescal" evidence, however, Howard regarded with skepticism the usual derivation of the peyote cult from Mexico via the Apache. Howard argued that the similarities of peyotism with the mescal bean cult indicate a derivation of the ritual content of peyotism from mescalism, and that the influences on ritual form would seem to be from north to south, contrary to the usual view. The present writer has replied to this by arguing (1) that the history and ethnology of peyotism proper already establish sufficiently a southern origin from Mexico via the Apache and other tribes of Texas and the eastern Southwest; (2) that the supposed similarities in ritual are limited, non-specific, and ambiguous; (3) that the botanical provenience of both *Lophophora* and *Sophora* are southern; and (4) that there are archaeological evidences of early date for the use of *Sophora* in southwest Texas (La Barre 1957a). This last argument has elicited further data from an archaeologist indicating abundant finds of *Sophora* in Texas sites (Campbell 1958). The present writer still looks to the south for the origins of both mescalism and peyotism, maintaining that the Plains Siouan and Algonkian mescalists who *late* and *historically* received peyote from southern tribes could hardly have shaped the original southern rite—even though an attenuated and earlier mescalism had come to them, *also* from the south. What we should look for is an earlier Red Bean Cult in Texas, among Apache tribes, and in Mexico, which, on this time level, might indeed have influenced the ritual content of Apache-Kiowa-Comanche peyotism, though this is still to be demonstrated.

NEW SUBSTANTIVE DATA ON THE PEYOTE RITE

Although the Plains rite is highly standardized and has been voluminously reported in tribal monographs since the classic account of Kroeber for the Arapaho (1907) and of Mooney for the southern Plains (1896), and although peyotism itself has since been monographed by La Barre, Gusinde, and Slotkin, there still remain a number of contributions to substantive detail. Howard has written on a Comanche spearpoint used in a Kiowa-Comanche ceremonial (1950). This was an item in the ritual paraphernalia of the road chief Levi Whitebear (a half-Negro, quarter-Kiowa, quarter-Comanche of Lincoln, Nebraska) to symbolize the old way of life in which hunting was important and as a token of thanksgiving. The spearpoint was placed, in order from the "moon," eagle wingbone whistle, spearpoint, staff. Howard regards this as "an intrusive element of recent origin" (1950: 5), but has since pointed out in correspondence that several other "fireplaces" use it, most of them apparently of Kiowa or Comanche origin, and that while he earlier believed it to be an otherwise functionless fetish, he has found it used in doctoring for bloodletting. Howard has also written about a Tonkawa peyote legend (1951); this is the standard and familiar stress-origin legend of peyote, except for the etiological rationalization of why the Tonkawa are called "cannibals" by other Indians. He has also described the "fireplace" of the Oto leader, Charles Whitehorn, since 1946 in the keeping of an Omaha, George Phillips; it is said to have been obtained by Whitehorn in a vision, but it is indistinguishable from the standard Kiowa-Comanche altar except for a heart under the fire and a transverse line from horn to horn of the "moon" (1956). Indeed, it is similar to an earlier Caddo-Delaware moon (La Barre 1938: 75, Fig. 4b)— a measure of the "originality" to be expected in peyote rites.

Probably the most significant recent contribution to our knowledge of early peyotism is that of Brant. In his study of peyotism among the Kiowa Apache (1950), he adds the valuable new historical detail that a Mescalero or Lipan Apache named Nayokogał brought peyotism to the Kiowa Apache about 1875. Since the Kiowa themselves obtained peyote about 1880, it may very well be that the Kiowa Apache were a link between the Kiowa and the other Apache tribes of Mexico and the Southwest. Brant's data are in any case entirely consistent with Morris Opler's southern Athapaskan ethnography and La Barre's southern Plains data on early peyotism. Brant adds another interesting detail that the Kiowa Apache ritual breakfast sometimes consists of pemmican and corn gruel. Since the original Mexican rite had boneless deer meat and parched corn in sugar-water— and some much later northern rites had canned corn beef and Cracker Jack—one can only remark that *plus ça change, plus c'est la même chose!*

The Cheyenne and Menomini, like the Winnebago, have long been known to celebrate a somewhat Christianized version of the old aboriginal rite. Spindler, in a preliminary paper on his Menomini studies (1951), adds the confirmatory details that the tepee poles represent Jesus and his disciples; the leader's staff is carved with crosses, and the leader makes the sign of the cross;

the ashes are shaped into the form of a "dove"; and there is a small pedestal on the moon for the "Master" Peyote—some of these apparently derivative from Christianity. "But," he adds, "the basic concepts and premises of the cult are native-oriented though modified and perverted to meet the unique needs of the participants." The same author states that the Menomini got peyote from the Potowatomi via J. M. Mitchell in 1914, and were influenced by the Winnebago, though they rejected some of John Rave's Christian elements; the purposes of 'meetings were "salvation" and prophetic visions, and one old woman kept a supply of peyote on hand to "get a vision for a design" for her beadwork when she tired of the old designs—which might be compared with the older Menomini pattern for song- and design-getting (Spindler 1950).

Other new data include those of Tax on Fox peyotism (1955). The volume *Iowa* (1949: 473–74), in the "State Guide Series" also indicates that the Sac and Fox of Iowa have obtained peyotism and now get their buttons direct from Texas. As reported in Canadian newspapers, peyote has now spread to the Saulteaux of Manitoba near Fort Qu'Apelle and Portage la Prairie; and, as reported in early December of 1956, peyote was spreading in northern Saskatchewan and Alberta as well.

Malouf indicates in his study of Gosiute peyotism (1942) some of the problems of establishing dates. La Barre had placed the origin in 1921 and Hayes in 1925 (Hayes 1940) when a Sioux, Sam Lone Bear, brought to the Gosiute the "Western Slope Way" (which eschewed tobacco), although the orthodox "Tipi Way" supplanted this in a short time. According to Hayes there were less than a dozen users before 1925; Malouf says his informants vaguely estimated that it got established sometime between 1925 and 1928. These data, not really inconsistent with one another, raise the question whether one should indicate the introduction or the *floruit* of the cult in stating origins. Indeed, Hayes mentions that Gray Horse, a Washo from Fallon, Nevada, and a great leader in the western Basin, had in 1940 used Peyote for twenty-five years, that is, since 1915. Malouf considers that Sam Lone Bear (or Roan Bear) may be the Ute Ralph Kochampaniskin or "Lone Bear" who had held Washo meetings as early as 1932. Since M. K. Opler ✩ agrees with Malouf's interpretation of the Ute origin of Sam Loan Bear, and since Aberle and Stewart (1957) have definitively discussed the question, the identification as "Sioux" by La Barre's informant must now be regarded as superseded. In any case, the Washo and the Gosiute have now an entirely standard Plains rite.

The Navaho have a long history of factionalism, in part arising over peyotism. Kirk reports that peyotism was strenuously resisted around 1932. The Charter of Incorporation in New Mexico of the Native American Church is dated July 15, 1945, with respect to Navaho peyotists. But in 1947 there were five or six thousand participants, that is, 35% of the population in the Shiprock region, which accounts for one-third of the area of the Navaho Reservation (Kirk 1947). Further discussion of the Navaho and peyote will be deferred until we deal below with the able monograph treatment of Aberle and Stewart on Ute-Navaho peyotism.

PROBLEMS OF DIFFUSION

Morris Opler has contributed a valuable description of a Tonkawa peyote meeting held in 1902 (1939a). Obtaining what are probably the last ethnographic materials available from this group, he states that the Tonkawa were taught peyotism by the Carrizo, and that a Chiricahua Apache visited the Tonkawa meeting of 1902. These data are consistent with those cited in Opler's standard and authoritative review of *The Peyote Cult* (1939b) that peyotism came to the Lipan and Tonkawa via the Tamaulipecan-Carrizo tribes; that the Mescalero received peyote before 1870; and that the Kiowa-Comanche got it between 1870 and 1880. Opler has also written on the use of Peyote by the Carrizo and the Lipan Apache. His description of a Carrizo peyote meeting, which included shamanistic tricks, indicates diffusion to the Tonkawa and Lipan Apache as well (1938). The material culture of Carrizo peyotism fits the later rite well, the shaman's bow pointing backward to the Mexican first-fruits hunting rite (as also does the Comanche spearpoint mentioned by Howard?) and forward to the leader's staff in the standard Plains rite. Opler mentions also that for these tribes the "male" peyote blossoms red and the "female" white, a belief that fits well transitionally between the notions of plant sexuality held in Mexico and the southern Plains belief that Peyote Woman can be heard singing when one has eaten a female peyote button.

Some special problems of diffusion are discussed in Merriam and D'Azevedo's study of Washo peyote songs (1957). In 1957 Washo peyotism was scarcely more than twenty years old, having been introduced by the Washo, Ben Lancaster, who had lived among the eastern and southern tribes. He began proselytizing in 1936, and by 1939 had obtained an enthusiastic group of Washo and Paiute adherents. But in 1940 his meeting was largely defunct; he built an octagonal church (of Osage origin?) and presided over the remnants. The reasons for the decline were partly the clash of conflicting ritual "ways" and partly the conflict of peyotist theology with the spirit-guidance concepts of the Washo; possibly, too, the rivalry between the old shamans and the new peyotists was involved.

The most thorough studies on the diffusion of peyotism in single tribes have been those of the Spindlers on Menomini, and of Aberle and Stewart on Navaho and Ute. In a paper on "Male and Female Adaptations in Culture Change," Louise and George Spindler (1958) introduced a new dimension into peyotist studies with their discussions of differential diffusion and acculturation, and then elaborated in their later studies.[3] Louise Spindler also discussed the problems of peyote and witchcraft in Menomini acculturation (1952), and at the same date George Spindler and Walter Goldschmidt (1952) published a preliminary programmatic discussion of the method Spindler was to use in his 1955 doctoral thesis. In this they discussed the problem of sociological and psychological variables among the Menomini and presented a graph on which the levels of socio-economic status of groups varied vertically and the degree of acculturation horizontally.

In *Sociocultural and Psychological Processes in Menomini Acculturation* (1955), George Spindler produced at the same time one of the ablest papers on acculturation and one of the most minutely researched documents on projective techniques in the culture-and-personality field. Spindler's problem was to study the differential acculturation of each of five discernible groups of individuals among the Menomini; his method was to make extensive Rorschach-test samples of individuals in each of these five groups. Members of the Menomini native-oriented Dream Dance group were the least acculturated and were roughly similar in personality structure to their Algonkian relatives, the Ojibwa. The Peyote Cultists, with an intermediate Kiowa-Comanche and Winnebago Christianized version of the cult, showed a systematic deviation from the other Menomini groups, based on their identification with the closely knit cult group of peyotists. The Transitionals, with both native and White culture experiences, the lower-class acculturated, and the middle-class acculturated were the other groups, the last being at the opposite extreme of a continuum from the Dream Dance group and showing basic personality reformulation. Spindler has shown precisely the context of the Menomini peyotists (p. 207):

> The systematic deviation in psychological processes demonstrated for the Peyote Cult consists of a relatively high degree of self-projective fantasy in a setting of anxiety, conflict, awareness, and introspection. This is accompanied by relative looseness of affect control and a possible decrement in reality control. This systematic deviation is represented statistically by consistent difference between the Peyotists as a group and all other Menomini categories, but the characteristics last named are shared with the transitionals.

The work of Aberle and Stewart on the diffusion of peyotism from the Ute to the Navaho is also admirable methodologically (1957). As early as 1954 Kluckhohn stated that, "Aberle and Moore in their studies of Navaho peyote use have also employed random sampling" (1954: 691). Kluckhohn and Leighton had noted in 1946 that, "The peyote and certain other religious cults flourish here" among the Navaho of Shiprock (1946: 125), long a center of anti-White feeling, and Thompson had included the Navaho in her discussion of the problems of acculturation in various tribes (1948). Aberle and Stewart attacked the problem systematically and statistically, giving careful attention to both geographic and psychological details. Despite continuous opposition from the Navaho tribal council, peyotism spread, in the authors' opinion, with respect to communications and geographic availability, although they regard the disgruntlement arising from the stock-reduction campaign as an important additional impetus to its spread. The present writer has reviewed this work elsewhere (1958) and will not deal with it further here; Morris Opler (1958) has also reviewed the work of Aberle and Stewart.

The same problem of differential diffusion has preoccupied other students, among them the distinguished sociologists Lasswell, Barber, and Shonle. Lasswell wrote on "Collective Autism as a Consequence of Cultural Contact: Notes on Religious Training and the Peyote Cult at Taos" (1935). In the opinion of the present writer, however, Lasswell attended too little to comparative ethnography and has perhaps been misled in his interpretations within this narrow framework of reference that he has chosen; but a historically longitudinal study of peyotism at Taos since colonial times is still worth doing. Barber points out the close temporal succession of Peyotism upon the Ghost Dance, and discusses John Wilson and the Kiowa shaman Baigya, both of whom bridged the two phenomena in time (1941). Barber concludes (pp. 674–75) that:

> The Ghost Dance and the Peyote cult, then, may in part be understood as alternative responses to a similar socio-cultural constellation. As such a response, the Peyote cult performs certain adaptive functions. On those whom it honors with leadership, it bestows prestige and status, serving as a path to social advancement. Public confession of sins in Peyote ceremonies is at once a mechanism for the dissolution of individual anxieties and a mode of social control. Like the old buffalo societies of the Teton Sioux, the cult can become a focus of tribal ceremonial and social activity. This interpretation, however, does not pretend to exhaust the possible understanding of the phenomena. It does not preclude the necessity for understanding the particular cultural patterns to which peyotism diffused and tracing their influence in the process of its assimilation. It does indicate the socio-cultural situation from which the Peyote cult was precipitated.

The usual psychological-ethnological explanation for the spread of peyote has been that of Shonle, who pointed out that peyote was diffusing in the same regions that had the old Plains vision quest (1925) and, indeed, the subsequent spread of peyotism has largely confirmed Miss Shonle's predictions. Barber writes (1941: 675) that:

> There may or may not be some relation between the importance of the vision in Plains culture and the Peyote cult. Shonle, for example, thinks there is. Petrullo [1934] criticizes the theory that Peyote is a substitute for the fasting and self-torture employed by the Plains Indians seeking a vision. I should say that the vision is an important element in the culture to which Peyote was assimilated, and, as such, exerted its influence, but that this cannot explain the particular occasion of the widespread diffusion of Peyote.

The present writer would point out in defense of Shonle that even among the Caddo-Delaware whom Petrullo studied, the peyote meeting was in the context of an ordeal or an endurance contest; that despite their closeness to the source of peyote, the Pueblos (with the exception of Taos, the most "Plains-like" of the Pueblos) have not accepted peyotism; that even at Taos peyotism has long had a difficult time; and, finally, that peyotism is still a very controversial subject among the Pueblo-influenced Navaho, despite the latter's common origin with the Apache, who were the major vehicle for the Mexico-Plains spread of the cult. It is probable that most contemporary students would agree with Shonle and Barber that prior culture did have some significance in the diffusion, both positively and negatively, rather than with Petrullo. Barber also asks the interesting question, "Do the leaders of the new cult come from among the old elite?" The answer would perhaps be negative for Taos and other fringe areas, but affirmative for the Plains, again indicating the significance of prior culture in the differential spread. Probably still

more work remains to be done on the problem of differential diffusion, with respect both to individuals and to tribes, and, since peyotism is a contemporary phenomenon, perhaps such studies might serve to clarify some general problems of diffusion.[4]

Dittman and Moore have studied disturbance in dreams as related to peyotism among the Navaho, believing that "a resort to peyotism might be connected with a breakdown of traditional methods of problem solving" (1957: 643) and concluding that peyotists have more "bad dreams" according to their indices than do the non-peyotists, and that the peyotists are disapproved by the majority of the people. Newcomb, writing on Cherokee-Delaware "Pan-Indianism," says (1955: 1044) that:

> As the old culture declined and Delaware society disintegrated the void was partly bridged with a *mélange* of traits which are Indian. The peyote cult was perhaps the first, and is still one of the strongest elements- furthering and cementing the bonds of Cherokee-Delaware Pan-Indianism.

Newcomb cites Devereux (1951) regarding Devereux's thesis that the common denominator of a real culture in various tribes constitutes a refractory remnant after tribal deculturation and, as such, aids the mutual reinforcement of Pan-Indianism in the separate tribes. The Pan-Indian character of peyotism has been stressed by both Slotkin and La Barre as well as other students of the cult, and would thoroughly support the position of Newcomb and Devereux. Jones's (1957) emphasis on the fact that among the Ute it was specifically the full-bloods identified with the old culture who were the peyotists, who were anti-White, and who resisted the agents' acculturative attempts, would also seem to support this contention.[5] In the Plains, however, peyotism is largely accommodative, in contrast to the Ghost Dance; and in some tribes, as in Menomini, the peyotists are at best a transitionally-acculturated group. Arth (1956) suggests an interesting refinement and thinks that the function of peyotism (and hence the differential facilitation of its spread) may be different for different age, sex, and other groups: the elderly may be concerned with health and peyote's curing function, the conservative may value its vision-producing power; the confused and half-acculturated older people may find in it a focus of resistance to the Whites; for some it may be social and recreational; and for others it may be connected with the breakdown of the Omaha male role. Newcomb (1956) has elsewhere written on the differential acculturation of the Delaware; Voget (1957) has criticized some of his conclusions in a review.

SCHOLARLY CONTROVERSIES OVER INTERPRETATIONS

The most vigorous controversialists among students of peyotism have been Stewart and Slotkin.[6] In an important tribal study of Ute peyotism, Stewart (1948) takes issue with the common belief that the peyote cult was basically aboriginal, with only secondary and adventitious accretions from Christianity. Stewart takes the view that Christian elements were early, integral, basic and essential, and diffused with the rite itself. It is possible that the specific tribe studied may give the field worker differing opinions on this matter (though it is a little surprising perhaps that the Ute are so notably Christian). The matter may be fairly viewed only by the interested student's first-hand examination of Stewart's work. But Marvin Opler (1940) has offered an equally vigorous rebuttal to Stewart's position in a paper on the character and history of the Southern Ute peyote rite. Stewart in turn replied with a communication on the Southern Ute peyote cult (1941), and Opler again with "Fact and Fancy in Ute Peyotism" (1942). Perhaps the final solution to the problem must be left to specialists on the Ute, although historical evidence from other tribes would appear to support Opler concerning the secondary nature of Christian influences on peyotism in general.

In his 1948 monograph (p. 3), Stewart gives the interesting item that:

Modern scientific interest in peyote was first aroused by Mrs. Anna B. Nickels, of Laredo, Texas, about 1880. From the Indians she learned of its supposedly marvelous therapeutic properties and sent samples to Parke, Davis and Co., drug manufacturers, and subsequently to scientists in Washington, D. C., Germany, France, and England for detailed and exhaustive study.

Slotkin (1955: 208, 222) disputes this and states that:

Modern pharmacological and psychological research on peyote was begun by Briggs (1887). . . . That Briggs was the pioneer is based upon the following evidence: (a) The files of Parke, Davis & Co. on the subject of peyote begin with a clipping of his 1887 article. (b) Lewin (1888) stated that the peyote he received from Parke, Davis & Co. was obtained from Mexico. Brigg's brother lived there, and it was from him that Briggs received his own supply. (c) Lewin used the unusual form "muscale button," as did Briggs. Mrs. Anna B. Nickels is usually credited with having brought peyote to the attention of Parke, Davis & Co. I reject this for the following reasons: (a) W. P. Cusick of that company informs me that "we are unable to locate any records . . . connected with Mrs. Nickels" (personal communication). (b) Mrs. Nickels lived in Laredo, Texas. (c) She used the common form "mescal button."

Apparently her spelling, residence, and the loss of records must deprive Mrs. Nickels of the distinction of first arousing scientific interest in peyote, despite her priority in time.

Another important tribal monograph on peyote by Stewart (1944) is his *Washo-Northern Paiute Peyotism*. Stewart considers peyotism here to be purely a healing cult and cautions against "the purely sociological explanation of acculturation." His major argument in this work is a rebuttal of the cultural thesis of diffusion (1944: 94, 98):

What is, then, the reason for diffusion? In the case of the Washo-Paiute, the individual, at times with economic motives, looms as a determining element. . . . In Ben [Lancaster], that is, the individual, rests the crucial factor in Washo-Paiute peyotism. . . . With faith shaken that cultural autopsy can adequately expose reasons for behavior and noting that in all groups there are remarkably distinct personal reactions toward introduced cults, proselytizers and their motives assume new significance. . . . Since those who decided in favor of peyote and believed it to be of great worth for curing, for salvation, and for better living had no cultural, social, or psychological status in common, but were definitely representative of all elements in the population,

it is evident that each reacted as an individual, for purely personal reasons.

Since Omer Stewart is in disagreement with earlier writers on peyote in a number of particulars, his work deserves extended discussion. Stewart says that "all Peyote rituals north of the Rio Grande . . . appear universally to include elements of Christian theology and ritual integrated with aboriginal elements" although "Radin, Opler, Petrullo, La Barre, and others consider Christian elements recent additions" whereas "evidence to the contrary is presented in my Ute Peyotism" (1944: 64). La Barre, however, in a review (1946: 633), countered:

What are these "Christian" elements anyway? *Prayers* to peyote, or via peyote to the Great Spirit? An earthen *altar?* Sage *incense?* An eagle wing-bone *whistle* (equated with the Catholic bell)? *Baptism* in the drum water? I cannot find a single demonstrably Christian element in Stewart's list of 265 traits, nor does he discuss any. Great Basin peyotism, which is recent, is not the best evidence to substantiate an argument for the near-aboriginality of Christian elements; Mexican or transitional Apache data would be more critical. Both Opler and Lumholtz are unimpressed by Christian elements in peyotism [and missionaries, from colonial times to the present, have uniformly combatted peyotism]. It is hard to see in them more than window-dressing for a proselytizing cult; considering some of the tribes' historical exposure to Christianity, it is surprising its influence is not greater.

Stewart (1944: 86) considers Shonle mistaken in her thesis that "the underlying belief in the supernatural origin of visions is important among the factors contributing to the diffusion of peyote and in a general way defines the area of its probable spread." By contrast, Stewart espouses the botanist Schultes' view that peyote's therapeutic power is more important and that "the peyote vision is incidental and of little significance" (Schultes 1938b in Stewart 1944: 86). But La Barre (1939) had already shown that Schultes was naïvely conceptualizing in terms of White ideology about "medicine" and that Schultes' unwitting dichotomy of "medicine power" into therapeutic pharmacodynamics and the supernatural vision created only a pseudo-problem. Plains "medicine power" is supernatural in origin (the vision), not pharmaceutical. If peyote did not cause visions, would new adherents to the cult be so ready to believe that it cures (has "medicine power")? *Of course* people take peyote partly to cure ills—*because* a vision-producing plant obviously has medicine power. La Barre further pointed out (1939: 634) that:

For the rest, the stubborn distributional fact remains that peyotism historically has spread much as Shonle's thesis would predict: we still await in vain reports of Pueblo peyotism, except in the case of the most Plains-like, Taos. La Barre is nevertheless in error (page 90ff.) in emphasizing the "cultural compatibility" explanation of peyotism's differential diffusion. No more applicable is Kroeber's "cultural disintegration theory," which says that peoples experiencing cultural disintegration and degradation will readily accept new religions, especially those which promise the miraculous restoration of former conditions of life" (page 90). Equally unacceptable, perhaps, would be a combination of these, to the effect that peyotism was successful as a "new" Indian religion precisely because it was already compatible with the threatened aboriginal beliefs in disintegrating cultures.

When prior culture is not significant, its current disintegrated status unimportant, and Christian influences (ancient or modern) undiscussed, one wonders why indeed this is called "a study in acculturation."

Stewart seems unjust, also, in accusing earlier students of peyotism of studiously ignoring the individual. Radin's *Crashing Thunder,* after all, was first published in 1920; and La Barre wrote in *The Peyote Cult* that, "A descriptive account of a ritual pattern, however meticulously detailed it be, must always fall short of reality unless supplemented by further information regarding its functioning in individuals" (1938: 93), when introducing a chapter on the "Psychological Aspects of Peyotism" which was surely not unfriendly to the study of individual motivations. The major motivation of the proselytizer Ben Lancaster, to take money, was certainly not going to be realized if a sufficient number of cult participants were not culture-psychologically willing to give the money. Furthermore, if Ben Lancaster had motivations, do not other persons also have them? Are there not common Washo or Ute cultural assumptions basic to these motives and to the cult itself? Is not belief in the peyote cure itself cultural? The unfortunate thing is that Stewart is right so far as he goes: the individual *is* important. That Ben Lancaster was an exploiter of peyotism economically, and John Wilson was too, is interesting and significant. But to leave it at that is to perpetuate the devil theory of history-by-plot. There are also Bert Crowlance and Mary Buffalo and Jack Bear Track to be considered as well, if we are to avoid a *Führerprinzip* theory of ethnological history. The franchise of being psychologically motivated must be extended equally to the new cult's opponents and adherents too, as well as to Ben Lancaster. On this larger scale, the past nature and the current acculturative state of the culture, and various individual relationships to both, may then not seem so unimportant. The "Great Man" theory is as inadequate to explain the history of peyotism as it is of any other history, when taken alone.

Of all the students of peyotism, Slotkin was the most industrious in rediscovering colonial documents, but his supposition that they all refer to peyote has sometimes been disputed. For example, in a 1951 paper, "Early Eighteenth Century Documents on Peyotism North of the Rio Grande," he said (p. 420) with respect to an obviously unidentified tribe he specified as Comanche,

One of these manuscripts, a report dated 1716, states that peyote was used by unspecified tribes in Texas. Another is the record of a trial held in Taos in 1720. During the proceedings it developed that an Isleta, who lived among the Hopi after the Pueblo Revolt, and now resided in Taos, had brought peyote with him from the Hopi.

This source, and this reasoning, however, are not sufficient to establish the existence of peyotism among the Comanche in 1760 nor, indeed, the cannibalism that is inferred from their *mitote*. On the contrary, if cannibalism on the part of the unspecified tribe is accepted from this tendentious colonial Spanish document, a far more plausible tribal identification would be the Tonkawa, who were known to have had peyote at an early date, and who were cannibals at least by repute.

Nor do we have any reason to infer the use of peyote at Isleta Pueblo at this or any other date, at least not on the basis of these documents. Beaver also scouts Slotkin's assertion that the Hopi ever had peyote (1952: 120):

The major idea of the article was to show the earliest mention of the use of peyote north of the Rio Grande, and to give evidence that an Isleta had brought the peyote to Taos from the Hopi. It would seem that both Slotkin and the Spanish could not distinguish peyote from jimson weed, or if it really was peyote that these Indians were using, they did not tell the truth as to its source. The Hopi were ignorant of the use of peyote and the older generations still are today.

Indeed, the phrases "the herb from Moqui" and "the herb from Aguatubi [Awatovi]" mentioned in the documents are inadequate to establish the plant involved as being specifically peyote.

Not one ethnologist working among the Hopi has ever mentioned the use of peyote among them. Another very important factor is that the cactus does not grow in the Hopi country, nor does it grow in the country of any tribe that surrounds the Hopi. The use of the jimson weed as a medicine and by the doctors as a means of diagnosing a sickness, however, has its distribution westward to California.

The early sporadic use of peyote at Taos is also open to further research and verification; but the present documents surely do not establish the use of *Lophophora williamsii* at these dates either among the Comanche, the Isleta, or the Hopi.

Slotkin continued his researches on early documents in his paper on "Peyotism, 1521–1891" (1955). This study contains a number of valuable new references to colonial documents, but Slotkin's use of them is again open to criticism. He states (p. 202) that:

In 1954 I had occasion to review the literature on the early history of peyotism, i.e., the use of peyote. The deeper I delved into the subject, the more unsatisfactory did the state of our knowledge appear. Consequently, it seemed useful to make a critical re-examination of the sources, so that future research might proceed on a sounder basis.

He begins his paper with a section on the "Identification of Peyote," quite as if La Barre (1938) had never devoted four appendices to the botanical identification of *Lophophora williamsii* or peyote, and the plants confused with them. Thereafter his use of documents at times only compounds confusion. For example, his inference that the Caddo (mapped as overlapping the Oklahoma-Arkansas-Louisiana-Texas border region) had peyote as early as 1709–16 is based on the bland formula that, "For purposes of this paper I attribute all 'Texas' material to the Caddo" (1955: 206). In his 1951 (p. 421) paper the unidentified tribe was Comanche! Both are wholly unwarranted, for Morris Opler's repeated studies on Texas peyotists in early times would surely have led one first to rule out such Texas tribes as the Tonkawa, Carrizo, and Lipan—and perhaps, because of the uncertain area of "Texas" in these documents, also the Coahuilteco, Jumano, and even the Tamaulipeco. Slotkin's list of the "Uses of Peyote" by various tribes is useful for its sources; but, again, this is not the first such study; and these sources should be used critically and with caution. Slotkin concludes (1955: 208 and 210):

The most significant result of this analysis is that the individual uses (to reduce fatigue and hunger, as a medicine, to induce "visions" for purposes of supernatural revelation, as an amulet, and as an intoxicant), and the collective use in tribal rites, all seem equally old and part of a single trait complex. Only the collective cult seems recent.

The present writer is at a loss to understand how, if the individual and collective uses in tribal rites are equally old, only the collective cult can then be recent. In the section on the "History of Peyotism," Slotkin cites peyotism for the Queres, Hopi, Isleta, Taos, Pima, Coahuilteco, and Caddo—quite as if Beaver and others had not brought some of these into grave question—and on this basis argues that "there seems to be no reason why peyotism in the north should not be as old as in the south—or at least pre-Conquest" (1955: 210). For the Coahuilteco, who live, in part, in regions where peyote grows, possibly; for the others, surely the Scottish verdict "not proven!" Perhaps it was another Texan tribe.

A minor disagreement arose over the botanist Schultes' paper on "The Appeal of Peyote (*Lophophora williamsii*) as a Medicine" (1938b). Schultes argued that the major reason for the spread of peyotism was its use as a "medicine" and not with reference to its vision-giving power. La Barre (1939) pointed out that Schultes' misunderstanding of the sources arose from his unawareness that "medicine" in reference to American Indians has by usage supernatural connotations, and that the *medicinal* virtues imputed to peyote were in fact based both on the visions it induces and on the "power" that the Indian thus infers is in it. The problem is purely a semantic one. Johnson (1940), incidentally, has criticized La Barre (1939) for awarding the credit for the rediscovery of *teonanacatl* to Dr. Richard E. Schultes, now Curator of the Oakes Ames Herbarium in the Harvard Botanical Museum. Johnson states that a linguist, Mr. R. J. Weitlaner of Mexico City, Johnson's father-in-law, found some mushrooms used by the Mazatec and, "recognizing the mushrooms as *teonanacatl*" of the Aztec, sent them to Dr. B. P. Reko, "who sent the specimens to botanists for identification" (1940: 549). Now, Mr. Weitlaner is certainly to be credited for his perspicacity in suspecting that the mushroom used in modern Mazatec witchcraft was probably the Aztec narcotic mushroom. But since Schultes was the first to identify the mushroom botanically as a *Basidiomycete* and to publish his results, the scientific credit would seem ultimately to be his. Perhaps this is another purely semantic problem. Can the matter be fairly stated thus: "Dr. Schultes was the first botanist to identify *teonanacatl* scientifically as a *Basidiomycete* and to publish his results"? As for Reko, he apparently misidentified *teonanacatl* with *ololiuhqui*, which is another plant, and did not himself establish the botanical identity of either.

Another point has arisen with respect to appropriate recommended usage in discussing drugs. Barber (1959) agrees with La Barre, Slotkin, and others, that peyote is not, technically, a "narcotic" since it is neither soporific nor addictive; but to remove it from the context of American Indian drug use, he thinks, is to lose the advantage of such ethnographic association. His point is well taken. Perhaps we might suggest the general term "psychotropic" for such specialized ethnographic use. In this connection it may be well to note the "mescalinismo" recently described for northern Peru by Gutérriez-Noriega (1950). The cortex of "Opuntia cylindrica 'San Pedro'" contains mescaline, for which reason the cactus has come to be used by medicine men; there is no public group ritual involved.

PEYOTE MUSIC AND ART

The major work on *Peyote Music* is by McAllester (1949). It is an excellent technical work and authoritative in its field. McAllester has also published on Menomini peyote music (1952). For technical reasons, music is an excellent way of tracing provenience and tribal influences. For example, "when peyote music [heard by McAllester in a ceremony near Window Rock] is sung by the Navaho it is rendered in the Ute musical style rather than the Navaho musical style" (Moore 1956: 220). The soundness of this method is demonstrated in the fact that the spread of peyotism from the Ute to the Navaho is thoroughly well documented for historic times by contemporary specialists on the Ute and Navaho, Stewart and Aberle, respectively. Kurath, in a review (1953: 113) of Concha Michel's *Cantos Indígenas de México* of 1951; has remarked that, "The most interesting are probably the Tarahumara sections, notably the *Canto del Peyote*, which the reviewer has found among the Navaho and the Cheyenne." Musicological evidence is thus an important adjunct to other ethnological and historical data in tracing the origins of peyotism; at the same time, the remarkable fact that the recognizably same song is found among the Tarahumara, Navaho, and Cheyenne is supported by the similar fact that in the peyote ritual meal, from ancient Mexico to modern Manitoba, the foods are always some form of boneless meat, fruit, and sweetened corn—a remarkable culture-continuity in both cases (see p. 49). Nettl (1958), in a valuable paper, has pointed out that McAllester's musicological evidence indicates the Peyote style came from the Apache to the Plains. The conclusions both of Nettl and of McAllester support the generally accepted theory of peyote's diffusion; but Nettl has also introduced an interesting principle of the differential survival of the specialized and the unspecialized that might well find application and testing in other fields of ethnography (1958: 523):

It [the Peyote style] retained a feature of Apache music, the use of restricted rhythmic values (only two note-lengths are usually found), but in the Plains it evidently acquired the cascadingly descending, terrace-shaped melodic contour. Possibly the forces described above operated here; the melodic contour of the Plains, a specialized and rather highly developed type, was strong enough to encroach on the Peyote style, but the more generalized rhythmic structure of the Plains was not strong enough to alter the specialized rhythmic organization derived from the Apache.

Nettl (1953) has also published some interesting observations on meaningless peyote song texts which probably have linguistic and diffusionist bearing. Rhodes (1958) has published on an individual peyote song, a kind of study that is rarely done.

Without doubt the most indefatigable collector of Indian songs was the late Frances Densmore. Some of her studies have relevance to peyotism. In 1938 she wrote a paper concerning the influence of hymns on the form of Indian songs. Paired phrases, characteristic of Protestant hymns, she found in thirteen (plus six in modified form) of twenty-two Wisconsin Winnebago songs that she transcribed; paired phrases were not characteristic of the 340 Chippewa songs that have been analyzed. Densmore believed that the difference is owing to the influence of the simple flowing melodies of the Catholic Church on the Chippewa, versus the Protestant missionary influence on the Winnebago. Densmore's musicological evidence is thus consistent with the belief of Mooney, Radin, and other ethnologists that the Winnebago cult represents a more Christianized form of the peyote religion. In another paper, Densmore (1941) demonstrated on musicological grounds the syncretism of Christianity with peyotism in the Winnebago Native American Church. The marked, but atypical, position of the Winnebago and the tribes influenced by them with regard to the Christian elements in their rite must now be accepted as established by her additional evidence; but Miss Densmore was surely mistaken in her historical perspective when she argued (1941: 80), on Winnebago grounds, that:

The peyote cult came to the Plains from other tribes and did not bring with it a ceremonial ritual. This was developed chiefly by adaptations of the customs of Christian worship.

This unfortunate error is another example of the danger of asserting propositions about peyotism at large on the basis of information from a single tribe.

The most recent work on peyote music is that by Merriam and D'Azevedo (1957) on Washo peyote songs. Some of their data on musical instruments, e.g., on the peyote rattle, are new; the description of vocal style is interesting; and their recording of songs and technical analysis of them are both competent and useful.

As is well known to ethnographers of the region, a number of American Indians in Oklahoma and the Southwest have in recent times become competent artists, quite commonly in *gouache* paintings (La Farge 1957). Some of those in Oklahoma, such as Ernest Spybuck, Stephen Mopope, and Monroe Huntinghorse (Tsa Toke), have been directly inspired in their paintings by peyotism. Recently a superb collection of Tsa Toke's paintings has been published by Denman (1957) in a limited edition by the Grabhorn Press. Monroe Huntinghorse (1904–37) was born near Saddle Mountain, Oklahoma, his grandmother being a captive White woman. He went to school at the College of Bacone at Muskogee. Huntinghorse's explanations of his pictures contain an explicit bird symbolism: the cormorant is the Water Bird of the morning ritual; the male and female yellowhammer or flicker is the Fire Bird; a parrot or a macaw, the Dawn Bird; the scissorstail or swallow, the peyote singers; while the eagle is representative of purity and love. Other information in this somewhat inaccessible and expensive ($32.00) book is worth recording here: Ida Lone Wolf, widow of the Kiowa warrior De Los Lone Wolf, said that sometimes in the old days, toward morning, if a man had great reverence, he

might dance in a peyote meeting. Is this a dim echo of dancing in the peyote rituals of early Texas and colonial Mexico?

White artists have also been inspired by peyote. In Gallery One in Soho, London, in the Autumn of 1957, twenty-two fine-nibbed pen drawings were shown by the French artist, Henri Michaux, portraying visions and made after taking mescaline (*Observer* 1957). In early 1953, a German photographer named Leif Geiges sent to America a number of *Surréaliste* composite photographs that simulate mescaline intoxication, six of which were published in an American weekly magazine (*Newsweek* 1953).

POPULAR ACCOUNTS OF PEYOTE AND PEYOTISM

Several recognized ethnographers have published popular accounts relating to peyote. One of the most charming of these is a recounting by Alice Marriott in the *New Yorker* (1954) of her peyote experiences on a field trip in South Dakota. Hoebel (1949) also wrote of "The Wonderful Herb" in a literary and humanities review, describing an Indian cult vision experience among the Cheyenne of Montana. Stewart's "Three Gods for Joe" (1956) is an amusing story of a Northern Paiute who is at once a *pohari* (shaman), a peyotist, and an Episcopalian. In the same periodical is a description of "The Peyote Way" by Slotkin (1956*b*). Howard wrote on peyote in the Pan-Indian culture of Oklahoma, in an article intended for the general reader (1955). Kamffer's article on *Plumed Arrows of the Huicholes of Western Mexico* (1957) is a pleasant well-illustrated piece, including data on Huichol peyotism. Bromberg's "Storm over Peyote" (1942) was based chiefly on La Barre, and was later summarized by Schultes (1937).

Among non-anthropologists who have recently written on peyote, the most prominent and publicized undoubtedly has been the British novelist and literary man, Mr. Aldous Huxley. In recent years Huxley has become a mystic and has read widely on oriental religions and on occidental psychic research. His book, *The Doors of Perception*, appeared in 1954 and reported his experiences with mescaline. Apart from its irritating habit of inaccuracy ("[mescaline] is less toxic than any other substance in the pharmacologist's repertory" and "Professor J. S. Slotkin, one of the very few white men ever to have participated in the rites of a Peyotist congregation"), the work is highly articulate in expressing Mr. Huxley's mystical views (p. 16):

The other world to which mescalin admitted me was not the world of visions; it existed out there, in what I could see with my eyes open. The great change was in the realm of objective fact. What had happened to my subjective universe was relatively unimportant.

These statements are not literary hyperbole for Huxley, for he believes that in mescaline intoxication he is discovering a larger *Istigkeit*. His book was somewhat variously reviewed, but provoked a symposium in the *Saturday Review* entitled "Mescalin—An Answer to Cigarettes?" by Huxley, Slotkin (who was dubious about peyote in this context), and a physician, Dr. W. C. Cut-

203

ting, who was guarded in his opinion. Huxley came to Durham, North Carolina, to visit his friend, Dr. J. B. Rhine, and on the evening of October 5, 1954, gave the opening address of the Duke University Lecture Series, on the subject of "Visionary Experience, Visionary Art, and the Other World." Mescaline, Huxley believes, opens the doors to another world in the "antipodes of the mind" that is as objective as an undiscovered Australia.

One of the most widely read accounts of peyote was the article "Button, Button . . ." that appeared in *Time* magazine (1951). It is also one of the most error-ridden (there is no "dismal hangover" from peyote, the ritual breakfast is not "to help straighten them out," peyote is not the "fruit" of the "mescal cactus," peyote is not "the mescal cactus," nor, incidentally, is mescal a cactus). The opinions in this article are as tendentious as its statements are erroneous. It is unfortunate that so many persons should obtain their notions about peyote from so irresponsible a source.

Journalistic surveys, often well-informed, of local or regional peyote rites have appeared increasingly in American and Canadian newspapers. One of the most workmanlike is "Indian Drums Beat Throughout Night: Peyote Users Faithful to Their Religion" (*Omaha Evening World-Herald* 1938), in which the reporter's integrity matches his knowledgeability. Aberle ✩ says that the *Phoenix Republican* has also maintained a high order of journalistic accuracy in articles on peyotism. By contrast, Olcott's brochure, *The Enchanted Hills* (1948), describes peyote so misleadingly ("shaped like a prickly pear," "this pear shaped bud . . . cut from the plant," etc.) that it is clear that she has never seen a peyote plant. Other popular accounts have been of similar level, though they appeared in widely disseminated media. A Sunday supplement article, "Sent to an Artificial Paradise by the Evil Cactus Root" (*American Weekly* 1941), was based on Petrullo's *The Diabolic Root*. Perhaps the nadir has been reached in DeJacques' piece on "America's Newest Dope Horror" (1955), in which one searches with difficulty for even one accurate statement.

FUTURE STUDIES

A FEW concluding remarks might be made concerning future studies in peyotism. Detailed tribal surveys, so well begun by Kroeber and so ably continued by Aberle and Stewart and by the Spindlers, still need to be made, in particular with respect to historical diffusion, merely blocked out in large by La Barre. Both the Navaho-Ute and the Menomini studies present valuable innovations in methodology with considerable applicability to other modern field problems, and remind us that a contemporary complex such as peyotism is highly available and useful for the testing of hypotheses concerning method, diffusion, psychological and cultural issues, and the like. Problems of Pan-Indianism and acculturation will certainly continue to have relevance to peyotism in the future. Detailed psychological studies of individual and tribal peyote "theology" and related ideologies (perhaps in conjunction with the Thematic Apperception Test and other projective techniques) can still uncover for us many matters of cultural importance. Musicologists, archaeologists, and linguists are greatly needed to help solve several knotty problems. For example, we still do not know, specifically, in what area the form of the ritual first took shape, and under the influence of what tribal cultural contexts, though most experts are now agreed that peyotism first arose in the general area of the botanical provenience of peyote. Questions of differential diffusion, in particular in the Southwest, remain to be studied, perhaps in terms of the formulations of Shonle and Benedict. A putative "Red Bean Cult" as a forerunner of peyotism, early suggested by La Barre and recently reintroduced by Howard, awaits future research and definition ethnographically and historically; however, a better substitute for the unfortunate term "mescalism" could probably be found, since "mescal" (once quite erroneously confused with a narcotic mushroom) now refers confusingly to a bean, a cactus, and a succulent xerophyte, as well as to distilled pulque. And, finally, pharmacological research, now abundant on mescaline, might well be continued on the eight other alkaloids present in panpeyotl.[7, 8]

Notes

1. This is true of both Protestant and Catholic missionaries, but Aberle✩ points out that, among the Navaho, Catholic missionaries have been "particularly lenient" toward the controversial peyotism of the Navaho.

2. DAVID F. ABERLE:✩ This source "has some very sage comments on the notion of 'model' psychoses, essentially taking the position that (a) the similarity of the conditions produced by mescaline, LSD [lysergic acid di-ethyl amide], etc., to the functional psychoses is doubtful, but (b) the gross changes of affect, sensorium, motor activity, and so on created by mescaline and other substances remain very important subjects for experimentation in understanding the functioning of the nervous system, psychological processes, etc. He [Wikler] also attempts a rather thorough coverage of this type of work."

3. LOUISE SPINDLER:✩ "It might be useful to offer a few additional notes on Menomini peyotism and raise some questions on the basis of them. These notes pertain to the role of women

members of the cult, which does not receive much explicit attention in the literature (but see L. Spindler 1956).

"(a) Relatively few female members attend meetings regularly and have vision experiences (three, in contrast to the 13 males). The Menomini peyote cult was originally for males only, and at present all important positions except one are held by males. Is it generally true that the cult is so male-dominated?

"(b) Many marginal female peyote-cult members use peyote in a very secular and rational manner—e.g., as medicine for earache, childbirth, etc.—with no reference to, or understanding of, its religious meaning. Others use peyote for inducing visions that furnish designs for beadwork or embroidery. These women lack identification with the cult as members, and have little involvement with the cult as a set of values and patterns for behavior. Do women peyotists elsewhere tend to be so practical and non-sacred in their point of view?

"(c) The female peyote-cult members comprise the only group, in the Menomini study, which is statistically differentiated from all other acculturative groups of women in specific Rorschach indices. Is there evidence that female peyotists elsewhere are psychologically distinct in any way from non-peyotists in the same tribal community?

"(d) The Menomini women peyotists show striking differences from the men. The men represent an introspective, almost schizoid personality type. On the other hand, the women are outward-oriented, and not very introspective. Furthermore, their Rorschach responses suggest that they have greater control over their emotions than do the peyote men, and that they are less tense. Are male and female peyotists psychologically different elsewhere?"

4. ÅKE HULTKRANTZ:✩ "It is surprising that Miss Shonle's viewpoint on the spread of peyotism, though shared by most anthropologists, has not given impetus to further investigations. I think

her theory is brilliant, and that the integration of the peyote cult with the Plains vision complex can be explained by three main conditions: (1) the old-fashioned visions—especially in correlation with dreams—could not be experienced in a society where religious doubts had resulted from the clash with White civilization, and where the natural environment, the setting for the vision quest, was encroached upon by the Whites (precisely this latter point was made by my Shoshoni informants!); (2) the peyote visions are stronger, more compelling, to the skepticist than are Plains visions (note, by the way, La Barre's quotation from Huxley, whose experiences vividly show that visions at peyote meetings are, or can be, truly hallucinatory, and are no pseudo-hallucinations like earlier visionary dreams); (3) peyote visions may be experienced by almost anybody, whereas in the old days a high percentage of Indians sought visions without success."

5. MARVIN K. OPLER:✩ "I agree with Jones's (1957) stress on cultural revivalistic elements of peyotism, which I also stressed in my Southern Ute study of 1940 and 1942. In the volume edited by Ralph Linton, *Acculturation in Seven American Indian Tribes* [New York: Appleton-Century-Crofts, 1940], I emphasized this aspect also in my chapter on the Southern Ute. This brings me to the commentaries on Omer Stewart's interpretation of the Christian elements in peyotism as being early, essential, and basic. There is a difference in the two cults on the two sides of the Southern Ute reservation, as I reported both in the *American Anthropologist* [1940a] and in the Linton volume in 1940 and 1942. I think it is clearly the case that Stewart has not only been, as La Barre points out, a chief controversialist representing a minority position, but that the position has added up to a curious kind of ethnocentrism in interpreting peyotism in a Christian fashion. Anthropologists are often alarmed when they find non-anthropologists guilty of this

practice. It is possible that as peyotism continues in the American scene under conditions of further acculturation it will become, as it appears to have in certain places, a more Christianized cult. But these are comments only upon the pace of acculturation. The early Southwestern and Basin instances seem to have been culturally revivalistic according to practically all other scholars. This is even the case where the cult was rather abortive, as in certain Ute settings. However, this does not preclude later studies discovering a stronger element from Christian settings. My own studies appeared before Stewart's and referred to field work primarily in 1936 and 1937. Any later studies, for instance today, might have to reckon with an increased pace of acculturation."

6. AKE HULTKRANTZ:☆ "The discussion surrounding peyote would probably have faded away were it not for the controversies engendered by Stewart and Slotkin. La Barre has ably characterized those controversies, and exhibited a no way unfair reaction to Slotkin's papers, which in a way usurp on his own contributions. Slotkin's monograph, being basically a manual for peyotists, is not entirely on the same level with La Barre's book; still, La Barre does not stress the somewhat dogmatic character of Slotkin's opus, but justly criticizes its shortcomings in the reconstruction of paths of diffusion, and praises it as a source of legal documents and of administrative reports on the Native American Church. Many of the controversies do seem referrable to the fact that, as La Barre points out, anthropologists have asserted general propositions on the basis of data from single tribes. Further, several earlier students of peyotism never witnessed a peyote meeting, partly because the more conservative tribes resisted their presence at meetings."

7. ÅKE HULTKRANTZ:☆ "Looking to the future, I think there are two important tasks for ethnologically trained students of peyotism. First, the relations between the Mescal Bean Cult and peyotism should be further investigated. Second, research should now concentrate on the character of the peyote belief-systems, which has been very much neglected by American anthropologists, and not only in this connection; see, for example, the (in themselves excellent) studies on the Plains Indian Sun Dance, wherein beliefs have, with few exceptions, been scarcely touched on. That religious beliefs play an active role in the diffusion of peyotism has been convincingly shown by Merriam and D'Azevedo in their paper on Washo peyote songs (1957). Perhaps I should add that my interest in the *Glaubensinhalt* of peyotism is an interest also in this phenomenon per se: after all, I am looking at peyotism with European eyes."

8. GEORGE SPINDLER:☆ "La Barre's paper stimulates me to raise some questions for future research.

"First, how deep are the psychological consequences of participation in the peyote cult? Among the Menomini, the peyote complex goes very deep in the emotional, cognitive, and perceptual structuring of individual members. In ritual and its symbolism, in the supporting ideology, in conversion experiences, in art work by peyotists, and in Rorschach-test responses, there is impressive continuity and consistency. To the extent that such consistency is characteristic of other peyote groups, future research cannot ignore the psychological, as well as the social and cultural, significance of peyotism.

"Second, how widespread are the elements of peyote, or of any, ideology? Can peyotism diffuse, and be accepted, without supportive ideology? How much is the ideology reworked to fit a tribal culture, and the unique demands of each contemporary tribal community? Is the ideology reworked without major changes in ritual symbolism? The literature contains some suggestive materials relevant to these questions, but we need much more, done more systematically.

"The third problem has to do with particular combinations of events and forces operating to hinder or enhance acceptance and growth of peyotism in specific cases. La Barre mentions several of the explanations so far advanced for the diffusion of peyote, but some are essentially uni-causal in type, and others take only limited account of what seem to be essential factors. In the Menomini situation, uni-causal explanations are totally inadequate, since Menomini peyotism started with an historical accident, got under way because a few individuals were in a ready state, and finally became firmly established not from any single cause but from a combination of factors. One of these factors, for example, was a contemporary change in traditional culture which relates closely to psychology: persons possessing powers to combat witchcraft were dying out, such that other persons who were in fear of sorcery turned instead to the peyote cult for protection.

"In short, future research on peyotism must operate in several dimensions —the historical, cultural, ideological, psychological, and social—if it, or any so-called 'nativistic movement,' is to be understood."

Bibliography

This Bibliography aims at comprehensiveness only with respect to significant ethnological articles appearing since 1938, but is not exhaustive of medical articles, colonial documents published since that time, etc., since bibliographies on these are easily accessible in Abramson (1956), Cholden (1956), Kline (1956), and Slotkin (1955, 1956a).

ABERLE, DAVID F., and OMER C. STEWART. 1957. *Navaho and Ute peyotism: A chronological and distributional study.* University of Colorado Studies, Series in Anthropology, No. 6. 129 pp.

ABRAMSON, H. A. (Ed.) 1956. *Neuropharmacology.* New York: Josiah Macy Foundation.

AGUIRRE BELTRÁN, GONZALO. 1952. La magia del peyotl. *Universidad de Mexico, Organo Oficial de la Universidad Nacional Autonoma de Mexico* 6, No. 68:2–4.

American Weekly. 1941. Sent to an artificial paradise by the evil cactus root.

ANONYMOUS. 1959. For those interested in peyotl. *Intercambio: Organo de la British Chamber of Commerce* 188:45–51. Mexico, D.F.

ARTH, MALCOLM J. 1956. A functional view of peyotism in Omaha culture. *The Plains Anthropologist* 7:25–29.

ASSOCIATED PRESS. 1948. Press release on American Medical Association committee report to U. S. Secretary of the Interior Krug, Nov. 25.

BARBER, BERNARD. 1941. A socio-cultural interpretation of the peyote cult. *American Anthropologist* 43:673–75.

BARBER, CARROLL C. 1959. Peyote and the definition of narcotic. *American Anthropologist* 61:641–46.

BEAVER, WILLIAM T. 1952. Peyote and the Hopi. *American Anthropologist* 54:120.

BIRD, PAUL. 1957. Review of: *Mushrooms, Russia and history,* by V. P. and R. G. WASSON (New York: Pantheon, 1957). *New York Times Book Review* (July 14), p. 30.

BRAASCH, W. F., B. J. BRANTON, and A. J. CHESLEY. 1949. Survey of medical care among the upper midwest Indians. *Journal of the American Medical Association* (Jan. 22) 139:220–25.

BRANT, CHARLES S. 1950. Peyotism among the Kiowa-Apache and neighboring tribes. *Southwestern Journal of Anthropology* 6:212–22.

BROMBERG, WALTER. 1942. Storm over peyote. *Nature Magazine* 35:410–12.

CAMPBELL, T. N. 1958. Origin of the mescal bean cult. *American Anthropologist* 60:156–60.

CANADIAN PRESS ASSOCIATION. 1956. Indians using drug peyote. Press release, Dec.

CARLSON, G. G., and V. H. JONES. 1939. Some notes on uses of plants by the Comanche Indians. *Papers of the Michigan Academy of Science, Arts, and Letters* 25:517–42.

CHOLDEN, LOUIS (Ed.) 1956. *Proceedings of the round table on lysergic acid diethylamide and mescaline in experimental psychiatry, held at the annual meetings of the American Psychiatric Association, Atlantic City, New Jersey, May 12, 1955.* New York: Grune & Stratton.

CLAUDE, H., and H. EY. 1934. La mescaline, substance hallucinogène. *Comptes-Rendus de la Société de Biologie* 115:838.

DANGBERG, GRACE M. 1957. Letters to Jack Wilson, the Paiute prophet, written between 1908 and 1911. *Bulletin, Bureau of American Ethnology*, Nos. 49–56.

DEJACQUES, WILLIS. 1955. America's newest dope horror. *Man to Man, the Stag Magazine*, July, pp. 8–9, 62–63.

DENBER, HERMAN C. B. 1955. Studies on mescaline III action in epileptics: Clinical observations and effects on brain wave patterns. *Psychiatric Quarterly* 29:433–38.

DENBER, HERMAN C. B., and SIDNEY MERLIS. 1954. A note on some therapeutic implications of the mescaline-induced state. *Psychiatric Quarterly* 28:635–40.

———. 1956a. Studies on mescaline I: Action in schizophrenic patients before and after electroconvulsive treatment. *Psychiatric Quarterly* 29:421–29.

———. 1956b. "Studies on mescaline IV: Antagonism between mescaline and chlorpromazine," in *Psychopharmacology* (ed. NATHAN S. KLINE). American Association for the Advancement of Science, Publ. No. 42. Washington, D.C.

DENMAN, LESLIE VAN NESS (Ed.) 1957. *The peyote ritual.* San Francisco: Grabhorn Press.

DENSMORE, FRANCES. 1938. The influence of hymns on the form of Indian songs. *American Anthropologist* 40:175–77.

———. 1941. Native songs of two hybrid ceremonies among the American Indians. *American Anthropologist* 43:77–82.

DEVEREUX, GEORGE. 1951. *Reality and dream, the psychotherapy of a Plains Indian.* New York: International Universities Press.

DITTMANN, ALLEN T., and HARVEY C. MOORE. 1957. Disturbance in dreams as related to peyotism among the Navaho. *American Anthropologist* 59:642–49.

Documents on Peyote. 1937. Statements by F. Boas, A. L. Kroeber, A. Hrdlička, J. P. and M. R. Harrington, W. La Barre, V. Petrullo, R. E. Schultes, Elna Smith, and Chief Fred Lookout (Osage) against U. S. Senate Bill 1399 (Feb. 8), Seventy-fifth Congress, first session. Mimeographed, 137817. Washington, D.C.: Government Printing Office.

DOUGLAS, F. H., and R. D'HARNONCOURT. 1941. *Indian art of the United States.* New York: Museum of Modern Art.

FABING, HOWARD D. 1957. Toads, mushrooms, and schizophrenia. *Harper's Magazine* 214, No. 1284:50–55.

FREEDMAN, D. X., G. K. AGHAJANIAN, E. M. ORNITZ, and B. S. ROSNER. 1958. Patterns of tolerance to lysergic acid diethylamide and mescaline in rats. *Science* (May 16) 127:1173–74.

GARATTINI, S., and V. GHETTI (Eds.) 1957. *Psychotropic drugs. Proceedings of the International Symposium on Psychotropic Drugs (Milan, May 9–11, 1957).* Amsterdam, London, New York, Princeton: Elsevier.

GRAVES, ROBERT. 1957. Review of: *Mushrooms, Russia and history*, by V. P. and R. G. WASSON (New York: Pantheon, 1957). *Saturday Review* (May 11) 39:21–22, 47.

GUSINDE, MARTIN. 1939. "Der Peyote-Kult, Entstehung und Verbreitung," in *Festschrift zum 50 jahrigen Bestandsjubilaum des Missionshauses St. Gabriel Wien-Mödling* (No. 8, St. Gabriel Studien), pp. 401–99.

GUTERRIEZ-NORIEGA, CARLOS. 1950. Área de Mescalinismo en el Perú. *America Indigena* 10:215–20.

GUTTMANN, ERICH. 1936. Artificial psychoses produced by mescaline. *Journal of Mental Science* 82:1–19.

GUTTMANN, ERICH, and W. S. MACLAY. 1936. Mescalin and depersonalization, therapeutic experiments. *Journal of Neurology and Psychopathology* 16:193–212.

HALLOWELL, A. IRVING. 1940. Review of: *The peyote cult*, by WESTON LA BARRE (Yale University Publications in Anthropology No. 19 [1938]). *Psychiatry* 3:150–51.

HAYES, ALDEN. 1940. Peyote cult on the Goshiute reservation at Deep Creek, Utah. *New Mexico Anthropologist* 4:34–36.

HIJAR Y HARO, LUIS. 1937. Viajes por America, 3 parte, El peyote al traves de los siglos. *Revista Mexicana de Ingeneria y Arquitectura* 15:543–63, 665–92. ("3 parte, El peyote al traves de los siglos" republished in *Viajes por America* [Mexico, D.F., 1940], by LUIS HIJAR Y HARO, pp. 60–108.)

HIMWICH, H. E. 1958. Psychopharmacologic drugs. *Science* 127:59–72.

HOCH, P. H. 1952. "Experimental induction of psychoses," in *The Biology of Mental Health and Disease* (ed. S. COBB), pp. 539–47. New York: Hoeber.

HOEBEL, E. ADAMSON. 1949. The wonderful herb, an Indian cult vision experience. *Western Humanities Review* 3:126–30.

HOWARD, JAMES H. 1950. A Comanche spear point used in a Kiowa-Comanche peyote ceremonial. *Museum News, University of South Dakota* 7:3–6. Mimeographed.

———. 1951. A Tonkawa peyote legend. *Museum News, University of South Dakota* 12:1–4. Mimeographed.

———. 1955. Pan-Indian culture of Oklahoma. *Scientific Monthly* 81:215–20.

———. 1956. An Omaha-Oto peyote ritual. *Southwestern Journal of Anthropology* 12:432–36.

———. 1957. The mescal bean cult of the central and southern Plains: An ancestor of the peyote cult? *American Anthropologist* 59:75–87.

HUXLEY, ALDOUS. 1954. *The doors of perception.* New York: Harpers.

Iowa. 1949. *Iowa.* ("State Guide Series.") New York: Hastings House.

JACOBSON, O. B., and J. D'UCEL. 1950. *Les peintres indiens d'Amérique.* Nice: Szwedzicki.

JOHNSON, J. B. 1940. Note on the discovery of teonanacatl. *American Anthropologist* 42:549–50.

JONES, J. A. 1957. The sun dance of the northern Ute. *Anthropological Papers, Bulletin of the Bureau of American Ethnology,* 47:203–63.

KAMFFER, RAÚL. 1957. Plumed arrows of the Huicholes of western Mexico. *The Americas,* June, pp. 12–16.

KANT, F. 1931. Uber Reaktionsformen im Giftrausch. *Archive für Psychiatrie* 91:694.

KIRK, RUTH F. 1947. Aspects of peyotism among the Navaho. Paper read at the 46th Annual Meeting of the American Anthropological Association, Albuquerque, Dec. 29.

KLINE, NATHAN S. (Ed.) 1956. *Psychopharmacology.* American Association for the Advancement of Science, Publ. No. 42. Washington, D.C.

KLUCKHOHN, CLYDE. 1954. Southwestern studies of culture and personality. *American Anthropologist* 56:685–97.

KLUCKHOHN, CLYDE, and DOROTHEA LEIGHTON. 1946. *The Navaho.* Cambridge, Mass.: Harvard University Press.

KROEBER, ALFRED L. 1907. *The Arapaho.* American Museum of Natural History Bulletin 18. New York.

KURATH, GERTRUDE. 1953. Review of: *Cantos indigenas de Mexico,* by CONCHA MICHEL (Mexico, D.F.: 1951). *American Anthropologist* 55:113.

LA BARRE, WESTON. 1938. *The peyote cult.* Yale University Publications in Anthropology No. 19. New Haven, Conn. (Reprint ed.; Hamden, Conn.: The Shoestring Press, 1960.)

———. 1939. Note on Richard Schultes' "The Appeal of Peyote." *American Anthropologist* 41:340–42.

———. 1946. Review of: Washo-Northern Paiute peyotism: A study in acculturation, by OMER C. STEWART (*University of California Publications in American Archaeology and Ethnology* [1944] 40:63–142). *American Anthropologist* 48:633–35.

———. 1947. Primitive psychotherapy in native American cultures: Peyotism and confession. *Journal of Abnormal and Social Psychology* 24:294–309.

———. 1957a. Mescalism and peyotism. *American Anthropologist* 59:708–11.

———. 1957b. Review of: *The peyote religion,* by JAMES S. SLOTKIN (Glencoe, Ill.: Free Press, 1956). *American Anthropologist* 59:359–60.

———. 1958. Review of: *Navaho and Ute peyotism: A chronological and distributional study,* by DAVID F. ABERLE and OMER C. STEWART (University of Colorado Studies, Series in Anthropology, No. 6 [1957]). *American Anthropologist* 60:171.

LA BARRE, WESTON, DAVID P. McALLESTER, JAMES S. SLOTKIN, OMER C. STEWART, and SOL TAX. 1951. Statement on peyote. *Science* 114:582–83.

LA FARGE, OLIVER. 1957. Review of: *The peyote ritual,* by LESLIE VAN NESS DENMAN (San Francisco: Grabhorn Press, 1957). *The New York Times Book Review,* Nov. 17, p. 30.

LASSWELL, H. D. 1935. Collective autism as a consequence of cultural contact: Notes on religious training and the peyote cult at Taos. *Zeitschrift für Sozialforschung* 4:232–47. Paris.

LEIGHTON, DOROTHEA, and CLYDE KLUCKHOHN. 1947. *Children of the people.* Cambridge, Mass.: Harvard University Press.

LEONARD, IRVING A. 1942. Peyote and the Mexican inquisition. *American Anthropologist* 44:324–26.

Life. 1959. Article on Wasson, illustrated, May 13.

LINDEMANN, E., and W. MALAMUD. 1933. Experimental analysis of the psychopathological effects of intoxicating drugs. *American Journal of Psychiatry* 13:853–81.

MALOUF, CARLING. 1942. Gosiute peyotism. *American Anthropologist* 44:93–103.

MARRIOTT, ALICE. 1954. The opened door. *New Yorker,* Sept. 25, pp. 80–82, 85–89.

McALLESTER, DAVID P. 1949. *Peyote music.* Viking Fund Publications in Anthropology No. 13.

———. 1952. "Menomini peyote music," in *Menomini Peyotism,* by J. S. SLOTKIN (Transactions of the American Philosophical Society 43, Pt. 4), pp. 681–700.

MERLIS, S., and W. HUNTER. 1954. Studies on mescaline II: Effects of administration after electric convulsive treatment of schizophrenic patients. *Psychiatric Quarterly* 29:430–32.

MERRIAM, ALAN P., and WARREN L. D'AZEVEDO. 1957. Washo peyote songs. *American Anthropologist* 59:615–41.

MOONEY, JAMES. 1896. The mescal plant and ceremony. *Therapeutic Gazette* 12:7–11.

MOORE, HARVEY C. 1956. Review of: *Enemy way music: A study of social and esthetic values as seen in Navaho music,* by DAVID

P. McAllester (Reports of the Rimrock Project, Values Series No. 3, Papers of the Peabody Museum of American Archaeology and Ethnology [1954]). *American Anthropologist* 58:220.

Nettl, Bruno. 1953. Observations on meaningless peyote song texts. *Journal of American Folklore* 66:161–64.

———. 1958. Historical aspects of ethnomusicology. *American Anthropologist* 60:518–32.

Newcomb, William W., Jr. 1955. A note on Cherokee-Delaware pan-Indianism. *American Anthropologist* 57:1041–45.

———. 1956. The culture and acculturation of the Delaware Indians. *Anthropological Papers, Museum of Anthropology, University of Michigan*, 10:113–22.

Newsweek. 1953. Mescal madness. Illustrated. Feb. 23, pp. 92, 93–94.

New York Times. 1954. Narcotics in rites stir Navajo issue. July 6.

Niedhammer, Matthew (O.F.M. Cap.) n.d. Statement on peyote (prepared for his ecclesiastical superiors at Saint Labre Indian Mission to the Cheyenne of Tongue River Reservation). MS., pre-1941. 164 pp.

Observer [London]. 1957. Article on Michaux pen drawings. Oct. 20.

Olcott, Deana. 1948. *The enchanted hills.* Pawhuska: The author.

Omaha Evening World-Herald. 1938. Indian drums beat throughout night: Peyote users faithful to their religion. Dec. 5.

Opler, Marvin K. 1940a. The character and history of the southern Ute peyote rite. *American Anthropologist* 57:463–78.

———. 1940b. Review of: *Der Peyote Kult,* by Martin Gusinde (Wien-Mödling: Missionsdruckerei St. Gabriel, 1939). *American Anthropologist* 42:667–69.

———. 1942. Fact and fancy in Ute peyotism. *American Anthropologist* 44:151–59.

Opler, Morris E. 1938. The use of peyote by the Carrizo and Lipan Apache tribes. *American Anthropologist* 40:271–85.

———. 1939a. A description of a Tonkawa peyote meeting held in 1902. *American Anthropologist* 41:433–39.

———. 1939b. Review of: *The peyote cult,* by Weston La Barre (Yale University Publications in Anthropology No. 19 [1938]). *American Anthropologist* 41:478–79.

———. 1958. Review of: *Navaho and Ute peyotism,* by David Aberle and Omer C. Stewart (University of Colorado Studies, Series in Anthropology, No. 6 [1957]). *Ethnohistory* 5:180–82.

Petrullo, Vincenzo. 1934. *The diabolic root: A study of peyotism, the new Indian religion, among the Delawares.* Philadelphia: University of Pennsylvania Press.

Radin, Paul. 1926. *Crashing Thunder.* New York: Appleton. (First published in 1920 as *Crashing Thunder: The autobiography of a Winnebago Indian* [University of California Publications in American Archaeology and Ethnology 16, No. 7].)

Regina Leader-Post [Saskatchewan]. 1954. Psychiatric research utilizes Indian drug. Dec. 6, p. 1.

Reh, Emma, and D'Arcy McNickle. 1943. Peyote and the Indian. *Scientific Monthly* 57:220–29.

Rhodes, Willard. 1958. A study of musical diffusion based on the wandering of the opening peyote song. *Journal of the International Folk Music Council* 10:42–49.

Ropp, Robert S. de. 1957. "The mind and mescaline," Chap. 2 in *Drugs and the Mind,* pp. 27–60. New York: St. Martin's Press.

Schultes, Richard E. 1937. Peyote cult from *Nature Magazine. Literary Digest* (Nov. 13) 124:24ff.

———. 1938a. Peyote: An American Indian heritage from Mexico. *El Mexico Antiguo* 4:199–208.

———. 1938b. The appeal of peyote (*Lophophora williamsii*) as a medicine. *American Anthropologist* 40:698–715.

———. 1939. The identification of Teonanacatl, a narcotic Basidiomycete of the Aztecs. *Plantae Mexicanae II.* [Harvard] Botanical Museum Leaflets 7, No. 3:37–54.

———. 1940a. The aboriginal therapeutic uses of *Lophophora williamsii. Cactus Succulent* [Society of America] *Journal* 12:177–81.

———. 1940b. Teonanacatl: The narcotic mushroom of the Aztecs. *American Anthropologist* 42:429–43.

Scully, Bede (O.F.M. Cap.) 1941. The Cheyenne and peyote. *Mission Almanac* [of the Seraphic Mass Association], May, pp. 6–14. Ashland, Montana: St. Labre Mission.

Shonle, Ruth. 1925. Peyote, the giver of visions. *American Anthropologist* 27:53–75.

Siskin, Edgar E. 1941. The impact of the peyote cult upon shamanism among the Washo Indians. Unpublished Ph.D. dissertation, Yale University (Department of Anthropology), New Haven.

Slotkin, James S. 1951. Early eighteenth century documents on peyotism north of the Rio Grande. *American Anthropologist* 53:420–27.

———. 1952. *Menomini peyotism, a study of individual variation in a primary group with a homogeneous culture.* Transactions of the American Philosophical Association 42, No. 4.

——. 1954. Mescalin: A substitute for tobacco? III The anthropologist. *Saturday Review* (Feb. 6) 37:14.

——. 1955. Peyotism, 1521–1891. *American Anthropologist* 57:202–30.

——. 1956a. *The peyote religion*. Glencoe, Ill.: Free Press.

——. 1956b. The peyote way. *Tomorrow, Quarterly Review of Psychical Research* 4:64–70.

SLOTTA, K. H., and G. SZYSZKA. 1933. Neue Darstellung von Meskalin. *Jahrbuch für praktische Chemie* 137:339.

SPINDLER, GEORGE. 1951. Psychological aspects of Menomini peyotism. Paper read at the Annual Meeting of Western States Branch, American Anthropological Association, Eugene, Ore., Dec. 28.

——. 1952. Personality and peyotism in Menomini Indian acculturation. *Psychiatry* 15:151–59.

——. 1955. *Sociocultural and psychological processes in Menomini acculturation*. University of California Publications in Culture and Society 5.

——. 1956. Personal documents in Menomini peyotism. *Primary Records in Culture and Personality* (ed. BERT KAPLAN), Vol. 2. Lawrence, Kansas: Microcard Foundation Publications.

SPINDLER, GEORGE, and WALTER GOLDSCHMIDT. 1952. Experimental design in the study of culture change. *Southwestern Journal of Anthropology* 8:68–83.

SPINDLER, LOUISE. 1952. Witchcraft in Menomini acculturation. *American Anthropologist* 54:593–602.

——. 1956. Women and culture change: A case study of the Menomini women. Unpublished Ph.D. dissertation, Stanford University.

SPINDLER, LOUISE, and GEORGE SPINDLER. 1958. Male and female adaptations in culture change. *American Anthropologist* 60:217–33.

STEWART, OMER C. 1939. Washo-Northern Paiute peyotism: A study in acculturation. *Proceedings of the 6th Pacific Science Congress* 4:65–68.

——. 1941. The Southern Ute peyote cult. *American Anthropologist* 43:303–308.

——. 1944. *Washo-Northern Paiute peyotism: A study in acculturation*. University of California Publications in American Archaeology and Ethnology 40, No. 3:63–141.

——. 1948. Ute peyotism. *University of Colorado Studies, Series in Anthropology* 1:1–42.

——. 1953. Review of: *Menomini peyotism*, by J. S. Slotkin (Philadelphia: American Philosophical Association, 1952). *American Anthropologist* 55:586–87.

——. 1956a. Peyote and Colorado's Inquisition law. *Colorado Quarterly* 5:79–90.

——. 1956b. Three gods for Joe. *Tomorrow, Quarterly Review of Psychical Research* 4:71–76.

TAX, SOL. 1955. "The social organization of the Fox Indians," in *Social Anthropology of North American Tribes* (ed. FRED EGGAN), pp. 243–82. Chicago: University of Chicago Press.

THOMPSON, LAURA. 1948. Attitudes and acculturation. *American Anthropologist* 50:200–15.

Time. 1951. Button, Button. . . . June 18, Vol. 57, pp. 82–83.

——. 1954. Untitled item on Aldous Huxley in section on "Religion." Sept. 27, Vol. 64, p. 84.

UNDERHILL, RUTH M. 1952. Peyote. *Proceedings of the XXXth International Congress of Americanists*, London, 1952, pp. 143–48. (Same as *San Vincente Foundation Publ. No. 2*, pp. 1–14 [n.d., mimeographed].)

——. 1954. Intercultural relations in the greater Southwest. *American Anthropologist* 56:645–62.

VOGET, FRED W. 1956. The American Indian in transition. *American Anthropologist* 58:249–63.

——. 1957. Review of: *The Culture and Acculturation of the Delaware Indians*, by William W. Newcomb, Jr. (Papers, Museum of Anthropology, University of Michigan, 10 [1956]). *American Anthropologist* 59:360–61.

WALLACE, ANTHONY F. C. 1959. Cultural determinants of response to hallucinatory experience. *A.M.A. Archives of General Psychiatry* 1:58–69.

WASSON, R. GORDON. 1956. "Lightning-bolt and mushrooms: An essay in early cultural exploration," in *For Roman Jacobson* (ed. MORRIS HALLE), pp. 605–12. The Hague: Mouton.

WASSON, VALENTINA P., and R. GORDON WASSON. 1957. *Mushrooms, Russia, and history*. New York: Pantheon.

WERTHAM, FREDERICK. 1952a. A study of pain. *Atlantic Monthly* (March) 189:52–55.

——. 1952b. "A psychosomatic study of myself," in *When Doctors Are Patients* (ed. MAX PINNER and BENJAMIN F. MILLER), pp. 102–18. New York: Norton.

WIKLER, ABRAHAM. 1957. *The relation of psychiatry to pharmacology*. Baltimore: Williams and Wilkins.

WILSON, A. J. C. 1949. Ayahuasca, Peyotl, Yagé. *Proceedings of the Society for Psychical Research* 48:353–63.

ZAEHNER, R. C. 1957. *Mysticism, sacred and profane*. New York: Oxford University Press.

P. McAllester (Reports of the Rimrock Project, Values Series No. 3, Papers of the Peabody Museum of American Archaeology and Ethnology [1954]). *American Anthropologist* 58:220.

Nettl, Bruno. 1953. Observations on meaningless peyote song texts. *Journal of American Folklore* 66:161–64.

———. 1958. Historical aspects of ethnomusicology. *American Anthropologist* 60:518–32.

Newcomb, William W., Jr. 1955. A note on Cherokee-Delaware pan-Indianism. *American Anthropologist* 57:1041–45.

———. 1956. The culture and acculturation of the Delaware Indians. *Anthropological Papers, Museum of Anthropology, University of Michigan,* 10:113–22.

Newsweek. 1953. Mescal madness. Illustrated. Feb. 23, pp. 92, 93–94.

New York Times. 1954. Narcotics in rites stir Navajo issue. July 6.

Niedhammer, Matthew (O.F.M. Cap.) n.d. Statement on peyote (prepared for his ecclesiastical superiors at Saint Labre Indian Mission to the Cheyenne of Tongue River Reservation). MS., pre-1941. 164 pp.

Observer [London]. 1957. Article on Michaux pen drawings. Oct. 20.

Olcott, Deana. 1948. *The enchanted hills.* Pawhuska: The author.

Omaha Evening World-Herald. 1938. Indian drums beat throughout night: Peyote users faithful to their religion. Dec. 5.

Opler, Marvin K. 1940a. The character and history of the southern Ute peyote rite. *American Anthropologist* 57:463–78.

———. 1940b. Review of: *Der Peyote Kult,* by Martin Gusinde (Wien-Mödling: Missionsdruckerei St. Gabriel, 1939). *American Anthropologist* 42:667–69.

———. 1942. Fact and fancy in Ute peyotism. *American Anthropologist* 44:151–59.

Opler, Morris E. 1938. The use of peyote by the Carrizo and Lipan Apache tribes. *American Anthropologist* 40:271–85.

———. 1939a. A description of a Tonkawa peyote meeting held in 1902. *American Anthropologist* 41:433–39.

———. 1939b. Review of: *The peyote cult,* by Weston La Barre (Yale University Publications in Anthropology No. 19 [1938]). *American Anthropologist* 41:478–79.

———. 1958. Review of: *Navaho and Ute peyotism,* by David Aberle and Omer C. Stewart (University of Colorado Studies, Series in Anthropology, No. 6 [1957]). *Ethnohistory* 5:180–82.

Petrullo, Vincenzo. 1934. *The diabolic root: A study of peyotism, the new Indian religion, among the Delawares.* Philadelphia: University of Pennsylvania Press.

Radin, Paul. 1926. *Crashing Thunder.* New York: Appleton. (First published in 1920 as *Crashing Thunder: The autobiography of a Winnebago Indian* [University of California Publications in American Archaeology and Ethnology 16, No. 7].)

Regina Leader-Post [Saskatchewan]. 1954. Psychiatric research utilizes Indian drug. Dec. 6, p. 1.

Reh, Emma, and D'Arcy McNickle. 1943. Peyote and the Indian. *Scientific Monthly* 57:220–29.

Rhodes, Willard. 1958. A study of musical diffusion based on the wandering of the opening peyote song. *Journal of the International Folk Music Council* 10:42–49.

Ropp, Robert S. de. 1957. "The mind and mescaline," Chap. 2 in *Drugs and the Mind,* pp. 27–60. New York: St. Martin's Press.

Schultes, Richard E. 1937. Peyote cult from *Nature Magazine. Literary Digest* (Nov. 13) 124:24ff.

———. 1938a. Peyote: An American Indian heritage from Mexico. *El Mexico Antiguo* 4:199–208.

———. 1938b. The appeal of peyote (*Lophophora williamsii*) as a medicine. *American Anthropologist* 40:698–715.

———. 1939. The identification of Teonanacatl, a narcotic Basidiomycete of the Aztecs. *Plantae Mexicanae II.* [Harvard] Botanical Museum Leaflets 7, No. 3:37–54.

———. 1940a. The aboriginal therapeutic uses of *Lophophora williamsii. Cactus Succulent* [*Society of America*] *Journal* 12:177–81.

———. 1940b. Teonanacatl: The narcotic mushroom of the Aztecs. *American Anthropologist* 42:429–43.

Scully, Bede (O.F.M. Cap.) 1941. The Cheyenne and peyote. *Mission Almanac* [of the Seraphic Mass Association], May, pp. 6–14. Ashland, Montana: St. Labre Mission.

Shonle, Ruth. 1925. Peyote, the giver of visions. *American Anthropologist* 27:53–75.

Siskin, Edgar E. 1941. The impact of the peyote cult upon shamanism among the Washo Indians. Unpublished Ph.D. dissertation, Yale University (Department of Anthropology), New Haven.

Slotkin, James S. 1951. Early eighteenth century documents on peyotism north of the Rio Grande. *American Anthropologist* 53:420–27.

———. 1952. *Menomini peyotism, a study of individual variation in a primary group with a homogeneous culture.* Transactions of the American Philosophical Association 42, No. 4.

PEYOTE STUDIES, 1958–1963

ETHNOGRAPHY

The years 1958-1963 have produced new field work data limited in amount but excellent in quality. Dustin, in particular, has filled in one important gap in our knowledge: the history and present status of Taos peyotism. About 1910, several Indians who had participated in Oklahoma meetings brought back peyote to Taos. The religious hierarchy of the pueblo resisted the new cult, saying, "It does not belong to us. It is not the work given to us. It will stop the rain. Something will happen." But in the drought of 1922 the "peyote boys" were quick to say, "Now it is so dry this summer because the peyote boys can't have their meetings; they used to bring so much rain." In the early 1930's Parsons was dubious about any wider spread of peyotism at Taos, but it has since flourished, cult members increasing from about 130 in 1936 to approximately 300 in 1960, out of a total population of some 900. Once outcasts, peyotists now command the most important religious and civic offices of the pueblo, including that of Governor. Taos is the only pueblo with any considerable cult, although individuals from Santo Domingo and Acoma pueblos frequently attend Taos peyote meetings.

La Barre had listed the Blackfoot among non-users as of 1922, citing in evidence the then national president of the Native American Church, the Cheyenne leader Alfred Wilson; but LaBarre considered the negative evidence in this case both surprising and unsatisfactory — especially since Wissler had once told him that in 1913 Wissler had heard peyote drumming on the Blackfoot reservation at the same moment the agent was denying its existence to him. Davis has partly resolved the problem, at least for the Piegan or southern Blackfoot. Davis believes that "The most intensive period of solicitation by non-Piegan peyotists appears to have occurred from about 1941 to 1948." His method of establishing this point is interesting: data were obtained from a predominantly male population of one-half or higher blood quantum, and four population-nuclei were examined for distributional purposes and found to show increased knowledge of peyote in direct proportion to their distance from Browning, Montana. Of the age-groups examined, those "over 45" had the highest percentage of "knowledge of peyote" while three times as many "no knowledge" responses were recorded for the age groups under 45. These statistical data appear to agree with what little direct knowledge we have: "About 1941-42 two Indians of unknown tribal affiliation walked into the Piegan Agency jail carrying a tape recorder and played peyote songs, asking that the people learn them. Also during this period a non-Piegan man asked two Piegan police officers, full-bloods who 'liked that stuff (referring to those who preferred the "old way" of life),' to help get the people interested. An Indian drifter from around Fort Benton was said to have attempted the introduction of peyote. In 1947-48 an Oklahoma Indian was 'peddling peyote.' Mexican sheep herders, evidently using peyote in a non-religious context, were said to have corrupted a number of young Piegan females" (Davis, *Mss.*, p. 3).

In field work during the summer of 1962, Kiste found that "Peyotism is well established among the Crow. Of some 3200 Crow resident on the reservation, approximately one half are involved in peyotism to some extent." It is interesting that there are two major leaders in Crow peyotism, one who has been prominent in the affairs of the national organization of the Native American Church, and another who had been state president of the Montana church only. It is the latter, nevertheless, who has the greater influence in Crow peyotism; the national leader's "lack of adherence to traditional values, especially that of generosity, is the *primary* factor which accounts for his failure to obtain the position to which he aspires." The state leader by contrast, at both the annual Sheridan (Wyoming) and Crow Indian fairs and rodeos, "erects a pavilion-like canopy adjacent to his tipi which serves as a cooking and dining area in which he and his wife provide meals for a great number of friends and relatives. The expenditure for such an undertaking is not slight; during the Crow Fair Russell had to secure a loan from a local bank in order to maintain his establishment" (Kiste, *Mss.*, pp. 4-5). There are 24 road chiefs among the Crow; those who are generous with their time and energy and indulge in "conspicuous giving" rank higher than those who do not.

Among other Siouan-speaking tribes, some new information on the Dakota is available. Included in Stephen Feraca's study of Teton Dakota contemporary religion is a section on Teton peyotism (pp. 48-57); and Mrs. Alice Kehoe at Harvard University and Dan Beveridge at the University of Saskatchewan are both working on peyotism among the Canadian Dakota, Mr. Beveridge around Moose Woods, Round Plains, and Standing Buffalo Reserves. Mrs. W. D. Wallis reports that around Griswold, according to the Dakota-speaking Father Gontran La Violette, "about eight families, including leaders of Catholic and Anglican churches" are peyotists, as are three more families at Oak Lake or Pipestone Reserve (Wallis, 1963). An American field worker, coming down U. S. Route One from Maine, far outside the usual domain of peyote or of peyotism, had an amusing experience: at a roadside trading post near Danvers, Massachusetts, he found a number of little boxes of cacti such as one can buy for a dollar in the West. "I was delighted to discover," he wrote, "that each box had at least one peyote plant, in good condition, already to plant in your window box . . . made up by [a company in] Arizona . . . [and] on the box is some botanical information on the various species in the little collection, but they don't mention the peyote" (McAllester, 1960).

Among ethnographic studies not reported in my earlier comparative surveys of peyotism, I would wish especially to draw attention to the items in the appended bibliography: Ruth Underhill on a Cheyenne-Arapaho meeting; Harrington on Lenape peyotism; Morris Opler on a Mescalero Apache origin legend which says that the Lipan were the first to have peyote, possibly not true literally but a plausible and valuable diffusionist datum; Stenberg on Wyoming Indian cultists; and Wallace and Hoebel on the standard Comanche rite (compare also Carlson and Jones). Hollander, in 1935, wrote in Dutch a survey article on peyotism which had heretofore escaped my notice; and Lowie, another, in an encyclopedia. Aguirre Beltran has a summary chapter on peyote in his book *Medicina y Magia*; and a chapter on peyotism in Vittorio Lanternari's *Movimento religiosi di libertà e di popoli oppressi* is now available in English. Older ethnographic items not listed in earlier bibliographies include articles by Boyer, Cazeneuve, Diguet, Geare, Ireland, Llewellyn, McNickle, and Putt.

PROBLEMS OF ACCULTURATION AND DIFFUSION

Camille Orso, an anthropology student at Bucknell University, has written "The Chapter that La Barre Didn't Write" on acculturational aspects of peyotism, attempting specifically to answer the question, "How did the Plains Indian culture, which was on the brink of extinction as a result of White policy, manage to reunify and strengthen itself through the incorporation of the Peyote Cult?"[1] Miss Orso regards the inter-tribal pan-Indianism of the peyote cult as the major cause. The paper of Wesley Hurt should also be consulted in this connection.

A study of "Western Navajo Peyotism" was presented by J. E. Levy at the San Francisco meeting of the American Anthropological Association in 1963. Levy noted three interesting phenomena: "*A*. A very rapid spread of peyotism into western [Navaho] communities which have resisted its intrusion for over thirty years.

---

[1] One reason, perhaps, is that thirty years ago young students still regarded themselves as collecting primary ethnographic material from old folks who had been active participants in the old native culture. Another reason is that the late and respected dissertation advisor of *The Peyote Cult* had repeatedly and vehemently gone on record, before 1937, as stating that acculturation studies (then just beginning to appear) were "not anthropology" — and so they well might have been regarded in terms of his own field work forty years ago. Nevertheless, those who can muster sympathy with a doctoral candidate might point out that acculturation was touched on in an Appendix on Christian elements, and that the same conclusion as Miss Orso's was reached on page 113 of *The Peyote Cult*.

B. An erratic development of cult forms exhibiting such great variety that some observers question the relationship to the Native American Church. *C.* A separate line of development which involves the use of peyote by traditional ceremonialists who have incorporated it into the pre-existing pharmacology and use it in a manner analogous to the use of Jimson weed (datura)." That peyotism came from many sources explains ritual variation, in Levy's opinion, while poverty and geographic distance are secondary factors. For example, Navaho peyote meetings may be held without drum, eagle wingbone whistle, or fan, although the chief peyote, staff, rattle, cedar, and smoking paraphernalia are usual. Altars vary from the common crescent or horseshoe to a right-angle chevron and, in one case, to a round disc; some meetings even lack an altar altogether. Women may or may not sing, and the number of assistant chiefs may vary. "As many converts are still novices it is not surprising that they do not yet know how to sing or drum and do not own their own blankets, fans, or rattles. Remarkably few Navajo songs are heard. Plains songs, especially Kiowa, sometimes Sioux, are heard. Ute song style is heard frequently. The most common song is the nonsense syllable set to Plains Music" (Levy, December 1963 *Mss.*, pp. 4-5).[2] Ritually, peyotism seems to be assimilated especially into the Navaho Sucking Way, itself borrowed, and perhaps also into the Stargazing Way. In an earlier study (Levy, *Mss.*, March 1963, p. 2), another point concerning Navaho diffusion is noted: "While Aberle and Stewart had emphasized the contact-distance correlation in the diffusion of peyotism among Navajo and Ute, Hurt denied such a correlation for Plains tribes in North Dakota." Navaho cultists evidently still use, however, an old defensive argument: "Peyotists eschew the use of alcohol with religious fervor. Many Navajos have become peyotists for the express purpose of solving their drinking problems" (Levy, *Mss.*, March 1963, p. 11).

Diffusionist problems are also evident in the peyotism of the Fox of Tama, Iowa.

[2] Although Apache and Navaho are both Southern Athapaskan linguistically, on musicological grounds alone future students might (quite correctly) infer that the Navaho got peyotism late from Ute and Kiowa sources, and not early from their nearby linguistic congeners, the Apache, who had been intermediaries between Mexican and Plains peyotism. As Nettl writes (p. 114), "The Peyote songs found primarily in the Plains-Pueblo are evidently related to the Athabaskan area also, both stylistically and historically. The Peyote religion was spread among the Plains-Pueblo tribes by the Apaches, either directly or deviously. Some Apache musical traits carried over into the Plains-Pueblo adaptations of the Peyote songs. The songs are now composites of both styles: they have the durational values and the predominant thirds and fifths of the Apaches, plus the tile-type melodic contour, incomplete repetitions, and isorhythmic tendencies characteristic of Plains-Pueblo music. The Peyote vocal technique is closer to the Athabaskan than to the Plains-Pueblo one, and the Peyote cadential formula may be another Athapaskan feature."

As Fugle writes (p. 33), "it is said that a Mesquakie belonging to both the Peyote religion and the Mesquakie clan religion can be helped by neither because it is impossible for him to have faith in both religions." To some degree, such "diffusion" is in fact an "acculturation" on the Indian level; indeed, Siegel and Beals have reported a "pervasive factionalism" over peyote at Taos in the interim before the peyotists, at least temporarily, seem to have achieved power. In 1962 Howard discussed Potawatomi mescalism and its relation to the diffusion of peyotism. Around 1961 it was reported to Brunner regarding the Mandan that "the Native American Church, the peyote cult, has been revived within the last few years. These developments will undoubtedly lead to vast changes in Berthold society and culture, but it is too early to assess their precise nature" (Brunner, p. 191).

On the basis of field work among the Gosiute, Carling Malouf (Letter, 1960) concludes that Christianity is there more than a matter of apologetics or propagandist veneer: "I am inclined more towards Omer Stewart's ideas on the matter, although I arrived at my own conclusions independently;" it is possible, he thinks, that this attitude toward Christianity may be characteristic of the Basin in general. Curiously, however, "In Montana, especially among the Rocky Boy reservation Cree, there are some definite anti-white elements. In recent years these, as well as other people in the State, won't even pray in English. 'It is better to pray in Indian,' they say." Louise Spindler has reported extensively on Menomini men and women, peyotists and non-peyotists, with respect to differential degrees of acculturation in each group.

THE NATIVE AMERICAN CHURCH

Dustin has written (p. 9) a succinct and valuable summary of the early history of this organization which deserves quotation:

By 1906 a loose intertribal association of local Peyote groups, known as the "Mescal Bean Eaters," had spread from Oklahoma in the south to Nebraska in the north. In 1909, in an attempt to accommodate White patterns of religious organizations, the "Mescal Bean Eaters" was changed into the "Union Church." The year 1918 brought a determined effort by the Bureau of Indian Affairs to have an anti-Peyote law passed by Congress. As a result, intertribal conferences were held in Oklahoma during the summer to discuss incorporating a Pan-Indian Peyotist association as a defense measure.

With the advice and assistance of James Mooney, one of the leading ethnologists of the Smithsonian Institution, who was studying Kiowa Peyotism at the time, the "Native American Church" incorporated in Oklahoma on October 10, 1918. In 1944 the articles of incorporation were amended so that the association became a national organization with the name, "The Native American Church of the United States." With the spread of Peyotism into Canada in 1955, the name was again changed to "The Native American Church of North America."

217

On June 23-26, 1960, nearly two hundred members of the Native American Church met at Greenwood, South Dakota, to reorganize and include the Yankton, Rosebud, and Pine Ridge groups under the state charter of the Native American Church of South Dakota, Inc.; Senator J. E. Lehman, Dr. Robert Hall of the Institute of Indian Studies, and Frank Takes Gun of Lodge Grass, Montana, president of the Native American Church of North America, Inc., were speakers. At Potato Creek, South Dakota, the state organization held its 40th annual convention on June 14-17, 1962 (*Institute of Indian Studies*, Nos. 13 and 15).

MESCALISM

R. C. Troike has made a careful study which discriminates four types of "mescal" (i. e. *Sophora secundiflora*) complex, and thereby advances our understanding considerably. Troike concludes (p. 949) that "the mescal bean medicine society complex was of relatively late origin and confined to the Plains, whereas mescalism itself has a far longer history, primarily in the area south of the Plains." Troike brings together data to show that the Tonkawa and Jumano (and also Coahuiltecan?) were probably the source of Caddo mescal ritualism. Certainly Campbell has demonstrated archeologically that *Sophora* was used in southwest Texas for several thousand years; and Troike, on good ethnographic grounds, shows that this use was quite probably associated with hunting ceremonialism. Troike concludes that "[ritual features] certainly do not indicate a derivation of peyotism from mescalism, but simply show that there was a selective adaptation of Mexican peyote practices to Plains ceremonial patterns. . . . It is evident that the mescal bean is simply a functional substitute for peyote in a basic deer or hunting cult, which was an important element in much North Mexican ceremonialism. . . . The Caddo were directly responsible for the diffusion of mescalism to their Plains relatives, along with much of the ritual context for the use of the mescal bean. The ultimate origins of mescalism *per se* unquestionably lie in the area of south Texas and northeastern Mexico where the plant, *Sophora secundiflora*, is indigenous" (Troike, pp. 959-960). This author proposes the more accurate term "sophorism," but is probably right in believing that the older, though inaccurate, term "mescalism" — which, strictly speaking, would refer to still a third plant, *Agave Americana*[3] —

[3] It is amusing that, as late as 1947, because of the persisting confusion, the Montana State Legislature has inadvertently also prohibited what might be dubbed "agavism," surely non-existent in Montana: "Senate Bill No. 102 to amend Section 94-35-123 of the Revised Codes of Montana, 1947, UNLAWFUL TO DISPENSE MESCAL BUTTON. That it shall be unlawful for any person, firm, corporation or association to sell, furnish or give away, or offer to sell, furnish, or give away, or have in his possession Peyote (Pellote), botanically known as Lophophora Williamsii; or Agava [sic] Americana, commonly known as the Mescal Button . . ."

is now too well established to be replaced. Perhaps "mescalism" will do, so long as the misnamed "mescal bean" is remembered to be *Sophora secundiflora,* and not peyote, *Lophophora williamsii,* and certainly not the century plant or American aloe, *Agave Americana,* source of pulque and tequila. J. H. Howard presents modified opinions on the relationship of peyotism and "mescalism" in general, and again in a paper on Potawatomi mescalism and peyotism in particular.

Dr. Richard Schultes, curator of the Harvard Botanical Museum, is probably the ranking botanical authority on hallucinogenic plants of the New World. His careful summary of the subject in a recent *Harvard Review* is consistent with the opinions of the ethnologists Troike and La Barre, and with those of the authority on Texan archeology, Dr. T. N. Campbell. Schultes writes:

One of the characteristic plants of the drier parts of Texas, the Southwest, and adjacent Mexico is the shrubby legume *Sophora secundiflora,* the dark red seeds of which are known as mescal beans or, in Mexico, as *frijolitos.* The seeds of *Sophora secundiflora* contain cytisine, a highly poisonous alkaloid of the nicotine group. Its toxic action is characterized by nausea, convulsions and eventual death from respiratory failure.

Indian groups of Texas and northern Mexico formerly took these narcotic seeds in the ceremonial Red Bean Dance. Various Plains Indians likewise employed mescal beans in distinct patterns of use: as an oracular or divinatory medium, to induce visions in initiation rites or as a ceremonial emetic and stimulant. The Kiowa and Comanche employ it today as part of the ornamental dress of the leader of the peyote ritual, pointing to its earlier use as a narcotic, a role which it lost with the arrival of the much safer and much more spectacular hallucinogenic peyote.

Our earliest reference to the mescal beans goes back to 1539, when Cabeza de Vaca mentioned them as articles of trade amongst the Texas Indians. The Stephen Long Expedition in 1820 reported the Arapaho and Iowa tribes using large red beans as a medicine and narcotic.

MESCALINE AND ITS EXPERIMENTAL USES

The chemistry and synthesis of mescaline and the other pan-peyotl alkaloids are now fully known, through work listed in earlier bibliographies in this volume and the work (additionally listed in the bibliography of the present appendix) of Banholzer *et al.,* Bennington *et al.,* Dessi, Dornow and Petsch, Ducloux, Fernandez, Hahn and Wassmuth, Heffter, Hey, Iwamoto, Jensch, Kindler and Peschke, Morin *et al.,* Nakada, Rosenthaler, Slotta *et al.,* Spaeth *et al.,* and Tsao. The pharmacognosia of peyote alkaloids has also been contributed to massively by such workers as Alles, Bard, Beccari, Block, Chaumerliac and Roche, Clark, Clerc and Paris, Colomb, Delay and Gerard, Denber *et al.,* De Nito, Garattini and Ghetti, Geesink and Den Hartog Jager, Janot and Bernier, Jantz, Lebeau, Marinesco, Marrazzi and Hart, Metzner, Popoff, Raymond-

Hamet, Reutter, Rinaldi and Himwich, Robles and Gomez, Speck, Sturtevant and Drill, Supniewski, Tarsitano, Thuillier, and Wolbach *et al.* The metabolism of mescaline has been partly established by Frederick and Mary Bernheim, Blaschko, Wolfram and Katarina Block, Cochin *et al.*, Friedhoff and Goldstein, Lewis and McIlwain, Osmond, Patzig, Polono and Maffezzoni, Smolska, Spector, Vogt, and Woods *et al.* A convenient summary of the *Pharmacology and Metabolism of Mescaline* has been made by Roland Fischer.

An extraordinary spate of research has accompanied discovery of the clinical relationships of lysergic acid and mescaline, their reactions to the powerful physiological substances serotonin and adrenochrome, and the relation of all four of these to the tranquilizing drugs reserpine (itself long used in the folk medicine of India) and chlorpromazine. This work is significant because it seemed to promise an understanding of the chemistry and cure of schizophrenia. The history and rationale of this research can be briefly summarized. Taylor tells (p. 307) of the dramatic discovery of lysergic acid:

The drug, analogous to mescal, but much more powerful, had been discovered in 1934 by a Swiss chemist, Albert Hofmann. Hofmann had been investigating substances analogous to mescal one day, when he began to feel sensations of unreality; on getting back home, he lay down and proceeded to experience a series of extraordinary hallucinations. Next day, he woke, feeling tired but otherwise normal. Back at the lab, he looked at the substances he had been synthesizing and decided he must have absorbed through his skin a small amount of a substance entered in his lab-book as LSD 25, an abbreviation for lysergic acid diethylamide, plus the date. He therefore took by mouth what he supposed to be a minimally small dose. He did not know that the substance was a thousand times stronger than mescal, and he had actually taken several times the maximum dose. Before long, he felt extreme sensations of unease and depersonalization, disruption of the time sense, and so forth. He was driven back home, where a series of fantastic hallucinations beset him, with some nausea. He felt sure that he had gone out of his mind and that he would never be able to report his discovery. Next day, however, he was all right again.

Subsequently he extracted a similar drug from mushrooms used by Mexican Indians in religious ceremonies, analyzed and synthesized it: it was named Psilocybin.

Hallucinatory experiences like Hofman's rather resemble certain forms of schizophrenia — hence the name psychotomimetic for such drugs — and raised the hope that this form of insanity might be understandable in chemical terms.

The biochemical and psychiatric reasoning surrounding subsequent research has been succinctly summarized by Jackson (pp. 68-69):

The most notable surge of effort along these lines has surrounded the role of serotonin in the biochemistry of the human organism. This substance, originally discovered in the lining of the intestine, was found to play an important part in the function of the smooth (involuntary) muscle. Eventually it was isolated from various sites in the central nervous system, in particularly high concentration from certain parts of the brain stem. Some investigators then measured serotonin in schizophrenics and reported it to be high, although a few others found it to be low.

What brought serotonin to the center of the stage in biochemical studies of schizophrenics was the finding that lysergic acid diethylamide (LSD) is antagonistic to serotonin in its action on smooth muscle. LSD had already attracted attention because it produced hallucinations and other symptoms in volunteer subjects; investigators were encouraged to believe that they had come on a means to induce "experimental psychoses". It was postulated that LSD might produce its peculiar effects by competition with serotonin in the central nervous system. This idea acquired even more stirring implications from the finding that reserpine, a tranquilizer already in wide use in mental hospitals, apparently produced its effects by a parallel sort of action. It was only one more step to the conclusion that schizophrenia was a disorder of serotonin metabolism and another step to the use of serotonin in the treatment of schizophrenics. Some investigators went so far as to inject the substance into the ventricles of patients' brains, a rather difficult neurosurgical procedure.

The enthusiasm over serotonin was heightened by the discovery of a breakdown product of adrenalin called adrenochrome. This substance bears a structural resemblance to LSD and to mescaline, the active ingredient in the hallucinatory mushrooms and peyote cactus employed in religious rituals by the Indians of the U. S. Southwest and Mexican highlands. The discoverers of adrenochrome found that it induced hallucinations when they administered it to themselves. They proposed, therefore, that an excess of adrenochrome in the biochemistry of schizophrenics brings on their psychotic symptoms.

Further research has failed to sustain these ideas and the hopes they excited. The function of serotonin in the central nervous system remains unknown. A serotonin antagonist called 2-bromo-lysergic acid produces none of the mental symptoms characteristic of LSD. Chlorpromazine, a tranquilizer more effective than reserpine in quieting schizophrenics, shows no signs of biochemical competition with serotonin. Adrenochrome has yet to be found in the body and has been labeled a laboratory artifact. A painstaking study of the turnover of adrenal substances in the bodies of normal and schizophrenic women by direct measurement from the adrenal arteries and veins has shown no detectable differences. Finally, the much heralded experimental psychoses have turned out to be nothing other than "toxic psychoses," familiar to clinicians for many years and clearly differentiated from schizophrenic states.

The physiology and chemistry of schizophrenia, which has baffled thousands of determined investigators over the last century, therefore still remains a mystery. The psychological and psychiatric investigation of mescaline, in an appended comprehensive though surely not exhaustive additional bibliography, has been done by such workers as: Aleksandrovskii *et al.*, Adler and Poetzl, (the co-workers in the Boston Psychopathic Hospital report), Bridger and Gantt, Bromberg and Tranter, Camisaca, Cattel, Cholden, Chweitzer, Geblewicz and Liberson, Crema, Cucchi, De Jongh, Delay *et al.*, Denber and his colleagues, Desoille, Duc, Endo, Ey and Rancoulle,

Favilli and Heymann, Feigen and Alles, Fischer and his colleagues, Franke, Frederking, Frisch and Waldmann, Georgi and Weber, Guillarmot, Guttman, Himwich, Hoch and his colleagues, Hollister and Hartman, Hori, Isibasi, Jantz, Klüver, Krapf, Landis and Clausen, Maclay, Marschall, Mátéfi, Mayer-Gross and his colleagues, McKellar, Merlis and co-workers, Möller, Morselli, Noteboom, Osmond and Smythies, Palmieri and Lacroix, Pap, Patzig and Block, Pennes, Rinaldi, Rinkel, Roberti and Heymann, Rotondo, Rouhier, Salomon and his colleagues, Sava, Schueler, Simpson and McKellar, Stockings, Szara, Teirich, Thale and Gabrio, Unger, Waeber, Wheatley, Wikler, Wilcox, Wolf, Woolley and Shaw, and Zucker. Early in 1961, at the Psychopharmacology Service Center at the National Institute of Mental Health, a project on Cross-Cultural Psychopharmacology, enlisting the aid of anthropologists, ethnobotanists and pharmacognosists, was planned under the direction of Dr. G. J. Cosmides; out of this has grown an International Conference on the Ethnopharmacologic Search for Psychoactive Drugs, to be held at the New York Academy of Medicine on 18-21 September 1964. In January of 1961, Dr. Timothy Leary of Harvard was organizing a symposium for the September meetings of the American Psychological Association on the subject of "Empirical Mysticism."

PEYOTE AS A "NARCOTIC"

In discussing a book by D. W. Maurer and V. H. Vogel on *Narcotics and Narcotic Addiction* published in 1954, C. G. Barber (as reported earlier in the present volume) had raised the question of "Peyote and the Definition of Narcotics" in an article published in 1959. Barber had objected to the inclusion, by implication he thought, of peyote as a narcotic substance. In a reply in 1960, in his article, "Peyote is Not a Drug of Addiction," Maurer disclaimed having stated that peyote is either addictive or narcotic, and rejected as inadequate Barber's definition of narcotic as "a substance which can alter or distort the user's perception of himself and of the external world, and which is taken or administered primarily for that purpose," arguing that this definition would include tobacco, aspirin, ether, adrenalin, insulin, sugar, carbonate of soda, and a host of other substances, and stating that all drugs of addiction bring euphoria, although euphoria is not brought on only by such drugs. Maurer suggested that to discover and report these effects is a sufficient task for the field ethnographer. In a rejoinder to Maurer, Barber rejected addiction-production and euphoria as adequate in defining a narcotic, and deplored the "apparent lack of enthusiasm for anthropological research in the field of narcotic use" (Barber, 1960, p. 687). La Farge subsequently addressed himself to the important question of the political effects of the definition of narcotics, stating that "La Barre (1960: 54) mentions Barber's

222

paper and, without commenting on his suggestion, seems to counter it by proposing the term 'psychotropic' for the use to which Barber would put narcotic. This term meets the need that the latter writer has stated, without creating any possibility that, by misrepresentation, anthropologists could be made to appear as supporters of either side in a politico-religious controversy" (La Farge, p. 689). Gorton, a neurologist and psychiatrist who had worked with mescaline at the New York Psychiatric Institute in 1952-1953, wrote, "it is my opinion that mescaline (which is the chief active constituent of peyote), is definitely not a narcotic, in the sense that it is a physically addicting drug, creating a physical dependency after prolonged use, as is the case with the opium alkaloids" (Gorton, p. 1335). Gorton agreed with Maurer and rejected Barber's definition of narcotic, as this would include even ethyl alcohol. Gorton added (p. 1335) that "the decisive question is whether a drug creates physical dependency, and only if this occurs is it to be regarded as a narcotic. I may add that Dr. Paul Hoch, who is one of the world's leading authorities on psychopharmacology, definitely states that mescaline is not a narcotic." The position is thus summarized by Jerrold Levy, an anthropologist working at the U. S. P. H. S. Indian Hospital at Tuba City, Arizona: "Recent research on mescaline in no way changes the conclusions drawn by anthropologists in respect to its non-harmfulness when used by normal subjects." This opinion reiterates that of Boas and his associates in a statement to Congress many decades before in 1937, and that of La Barre and his associates in 1951. In 1961, a careful statement prepared by MacGregor, with the aid of La Farge, was passed by the Board of Directors of the Association on American Indian Affairs, and published in *Indian Affairs* as the official position of the Association. It is firmly protective of the Indian peyote religion.

PEYOTE AND THE LAW

It was the State of Oklahoma, stimulated by the Agent of the Cheyenne and Arapahoe Agency, which first outlawed the use of peyote, in its Sessions Laws of the year 1899. In 1907, three Indians were found guilty under this law and fined $25 each and costs. After the famous Comanche chief Quanah Parker testified before the legislature, the anti-peyote law of Oklahoma was repealed in 1908, and failed of re-enactment in 1909 and again in 1927. There were then no clear legal restrictions on the use of peyote in force between 1908 and the passage of state anti-peyote laws in 1917 in Colorado, Utah and Nevada. In 1907, a group of Indian agents had petitioned Congress for the passage of a law prohibiting the use of peyote, but the bill was never sent to Congress; the Bureau of Indian Affairs then itself drafted a bill in 1910, but for some reason it, too, was never submitted to Congress. In 1916 Senator Thompson

223

of Kansas and Representative Gandy introduced a bill in the 64th Congress, 1st Session, to prohibit the use and transportation of peyote in interstate commerce. This bill was defeated, as were similar bills introduced in 1917, 1918, 1919, 1921, 1922, 1924, 1926, and 1937. No Federal legislation exists, prohibiting the Indian religious use of peyote. "Peyotl is not regarded as a narcotic drug, and its use is not prohibited by the Federal Government" (*Bulletin on Narcotics*, IX, #2, April-June, 1959, p. 18). In October 1962, amendments to the Federal Food and Drug Act brought psilocybin and LSD under stricter control, but did not include peyote. In Canada, on the other hand, Indians can legally obtain peyote only by medical prescription; in November 1954, some Indians from Long Plains Reserve in Manitoba were arrested at the North Dakota border for bringing in an undeclared parcel of peyote buttons, under the Canadian narcotic law against the use of peyote.

State anti-peyote laws, however, have been passed in Colorado, Utah, and Nevada (1917), Kansas (1920), Arizona, Montana, South Dakota, and North Dakota (all in 1923), Iowa (1924), Wyoming and New Mexico (1929; but in 1959 the New Mexico legislature passed an amendment permitting the ritual use of peyote), Idaho (1935), and Texas (1937). Non-enforcement and subsequent legal actions have made the law a dead letter in Arizona and New Mexico; in 1926, Big Sheep was prosecuted and convicted under the Montana state law, but an amendment has since legalized the use of peyote in worship there. In 1957, acting on information sent by the inspector at Laredo, California state and district officers confiscated an express parcel containing 20 pounds of peyote (*Monthly Narcotics Intelligence Bulletin*, 15 September 1957), under a California law which classes peyote with heroin and marijuana as a banned drug.

The legal action most likely to set precedent, however, is the disposition of the case against Mary Attakai, a member of the Navaho Native American Church, under an anti-peyote ordinance of the Navaho Tribe. The local judge in Flagstaff, Arizona, H. L. Russell, disqualified himself, whereupon the Hon. Yale McFate was sent from Phoenix to preside over the case in the Superior Court of Coconino County in Flagstaff. In a notably lucid and well-informed opinion, rendered on 26 July 1960, the Court held that:

Peyote is not a narcotic. It is not habit-forming. . . . There are about 225,000 members of the organized church, known as the Native American Church, which adheres to this practice. . . . The use of peyote is essential to the existence of the peyote religion. Without it, the practice of the religion would be effectively prevented. . . . It is significant that many states which formerly outlawed the use of peyote have abolished or amended their laws to permit its use for religious purposes. It is also significant that the Federal Government has in nowise prevented the use of peyote by Indians or others."

Inasmuch as the statute under which Mary Attakai was convicted of illegal possession is contrary to both the 14th Amendment of the Federal Constitution and Article II, Sections 4, 8, 12, and 13 of the Arizona Constitution, the Court found the statute unconstitutional, exonerated the bond, and dismissed the case. Expert opinion has widely admired the decision of Judge McFate.[4]

Among American Indians, all psychotropic drugs (including tobacco) were invariably used only in religious or sacred contexts, because of the belief that the effects of using these substances were evidence of supernatural "power" in them. As Schultes has remarked (p. 143), "It is interesting here to note that when problems do arise from the employment of narcotics, they arise after the narcotics have passed from ceremonial to purely hedonic or recreational use." Although problems come up concerning American Indian peyotism, these have arisen largely because the Indian use of peyote has been judged, or misjudged, only on the basis of a cross-cultural view of "narcotic" drugs as they are used in western societies. But religious freedom and medical value in the use of peyote are two separate issues. In Paris, in 1959, a handbill appeared in which the secular, allegedly medical and psychiatric, use of peyote is at least dubious in this latter context, given pharmacologists' negative opinion of the usefulness of pan-peyotl. The handbill for "Peyotyl R. D." (evidently a proprietary name) is as follows:

LE PEYOTYL R. D.

Le "PEYOTYL R. D.", produit naturel n'ayant subi aucune transformation ou altération chimique conserve, vivantes, toutes les propriétés merveilleuses du Peyotl

---

[4] Omer C. Stewart, an authority on Ute and Navaho peyotism, and Dr. B. E. Gorton, a psychiatrist from Phoenix who had studied with the psychopharmacological authority Dr. P. H. Hoch, were expert witnesses at this trial, and adduced Slotkin's book on *The Peyote Religion* in evidence. The defense attorney, Herbert L. Ely, was retained and sent to Flagstaff by the American Civil Liberties Union at the request of the Indians, led by Mr. Frank Takes Gun, President of the Native American Church. Stewart's article on "The Native American Church (Peyote Cult) and the Law" is the most compendious source available on recent legal questions. Carling Malouf testified on behalf of the amendment to the Montana state law. It is interesting that, so far as the present writer's information goes, anthropologists as expert witnesses have, without exception, testified in favor of peyotists. In April 1962, three Navaho peyotists were arrested near Needles, California, and given suspended sentences of two to ten years. Judge Carl B. Hilliard of the San Bernardino County Superior Court based his decision on the United States Supreme Court decision of 1879, which held polygamy unlawful even though it was a feature of Mormon religious faith. On 7 May 1963, the American Civil Liberties Union asked the California Court of Appeals to overrule the conviction, on the ground of differences between polygamy and peyotism.

(Lophophora williamsii). Cette plante est connue et utilisée depuis des siècles par les indiens du Mexique pour ses vertus thérapeutiques, à la fois *toniques* et *sédatives* qui en font l'un des meilleurs reconstituants naturels et l'arme la plus sûre contre la douleur. C'est également un *antispasmodique* remarquable et le *spécifique*, par excellence, *de toutes les névroses.*

Les recherches scientifiques les plus récentes permettent d'affirmer que le PEYOTYL R. D., substance même du Peyotl, n'a aucun effet intoxicant sur l'organisme et n'est contre-indiqué en aucun cas. Il diffère fondamentalement des excitants ou des calmants ordinaires, a l'effet d'ailleurs fugace, en ce que son emploi peut être prolongé sans trouble ni accoutumance. *Le "Peyotyl R. D." pris régulièrement ramène l'équilibre et le calme et favorise en plein épanouissement des facultés de l'individu.*

INDICATIONS: Asthénie, Convalescences, Surmenage physique et intellectuel, Dépression nerveuse, Neurasthénie, Insomnie, Migraines, Névralgies, Douleurs abdominales et rhumatismales, Asthme, Dyspnée, Hystérie, Toux d'irritation.

DOSE: 2 à 4 dragées par jour avant les repas.
Contre l'insomnie: 1 ou 2 dragées avant de se coucher, à une heure d'intervalle.

PAS D'ACCOUTUMANCE

Le Flaçon de 20 dragées en vente au prix imposé 14 fr. 95, impôt.
Une Brochure détaillée sur le Peyotl est envoyée sur simple demande.

The varied claims for peyote in this handbill seem extravagant; certainly one would not expect a substance that keeps one awake all night to be good for insomnia! Nor is it clear how a substance containing strychnine-like alkaloids would be anti-spasmodic; that it is the specific for all neuroses can be flatly doubted.

Because of its production of predominantly visual hallucinations in color, mescaline, the main psychotropic alkaloid of peyote, has been much used experimentally by psychologists and psychiatrists on artist-subjects, psychotics, and themselves. Reitman summarized these materials in 1950 in a book on Psychotic Art (p. 35):

Maclay studied the mescalin hallucinations of subjects able to draw. He asked them to sketch their hallucinations instead of giving a verbal account of them. They appeared fleeting in shape, position and colour, and all the shapes tended to elongation and reduplication. Reduplicated zigzag lines were frequent. Another fairly common character of the visual hallucinations was a "tapestry pattern." Knauer and Maloney's subjects reported mosaics and ornaments, spiral and windmill and carpet patterns; other workers have found that colour in mescalin hallucinations becomes dissociated from form. When Maclay studied the drawings of his subjects, he observed that the "tapestry" pattern was probably the reproduction of the choroid or intermediate coat of the subject's eyeball which were perceived and then painted. Fig. 8 is a painting by one of Maclay's mescalin subjects representing the choroid in an artistic elaboration. Fig. 9 is an interesting parallel. This picture was painted by a schizophrenic patient under the following conditions: she was gazing out of the window absentmindedly, when she started to sketch the background, and the flowerpot was elaborated later. Probably she experienced her choroid as an after-sensation and incorporated it into the picture which, with some phantasy, represents her two eyes and her nose. The point to emphasize, however, in both examples is the strongly physiological perceptual impetus which moulds the "artistic" expression. Maclay speculated on the psychological versus the physiological theories of hallucinations and concluded that at least in mescalin the hallucinations are physiological in origin, but that their content is determined psychologically.

Maclay and Guttman had reported on "Mescaline Hallucinations in Artists," in 1941, and Mátéfi on self-experiments using mescaline with special consideration of a drawing test. A discernible difference between these early and later uses of mescaline is that the former represent serious scientific investigations with an articulate experimental rationale, whereas later ones represent primarily private experiential and hedonistic indulgence.

CHEMICAL MYSTICISM

American anthropologists first learned of peyote from a series of scholarly articles and books published in the 1890's by two of the most sober and respected ethnographers of their generation: James Mooney, on American, and Carl Lumholtz, on Mexican Indians. In America there has always been a marked puritanical strain in the anti-peyote attitudes of the larger lay public. Anthropologists, on the other hand, have consistently tended to a protectionist stand, from Mooney and Boas to La Barre's monographing of *The Peyote Cult* in 1938 — and eighteen years later, Slotkin had even become a member and protagonist of *The Peyote Religion* of 1956. Elsewhere, however, as in all matters concerning "red Indians," others looked upon the new plant with the Romanticism-ensorcelled eyes of Europeans.

As early as 1898, Havelock Ellis, a British sexologist, wrote about "a new artificial paradise" produced by eating certain cactus buttons from the American Indian Southwest. German scholars first knew widely of this from Lewin's *Phantastika*, portentively subtitled "narcotic and stimulating drugs for doctors and non-doctors" *(betäubenden und erregenden Genussmittel für Ärzte und Nichtärtze)*, published in Berlin in 1924 and translated into English in a New York and London edition of 1931 —(although of equal importance in spreading knowledge of the new plant-marvel was Klüver's workmanlike little book on *Mescal*, "the divine plant," appearing in London in 1928). French savants knew of it from Rouhier's monograph on *Peyotl*, first published in 1926 and republished a year later as *The Plant that Makes the Eyes Enmarvelled*; and in 1936 Philippe de Félice produced his book *Poisons sacrés, ivresses*

227

divines, subtitled "an essay on some lower forms of mysticism." This tradition continued in Williams' *Many Dimensions* of 1931 and Taylor's "Come and Expel the Green Pain" of 1944.

But the greatest impetus to a titillated lay interest in peyote was provided by a widely publicized and rather absurd book of 1954 by the novelist and mystic Aldous Huxley, entitled *The Doors of Perception*, wherein peyote — which Huxley persisted in calling by the long-discarded and quite incorrect name "mescal" — was touted as a chemical key to the mystical state, a sort of instant Zen.

> The other world to which mescalin admitted me was not the world of visions; it existed out there, in what I could see with my eyes open. The great change was in the realm of objective fact. What had happened to my subjective universe was relatively unimportant. (p. 16)

— not literary hyperbole for Huxley, but the objective discovery of a new *Istigkeit*. Jean Cazeneuve explained this later in the *Revue Philosophique* (p. 179):

> The explication which [Huxley] proposes is founded in part on the fact that the system of enzymes regulating the distribution of glucose in the cells of the brain is disturbed by mescaline. Having recourse to the Bergsonian theory, according to which the brain would have, in perception as in memory, an eliminative function, that is to say divesting "pure perception" of all that which is not useful, Huxley thinks that the deprivation of sugar following the ingestion of mescaline could, by inhibiting the normal action of that function of the brain, re-endow sensation with its original purity.

Assuming for the moment the reality of this implied physiology in which impaired functioning somehow becomes its opposite, a non-mystic might of course offer an alternative hypothesis: that the disturbing effect of mescaline might represent not a heightening of the perceptual but a lowering of the critical powers of the mind. In France, Henri Michaux continued nevertheless in the mystic vein in his *Misérable Miracle* of 1956, *L'Infini Turbulent* of 1957, and *Connaissance par les Gouffres* of 1961, all such dreadful knowledge from the infinite abyss being derived from the use of mescaline. Zaehner criticized the Huxleyan view in a book on *Mysticism Sacred and Profane: An Inquiry into Some Varieties of Praeternatural Experience*; in the same year 1961 a chapter on mescaline appeared in Laski's *Ecstasy, A Study of Some Secular and Religious Experiences* (pp. 263-273); Alan Watts experimented with mescaline, among other drugs, as described in his book, *The Joyous Cosmology*, published in 1962.[5]

---

[5] Psilocybin research has undergone a development identical to that of research on mescaline. First came the precise and scholarly work of Valentina and Gordon Wasson on the ethnographic rediscovery of *teonanacatl*, the psychotropic mushroom of the ancient Aztec known from colonial Spanish sources but misidentified by Safford with peyote (who also misidentified *ololiuqui* with

On 26 April 1959, the *San Francisco Sunday Chronicle* represented, by name and by picture, that the then-top male movie star had been administered "a synthetic of the drug mescalin"[6] by a therapist who also treated a number of other film celebrities; the therapist had recently been an associate in the conservative Psychiatric Institute of Beverly Hills, which denied full membership to several such practitioners.

I have just been born again [said the film star]. I have just been through a psychiatric experience that has completely changed me. It was horrendous. I had to face things about myself which I never admitted, which I didn't know were there. Now I know that I hurt every women I loved. I was an utter fake, a self-opinionated boor, a know-all who knew very little. . . . That moment when your conscious meets your subconscious is a helluva wrench. You feel like the whole top of your head is lifting off. . . . I have been married three times, but never had a child. Now I am fit for children. . . . I was always searching for peace of mind, I'd half messed around with Yoga, hypnosis and religion and made sporadic attempts at mysticism. Nothing seemed to really give me what I needed until this last treatment.

Under such prestigious auspices, the movement of "chemical mysticism" was now in full career.

The best known of the beatnik poets, Allen Ginsberg of *Howl*, experimented with writing poetry under the influence of various psychotropic drugs, including peyote — an innovation copied by a number of lesser literary figures. Jack Green reported a peyote experience in the Krim-edited book on *The Beats: A Gold Medal Anthology* in 1960; and an appendix to W. S. Burroughs' *Naked Lunch* (1962) concerns a peyote experience (see also McClure, and Ebin's anthology). John Wilcock devoted his column, *the village square*, in the 27 July 1961 [Greenwich] *Village Voice*, to a résumé of peyote, and on 3 August 1961, to the "fifth freedom . . . [to] unplug the neural centers which censor, limit, and control a vast network of brain cells." The puritanical Freudian thesis that humans *need* such forebrain inhibition of raw hind-

datura) — an error already questioned on textual and linguistic grounds by La Barre in 1938; the ethnobotanical identifications of *teonanacatl* by Schultes at Harvard and Roger Heim in Paris; and the elegant isolation and chemical synthesis of psilocybin by Hofmann — only to be followed by *The Sacred Mushroom: Key to the Door of Eternity* by Andrija Puharich, in his "offbeat polemic on *Amanita muscaria* as a valuable aid to extrasensory perception, built around the case history of a man who supposedly described (using hieroglyphics and 'the vocalized ancient Egyptian language') ancient Egyptian ritual uses of the mushroom" (D. B. Heath, personal letter) — and finally the controversial research of Leary and Alpert at Harvard, and the promiscuous use of psilocybin by various lay persons in the 1960's. Meanwhile, valuable and still incompletely explored ethnological insights remain embedded in the work of the Wassons.

[6] On the basis of Kobler's article (p. 39) this substance would seem to be LSD-25, but journalistic sources are not always discriminating in such matters.

brain impulse, in order to achieve civilization or indeed any kind of culture, was ignored or jettisoned by those intent on a psychedelic spree. Peyote and mescaline were now becoming well known to every practicing bohemian and beatnik.

In May of 1960, two Federal agents seized 311 pounds of buttons and 145 capsules of powdered panpeyotl from Barron Bruchlos, a twenty-eight year old ex-Harvard student, at that time the bearded and barefoot proprietor of The Dollar Sign Coffee House, on 306 East Sixth Street in New York's lower East Side. The café had a $ sign over the door but no other identification except a cage of monkeys in the window. This Federal action was quite unexpected, because Bruchlos had paid $350 to cactus companies that leased Government lands in Texas and that also got it at Federal auctions of cactus on lands recently taken over by the Government; the legally mailed peyote containers bore seals of the Department of Agriculture declaring the contents to be free of harmful insects. Narcotics agents, however, operate under the Department of the Treasury; but no Federal law against the transportation, sale and use of peyote existed on the statute books. Mr. Bruchlos said he would have netted two to five thousand dollars, if he had processed and sold all the peyote ground up in capsules, selling them at fifty to seventy-five cents each to the beatniks and college students who were his clients. Bruchlos was disturbed over the fact that his competitors, who had bought hundreds of capsules from him wholesale before the seizure, were still busily selling the ground-up panpeyotl, and some of them had even advertised in the classified columns of several college newspapers. No ruling could be obtained from the Federal Government, which brought no charges against Mr. Bruchlos but nevertheless kept the confiscated shipment.[7]

AN ACADEMIC DEBACLE

On 27 May 1963, President Pusey of Harvard announced that an assistant professor of clinical psychology, Dr. Richard Alpert of the Social Relations Department, had been fired. It was a thing unheard of at Harvard, the first such action in the ten years of Pusey's presidency, and was obviously done under sore duress and after extraordinary attempts at leaning over backward in the interest of academic freedom.

[7] The legal basis of this Government seizure remains obscure and may never be known. About a month afterward Bruchlos gave up The Dollar Sign and set up a new place called The Cart Wheel at 64 East Seventh Street, where the present writer and his collegian son visited and talked with him. But late on the night of 6 December 1960, a friend found Bruchlos dead, sprawled on a bed in his basement room. There were no signs of violence, and police did not regard as a suicide note a beatnik poem found nearby containing the line "If leukemia kills me . . ." Death was apparently from natural causes, although Bruchlos's father, a trade magazine publisher, requested an autopsy and said that his son had not been ailing. I am indebted to Dr. Paul Gebhard for originally locating The Dollar Sign for me.

230

Alpert had done able work in child psychology in Iowa and was the son of a former president of the New Haven Railroad. Supported by the Harvard Center for Research in Personality, Alpert and his associate, Dr. Timothy Leary, had been studying the effects of psychotropic drugs, including mescaline, psilocybin, and LSD-25. The possession of mescaline or peyote by other than qualified researchers is a felony under Massachusetts law; the law does not, however, define who qualified persons are, and several American chemical companies could supply mescaline at about $4.00 a dose; while Sandoz, a Swiss company for whom the original synthesizer, Hofmann, worked, supplied psilocybin and LSD-25 free or at nominal prices.

Timothy Leary, Alpert's colleague, had a doctorate in psychology from the University of California, had written a reputable text on a functional theory and method of personality diagnosis published in 1957, and was a lecturer in clinical psychology at Harvard. Leary had first encountered psychotropic drugs in Mexico at a "mushroom party" where friends had persuaded him to eat the phenomenal number of nine of the psilocybin-containing fungi. He was greatly impressed by the "consciousness-expanding" effects of the drug, an opinion similar to that of Huxley concerning the action of "mescal" and mescaline. Later, Huxley himself was included with Allen Ginsberg and William Burroughs as one of the "outstanding creative intellectuals" invited to undergo experiments at Harvard. Alpert and Leary, in their mimeographed reports, were soon predicting the usefulness of psilocybin in psychotherapy, and in 1961 they began to test the new therapy on the inmates of a nearby prison.

Colleagues among professional psychologists were quick to criticize the Alpert-Leary methodology, alleging that the psychotropic substances were given in sessions resembling cocktail parties, and that the researchers were necessarily slipshod in collecting and recording data inasmuch as they themselves took the drug at the same time as their subjects did. Experiments on the original 38 subjects were meanwhile becoming known, and more and more undergraduate students sought to ferret out the sources of the drugs. Some succeeded: one chemical supply house in Manhattan sold mescaline at $35 a gram (roughly two doses), more than four times the regular trade price, and another New York firm sold it to undergraduates at regular prices. One student obtained a quantity of buttons from Texas and sold them to classmates at reasonable rates. A box of LSD-impregnated sugar cubes from New York sold for $1.00 each on the Harvard Square black market. Replying to critics, Leary and Alpert argued that no government had the right to forbid citizens the freedom to explore their own inner consciousness.

Local mescaline and psilocybin research was given its first open publicity in an article published in the 20 February 1962 issue of *The Harvard Crimson*, the undergraduate daily newspaper, to which Alpert and Leary replied with a letter to the

Editor of the *Crimson*. A few days later, a responsible psychiatrist, Dr. Dana L. Farnsworth, Director of the Harvard University Health Service, wrote a letter to the *Crimson* suggesting that mescaline could do real psychiatric damage to borderline personalities: "Actually, the ingestion of the drug can precipitate psychotic reactions in some apparently normal persons. It has been known to increase slight depressions into suicidal ones and to produce schizophreniclike reactions" (Weil, p. 44). A private meeting of all members of the Center for Research on Personality was called for 14 March 1962; the researchers were not aware that a reporter from the *Crimson* was also quietly sitting in the room. Dr. Herbert C. Kelman, a social psychologist, summed up the objections of the other psychologists by saying that "The program has an anti-intellectual atmosphere. Its emphasis is on pure experience, not on verbalizing findings" (Weil, p. 44). The psychologists also objected that graduate students in the experiment were becoming sect-like insiders who considered non-cultists "squares."

The *Crimson's* account of this troubled meeting touched off violent debate. On 20 March, the Massachusetts State Food and Drug Division announced an investigation of the research to ascertain whether the state law had been violated. In mid-April the state decided that research could continue if a simple precaution — that a licensed physician (promptly dubbed the "ground-control man" by hipsters) always be present — were observed; it dropped the threatening earlier question of the legality of work done before March 1962.

In the summer of 1962, Leary and Alpert and some friends went to Mexico and rented the Catalina Hotel at Zihuatenejo, a seaside resort near Acapulco, where some Harvard students and other persons joined them. In the fall, Alpert and Leary returned to Harvard, attacking the restrictions on their mind-liberating research and predicting that this would be a major civil liberties issue in the next decade. "Consciousness expansion" was the chief table conversation at Harvard. Some undergraduates enrolled in a notoriously difficult course in organic chemistry solely to develop the skill to synthesize mescaline; and a new figure appeared in the Square, a professional "junk" peddler selling high-grade mescaline and sugar cubes each containing a drop of LSD. Leary and Alpert vigorously attacked the subsequent stern warning of Dean Monro and Dr. Farnsworth as being scientifically irresponsible.

In October of 1962, Leary announced the formation of IFIF, the "International Federation for Internal Freedom" (dues $10 a year) and the continuation of the "Freedom Center" in Mexico during the summer of 1963 ($200 a month for room and board, half-rates for children). Soon an IFIF-Los Angeles center was opened, and two other experiments in multi-family living (an idea derived from Huxley's Utopian novel *Island*) were begun in suburban Newton, Massachusetts, in two houses, one of which had an India-print-draped meditation room accessible only by trapdoor. Despite the freely expressed attacks of the IFIF group, the Harvard Corporation nevertheless scrupulously voted on 7 January to honor an overlooked verbal promise by the Dean of the Graduate School of Education of a one-year extension of Alpert's appointment. In February of 1963, IFIF literature began to appear, mailed to undergraduates and any other interested persons.

In Cambridge one could now arrange to buy mescaline in local sandwich shops, and a new fad in the spring was to buy packets of morning-glory seeds, because these were thought to be the basis of the ancient Aztec *ololiuqui*. In April, Leary disappeared from classes, allegedly without prior notice, and turned up in Los Angeles. The Corporation, consulted by President Pusey and the Dean of the Faculty, promptly relieved Leary of his teaching duties and stopped his salary. Alpert admitted to the President on 14 May that he had broken an agreement not to give the drugs to undergraduates, and on 27 May the Corporation voted on these grounds to terminate Alpert's services immediately. Leary was now reported to be in Mexico. In June, responding to allegedly odd happenings at Zihuatanejo, the Mexican Government gave the entire IFIF group five days to leave the country. In November of 1963 they were reported to have bought a small uninhabited island in the British West Indies as a possible refuge; in December, Alpert and Leary were settled in a rented 53-room mansion on a 2,500-acre estate near the village of Millbrook in Dutchess County, New York; authorities at the neighboring Bennett College for girls promptly declared the estate out-of-bounds for its students.

In the summer of 1963 a new quarterly, the *Psychedelic Review* (the term, which means "mind-expanding," is taken from Osmond [1957]), began publication in Cambridge, Massachusetts, with Alpert and Leary on the board of editorial consultants. The first issue contained an article by Metzner on the pharmacology of various psychotropic drugs, including mescaline. The fall number of the *Review*, in an editorial, stated that

This second issue of *The Psychedelic Review* marks a major change in organization and policy. The journal is no longer published or sponsored by the International Federation for Internal Freedom. The leaders of that organization, Dr. Timothy Leary and Dr. Richard Alpert, do not continue as members of the *Review's* Board of Editors, and no continuing members of the Board are members of IFIF. The point of this sharp separation is to avoid the identification of *The Psychedelic Review* with any single socio-ideological group or perspective. Amid the controversy — scientific, philosophical, legal — that rages around psychedelics, the *Review* seeks to be an independent, non-partisan voice.

The second issue contained an interesting and provocative article by J. K. Adams on "Psychosis: 'Experimental' or Real," a short study by G. Fisher on proper dosages of psychotropic substances, a scholarly survey by R. E. Schultes, Curator of Economic Botany at the Harvard Botanical Museum, of "Botanical Sources of the New World Narcotics" (with data on peyote on pp. 156-157), and a paper on "Psychometabolism" by Sir Julian Huxley, distinguished biologist and brother of the late novelist Aldous Huxley.

The Summer, 1963 number of *The Harvard Review* was devoted to "Drugs and the Mind". A major article in it is on "The Politics of Consciousness Expansion," written by Richard Alpert and Timothy Leary in a curiously telegraphic though quite clear style:

> Establishment controls vision. Vision bursts establishment. . . . The university is the Establishment's apparatus for training consciousness-contractors. The intellectual ministry of defense . . . Internal politics . . . LSD is more frightening than the Bomb! . . . We are, in a real sense, prisoners of our cognitive concepts and strategies . . . psychedelic compounds. Cortical vitamins . . . The game is about to be changed, ladies and gentlemen . . . The verbal dam is collapsing. Head for the hills, or prepare your intellectual craft to flow with the current (pp. 33-35).

Reprinted and adapted from the *Botanical Museum Leaflets of Harvard University* is a valuable summary of the ethnobotany of *teonanacatl* by Gordon Wasson. The issue also contains a report by Jones of a psilocybin experience, and "An Artist's View" by Richard Hoener, including two watercolors and two sketches by the author. In a brief history of narcotics in the United States, Zinberg makes the surprising point that consciousness of the danger of drug addiction is relatively new in America. "The remarkable fact is that at the turn of the century over four percent of the population of the United States was addicted to narcotics," largely through the use of popular proprietaries containing opium, morphine, codeine, and heroin (p. 57).

In 1963 the use of psychotropic drugs by college students was the object of aroused concern. E. A. Grossman wrote on the matter in the *Harvard Alumni Bulletin,* and the next issue of the *Bulletin* contained a similar article by H. K. Beecher, reprinted in the *Medical Tribune.* The 1963 issues of the *Harvard Crimson* were full of the controversy. In a leading editorial, Dr. Roy R. Grinker, Editor of the *Archives of General Psychiatry,* warned psychiatrists and others against the experimental use of LSD-25 and other psychotomimetic drugs; and in the same issue, Drs. Sidney Cohen and Keith Ditman of the Veterans' Administration Hospital in Los Angeles wrote of the increasing number of adverse reactions to the drugs. Elizabeth Mirel summarized these warnings of the "Danger in 'Happy Drugs'" in a widely syndicated Science Service release to newswriters, and the senior scientific reporter of the *New York Times,* William L. Laurence, wrote "On Hallucinogens: Warning Issued over the Dangers of Improper Use of LSD-25."

Peyote and mescaline already seem destined to be *passé* among both mystics and beat hipsters. It is likely, in any case, that peyote as used by Indians will never constitute a significant danger; the action of panpeyotl is relatively very feeble, and its alkaloids are antagonistic to one another in their effect. Synthetic mescaline, the dispensing of which can be more easily controlled, is a more serious and controversial issue. The real danger lies rather in LSD-25 and psilocybin, both of which are many hundreds of times as potent as the peyote alkaloids. And, indeed, it was psilocybin and LSD-25 that primarily figured in the experiments both at Harvard and among the beatnik Bohemians and the lunatic fringe of Los Angeles "therapists."

David Ricks, in his "Mushrooms and Mystics: A Caveat" in the *Harvard Review* issue on "Drugs and the Mind," arrives at what is probably a consensus among many people concerning lay use of psychotropic drugs:

Most of the individual research on the drugs was badly designed and poorly executed, and some was irresponsible. . . . The issue is whether one has any right to do something that might be harmful when he is in no position to pick up the pieces . . . It is also necessary to consider who takes the drugs and why . . . some . . . [do] for "kicks". . . . And although armchair pilgrims and parlor game mystics may not be exemplary people, there is still something honest and admirable about their search for raw experience. . . . One must have an unusually strong passive component in his make-up if he is to see any sense in seeking his own personal Everest in a pill. In the drug user, as in the alcoholic, this optimism toward the other world of expanded consciousness is often combined with a profound pessimism about the prospects of satisfaction in the world of everyday experience. . . . To cater to this passivity and despair, rather than to help young people develop means of combating it, goes against some of the most basic values of education. . . . A society which forces intelligent and informed people into stuporous retreat is not completely healthy. Most of us may not want to follow them into their illusory Utopias, but the fact that they find that retreat necessary should shake our complacency to its deepest roots.

It is perhaps fitting to end with the "Reflections of a Peyote Eater" himself. Chase Mellen III, an English major at Harvard, attended a Native American Church meeting one recent summer on a Montana reservation, where he partook of a boiled decoction of peyote. Mr. Mellen's attitude toward the Indians is sympathetic and humane; and he writes a competent, intelligent, and articulate report on a peyote experience (but this has now been done so many times!). In the *Harvard Review* (p. 67) he writes:

The drug experience is of value as a method in scientific research (where it may lead to an understanding of the chemistry of the mind) and as a purely hedonic escape from the routine of daily life. To think of it as anything more is unwise.

But even this judgment may be over-generous. The promise of an understanding of schizophrenia — at least so far as experiments with mescaline are concerned — has now, according to the experts, largely faded away. As for hedonic escapes, western man already complacently accepts (since it is ours) the mass use of substances such as tobacco and alcohol which, to physical health, can be far more dangerous than a weekly Indian use of a feebly psychotropic desert plant. And as for his mental health, western man is already embedded in narcotic institutions such as advertising, television, and movies—which invite illusions about ourselves fully as dangerous as any Indian religious cult.

NOTE

While this edition is in press, word has been received that California's Fourth District Court of Appeals has ruled that

. . . the use of peyote in Indian religious ceremonies constitutes enough of a threat to public safety to make the act illegal without violating constitutional rights of religious freedom. The ruling affirmed the conviction of three Navajo Indians who had appealed on the grounds of violation of religious freedom. In an 18-page opinion, the court pointed out that there are precedents for the use of the state's police power in the area of religion where the health, safety or welfare of the general public is endangered. . . . The court decision noted that this group has no rules of membership nor formal restriction of its ceremonies to members. Given the right to use peyote would lay open the drug to "that segment of our society whose conduct persistently reflects the bizarre," the decision stated.*

This action raises a number of legal and social questions: what constitutes "enough" to set aside constitutional rights; how it is possible that religious rights can be withdrawn without violating religious freedom; and whether the police power of the state is here properly invoked against a bona fide and long-established American Indian religious group. It is unclear why the court should arrogate to itself the giving or the withholding of a right to freedom of religion which the U.S. Constitution already explicitly guarantees; why the religious users should be directly penalized in the alleged indirect interest of other potential users *ultra vires* and beyond the question; why the use of peyote should have been adjudged harmful in the face of a massive contrary consensus of experts on the matter — and, indeed, why in an open and democratic society non-conformity, even to the point of conduct

* "Peyote Ruled Illegal in California," *Institute of Indian Studies* (Vermillion, South Dakota) Series LXIV, Bulletin No. 28 [February 1964] News Report No. 19.

adjudged by some "bizarre," should now become illegal. Carried to its logical conclusion, this reasoning would hold that any departure from conformity to any orthodoxy
is illegal. The judgment would appear to be inconsistent with decades of liberal interpretation of the rights of this religious minority, and even appears to run counter to
the precedent set by the Hon. Yale McFate in the neighboring state of Arizona, with
whose notable opinion experts both in peyotism and in pharmacology have with una-
nimity concurred.

BIBLIOGRAPHY

ADAMS, J. K., Psychosis: "Experimental" and Real, *Psychedelic Review*, 1 (1963) 121-144.

ADLER, A. & POETZL, O., Ueber eine eigenartige Reaktion auf Meskalin bei einer Kranken mit doppelseitigen Herden in der Sehsphäre, *Jahrbuch für Psychiatrie und Neurologie*, 53 (1936) 13-34.

AGUIRRE BELTRAN, GONZALO, *Medicina y Magia*, Mexico: Instituto Nacional Indigenista, 1963 (Ch. 7, "Peyotl Zacatequensi," pp. 140-162).

ALEKSANDROVSKII, A. B., BABSKII, E. B. & KRYAZHEV, V., [Local parabiotic changes in the brain produced by mescaline poisoning] *Arkhiv Biologischeskikh Nauk* 42 (1936) 147-173.

ALLES, G. A., Some relations between chemical structure and physiological action of mescaline and related compounds, in Abramson, H. A. (ed.), *Neuropharmacology*, New York: Macy Foundation, 1957, pp. 181-267.

ALPERT, R. & LEARY, T. The Politics of Consciousness Expansion, (Drugs and the Mind Issue) *The Harvard Review* 1 (1963) 33-37.

AMERICAN ASSOCIATION FOR THE ADVANCEMENT OF SCIENCE, Publication 42, *Psychopharmacology*, Washington, 1956, 175 pp.

AMERICAN CIVIL LIBERTIES UNION, *40th Annual Report*, 1960, p. 55.

ANONYMOUS, Estudio relativo al peyote, *Instituto médico nacional de México*, 1913.

ANONYMOUS, Hallucinations, *Lancet*, 240 (1941), p. 421.

ANONYMOUS, Is Peyote Narcotic? No, say Indians, *Southwesterner*, 2 (1963 #7 (Reprinted in *Newsletter* of Bureau on Alcoholism, Health and Welfare Building, Regina, Saskatchewan, Canada, 11 March 1963, mimeographed).

ANONYMOUS, Mescaline in psychiatric research, *Lancet*, 1 (1936), p. 553.

ANONYMOUS, Peyotes datos para su estudio, *Anales del Instituto médico nacional de México*, 4 (1899) 203-214.

ANONYMOUS, The phenomenon of mescal intoxication, *New York Medical Journal*, 65 (1897) 882-884.

ARTHUR, W. R., *Law of Drugs*, St. Paul: West Publishing Co., 1940, (*Vide sub* Poison, Use of peyote, pellote, regulated by statute).

BANHOLZER, K., CAMPBELL, T. W. & SCHMID, H., Notiz ueber eine neue Synthese von Mezcalin, N-methyl- und N-dimethyl-mezcaline, *Helvetica chimica Acta*, 35 (1952) 1577-1581.

BARBER, C. G., Rejoinder to Maurer, Letters to the Editor, *American Anthropologist*, 62 (1960) 685-687.

BARD, L., "El peyote," algunas observaciones clinicas sobre sus efectos, *Revista médica latino-americana* (B. A.), 26 (1941) 471-487.

BARNARD, MARY, The God in the Flowerpot, *American Scholar*, 32 (1963) 578-586 (Reprinted in *Psychedelic Review*, 1 [1963] 244-251).

BARRON, F., JARVIK, M. E. & BUNNELL, S., The Hallucinogenic Drugs, *Scientific American*, 210 (1964) 29-37.

BECCARI, E., Farmacognosia del Peyotl, *Archivio di farmacológia sperimentale e scienze affini*, 61 (1936).

BEECHER, H. K., Science, drugs, students, *Harvard Alumni Bulletin*, 65 (2 February 1963), p. 338 (Reprinted as Editorial in *Medical Tribune*, 4 [12 April 1963] p. 11).

BENNINGTON, F. & MORIN, R. D., An improved synthesis of mescaline, *Journal of the American Chemical Society*, 73 (1951) p. 1353.

BENNINGTON, F., MORIN, R. D. & CLARK, L. C. JR., Mescaline analogs. IV Substituted 4,5,6-tri-methoxynindoles, *Journal of Organic Chemistry*, 20 (1955) 1454-1457.

BERNHEIM, F. & BERNHEIM, M. L. C., The oxidation of mescaline and certain other amines, *Journal of Biological Chemistry*, 123 (1936) 317-326.

Birth, 3 (1960) 64-80 [various quotations on peyote from diverse sources].

BLASCHKO, H., Enzymic oxidation of mescalin in the rabbit's liver, *Journal of Physiology*, 103 (1944-45) Proc. 13 P.

BLOCK, W., Pharmacological aspects of mescaline, in Rinkel, M. & Denber, H. C. B. (eds.), *Chemical Aspects of Psychosis*, New York: McDowell, 1958, pp. 108-119.

BLOCK, W., Zur Physiologie des ^{14}C-radioaktiven Mescalins in Tierversuch, IV. Vergleichende Untersuchungen mit ^{14}C-Mescalin und ^{14}C-β-Phenyl-äthylamine, *Zeitschrift für Naturforschung*, 8b:8 (1953) 440-444.

BLOCK, W., *In vitro* Versuche zum Einbau von ^{14}C-Mescalin und ^{14}C-β-Phenyl-äthylamine in Proteine, I. Mitteilung. Der enzymatische Vorgang, *Zeitschrift für physiologische Chemie*, 294 (1953) 1-12; II. Mitteilung. Einflüsse der Aminoxydase, *ibidem*, pp. 49-56; III. Mitteilung, *In vitro* Versuche zum Einbau von ^{14}C-Mescalin und ^{41}C-β-Phenyl-äthylamine in Proteine, *ibidem*, 296 (1954) 1-10.

BLOCK, W. & BLOCK, K., La distribution de la méscaline marquée (^{14}C-radioactif) dans l'organisme animal et son association avec les protéines du foie, *2e Congrès international de Biochimie*, Paris, 1952, p. 429.

BLOCK, W., & BLOCK, K., Synthese von ^{14}C-radioaktivem Mescalin, *Chemische Berichte*, 85 (1952) 1009-1012.

BLOCK, W., BLOCK, K., & PATZIG, B., Zur Physiologie des ^{14}C-radioaktivem Mescalins in Tierversuch. I. Fermentversuch und Ausscheidungsprodukte, *Zeitschrift für physiologische Chemie*, 290 (1952) 160-168; II. Verteilung der Radioaktivität in den Organen in Abhängigkeit von der Zeit, *ibidem*, 230-236; III. Mescalineinbau in Leberprotein, *ibidem*, 291 (1952) 119-128.

Boston Globe, 1962: 12 December; 1963: 14, 15 March; 17 April; 13 May.

BOSTON PSYCHOPATHIC HOSPITAL, Experimental Psychoses (LSD-25), *Scientific American*, 192 (1955) 34-39.

BOYER, J., Le peyotl, cactus mexicain qui provoque des rêves visuels merveilleux, *Nature* (Paris), 55 (1927) 403-406.

BRIDGER, W. H. & GANTT, W. H., The effect of mescaline on differentiated conditional reflexes, *American Journal of Psychiatry*, 113 (1956) 352-360.

BROMBERG, W. & TRANTER, C. L., Peyote intoxication: some psychological aspects of peyote rite, *Journal of Nervous and Mental Disease*, 97 (1943) 518-527.

BRUNNER, E. M., *Mandan*, [Ch. IV] in E. H. Spicer (ed.), *Perspectives in American Indian Culture Change*, Chicago: University of Chicago Press, 1961, pp. 187-277.

BULLETIN ON NARCOTICS, 9 #2 (April-June 1959), p. 18; also Fig. 7, Handbill on "Peyotyl."

BURROUGHS, W. S., *Naked Lunch*, Paris: Olympia Press, 1962 (Also New York: Grove Press, 1962).

CAMISACA, L., L'azione della mescalina sull'apparato vestibolare, *Oto-rino-laringologia italiana*, 18 (1949) 90-107.

CANADIAN MENTAL HEALTH ASSOCIATION, The Strange Case of Mr. Kovish, Regina, Saskatchewan, ? 1963 (brochure).

CARLSON, G. G. & JONES, V. H., Some Notes on Uses of Plants by the Comanche Indians, *Michigan Academy of Science, Arts and Letters*, 25 (1939) 517-542, pp. 537-538 & 540.

CATTELL, J. P., Influence of mescaline on psychodynamic material, *Journal of Nervous and Mental Disease*, 119 (1954) 233-244.

CAZENEUVE, J., Le peyotisme au Nouveau-Mexique, Notes sur une nouvelle Religion, *Revue Philosophique*, 171-182.

CHAUMERLIAC & ROCHE, Un vasodilateur inattendu, la mescaline, *Bulletin de la société d'ophtalmologie de Paris*, (1948) 800-802.

CHOLDEN, L. (ed.), *Lysergic acid diethylamide and Mescaline in Experimental Psychiatry*, New York & London: Grune & Stratton, 1956.

CHWEITZER, A. & GEBLEWICZ, E., L'action de la mescaline sur la coloration du Cyprin bronzé, *Sociéte de biologie, Comptes rendus*, 128 (1938) 867-868.

CHWEITZER, A., GEBLEWICZ, E. & LIBERSON, W., Etude de l'electrencéphalogramme humain dans un cas de l'intoxication mescalinique, *Année psychologique* (Paris), 37 (1936) 94-119.

CHWEITZER, A., GEBLEWICZ, E. & LIBERSON, W., Action de la mescaline sur les ondes α (rythme de Berger) chez l'homme, *Société de biologie, Comptes rendus*, 124 (1937) 1296-1299.

CLARK, L. C., FOX, R. P., BENNINGTON, F & MORIN, R. D., Effects of mescaline, lysergic acid diethylamide, and related compounds on respiratory enzyme activity of brain homogenates, *Federation Proceedings*, 13 (1954) 27.

CLERC, A., PARIS, R. & JANOT, M. M., Contribution à l'étude experimentale du sulfate de mescaline, *Société de biologie, Comptes rendus*, 121 (1936) 1300-1302.

COCHIN, J., WOODS, L. A. & SEEVERS, M. H., The absorption, distribution, and urinary excretion of mescaline in the dog, *Journal of Pharmacology and Experimental Therapeutics*, 101 (1951) 205-209.

COHEN, S., Notes on the hallucinogenic state, *International Record of Medicine*, 173 (1960) 380-387.

COLOMB, D., *Contribution à l'étude pharmacologique de la mescaline*, Lyon, 1939, 80pp.

CREMA, A., Valutazione quantitativa dell'azione dei farmaci sulla funzionalità vestibolare, III. Neurotossicita della mescalina, *Bolletino della società italiana di biologia sperimentale*, 29 (1953) 1520-1522.

CROIZAT, L., A study of the genus Lophophora Coulter, II. *Desert Plant Life*, 15 (1943) 152-154.

CRUSE, R. R., Chemurgic survey of desert flora in the American Southwest, *Economic Botany*, 3 (1949) 111-131.

CUCCHI, A., Azione della mescalina sul profilo psicologico, *Rivista sperimentale di Freniatria*, 63 (1939) 393-404.

DAVIS, L. B., Peyotism and the Blackfeet Indians of Montana: An Historical Assessment, *Studies in Plains Anthropology and History*, #1 (Mimeographed), Browning, Montana, 1961.

DE JONGH, H. H., *Experimental Catatonia*, Baltimore: Williams & Wilkins Co., 1945.

DELAY, J., DENIKER, P., ROPERT, M. & THUILLIER, J., Antagonisme de la mescaline et de la chloropromazine, *Société de Biologie, Comptes rendus*, 150 (1956) 512-513.

DELAY, J. & GERARD, H. P., Les illusions de la mescaline, *Encéphale*, 39 (1950) 55-63.

DELAY, J. & GERARD, H. P., L'intoxication mescalinique expérimentale, *Encéphale*, 37 (1948) 196-235.

DELAY, J., GERARD, H. P. & HALLAIX, D., Illusions et hallucinations de la mescaline, *Press médicale*, 57 (1949) 1210-1211.

DELAY, J., GERARD, H. P. & RACAMIER, P. C., Les synesthésies dans l'intoxication mescalinique, *Encéphale*, 40 (1951) 1-10.

DELAY, J., PICHOT, P. & THUILLIER, J., Les nouvelles chimothérapies de l'alcoolisme, *Annales médico-psychologiques*, 2 (1949) 427-429.

DENBER, H. C. B., Drug-Induced States resembling Naturally Occurring Psychoses, in S. Garattini & V. Ghetti (eds.), *Psychotropic Drugs*, New York, 1957, pp. 26-35.

DENBER, H. C. B., Studies on mescaline, XI. Biochemical findings during the mescaline-induced state, with observations on the blocking action of different psychotropic drugs, *Psychiatric Quarterly*, 35 (1961) 18-48. [For other studies by Denber, see Bibliography in La Barre, W., *Current Anthropology*, 1 (1951) p. 58; see also under Merlis in the present Bibliography].

DENBER, H. C. B., Studies on mescaline, VII. The role of anxiety in the mescaline-induced state and its influence on the therapeutic result, *Journal of Nervous and Mental Disease*, 124 (1956) 74-77.

DENBER, H. C. B. & MERLIS, S., Studies on mescaline, I. Action in schizophrenic patients, *Psychiatric Quarterly*, 29 (1955) 421-429.

DENBER, H. C. B. & MERLIS, S., Studies on mescaline, VI. Therapeutic aspects of the mescaline-chlorpromazine combination, *Journal of Nervous and Mental Disease*, 122 (1955) 463-469.

DENBER, H. C. B., MERLIS, S. & HUNTER, W., Studies on mescaline: its action on the clinical and brainwave patterns of schizophrenic patients, *Journal of Nervous and Mental Disease*, 120 (1954) p. 87 [abstract].

DENBER, H. C. B., TELLER, D. N., RAJOTTE, P. & KAUFFMAN, D., Studies on mescaline, XIII. The effect of prior administration of various psychotropic drugs on different biochemical parameters: a preliminary report, *Annals of the New York Academy of Science*, 96 (1962) 14-36.

DE NITO, G., Richerche tossicologiche e farmacologiche sulla mescalina, *Rassegna de terapia e patologia clinica*, 6 (1934) 577-594. [Abstract in *Berichte über die gesamte Physiologie und experimentelle Pharmacologie*, 84 (1935) p. 511].

DESOILLE, H., Remarque sur le mode de formation des hallucinations provoquées par le peyotl (expériences personnelles), *Revue d'oto-neuro ophtalmogie*, 16 (1938) 136-138.

DESSI, P., Sul dosaggio fotometrico della mescalina e simpanina col reattivo di Richter, *Farmaco Scienze e technica*, 5 (1950) 32-38.

DESSI, P. & FRANCO, T., Applicazione della reazione de Beyer e Skinner al dosaggio fotometrico della mescalina e dell'istamina, I. Curvo d'assorbimento nel visibile, *Bolletino della Società Italiana di biologia sperimentale*, 25 (1949) 1368-1369.

DIGUET, L., Contribution à l'étude ethnographique des races primitives du Mexique: la Sierra du Nayarit et ses indigènes, *Nouvelles Archives des Missions scientifiques et littéraires*, 9 (1899) 621-625.

DIXON, W. E., A preliminary note on the pharmacology of the alkaloids derived from the mescal plant, *British Medical Journal*, 2 (1898) 1060.

DORNOW, A. & PETSCH, G., Notiz zur Darstellung des β-Oxy β-(3,4,5-trimethoxy-phenyl)-aethylamins ("Oxymezcalin"), des Bis-[β-3,4,5-trimethoxy-phenyl)-aethyl]-amine ("Dimezcalin") und des β-(3,4,5,-trimethoxyphenyl) aethylamine ("Mescalin"), *Archiv der Pharmazie*, 284 (1951) 160-163.

DORNOW, A. & PETSCHE, G., Ueber die Darstellung des Oxymezcalins und Mezcalins, II, *Archiv der Pharmazie*, 285 (1952) 323-326.

DORVAULT, Peyotl, *L'officine*, 1945, p. 1306.

DUC, C., Sintomi visivi nell' intossicazione mescalina, *Bolletino di oculistica*, 15 (1936) 745-760.

DUCLOUX, E. H., Algunas reacciónes microquímicas de la mescalina, *Revista Farmaceutica* (B. A.), 74 (1931) 87-99.

DUCLOUX, E. H., *Notas Microquimicas sobre "Doping"*, Buenos Aires, 267 pp.

DUSTIN, C. B., Peyotism and New Mexico, Farmington, N. M., 1960, 51 pp. (brochure).

EBIN, DAVID (ed.), *The Drug Experience*, New York: Orion, 1961.

ENDO, K., Experimental Study of mescalin intoxication on relation between clinical picture and EEG in man, *Folio psychiatrica neurotica japonica*, 6 (1952) 104-113.

EY, H. & RANCOULE, M., Hallucinations mescaliniques et troubles psychosensoriels de l'encéphalite épidémique chronique, *Encéphale*, 33 (1938), pt. II, 1-25.

FAVILLI, M., La percezione del tempo nell' ebbrezza mescalinica, *Rassegna di studi psichiatrici*, 26 (1937) 455-462.

FAVILLI, M. & HEYMANN, H., Sull'alcune modificazioni psichiche da intossicazione mescalinica, *Rassegna di studi psichiatrici*, 26 (1937) 191-212.

FEIGEN, G. A. & ALLES, G. A., Physiological concomitants of mescaline intoxication, A study of the effects upon normal subjects tested with submaximal doses, *Journal of Clinical and Experimental Psychopathology and Quarterly Review of Psychiatry and Neurology*, 16 (1955) 167-178.

FELICE, PHILIPPE DE, *Poisons sacrés, ivresses divines*, Paris: A. Michel, 1936.

FERACA, S. E., Wakinyan: Contemporary Teton Dakota Religion, *Studies in Plains Anthropology and History*, #2, Browning, Montana, 1963, pp. 48-57.

FERNANDEZ, V., Análisis qualitiva y cuantitativa del mezcal, *Monografías mexicanas de matéria médica*, (1890) 173-190.

FISCHER, R., Factors involved in drug-produced model psychoses, *Experientia*, 10 (1954) 435-436 [Also in *Journal of Mental Science*, 100 (1954) 623-631].

FISCHER, R., Pharmacology and Metabolism of Mescaline, *Revue Canadienne de Biologie*, 17 (1958) 389-409.

FISCHER, R., Possible biosynthesis of D-lysergic acid diethylamide-like compounds from mescaline, *Experientia*, 11 (1955) 162-163.

FISCHER, R., Selbst-beobachtungen im Mezkalinrausch, *Schweitzerische Zeitschrift für Psychologie*, 5 (1946) 308-313.

FISCHER, R. & AGNEW, N., On drug-induced experimental psychoses, *Naturwissenschaften*, 41 (1954) 431-432.

FISCHER, R., GEORGI, F. & WEBER, R., Psychophysische Korrelationen, VIII. Modellversuchen zum Schizophrenieproblem, Lysergsäurediäthylamid und Mezcalin, *Schweitzerische medizinische Wochenschrift*, 81 (1951) 817-819 & 837-840.

FISCHER, R., GRIFFIN, F. & LISS, L., Biological Aspects of Time in Relation to (Model) Psychoses, *Annals of the New York Academy of Science*, 96 (1962) 44-64.

FISHER, G., Some Comments Concerning Dosage Levels of Psychedelic Compounds for Psychotherapeutic Experiences, *Psychedelic Review*, 1 (1963) 208-219, pp. 214-215.

FORSTER, E., Selbstversuch mit Meskalin, *Zeitschrift für die gesamte Neurologie und Psychiatrie*, 46 (1919).

FRANKE, G., Variierte Serienversuche mit Meskalin, *Zietschrift für die gesamte Neurologie und Psychiatrie*, 150 (1934) 427-433.

FREDERKING, W., Ueber die Verwendung von Rauschdrogen (Mescaline und Lysergsäurediäthylamid) in der Psychotherapie, *Psyche* (Stuttgart), 7 (1953) 342-364. [See also Intoxicant Drugs (mescaline and lysergic acid diethylamide) in psychotherapy, *Journal of Nervous and Mental Disease*, 121 (1955) 262-266].

FRIEDHOFF, A. J. & GOLDSTEIN, M., New Developments in metabolism of mescaline and related amines, *Annals of the New York Academy of Science*, 96 (1962) 5-13.

FRISCH, H. & WALDMANN, E., Darstellung von β (3,4,5-Trimethoxyphenyl)-β-aminoethan, *Chemisches Zentralblatt*, 1-2 (1932) 2867.

FRISCH, H. & WALDMANN, E., Mescaline, *Austrian*, 125,694, 15 July 1931.

FUGLE, E., Mesquakie Witchcraft Lore, *Plains Anthropologist*, 6 (1961) 31-39 [Mimeographed].

GARATTINI, S. & GHETTI, V., *Psychotropic Drugs*, Milan: Proceedings of the International Symposium on Psychotropic Drugs, 1957.

GEARE, R. L., The consumption of peyote among the Indians, *Merck's Report* (New York), 22 (1913) 9.109.

GEBHARD, P., *Letter*, 26 January 1960.

GEESINK, A. & DEN HARTOG JAGER, W. A., Influence de la mescaline (trimethoxy-β-phényl-éthylamine) et de la diméthoxy-β-phényl-éthylamine sur la tension artérielle, *Archives néerlandaises de physiologie*, 24 (1939) 79-82.

GEORGI, F., FISCHER, R. & WEBER, R., Psychophysische Korrelationen, 6. Modellversuche zum Schizophrenieproblem, Mescalintoxikose und Leberfunktion, *Schweitzerische medizinische Wochenschrift*, 79 (1949) 121-123 [See also *Excerpta Medica*, sect. 8, 2 (1949) 951].

GERSHON, S. & OLARIU, J., JB 329, A New Psychotomimetic, its antagonism by tetrahydroaminacrin and its comparison with LSD, Mescaline and Sernyl, *Journal of Neuropsychiatry*, 1 (1960) 283-292.

GORTON, B. E., Peyote and the Arizona Court Decision, Letters to the Editor, *American Anthropologist*, 63 (1961) 1334-1335.

GREEN, JACK, Peyote, in Seymour Krim (ed.), *The Beats*, Greenwich, Conn.: Fawcett Publications, 1960, pp. 94-107.

GRINKER, ROY, Editorial, *Archives of General Psychiatry*, 9 June 1963.

GROSSMAN, E. A., The undergraduate: some aspects of consciousness at Harvard, *Harvard Alumni Bulletin*, 65 #7 (12 January 1963) 304-305, 311.

GUILLARMOT, J., La Pellotine chez les aliénés, Thèse Doct. Méd., Lausanne, 1897.

GUTTMANN, E., Experimentelle Halluzination durch Anhalonium lewinii, *Berliner klinische Wochenschrift*, 68 (1921) 235, 816 [See also *Deutsche medizinische Wochenschrift*, 47 (1921) 145].

GUTTMAN, E. & MACLAY. W. S., Mescaline and depersonalization: therapeutic experiments, *Journal of Neurology and Psychopathology*, 16 (1936) 193-212.

HAHN, G., Synthese des Mescalins (Entgegnung auf die "Berichtigung" von K. H. Slotta und G. Szyszka), *Berichte der deutschen chemischen Gesellschaft*, 67 B (1934) 1210-1211.

HAHN, G. & WASSMUTH, H., Ueber β-[Oxyphenyl] äthylamine und ihre Umwandlungen, 1. *Berichte der deutschen chemischen Gesellschaft*, 67 B (1934) 696-708.

HAMET, R., Neue Beobachtungen über die physiologische Wirkung des Mescalins, *Archiv für experimentelle Pathologie und Pharmacologie*, 169 (1933) 97-113.

HARRINGTON, M. R., Religion and Ceremonies of the Lenape, *Indian Notes and Monographs* (Heye Foundation) Museum of the American Indian, 1921, 185-190.

Harvard Crimson, 1962: February 20, 21, 28; March 15, 16, 17, 19, 21, 22, 23, 28; April 16, 23; May 28; October 22, 25; December 13. 1963: January 16; February 14, 20, 28; March 1, 15, 19; May 1.

HAVENS, J., A Memo to Quakers on Consciousness-changing Drugs (LSD, Mescaline, Psilocybin), *Mss.* 1963.

HEFFTER, A., Beiträge zur chemischen Kenntnis der Cactaceen, *Apotheker Zeitung*, 11 (1896) 746.

HEY, P. The synthesis of a new homologued mescaline, *Quarterly Journal of Pharmacy*, 20 (1947) 129-134.

HIMWICH, H. E., Psychopharmacologic Drugs, *Science*, 127 #3289 (10 January 1958) 59-72.

HOCH, P. H., Experimentally produced psychoses, *American Journal of Psychiatry*, 107 (1951) 607-611; *ibidem*, 108 (1952) 579.

HOCH, P. H., CATTELL, J. P. & PENNES, H. H., Effects of drugs: theoretical considerations from a psychological viewpoint, *American Journal of Psychiatry*, 108 (1952) 585-589.

HOCH, P. H., CATTELL, J. P. & PENNES, H. H., Effects of mescaline and lvsergic acid (d-LSD-25), *American Journal of Psychiatry*, 108 (1952) 579-584.

HOENER, A., An Artist's View, [Drugs and the Mind Issue] *Harvard Review*, 1 (1963) 44-50.

HOFFER, A., OSMOND, H. & SMYTHIES, J., Schizophrenia: A new approach, II. Result of a year's research, *Journal of Mental Science*, 100 (1954) 29-45.

HOLLANDER, A. N. J., De Peyote-cultus der Noord-amerikaanise indianen, *Mensch en Maatschappij*, 11 (1935), #1-2.

HOLLISTER, L. E. & HARTMAN, A. M., Mescaline, LSD, and psilocybin: comparison of clinical syndromes, effects on color perception and biochemical measures, *Comprehensive Psychiatry*, 3 (1962) 235-241.

HORI, K., Ueber experimentelle Mescalinvergiftung: Versuch am Menschen, *Psychiatria et neurologia japonica*, 41 (1937) 13; Versuch an Tieren, *ibidem*, 42 (1938) 4.

HOWARD, J. H., Mescalism and Peyotism Once Again, *Plains Anthropologist*, 5 (1960) 84-85 [Mimeographed].

HOWARD, J. H., Potawatomi Mescalism and its Relationship to the Diffusion of the Peyote

Cult, *Plains Anthropologist*, 7 (1962) 125-135 [Mimeographed].

HURT, W. R., Factors in the Persistence of Peyote in the Northern Plains, *Plains Anthropologist*, 5 (1960) 16-27 [Mimeographed].

HUXLEY, A., *The Doors of Perception* and *Heaven and Hell* [both books now published as one], New York: Harper Colophon Books.

HUXLEY, A., Drugs that shape men's minds, *Saturday Evening Post*, 231 (18 October 1958) 28ff.

HUXLEY, A., Human Potentialities, in S. M. Farber & R. H. L. Wilson (eds.), *Control of the Mind*, New York: McGraw-Hill, 1961, pp. 60-76 [also in paperback].

HUXLEY, A., *Island*, New York: Harper, 1962.

HUXLEY, A., Mescaline and the "Other World," in L. Cholden (ed.), *op. cit.*

HUXLEY, A., Visionary Experience, in G. S. Nielsen (ed.), *Clinical Psychology*, vol. 4, Copenhagen: Munksgaard, 1962.

HUXLEY, J., Psychometabolism, *Psychedelic Review*, 1 (1963) 183-204, p. 199.

Indian Affairs, News Letter of the American Indian Fund and the Association on American Indian Affairs, Inc., Peyote and the Native American Church of the United States, #41A (Supplement), 1961.

Institute of Indian Studies, State University of South Dakota, Vermillion, S. D., #13 (15 August 1960) "NAC Groups Reorganize at State Meet"; LXII, Bull. #21 (August, 1962), News Report #15, "Native American Church of South Dakota, 40th Annual Convention."

International Federation for Internal Freedom, A Bibliography of Psychedelic and Related Research, #1, May 1963, 10 pp.

International Federation for Internal Freedom, Newsletter, May 1963; November 1963.

IRELAND, E. J., Peyote, divine plant of the South-western Indians, *Journal of the New Orleans College of Pharmacy*, 6 (1940-1942) 4.

ISIBASI, T., Beitraege zur Kenntniss der experimentellen Meskalinvergiftung an Normalen, *Psychiatria et neurologia Japonica*, 41 (1937) 38.

IWAMOTO, H. K., The synthesis of analogs of mescaline, Thesis, Graduate School of the University of Maryland, 1942-1944, 43 [Abstract].

JACKSON, D. D., Schizophrenia, *Scientific American*, 207 (1962) 65-72, 74, pp. 68-69.

JANOT, M. M. & BERNIER, M., Essai de locali-

sation des alcaloïdes dans le peyotl, *Bulletin des sciences pharmacologiques*, 40 (1933) 145-153.

JANTZ, H., Zur Pathophysiologie des Meskalinrausches, *Klinische Wochenscrift*, 19 (1940) 774; also *Medizinische Klinik* (Berlin), 36 (1940) 790.

JANTZ, H., Veränderung des Stoffwechsels im Meskalinrausch beim Menschen und im Tierversuch, *Zeitschrift für die gesamte Neurologie und Psychiatrie*, 171 (1941) 28-56.

JENSCH, H., Zur Synthese des Mezcalins, *Medizin und Chemie*, 3 (1936) 408-411.

JOEL, E., Peyotl, *Die medizinische Welt*, 3 (1929) 265-267.

KAHAN, MRS. F. H., Letter, 8 June 1959, Regina, Saskatchewan.

KELSEY, F. D., The Pharmacology of Peyote, *South Dakota Journal of Medicine and Pharmacy*, 12 (1959) 231-233.

KINDLER, K. & PESCHKE, W., Ueber neue über verbesserte Wege zum Aufbau von pharmakologisch wichtigen Aminen, VI. Ueber den Synthesen des Meskalins, *Archiv der Pharmazie*, 270 (1932) 410-413.

KINSKA, E., Mescaline, *Chemisky Obzor*, 22 (1947) 77-79.

KISTE, R. C., Preservation of Aboriginal Values as Evidenced by Crow Peyote Leaders, Paper delivered at the Northwestern Anthropological Conference, 26-27 April 1963, Eugene, Oregon.

KLINE, N. S. (ed.), *Psychopharmacology*, Washington: American Association for the Advancement of Science, #42, 1956.

KLUEVER, H., Mechanisms of Hallucinations, in *Studies in Personality: Essays in Honor of Lewis M. Terman*, New York: McGraw-Hill, 1942, pp. 175-207.

KNAUER, A. & MALONEY, W., A Preliminary Note on the Psychic Action of Mescalin, *Journal of Nervous and Mental Diseases*, 72 (1930) 397.

KOBLER, JOHN, The Dangerous Magic of LSD, *Saturday Evening Post*, 236th yr., #38 (2 November 1963), 30-32, 35-36, 39-40.

KRAPF, E. E., Experimentos com venènos embriagadores: seu valor para a patopsicologia y a clinica psiquiatrica, *Neurobiologia* (Recifa, Brazil), 14 (1951) 99-108.

KRIM, S. (ed.), *The Beats: A Gold Medal Anthology*, Greenwich (Conn.): Fawcett Publications, 1960.

LA FARGE, O., Defining Peyote as a Narcotic, Letters to the Editor, *American Anthropologist*, 62 (1960) 687-689.

LANDIS, C. & CLAUSEN, J., Certain effects of mescaline and lysergic acid on psychological functions, *Journal of Psychology*, 38 (1954) 211-221.

LANTERNARI, V., *The Religions of the Oppressed: A Study of Modern Messianic Cults*, New York: Knopf, 1963, (tr. L. Sergio), pp. 63-113.

LASKI, M., *Ecstasy: A Study of Some Secular and Religious Experiences*, London: Cresset, 1961 [Ch. 24, "Mescalin and Ecstasy," pp. 263-273].

LAWRENCE, W. L., On Hallucinogens: Warning Issued over the Dangers of Improper Use of LSD-25, *New York Times*, 9 June 1963, p. E-11.

LEBEAU, P. & JANOT, M. M., *Traité de pharmacie chimique*, Paris, 1955, vol. 4, p. 3135.

LECLERC, H., La plante qui fait les yeux émerveillés, *Presse médicale*, 34 (1926) 1581.

LEVY, J. E., Navajo Use of Native Psychoactive Drugs, *Mss.*, March 1963.

LEVY, J. E., Western Navajo Peyotism, Paper presented at the San Francisco Meeting of the American Anthropological Association, November 1963.

LEWIN, L., Ueber Anhalonium Lewinii und andere giftige Cacteen, *Berichte der deutschen Gesellschaft*, 12 (1894) 283-290.

LEWIS, J. L., & MCILWAIN, H., Action of some ergot derivatives, mescaline, and dibenamine on the metabolism of separated mammalian cerebral tissues, *Biochemical Journal*, 57 (1954) 680-684.

LLEWELLYN, J. F., Mescal buttons, *Proceedings, Missouri Pharmaceutical Association*, 20 (1900) 58-62.

London Observer, 2 February 1964, p. 23 [Article on mescaline, LSD, Cannabis, Banisteriopsis, etc.].

LOWIE, R. H., Peyote Rite, *Hastings Encyclopedia of Religion and Ethics*, Edinburgh and New York: Macmillan, 1908-1927, 4:735-736, 9:815.

MACLAY, W. S., & GUTTMANN. E., Mescaline hallucinations in artists, *Archives of Neurology and Psychiatry*, 45 (1941) 130-137.

MALOUF, C., Letter, 3 February 1960, Missoula, Montana.

MARINESCO, G., A propos de l'audition colorée, *Presse médicale*, 40 (1931) 743-744.

MARINESCO, G., Recherches sur l'action de la mescaline, *Presse médicale*, 74 (1933) 1433-1437.

MARINESCO, G., Visions colorées produites par la mescaline, *Presse médicale*, 92 (1933) 1864-1866.

MARRAZZI, A. S., & HART, E. R., Mescaline — Pharmacology of the nervous system, *Progress in Neurology, Psychology*, 8 (1953) 69-88.

MARRAZZI, A. S. & HART, E. R., Relationship of hallucinogens to andrenergic cerebral neurohumors, *Science*, 121 (1955) 365-367.

MARSCHALL, C. R., An inquiry into the causes of mescal visions, *Journal of Neurology and Psychopathology* (London), 17 (1936-1937) 289-304.

MATEFI, L., Mezcalin und Lysergsäure diäthyl-amid-Rausch: Selbstversuche mit besonderer Berücksichtigung eines Zeichentests, *Confinia Neurologica*, 12 (1952) 146-177.

MAURER, D. W., Peyote is Not a Drug of Addiction, Letters to the Editor, *American Anthropologist*, 62 (1960) 684-685.

MAURER, D. W. & VOGEL, V. H., *Narcotics and Narcotic Addiction*, Springfield (Ill.): Charles C Thomas, 1954.

MAYER-GROSS, W., Ueber Synaesthesien im Meskalinrausch, in G. Anschütz (ed.), *Farbe-Ton-Forschungen*, vol. 3, Hamburg, 1931.

MAYER-GROSS, W. & STEIN, H., Experimental Psychoses and other mental abnormalities produced by drugs, *British Medical Journal*, 2 (1951) 317-321.

MAYER-GROSS, W. & STEIN, H., Veränderte Sinnestätigkeit im Meskalinrausch, *Deutsche Zeitschrift für Nervenheilkunde*, 89 (1926) 112-118.

MCALLESTER, D., Letter, 9 September 1960, Middletown, Conn.

MCCLEARY, J. A., SYPHERD, P. S. & WALKINGTON, D. L., Antibiotic Activity of an Extract of Peyote *(Lophophora williamsii)*, *Economic Botany*, 14 (1960) 247-249.

MCCLURE, M., *Meat Science Essays*, San Francisco: City Lights Books, 1963.

MCFATE, YALE, Decision of the Honorable Yale McFate in the Case of the State of Arizona vs. Mary Attakai, No. 4089, Superior Court, Coconino County, Flagstaff, Arizona, July 26, 1960, 3:00 p.m., *American Anthropologist*, 63 (1961) 1335-1337 [Also Mimeographed].

MCKELLAR, P., Mescaline and Human Thinking, in Crocket, Sandison and Walk (eds.), *Hallucinogenic Drugs and Their Psychotherapeutic Use*, Springfield (Ill.): Charles C Thomas, 1963.

MCNICKLE, D. A., Peyote and the Indian, *Scientific Monthly*, 57 (1943) 220-229.

MELLEN, C., Reflections of a Peyote Eater, (Drugs and the Mind Issue), *Harvard Re-*

view, 1 (1963) 63-67.

MERLIS, S. & DENBER, H. C. B., Studies on mescaline, V. Electroencephalographic evidence for the antagonism between mescaline and chlorpromazine hydrochloride, *Journal of Nervous and Mental Disease*, 123 (1956) 542-545.

METZNER, R., The Pharmacology of Psychedelic Drugs, *Psychedelic Review*, 1 (1963) 69-100.

MICHAUX, H., *Connaissance par les Gouffres*, Paris: Gallimard, 1961.

MICHAUX, H., *L'Infini Turbulent*, Paris: Mercure de France, 1957 (chs. I-III).

MICHAUX, H., *Misérable Miracle*, Monaco: Rocher, 1956.

MIREL, E., Danger in "Happy Drugs," *Science Service*, Feature packet for 17 August 1963.

MOLLER, A., Einige Meskalin Versuche, *Acta psychiatrica et neurologica*, 10 (1935) 405-442.

MORIN, R. D., BENNINGTON, F. & CLARK, L. C., JR., Synthesis of 5,6,7-trimethoxyindole, a possible intermediary metabolite of mescaline, *Journal of Organic Chemistry*, 22 (1957) 331-332.

MORSELLI, G. E., Contribution à la psychopathologie de l'intoxication par la mescaline, *Journal de psychologie normale et pathologique*, 33 (1936) 368-392.

MORSELLI, G. E., Mescalina e schizofrenia, *Rivista di psicologia*, 40-41 (1944-1945) 1-23.

NAKADA, T. & NASHIHARA, K., Syntheses of anhalonium bases, I. Synthesis of carnegine and pellotine methyl ether, *Journal of the Pharmaceutical Society of Japan*, 64 (1944) 74-76.

NETTL, B., Observations on meaningless peyote song texts, *Journal of American Folklore*, 66 (1953) 161-164.

NEVOLE, S., [Concerning Four-dimensional sight: a physio-pathological study of space-perception, with special reference to experimental poisoning with mescaline], *Lékarského Khihkuspectvi a Nakladatelstvi*, 1947.

NEWBERNE, R. E. L., Peyote, An insidious evil, *Indian Rights Association*, #114, 1918.

New York Journal-American, 7 December 1960, p. 4, Harvard-Bred Beatnik Found Dead in Village.

New York Post, 7 December 1960, Coffee House Owner Dead.

New York Times,
23 June 1960, Peyote Peddler at Odds with U. S.
7 December 1960, Cafe Owner Found Dead. Use.

14 November 1962, Indian Drug Rite Backed on Coast.
15 November 1962, Court Considering Use of Drug in Indian Rite.
30 November 1962, Indians on Coast Lose Peyote Case.
7 May 1963, Group Backs Indian Drug Use.
29 May 1963, Ousted Educator Rebuts Harvard.
9 June 1963, On Hallucinogens [W. L. Lawrence].
15 December 1963, Psychic-Drug Tests Put Data in Shape.

New York Tribune, 3 June 1963, Editorial, "Harvard Bites the Mushroom."

Newsweek, 6 August 1962, 'Right' to Hallucinate.

NOTEBOOM, L., Experimental catatonia by means of derivatives of mescaline and adrenaline, *Proceedings of the Royal Academy of Sciences of Amsterdam*, 37 (1934) 562-574.

NOTEBOOM, L., Experimental catatonia produced with synthetic preparations of mescaline and adrenaline, *Nederlandsch Tijdschrift voor Geneeskunde*, 76 (1932) 517-518, 2860-2862.

OPLER, M. E., A Mescalero Apache Account of the Origin of the Peyote Ceremony, *El Palacio*, 52 #10 (October 1945) 210-212.

ORLOWSKI, P. Ueber Meskalin, *Apotheker Zeitung*, 4 (1952) 124-126.

ORSO, CAMILLE, The Chapter That La Barre Did Not Write, *Mss.*, Bucknell University, Lewisburg, Penna., 1963.

OSMOND, H., On Being Mad, *Saskatchewan Psychiatric Services Bulletin*, 1:2 (Sept. 1952).

OSMOND, H., A Review of the chemical effects of psychotomimetic agents, *Annals of the New York Academy of Science*, 66 (1957) 418-434.

OSMOND, H., That Night in the Tepi, *Twentieth Century*, 170 (1961) 38-50.

OSMOND, H. & SMYTHIES, J., Schizophrenia: a new approach, *Journal of Mental Science*, 98 (1952) 309-315.

PALMIERI, V. M. & LACROIX, G., Ulteriori ricerche sull'intossicazione da mescalina, *Atti Congresso de medicina legale*, 8, 1940 (1941) 540-549.

PAP, Z. VON, Einwirkung des Meskalinrausches auf die post-hypnotischen Sinnestäuschungen, *Zeitschrift für die gesamte Neurologie und Psychiatrie*, 155 (1936) 655-664 [See also *Orvosi hetilap*, 80 (1936) 75-78].

PATZIG, B. & BLOCK, W., Zur Auffassung des schizophrenen Prozessgeschehens nach Tierversuchen mit ^{14}C-radioaktivem Meskalin, *Naturwissenschaften*, 40 (1953) 13-17.

PENNES, H. H., Clinical reactions of schizophrenics to Sodium Amytal, Pervitin Hydrochloride, Mescaline Sulfate, and D-Lysergic Acid Diethylamide (LSD-25), *Journal of Nervous and Mental Disease*, 119 (1954) 95-112.

POLONO, A. & MAFFEZZONI, G., Le variazione dell' attività colinergica del tessuto cerebrale per effetto della bulbocapnina, della mescalina e della dietilamide dell' acido lisergico, *Sistema nervoso*, 4 (1952) 578-581.

POPOFF, E. I., K farmakologii pellotina, *Vrach* (St. Petersburg), 28 (1897) 1361.

PORTELL VILA, J., La mescalina y la banisterina como dos nuevos azotes de la humanidad, *Cronica médicoquirúrgica de la Habana*, 58 (1932) 87-94.

Psychedelic Review, Cambridge, Massachusetts, vol. 1, no. 1 (Summer, 1963) —.

PUHARICH, A., The Sacred Mushroom: Key to the Door of Eternity, Garden City: Doubleday & Co., 1959.

PUTT, E. B., Mescal, *Report, Office of Indian Affairs*, Department of the Interior, Washington, D. C., 1911.

REITMAN, F., *Psychotic Art*, London: Routledge & Kegan Paul, 1950, p. 35.

RETI, I. & CASTRILLON, J. A., Cactus alkaloids, *Journal of the American Chemical Society*, 73 (1951) 1767-1769.

REUTTER, L., Du Peyolt [sic], comme drogue sensorielle, *Schweizerische Apotheker-Zeitung*, 62 (1924) 441-443.

RHO, F., Peyotl (pellote) o mescal (la planta che riempie gli occhi di meraviglie), *Annali di medicina navale e coloniale*, 38 (1932) 92-99.

RHODES, W., Acculturation in North American Indian Music, *Proceedings of the 29th International Congress of Americanists*, 1952, Vol. II, pp. 127-132.

RICHARDSON, D. A., Anhalonium Lewinii mescal button, a report of five cases, in which the tincture was exhibited in four-drop doses daily, *Denver Medical Times*, 16 (1896-1879) 213-217.

RICKS, D. F., Mushrooms and Mystics: A Caveat, (Drugs and the Mind Issue), *Harvard Review*, 1 (1963) 51-55.

RIGNEY, F. J. & SMITH, L., *The Real Bohemia*, New York: Basic Books, 1961.

RINALDI, F. & HIMWICH, H. E., The cerebral electroencephalographic changes induced by

LSD and mescaline are corrected by frenquel, *Journal of Nervous and Mental Disease*, 122 (1955) 198-199.

RINKEL, M. & DENBER, H. C. B. (eds.), *Chemical Concepts of Psychosis*, New York: McDowell, 1958.

RINKEL, M., DESCHON, H. J., HYDE, R. W. & SOLOMON, H. C., Experimental Schizophrenia-like symptoms, *American Journal of Psychiatry*, 108 (1952) 572-578.

ROBERTI, C. E. & HEYMANN, H., Dell' allucinazioni, *Rassegna di studi psichiatrici*, 26 (1937) 245, 353.

ROBLES, C. & GOMEZ ROBLEDA, J., Trabajo inicial acerca de la acción fisiológica clorhidrato de peyotina, *Anales del Instituto de biologia* (México), 2 (1931) 15-46.

ROSENTHALER, L., Detection of organic compounds: microchemical reactions of mescalin, *Pharmaceutische Zeitung*, 76 (1931) 653-654.

ROTONDO, H., Fenomenología de la intoxicación mescalinica y análisis funcional del pensamiento en su decurso, *Revista de neuropsiquiatria* (Lima), 6 (1943) 58-143.

SALOMON, K., THALE, T. & GABRIO, B. W., Investigation of the psycho-chemical basis of visual hallucinations produced by mescaline, *Federation Proceedings*, 6 (1947) 367-368.

SALOMON, K. & BINA, A. F., Ultraviolet absorption spectra of mescaline sulfate and β-phenylethylamide sulfate, *Journal of the American Chemical Society*, 68 (1946) 2403.

SALOMON, K., GABRIO, B. W. & THALE, T., A study of mescaline in human subjects, *Journal of Pharmacology and Experimental Therapeutics*, 95 (1949) 455-459.

San Francisco Sunday Chronicle, 26 April 1959, J. Hyams, "I was a Boor . . . An Utter Fake."

SAVA, V., Recherches sur l'audition colorée et l'intoxication expérimentale par la mescaline, Thèse doctorale de Médicine, Bucharest, 1929.

SCHUELER, F. W., The effect of succinate in mescaline hallucinations, *Journal of Laboratory and Clinical Medicine*, 33 (1948) 1297-1303.

SCHULTES, R. E., Botanical Sources of the New World Narcotics, *Psychedelic Review*, 1 (1963) 145-166, pp. 156-157.

SCHULTES, R. E., Hallucinogenic Plants of the New World, (Drugs and the Mind Issue), *Harvard Review*, 1 (1963) 18-32, pp. 25-26.

SCHULTES, R. E., Native Narcotics of the New World, *Pharmaceutical Sciences*, 3rd Lecture Series (1960) 142-185, pp. 154-156.

Schumann, K., Blühende Kakteen, *Iconographia Cactacearum*, 1913, No. 38.

Schumann, K., Echinocactus Williamsii Lem., *Monatschrift für Kakteenkunde*, 4 (1894) 36-37, 159; 5 (1895) 11, 14, 94; 6 (1896) 15 [= *Lophophora williamsii* (Lemaire) Coulter].

Schumann, K., Die Gattung Ariocarpus (Anhalonium), *Botanische Jahrbücher für Systematik, Pflanzengeschichte, und Pflanzengeographie*, 24 (1898) 551.

Schumann, K., Gesamtbeschreibung der Kakteen, *Monographia Cactacearum*, 1899, p. 318.

Siegel, B. J. & Beals, A. R., Pervasive Factionalism, *American Anthropologist*, 62 (1960) 394-417, pp. 397-398.

Simpson, L. & McKellar, P., Types of Synaesthesia (mescal experiments), *Journal of Mental Science*, 101 (1955) 141-147.

Slotta, K. H. & Heller, H., Ueber β-Phenyläthylamine, 1. Mezkalin und Mezkalin-ähnliche Substanzen, *Berichte der Deutschen chemischen Gesellschaft*, 63 (1930) 3029-3044.

Slotta, K. H. & Mulier, J., Ueber den Abbau des Meskalins und meskalin-ähnlicher Stoffe im Organismus, *Zeitschrift für physiologische Chemie*, 238 (1936) 14-22.

Slotta, D. H. &·Szyszka, B., Ueber β-Phenyläthylamine, 3. Neue Darstellung von Mescalin, *Journal für praktische Chemie*, 137 (1933) 339-350.

Slotta, D. H. & Szyszka, G., Synthese des Meskalins (Eine Berichtigung der gleichlautenden Arbeit von G. Hahn und H. Wassmuth), *Berichte der Deutschen chemischen Gesellschaft*, 67 (1934) 1106-1108.

Smolska, B., Ueber mikroskopische Veraenderungen der inneren Organe der weissen Maus nach akuten und sub-akuten Meskalinvergiftungen, *Deutsche Zeitschrift für die gesamte gerichtliche Medizin*, 18 (1932) 91-95.

Smythies, J. R., The Mescaline Phenomena, *British Journal for the Philosophy of Science*, 3 (1963) 339-347.

Smythies, J. R., Mode of Action of Mescaline, in Crocket, Sandison and Walk (eds.), *Hallucinogenic Drugs and Their Psychotherapeutic Use*, Springfield (Ill): Charles C Thomas, 1963.

Spaeth, E., Ueber die Konstitution von Pellotin und Anhalonidin, *Berichte der Deutschen chemischen Gesellschaft*, 65 (1932) 1778-1785.

Spaeth, E. & Becke, F., 11. Mitteilung ueber Kakteen-Alkaloide. Eine neue Synthese des Pellotins, *Berichte der Deutschen chemischen Gesellschaft*, 67 (1934) 266-268; 12. Die Konstitution des Anhalamins, *ibidem*, 67 (1934) 2100-2102.

Spaeth, E. & Becke, F., 15. Mitteilung ueber Kakteen-Alkaloide. Ueber die Trennung der Anhaloniumbasen, *Monatshefte für Chemie*, 66 (1935) 327-336.

Spaeth, E. & Boschan, F., 10. Die Konstitution des Pellotins und des Anhalonidins, *Monstshefte für Chemie*, 63 (1933) 141-153.

Spaeth, E. & Bruck, J., 18. Ueber ein neues Alkaloid aus den Mescal buttons, *Berichte der Deutschen chemischen Gesellschaft*, 70 (1937) 2446-2450; *idem*, 19. N-Acetylmezkalin als Inhaltstoff der Mezcal buttons, *ibidem*, 71 (1938) 1275-1276.

Speck, L. B., Toxicity and effects of increasing doses of mescaline, *Journal of Pharmacology and Experimental Therapeutics*, 119 (1957) 78-84.

Spector, E., Identification of 3,4,5-trimethylphenylacetic acid as a major metabolite in the dog, *Nature*, 189 (1961) 751-752.

Spindler, L. S., Menomini Women and Culture Change, *Memoir 91, American Anthropological Association*, 1962, pp. 62-69.

Steiner-Bernier, M., Contribution à l'étude du peyotl (Echinocactus Williamsii Lem.), *Thèse Doctorale de Pharmacie*, Paris, 1936, 70 pp.

Stenberg, M. P., The Peyote Cult among Wyoming Indians, *University of Wyoming Publications*, 12 (1946) 85-156.

Stewart, O. C., The Native American Church (Peyote Cult) and the Law, *Denver Westerners Monthly Roundup*, 17 (1961) np.

Stewart, O. C., Peyote and the Arizona Court Decision, *American Anthropologist*, 63 (1961) 1334.

Stockings, G. T., A clinical study of the mescaline psychosis with special reference to the mechanism of the genesis of schizophrenia and other psychotic states, *Journal of Mental Science*, 86 (1940) 29-47.

Sturtevant, F. M. & Drill, V. A., Effects of mescaline in laboratory animals and influence of ataraxics on mescaline-response, *Proceedings of the Society for Experimental Biology and Medicine*, 92 (1956) 383-387.

Supniewski, J. V., [Pharmaceutical properties of synthetic alkaloids of peyotl], *Polska Gazeta Lekarska*, 9 (1930) 449-454, 737-740.

Supniewski, J. V., [Pharmacologic properties of synthetic alkaloids derived from mescaline], *Polska Gazeta Lekarska*, 9 (1930)

287-293; 10 (1931) 961-964.

SZARA, S., Comparison of the psychotic effect of tryptamine derivatives with the effects of mescaline and LSD in self-experiments, in S. Garrattini and V. Ghetti (eds.), *Psychotropic Drugs*, New York: Elzevier, 1957. 460-463.

SZUMAN, S., Analiza formalna i psychologiszna widzen meskalinowych, *Kwart. Psychol.*, 1 (1930) 156-212 [Summary in German, pp. 214-220].

TARSITANO, F., La ricerca tossicologica della mescalina, *Folia Medica*, 30 (1947) 340-344; *Bolletino della Società italiana di biologia sperimentale*, 20 (1945) 762-763.

TAYLOR, N., Come and Expel the Green Pain, *Scientific Monthly*, 58 (1944) 176-184.

TAYLOR, RATTRAY, *The Science of Life*, New York: McGraw-Hill, 1963, p. 307.

TEIRICH, H. Ueber eine Meskalinschädigung, *Psyche* (Stuttgart), 7 (1954) 637-640.

THALE, T., GABRIO, B. W. & SALOMON, K., Hallucination and imagery induced by mescaline, *American Journal of Psychiatry*, 106 (1950) 686-691.

THUILLIER, J., Suppression par la chlorpromazine des contractions utérines provoquées par la mescaline, *Comptes rendus de la Société de Biologie*, 150 (1956) 1150-1151.

TROIKE, R. C., The Origin of Plains Mescalism, *American Anthropologist*, 64 (1962) 946-963.

TSAO, M. U., A new synthesis of mescaline, *Journal of the American Chemical Society*, 73 (1951) 6495-6496.

UNDERHILL, R. M. PEYOTE, *Proceedings of the 30th International Congress of Americanists, Cambridge, 1952*, London: Royal Anthropological Institute, 1952, 143-148.

UNGER, S. M., Mescaline, LSD, psilocybin and personality change: a review, *Psychiatry*, 26 (1963) 111-125.

UNITED NATIONS, *Bulletin on Narcotics*, Vol. IX, no. 2 (April-June 1959) 16-41.

UNITED STATES TREASURY BUREAU, *Monthly Narcotics Intelligence Bulletin*, 15 September 1957.

URBINA, M., El peyote y el Ololiuhqui, *La Naturaleza* (México), 3 (1912) 131.

VOGT, M., Die Verteilung von Arzeneistoffen auf verschiedene Regionen des Zentralnervensystems, Zugleich ein Beitrag Zu Ihrer quantitativen Mikrobestimmung im Gewerbe Chinin und Mezkalin, *Archiv für experimentelle Pathologie und Pharmakologie*, 178 (1935) 560-576.

WAEBER, A., Zur Wirkung von Anhalonium lewinii, *St. Petersburg Medizinische Zeitschrift*, 37 (1912) 17-20.

WALLACE, E. & HOEBEL, E. A., *The Comanches: Lords of the South Plains*, Norman (Oklahoma), 1952, 331ff.

WALLIS, MRS. W. D. Letter, 4 December 1963.

Washington Post, 20 January 1964, 300 Oxonians using Drugs, Weekly [*Isis*] says.

WASSON, R. G., The Mushroom Rites of Mexico, (Drugs and the Mind Issue), *Harvard Review*, 1 (1963) 7-17.

WATTS, ALAN, *The Joyous Cosmology*, New York: Pantheon, 1962.

WEIL, A. T., The Strange Case of the Harvard Drug Scandal, *Look*, vol. 27, #22 (5 November 1963), 38, 43-44, 46, 48 [the most complete available source].

WEST, L. J., (ed.), *Hallucinations*, New York & London: Grune & Stratton, 1962.

WHEATLEY, M. D. & SCHUELER, F. W., A synergism between mescaline and rhythmic stimulation by light [Abstract], *Electroencephalography and Clinical Neurophysiology*, 2 (1950) 226.

WIKLER, A., Clinical and electroencephalographic studies on the effects of Mescaline N-allylnormorphine and morphine in man, *Journal of Nervous and Mental Disease*, 120 (1954) 157-175.

WIKLER, A., Mechanisms of action of drugs which modify personality function, *American Journal of Psychiatry*, 108 (1952) 590-599.

WILCOCK, J., the village square, [Greenwich] *Village Voice*, #294 (27 July 1961); #295 (3 August 1961).

WILCOX, R. W., Pellotine, *New York Lancet*, 1898, p. 81.

WILLIAMS, C., *Many Dimensions*, London, 1931.

WOLBACH, A. B., ISBELL, H. & MINER, E. J., Cross-tolerance between mescaline and LSD-25, with a comparison of the mescaline and LSD reactions, *Psychopharmacologia*, 3 (1932) 1-14.

WOLF, R., Das Raum- und Zeiterleben unter abnormalen Bedingungen, besonders im Meskalinrausch, *Deutsche Medizinische Wochenschrift*, 77 (1952) 168-170.

WOODS, L. A., COCHIN, J., FORNEFELD, E. J., McMAHON, F. G. & SEEVERS, M. H., Estimation of amines in biological materials with critical data for cocaine and mescaline, *Journal of Pharmacology and Experimental Therapeutics*, 101 (1951) 188-199.

WOODS, L. A., COCHIN, J. & SEEVERS, M. H.,

Fate of mescaline in serum, plasma and blood, *Federation Proceedings,* 9 (1950) 326.

WOOLLEY, D. W. & SHAW, E., A biochemical and pharmacological suggestion about certain mental disorders, *Proceedings of the National Academy of Sciences* (Washington, D. C.) 40 (1954) 228-231.

ZAEHNER, R. C., *The Menace of Mescaline,* Blackfriars, 1954.

ZAEHNER, R. C., *Mysticism, Sacred and Profane: An Inquiry into Some Varieties of Praeternatural Experience,* New York: Galaxy Books, 1961.

ZINBERG, N. E., Narcotics in the United States: A Brief History (Drugs and the Mind Issue), *Harvard Review,* 1 (1963) 56-62.

ZUCKER, K., Experimente über Sinnestäuschungen, *Archiv für Psychiatrie,* 83 (1928) 706-754.

ZUCKER, K., Ueber die Zunahme spontaner Halluzinationen nach Meskalin, *Zentralblatt für die gesamte Neurologie und Psychiatrie,* 56 (1930) 447-448.

PEYOTE STUDIES, 1963-73

Peyote continues to be studied with an apparently inexhaustible interest by a variety of disciplines. The decade indicated includes several new breakthroughs, concerning which students who wish to be *au courant* will want to be familiar.

BOTANY

The older view that *Lophophora* existed in two species, *Anhalonium lewinii* and *Anhalonium williamsii* (e.g., Ramirez, 1900), was largely discarded by botanists who regarded these as mere vegetative or age-variants, especially since both "species" have been observed growing from the same root-stock. As a result,

It has long been thought that the genus [*Lophophora*] might be monotypic, but recent botanical and chemical studies indicate that there may be a second species—*L. diffusa*—endemic to a small area of central Mexico (Schultes, in Snieckus, 1972: 6).

Anderson, who is largely responsible for the changed view, notes that

The former [*L. williamsii*] is both wide-ranging and highly variable morphologically [whence the earlier, but no longer accepted, "species"], whereas the latter [*L. diffusa*] consists of a single, fairly small population restricted to the State of Querétaro (Anderson, 1969: 299).

Genetically, Boke and Anderson (1970: 569) regard *L. diffusa* as the ancestral type; perhaps the ecological adaptiveness of the mutant *L. williamsii* accounts for its wider geographic range. Anderson and Stone (1971: 77) give a map of the distributions, and pictures (Figs. 2, 3) of the two species.

Peyote is not a rare cactus and in many localities is quite abundant, often forming clumps under most sizable shrubs. Caespitose [low turflike patches] individuals or even large clones [vegetatively but not genetically individuated] are common, although single-headed plants are present in each locality as well. Injury or harvesting by man induces the formation of many stems from a single root-stock. Single clones more than 1.5m across have been observed in San Luis Potosí (Anderson, 1969: 302).

Soil tests do not show differences in the two limestone-soil locales of the two species. Morphologically,

In the extensive northern population (Texas along the Río Grande to San Luis Potosí in Mexico) the tubercles are usually arranged as distinct ribs or elevated podaria, whereas in the restricted southern population (limited to the Mexican State of Querétaro) podaria and ribs are poorly developed or lacking and there are also differences in pollen structure (Boke and Anderson, 1970: 569).

The key to the species may be summarized as follows. *L. williamsii* plants are blue-green, usually with well-defined ribs and furrows, tufts of trichomes usually equally spaced on the ribs, flowers pinkish or rarely whitish, not found in Querétaro; *L. diffusa* plants are yellow-green, usually lacking well-defined ribs and furrows, tufts of trichomes usually spaced unequally on prominent podaria, flowers commonly whitish to yellowish white, found in Querétaro (Anderson, 1969: 304). This taxonomist (Anderson, 1969: 305–10) gives an exhaustive discussion of synonyms, e.g., *Echinocactus, Anhalonium,* and excluded names and taxa of uncertain status, including *nomina nuda* (names unverified by collected specimens). Following Tsukada, Anderson and Stone (1971: 82) consider that "small tricolpate grains are probably more typical of the ancestors of the Cactaceae and the more elaborate geometric designs of the northern pollen of *Lophophora williamsii* represent greater evolutionary divergence and specialization." Other authorities (Schultes and Hofmann, 1973: 129–33; Bravo, 1967) follow the re-monographing of *Lophophora* into two species. Besides morphological and pollen differences, the presence or absence of mescaline, lophophorine, and pellotine is also diagnostic. Other botanical works of interest are by Emboden (1972); Schleifer (n.d.); Schultes (1961ab, 1963ab, 1965a, 1966, 1967, 1969, 1969–70, 1970abc, 1972); Schultes and Vestal (1939); and Weniger (1971); and by Furst (1971a) on the "false peyote" *(Ariocarpus retusus)* of Huichol tradition.

CHEMISTRY AND PHARMACOLOGY

New substances continue to be isolated from *Lophophora williamsii*—among them, anhalotine, lophotine, and peyotine (Kapadia, Shah, and Zalucky, 1968), peyonine (Kapadia and Highet, 1968), peyophorine (Kapadia and Fales, 1968a), and various N-methylated tyramine derivatives (McLaughlin and Paul, 1966). Kapadia and Fales (1968b) have identified fourteen new peyote alkaloid amides, their research being much facilitated by gas chromatography (Lundström and Agurell, 1968). The biosynthesis of peyote alkaloids has been studied by Leete (1966); the chemistry, biogenesis, and biological effects by Kapadia and Fayez (1970); and an improved synthesis of mescaline has been described by Benington and Morin (1951). As Schultes remarks,

The peyote cactus is a veritable chemical factory. More than 30 alkaloids and amine derivatives—many, to be sure, in minute amounts—have been isolated from the plant. Most of them are undoubtedly biodynamically active, but, with the exception of several, their effects are not well understood. They belong mainly to the phenylethylamines and the biologically related isoquinolines. The most thoroughly investigated is mescaline, a phenylethylamine (3, 4, 5-trimethoxyphenylethylamine), which is known to be responsible for the extraordinary visual hallucinations (Schultes, in Scnieckus, 1972: 6).

Representative experiments on peyote are by McGlothlin (1965) and on mescaline by P. B. Smith (1959). Mescaline is highly toxic in the technical sense, that is, in large doses the fourth level of EEG response with sudden spastic jerks and the fifth level of epileptoid convulsions followed by death may be reached, whereas, despite its very great pharmacodynamic potency, only the third or hallucinatory EEG level is reached with LSD, and no deaths, though long-lasting psychoses from its use are authenticated (McGlothlin, Cohen, and McGlothlin, 1967; see also Cohen, in Hicks and Fink, 1969; Frosch, Robbins, and Stern, 1965; Smart and Bateman, 1967; Ungerleider, Fisher, and Fuller, 1966).

Mescaline, like LSD, has been reported to be teratogenic (Geber, 1967), that is, it appears to affect the germ cells and to produce congenital malformations or monstrous births. The original problem was raised by Zellweger, McDonald, and Abbo (1967), by Cohen, Marinello, and Back (1967), by Auerbach and Rugowski (1967), by Dipallo (1967), and others. Later work by Smart and Bateman (1968) and by Hsu, Strauss, and Hirschhorn (1970) has solidified medical opinion on the dangers of parental use of LSD; see also Hall, Weise, and Busse (1973). Analysis of "street drugs" at the New Jersey Neuro-Psychiatric Institute near Princeton showed that very few, if any, alleged specimens were genuine mescaline, but rather mixtures of LSD, strychnine, and other deleterious substances; of samples gathered in the Yorkville area of Toronto and other Canadian cities *not one* of the 58 samples so designated tested out as mescaline (Marshman and Gibbons, 1970)—a result that youthful users express in the truism that "mescaline and psilocybin are impossible to get" (although psilocybin is far less toxic than mescaline, Sandoz, the only pharmaceutical house that synthesizes psilocybin, has refused its distribution in the United States except through federal government auspices, currently to six scientific programs, only two of which experiment on humans). Besides its toxic effects, pure synthetic mescaline is often severely nauseating for periods up to ten hours, which greatly reduces its "psychedelic" attractiveness; and if, in addition, alleged "mescaline" is actually teratogenic LSD, the informed have come to avoid it. On present and extensive information, the teratogenic effects of LSD appear to operate both upon the germ cells of both parental users and on the embryo as it develops in the mother. The use of synthetic mescaline has ceased and the taking of alleged "mescaline" seems to be declining among youthful experimenters.

The hypothetical basis of the schizophreniform "model psychosis" has come under severe criticism by psychiatrists (e.g., Jackson, 1962; pp. 220–21 in the present volume; experiments specifically on mescaline, pp. 221–22). Since the first report suggesting use of the new synthetic hallucinogens in psychotherapy (Busch and Johnson, 1950), the American Psychiatric Association met in 1955 in a round-table symposium for assessment of psychotomimetics in psychotherapy (Cholden, 1956; Wikler, 1957). Of the enormous literature, the following are the best summaries: Abramson (1967); Buckman, in Hicks and Fink (1969: 217–25); Osmund, in Hicks and Fink (1969: 217–25); Salzman, in Hicks and Fink (1969: 23–32); Cohen, in Ungerleider, (1970: 22–44); Cole and Katz (1964); Crocket, Sandison, and Walk (1963); Hollister (1968); Malitz (1966); May and Wittenborn (1969); Rinkel, in Cholden (1956); Savage, Savage, Fadiman, and Harman (1964); and Smart (1970). Useful bibliographies, arranged in chronological order, on the employment of mescaline and other hallucinogens in psychotherapy have been compiled at the National Institute of Mental Health by Unger (1963ab, 1964). Except for psilocybin, the prospects appear unpromising; no current work on the therapeutic use of psilocybin is known to the present writer, which is an unfortunate experimental hiatus.

Psychotropics have by no means the same psychological effects, nor are they identical in toxicity or in potency: STP = DOM (2, 5-dimethoxy-4-methylamphetamine), for example, has psychotropic effects in humans between 60 and 100 times as potent as mescaline, but only 1/30–1/50 the effect of LSD (Idanpaan, McIsaac, Ho, and Tansey, 1969). Fischer, Marks, Hill, and Rockey (1968) have emphasized personality structure as the main determinant in drug-induced "model psychoses" (see also Thatcher, Kappeler, Wisecup, and Fischer, 1970). Freedman, Aghajanian, and Ornitz (1958) have studied patterns of tolerance to mescaline and LSD, and Balestrieri and Fontanari (1959), as well as Wolbach, Isbell, and Miner (1962), have investigated cross-tolerance between mescaline and LSD. Aboul-Enein (1973) have given a pharmacological profile on mescaline; see also Olney (1972). Cappell and LeBlanc (1971) have noted a conditioned aversion to saccharine in single administrations of mescaline and LSD, and Hebbard and Fischer (1966) the effects of mescaline and other hallucinogens on small involuntary eye movements; in earlier work, Adler and Pötzl (1936) had studied the effects of mescaline on patients with visual-lobe diplopia. Wolbach, Miner, and Isbell (1962) have compared the effects of mescaline in general with other psychotropic drugs.

Since the pioneer works on psychopharmacology by Ernst von Bibra (1855) and Louis Lewin (1931, reprinted 1964) and by Kurt Beringer (1927, reprinted 1969) and Heinrich Klüver on peyote (1928, reprinted in 1966 as *Mescal, and Mechanisms of Hallucination*), and a herein hitherto unnoted early article by Serko (1913) on peyote intoxication, a number of general works on hallucinogenic drugs have appeared. Perhaps the best and most accessible single article summarizing data on hallucinogens is by Barron, Jarvik, and Bunnell (1964). Authoritative on the botanical and chemical distribution of hallucinogens are the articles by Schultes (1970b, 1969–70). Hoffer and Osmund (1967) are useful on the hallucinogens; and Efron, Holmstedt, and Kline (1967) on the ethnopharmacologic search for psychoactive drugs. An informative and handsomely illustrated book on

Narcotic Plants is by Emboden (1972). The authority in its field is *The Botany and Chemistry of Hallucinogens* by Schultes and Hofmann (1973).

Polish scholars have become interested in peyote and mescaline in recent years (Prajer, 1968ab, 1969; Szuman, 1930; Witkiewicz, 1932). In Italian, Bernabai (1966) compares mescaline and psilocybin. The best source in French on hallucinogenic plants is by Schultes (1969–70). In German, Wagner has data on "peyotl-mescalin" (1969: 85–91); in Spanish, Pérez Cirera on peyotl and teonanacatl (1966), and Guerra (1967) on early ethnobotanical sources on Mexican phantastica. In Switzerland, "A Genevese pharmacy embarked on a large-scale advertising campaign for a product named Peyotl, for which it claimed remarkable properties . . . Subsequently, the Swiss Federal Public Health Service stated that 'it would be advisable to allow Peyotl to be supplied only on medical prescription' " (Anonymous, 1959: 26). In Russia, the often-stated major problem is alcoholism, and draconian law enforcement has made hallucinogens virtually unknown (personal information from psychiatrists in Russia, 1972). In most European countries, in Africa, and in Latin America, the use of hallucinogens in general is vigorously repressed.

One of the most interesting discoveries is that of the antibiotic activity of a solution of panpeyotl in alcohol. "In Beals it is stated, p. 61, ethanol tincture of peyote inhibits a wide spectrum of bacteria including inhibitory action against 18 strains of penicillin-resistant *Staphylococcus aureus* and one strain of pathogenic fungus. Experiments with white mice and this 'peyocactin,' all treated animals survived otherwise fatal doses of staphylococcus, all controls died within 60 hours" (McCleary, Sypherd, and Walkington, 1960). In 1939, the present writer (La Barre, 1939) pointed out Schultes' argument that "the appeal of peyote as a medicine" was based on the inadmissable substitution of the western pharmacological concept of medicine in place of the native idea of supernatural "medicine" and that it was the hallucinogenic earnest of "medicine power" in peyote that motivated native use in shamanic curing. The *de jure* ethnological argument still stands on good native grounds; on the *de facto* value of peyote as a pharmaceutical substance, the present writer yields.

Another interesting question is "Why do plants produce drugs?" or "What is their function in plants?" (Bever, 1970). Adaptively, the mere presence of drugs as metabolic end products would be a less-impressive explanation than that they perform protective functions for the plant against insect and other predators (as with nicotine, rotenone, cedar oil, pine tar). Another broadly interesting problem is the use of hallucinogens by fish, birds, and mice, as well as by man (Siegel, in Vinar, Voltava, and Bradley, 1971), and the ethological bases for self-administration of hallucinogens in a wide variety of non-human animals (Siegel, 1973). Of similar broad interest is the theory of hallucinosis in drug-induced states of the central nervous system, by Winters and Wallach (in Efron, Holmstedt, and Kline, 1967: 193–228). The republication of Klüver's classic paper on the mechanisms of hallucination (1966) reminds us of ongoing research on form constants in hallucinosis (Siegel and West, in press). Marshall (1935, 1937) considers that form constants in peyote visions derive from actual eye anatomy—including structures *behind* the retina—hence that "the rods and foveal cones can look backwards" and, under certain conditions, actually can see retinal pigment, choriocapillary circulation, and the like themselves. Additionally, of course, pre-retinal secretions on the cornea, moving particles in the vitreous humor, the network of retinal vessels, and various properties and states of the cornea, lens, or other structures within the eye would quite ordinarily be projected onto the retina and be seen (Klüver, 1966: 69). Some "visions" therefore are a witnessing of phenomena within the eye itself.

Of botanico-chemical as well as ethnographic interest is the discovery of mescaline in several South American cacti. John Gillin (1945)—who was the first to record native use of the hallucinogenic "San Pedro" cactus in Peru—later studied in folk medicine as the drink *cimora* made from "Opuntia cylindrica" (Cruz Sánchez, 1948a), mapped the ethnographic area of the drug's use (Gutiérrez-Noriega, 1950), and studied in pharmacodynamically (Gutiérrez-Noriega and Cruz Sánchez, 1947; Cruz Sánchez, 1948b). The French ethnobotanist Friedberg submitted one of her voucher specimens to the Parisian pharmacologist Poisson, who identified mescaline as the active principle (Poisson, 1960; verified by Gonzalez Huerta, 1960, and Turner and Heyman, 1961). Friedberg published further (1964) on the cactus ethnobotanically, followed by Sharon (1972) and Dobkin de Rios (1968ab, 1969abc) on its folk-medicine uses. Properly *Trichocereus pachanoi*, the cactus is known as *aguacolla* in Ecuador and as "San Pedro" in Peru. According to Furst, *Trichocereus pachanoi* may have been used as early as 3,000 years ago—based on the finding of Chavín-period textiles and ceramics in Peru that depict it, for example, in connection with the jaguar deity (Sharon, in Furst: 1972, Fig. 21, p. 115)—and certainly it is widely cultivated in Andean Ecuador, Peru, and probably Bolivia (Schultes and Hofmann, 1973: 133–35). *Trichocereus tersheckii* ([Parmentier] Britton and Rose) and also other *Trichocereus* species contain mescaline (Reti and Castrillon, 1951; Schultes, in Scnieckus, 1972), including *T. macrogonus* and *T. werdermannianus* (Emboden, 1972: 56).

ETHNOGRAPHY

Modern information on Huichol peyotism is of major significance, since this west Mexican group has a ritual closest to the pre-Columbian of any extant tribe; and, geographically remote, the Huichol have remained almost wholly uninfluenced by Christianity. Of particular importance to an understanding of peyotism are the rich materials on Huichol symbolism collected by Furst. The Huichol origin myth indicates the crisis cult ubiquitous in religious origins. The ancient gods had come together in the first *tuki* or sanctuary-retreat made by Tatewari, "Our Grandfather," or deified Fire. When met together, the gods discovered that all were ill, one with a pain in his chest, another in the stomach, others in the eyes, legs, and so forth. Those responsible for rain were giving no rain; the masters of animals, no game. "It was a time of general malaise in the Sierra, and none knew how 'to find his life' " (Furst, in Furst, 1972: 145).

Into this assembly came Grandfather Fire, Mara'akáme the First Shaman, who told them they must undertake an arduous journey to the sacred peyote land to the east where the Sun was born. Not all the divine seekers succeeded in making the journey, some dropping out from hunger and thirst or sheer exhaustion. But the chief male gods and the Rain and Earth Mothers followed Tatewari to the sacred mountains of Wirikuta, on "the fifth level" at the end of the world, where Deer-Peyote revealed himself in the ceremonial quest, and the gods "found their life." So too the present-day Huichol may reach sacred myth-time once more by performing the difficult pilgrimage–hunt ritual.

It is a "hunt" in the literal sense, because to the Huichol, peyote and deer are synonymous. The first of the sacred plants to be seen by the leader of the hunting party contains the essence of Elder Brother Wawatsári, "master" of the deer species, and manifests itself as deer, which in turn explains why it is first "shot" with bow and arrow before being dug from the ground and ritually divided among the participants in the hunt. At the same time Deer-Peyote embodies the equally sacred and life-giving Maize, so that deer, peyote, and maize together form a symbol complex. On the peyote pilgrimage, or "hunt," these three elements become fused, the mythic "first times" that existed before the separation of man, plants, animals, and "gods" are re-created, man reunites with his ancestors, and contradictions between what is and what is thought to be or desired, between life and death, and between the sexes are resolved, bringing about that state of unity and continuity between past and present, "between man, nature, society, and the supernatural," that epitomizes the Huichol view of "the good". . . This is what the Huichol mean when they say that on the peyote hunt "we go to find our life" (Furst, in Furst, 1972: 141–42; compare Furst and Myerhoff, 1971).

In symbolic detail, the unacculturated myths of the Huichol contain embedded in them elements of manifestly very great antiquity, some harking back to the mesolithic horizons of the paleo-Siberian migrants who became the American Indians: the special connection of shamans with fire; the shamanic wearing of deer antlers; the spirit-familiar (Wawatsári) as "master of animals"; the shaman as weather-mage, psychopomp, or spirit guide; ritual confession (a pan-American trait); "backward talking"; the rainbow as cosmic soul; the rite at the hunt site so that the prey can rise again from its bones; obligatory sharing of the kill; and so forth. (La Barre, 1970: *passim*). Huichol myths at times seem merely to recombine and reconfigurate motifs of great antiquity, as when a deer-horned shaman initiates novices with his musical bow or shamanic drum into his "medicine society" by sharing his ritual visionary secret, and transforms the novices into bird-spirits, which, with the help of his animal-familiar or "master of animals," he leads through dangers on the shamanic journey through the sky (Furst, 1972: 148–50). Taken as a whole, the Huichol is almost the ideal type of the mesolithic shamanic myth.

Furst (1972: 143) even cites archeological evidence to suggest connection of west Mexican tribes with the south Mexican and Guatemalan cult of the hallucinogenic mushroom. In general, ethnologists are coming to agreement on the great age of hallucinogens and other shamanic motifs in the New World (see La Barre on "Hallucinogens and the Shamanic Origins of Religion," in Furst, 1972: 261–78; and Harner's anthology, *Hallucinogens and Shamanism,* 1973). Archeology has repeatedly confirmed ethnological opinion. For example, from some of the stratigraphically and chronologically best-controlled sites in northeastern Mexico, the oldest presently known Amerindian hallucinogen, *Ungnadia speciosa,* or Texas buckeye, has been Carbon[14]-dated at about 10,500 B.P. The red bean, *Sophora secundiflora,* has been found (Bonfire Shelter, 8440–8120 B.C.) in association with Folsom and Plainview projectile points, the red bean continuing to the topmost level (A.D. 420–1040). Peyote, *Lophophora williamsii,* lacking at Frightful Cave (7500 B.C.–A.D. 570), is found at Cuatro Cienagas in an A.D. 810–1070 horizon.

All of the above data seem to indicate that the regular use of psychotropics is established in the northeastern Mexico/Trans-Pecos Texas area by *ca.* 8500 B.C. The earliest plants would appear to be the buckeye and the red bean, though the frequency of the former is much greater than the latter in early contexts. Later, the use of the red bean became more common while the buckeye declines. At some point, as yet undetermined with precision, the use of the red bean likewise declines and peyote becomes the favored plant. This supports the view of La Barre and others that a widespread red bean cult preceded the use of peyote in the area under discussion . . . Considerable, though wholly circumstantial evidence, suggests the use of the buckeye and the red bean may be part of a hunting cult. The cache items from Texas, and what may be another antler headdress from Mexico are but a few of the more direct hints of such a cult (Adovasio and Fry, 1972).

Because of the great toxicity of *Ungnadia speciosa,* Schultes, the ethnobotanical authority on American hallucinogens, has questioned (personal communication) its ritual use. The archeological evidence, however, is impressive: Horseshoe Cave, for example, contained a pint of buckeye and red beans *mixed together.*

Specifically, the Mexican buckeye is often found in large quantities literally sealed in plaited or twilled baskets, entrance to which can be made only by tearing open the container. One such cache contained eleven pounds of the plant. No other plant in this or the other Coahuila sites was similarly stored except the red bean (Adovasio and Fry, 1972).

The quantitative-stratigraphic evidence is that earlier-used but highly toxic plants were gradually supplanted by later-discovered and less toxic species, in the sequence buckeye–red bean–peyote. The place of teonanacatl, the least toxic, in this series is unknown, although Guatemalan "mushroom stones" also have a respectable antiquity (conservatively, 1000 B.C.); and the red bean (Cabeza de Vaca, 1539), teonanacatl (frescoes from central Mexico, A.D. 300, and in colonial sources, e.g., Hernandez, 1651), and peyote (middle sixteenth-century sources) were all known in post-Columbian ethnographic use, whereas the buckeye to date is not. For other relevant archeological data, see Taylor (1948, 1956; Taylor, in Eckholm and Wiley, 1966), and Story and Bryant (1966), in addition to earlier-cited reports by Campbell (1958) and Troike (1962) on the red bean.

The deer–maize–peyote symbol-complex among the Huichol, originally noted by Lumholtz, has been greatly enriched by the work of Barbara Myerhoff, who analyzes the complex in a Geertz–Turner–Lévi-Straussian framework emphasizing the resolution of societal, historical, and ideological conflicts in Huichol life (Myerhoff, 1968ab, 1972). Her data may also be viewed in terms of the "oceanic feeling" or "regression in the service of the ego" to the timeless, ritual id- or "alcheringa-time" that both ethnographers and psychopharmacologists have noted as characteristic of hallucinogenic states. Marino Benzi (1969) has described Huichol visions under the influence of peyote. In this article he considers that peyotism originated in this isolated group, the only one keeping to its aboriginal form, and he stresses the remarkable coherence and uniformity of Huichol peyotism and its continuity (see also a review of this article in *Transcultural Psychiatry Research Review* [April 1971: 79–80]). Benzi later (1972) published a book on *Les derniers adorateurs du Peyotl.* In a review of Benzi, Jilek (1973) states that

Benzi has presented much more than an ethnographic report. His book is a mine of data which are of interest not only to the student of anthropology and comparative psychiatry, but also the psychoanalyst, the ethnopharmacologist, and the historian of religion.

In Dutch we also have a treatment of Mexican peyotism by Charleux (1928), and in Spanish, by Benitez (1968). In this connection we might state that John Tate Lanning, a historian of Latin America at Duke University, has an incomparable knowledge of colonial documents, many of them on early peyotism.

Our knowledge of Huichol peyotism is all the more valuable, inasmuch as the cult is extinct among the Mescalero Apache (Boyer and Boyer, 1967: 7), the tribe long regarded as the transitional bearer of peyotism to the Southern Plains Kiowa and Apache. Already described by Opler (1936) as "a tribe of shamans, active or potentially active," the Mescalero "peyote meetings became places in which shamanistic rivalries and witchcraft flourished. Disruption resulted, rather than cohesiveness through shared experience" (Boyer, Boyer, and Basehart, in Harner, 1973: 56).

In general, the dates of the introduction of peyotism into the Southern Plains tend to have been pushed farther back from the present writer's earlier, somewhat conservative dates. Nor should the possibility of multiple influences from Texas as well as from the Southwest be ignored. "One peyote chief claims that the Kiowa Apache had, on occasion, obtained the cactus from the Tonkawa and used it as a medicine and as a part of shamanism prior to 1875; and perhaps prior to the time of reservationism in 1868" (Beals, 1971: 45). This author gives a Tonkawa origin legend and notes that they had no drum or gourd, but used the musical bow, which is consistent with Mexican evidence. "The use of peyote as a focus of a religion is said to have originated with a visit of [dà yaî gáł] who was either Mescalero or Lipan" (Beals, 1971: 45). Since the small Athapaskan tribelet of the Kiowa Apache had the position of a band among their protectors, the Kiowa, the possibility exists that they may have been the medium of introduction from other Apache, whether Mescalero or Lipan. The oldest historical report on the use of peyote on the Kiowa–Comanche–Apache reservation is that of the Indian agent, J. Lee Hall, on August 6, 1886 to the Commissioner of Indian Affairs; the next report mentioning the use of peyote was that of his successor, E. E. White, on August 18, 1888 (Beals, 1971: 48). The Indians' reaction to repression was the modification of the ritual by Apache John, Old Man Archutah, and Saddleblanket, who excluded shamans, e.g. Dabeko, from the meetings about 1890. The efforts at repression reached a peak about 1918.

A visit to the area by James Mooney during the time was instrumental in the organization of the [Native American] Church. An intertribal conference was held at El Reno, Oklahoma, with one of the participants being Apache Ben. An Oklahoma charter of the articles of incorporation was granted on October 10, 1918 (Beals, 1971: 51).

Before the time of Christian syncretism, the ritual fire was extinguished at midnight, followed by shamanistic exhibitions. But in 1960 the Kiowa Apache revived the Manatidie as their most important ceremony, and Beals believes that since that date both the frequency of peyote meetings and their general importance declined among the Kiowa Apache (Beals, 1971: 52; see also Hill and Beals, 1966).

In an important paper on "The Peyote Religion and the Ghost Dance," Omer C. Stewart (1972) maintains that peyotism was already established in Texas and Oklahoma by the time of the 1890 Ghost Dance, and he faults Mooney, prestigious authority on both religions, for misleading Slotkin, Shonle, Barber, Underhill, and others. Stewart carefully marshalls his evidence (cited from ethnographers including La Barre) that "many Texas and Oklahoma [some twenty] tribes knew Peyotism before they knew the Ghost Dance" (Stewart, 1972: 28–29), and quotes La Barre (1938: 43) that *"in the Plains* [my emphasis added], peyotism largely followed the Ghost Dance" and Barber (1941: 671) that "the Peyote cult as a significant nativistic movement came in approximate temporal succession to the Ghost Dance of 1890." In its major spread northward, peyotism was in fact post-Ghost Dance, but students of peyotism will be grateful to Stewart for the changed historical emphasis.

The most compendious new monograph on a single tribe is Aberle's on *The Peyote Religion among the Navaho* (1966). Jorgensen (1969) argued that F. Voget, a reviewer of the book, did not attend sufficiently to Aberle's "relative deprivation" theory but was preoccupied with his own acculturational view; Voget (1969) replied by pointing out the individual–group problems in such a "psychological" explanation as Aberle's, which Aberle and Voget had both agreed was inadequately demonstrable. Wagner (1968) has studied variations in the Navaho peyote ritual. The first psychiatrist to publish on Navaho peyotism (Bergman, 1971) was reviewed by Jilek (1972), who states that

Group-therapeutic factors are operant in the meetings of the congregation whose members derive considerable benefit from ego-strengthening support . . . a valuable assistance for many Indian people threatened with identity diffusion. It provides help in crises situations and is especially beneficial to Indians with drinking problems. The paper's discussant, Karl Menninger, who for many years has had a part in Supreme Court repeals of anti-peyote legislation, is in full agreement. He considers peyote "a better antidote to alcohol than anything the missionaries, the white man, the American Medical Association, and the public health services have come up with" (Jilek, 1972).

Elsewhere in the Southwest, Collins (1967, 1968, 1969) has discussed peyotism at Taos Pueblo, long an area of factionalism: here, interestingly, "Each individual owns a 'peyote chief,' and often employs it in the world of the profane to ward off evil and to bring good luck" (Collins, 1968: 431). The peyote question at Taos has also been discussed by Waters (1971).

The Western Shoshone, a tribe with "pervasive factionalism," have also, as one bone of contention, disagreed on peyote, whose power, anti-peyotists claim, comes from the rattlesnake or coyote rather than being inherent in peyote, as peyotists claim; in the traditional tribal view, peyotists are therefore equated with witches (Lieber, 1972). The Washo have also had conflict over the new religion. Although some Washo may have known peyote in 1920, the Ute shaman Lone Bear brought the ceremony in 1932, followed in 1938 by Franklin York, who exploited it economically.

In a sense peyote gave the Washo a sense of identity. In defying the white law and white disapproval and conducting peyote services, they were asserting themselves as Indians. Because peyote meetings were intertribal they were conducted in English and gave the Washo a sense of identity with other Indians. Most important was the fact that aboriginal religious practices, as meager and informal as they were, tended to disappear almost completely . . . Washo religious energy was devoted to the peyote cult. Even people who did not attend meetings became believers and peyote became the most powerful figure in Washo supernatural world . . . Today, because the Washo peyote meetings are the nearest ones to the urban centers of the San Francisco Bay area, the Washo country has become a center of peyote activity for Indians of many tribes. Indians living in the cities regularly make weekend trips to the Washo country to attend meetings. There they appear to renew their Indian self-image which enables them to return to the city and adjust to urban life for a time before they once again seek renewal (Downs: 1966: 103-4).

The Spindlers (1971: 94–140) see peyotism among the Menomini "dreamers without power" as adaptive, reducing cognitive and emotional dissonance between Menomini and white cultures. Although peyote shamans still doctor with redhot coals in their mouths, the cult itself is highly Christianized. The Spindlers' work is valuable because of their psychological approach, and discrimination among the acculturated and the less acculturated, men versus women, and so on;

Rorschach tests show peyotists as highly deviant among the Menomini, though homogeneous among themselves. The Ritzenthalers have also discussed Woodlands peyotism. "From the Winnebago, who are still the chief advocates of the cult, it spread to the Forest Potawatomi [about 1908], the Sauk and the Fox, while only feeble inroads were made among the Chippewa" (R. E. and P. Ritzenthaler, 1970: 93–94). Bee (1966) stresses the influence of traditional patterns in Potawatomi peyotism; see also the more general treatment of peyotism by Bee (1965).

Since Petrullo's (1940) paper on peyotism as an emergent Indian culture, Voget (1957) has analyzed the social and ceremonial systems of three movements—Pacific Northwest Shakerism, the Iroquois "Great Message," and Plains peyotism—"in the light of the role they played in furnishing social approval and relatively new sets of statuses in periods of social and cultural disorganization . . . in the framework of role theory, dealing with the renewal of the 'self' as a function of improvement in social status" (L. and G. Spindler, in Siegel, 1959: 54). Herzberg has also discussed peyotism in her book on modern pan-Indian movements (Herzberg, 1971: Ch. III). Wiener has a typical brief résumé of peyotism, based on Schultes, in a book on Indian medicines and foods (1972: 98–99).

A treatment of peyotism by the sociologist B. R. Wilson (1973: Ch. 13) must be taken severely to task. Having no adequate ethnographic background, Wilson commits many errors of interpretation. His "introversionist" peyotists can hardly have "withdrawn" from a white world they never belonged to; their seeking of visions is no earnest of "Christian quietism" since visions are deep in their ethnographic background, not "a strong pietistic current." "The exact properties of peyote . . . have been disputed" but not by informed persons; the variants in peyote ritual were hardly "rival" in Wilson's sense; he confuses John Wilson, the Caddo-Delaware peyotist, with Jack Wilson (Wovoka), the Paiute Ghost Dance messiah; peyotism as "essentially Christian faith, adapted to traditional Indian beliefs and practices" is nonsense, since it is basically an ancient aboriginal rite and *differently integrated* into various tribal traditions. The statement that "Peyote is a contemplative religious movement, in which men emphasize their spiritual inadequacy" misapprehends the conventions of the aboriginal vision-quest. Navaho peyotism is not "basically a response of withdrawal from involvement" with a "new internalized ethic" in a "matrix of the rejection of the wider world." Wilson criticizes Aberle for not discriminating between "conversionist" and "introversionist" sects, calling all of them "redemptionist"—which hardly touches this authority since both European categories are irrelevant to Navaho peyotism —and condescends to La Barre as "not necessarily wrong" while confusing John Wilson and Jack Wilson in his argument. "The ambitious work by Vittorio Lanternari . . . by no means always accurate . . . lacks a coherent analytical procedure, and even the order of presentation of material seems to me likely to mislead the reader." All these may be the case. But the same criticisms and more apply to Wilson's unfortunate work.

Polish scholars have recently become interested in peyotism, as shown in a volume edited by Anny Kutrzeba-Pojnarowej (1972). The articles by Barbara Walendowska and Ewa Nowicka seem to me to have a good sense of proportion of the survival and strength of native components, but that by Mirosława Posern-Zielínska perhaps overemphasizes the Catholic component in peyotism; Krystyna Bidwell's summary of it (Kutrzeba-Pojnarowej, 1972: 243–49) is competent and clear.

Brant (1963) gives us Joe Blackbear's story of the origin of peyotism, and Howard (1962) an article on peyote jokes; however, Howard appears to be unfamiliar with the wider relevance of tricksters and ceremonial clowns in American Indian religion. Howard (1960) also reopens the question of mescalism and peyotism on which he had disagreed earlier with La Barre; however, the use of ritual fire, the shaman's bow, and mescal-bean necklaces hardly militates against but rather re-emphasizes a Mexican provenience. The use of a spear point, apparently in Kiowa- and Comanche-derived rituals, as part of the Road Chief's paraphernalia (to emphasize the old way of life) has also been reported on by Howard (1950); other peyote-relevant papers, heretofore unlisted by the present writer, are those by Mooney (in Hodge, 1907–10, 2:237), D. Collier (1929) and J. Collier (1952), Radin (1950), Blair (1921), and M. G. Smith on a Negro peyote cult (1934). In his standard work on the *Indians of North America* (Driver, 1969), Driver and Massey have a very useful Map 13, indicating not only the source area for peyote, but also areas in which peyotism was first reported, successively in the sixteenth, seventeenth, eighteenth, nineteenth, and twentieth centuries, thus giving a clear panoramic sweep of the tribe-by-tribe diffusion of peyotism. Their Map 14 further gives the areas of aboriginal use of the black drink, the mescal bean, jimsonweed, teonanacatl, and ololiuqui.

THE NEW WORLD NARCOTIC COMPLEX

In noting the prevalence of shamanism among hunting peoples, La Barre has repeatedly pointed out the relationship of various hallucinogens to the shamanic supernatural-"power" vision quest or religious revelation, that is, the importance of actual psychotropic material substances in shaping shamanism, an archaic form which perhaps underlies, in time, all religions—both of the Old World and the New—and, because of the many such substances used, suggests the existence of a very old, multiple-culture-area "narcotic complex" in the New World (La Barre, 1964abc; see also, La Barre, 1938:131–37). The presence of essential shamanism in crisis cults such as the Ghost Dance, and the significance of psychotropic plants in some of these, was later compendiously treated in a monograph (La Barre, 1970, 1972ab). Still again, in "Hallucinogens and the Shamanic Origin of Religion" (La Barre, in Furst, 1972: 272), he maintained that, in the New World especially, "ecstatic-visionary shamanism is, so to speak, *culturally programmed for an interest in hallucinogens and other psychotropic drugs,*" and proceeded to give numerous illustrations in aboriginal American Indian religion. The "narcotic complex" was accepted on botanical grounds by Schultes (1960a: 143), and on ethnographic grounds by Furst (1972: vii–xvi) and—although the subject has hardly been as neglected as Harner states—by Harner (1973: vii–viii).

As early as 1963, Schultes had noted that "it is of interest that the New World is very much richer in narcotic plants than the Old and that the New World boasts at least 40 species of hallucinogenic or phantastica narcotics as opposed to half a dozen species native to the Old World" (Schultes, 1963b: 147). Indeed, and largely owing to his own new discoveries, the botanical discrepancy increased: later, sixty species were cited (Schultes, 1967:36), and currently (Schultes, 1973: 543), "From 90 to 100 [hallucinogenically employed] species are now known to be used in the Western Hemisphere as against a dozen or so in the Eastern." Biochemically, plant hallucinogens are often alkaloids, but four or five thousand species are now known to be alkaloidal; and, besides alkaloids, other constituents (glycosides, resins, essential oils) may also be responsible for narcotic activity—but both alkaloidal and non-alkaloidal psychotropic plants are presumably distributed equally in both hemispheres.

The reason for this marked discrepancy is by no means immediately apparent. In point of fact, one might reasonably suppose that the reverse would be the case. That is, the Old World has a far greater land mass than the New and certainly as varied climates, and hence the apparent possibility of a greater number and variety of plants. Furthermore, men and proto-men who might have discovered the properties of those plants that are narcotic have existed for an incomparably longer period (from the Australopithecines and *Homo habilis* onward) in the Old World than in the New (only from the late Paleolithic and Mesolithic onward). Thus, on geographic-ecological and botanical and also on anthropological grounds, the Old World *prima facie* should hold more psychotropic plant species than the New—which is quite contrary to the apparent facts (La Barre, 1970b: 73).

It can scarcely be maintained that our scientific knowledge on New World botany is more complete than that on the Old; paradoxically, as Schultes and others increase that knowledge, the statistical discrepancy only increases.

Returning to the problem, the distinguished ethnobotanist queried: "Is there any reason to presume that man in a primitive state of culture possesses any peculiar intuition enabling him to uncover more efficiently than his more civilized counterpart those plants that nature has endowed with physiologically active principles?" (Schultes, 1966: 295). This explanation seems psychologically dubious (though a psychological explanation may be possible); besides, it does not explain the Old World–New World statistical discrepancy. To this statistical question in botany, the anthropologist can offer an ethnological reply (La Barre, 1970b)—essentially, that the New World peoples remained closer in ethos to their earlier Mesolithic hunting ecologies, which are functionally related to shamanism, and that shamanic visions and the use of hallucinogens are culturally related.

THE NATIVE AMERICAN CHURCH AND THE LAW

In reply to the overstated criticisms of anthropologists by Indian activists such as Vine Deloria, Omer Stewart points out that when the Native American Church was under attack in the Chavez Bill of 1937, the anthropologists Boas, Kroeber, Hrdlicka, J. P. and M. R. Harrington, La Barre, Petrullo, Elna Smith, and Donald Collier volunteered expert defense. Again, in 1951 a "Statement on Peyote" appeared in *Science,* signed by La Barre, McAllister, Slotkin, Stewart, and Tax, in defense of the peyote religion. Indeed, during the 1962–72 period, Stewart himself, as did Slotkin, repeatedly testified in court cases, including the important one that reached the California Supreme Court, and also in critical Navaho cases in Arizona. In April–May 1968, Sam Houston Clinton, Jr., an American Civil Liberties Union attorney, *in re* No. 12,879 (49th Judicial District Court of Webb County), *The State of Texas v. David S. Clark,* won the case for the defendant, in a proceeding in which La Barre made a lengthy written deposition, as did McAllister. This case tested the constitutionality of *60th Legislature of Texas (January 10–May 29, 1967, Chapter 720, S. B. No. 17,* which was here found inapplicable to the Native American Church. On June 4, 1969, the Texas Legislature amended Sections 1–2, Ch. 425, *Acts of the 56th Legislature, Regular Session, 1959,* to specify that the law "does not apply to its use in bona fide religious ceremonies of the Native American Church (NAC Newsletter, April 1970). In the State of South Dakota Drugs and Substances Control Law of 1970 (Sec. 8, Schedule 1, subsection 9a) the exception is stated as part of the law itself: "Peyote, when used as a sacrament in services of the Native American Church in a natural state which is unaltered except for drying or curing or slicing, is hereby excepted." In 1970, of seventeen states with anti-peyote laws, only five did not provide specific exemption for Indians, and the President of the Native American Church, Leonard Springer, an Omaha, was seeking redress of these when he died on July 28, 1971. On June 7, 1971, the Minnesota Legislature amended Minnesota Statutes, Chapter 152, by adding Sec. 12, 152.02 stating that the law "does not apply to the nondrug use of peyote in bona fide religious ceremonies of the Native American Church," partly as the result of anthropologists serving as expert witnesses. Again, in the *Federal Register* of March 13, 1971, the "Comprehensive Drug Abuse Prevention and Control Act of 1970" subsequent to testimony by La Barre was amended in Section 307.31 to exempt members of the Native American Church (NAC Newsletter, August 1971). "It is therefore neither fair nor accurate to allege that anthropologists (who paid informants for their time) were uniformly 'colonial' exploiters of Indians, presumably for the vast sums to be earned by their scholarly and obscure monographs" (Stewart, in Officer, 1973: 41). In any case, Stewart (1961, 1970; Stewart, in Walker, 1972) is the undisputed authority on peyote legislation. Wax (1971: 141–44) has a not-very-adequate summary on the Native American Church, and raises the "moot question" of accommodation of peyotists to the American work week, really a bogus issue since peyote meetings are usually held on Saturday nights.

PEYOTE IN ART, MUSIC, LITERATURE, AND DRAMA

The gifted modern American composer Ned Rorem has described convincingly his emotionally profound experience with mescaline, which he considered one of the most important experiences of his life (Rorem, 1967: 159–69). Artaud, the tortured and talented French actor, fled France after the failure of his production of *The Cenci* to live with the Tarahumare Indians of Mexico and there to partake of their sacred *hikuli* (peyote). He returned to Europe a year later with a new addition to his old opium addiction (De Gramont, 1970). Philip Lamantia has a section in his brochure *Narcotica* (1959) translated by L. Dejardin from the French of Artaud.

Natachee Scott Momaday, a Kiowa assistant professor of English in the University of California at Santa Barbara, won the Pulitzer Prize for his *House Made of Dawn*, called "a novel of exceptional beauty" by the *Wall Street Journal*. In it he summarizes a standard peyote meeting (Momaday, 1968: 110–14), including the prayers of four participants (pp. 113–14), and quoting a speech of "Tosomah, orator, physician, Priest of the Sun, son of Hummingbird" from the first two paragraphs of La Barre (1938: 7). Michael McClure's *Hymns to St. Geryon, and Other Poems* includes among them a "Peyote Poem" (1959: 39–50).

Bernard Roseman (1968) tells *The Peyote Story* in a handlettered text published in Hollywood. *Birth* (1960), a pastiche of articles and quotations on psychedelics, contains a "Peyote Section" (pp. 64–80), including sections on peyote eating from Allen Ginsberg's *Journals*. Jerome Rothenberg edited *Shaking the Pumpkin* (1972), an anthology of traditional poetry of the Indians of North America, which contains peyote visions of the Winnebago (pp. 358–61) and of the Huichol (pp. 362–65). Harold Heifetz in *Jeremiah Thunder* (1968: Chs. 12–13) mentions peyote (p. 163) as a "turgid plumlike cactus" and the description of a peyote ritual is equally improvised, mixing the shofar and Moses' rod, Puebloid and peyotist motifs with the Mexican Penitentes.

One of the famed Kiowa artists, Monroe Tsa To ke (Huntinghorse, 1904–37), wrote and illustrated *The Peyote Road, Visions and Descriptions* (1957), unfortunately in an edition of only 325 copies. Pieri Scanziani of Rome, in 1969 was writing an article for the periodical *Tempo* (Milan), in part on Tsa To ke and peyotism, and later planned a book, but neither of these has been located. Jack Hokeah, another of the original "Five Kiowa" painters, has had his *Peyote Chief* gouache (c. 1930) handsomely reproduced from the collections of the Museum of the American Indian (Heye Foundation) as a folding correspondence card. Woody Crumbo, an Indian artist who lectures on peyote, is said to have written a book on peyotism in the late 1960s.

Savage, a play written and directed by Maxine Klein, opened in the Boston

University Theater in January of 1971, before a stay at La Mama, an off-Broadway theater in New York. The first act is structured as a social-protest peyote meeting, in which an Indian under the influence of peyote travels psychologically through history, witnessing the uncountable wrongs done to his people, and in a stylized ritual he then kills two whites (Sterritt, 1971).

Leonard Crow Dog, a Sioux shaman and peyote leader from Rosebud, South Dakota, recorded an album called *Crow Dog's Paradise* (Elektra, 1972) with his father Henry Crow Dog. The younger Crow Dog has performed as a dancer at the "Electric Circus" in New York, the "Electric Factory" in Philadelphia, and the anti-poverty demonstration at Resurrection City in Washington, D.C. (Cott, 1972).

One of the best ethnographic movies ever made is *To Find Our Life: The Peyote Hunt of the Huichols of Mexico,* by the anthropologist Peter T. Furst (reviewed by La Barre, 1970c). This is a sound movie, in full color, of an actual ritualized journey of the Huichol to find their sacred deer–maize–peyote in the ancient symbolic hunt. The remarkable narration of the movie consists of texts directly translated from the Huichol; and the incidental art work consists in the astonishing and brilliant wax-and-yarn peyote "paintings" made by Huichol artists. Some of the peyote myths have been made into yarn paintings, coiled and embedded in beeswax in the *nearika* technique, an indigenous folk art marketed in Guadelajara. The yarn mosaics are composed in brilliant contrastive colors; according to the late Ramón Medina Silva, a Huichol shaman-artist, the more brilliant the colors the more nearly they resemble what one sees after eating peyote (Furst, 1968: 20). Furst, incidentally, has been one of the most perceptive and convincing students of Mexican archeological art with respect to the ethnography both of shamanism (Furst, 1965, 1968a: 143–78; Haekel, 1968) and of hallucinogens *(Psychotropic Flora and Fauna in pre-Columbian Art,* Furst, in press; compare Dobkin de Rios, 1974).

In the spring of 1972, the Smithsonian Institution produced an imaginative and well-planned exhibition of psychotropic drugs, in connection with a number of scientific symposia and television broadcasts. The Botanical Museum of Harvard University had an exhibit on *The Transcultural Significance of Magic Plants* (brochure by Schultes, 1965); and an exhibit on hallucinogenic drugs was arranged at the meetings of the American Psychiatric Association by the Committee on Transcultural Psychiatry (brochure, Rinkel and Schultes, 1965).

STUDENTS

During the National Symposium on the Psychedelic Drugs and Marihuana, sponsored by the Illinois State Medical Association in Chicago in 1968, James R. Gamage, a student at Beloit College, proposed formation of the Student Association for the Study of Hallucinogens. This was a serious and thoughtful group whose motto was "Respect for drugs through education" and they quickly obtained the formal consultant services of a distinguished group of psychiatrists, anthropologists, sociologists, religionists, philosophers, and medical men. On

October 2-4, 1969, STASH held its first semi-annual symposium in Beloit on "Problems and Prospects of Research with Psychoactive Drugs" which was addressed by a number of nationally known medical researchers. The association has been especially successful in its bibliographic work and has performed a genuine service for researchers and other interested persons. In the fall of 1968, as an outgrowth of the Psychedelic Information Center in Cambridge, Massachusetts, an organization was proposed by Lisa Bieberman for "the development of a non-Indian psychedelic religious group . . . to carry out a long-term religious experiment in systematic use of psychedelics, to be known as Phanerothyme Center."

According to Hinkle's account (in Cantor and Wertham, 1968: 777–80), "the first psychedelic drug to reach the Village in any quantity was peyote," cheaply and plentifully obtainable from Laredo at ten dollars for a hundred buttons. In late 1957 natural peyote was widely used and, in the summer of 1958, mescaline, the first synthetic hallucinogen (LSD did not arrive in the Village in any quantity until the winter of 1961–62, and in the Bay Area not until the summer of 1964). Later, a great variety of psychotropic drugs were used, including morning glory seeds, Hawaiian wood rose seeds, and Mexican mushrooms. More especially, however, the smoking of marihuana spread with youthful rock-and-roll musicians to use even by middle-class, largely urban, adults. But the original centers were dispersing. In October 1967 a hundred persons held a mock funeral of the "death of the hippie" in Haight-Ashbury. Jefferson Airplane and the Grateful Dead had long since moved away, and many of the "flower children" had fled to the Sierras, Vancouver, La Paz, Europe, and India (*Newsweek*, December 2, 1968).

In the autumn of 1968 Timothy Leary, self-styled leader of the "League for Spiritual Discovery," published his autobiographical *High Priest*. He was subsequently arrested with his daughter on returning from Mexico. In September 1970, after serving six months of a maximum ten-year sentence for the possession of marihuana, Leary escaped from a minimum-security farm in California and fled to Algeria, where Eldridge Cleaver and other Black Panthers were stationed. Encountering some difficulties in Algeria, Leary went to Switzerland; but after six months there, he was asked to leave. Next, after a brief stay in Vienna, Leary made his way to Afghanistan, but the government authorities extradited him back to Los Angeles in January 1973. Although many said he had been arrested, and even persecuted, on the wrong charge—possession of marihuana—Leary's major proselytization on behalf of LSD gradually lost student support for him, and it was an earlier and older figure, Allen Ginsberg, who remained leader of the "movement to legalize pot." Leary's former colleague Richard Alport, fired from Harvard with him in 1963, went to India for a winter of study with a guru in a small temple in the Himalayas. Returned as Baba Ram Das, he became a minor influence in the movement to seek spiritual enlightenment without the use of psychedelic drugs.

Since the mid-sixties, the use of various psychotropic drugs spread widely among middle-class college populations in all regions of the country. Many articles and books of varying competence appeared, among the best-informed being Farnsworth (1963), Gordon (1963), McGlothlin and Cohen (1965), Cary (1968), Imperi, Kleber, and Davie (1968), Pearlman (1968), Nowlis (1969), Cerletti and Bové (1969), H. and O. J. Kalant (1971), and Hoover (1972). Of particular alarm to parents was the spread of drug use to younger high school "teeny-boppers" and even into grade schools (*Newsweek,* April 2, 1969), and at a time when drugs were already beginning to lose popularity among college youth.

One of the most notorious and alarming events of 1969 was the bloody murder of five persons early on August 9 at the home of Sharon Tate, movie actress wife of the director Roman Polanski, by several individuals said to belong to a satanic drug cult. Curiously, one of the murder victims, a handsome and impetuous Pole named Voityek Frokowsky, social center of the Tate group, was said himself to be on the fifth day of a planned eight- or ten-day experiment with mescaline intoxication (Washington Post–Los Angeles Times News Service, August 27, 1969).

This and other drug cases led to aroused public support of an active Bureau of Narcotics and local law enforcement agencies. A characteristic action was the seizure of the largest amount of peyote ever made in the state of North Carolina. On the first of June 1971, the vice squad of the Durham police arrested a local college flunk-out, originally from Los Angeles, and seized twenty pounds of peyote, along with marihuana, hashish, and LSD. Again, on September 14, 1972, three persons, two of them college students, were arrested in Westbury, Long Island, for possession of nearly seventy pounds of peyote, brought by car from Arizona—some 3,000 buttons, each retailing for three dollars. The Bureau of Narcotics said this was the largest seizure of peyote in the East.

The Federal narcotics agents, after a year of investigation in what was said to be "the largest coordinated police effort against illegal narcotics trafficking" (*New York Times,* August 6, 1972, p. 1), seized thirty-nine members of the "Brotherhood of Eternal Love" in pre-dawn raids in California and Oregon. This group was an offshoot of Leary's "League for Spiritual Discovery" through his "Mystic Arts World Psychedelic Shop" in Laguna Beach. The major target was a ranch in the San Jacinto mountains east of Los Angeles, said to be the site of the largest manufacture of LSD in the world. Two hashish laboratories were seized as well; the Brotherhood was alleged by the Bureau of Narcotics also to be the largest importers of hashish, of which 1000 pounds had been smuggled in, largely from Afghanistan.

Much of the above has the ring of remote past history. It is difficult to conceive of anything so grotesquely outdated in any year as last year's student attitudes and behaviors. In late 1972, the use of hard drugs was fading on twenty-six campuses studied in the New York–New Jersey–Connecticut area—though the sale and use of soft drugs (marihuana, hashish, barbiturates, and a "downer" known as Quaalude) had become virtually institutionalized (McFadden, 1972; see also Goodman, 1974; and *Journal* [of the Addiction Research Foun-

dation], 1973). Use of mescaline, LSD, amphetamines, and heroin had sharply
dropped; the only hard drug in moderate supply and demand was cocaine, largely
sniffed. Students were turning to beer, wine, and liquor, often with the coopera-
tion of university officials who provided housing for new drinking places, and
small-scale trade in cannabis was becoming casual and well-nigh universal. But
prices were up: marihuana ranged from fifteen to fifty dollars an ounce, cocaine by
a [quarter-]"spoonful" from twenty to forty dollars, and Quaalude pills (popular
at girls' schools until it was suspected that they were teratogenic) from thirty-five
cents to a dollar each. At Princeton and other eastern campuses, the use of all
drugs had become passé, in part because the earlier wealthy and middle-class
"preppies" had been considerably replaced by an almost ferociously upward-
mobile and competitive meritocracy. And at Yale, the authorities, perhaps gratefully, had returned to worry about the injudicious overconsumption of
alcohol.

JOURNALISM

With the massive change in student culture, peyote has become much less of
a journalistic sensation, though various studies continue to be published as news.
The periodical *Newsweek* (1973) contains a sober and informed article on the
peyote religion as a focus for Indian identity, in contrast with earlier articles such
as that in the Canadian edition of *Time* (1954) on a Christianized Iowa meeting.
Nevertheless, poorly informed and less ably researched articles continue to appear. In "The Peyote Road," former Sante Fe newspaperman Peter Nabokov *(New
York Times Magazine,* 1960), states—in an otherwise colorful article on a Navaho
meeting—that the button is a "blossom cut from the top of a peyote plant," which
is consistent neither with the later statement that "the buds are sliced" nor with the
actual fact.

F. X. Tolbert (1972), by contrast, contains interesting new information that "El
Peyote Ranch" (between Mirando City and Hebbronville in Texas) was formerly a
mecca for various "peyotists." The four licensed dealers in Mirando City and
nearby Oilton were required by the Federal government to keep careful records of
sales. But there are peyote rustlers nowadays. In the Laredo District Attorney's
office it was said that "many cowboys go armed while working on ranches where
peyote grows, for in several cases the trespassers carried weapons and reacted
violently when caught at their harvest."

Intercambio (1959) contains yet another layman's description of the effects of
eating peyote; see also Schleifer (1960). Stewart Brand's (1967) miscellaneous
account has confused the peyote meeting plan with a pretentious and absurd
Hindu-Jungian "mandala" of which it is safe to say no Indian peyotist ever heard.
Cardon's (1963) article is largely an excerpting of Marriott's "Opened Door" in the
New Yorker (1954). In discussing Indian resistance, Marriott and Rachlin are said
(New Yorker, 1969) to disapprove of the Native American Church "as a kind of

drugged surrender." These authors' (1971) careless, short, somewhat literary paperback on *Peyote* is unfortunately sometimes improvised and full of inaccuracies.

CASTANEDA

One of the literary sensations of the decade was the Castañeda phenomenon. A man in his mid-thirties of uncertain origin, Carlos Castañeda was an undergraduate student planning graduate work in anthropology at the University of California at Los Angeles. In 1960, in an Arizona bus station, he met Juan Mathus, a half-Yaqui, half-Yuma Indian from Sonora. Although the old man attempted to avoid him, Castañeda persisted and, despite much apparently contemptuous putting down, later followed Mathus to Mexico to learn the secrets of "mescalito" and, eventually, of Jimsonweed and psilocybin as well. Castañeda's subsequent first book, *The Teachings of Don Juan* (1968), contains a preposterous appendix purporting to be "A Structural Analysis" that shows an abrupt change of style from the romantic to the reassuringly pedantic, tacked on at the suggestion of a well-meaning sociologist in order to make scientific an otherwise woefully inadequate ethnography. This tedious attempt to play dutiful Lévi-Straussian games can have satisfied neither Castañeda's professors nor the general reader. But its dullness did mislead some readers with its implication of scholarship.

Charles Simmons, a professional book reviewer for the *New York Times*, was modest, puzzled, and canny, wondering gingerly whether he was really treating "not of a novel but of a doctoral thesis . . . a book I don't have the background to judge as anthropology . . . [but] if it had been published as a novel it would be, I think, destined for fame" (Simmons, 1968). His book-sense was accurate: *Teachings* promptly became a best-seller and a bible of the young.

In a later review of *A Separate Reality*, Wasson (1972) wrote that when *Teachings* first appeared, he thought he "smelled a hoax." But correspondence with the author revealed field notes in Spanish, and the older scholar kindly wrote advice, which the younger man failed to follow. A fastidious writer, Wasson found Don Juan often out of character and noted "many vulgarisms in the conversation that smack only of cheap talk of under-educated North Americans." His final judgment was astringent. "Occasionally there is a faint trace of authenticity in these pages, submerged in a welter of science fiction badly written." Wasson wondered whether "perhaps the University of California Press did a re-writing job in the former book." Nevertheless, an anthropologist would have assured him, the academic credentials of Castañeda seemed authentic. Had he not, after all, presented a paper on "The Didactic Uses of Hallucinogenic Plants: An Examination of a System of Teaching" at the annual convention of the American Anthropological Association in 1968?

In the summer of 1972, *The New York Times* asked me to review *A Separate Reality*. The editors found the review too caustic to print but, with the customary grace of the *Times*, nevertheless paid for the rejected manuscript. The review said, in part (quoted with permission):

All men seek some touchstone for the validity of their beliefs, whether that authority be of persons (tribal or historic tradition or individual visionary experience, immediate or borrowed), or of things (the scientific reference to validation by impersonal nature). For those inexperienced in the use of this last technique, and for those alienated from their own society and culture, it is all too easy to think they find that authority for belief or world-view in still another tribe. Thus, scientifically uneducated youngsters move easily, in a matter of mere years, from Zen Buddhism to Hindu Vedantism, in their quest for some impressive cultural authority, and even turn on soon again as "Jesus freaks."

One can be sympathetic with other world-views and yet ask the question: Is not the endless quest for a *guru* in fact diagnostic of the authoritarian personality, a sign of eternal adolescence in the seeker? That is, such persons dependently seek in the mere authority of other persons what can only be found in fresh inquiries of That Which Is, reality. The purpose of comparative culture studies is properly to discover the nature of culture itself, not to indulge in individual daisy-picking over the problem of "what can a man believe." As for finding cosmic truth by searching "inner space"—often deplorably unfurnished—with the aid of drugs, this epistemology is too noodleheaded and naive to merit comment.

Having made out with a good thing in *The Teachings of Don Juan: A Yaqui Way of Knowledge*, Carlos Castañeda now writes a kind of "Don Juan Revisited." There is a certain poignancy in the picture of a raw young anthropologist in his encounter with a wise old man of another culture, and in both books Castañeda has played this for all it is worth, even to his own indignity. But no professional anthropologist who read the first book was ever able to suppose it made any contribution to Yaqui ethnography. . . .

The long disquisition of Don Juan and the detailing of each confused emotional reaction of the author, in the present volume, imply either total recall, novelistic talent, or a tape recorder. No banality goes unrecorded, nothing is summarized, nothing is spared us, and yet the nourishment of it all hardly matches that in Jello. The total effect is self-dramatizing and vague, and Castañeda curiously manages to be at once disingenuous and naive. Even as belles lettres the book is wanting, for the writing is pretentious (twice we read of "insidious hair," as though the writer were enamoured of his concoction). The *smoking* of the "psilocybe" (mushroom) raises some wonder too.

There seems to exist a sizeable public with a taste for the plastic flowers of science-writing in Ardrey, Heyerdahl, and Desmond Morris, and that public will no doubt be pleased with this new production. One longs for sheer information on datura and narcotic mushrooms beyond the oblique words of Don Juan and the empty feelings of the acolyte, and both books together advance our knowledge of peyotism not a whit. But perhaps it is unfair to expect this of an ego trip. Everything is smarmy with self-important and really quite trivial feelings and narcissistic self-preoccupation.

One's impatience is aroused by the most obvious questions being left unasked. For example, is "a separate reality" the same for every society, or even for two individuals? And is a toxic state of the brain any earnest for the existence of another "reality"? The book is pseudo-profound, sophomoric and deeply vulgar. To one reader at least, for decades interested in American hallucinogens, the book is frustratingly and tiresomely dull, posturing pseudo-ethnography and, intellectually, kitsch. (La Barre, 1972.)

The *Times* subsequently found a reviewer for all three Castañeda books in Paul Riesman, a young professor at Carleton College whose opinions were manifestly closer to a consensus of readers than were mine. Riesman considers that we are incredibly fortunate to have Carlos Castañeda's books . . . The "structural analysis," the second part of the book, is awful . . . a pathetic denial of the reality of the experience presented in the first part of the book . . . it is because of the collaborative nature of the work that it is appropriate, I think, to call it science . . . I can't even begin to point out all the delights to be found in these books. In any case, the excellence of Castañeda's writing ensures, I believe, that readers will discover these things for themselves (Riesman, 1972).

Yet other writers had different reactions. The distinguished novelist Joyce Carol Oates, in a letter to the *Times*, wondered, "is it possible that these books are non-fiction? I realize that everyone accepts them as anthropological studies, yet they seem to be remarkable works of art" (Oates, 1972). Another letter writer, replying to Oates, put *Journey to Ixtlan* "on the fiction side [since] the 'wrestling with the ally' sequence . . . seems to be an imitation of Jacob wrestling with the angel and asking for a blessing; and the 'stopping of the world' scene, which appears to be a travesty of the Transfiguration, involving a coyote" (Gregory, 1973). Still another, who felt that Castañeda's books successively deteriorated, wrote that "This, interestingly enough, is just about the way the quality of psychedelic experience deteriorates when occultist 'power,' rather than enlightenment, is the objective . . . These things Castañeda writes about *could* have happened. I just don't think they did" (Kleps, 1973). And a professor of English wrote that "billed as anthropology . . . *Journey* reads nevertheless like a novel. Its classic form is the tale of initiation" and compares it with Huck Finn, floating with Jim on a raft down the Mississippi, and with Hemingway's Nick Adams learning Indian lore in the north woods—though Castañeda "seems only too willing to suspend disbelief" (Howes, 1973). Indeed, one professional reviewer felt that, when Castañeda stopped taking field notes, "anthropology's loss has become literature's gain" (Jellinek, 1971).

There was meanwhile a growing interest in Carlos Castañeda as a person. But he remained curiously elusive, whether upon advice or by his own inclination.

To compensate for his growing image and legend, Carlos Castañeda erases his personal history and deliberately withholds information that would destroy the anonymity he needs so that he can wander freely in whatever worlds there are or may be. When he is caught in the official world, where withholding information is tantamount to treason, he may give his name, rank and serial number. Then, like the Lone Ranger, he disappears in a cloud of rumor (Keen, 1972).

In this same interview, curiously devoid of biographical detail, appeared the celebrated drawing by Oden, half-erased by the "psychonaut" himself.

In his review of the three books, "Upward and Juanward" in *The Village Voice*, the novelist Sukenick wondered whether Castañeda were perhaps a "new Ossian" and revealed the fascinating information that it was Anaïs Nin—more than any other the writer "who has over the years insisted on the continuity of dream and reality" (Sukenick, 1973)—who helped Castañeda secure a publisher for *Teachings* when he was having difficulty finding one.

Bruce Cook published the first overtly skeptical study, "Is Carlos Castañeda for Real?" in *The National Observer*. In late 1971 or early 1972, Cook had had an interview with Castañeda in Los Angeles when *A Second Reality* appeared. But Cook did not publish the interview.

Why then didn't I write up the interview with him at the time? Because there were inconsistencies in his story . . . and a curious reticence on corroborating details and evidence of any sort to back him up. In short, I wasn't sure he was completely on the level. . . . I don't believe he is who he says he is. . . . After talking with him about two hours I came away convinced that he could not have written the books he says he has. It is not that his command of spoken English seems imperfect—they say Joseph Conrad spoke with a thick accent all his life—but because the English he speaks is so laden with the jargon of sociology and anthropology and his syntax so academic that he could not have executed the excellent narratives. I'm suggesting a collaborator. . . . No, not Don Juan, someone rather with skill in the narrative form, one who has written novels himself and might take Castañeda's field data and turn them into the three absorbing books that have now so far appeared. Clifford Irving, perhaps? (Cook, 1973)

Parodies of the highly vulnerable Castañeda style soon appeared. "The Teachings of Joe Pye (Field Notes for Carlos Castañeda's Next Epiphany)" in the *New Yorker* copied the bathetic pseudo-naiveté of the books—but "Joe" warned "that if I neglected to cut him in on the royalties there would be trouble" (Tomkins, 1973). In *Harper's*, the article "Talking to Power and Spinning with the Ally: The Glossed Carlos Castañeda" by Gwyneth Craven (1973) is generally sympathetic but also gently ironic. But finally in *The New York Times* itself, "The Teachings of Don B: A Yankee Way of Knowledge" by the novelist Donald Barthelmé is a wildly raucous lampoon on the author's learning of Yankee culture from a Village character, mimicking the flat-footed banality of Castañeda's style and the Zen-like answers of Don B. After imbibing psychotropic ethanol, a profound warmth or yellow sadness merged with an indescribable anguish or pink luminosity, and he hallucinated:

A truly monstrous thing! Never in the wildest fantasies of fiction had I encountered anything like it. I looked at it in complete, utter bewilderment. It was strange and eerie, and yet familiar. Then I realized with a shock of horror, terror and eeriness that it was a colossal Publisher, and that it was moving toward me, wanted something from me. I fainted. When I revived, it took me to lunch at Lutèce and we settled on an advance in the low 50's, which I accepted even though I was not yet, in the truest sense, a man of knowledge (Barthelmé, 1973).

But the final accolade arrived when Castañeda became the cover man on *Time*. At least a psychedelic Daliesque transparency of him did; for most of the photographs show only an eye between fingers, eyes beneath a hat brim and half hidden by a book, or a hand atop a hat. One story is that he was born in São Paolo on Christmas Day, 1935 to teenage parents of "well-known" family but, because his parents were so immature, he was sent to live with his maternal grandparents in a back country chicken farm in Brazil. When he was six, his parents took their only child back and lavished their guilty affection on him. But his mother died a year later and he was left alone with his father, whom he mentions in his books with fondness and pity mixed with contempt. He was put in the very proper Avellaneda boarding school in Buenos Aires, but when about fifteen he became uncontrollable and was placed by an uncle with a foster family in Los Angeles. In 1951 he enrolled at Hollywood High; and two years later took a course in sculpture at the Milan Academy of Fine Arts, but "I did not have the sensitivity or the openness to be a great artist." Returned to Los Angeles, he started in social psychology at UCLA, later shifting to anthropology, and in 1959 formally changed his name to Castañeda.

This story, however, is at least partly untrue; for during the years 1955–1959 Carlos Castañeda, under that name, was enrolled as a pre-psychology major at Los Angeles City College, where he took two courses in creative writing and one in journalism. And immigration records show that a Carlos César Arana Castañeda did enter the United States at San Francisco, as he says he did, in 1951. But he was a Peruvian, born on Christmas Day, 1925 in the old Inca town of Cajamarca—which made him 48, not 38, in 1973. After high school in the village, he moved in 1948 with his parents to Lima where he was graduated from the Colegio Nacional de Nuestra Señora de Guadelupe, and then studied painting and sculpture at the National School of Fine Arts in Peru—his father a goldsmith and watchmaker named Burungaray, rather than the academic man and author of other versions. José Bracamonte, a friend who knew him in Peru, says Carlos had lived there mainly off gambling on cards, horses, and dice—"witty, imaginative, cheerful, a big liar"—a description that Castañeda seems to confirm in the self-description of "O, how I love to throw the bull around." The same may be true concerning his Yaqui fieldwork, for Jésus Ochoa, head of ethnography at the National Museum of Anthropology in Mexico, believes that "basically the work has a very high percentage of imagination." At present Castañeda is finishing *Tales of Power*, the fourth and last volume in the Don Juan cycle.

The friendly *Time* correspondent, Sandra Burton, who spent many hours over several weeks with Castañeda, was troubled by the flamboyant inconsistency of his many autobiographies. It does not matter. For the historic Carlos, whoever he was, has long since been transmogrified by pseudologia phantastica into lunar myth, a folk hero.

BIBLIOGRAPHY

ABERLE, DAVID, The Peyote Religion Among the Navaho, Chicago: Aldine, 1966.

ABOUL-ENEIN, H. Y., Mescaline: A Pharmacological Profile, *American Journal of Pharmacology*, 145, #4 (1973) 125–28.

ABRAMSON, H. A. (ed.), *The Use of LSD in Psychotherapy and Alcoholism*, Indianapolis: Bobbs-Merrill, 1967.

ADLER, A. & O. PÖTZL, Uber eine eigenartige Reaktion auf Meskalin bei einer Kranken mit doppelseitigen Herden in der Sehsphäre, *Jahrbücher für Psychiatrie und Neurologie*, 53 (1936) 13–34.

ADOVASIO, JAMES M. & G. F. FRY, Prehistoric Psychotropic Drug Use in Northeastern Mexico and Trans-Pecos Texas, *Paper, 71st Annual Meeting of the American Anthropological Association*, Toronto, 1972 [mimeo].

Alcohol and Health Notes, 1, #1 (December 1970) 5, "Russians Taking Hard Line on Use of Alcohol Drinks," Washington, D.C.: Department of Health, Education and Welfare, National Institute on Alcohol Abuse and Alcoholism, National Institute for Mental Health.

ANDERSON, EDWARD F., The Biogeography, Ecology, and Taxonomy of Lophophora (Cactaceae), *Brittonia*, 21, #4 (October-December 1969) 299–310.

ANDERSON, EDWARD F. & MARGARET S. STONE, A Pollen Analysis of Lophophora (Cactaceae), *Cactus and Succulent* [Society of America] *Journal*, 43 #2 (March–April 1971) 77–82.

ANONYMOUS, *Bulletin on Narcotics*, 9, #2 (April–June 1959) 26.

ARTAUD, ANTONIN, Letter, translated by L. Dejardin, in Philip Lemantia, *Narcotica*, San Francisco: Auerhahn Press, 1959.

AUERBACH, R. & J. A. RUGOWSKI, Lysergic acid diethylamide: Effects on Embryos, *Science*, 157 (1967) 1325–26.

BALESTRIERI, A. & D. FONTANARI, Acquired and Cross Tolerance to Mescaline, LSD-25, and BOL-148, *Archives of General Psychiatry*, 1 (1959) 279–82.

BARRON, FRANK, MURRAY E. JARVIK, &

STERLING BUNNELL, JR., The Hallucinogenic Drugs, *Scientific American*, 210, #4 (1964) 29–37.

BARTHELMÉ, DONALD, The Teachings of Don B.: A Yankee way of knowledge, *New York Times Magazine* (February 11, 1973) 14–15, 66–67.

BEALS, KENNETH, The Dynamics of Kiowa Apache Peyotism, [University of Oklahoma] *Papers in Anthropology*, 12, #1 (Spring 1971) 35–89.

BEE, R. L., Peyotism in North American Indian Groups, *Transactions of the Kansas Academy of Science*, 68 (1965) 13–61.

———, Potawatomi Peyotism: The Influence of Traditional Patterns, *Southwestern Journal of Anthropology*, 22, #6 (Summer 1966) 194–205.

BENINGTON, F. & R. D. MORIN, An Improved Synthesis of Mescaline, *Journal of the American Chemistry Society*, 73 (1951) 1353.

BENITEZ, FERNANDO, *En la Tierra Magica del Peyote*, Mexico: Biblioteca Era, 1968.

BENZI, MARINO, *Les derniers adorateurs du peyotl*, Paris: Gallimard, 1972.

———, Visions des Huichols sous l'effet du Peyotl, *Hygiene Mentale*, 3 (1969) 61–97 [reviewed in *Transcultural Psychiatry Research Review*, 8 (April 1971) 79–80].

BERGMAN, ROBERT L., Navajo Peyote Use: Its Apparent Safety, *American Journal of Psychiatry*, 128, #6 (1971) 695–99.

BERINGER, K., *Der Meskalinrausch*, reprinted, New York: Springer-Verlag, 1969.

BERNABAI, A., Plante magiche Americana (Psilocybe-Stropharia-Anhalonium), *Ann. Sanità Pubblica*, 27 (Noviembre-Diciembre 1966) 1265–96.

BEVER, O., Why do plants produce drugs? Which is their function in the plants?, *Quarterly Journal of Crude Drug Research*, 10 (1970) 1541–49.

BIBRA, ERNST VON, *Die Narkotischen Genussmittel und der Mensch*, Nürnberg: Verlag von Wilhelm Schmid, 1855.

BIDWELL, KRYSTYNA, Peyotism, Religion of the North American Indians [Summary of Mirosława Posern-Zielińska, *Peyotzym*

Religia Indian Ameryki Połnocnej, in Anny Kutrzeba-Pojnarwej, 1972].

BLAIR, THOMAS S., Habit Indulgence in Certain Cactaceous Plants Among the Indians, *Journal of the American Medical Association*, 76 (April 9, 1921) 1033–34.

BOKE, NORMAN H. & EDWARD F. ANDERSON, Structure, Development, and Taxonomy in the Genus Lophophora, *American Journal of Botany*, 57, #5 (1970) 569–78.

BOYER, L. B. & RUTH M. BOYER, A Combined Anthropological and Psychoanalytical Contribution to Folklore, *Psychopathologie Africaine*, 3 (1967) 333–72.

BOYER, L. B., RUTH M. BOYER, & HARRY W. BASEHART, Shamanism and Peyote Use Among the Apaches of the Mescalero Indian Reservation, in Michael J. Harner (ed.), *Hallucinogens and Shamanism*, New York: Oxford University Press, 1973, pp. 53–66.

BRAND, STEWART, The Native American Church Meeting, *Psychedelic Review*, #9 (1967) 21–35.

BRANT, CHARLES S., Joe Blackbear's Story of the Origin of Peyote Religion, *Plains Anthropologist*, 8, #21 (August 1963) 180–81.

BRAVO, H., Une revisión del género *Lophophora, Cactaceas y Succulentes Mexicanas*, 12 (1967) 8–17

BRILL, L. & L. LIEBERMAN, *Authority and Addiction*, (Boston: Little, Brown, 1964).

BUCHANAN, D. N., Mescaline Intoxication, *British Journal of Medical Psychology*, 9 (1929) 67–88.

BUCKMAN, JOHN, Psychedelic Drugs as Adjuncts in Analytic Psychotherapy, in R. D. Hicks and P. J. Fink (eds.), *Psychedelic Drugs*, New York: Grune & Stratton, 1966, pp. 217–25.

BURSCH, W. K. & W. C. JOHNSON, LSD-25 in Psychotherapy, *Diseases of the Nervous System*, 11, #8 (August 1950) 241–43.

CANTOR, NORMAN F. & MICHAEL S. WERTHMAN, *The History of Popular Culture* (New York: Macmillan, 1968).

CAPPELL, H. & A. E. LEBLANC, Conditioned aversion to saccharine by single administrations of mescaline and d-amphetamine, *Psychopharmacologia* [Berlin], 22 (1971) 352–56.

CARDON, B. P., Peyote and the Native American Church, *Journal of Psychedelic Drugs*, 1, #2 (1963) 72–76.

CARY, J. T., *The College Drug Scene*, Englewood Cliffs, N.J.: Prentice-Hall, 1968.

CASTAÑEDA, CARLOS, The Didactic Uses of Hallucinogenic Plants: An Examination of a System of Teaching, *Paper, 67th Annual Meeting of the American Anthropological Association, 1968, "Abstracts,"* pp. 21–22.

———, *The Teachings of Don Juan: A Yaqui Way of Knowledge*, Berkeley: University of California Press, 1968.

———, *Journey to Ixtlan: The Lessons of Don Juan*, New York: Simon & Schuster, 1972.

———, *A Separate Reality: Further Conversations with Don Juan*, New York: Simon & Schuster, 1972.

CERLETTI, A. & F. J. BOVÉ, *The Present Status of Psychotropic Drugs*, Amsterdam: Excerpta Medica Foundation, 1969 [Proceedings of the Sixth International Conference of the Collegium Internationale Neuropharmacologicum, Terragona, Spain, April 24–27, 1968].

CHARLEUX, A., Een botanische curiositeit, *Indische Cult.* [Teysmannia], 13 (January 1, 1928) 18–20.

CHOLDEN, LOUIS (ed.), *Lysergic Acid Diethylamide and Mescaline in Experimental Psychiatry*, New York: Grune & Stratton, 1956.

COHEN, M. M., M. J. MARINELLO, & N. BACK, Chromosomal Damage in Human Leucocytes induced by Lysergic acid diethylamide, *Science*, 155, #3768 (1967) 1417–19.

COHEN, SIDNEY, The Personality of the User—Before and After, in R. D. Hicks and P. J. Fink (eds.), *Psychedelic Drugs*, New York: Grune & Stratton, 1969, pp. 76–82.

———, A Quarter Century of Research with LSD, in J. Thomas Ungerleider (ed.), *The Problems and Prospects of LSD*, 2nd ed., Springfield, Ill.: Charles C Thomas, 1970, pp. 22–44.

COLE, J. O. & M. M. KATZ, The Psychotomimetic Drugs: An Overview, *Journal of the American Medical Association*, 189 (1964) 758–61.

COLLIER, DONALD, Peyote, A General Study of the Plant, the Cult, and the Drug, (U.S.

Congress) *Senate Committee on Indian Affairs*, 34 (1929) 18234–55.

COLLIER, JOHN, The Peyote Cult, *Science*, 115 (1952) 503–4.

COLLINS, JOHN JAMES, A Descriptive Introduction to the Taos Peyote Ceremony, *Ethnology*, 7 (1968) 427–49.

———, Peyotism and Religious Membership at Taos Pueblo, New Mexico, *Southwestern Social Science Quarterly*, 48 (1967) 183–91.

COOK, BRUCE, Is Carlos Castañeda for Real?, *The National Observer*, (February 24, 1973).

COTT, JONATHAN, Music to Enhance Life? *The New York Times*, (February 13, 1972).

CRAVENS, GWYNETH, Talking to Power and Spinning with the Ally, The Glossed Carlos Castañeda, *Harper's*, (February 1973) 91.

CROCKET, R., R. A. SANDISON, & A. WALK (eds.), *Hallucinogenic Drugs and their Therapeutic Use*, Springfield, Ill.: Charles C. Thomas, and London: H. K. Lewis, 1963 [Proceedings of the Quarterly Meeting of the Royal Medico-Psychological Association, London, 1961].

CRUZ SANCHEZ, G., Aplicaciones populares de la cimora en el norte del Perú, *Revista de Farmacología y Medicina Experimental* [Lima], 1 (1948a) 253ff.

———, Farmacología de *Opuntia cylindrica*, *Revista de Farmacología y Medicina Experimental* [Lima], 1 (1948b) 143ff.

DENBER, H. C., Studies with mescaline, *Rivista Neurobiologica*, 10 (1964) 1157–68 [Supplement].

DIPALLO, J. A., LSD: Effects on Offspring, *Science*, 158, #3800 (1967) 522.

DOBKIN DE RIOS, MARLENE, Folk Healing with a Mescaline Cactus in North Coastal Peru, *Paper, 67th Annual Meetings of the American Anthropological Association*, 1968a, "Abstracts," pp. 34–35.

———, Trichocereus pachanoi—A Mescaline Cactus Used in Folk Healing in Peru, *Economic Botany*, 22, #2 (April–June 1968b) 191–94.

———, Folk healing with a psychedelic cactus in north coastal Peru, *International Journal of Social Psychiatry*, 15, #1 (Fall–Winter 1969a) 23–32.

———, Fortune's Malice, Divination, Psychotherapy, and Folk Medicine in Peru, *Journal of American Folklore*, 82, #324 (April–June 1969b) 132–141.

———, Curanderismo Psicodelico en el Peru: Continuidad y Cambio, in *Mesa Redonda de Ciencias Prehistoricas y Antropológicas*, Lima: Universidad Catolica, 1969c.

———, The Influence of Psychotropic Flora and Fauna on Maya Religion, *Current Anthropology*, 15, #1 (February 1974).

DOWNS, JAMES F., *The Two Worlds of the Washo*, New York: Holt, Rinehart & Winston, 1966.

DRIVER, HAROLD E., *Indians of North America*, Chicago: University of Chicago Press, 2nd rev. ed., 1969.

EFRON, D. H., B. HOLMSTEDT, & N. S. KLINE (eds.), *Ethnopharmacologic Search for Psychoactive Drugs*, Washington: Public Health Service Publication No. 1645, 1967.

ECKHOLM, G. F. & G. R. WILLEY (eds.), *Handbook of Middle American Indians*, Vol. 4, Archeological Frontiers and External Connections (25 vols.), General Editor, Robert L. Wauchope, Austin: University of Texas Press, 1966.

EMBODEN, W. A., *Narcotic Plants*, New York: Macmillan, 1972.

FARNSWORTH, D. L., Hallucinogenic Agents, *Journal of the American Medical Association*, 185, #11 (1963) 878–80.

FARNSWORTH, NORMAN R., Hallucinogenic Plants, *Science*, 162 (1968) 1086–92.

FISCHER, R., P. MARKS, R. HILL, & M. ROCKEY, Personality Structure as the Main Determinant of Drug-induced (Model) Psychoses, *Nature* [London], 218 (1968) 296.

FREEDMAN, DANIEL X., GEORGE K. AGHAJANIAN, EDWARD M. ORNITZ & B. S. ROSNER, Patterns of Tolerance to Lysergic Acid Diethylamide and Mescaline in Rats, *Science*, 127 (May 16, 1958) 1173–74.

FRIEDBERG, CLAUDINE, Utilisation d'un cactus à mescaline au nord de Pérou (*Trichocereus pachanoi*, Britton & Rose), *Proceedings of the Sixth International Congress of Anthropological and Ethnological Sciences*, II, part 2 (1964) 21–26.

FROSCH, W. A., E. S. ROBBINS, & M. STERN, Untoward Reactions to Lysergic Acid Diethylamide (LSD) Resulting in Hospitalization, *New England Journal of Medicine*, 273 (1965).

FURST, PETER T., West Mexican Tomb Sculpture as Evidence for Shamanism in Prehispanic Mexico, *Antropológica* [Caracas], 15 (1965) 29–60.

———, The Olmec Were-Jaguar Motif in the Light of Ethnographic Reality, *Dumbarton Oaks Conference on the Olmec* (Washington, D.C.: Trustees of Harvard University, 1968a), pp. 143–78.

———, Myth in Art: A Huichol Depicts his Reality, *Los Angeles County Museum of Natural History Quarterly*, 7, #3 (Winter 1968-69) 16–25 [Reprint No. 11, Latin-American Center, University of California at Los Angeles, 1968b].

———, *Ariocarpus retusus*, the 'false peyote' of Huichol Tradition, *Economic Botany*, 25 (1971a) 182–87.

———, Psychotropic Flora and Fauna in Pre-Columbian Art, in *Symposium on the Prehistoric Arts of Arid America*, Lubbock: Texas Tech University, 1971b.

———, To Find Our Life: Peyote among the Huichol Indians of Mexico, in P. T. Furst (ed.), *Flesh of the Gods: The Ritual Use of Hallucinogens*, New York: Praeger, 1972, pp. 136–84.

———, West Mexican Art: Secular or Sacred?, in *The Iconography of Middle American Sculpture*, New York: Metropolitan Museum of Art, 1973, pp. 98–133.

FURST, PETER T. & BARBARA MYERHOFF, El mito como historia: ciclo del peyote y del datura entre los Huicholes de México, in *Coras, Huicholes y Tepehuanos*, México: Instituto Nacional Indigenista, 1971.

GEBER, W. G., Congenital Malformation produced by Mescaline, Lysergic diethylamide and Bromolysergic Acid in a Hamster, *Science*, 158, #3798 (1967) 265–67.

GILLIN, JOHN, *Moche: A Peruvian Coastal Community*, Washington, D.C.: Smithsonian Institution, 1945.

GONZALEZ HUERTA, INES, Identificación de la Mescalina Contenida en el *Trichocereus pachanoi* (San Pedro), *Revista del Viernes Médico* [Lima], 11, #1 (1960) 133–37.

GOODMAN, GEORGE, Students See a Shift from Drugs to Drink, *The New York Times*, (February 2, 1974).

GORDON, N., The Hallucinogenic Drug Cult, *The Reporter*, (August 15, 1963), 35–43.

GRAMONT, SANCHE DE, A Vocation for Madness, *Horizon*, 12, #2 (Spring 1970) 48–55.

GREGORY, HORACE, Journey to Ixtlan [Letter to] *The New York Times* (January 7, 1973).

GUERRA, F., Mexican Phantastica—A Study of the Early Ethnobotanical Sources on Hallucinogenic Drugs, *British Journal of the Addictions*, 62 (March 1967) 171–87.

GUTIÉRREZ-NORIEGA, CARLOS, Area del mescalinismo en el Perú, *América Indigena*, 10 (1950) 215.

GUTIÉRREZ-NORIEGA, CARLOS & G. CRUZ SÁNCHEZ, Alteraciones mentales producidas por la *Opuntia cylindrica*, *Revista de Neuropsiquiatrica* [Lima], 10 (1947) 422ff.

HAEKEL, JOSEF, Ethnology Interprets Archaeology, *Review of Ethnology*, 1 (August 5, 1968) 1–3.

HALL, R. J., C. E. WEISE, & S. BUSSE, *Teratogenic and Chromosomal Damaging Effects of Illicit Drugs*, Toronto; Addiction Research Foundation, 1973.

HARNER, MICHAEL J. (ed.), *Hallucinogens and Shamanism*, New York: Oxford University Press, 1973.

HEBBARD, F. & R. FISCHER, Effects of Psilocybin, LSD and Mescaline on small, involuntary eye movements, *Psychopharmacologia* [Berlin], 9 (1966) 145–56.

HEIFETZ, HAROLD, *Jeremiah Thunder*, New York: Doubleday, 1968.

HERTZBERG, HAZEL W., *The Search for an American Indian Identity: Modern Pan-Indian Movements*, Syracuse, N.Y.: Syracuse University Press, 1971 [Ch. III, "Religious Pan-Indianism, The Peyote Cult, The Native American Church"].

HICKS, R. D. & P. J. FINK (eds.), *Psychedelic Drugs*, New York: Grune & Stratton, 1966.

HILL, TOM & KENNETH BEALS, Some Notes on Kiowa-Apache Peyotism with Special Reference to Ethics and Change, Norman [University of Oklahoma]: *Anthropological Papers*, Spring 1966.

HINKLE, WARREN, A Social History of Hippies, *Ramparts*, 5#9 (March 1967) 9-10, 17-19.

———, The Hippies' World, in N. F. Cantor and M. S. Wertham (eds.), *The History of Popular Culture*, New York: Macmillan, 1968.

HODGE, F. W. (ed.), *Handbook of Indians North of Mexico*, Washington, D.C.: Bureau of American Ethnology, Bulletin 30, 2 vols., 1907–1910.

HOFFER, A. & H. OSMUND, *The Hallucinogens*, New York: Academic Press, 1967.

HOKEAH, JACK, Gouache painting, "Peyote Chief" (ca. 1930), Museum of the American Indian (Heye Foundation), #15–120.

HOLLISTER, LEO E., Chemical Psychoses: LSD and Related Drugs, Springfield, Ill.: Charles C Thomas, 1968.

HOOVER, J. P., College Drug Scene: As It Is, *New York State Journal of Medicine*, 16 (1972) 1866–72.

HOWARD, JAMES H., A Comanche Spear Point Used in a Kiowa-Comanche Peyote Ceremonial, [Vermillion]: *Museum News University of South Dakota*, 12, #2 (December 1950) 3–6 [mimeo].

———, Mescalism and Peyotism Once Again, *Plains Anthropologist*, 5, #10 (November 1960) 84–85.

———, Peyote Jokes, *Journal of American Folklore*, 75, #296 (1962) 10–14.

HOWES, VICTOR, Desert Meditation, or Back Home to L.A., *Christian Science Monitor* (January 24, 1973).

HSU, LILLIAN Y., LOTTE STRAUSS, & KURT HIRSCHHORN, Chromosome Abnormality in Offspring of LSD User, *Journal of the American Medical Association*, 211, #6 (February 8, 1970) 987-90.

IDANPAAN, JUHANA E., W. M. MCISAAC, BENG T. HO, & L. WAYNE TANSEY, Relation of Pharmacological and Behavioral Effects of a Hallucinogenic Amphetamine to Distribution in Cat Brain, *Science*, 164 (1969) 1085–87.

IMPERI, L. L., H. D. KLEBER, & J. S. DAVIE, Use of Hallucinogenic Drugs on Campus, *Journal of the American Medical Association*, 204 (1965) 1021–24.

JELLINEK, R., The Education of a Shaman, *The New York Times* [Books of the Times] (May 14, 1971).

JILEK, W. G., Review of Robert L. Bergman, Navaho Peyote Use, in *Transcultural Psychiatry Research Review*, 9 (October 1972) 158–61.

———, Review of Marino Benzi, Les derniers adorateurs du peyotl, in *Transcultural Psychiatry Research Review*, 10 (April 1973) 59–63.

JONES, WILLIAM K., Notes on the History and Material Culture of the Tonkawa Indians, *Smithsonian Contributions to Anthropology*, 2, #5 (1969) 65–81.

JORGENSEN, JOSEPH G., Voget's Review of *The Peyote Religion: A Comment*, *American Anthropologist*, 71 (1969) 909–11.

Journal [of the Addiction Research Foundation, Toronto], "On U.S. College Campuses Cannabis Use 'an Institution,' ", 2, #3 (March 1, 1973) 16.

KALANT, HAROLD & O. J. KALANT, *Drugs, Society and Personal Choice*, Don Mills, Canada: General Publishing Co., 1971.

KAPADIA, G. J. & H. M. FALES, Peyote Alkaloids VI. Peyophorine, a tetrahydroisoquiniline cactus alkaloid, containing an N-ethyl group, *Journal of Pharmacological Science*, 57 (1968a) 2017–18.

———, Krebs Cycle Conjugates of Mescaline, Identification of fourteen new alkaloid amides, *Chemical Communications*, 1968 (1968b) 1688–89.

KAPADIA, G. J. & M. B. E. FAYEZ, Peyote Constituents: Chemistry, Biogenesis, and Biological Effects, *Journal of Pharmacological Science*, 59 (1970) 1699–1727.

KAPADIA, G. J. & R. J. HIGHET, Peyote Alkaloids IV. Structure of peyonine, novel β-phenethylpyrrole from *Lophophora williamsii*, *Journal of Pharmacological Science*, 57 (1968) 191–92.

KAPADIA, G. J., N. J. SHAH, & T. B. ZALUCKY, Peyote Alkaloids II. Anhalotine, lophotine, and peyotine, the quaternary alkaloids of *Lophophora williamsii*, *Journal of Pharmacological Science*, 57 (1968) 254–62.

KEEN, SAM, Sorcerer's Apprentice, *Psychology Today* (December 1972), 90–102.

KLEPS, ART, Castañeda (Continued), [Letter to] *The New York Times* (February 4, 1973).

KLÜVER, H., Mechanisms of Hallucinations, in Q. McNemar and M. A. Merrill (eds.), *Studies in Personality*, New York: McGraw-Hill, 1942, pp. 175–207.

———, *Mescal and Mechanisms of Hallucina-*

tions, Chicago: University of Chicago Press, 1966.

———, Discussion [of Edward V. Evarts, "Neurophysiological Correlates of Pharmacologically Induced Behavioral Disturbances"], in *The Brain and Human Behavior* (Research Publications of the Association of Nervous and Mental Diseases, 36 [1958] 376–77).

KUTRZEBA-POJNARWEJ, ANNY (ed.), *Peyotzym Religia Indian Ameryki Połnocnej*, Warsaw: Biblioteka Etnografii Polskie, #25, 1972.

LA BARRE, WESTON, Le complexe narcotique de l'Amérique autochtone, *Diogène*, 48 (1964a) 120–34.

———, El Complejo Narcótico de la America autóctona, *Diógenes*, 48 (1964b) 102–12.

———, The Narcotic Complex of the New World, *Diógenes*, 48 (1964c) 125–38 [also *Bobbs-Merrill Reprint Series in the Social Sciences*, A-429]

———, *The Ghost Dance: Origins of Religion*, New York: Doubleday, 1970a; London: Allen & Unwin, 1972; revised ed., New York: Delta Books, 1972.

———, Old and New World Narcotics: A Statistical Question and an Ethnological Reply, *Economic Botany* 20, #1 (1970b) 73–80.

———, To Find Our Life: The Peyote Hunt of the Huichols of Mexico, *American Anthropologist*, 62, #5 (1970c) 1201.

———, Review of Carlos Castañeda, A Separate Reality: Further Conversations with Don Juan, *Manuscript* (November 19, 1972).

———, Hallucinogens and the Shamanic Origins of Religion, in P. T. Furst (ed.), *Flesh of the Gods: The Ritual Use of Hallucinogens*, New York: Praeger, 1972, pp. 261–78.

LAMANTIA, PHILIP, *Narcotica*, San Francisco: Auerhahn Press, 1959.

LANNING, JOHN TATE, Manuscript Notes on Spanish Colonial Sources for Mexico, Duke University, 1973.

LEARY, TIMOTHY, *High Priest*, Cleveland: World Publishing Co., 1968.

LEETE, E., Biosynthesis of the peyote alkaloids, *Journal of the American Chemical Society*, 88, #18 (1966) 4218–21.

LEVI, A. W., Review of Casteñeda, *Saturday Review* (August 21, 1971).

LEWIN, LOUIS, *Phantastica: Narcotic and Stimulating Drugs*, tr. from 2nd German ed. by P. H. A. Wirth, New York: E. P. Dutton, 1931, reprinted 1964.

LIEBER, MICHAEL D., Opposition to Peyotism among the Western Shoshone: The Message of Traditional Belief, *Man*, 7, #3 (September 1972) 387–96.

LUNDSTRÖM, J. & S. AGURELL, Gas Chromotography of Peyote Alkaloids, *Journal of Chromatography*, 36 (1968) 105–8.

MALITZ, S., The Role of Mescaline and D-lysergic Acid in Psychiatric Treatment, *Diseases of the Nervous System*, 27, #7, pt. 2 (1966) 39–42.

MARRIOTT, ALICE & CAROL K. RACHLIN, *Peyote*, New York: Mentor, 1971.

MARSHALL, C. R., Entopic Phenomena Associated with the Retina, *British Journal of Ophthalmology*, 19 (1935) 177–201.

———, An Equiry Into the Causes of Mescal Visions, *Journal of Neurology and Psychopathology*, 17 (1937) 289–304.

MARSHMAN, JOHN & ROBERT J. GIBBINS, A Note on the Composition of Illicit Drugs, *Ontario Medical Review* (September 1970), 1–3.

MAY, PHILIP R. A. & J. R. WITTENBORN (eds.), *Psychotropic Drug Response: Advances in Prediction*, Springfield, Ill.: Charles C Thomas, 1969.

McCLEARY, JAMES A., PAUL S. SYPHERD, & DAVID L. WALKINGTON, Antibiotic Activity of an Extract of Peyote, *Lophophora williamsii* (Lemaire) Coulter, *Economic Botany*, 14 (1960) 247–49.

McCLURE, MICHAEL, *Hymns to St. Geryon and Other Poems*, San Francisco: Auerhahn Press, 1959.

McFADDEN, ROBERT D., Hard Drugs Fade on Campuses, *The New York Times* (November 20, 1972).

McGLOTHLIN, WILLIAM H., Hallucinogenic Drugs: A Perspective with Special Reference to Peyote and Cannabis, *Psychedelic Review*, 6 (1965) 16–57.

McGLOTHLIN, WILLIAM H. & S. COHEN, The Use of Hallucinogenic Drugs among College Students, *American Journal of Psychiatry*, 122 (1965) 572.

McGlothlin, W. H., S. Cohen, & M. S. McGlothlin, Long Lasting Effects of LSD on Normals, *Archives of General Psychiatry*, 17 (November 1967) 521–32.

McLaughlin, J. L. & A. G. Paul, The Cactus Alkaloids. I. Identification of N-methylated tyramine derivatives in *Lophophora williamsii*, *Lloydia*, 29 (1966) 315–327.

Miller, Peter S., Continuity and Change in Washo Peyotism: A Preliminary Report, *Paper, Great Basin Anthropological Conference*, September 4, 1964, University of Nevada.

Momaday, Natachee Scott, *House Made of Dawn*, New York: Harper & Row, 1968.

Mooney, James, Peyote, in F. W. Hodge (ed.), *Handbook of American Indians North of Mexico*, Washington, D.C.: Bureau of American Ethnology, Bulletin 30, 2 vols., 1907–10, 2: 237.

Myerhoff, Barbara, The "Deer-Maize" Peyote Complex among the Huichol Indians of Mexico, Doctoral Dissertation, University of California at Los Angeles, 1968a.

———, The Deer-Maize-Peyote Symbol Complex among the Huichol Indians of Mexico, *Paper, Annual Meeting of the American Anthropological Association*, November 21–24, 1968b, "Abstracts," pp. 96–97.

———, Return to Beginnings: Rituals of Opposition and Continuity, *Paper, 71st Annual Meeting of the American Anthropological Association*, Toronto, 1972, "Abstracts," p. 88.

Nabokov, Peter, The Peyote Road, *The New York Times Magazine* (March 9, 1960).

Newsweek, December 2, 1968, "Where Are They Now? The Haight-Ashbury Scene."

———, April 21, 1969, "The Drug Generation: Growing Younger."

Nowicka, Ewa. *See* Kutrzeba-Pojnarowej, Anny.

Nowlis, Helen H., *Drugs on the College Campus*, New York: Anchor Books, 1969.

Oates, Joyce Carol, Anthropology—Or Fiction? [Letter to] *The New York Times* (November 26, 1972).

Officer, James (ed.), *Anthropology and the American Indian*, San Francisco: Indian Historical Press, 1973.

Olney, R. K., Mescaline, *Texas Medicine*, 68, #7 (1972) 80–82.

Osmund, Humphrey, Psychedelic Drugs in the Treatment of Alcoholism, in R. D. Hicks and P. J. Fink (eds.), *Psychedelic Drugs*, New York: Grune & Stratton, 1929, pp. 217–25.

Pearlman, S., Drugs Use and Experience in an Urban College Population, *American Journal of Orthopsychiatry*, 38 (1968) 503–14.

Peiner, L., Peyote cult, mescaline hallucinations, and model psychosis, *New York Journal of Medicine*, 67 (November 1, 1967) 2838–43.

Perez Cirera, R. Plantas alucinógenes (Peyote y Hongos alucinógenos), *Acta Physiologica Latino-Americana*, 16, suppl. 2 (1966) 219–33.

Petrullo, V., Peyotism as an Emergent Indian Culture, in *Indians at Work*, 7, #8 (1940) 51–60.

Poisson, J., Présence de mescaline dans une Cactacée péruvienne, *Annales Pharmaceutiques Françaises*, 18 (1960) 764–65.

Posern-Zielińska, Mirosława, *Peyotyzm Religia Indian Ameryki Północnej*, in Anny Kutrzeba-Pojnarowej (ed.), Summarized by K. Bidwell, pp. 243–49, Warsaw: Zakład Narodowy Imienia Ossolińskich Wydawnictwo Polskiej Akademii Nauk, Institut Historii Kultury Materialnev, Biblioteka Etnografii Polskiev, 25, 1972.

Prajer, Z., Peyotl-Bog-Diabeł-czy tylko zwykły kaktus? *Informator Polskiego Towartzstwa Miłośników Kaktusów*, 1968a, pp. 22–29, 111–29.

———, Peyotl-przez 'mędrca szkielko' ", *Informator Polskiego Towarzystwa Miłośników Kaktusów*, 1968b, pp. 120–29.

———, Peyotl—przez 'mędrca skiełko', *Swiat Kaktusów*, 2 (1969) 35–43.

Radin, Paul, The Religious Experiences of an American Indian (John Rave), *Eranos Jahrbuch* [Zurich], 18 (1950) 249–90.

Ramirez, José, El peyote Anhalonium Lewinii y Anhalonium Williamsii, Cactaceas, *Instituto Medico Nacional de México Anales*, 4 (1900) 233–50.

Reti L. & J. A. Castrillon, Cactus Alkaloids, I. *Trichocereus terscheckii* (Parmentier) Britton and Rose, *Journal of the American Chemical Society*, 73 (1951) 1767–69.

Riesman, Paul, Review of Carlos Castañeda,

Journey to Ixtlan, A Separate Reality, and The Teachings of Don Juan, *The New York Times Book Review* (October 22, 1972).

RINKEL, M., Lysergic Acid Diethylamide and Mescaline in Experimental Psychiatry, in L. Cholden (ed.), *Lysergic Acid Diethylamide and Mescaline in Experimental Psychiatry*, New York: Grune & Stratton, 1956.

RINKEL, MAX & R. E. SCHULTES, *Transcultural Significance of 'Magic Plants,'* Brochure for Exhibit at Annual Meetings of the American Psychiatric Association, Atlantic City, 1965.

RITZENTHALER, R. E. & P. RITZENTHALER, *The Woodland Indians of the Western Great Lakes*, Garden City, N.Y.: Natural History Press, 1970, pp. 93–94.

ROREM, NED, The New York Diary of Ned Rorem, New York; Braziller, 1967, pp. 149–69.

ROSEMAN, BERNARD, The Peyote Story, Hollywood, Calif.: Wilshire Book Co., 1968.

ROTHENBERG, JAMES (ed.), *Shaking the Pumpkin: Traditional Poetry of the Indian North Americas*, Garden City, N.Y.: Doubleday, 1972.

SALZMAN, CARL, Controlled Therapy Research with Psychedelic Drugs, in R. D. Hicks and P. J. Fink (eds.), *Psychedelic Drugs*, New York: Grune & Stratton, 1966, pp. 23–32.

SAVAGE, CHARLES, ETHEL SAVAGE, JAMES FADIMAN, & WILLIS HARMAN, LSD: Therapeutic Effects of the Psychedelic Experience, *Psychological Reports*, 14 (1964) 111–20.

SCANZIANI, PIERO, Manuscript on Tsa To ke and Peyotism, for *Tempo* [Milan], *ca.* January 1969.

SCHLEIFER, MARC, States and Visions, *Birth*, no. 3, Bk. 1 (Autumn 1960) 79–80.

SCHLEIFER, HEDWIG, *Sacred Narcotic Plants of the New World Indians*, New York: Hafner Publishing Co., 1974.

SCHULTES, RICHARD EVANS, Native Narcotics of the New World, *Pharmaceutical Sciences*, 3rd Lecture Series (1960a) 142–85 [See also in *Texas Journal of Pharmacy*, 2 (1961a) 141–67].

———, Botany Attacks the Hallucinogens, *Pharmaceutical Sciences*, 3rd Lecture Series (1960b) 168–85 [See also in *Texas Journal of Pharmacology*, 2 (1961b) 168–85].

———, Hallucinogenic Plants of the New World, *Harvard Review*, 1, #4 (1963a) 18–32.

———, Botanical Sources of the New World Narcotics, *Psychedelic Review*, 1 (1963b) 145–66.

———, Ein halbes Jahrhundert Ethnobotanik Amerikanischer Halluzinogene, *Planta Medica: Zeitschrift für Artzeneipflanzenforschung*, 13 (1965a) 125–37.

———, The Transcultural Significance of 'Magic Plants,' Brochure for Exhibit, Botanical Museum of Harvard University, 1965b.

———, The Search for New Native Hallucinogens, *Lloydia*, 29 (1966) 293–308.

———, The Place of Ethnobotany in the Ethnopharmacologic Search for Psychotomimetic Drugs, in Efron, Holmstedt, and Kline (eds.).

———, *Ethnopharmacologic Search for Psychoactive Drugs*, 1967, pp. 33–57.

———, Hallucinogens of Plant Origin, *Science*, 163 (January 17, 1969) 245–54.

———, Le regne végétal et les substances hallucinogènes, *Bulletin des Stupéfiants*, 21, #3 (Juillet–Septembre 1969) 3–16; 21, #4 (Octobre–Décembre 1969) 17–30; 22, #1 (Janvier–Mars 1970) 25–53.

———, The Botanical and Chemical Distribution of Hallucinogens, *Annual Review of Plant Physiology*, 21 (1970b) 571–98.

———, The New World Indians and Their Hallucinogenic Plants, *Morris Arboretum Bulletin*, 21, #1 (March 1970c) 3–14.

———, The Plant Kingdom and Hallucinogens, *Bulletin on Narcotics*, 21, #3 (1969) 3–16, 21, #4 (1969) 15–27; 22, #1 (1970) 25–53.

———, Plant Hallucinogens and Their Role in American Indian Cultures, in V. Scnieckus (ed.), *Drugs and Society*, Ontario: University of Waterloo, 1972, pp. 3–15.

———, Tropical American Hallucinogens: Where Are We and Where Are We Going? *Ciencia e Cultura*, 25, #6 (Junho 1973) 543–61.

SCHULTES, RICHARD EVANS & ALBERT HOFMANN, *The Botany and Chemistry of Hallucinogens*, Springfield, Ill.: Charles C Thomas, 1973.

Scnieckus, V. (ed.), *Drugs and Society*, Ontario: University of Waterloo, 1972.

Serko, A., Im Mescalinrausch, *Jahrbücher für Psychiatrie und Neurologie*, 34 (1913) 355–66.

Sharon, Douglas, The San Pedro Cactus in Peruvian Folk Healing, in P. T. Furst (ed.), *Flesh of the Gods: The Ritual Use of Hallucinogens*, New York: Praeger, 1972, pp. 114–35.

Siegel, B. (ed.), *Biennial Review of Anthropology*, Palo Alto, Calif.: Stanford University Press, 1959.

Siegel, Ronald K., An Ethological Search for Self-Administration of Hallucinogens, *International Journal of the Addictions*, 8, #2 (1973) 373–93.

———, Studies of Hallucinogens in Fish, Birds, Mice and Men: The Behavior of "Psychedelic" Populations, in O. Vinar, Z. Voltava, and P. B. Bradley (eds.), *Advances in Neuro-Psychopharmacology*, Amsterdam: North Holland, 1971, pp. 311–18.

Siegel, R. K. & J. West (eds.), *Hallucination* (in press).

Simmons, Charles, The Sorcerer's Apprentice ["Books of the Times"], *The New York Times* (August 14, 1968).

Smart, Reginald G., Some Current Studies of Psychoactive and Hallucinogenic Drug Use, *Canadian Journal of Behavioral Science*, 2, #3 (1970) 232–45.

Smart, R. G. & K. Bateman, Unfavourable Reactions to LSD: A Review and Analysis of the Available Case Reports, *Canadian Medical Association Journal*, 97 (1967) 1214–21.

———, The Chromosomal and Teratogenic Effects of Lysergic Acid Diethylamide: A Review of the Current Literature, *Canadian Medical Association Journal*, 99 (1968) 805–10.

Smith, M. G., A Negro Peyote Cult, *Journal of the Washington Academy of Sciences*, 24 (1934) 448–53.

Smith, P. B., A Sunday with Mescaline, *Bulletin of the Menninger Clinic*, 23 (1959) 20–27.

Spindler, Louise & George Spindler, Culture Change, in B. Siegel (ed.), *Biennial Review of Anthropology*, Palo Alto, Calif.: Stanford University Press, 1959.

———, *Dreamers Without Power: The Menomini Indians*, New York: Holt, Rinehart &

Winston, 1971 (Ch. 3, The Peyote Road, pp. 94–140).

Sterritt, David, Maxine Klein and the Indians, *Christian Science Monitor* (February 24, 1971).

Stewart, Omer C., Anthropologists As Expert Witnesses for Indians: Claims and Peyote Cases, in James Officer (ed.), *Anthropology and the American Indian*, San Francisco: Indian Historical Press, 1973, pp. 35–42.

———, The Native American Church and the Law with Description of Peyote Religious Services, *Westerners Brand Book*, 17 (1961) 5–47.

———, The Native American Church and the Law, in Deward E. Walker (ed.), *The Emergent Native Americans, A Reader in Cultural Contact*, Boston: Little, Brown, 1972, pp. 282–97.

———, The Peyote Religion and the Ghost Dance, *Indian Historian*, 5, #4 (Winter 1972) 27–30.

Story, Dee Ann & Vaughan M. Bryant, Jr. (eds.), A Preliminary Study of the Paleoecology of the Amistad Reservoir Area, *Final Report Gs-667*, National Science Foundation, June 1966.

Sukenick, Ronald, Upward and Juanward, *The Village Voice* (January 25, 1973).

Szuman, St., Analiza formalna i psychologiczna widseń meskalinowych, *Kwartalnik Psychologiczny*, 1–2 (1930) 156–212.

Taylor, W. W., *A Study of Archeology*, Memoir 69, American Anthropological Association, 1948.

———, Some Implications of the Carbon 14 Dates from a Cave in Coahuila, Mexico, *Bulletin of the Texas Archaeological Society*, 27 (1956) 215–34.

———, Archaic Cultures Adjacent to the Northeastern Frontiers of Mesoamerica, in G. F. Ekholm and G. R. Willey (eds.), *Handbook of Middle American Indians*, vol. 4: 59–94, 1966.

Thatcher, K., T. Kappeler, P. Wisecup & R. Fischer, Personality trait-dependent performance under psilocybin, *Diseases of the Nervous System*, 31 (1970) 181–92.

Time, March 5, 1973, Behavior: Don Juan and the Sorcerer's Apprentice, pp. 36–38,

43–45 [Cover article on Castañeda: Magic and Reality].

TOMKINS, CALVIN, The Teachings of Joe Pye, *New Yorker,* 48, #50 (February 3, 1973) 37–38.

TSA TO KE, MUNROE [HUNTINGHORSE], The Peyote Ritual: Visions and Descriptions, San Francisco: Grabhorn Press, 1957.

TURNER, W. J. & J. J. HEYMAN, The Presence of Mescaline in *Opuntia cylindrica, Journal of Organic Chemistry,* 25 (1960) 2250.

TURNS, D. & H. C. DENBER, Mescalin und Psychotherapie, *Artzeneimittelforschung,* 16 (1966) 251–53.

UNGER, SANFORD M., LSD, Mescaline, Psilocybin and Psychotherapy: An Annotated Chronology, Washington: National Institute of Mental Health, 1963a.

———, Mescaline, LSD, Psilocybin, and Personality Change: A Review, *Psychiatry,* 26, #2 (May 1963b) 111–25.

———, LSD and Psychotherapy: A Bibliography of the English Language Literature, *Psychedelic Review,* 1, #4 (Summer 1964) 442–49.

UNGERLEIDER, J. T., D. D. FISHER, & M. FULLER, The Dangers of LSD, *Journal of the American Medical Association,* 197 (1966) 389.

VESTAL, PAUL A. & RICHARD EVANS SCHULTES, The Economic Botany of the Kiowa Indians as It Relates to the History of the Tribe, Cambridge, Mass.: Harvard Botanical Museum, 1939.

VINAR, O., Z. VOLTAVA, & P. B. BRADLEY (eds.), *Advances in Neuro-Psychopharmacology,* Amsterdam: New Holland, 1971.

VOGET, F., The American Indian in Transition: Reformation and Status Innovations, *American Journal of Sociology,* 62 (1957) 369–78.

———, Voget's Reply to Jorgensen, *American Anthropologist,* 71 (1969) 911.

WAGNER, HILDEBERT, *Rauschgift-Drogen,* Berlin-Heidelberg-New York: Springer-Verlag, 1969, pp. 85–91.

WAGNER, ROLAND M., A Study of Variation in Peyote Ritualism, With Appendix on New Syncretistic Ceremonies Developing on the Navaho Reservation, Unpublished manuscript, Department of Anthropology, University of Oregon, 35 pp., 1968.

WALENDOWSKA, BARBARA. *See* Kutrzeba-Pojnarwej, Anny.

WALKER, DEWARD E., JR. (ed.), *The Emergent Native Americans, A Reader in Cultural Contact,* Boston: Little, Brown, 1972.

WALLACE, A. F. C., Cultural Determinants of Response to Hallucinatory Experience, *Archives of General Psychiatry,* 1 (July 1959) 58–69.

WASSON, R. GORDON, Review of Carlos Castañeda, A Separate Reality, *Economic Botany,* 26 (January–March 1972) 98–99.

WATERS, FRANK, *The Man Who Killed the Deer,* New York: Simon & Schuster (Pocket Books), 1971.

WAX, MURRAY L., *Indian Americans,* Englewood Cliffs, N.J.: Prentice-Hall, 1971.

WEINER, MICHAEL A., *Earth Medicine—Earth Foods; Remedies, Drugs, and Natural Foods of the North American Indians,* New York: Macmillan, 1972.

WENINGER, DEL, *Cacti of the Southwest: Texas, New Mexico, Oklahoma, Arkansas, and Louisiana,* Austin: University of Texas Press, 1971.

WIKLER, ABRAHAM, *The Relation of Psychiatry to Pharmacology,* Baltimore: Williams and Wilkins, 1957.

WILSON, BRYAN D., *Magic and the Millennium, A Sociological Study of Religious Movements of Protest among Tribal and Third-World Peoples,* New York: Harper & Row, 1973.

WINTERS, W. D. & M. B. WALLACH, Drug induced States of CNS excitation: A Theory of Hallucinosis, in D. H. Efron (ed.), *Psychotomimetic Drugs,* New York: Raven Press, 1967, pp. 193–228.

WITKIEWICZ, S. L., *Nikotyna-alkohol-kokaina-peyotl-eter,* Warsaw, 1932.

WOLBACH, A., H. ISBELL & E. MINER, Cross-tolerance between mescaline and LSD-25, *Psychopharmacologia* [Berlin], 3 (1962) 1–14.

WOLBACH, A., E. MINER, & H. ISBELL, Comparison of psilocin with psilocybin, mescaline and LSD-25, *Psychopharmacologia* [Berlin], 3 (1962) 219–23.

ZELLWEGER, H., J. S. McDONALD, & G. ABBO, Is Lycergide a teratogen? *Lancet,* 2 (1967) 1066–68.

ZINGG, ROBERT, *The Huichols: Primitive Artists,* New York: Stechert, 1938.

PEYOTE STUDIES, 1974–1988

During the last dozen years the most important event in peyote studies has been the long-awaited publication of Omer Stewart's volume on *Peyote Religion*. When I first read the then-titled "History of the Peyote Religion" in 1981, the manuscript ran to 1,705 typed pages comprising 56 chapters. Despite its bulk, the manuscript published in 1987 was substantially unmodified save only for the usual copy-editing. As a result, *Peyote Religion* is unquestionably the fullest account available of the history and tribal diffusion of peyotism, much fleshing out La Barre's skeletal diffusion diagram in the present work, which is intended to be a fully comprehensive account of the ethnography, botany, chemistry, pharmacology, etc., of peyotism. Stewart is also the incomparable authority on laws regarding peyote. In recent years he and his colleague Aberle have been foremost with expert testimony in defense of the Indian religion, and with substantial success.

William L. Merrill's review of Marriott and Rachlin's monograph on *Peyote* rates it as,

disappointing. . . . poorly organized [and containing] some information that is patently incorrect, particularly in regard to botanical and pharmacological materials. . . . American Indian culture is misrepresented. By presenting peyotism as a release from reality, Marriott and Rachlin perpetuate the widely-held misconception that drug use in whatever form or cultural context equates with escapism. As a result, they contribute very little to a cross cultural understanding of the use of drugs . . . [G]eneral readers. . . . will be misled by the authors' distorted and pseudo-scientific presentation.

An anonymous commentator in *Behavior Today* states that the "special January–June issue of the *Journal of Psychedelic* [now *Psychoactive*] *Drugs* represents one of the three or four most important contributions ever made to the subject. Guest editor Jonathan Ott has rounded up major articles" by participants in the San Francisco Conference on Hallucinations in Native American Shamanism and Modern Life of 28 September through 1 October 1978— including Schultes, Wasson, Hofmann, and La Barre, dubbed the "Great White Shamans" in Stafford and Eisner's witty and accurate summary of the conference.

The best inexpensive and comprehensive volume on psychotropic drugs in general remains Schultes's *Hallucinogenic Plants*. For academic readers, Schultes and Hofmann's *Plants of the Gods* is equally excellent. In their second enlarged edition of *The Botany and Chemistry of the Hallucinogens*, Schultes and

Hofmann have achieved undoubted world authority. Schultes contributed "An Overview of Hallucinogens in the Western Hemisphere," and La Barre, "Hallucinogens and the Shamanic Origins of Religion," in Peter Furst's classic *Hallucinogens and Culture*. Classic also is Furst's *Flesh of the Gods: The Ritual Use of Hallucinogens*.

For general studies of hallucinogens, see also Aaronson and Osmund, *Psychedelics*; Du Toit, *Drugs, Rituals, and Altered States of Consciousness*; La Barre, "Psychedelics Galore"; Opler, "Cross Cultural Uses of Psychoactive Drugs"; Ott, *Hallucinogenic Plants of North America*; Perez de Barados, "Drogas alucinogenas"; Schultes, "The Unfolding Panorama of the New World Hallucinogens" in Gunkel; and Schultes, "Plants and Plant Constituents as Mind-altering Agents Throughout History," in Iverson, Iverson, and Synder. Stafford's *Psychedelic Encyclopedia* is a useful compendium. Stewart's articles in the *Encyclopedia Americana* and, with Slotkin, in the *Britannica* are standard sources. Journalistic accounts are to be found in *Newsweek* and *Time*, and, by Bergquist, in *Look*. Official policies are in Burke and in Collier. For other general accounts, see Bergquist, Cartwright, Cline, Douglas, and M. G. Smith.

On religion and hallucinogens we have La Barre, *The Ghost Dance: Origins of Religion*; his "Shamanic Origins of Religion and Medicine," in Ott (reprinted in Rossi, Buettner-Janusch, and Coppenhaver); his "Amerindian Religions," in Faruqi and Sopher; and his "Mouvements religieux nés de l'acculturation en Amérique du Nord," in the Encyclopédie de la Pléiade series. On peyotism and acculturation see also Barber, and Piscitelli.

On peyote in particular: La Barre, "Peyotegebrauch bei nordamerikanischen Indianern," in Völger and von Welck's comprehensive 3-volume work, *Rausch und Realität: Drogen in Kulturvergleich*; La Barre, "The Diabolic Root," in *New York Times Magazine*, 1 November 1964, reprinted, on pp. 193–97, in Wax and Buchanan, *Solving "The Indian Problem."* Ebin devotes pp. 223–307 specifically to peyote. Merrill has written a thesis on *Indigenous Drug Use in Aboriginal North America*, of which chapter 6 is on peyote. Stump, "Peyote"; Underhill, *Peyote* (1952); and Young, "The Magic of Peyote," are brief accounts.

Hultkrantz discusses "Conditions for the Spread of the Peyote Cult in North America"; La Barre, "Anthropological Perspectives on Hallucination and Hallucinogens"; Masters and Houston, *The Varieties of Psychedelic Experience*; and Morgan, "Man, Plant, and Religion: Peyote Trade in the Mustang Plains of Texas." On Texas tribes, see also Bollaert. Piscitelli writes on "Peyotism in Process: A Study of Diffusion and Acculturation"; Hesse on nonaddiction. An excellent historical summary is Bruhn and Holmstedt's "Early Peyote Research."

The botanist Anderson made an attempt at holism in *Peyote: The Divine Cactus* with some attention to medical, pharmacological, and chemical aspects, derivatively covering much earlier ground. He attended one peyote meeting. Anderson is the ranking taxonomic botanist on the genus *Lopho-*

phora, which he divides into the familiar *L. williamsii* and *L. diffusa*, the latter confined to Quarétaro. Anderson's work confirms the old native insistence on two varieties of peyote. On taxonomy, see also Boke and Anderson (1970).

The United Nations has officially adopted the term "psychotropic" advocated by Barber and La Barre, since Schultes objected to the mongrel term "psychedelic" and La Barre to the tendentious "entheogen" of Ruck and others.

The present monograph has been translated into Spanish as *El Culto del Peyote.*

PSYCHOLOGICAL STUDIES

Malcolm Bowie states that, "[Henri] Michaux has written more, and with more acute insight, about the psychological effects of drugs than any other European writer of the century." Whereas Aldous Huxley and others have superficially described euphoric and revelatory aspects of mescaline, Michaux emphasizes the terrors of the "bad trip." See Louise Varèse's translation of Michaux's *Miserable Miracle*, Michael Fineberg's translation, *Infinite Turbulence,* and Haakon Chevalier's translation, *Light Through Darkness*, of *Connaissance par les gouffres.* Michaux's long poem *Paix dans les brisements* and his book of 1966, *Les grandes épreuves de l'esprit,* are as yet untranslated.

Psychological effects of hallucinogens are discussed in Bowie, "Trajectories of a Mind in Crisis." Bourguignon discriminates hallucinatory (drug-induced) trance in males from possession trance (hysteroid) in females. Cohen describes the effects of *The Hallucinogens* in Clark and del Giudice. De Ropp is largely devoted to the historical discovery of various psychotropic drugs and to descriptions of the hallucinatory experience of early users; pp. 15–50 comprise his chapter on "The Mind and Mescaline." Devereux writes of an Indian woman patient with a degree in medical biology who nevertheless took her minor ailment to a peyote meeting for cure.

La Barre writes on anthropological perspectives on hallucinogens in Siegel and West, *Hallucinations: Behavior, Experience, and Theory;* Masters and Houston describe *The Varieties of Psychedelic Experience;* and Spindler gives the case of a "schizophrenic" Indian peyotist among the Menomini. *The Autobiography of a Kiowa Indian* is that of a longtime peyotist, Charley Apekaum, recorded by La Barre. There is some American Indian poetry in Brandon. Peyote painting, mostly done by Kiowa artists, is well represented by Tsa Toke (Monroe Huntinghorse). Among the Huichol, "Ramón [Medina] was the real innovator of the art of yarn-painting" (Furst, in Berrin). On peyote art, see also Snodgrass.

On the individual level, we have the Ebin anthology on *The Drug Experience: First Person Accounts.* Allen Ginsberg, for example, had his first peyote experience in the backyard of his family home; while on the Red Sea en route to Mombasa, he was much irritated in reading Zaehner's book on *The Menace of Mescaline* (1954). Antonin Artaud wrote ("General Security," 1925, in Sontag, p. 99): "Let the lost destroy themselves, we have better ways to occupy our time than to attempt a regeneration which is not only impossible but also pointless, *odious and harmful*. So long as we have failed to eliminate any of the causes of human despair, we do not have the right to try to eliminate those means by which man tries to cleanse himself from despair." In his *Voyage to the Land of the Tarahumare*, Artaud continues in the same vein: "All the laws, all the restrictions, all the campaigns against narcotics will only succeed in depriving all the most destitute cases of human suffering, who possess over society certain inalienable rights, of the solvent of their miseries, a sustenance for them more wonderful than bread, and the means of finally re-entering life." These opinions concerning peyote are perhaps not universally shared. After a frightening peyote meeting arranged by Harrington, Mable Dodge Luhan (a D. H. Lawrence figure married to a Pueblo Indian) telephoned John Collier for advice. Collier, then a New York social worker, later became Roosevelt's Commissioner for Indian Affairs. Then and later, Collier took the unusual position of defending the Indians' rights to their culture and political autonomy; indeed, Collier turned official policy toward peyotism entirely around, from conservative prohibition to liberal permissiveness. But Mrs. Luhan became "the most powerful, continuous, and disruptive influence against peyote" (Anderson).

In 1967 the elegantly edited *Journal of Psychedelic* [now *Psychoactive*] *Drugs* was founded by Haight-Ashbury Publications, in association with the Haight-Ashbury Free Medical Clinic, under the aegis of David E. Smith, M.D. It quickly became a respected and authoritative quarterly journal, at one time in association with the Wisconsin-based STASH (which, regretably, closed its doors in 1980). On 22 May 1976 a Society for the Study of Cultural and Historical Aspects of Psychotropic Drug Use was projected in San Francisco by J. C. Kramer, M.D., and the anthropologist Marlene Dobkin de Rios.

Timothy Leary and Richard Alpert (now "Ram Dass" after a visit to India) returned after twenty years to Harvard to present two lectures to a standing-room-only audience in Sanders Theater. Earlier both had been dismissed by President Pusey—Alpert for breaking his agreement not to use undergraduates in drug "experiments," and Leary for long, unauthorized absences from teaching. But Leary's advocacy of LSD did not achieve the onetime momentum of Ginsberg's advocacy of marihuana, which even won the sponsorship of the late Margaret Mead. In 1977, then somewhat in a minority, La Barre had declared that "medically, marihuana, in the respective amounts and manner of use, may be every bit as dangerous as tobacco" (*Culture in Context*, p. 105).

A complex but convincing psychiatric understanding of very old hunting symbolism and myth is provided in Merkur's brilliant study of "The Psychodynamics of the Navajo Coyoteway Ceremonial"—highly relevant to peyotism since peyotism also involves Coyote and very old hunting symbolism.

In an important article, Siegel and Jarvik raise the interesting psychophysiological question whether there are *formal visual constants* in drug-induced hallucinations, given by actual ocular- and neuro-anatomy, that transcend cultural and individual idiosyncracies. They well establish their case, verified in work by Knoll, Kugler, Hofer, and Lawder in "Effects of Chemical Stimulation"; Knoll, "Anregung geometrischer Figuren"; Kellogg, Knoll, and Kugler, "Form Similarity Between Phosphenes of Adults and Pre-School Children's Scribblings"; Knoll, Hofer, Lawder, and Lawder, "Die Reproductionsbarkeit"; and Knoll and Kugler, "Subjective Light Pattern Spectroscopy." On this subject see also Ardis and McKellar, "Hypnogogic Imagery and Mescaline"; some experienced users of psilocybin can summon hypnogogic hallucinations of intricate visual patterns at will; never the same alike, these patterns seem to be actual ever-changing reverse projections, from optic nerve to retina, of neuroelectrical brain states, ever unique. See also Reichel-Dolmatoff, "Subjective Seeing and Decorative Patterns," in his *Beyond the Milky Way: Hallucinatory Imagery of the Tukano Indians:* "The decorative patterns of the Tukano are almost wholly derived from drug-induced inner light [phosphene] experiences" (p. 47).

ECONOMICS

There have been few data in published documents of original fieldwork on *peyoteros*, or traders in peyote buttons, though the Texas-Mexican Railroad trade after 1881 was certainly based on earlier trade by other means. George H. Morgan has treated this neglected economic aspect of peyote in a competently and authoritatively written book derived from his 1976 doctoral dissertation, *Man, Plant, and Religion: Peyote Trade in the Mustang Plains of Texas.* It has been estimated that the traffic in peyote had a monetary value approaching $100,000 in the mid-1970s.

In a news article titled "In Hard-Hit South Texas, Dealing Peyote Can Still Turn a Profit," John MacCormack notes that three dealers in Webb County and five in Starr County have major control of the traffic in peyote, which grows in a limited area. Isobel Lopez of Oilton, in Webb County, paid about $4,000 a year to ranchers for peyote-gathering lease rights on their land. As a boy in Mirando City, Salvador Johnson harvested peyote at a dollar a thousand buttons for local dealers, but in 1986 the dealer price was $100 for a thousand green buttons and $20 per thousand more for sun-dried peyote. Johnson now has his own business. Since 1971 only dealers licensed with both the Texas Department of Public Safety and the Drug Enforcement Administration in Houston may conduct business with Indians. Since Castaneda's books were published, trespassing hippies seeking to gather peyote have been in conflict with both ranchers and the law: "There is little open land left for the Indians or anyone else to prospect for peyote growing wild" (MacCormack).

ARCHEOLOGY

An important archeological study, previously available only in manuscript, has now been published: J. M. Adovasio and G. F. Fry, "Prehistoric Psychotropic Drug Use in Northeastern Mexico and Trans-Pecos Texas." Frightful Cave, in which the evidence of human activities dates from 7500 B.C. to A.D. 570, yields the Texas Buckeye (*Ungnadia speciosa*) and the Red Bean (*Sophora secundiflora*) at all levels, as do Fat Burro Cave (3000 B.C.–A.D. 1070), Fate Bell Shelter, and others. "At CM79, yet another Cuatro Cienegas site, peyote in the form of a necklace has been found and dated between 810 and 1070 A.D." The oldest archeological specimen of *Lophophora* is from a burial cave in Coahuila of the same date, "one of the oldest materials ever submitted to alkaloid analysis" (Bruhn, Lindgren, and Adovasio). Bonfire Shelter (8440–8120 B.C.) yielded *Sophora secundiflora* beans "in direct association with Folsom and Plainview projectile points"; that shelter and Frightful Cave yielded "the earliest dated occurrence of psychotropic drugs in North America." These finds virtually touch the Mesolithic horizons in which Furst and La Barre find ethnographic hints of Old World provenience (deer-hunting associated with hallucinogens, thunder-engendered mushrooms, Thunderbird-eagle rainmaker, etc.). Deer-hunting and peyote are also firmly established New World associations: "Considerable, though wholly circumstantial evidence, suggests that the use of the buckeye and the red bean may be part of a hunting cult. The cache items from Texas and what may be an antler headdress from Mexico are but part of the more direct hints at such a cult" (Furst 1973).

Klaus Wellman proposes that aboriginal rock paintings in the Chumash-Yokuts area and in the lower Pecos region of Texas may have been produced by shamans while under the influence of hallucinogens, that is, *Datura* in California and the mescal bean, *Sophora secundiflora*, in Texas (see also Gowdy, Grant, Lee, Merrill, and Newcomb on this question). In California the polychrome paintings display designs similar to those visualized under *datura* intoxication; in Texas they display "conceptual analogues of the mescal bean (*Sophora secundiflora*) cult as practiced during historic times by Great Plains Indians." Kroeber had first suggested such a connection between *datura* and California rock paintings; and toloache does grow abundantly near the Chumash-Yokuts sites. In Texas rock art the elongated figures of shamans often wear horn or antler headdresses. The archeologist Campbell first suggested the connection of Texas rock paintings with the Red Bean cult. These conjectures by the physician Wellman and by the archeologist Campbell are lent countenance by the fact that the Panther Cave paintings include a leaping deer, which La Barre and Furst thought to be connected with the Red Bean cult, and La Barre with early peyotism in Mexico. Furst (in Bernal, et al., *The Iconography of Middle American Sculpture*) figures a life-size, horned effigy-head jar from Colima and notes that horned heads are widely associated with shamanism; he also reproduces a redware vessel decorated with four peyote cactus effigies, again from Colima. See also Dobkin de Rios, "Plant Hallucinogens, Out of Body Experiences, and New World Monumental Earthworks," in Du Toit.

Peter Furst and Gordon Wasson have been especially alert to illustrations of iconographic art relating to hallucinogens. In Mexico there is abundant evidence of *flowers* on representations of divinities related to ritual hallucinogens (Wasson, 1973).

Fintzelberg has written on "Peyote Paraphernalia" used in the rituals.

CHRISTIAN INFLUENCE

The degree of Christian influence on peyotism has long been disputed by Stewart and La Barre. There is no question of the real and early influence in Mexico, which was later even reinforced in some tribes in the United States, such as the Winnebago. Anderson notes a "Santa Niña de Peyotes" but with no reference to Franciscan sources. Anderson (1980) notes that in Coahuila there was a mission named "El Santo de Jesus Peyotes." Well taken is Stewart's contention that individual Indians may well embody several traditions simultaneously. But La Barre regards Christian ideological influence as superficial and often used mainly for protective purposes, for most certainly the implicit cultural nature of peyotism is authentically aboriginal, and the huge philosophical and theological background of Catholic belief is missing in the peyote religion.

On this question Piscitelli writes:

The obvious lack of completely integrated elements of Christian religion in peyotism is easily explained. The Indians feel, and rightly so, that peyote is the last real link with their aboriginal past and they are unwilling to abandon it. They are cognizant of the whites' desperate effort to destroy this last link with the past and convert the Indians to Christianity. Since peyote has contributed so greatly to a sense of solidarity and to the maintenance of morals, the Indians are prompted to employ every device at their command to defend this last stronghold of their aboriginal culture.

With regard to the Native American Church, Piscitelli writes:

This peyote organization was the result of a famous meeting at Calumet, Oklahoma, where important leaders of the Oto, Kiowa, and Apache gathered to discuss means of defending peyotism against white repressive measures. James Mooney also attended the council and was extremely influential in persuading the assembly to form a state-chartered organization.

Many of the group objected to the white religious elements implied in the title of Koshiway's First Born Church of Christ. Therefore, because the desire was to revert to a purer, more aboriginal type of peyotism, the more suitable title, Native American Church, was eventually decided upon.

The distinguished Americanist Åke Hultkrantz well expressed the complexity of the peyotist situation, caught as it is between White acculturational pressures and residues of aboriginal tribal pasts: "The peyote cult has its own theology, concentrated around the marvelous plant and with obvious traits of Catholic Christianity. On the other hand, the peyote movement tries to replace Christianity; God has sent Christ to the whites, peyote to the red man. At the same time the peyote movement has acted against the inherited, indigenous tribal religion, causing friction on reservations wherever it has appeared." The evidence for individual-tribal religious resistance is plentiful in the history of the diffusion of the new cult. The great strength of peyotism, however, is that no matter how the specific tribal culture may have suffered, peyotism is based on a *generic culture-areal foundation* (consistent certainly in the Plains culture area), so that separate tribes tend to reinforce one another toward a pan-Indian religion.

Hultkrantz writes that "Peyote provided the ideological foundation for the opposition to white supremacy. . . . It meets traditional Indian requirements in a way orthodox Christianity never does. . . . Altogether it is a question of an additive process, not a fundamental change of the ideological pattern" that was and is aboriginal.

La Barre supported Ruth Shonle's view (1925) that the diffusion of peyote was facilitated by the ancient and commonly held cultural ideology of the vision quest; Stewart argues that the diffusion resulted instead from the common attendance at Carlisle School of students from various tribes. Stewart also writes ("A Reply to La Barre's 'Retort Courteous,'" p. 114): "From the time Peyotism was officially reported on the Kiowa, Commanche [*sic*], and Wichita reservation in 1885 (Stewart 1974: 212), B[ureau of] I[ndian] A[ffairs] officials and denominational Christian missionaries, in official reports and testimony in support of laws to prohibit the use of Peyote in Indian religious rituals, recorded that they doubted the Indians' claim that Peyotism had, in fact, incorporated Christian elements and thus had the same rights to Constitutional protection as other religions." The fact is that Christians vigorously sought to *prohibit* peyotism, not that Indians were seeking escape from aboriginal patterns into Christianity. In any case, Christians are perhaps better judges of whether peyotism is Christian. At the same time, it seems an odd understanding of the Constitution to say that their being Christian is the reason for protection, although this may explain Stewart's well-meaning fervor to find peyotism "Christian."

Piscitelli remarks judiciously on the question of historic dates of first tribal contacts with peyotism: "La Barre and Shonle differ quite markedly on a number of [chronological] points. This, however, should not be regarded as an error on the part of either, for the former based his material on native information and the latter on official governmental reports. Therefore La Barre is probably dealing with the earliest contacts and introductions, while Shonle's generally later dates show recognition of the rite only after it flourished sufficiently to attract official attention." It is also to be anticipated that in many instances more detailed tribal studies will discover brief, tentative contacts earlier than the well-remembered major contacts noted by La Barre's informants.

LAW

The Firstborn Church of Christ Articles of Incorporation were filed with the Oklahoma secretary of state in Oklahoma City on 8 December 1914. Repeatedly, laws prohibiting peyote use had been passed in many states only to be found invalid or, upon litigation, making specific exception of American Indian use. La Barre gives typical cases ("A Step Backward" and "Religious Freedom of Indians Again Upheld"). While Anderson has a chapter on peyote legislation, the authority on the legal status of peyotism is Omer Stewart (in a forthcoming volume of *Handbook of North American Indians*, edited by Sturtevant). Houston Smith has articles on the religious and philosophical aspects ("Do Drugs Have Religious Import?" and "Mescalin and Metaphysics"). On legal issues, consult three "Anonymous" entries regarding Navaho and Taos in the bibliography below, and Barringer, Bates, the Collier entries, and Colton. On international policies, see United States Conference for the Adoption of a Protocol on Psychotropic Substances.

A group of young people from San Francisco went to Nevada and then to Santa Fe, incorporating as "The American Church of God" in 1968, and achieved a membership of 200 persons. One of several other non-Indian groups was the "Church of the Awakening" (Stewart, *Peyote Religion*, p. 326). These somewhat ad hoc groups have generally not fared well in the courts. For example, in 1968, Judge Gerhard Gesell of the United States District Court of the District of Columbia "denied the Neo-American Church the privilege of legal use of psychedelic drugs for religious purposes" (Stewart, *Peyote Religion*, pp. 325–26).

Stewart gives a clear view of official policy with respect to Indians:

[T]he Bureau of Indian Affairs constantly and vigorously opposed the Peyote religion from the time it was discovered in the United States in 1886 until the appointment of Commissioner John Collier in 1933. The Native American Church was incorporated under the laws of Oklahoma on October 10, 1918 by members of the Cheyenne, Oto, Ponca, Comanche, Kiowa, and Kiowa-Apache tribes. For consulting with and advising the Peyotists, ethnologist James Mooney of the Smithsonian Institute was ordered to return to Washington, D.C., by Smithsonian officials at the request of the commissioner of Indian Affairs. From 1916 to 1926 ten bills to prohibit the use of Peyote were presented to Congress at the request of the Bureau of Indian Affairs. None became law.

Under Commissioner Collier, the traditional role of the BIA of opposing all aboriginal religious ceremonialism was abandoned and the religious freedom for all Indian religions became the rule. Collier attempted to protect the Native American Church, the Sun Dance. . . . etc., but he did not sponsor any religion (Stewart, review of Milton, p. 239).

The opposition to all these native religions, including peyotism, was primarily Christian missionaries.

Mostly under state laws, non-Indians continued to be prosecuted for violations. A typical case was that of Duke University student Joe Blow of Pelham, New York, arrested on six counts after a raid by the vice and narcotics division of the Durham, North Carolina, Department of Public Safety, upon the discovery in his possession of 3-3/4 pounds of peyote buttons—a substance rare recently in this college town, although that was "probably the largest amount in the 1970s" (*Durham Morning Herald*, "Student Charged as Peyote Found," 25 February 1977). A faculty member defended a medical student arrested earlier on the dubiously drawn-up charge of *smoking* peyote, so that the vice squad itself began to behave more legally. This case was dismissed.

In October 1988 the Oregon Supreme Court ruled unanimously that Alfred Smith, a Klamath, and Galen Black, another Indian member of the Native American Church—both of whom had been fired and denied unemployment benefits—were protected by the U.S. Constitution's guarantee of religious freedom. It is to be hoped that other states will follow suit.

In August 1977:

The Central Intelligence Agency informed Princeton and 85 other institutions that they had been involved in secret research sponsored by the agency during 1953–64 in an attempt to develop ways to manipulate human behavior. The project, code-named MK-ULTRA, had included experiments with hallucinogens [including LSD-containing morning-glory seeds]. . . . Although most of the pertinent documents had long since been destroyed, evidence of the project was unearthed by the Rockefeller and Church investigations of 1975–76. Then, this past summer boxes of MK-ULTRA files were discovered in the CIA archives. The University immediately demanded access to the records, under the Freedom of Information Act, and received copies with the names of all individuals and institutions blotted out. The University was entirely unaware of what had been going on; it did not require disclosure of consultation with government bodies if these assignments did not take them away more than one day a week ("In the MK-ULTRA's Service," *Princeton Alumni Weekly*, 26 September 1977).

Such questionable and even illegal operations of the CIA have recently been disclosed somewhat more fully in the Iran-Contra affair, but the public was nevertheless much exercized because hallucinogenic drugs had been used, often on unsuspecting subjects.

The legal-anthropologist Lawrence Rosen raised the question, among others, of the disinterest of anthropological witnesses in a court of law (*American Anthropolgist*, 79 [1981] 555–78). In the same issue as Stewart's response (*ibid.*, pp. 114–15) to La Barre's "Retort Courteous" (*ibid.*, pp. 113–14), Stewart also attacked Rosen in "An Expert Witness Answers Rosen" (*ibid.*, pp. 108–11), to which Rosen made "Response to Stewart" (*ibid.*, pp. 111–13). The disagreement had begun from an article of Stewart's in Officer, 1973 (pp. 35–42), Stewart's critique of La Barre in a review in *American Anthropologist*, 81 (1979): 930–32. Neither defendant yielded.

TRIBAL STUDIES

The real core of peyote research is, of course, in tribal studies. The present discussion seeks only to supplement the rich materials in Stewart's mainly historical *Peyote Religion*, to draw attention to new studies from various sources, and to note peripheral non-diffusionist interests. For ease of reference, the sequence is roughly alphabetical.

Alaskan Eskimo. In early 1975 peyotism was proposed for the Alaskan Eskimo by a visiting archeologist as an antidote for their widespread alcoholism (in a letter to La Barre of 2 January 1975).

Aztec. Hultkrantz writes (1975: 246), "It is plausible, as Professor Linné has suggested to me, that the wild and colorful world of the Aztec gods was partly stimulated by visions aroused through the priests' peyote consumption." Furst earlier advanced the hypothesis that to a great extent Aztec religion was influenced by psychotropic experience (Furst, Introduction to Benitez, *Magic Land*, 1976); Geoffrey Gorer also thinks that "Aztec art is a mescaline-tinted vision" (quoted in Ebin). (Dobkin de Rios finds a similar influence of psychotropic plants in Maya religion.)

Blackfoot. See Davis, "Peyotism and the Blackfeet Indians of Montana: An Historical Assessment"; also Anonymous, "Peyote in Montana."

Caddo. John Wilson, formerly a Caddo after the Black Beaver Delaware merged with them in 1874, in 1893 was a recognized leader both in peyotism and in the Ghost Dance, influenced also by Catholicism (Thurman, pp. 280–85). He was killed, along with his Quapaw wife, while crossing the Flyer track in a wagon on 16 April 1901, his detractors said because he used religion to make money. For the early Caddo, see Elsie Clews Parsons, "Notes on the Caddo."

Cheraw. Jim Chavis, a 25-year-old quarter-Cheraw carpenter of Charlotte, who claimed to be president of the North Carolina Native American Church, announced he would hold a peyote meeting in July 1976. Peyote was banned by state law but permitted by federal regulation. Police threatened arrest and a fine for anyone possessing peyote at the meeting, but Chavis had the buttons from a state-regulated dealer in Texas and threatened suit if arrested (AP article on "Use of Peyote," 22 July 1976).

Cherokee. Fogelson writes that,

the modern diffusion of the Peyote Religion. . . . stops short at the borders of the Cherokee area of Oklahoma and that peyote is unknown in North Carolina. While the Peyote Religion is particularly strong among the Delawares occupying the northern portion of the former Cherokee Nation, and while a few Cherokee-Delawares and a few Cherokees in that region are Peyotists, it is no doubt culturally significant that, despite easy access, the overwhelming majority of Oklahoma Cherokees have rejected the Peyote Religion.

Fogelson believes that this resistance is owing to the survival of a concept of an *orenda*-like "power" among them that obviates peyote.

Cheyenne. Goggin contributes "A Note on Cheyenne Peyote."

Chippewa. Fred Blessing writes of the "Discovery of a Chippewa Peyote Cult in Minnesota."

Coast Salish. Jilek-Aall describes alcoholism and peyotism in this group.

Comanche. Because of his great importance for the early spread of peyotism, we should note here Tilghman's biography of *Quanah, The Eagle of the Comanche*. See also David E. Jones, *Sanapia, Comanche Medicine Woman*.

Delaware. Edmund Carpenter (personal communication, 5 January 1970) wrote: "The symbolism that Wilson sketched on the tent floor bears resemblances to the Delaware Big Horn Dance symbolism and this in turn bears resemblances to the design or Hopewellian sacred earth enclosures in Ohio— the square, corridor and circle or oval being common to all three—a point that didn't escape Speck" in Speck's article on John Wilson. Thus even aberrant peyote altars appear to have aboriginal roots. On the Delaware, see also Newcomb and Thurman.

Huichol. A lengthy report on Huichol peyotism by Preuss was lost in the World War II bombing of the publisher at Leipzig, and the only other copy, together with his field notes, was lost in the Allied raid on Berlin in March 1944 (Furst, "Introduction" to Benitez). Furst believes that "Huichol religion was at the very least far less modified by Spanish Catholicism than any other in Mexico." There are 20 pages of translations of Huichol poems and songs in Benitez. Furst also reports on the Huichol "parching of the maize," which is evidently a very ancient motif in the standard peyote breakfast. Benitez describes a kind of ritual clowning in the Huichol peyote quest that resembles the clowning in some Pueblo ceremonies. Benitez also lists the fourteen traditional stops on the Huichol peyote pilgrimage during the 300-mile walk between Jalisco and Catorce in San Luis Potosi. See also Myerhoff on the *Peyote Hunt*, which is symbolically a hunting as of Elder Brother Deer, in which the first peyote plant seen by the shaman is shot with a bow and arrow. Scott Robinson has a *Huichol Peyote Hunt* film of 1976. The usual matey first-person-alized travel talk of the *National Geographic* article by James Norman adds nothing to our knowledge of Huichol peyotism, but the article is accompanied by the usual superb photographs in this periodical (in this case by Guillermo Adema E.), including a fine wax-mosaic on the cover. These famed "yarn-paintings" of the Huichol are lavishly illustrated in Kathleen Berrin (ed.), *Art of the Huichol Indians* (note especially the chapters by Muller and by Eger). There are tape recordings by Ram Dass on *The Huichol Cosmology*, and by Don José of peyote songs.

Kiowa. Ruth Underhill (*Red Man's Religion*) suggests that the old Kiowa ceremony of the sacred stones placed on a crescent altar was one source (along with mescalism and the Mexican peyote rites) of the Plains ceremonial. On the Kiowa, see also Roy Benedict. La Barre has edited *The Autobiography of a Kiowa Indian*, Charley Apekaum, a prominent peyotist.

Kiowa Apache. Bittle writes on "The Peyote Ritual: Kiowa-Apache." Brant has edited *Jim Whitewolf: The Life of a Kiowa Apache Indian*, which contains new data on peyotism and the Ghost Dance.

Menomini. Slotkin is excerpted in Ebin (pp. 240–69) on Menomini peyotism. George Spindler writes carefully of a Menomini "schizophrenic" peyotist: "The meaning of peyotism for Joe Nepah is minimal if not non-existent. . . . He is mentally ill because he cannot recognize [the usual peyotist's] boundaries in time and social space and therefore cannot find meaning. The peyotists are not mentally ill because they also recognize boundaries [of peyotism] in time and space and do find meaning within these boundaries."

Navaho. Wagner states (p. 173) that Christian philosophy is not conspicuous in Navaho peyote, which in the post-midnight ritual emphasizes traditional native exorcism of witchcraft; at dawn the participants go outdoors to offer corn-pollen to the rising sun. The peyote ritual is assimilated to the "Star Way" or the "Star-Gazing Way" and was triggered after 1934 by John Collier's reduction of Navaho livestock. David Aberle, "One Anthropologist's Problems," is a thoughtful statement by an experienced fieldworker on some of the intellectual and moral dilemmas of an ethnographer of Navaho peyotism. On the conflicts over peyote, see also Mary Shepardson on "Navaho Factionalism and the Outside World," in Basso and Opler. Roland Wagner, who did doctoral research (University of Oregon, 1970) writes in a personal communication (1970):

Regarding the assertion [Slotkin's] that the Native American Church is replacing traditional Navaho religion, my research last summer [1969] indicated contrary conclusions. I found that within the past two years or so a new form of ritual syncretism has developed on the reservation. My informants felt that these new "double meetings" (peyote meetings combined with sand paintings and traditional chant elements) were in no way contradictory to either traditional religion or the peyote religion. The typical response is that "all of them are the same thing." I also had the impression that several road chiefs (peyote ritual leaders) are conversant with Navaho ceremonies and that they are continuing to perform both rituals, with no apparent conflict involved.

In the Navaho "V-Way Ceremony" the peyote-fire ashes are shaped into a V instead of the usual crescent moon. Some Navaho say this symbolizes the World War II "V for Victory"; others, Christ's victory over death. Anderson says that the Navaho ceremony stresses personal confession, but this is a near-universal aboriginal Amerindian culture trait, which at most melds with the newer Christian confession (which, however, is not performed in public). Weeping during prayer in meeting is aboriginal also in the vision quest. In one Navaho curing ceremony where a hot coal was held in the teeth, the road chief was a Kiowa. Anderson reproduces a membership card of the "Native American Church of Navajoland," signed by the President and Secretary of the church. Tom Bahti has a section on "Peyote" in *Southwestern Indian Ceremonies*. On Navaho litigation over peyote see Anonymous, "Coast Navajos Win Right to Use Peyote in Religious Rites"; Anonymous, "The Trial of Navajo Members of the Native American Church"; and John Collier, "Memorandum on Navaho Anti-Peyote Ordinance."

Northern Paiute. Michael Hittman wrote a Long Island University manuscript (1983) on "Opiates, Peyote, and Federal Dependence: Why the Smith and Mason Valley Numu (Northern Paiute) Rejected Peyotism."

Ponca. There is a section on religion in Howard's ethnography of *The Ponca Tribe*, including data on peyotism.

Potawatomi. Ruth Landes has a monograph on *The Prairie Potawatomi: Tradition and Ritual in the Twentieth Century* with data on peyotism.

Sioux. On Pine Ridge Sioux, see Stephen E. Feraca, "Peyotism."

Taos. The Southwestern Pueblos, despite their proximity to the source and their long contact with nearby tribes that used peyote, have consistently resisted the new religion, having strong and intact ceremonialisms of their own. The single exception is "the most Plains-like of the Pueblos," Taos (Leslie Spier, personal communication, c. 1937), even though Southern Athapaskan non-Pueblo tribes like the Mescalero Apache and the Navaho did take up peyotism. Ever since our first knowledge of Taos peyotism there has been conflict over it in this pueblo. We therefore welcome the doctoral dissertation (SUNY Buffalo, 1969) of John James Collins on "Peyotism at Taos Pueblo and the Problem of Ceremonial Description." Collins believes that Mabel Dodge Luhan should be "charged with being a major cause of the Peyote controversy" for twenty years. She required Antonio Luhan, a recognized leader of the peyote religion at Taos in 1916, to abandon it in order to marry her. Mrs. Luhan was behind the Chavis Bill S-1399 of 8 February 1937. On Taos factionalism see Fenton, the Collier "Statement," and Stewart, "Taos Factionalism."

Tarahumara. It is unreasonable to treat the fantasies of a gifted psychotic once in Rodez Asylum as authentic ethnography. In *The Peyote Dance*, Antonin Artaud believes the Tarahumara are "the direct descendants of the Atlanteans" and that only the "hermaphroditic" root (in the form of male and female organs) is used, in an orgiastic rite, etc. While the peyote religion was present in the time of Bennett and Zingg (before 1935), it has apparently fallen into desuetude among the Tarahumara. Merrill writes (personal communication, 9 September 1979): "There were no peyote ceremonies in the area in which I lived during the two years I was there, so I didn't get to see any. However, I was able to attend several ceremonies associated with a similarly treated plant called *bakanawi* (the identification of which is still unclear)." See Kennedy on the "Tesguino Complex: The Role of Beer in Tarahumara Culture" and Bye on their hallucinogenic plants. (See Vogt for the Ixcatec, p. 498; Highland Uto-Aztecans, p. 790; Huichol, pp. 806–808, 811; Tepecano, p. 820; and Tarahumara, pp. 864, 867).

Urban Peyotists. From about 1953 to 1966 peyote meetings were held in Camden, New Jersey, among Indians of advanced age, including Navaho, Lumbee, and on one occasion, Hopi. The wooden altar used "looked something like a piece of driftwood," according to the Navaho-Black informant, who attended from age five to age eighteen in her grandmother's house. The meetings were held in private homes, but were discontinued some years ago. Peyote rituals were also held in Atlanta, Georgia, the principals being Indians chiefly from the Southwest.

Stewart records: "I asked Truman Dailey about it, and he assured me that there was no such church, and that [the Kiowa novelist N. Scott] Momaday's [Urban Peyote] church was purely imaginary" (Omer Stewart 1987, p. 319). It was at the Millbrook (New York) estate of Thomas and William Hitchcock that the LSD "League for Spiritual Discovery" was formed in 1968, and soon afterward there the "Neo-American Church," which was still publishing a newsletter in 1976 (Stewart, personal communication, 1981). The church title, evidently modeled on the "Native American Church," would attempt to borrow constitutional support of authentic native peyotism. *The Psychedelic Review* published eleven numbers until 1971.

Washo. According to James E. Downs, in *The Two Worlds of the Washo* (1966):

Some Washo may have known of the cult in the 1920s, but it was not until 1932 that peyotism found its way into the Washo country by a Ute shaman named Lone Bear. Lone Bear made a few Washo converts and held some curing meetings, but he was a notorious drunkard, often in trouble with the law, and the Washo avoided his peyote meetings. Six years later, Franklin York [aka Ben Lancaster], a half-breed Washo and a sometime bootlegger who had traveled widely over the United States in medicine shows returned to his home country to preach the peyote doctrine. York was successful in spreading the peyote cult among the Washo and the neighboring Paiute. Soon his meetings were well attended and collections were often as high as $50.

But peyotism encountered problems with the law:

In the state of California the cactus was declared to be illegal [in a law which is presently being challenged in the courts], and frequently county welfare agencies in Nevada refused to assist members of the cult. Some older Washo, grown used to the dependent relationship between Indian and white society, opposed the cult because it offended the missionaries who would then refuse to give Christmas presents and the like to the Indians. . . . The progress of the cult was not smooth. From time to time meetings would almost cease and only a few devoted adherents would remain. Then, inexplicably a new burst of enthusiasm would swell the meetings.

It is possible, also, that because peyote had been declared illegal in California, many Indians from the San Francisco area flocked to the nearby Nevada Washo to renew their Indianness and thus to reinvigorate Washo peyotism. On Washo, see Downs; also D'Azevedo.

Western Shoshone. Michael Lieber writes that traditionalists in this tribe equate witchcraft with peyotism, the power of which they attribute to rattlesnake familiars or to Coyote, rather than to the plant itself as adherents maintain. The Shoshone have partly mythologized the conflict:

Indians have two souls (*mugaha*). When a person dies, one mugaha stays on earth as a ghost; the other goes to the land of the dead, the land of Wolf. Only good people go to Wolf's land. The *mugaha* of witches (*dizipuha*), their victims, and people who die by violence, are taken by coyote and they stay with him elsewhere on earth. Coyote wants more souls for himself. That's why he made witches. But he wasn't getting enough souls, so he created peyote (read peyotism). Now he gets the souls of peyotists too (Lieber 1972).

Yankton Sioux. George Morgan (*Ethnobotany*) reports that Asa Primeaux of the Yankton Sioux says *Calamus*, a psychotropic rhizome, was formerly given to Indian racing ponies, before they began to give them peyote preceding a race.

The belief in the anti-alcoholic potency of peyote dates at least to the time of Curtis (see Stafford, p. 47). The effect may be primarily psychological: Curtis reported on the "Peyote Experiences" of a Cheyenne and a Ponca, the first testifying how peyote had cured him of alcoholism, the second of a cure of tuberculosis by peyote. In any case, the distinguished American psychiatrist Karl Menninger, "who for many years has had a part in Supreme Court repeals of anti-peyote legislation, is in full agreement. He considers peyote 'a better antidote to alcohol than anything the missionaries, the white man, the American Medical Association, and the public health services, have come up with'" (Jilek).

Schultes writes that "There are probably 150 species [of hallucinogens] (including fungi) used in primitive societies in the Americas, and additions to the list are frequently being observed" (Schultes, *Iconography*, p. 81). In the last decades, this conservative authority has progressively increased his estimate, partly because of his own classic Amazonian researches. (See his "Botanical and Chemical Distribution of the Hallucinogens" and "Avenues for Future Ethnobotanical Research").

A Schultes 1977 title suggested that "Mexico and Colombia [were] Two Major Centers of Aboriginal Use of Hallucinogens" in the Americas. Schultes based his case on botanical grounds. On ethnographic grounds, La Barre fully agreed, suggesting the addition of a third center among the Quechua-Aymara of Peru and Bolivia (letters to the editor, *Journal of Psychedelic Drugs*, p. 351). For example, *Trichocereus pachanoi* (aguacolla, cimora, or "San Pedro") is a large columnar mescaline-containing cactus used by Peruvian shamans since pre-Columbian times (Schultes, "Iconography," pp. 96–97; Schultes and Hofmann, *Plants of the Gods*, pp. 58, 76–77, 81, 154–57, and *Botany and Chemistry*, pp. 225–37); and this Andean region is of course the *locus classicus* of aboriginal use of cocaine. Douglas Sharon has the most complete discussion of "The History of a Magical Plant" in his *Wizard of Four Winds;* see also his earlier "San Pedro Cactus" in Furst, *Flesh of the Gods*. STASH has a valuable brochure on *Mescaline and Peyote*.

Anderson (*Taxonomic Revision*) has botanically established two peyote species of *Lophophora*, viz. *L. williamsii* and *L. diffusa*, the latter found only in Querétaro; the two species are the only members of their genus. In 1971, Furst fully clarified "*Ariocarpus retusus*, the 'False Peyote' of Huichol Tradition." But Díaz discovered, among many other hallucinogens he discussed, five *Senecio* spp. of false peyote (see the present volume, Appendix 1, "Peyote in Mexico," pp. 124–25, for an earlier discussion of peyote nomenclature).

The Mescal Bean ("Red Bean" or *Sophora secundiflora*) has been widely used, primarily as a decorative bead (Merrill, *An Investigation*, 1977). But there is considerable ethnographic evidence (Murie, 1914; Skinner, 1915, 1926; Howard, 1953; and others), as well as archeological evidence (Adovasio, 1976; Campbell, 1958; Fry, 1976; Newcomb, 1956; and Troike, 1962) of a Red Bean cult in Mexico and in the Plains that preceded the peyote cult and may have contributed some traits to it. Indeed, Furst believes American Indians have used *Sophora* for ten thousand years:

At Fate Bell Shelter, for example, the psychoactive seeds of *Sophora secundiflora* and of another plant, *Ungnadia speciosa*, were found in all levels spanning the well-dated Trans-Pecos archeological Periods II through VI (7000 B.C. to A.D. 1000). Similarly, Eagle Cave, which has also been well-dated, yielded the two species in association in occupation levels dating from 7000 B.C. to the eleventh century A.D.

There is thus no doubt of a well-developed shamanistic, ecstatic-visionary complex involving *Sophora secundiflora*, and perhaps other psychotropic species, in the period immediately following the decline and extinction of Late Pleistocene big game (Furst, *Morning Glory and Mother Goddess*, p. 191).

Besides his own discoveries of ceramic and other picturing of peyote, the mescaline-containing *Trichocereus pachanoi*, and other psychotropic plants, Furst states elsewhere that

It was Weston La Barre who suggested on several occasions (e.g. 1972: 270–278) that the origins of the American Indian hallucinogenic complex had to be sought ultimately in ecstatic, vision-seeking Paleoasiatic shamanism, the fundamental religion of the pre-agricultural Paleolithic and Mesolithic hunting peoples of Siberia who presumably constituted the ancestral pool from which flowed the Late Pleistocene migrations into North America. La Barre's contention, which came to be increasingly shared by some of his colleagues in the study of aboriginal American religion and the botany and anthropology of hallucinogens, thus appears to be confirmed: the historic shamanistic "red bean" cult of the southern Plains is at least as old [elsewhere in America] as the big-game hunting phase of the terminal Pleistocene and thus appears to reach back toward a time when the peopling of North America across the Bering land bridge might still have been in progress (Furst, *Archaeological Evidence*, p. 25).

But Stewart nevertheless believes that "theorists have inflated the importance of this relationship between mescal beans and Peyote" (*Ethnohistorical Aspects of Peyotism and Mescalism*, p. 297). The resolution of this impasse must rest upon the judges' knowledge of the evidence, ethnographic and archeological.

In "Mescalism and Peyotism Once Again" (1960), in reply to La Barre's critique, Howard writes:

I would certainly agree that the practice of ceremonially eating the peyote cactus stems from Mexico. However, I doubt that certain features of the Plains Peyote rite, such as the ceremonial center fire, the leader's bow-like staff, the use of small gourd rattles, and the wearing of mescal bean bandoliers are derived from Mexican Peyote rituals. On the other hand, all of these elements were regularly present in the Plains Red Bean rites. . . . All of these items while shared by the Red Bean cult and the more recent Plains Peyote cult, are lacking in the Mexican Peyote rites (p. 84).

Howard's specifying (p. 85) that the feathers of "the flicker *Colaptes auratus* or *Colaptes caffer collaris* figure prominently in both the Red Bean cult and the Peyote religion" greatly strengthens his case for their historical connection. Indeed, in the art of the Kiowa painter Monroe Huntinghorse and other peyotist artists, this bird repeatedly is specifically drawn as the "water bird." Howard states:

In conclusion, my position on the Red Bean cult–Peyotism question would seem to be essentially the same as La Barre's namely that both the Red Bean cult and the Peyote religion spread from "south to north," the former entering the southern and central Plains several years before the latter. The earlier Red Bean cult seems to have paved the way for the later Peyote cult and perhaps contributed heavily to the form of the later Plains Peyote ceremony. Data from the Tonkawa, Comanche, and Oto describing the transitional type rites in which both red beans and peyote buttons were consumed indicate that in some cases the principal change-over involved the substitution of *Lophophora williamsii* or peyote for the more potent *Sophora secundiflora* or mescal bean (p. 85).

The new Texas-Mexican archeological data would appear to agree completely with Howard's sequence, Adovasio and Fry suggesting that the less-toxic plant was substituted for the earlier one.

With the antiquity of the Red Bean well established archeologically in Mexico and Texas by new C_{14} tests at the Smithsonian, the age of peyote increases also. Furst pictures a "Bowl with four peyote-like cactus effigies in high relief" from Colima, dating from *ca.* 100 B.C. to A.D. 200–300 (Furst, Hallucinogens in Precolumbian Art, fig. 6, p. 66), and an "Effigy snuffing pipe of burnished grey clay in the form of a deer holding a peyote cactus in his mouth, from Monte Alban, Oaxaca, Late Formative Monte Alban I–II, *ca.* 300–100 B.C." (Furst, *Archaeological Evidence*, plate 8, p. 21; see also "West Mexican Art"). Indeed, the well known Aztec statue of Xochipilli, "Prince of Flowers," is used by Wasson as a "cultural Rosetta Stone" by which he is able to demonstrate that flowers on the statue represent known hallucinogenic plants; furthermore, "flower" is a metaphor for hallucinogen in pre-Columbian Nahuatl poetry (see La Barre, review of Wasson's *The Wondrous Mushroom: Mycolatry in Mesoamerica*, in *Journal of Psychoanalytic Anthropology*, p. 318, for similar "kennings" in American Indian iconography).

New Amerindian hallucinogens continue to emerge as the subject is pursued. One, the rhizome of the "Sweet Flag" (*Acorus calamus*), was very widely used by Great Lakes Siouans, Central Algonkians, and Iroquoians eastward to Maine and northward into Canada as a medicine (Morgan, *Ethnobotany*, pp. 235–46), and even ceremonially by the Dakotas (Howard, 1965). In large quantities the sweet flag is alleged to be psychotropic (Hoffer and Osmund 1967; but see Schultes & Hofmann, pp. 320–21).

Of striking interest is the suggestion that some insects, such as cicadas and lantern flies, may have been used in Amerindian snuffs, since some *Fulgoridae* of the Old World are known to contain narcotic substances. In the district of Garhwal (Uttar Pradesh, India) smaller insects, such as *Phrommia marginella* Oliv., are reportedly consumed for their narcotic properties (Reichel-Dolmatoff, *Shaman and Jaguar*, pp. 199–200, 248). An unidentified Amazonian "bamboo grub" has also been implicated as narcotic (La Barre, *Anthropological Perspectives*, p. 52). A bird whose flesh has been reported to be narcotic, the red-and-black *pito* (Sp.) or *ocon3netl* (Mixe), has been known since it was reported as such in Tlaxcala in 1576 by Diego Munoz Camargo (F. J. Lippe in Anonymous, "Notes and News," *Ethno-Pharmacology Society Newsletter*, p. 10). The bird is thought to make its flesh narcotic by eating "poisonous" mushrooms and other substances. There is also a hallucinogenic "dream fish" (*Kyphosus fuseus*) caught off Norfolk Island by native Melanesians; at least four species of "goat fish" are known to cause "hallucinations and/or nightmares when eaten," although there appears to be some seasonality in this effect (letter from Matthew Bell, 9 September 1983). Many Japanese aficionados relish a fish that is hallucinogenic, though dangerously toxic:

The most potent poisons would be tetrodoxotoxins from puffer fish species. Many Haitians can distinguish three varieties and are well aware of their toxic nature: they are called *fou-fou* (*Diodon hystrix*), the *krapo mè* or "crapaud de mer" (*Sphaeroides testistineus*) and the *bilan* (*Diodon holacanthus*). Tetrodotoxins are among the most poisonous of all non-proteinaceous substances that induce coma, peripheral paralysis and greatly disturbed metabolic rates. There is a large body of literature, much of it in Japanese medical journals (Paul Farmer, Jr., letter of January 1986).

On this subject, see Findley E. Russell, "Marine Toxins" for four named species of narcotic mullet.

In 1979, William Emboden gave a lecture at Harvard on "Transcultural Uses of Water Lilies (*Nymphoidea*) as Ritual Narcotics." The subject is engrossing, since the lotus is sacred in Indian Buddhism and in ancient Egypt alike and may be the substance of the obscure Odyssean Lotus-Eaters. As to other important psychotropics, an excellent symposium on *Cannabis* is edited by Vera Rubin; comprehensive summaries are found in Schultes, "Man and Marihuana," and in La Barre, "History and Ethnography of *Cannabis*," pp. 93–107 in *Culture in Context*. With respect to psychotropic substances in general, *Recreational Drugs*, by Young, Klein, and Beyer, is billed to contain "everything you need to know about banana skins, belladonna, betel nuts, calamus, calea, california poppy, catnip, cimora, coleus, damiana, datura, dona ana, epena, Hawaiian baby wood rose, heliotrope, henbane, hydrangea, iboga, jimson weed, kola nuts, lettuce opium, lobelia, mandrake, mescal beans, morning glory seeds, nutmeg, ololiuqui, pemoline, yohimbé. . . ."

CHEMISTRY AND PHARMACOLOGY

La Barre had criticized Schultes for a culture-bound modern (pharmacodynamic) interpretation of the Indian usage of the term "medicine" (meaning for them supernatural-containing substances). Somewhat ironically, McLeary, Sypherd, and Walkington have discovered "antibiotic activity of an extract of peyote (*Lophophora williamsii* [Lemaire] Coulter)." La Barre concedes, pharmacodynamically only.

According to Anderson, the peyote cactus contains the greatest number of alkaloids known to occur in the Cactaceae, some of which are in only this genus, though others are fairly widespread: "These compounds present a fascinating challenge to biochemists who are trying to determine their biogenesis within the plant." Stafford says (p. 173) that there are at least 40 phenethylamine and simple isoquinoline alkaloids in *L. williamsii*. Curiously, the negative results of an earlier investigator (Heffter) with *Anhalonium williamsii* can be explained if we assume that his plant material was collected in Querétaro and was in fact *L. diffusa*," of which 90 percent of the alkaloids are pellotine, with almost no mescaline (Bruhn and Holmstedt, p. 385). This highly probable solution to a longtime puzzle is lent further countenance by the fact that in 1907, Diguet reported that in Querétaro peyote is called *señi*, a term Schultes recorded among the Kiowa in 1936 ("Peyote Intoxication," thesis; Harvard University, 1936), reminding us again that Indian peyotist informants in Oklahoma insisted to La Barre that there were two kinds of peyote, male and female (*L. williamsii*, "male," and *L. diffusa*, "female," in their folk taxonomy). See the present volume, pp. 12–14, 21, 106, 138, and 200, on alleged sex in plants.

The now earliest-known reference to peyote in English is in Bartlett's (3d edition, 1860) *Dictionary of Americanisms* as "whiskey-root"—cited by Sir Richard Burton in comparing peyote to fly-agaric, surely the first such comparison. The curious epithet may have derived because the Mexican peasant beer, "mescal," made from the mescal plant *Agave americana*, gave its name to the "mescal bean," *Sophora secundiflora*, as well as to the "mescal button" *Lophophora williamsii*—a connection complicated by the custom in some places of at times mixing buttons and/or beans with mescal (Aztec *mezcal, mexcalli metl*, "maguey liquor").

In 1937, W. G. Gerber reported on "Congenital Malformations produced by Mescaline, Lysergic acid diethylamide and Bromolysergic Acid in a Hamster," and that "mescaline, although a less potent teratogen as judged by the dose needed to produce abnormalities, is nevertheless equipotent in the type and number of abnormalities produced" (p. 266). Stenchever even reports "Chromosome Breakage in Users of Marihuana." Despite a perhaps legitimate suspicion that in the 1960s some persons may have overstated the case out of well-meaning tendentiousness, nevertheless, although no such results are known ethnographically, and although doses must be enormous to produce teratologies, pregnant women might well eschew the use of peyote.

The National Institute of Mental Health has a 31-page bibliography on the subject. The effect of mescaline on cats seems mainly to abolish their interest in catching mice (De Ropp, p. 49; see also V. S. Johnston, on rats). Lemberger and Rubin discuss in a monograph the *Physiological Disposition of Drugs of Abuse;* and Schultes, "The botanical and chemical distribution of hallucinogens." Caterina Bruhn has investigated the "Alkaloids and Ethnobotany of Mexican Peyote Cacti and Related Species." Mescaline crystals, in three stages of magnification, are pictured in an issue of *The Blotter* (No. 4, p. 59) inside the back cover.

Furst and Coe cautiously adduce Maya and Huastec parallels to a Huichol use of powdered peyote and water as an enema. That deer bone and deer bladder were used in making the enema syringe is undoubtedly of symbolic significance in native terms.

Crocket, Sandison, and Walk edited the papers of a symposium, *Hallucinogenic Drugs and Their Therapeutic Use* (1963); Litwin and Metzner write on "Reactions in Psilocybin Administered in a Supportive Environment"; and Lewis, on the treatment by a *yuwipi* shaman of the Oglala Sioux *wicinko* depressive symptom. Unger has an annotated chronology on "LSD, Mescaline, Psilocybin and Psychotherapy" (1963a); James Fadiman, an hour-and-one-half taped lecture, *Selective Uses of Psychedelic Drugs*; and the psychiatrist Wolfgang Jilek, an article on indigenous therapeutic ceremonies using psychotropic drugs. Albaugh and Anderson report on "Peyote in the Treatment of Alcoholism Among the American Indians": the authors do not propose that a peyote meeting is a cure for alcoholism; however, they do feel that it offers specific advantages in the treatment of the Indian alcoholic. The present writer believes that the prospects of the use specifically of psilocybin are good in compulsive-obsessive cases *when made simultaneously* with adequate psychotherapy.

Bruhn, Lindgren, and Adovasio report on "Peyote Alkaloids: Identification in a Prehistoric Specimen of *Lophophora* from Coahuila, Mexico." The specimen came from a burial cave in west central Coahuila associated with a C_{14} date of A.D. 810–1070—"one of the oldest materials ever submitted to alkaloid analysis" by thin-layer chromatography, gas chromatography, and gas chromatographic mass spectroscopy (see also Lundström and Augurell on "Thin-layer chromatography of the peyote alkaloids").

THE CASTANEDA PHENOMENON

The Castaneda imposture lingered on into the late 1970s with Carlos' fourth squeeze of the lemon in *The Second Ring of Power*. Persons with any firsthand information on peyote or peyotism remain baffled that such a patent and half-literate fraudulence could ever have passed muster. Carlos did not even do his library work adequately. He writes, for example, that "Mescalito (peyote) is a protector, a kind, gentle protector"—whereas mescaline notoriously causes severe stomach cramps, and even a single button can produce symptoms. William James was given five buttons by S. Weir Mitchell and wrote to his brother Henry James: "I ate one button three days ago, was violently sick for twentyfour hours, and had no other symptoms whatever except that and the Katzenjammer the following day. I will take the visions on trust" (De Ropp, p. 470).

An informed "higher criticism" of the very content of Carlos's fantasies soon encounters grave suspicion. For example, no Mexican who ever drank pulque (brewed from mescal, the ever-present giant *Agave americana* xerophyte) would ever improvise a *peyote* deity that he dubbed "Mescalito." But the ingenuousness of the young and the disingenuousness of some professional anthropologists together provided a trickster's highly lucrative hoax. The chicanery and the credulity of Castaneda's dupes can be relished especially in the second edition of DeMille's classic *Castaneda's Journey: The Power and the Allegory.* The saga illustrates again the social symbiosis of the shaman-trickster with the ignorant and devious, the bogus with the gullible.

The Castaneda imposture has been called the greatest hoax in anthropology since Piltdown Man, although it was instantly detected as forgery by two or three experts, if not by the committee that awarded him a UCLA doctorate for one of his fiction books. For a wide spectrum of opinions on Castaneda, see Basso, Beals, Bly, Bock, *Booklist,* Cook, Cravens, DeMille, Faber, Farren, First, Gill, Hippler, Hughes, Jellinek, Keen, Kleps, Krippner, La Barre (in DeMille), Lamb, Leach, Le Clair, Leonard, Levi, *Library Journal,* Madsden, Maquet, Mitgang, Noel, Oates, *Publishers Weekly,* Riesman, Siegel, Silverman, Spicer, Strachan, Taylor, Wasson, and Wilk.

The Internal Revenue Service has raised the question whether Castaneda's tax returns for 1976 and 1977 are fact or fiction also. The IRS refused to accept $76,500 claimed for "business cost" deductions, taken "mostly for research, including substantial payments to Mexican nationals." The probability is that a poor graduate student did not command this order of money to pay "informants"—if indeed they existed—certainly not until he had amassed undisclosed sums on his best-selling books. Castaneda is currently appealing the verdict to the Tax Court (*Wall Street Journal,* 1 October 1980).

BIBLIOGRAPHY

AARONSON, BERNARD, & HARVEY OS-MUND, *Psychedelics: The Uses and Implications of Hallucinogenic Drugs*, Garden City, N.Y.: Doubleday, 1970.

ABBOTT, L., The Menace of Peyote, *American Indian Magazine*, 5 #2 (1917) 134–36.

ABERLE, DAVID F., One Anthropologist's Problems, *Southwestern Anthropological Association Newsletter*, 19 #3 (August 1980) 1–5.

ABOUL-ENEIN, H. Y., Mescaline: A Pharmacological Profile, *Journal of Pharmacy*, 4 #4 (April 1978) 45–46.

ADOVASIO, J. M., & G. F. FRY, Prehistoric Psychotropic Drug Use in Northeastern Mexico and Trans-Pecos Texas, *Economic Botany*, 30 (January–March 1976) 94–96.

AKERS, B. P., Peyote and Peyotism (Mexico, United States), M.A. thesis, Western Michigan University, 1986.

ALBAUGH, BERNARD J., & PHILIPO ANDERSON, Peyote in the Treatment of Alcoholism Among the American Indians, *American Journal of Psychiatry*, 131 #11 (1974) 1247–50.

ALLAIN, PATRICIA, *Hallucinogènes et societé: cannabis et peyotl, phénomènes culturales et mondes de l'imaginaire* (Paris: Payot, 1973).

ALPORT, R., see Ram Dass.

ANDERSON, EDWARD F., *Peyote, the Divine Cactus* (Tucson: University of Arizona Press, 1980).

———, A Taxonomic Revision of Ariocarpus, Lophophora, Pelecyphora, and Obregonia, Ph.D. diss., Claremont College, 1961.

ANONYMOUS, Button Eaters, *Time*, 3 September 1964, 64.

ANONYMOUS, Coast Navajos Win Right to Use Peyote in Religious Rites, *New York Times*, 25 August 1964.

ANONYMOUS, Notes and News, *Ethno-Pharmacology Society Newsletter*, 3 #3 (Spring 1980) 10.

ANONYMOUS, The Peyote Cure, *Human Behavior*, 4 #4 (April 1975) 45–46.

ANONYMOUS, Peyote in Montana, *American Association of Indian Affairs*, 6 (24 March 1939).

ANONYMOUS, review of Merrill, Investigations, in *Ethnopharmacology Newsletter*, 1 #4 (Spring 1978) 3–4.

ANONYMOUS, review of the Ott-edited issue of the *Journal of Psychedelic Drugs*, in *Behavior Today*, 10 #39 (8 October 1979) 1.

ANONYMOUS, Trial of Navajo Members of the Native American Church, *New York Times*, 30 November 1962.

ANONYMOUS, United States Department of the Interior Secretary Ickes Moves to Protect Minority Religious Groups at Taos Pueblo, *Indians at Work*, 419 (1936) 8–13.

ANONYMOUS, *The Weewuk Tree* (San Francisco, American Indian Historical Society), No. 2, 1972.

ARDIS, J. A., & P. MCKELLAR, Hypnogogic Imagery and Mescaline, *Journal of Mental Science*, 102 (1956) 22–29.

ARTAUD, ANTONIN, *The Peyote Dance* (translation by Helen Weaver of *Les Tarahumaras*), New York: Farrar, Strauss, and Giroux, 1976.

———, *Les Tarahumaras*, Paris: Gallimard, 1971; also in *Oeuvres Completes*, vol. 12, Paris: L'Arbalete, 1966.

———, A Voyage to the Land of the Tarahumaras, pp. 379–91 in Sontag, p. 101.

ASSOCIATED PRESS, Use of Peyote as Religious Sacrament Eyed, 22 July 1976.

BAHTI, TOM, Peyote, pp. 58–61 in *South-western Indian Ceremonials*, Flagstaff, Ariz.: KC Publications, 1970.

BARBER, B., Acculturation and Messianic Movements, *American Sociological Review*, 6 (1941) 663–69.

BARRINGER, R. B., The Regulation of Psychedelic Drugs, *Psychedelic Review*, 1 #4 (1964) 394–441, pp. 405–406.

BARTLETT DICTIONARY OF AMERICANISMS, 3d edition, 1860.

BASSO, KEITH, Comment on Castaneda, *Annual Review of Anthropology*, 2 (1973) 246.

———, & MORRIS E. OPLER (eds.), *Apachean Culture History and Ethnology*, Anthropological Papers, No. 21, Tucson: University of Arizona Press, 1971.

BATES, R. C., Psychedelics and the Law, *Psychedelic Review*, 1 #4 (1964) 379–92, reprinted in *The Psychedelic Reader*, pp. 217–30.

BEALS, RALPH, Castaneda and Credibility, *Los Angeles Times*, 16 October 1977, p. 2.

———, Castaneda Clarified, *Los Angeles Times Book Review*, 17 July 1977.

———, ·Sonoran Fantasy or Coming of Age, *American Anthropologist*, 80 (1978) 355–62.

BEAN, L. J., & SYLVIA E. VANE, Shamanism: An Introduction, in BERRIN.

BEE, ROBERT L., Potawatomi Peyotism: The Influence of traditional patterns, *Southwestern Journal of Anthropology*, 22 #6 (Summer 1966) 194–205.

BENEDICT, ROY, Kiowa Untamed, Incorrigible, Civilized in Half a Century, *The American Indian*, 2 #s2–6 (October–February 1928).

BENITEZ, F., *In the Magic Land of Peyote*, trans. by John Upton, Austin: University of Texas Press, 1975.

———, *La Tierra Magica del Peyote*, Altos, Mexico: Biblioteca Era, 1961.

BERGQUIST, LAURA, Peyote: The Strange Church of Cactus Eaters, *Look*, 21 #24 (10 December 1957), pp. 36–41.

BERGQUIST, R., The Peyote Cult, *Wisconsin Archeologist*, n.s., 29 #2 (1948) 28–37.

BERNAL, IGNACIO, et al., *The Iconography of Middle American Sculpture*, New York: Metropolitan Museum of Art, 1973.

BERRIN, KATHLEEN (ed.), *Art of the Huichol Indians*, New York: Harry B. Abrams for the Fine Arts Museum of San Francisco, 1978.

BISCHOFF, R., The Peyote Cult, *Wisconsin Archeologist*, n.s., 29 #2 (1948) 28–37.

BITTLE, W. E., The Peyote Ritual: Kiowa-Apache, *Bulletin of the Oklahoma Anthropological Society*, 2 (March 1934) 69–78.

———, review of Brant, *Jim Whitewolf*, in *American Anthropologist*, 72 (1970) 884.

BLESSING, FRED K., Discovery of a Chippewa Peyote Cult in Minnesota, *Minnesota Archeologist*, 21 (1961) 1–8.

BLOTTER, 4:59.

BLY, ROBERT, Carlos Castaneda Meets Madame Solitude, review of *Second Ring*, *New York Times Book Review*, 22 January 1978, pp. 7, 22.

———, reply to Harner, Evers, and Walk, in Letters to the Editor, *New York Times Book Review*, 22 January 1978.

BOCK, ROBERT K., review of DeMille, *Don Juan Papers*, *American Anthropologist*, 83 (1981) 712–14.

BOLLAERT, W., Observations on the Indian Tribes of Texas, *London Ethnological Society Journal*, 2 (1950) 277.

BOOKLIST, review of Castaneda, *Second Ring*, 74 (1 December 1977) 599.

BOURGUIGNON, ERIKA, Hallucinatory (Drug-Induced) Trances Versus Possession Trances, Male and Female Forms of Altered States, *Abstracts, 71st Annual Meeting of the American Anthropological Association*, p. 28.

BOWIE, MALCOLM, Trajectories of a Mind in Crisis, [London] *Times Literary Supplement*, 15 October 1976, p. 1309.

BRANDON, WILLIAM, *The Magic World*, New York: Morrow, 1971.

BRANT, CHARLES S., *Jim Whitewolf: The Life of a Kiowa Apache Indian*, New York: Dover, 1969.

BRITO, S. J., The Development and Change of the Peyote Ceremony Through Time and Space, Ph.D. diss., Indiana University, 1975.

BROSIUS, S. M., The Ravages of Peyote, *Annual Report of the Indian Rights Association*, 74 (1916) 37–41.

BROWN, MEL, Viva Peyote! Magical Native American Cactus, *High Times* [Farmingdale N.Y.], 38 (October 1978) 80–82.

BRUHN, J. G., & CATERINA BRUHN, Alkaloids and the Ethnobotany of Mexican Cacti and Related Species, *Economic Botany*, 27 #2 (April–June 1973) 241–51.

———, & BO HOLMSTEDT, Early Peyote Research, *Economic Botany*, 28 #4 (1974) 353–90.

———, J. E. LINDGREN, & J. M. ADOVASIO, Peyote Alkaloids: Identification in a Prehistoric Specimen of *Lophophora* from Coahuila, Mexico, *Science* (1978).

BURKE, C., Peyote, *Annual Report of the Commissioner of Indian Affairs*, 1922, p. 20; 1923, p. 20; 1924, p. 21; 1925, p. 25.

BURTON, RICHARD, *The Look of the West—Across the Plains to California*, Lincoln: University of Nebraska Press, 1963.

BYE, ROBERT A., JR., Hallucinogenic Plants of the Tarahumara, *Journal of Ethnopharmacology*, 1 (1979) 23–48.

CARPENTER, EDMUND, personal communication, 5 January 1970.

CARTWRIGHT, W. D., The Peyote Cult, *Denver Art Museum Leaflet*, #105 (1950).

———, Ritual Equipment, *Denver Art Museum Leaflet*, #106 (1958).

CASTANEDA, CARLOS, Listen to the Lizards, in L. L. Langness.

———, *The Second Ring of Power*, New York: Simon & Schuster, 1977.

———, A Yaqui Way of Knowledge, in Ino Rossi, John Buettner-Janusch, & Dorian Coppenhaver.

CLARK, WALTER, *Chemical Ecstasy: Psychedelic Drugs and Religion*, New York: Sheed & Ward, 1969.

CLARK, W. G., & J. DEL GIUDICE (eds.), *Principles of Psychopharmacology*, New York: Academic Press, 1970.

CLINE, J. H., The Mescal Feast, *Western World*, 4 #1 (December 1904) 5–29; 5 #5 (September 1907).

COHEN, SIDNEY, The Hallucinogens, pp. 439–503 in CLARK & DEL GIUDICE.

COLLIER, JOHN, Discussion Concerning Peyote, Hearings of the House Subcommittee in Charge of Interior Department Appropriations Bill for 1936, April 1935, pp. 689–96.

———, *The Indians and Religious Freedom*, New York: American Indian Defense Association, Inc., 1924.

———, *The Indians of America*, New York: Norton, 1947, pp. 238–42.

———, Memorandum on Navaho Anti-Peyote Ordinance for Secretary Ickes, December 6, 1940, Documents 129020–21, Washington: Bureau of Indian Affairs, mimeographed.

———, Religious Freedom and Indian Culture, Circular 2970, Washington: Bureau of Indian Affairs, 3 January 1934; reprinted *United States Senate Committee on Indian Affairs: Survey of Conditions* (1937), pt. 34, 18319–20.

———, Statement on Peyote at Taos, Washington: *United States Senate Committee on Indian Affairs: Survey of Conditions* (1937), pt. 34, 18319–20.

COLLINS, JOHN JAMES, Peyotism at Taos and the Problem of Ceremonial Description, Ph.D. diss., State University of New York at Buffalo, 1969.

COLTON, DON E., Statement at Congressional Hearing Against Peyote, *Congressional Record*, 65 #2 (1924) 1421.

COOK, BRUCE, Is Carlos Castaneda for Real?, *National Observer*, 12 #8 (February 1973) 33.

CRAVENS, GWYNETH, The Arc of Light:

Reading Carlos Castaneda, A Primer on Shamanism, *Harper's*, 249 (September 1974) 43 ff.

———, Talking to Power and Spinning with the Ally, *Harper's*, 246 (February 1973) 91 ff.

CURTIS, EDWARD S., see Stafford (ed.).

DAILEY, TRUMAN, The Great Spirit and Peyote, 40-minute lecture by Native American Church spokesman, Pacific Tape Library, 5316 Venice Blvd., Los Angeles, Calif. 10019.

DAVIS, L. S., Peyotism and the Blackfeet Indians of Montana: An Historical Assessment, *Studies in Plains Anthropology* (Browning, Mont.), 1 (1961).

D'AZEVEDO, WARREN L., Delegation to Washington: A Peyotist Narrative, *Indian Historian*, 6 #2 (1972) 4–6.

———, Some Recent Developments in the Spread of the American Indian Native American Church (Peyotist) Among the Washo, paper delivered at 53d annual meeting of the American Anthropological Association, 28–30 December 1954.

DeMALLIE, RAYMOND, & DOUGLAS R. PARKS (eds.), *Studies in the Anthropology of the American Indian*, Bloomington, Ind.: American Indian Studies Research Institute.

DeMILLE, RICHARD, Las Aranas de Castaneda [in English], *Revista Española de Antropologia Americana* (Madrid: Universidad Complutense), 11 (1981) 328–33.

———, Castaneda: Fact or Fiction?, *High Times* (April 1977).

——— (ed.) *Castaneda's Journey: The Power and the Allegory*, Santa Barbara, Calif.: Capra Press, 1976.

———, (ed.), *The Don Juan Papers*, Santa Barbara, Calif.: Ross-Erikson, 1980.

———, review of Castaneda, Second Ring, *American Anthropologist*, 81 (1979) 188–89.

———, letter to editor, Castaneda and Credibility, *Los Angeles Times*, 16 October 1977, p. 2.

DER MARDEROSIAN, ARA H., Current Status of Hallucinogens in the Cactaceae, *American Journal of Pharmacy*, 136 (1966) 204–12.

DE ROPP, R. S., *Drugs and the Mind*, rev. ed., New York: Delacourt Press/Seymour Lawrence, New Era Editions, 1976.

DEVEREUX, GEORGE, Cultural Factors in Psychoanalytic Therapy, pp. 289–304 in Devereux, *Basic Problems in Psychotherapy*, Chicago: University of Chicago Press, 1980.

DÍAS, JOSÉ LUIS, Ethnopharmacology of Sacred Hallucinogenic Plants Used by the Indians of Mexico, *Annual Review of Pharmacology and Toxicology*, 17 (1977) 647–75.

DOBKIN DE RIOS, MARLENE, The Influence of Psychotropic Fauna and Flora on Maya Religion, *Current Anthropology*, 15 #2 (June 1974).

———, Plant Hallucinogens, Out of Body Experiences, and New World Monumental Earthworks, in Du Toit.

DON JOSÉ, *Huichol Ceremonial Chanting*, Workshop Cassette, Hot Springs Lodge, Big Sur, Calif. 93920.

DOUGLAS, F. H., & WILLENE CARTWRIGHT, The Peyote Cult, *Denver Art Museum Leaflets*, No. 105 (December 1950).

DU TOIT, BRIAN M. (ed.), *Drugs, Rituals, and Altered States of Consciousness*, Rotterdam: A. A. Balkema, 1977.

EBIN, DAVID (ed.), *The Drug Experience: First Person Accounts of Addicts, Writers, and Others*. New York: Orlon Press, 1960; Grove, 1961.

EGER, SUSAN, Huichol Women's Art, in Berrin.

EMBODEN, WILLIAM, *Narcotic Plants*, New York: Macmillan, 1973.

———, review of Anderson, Peyote the Divine Cactus, in *Ethnopharmacology Society Newsletter*, 4 #1 (Winter 1961) 11–12.

———, review of Merrill, An Investigation, *Ethnopharmacology Newsletter*, 1 #4 (Spring 1978) 3–4.

———, Transcultural Use of Narcotic Water Lilies in Ancient Egypt and Maya Drug Ritual, *Journal of Ethnopharmacology*, 3 #1 (1981) 39–83.

EVERS, L. M., letter to the editor, *New York Times Book Review*, 7 May 1978.

FABER, M. D., *Culture and Consciousness*, New York: Human Sciences Press, 1981.

———, Don Juan and Castaneda: The Psychology of Altered Awareness, *Psychoanalytic Review*, 64 #3 (Fall 1977) 323–79.

———, In Search of the Good Father: A Mystical Quest, I, Castaneda and Don Juan: An Unconscious Dimension of the Master-Pupil Relationship, and II, The Quest for Harmony, *Psychocultural Review*, 1 #3 (Summer 1977) 261–84, and 1 #4 (Fall 1977) 399–420.

FADIMAN, JAMES, *Selective Uses of Psychedelic Drugs*, Big Sur, Calif.: Pacifica Tape Library, No. 2840 (1971).

FARACA, STEPHEN E., Peyotism, *Pine Ridge Research Bulletin* (Aberdeen: South Dakota Department of Health, Education, and Welfare), 10 (August 1969) 34–45.

FARREN, DAVID, comment on Castaneda, *Los Angeles Times Book Review*, 5 March 1978, p. 4.

FARUQI, ISMA'IL, & D. K. SOPHER (eds.), *Historical Atlas of the Religions of the World*, New York: Macmillan, 1974.

FENTON, WILLIAM N., Factionalism at Taos Pueblo, New Mexico, in *Anthropological Papers*, Bureau of American Ethnology Bulletin 164, 297–344, Washington, 1957.

FIKES, J. C., Huichol Indian Identity and Adaptation, Ph.D. diss., University of Michigan, 1985.

FINTZELBERG, NICHOLAS, Peyote Paraphernalia, *Ethnic Technological Notes* (San Diego Museum of Man), No. 4 (1969).

FIRST, ELSA, Don Juan Is to Carlos Castaneda as Carlos Castaneda Is to Us, *New York Times Book Review*, 27 October 1974, pp. 35, 38, 40.

FIRSTBORN CHURCH OF CHRIST ARTICLES OF INCORPORATION, filed with Oklahoma Secretary of State, Oklahoma City, 8 December 1914.

FOGELSON, RAYMOND, Cherokee Notions of Power, pp. 185–94 in Fogelson and Richard N. Adams, *The Anthropology of Power*, New York: Academic Press, 1977.

FURST, PETER, Archaeological Evidence for Snuffing in Prehispanic Mexico, [Harvard] *Botanical Museum Leaflets*, 24 #1 (31 July 1974) 1–28.

———, The Art of Being Huichol, in BERRIN.

———, *Flesh of the Gods: The Ritual Use of Hallucinogens*, New York: Praeger, 1972.

———, *Hallucinogens and Culture*, San Francisco: Chandler and Sharp, 1976.

———, Hallucinogens in pre-Columbian Art, pp. 55–101 in King and Traylor.

———, Introduction to Benitez, *Magic Land*.

———, Morning Glory and Mother Goddess at Tepantitla, pp. 187–215 in Norman Hammond (ed.), *Mesoamerican Archaeology*, London: Dutton, 1974, p. 191.

———, The Parching of the Maize: An Essay of the Survival of Huichol Ritual, *Acta Ethnologica et Linguistica* (Vienna: Institut für Völkerkunde), 14.

———, *To Find Our Life: The Peyote Hunt of the Huichols of Mexico*, film, 1970.

———, West Mexican Art: Secular or Sacred?, in Ignacio Bernal et al.

——— & MICHAEL D. COE, Ritual Enemas, *Natural History*, 86 #3 (March 1977).

GILL, JERRY H., The World of Don Juan: Some Reflections, *Soundings* (1974).

GINSBERG, ALLEN, Experiences with Peyote, pp. 302–308 in Ebin.

———, *Journals: Early Fifties–Early Sixties*, ed. Gordon Hall, New York: Grove, 1977.

GOGGIN, J. M., A Note on Cheyenne Peyote, *New Mexico Anthropologist*, 3 (1939) 26–30.

GOWDY, J. M., Review of Symptomatology in 212 Cases, *Journal of the American Medical Association*, 221 (1972) 585–87.

GRANT, C., *The Rock Paintings of the Chumash: A Study of a California Indian Culture*, Berkeley: University of California Press, 1969, pp. 93–96.

GUNKEL, J. E. (ed.), *Current Topics in Plant Science*, New York: Academic Press, 1969.

HAMPTON, C. M., American Indian Religion Under Assault: Opposition to the Peyote Faith (Native American Church), Ph.D. diss., University of Oklahoma, 1984.

HARNER, MICHAEL, letter to the editor, *New York Times Book Review*, 7 May 1978.

HERSH, THOMAS, KEES BOLLE, M. DOBKIN DE RIOS, & LEWIS YABLONSKY, Carlos Castaneda: Stopping the World, lectures 9:00 A.M.–5:00 P.M., 22 January 1977, University of California at Los Angeles.

HESSE, ERICH, *Narcotics and Drug Addiction*, New York: R. West, 1946, pp. 76–87.

HIPPLER, ARTHUR, review of Castaneda, *Journal of Psychoanalytic Anthropology*, 1 #3 (Summer 1978) 384–86.

HITTMAN, MICHAEL, Opiates, Peyote, and Federal Dependence: Why the Smith and Mason Valley Numu (Northern Paiute) Rejected Peyotism, MS, Long Island University, 1983.

———, *The Yerinston Paiute Tribe* [Numu], edited by James D. Bednark, Yerinston, Nev.: Yerinston Paiute Council, 1984.

HODGES, D. H., Analysis of Southern Cheyenne Songs, Ph.D. diss., University of Oklahoma, 1980.

HOWARD, JAMES, Mescalism and Peyotism Once Again, *Plains Anthropologist*, 5 #10 (November 1960) 84–85.

———, Notes on the "Holy Dance" Medicines and Their Uses, *American Anthropologist*, 55 (1953) 608–609.

———, *The Ponca Tribe*, Bureau of American Ethnology, Bulletin 195, Washington, 1965.

HUERTA, INEZ GONZALES, Identificación de la Mescalina contenida en el *Trichocereus pachanoi* (San Pedro), *Revista del Viernes Médico*, 11 #1 (1960) 133–37.

HUGHES, R., Don Juan and the Sorcerer's Apprentice, *Time*, 101 #10 (1973) 36–38, 43–45.

HULTKRANTZ, ÅKE, Conditions for the Spread of the Peyote Cult in North America, in Haralds Bezais (ed.), *New Religions*, Stockholm: Almquist & Wiksell, 1975.

———, Pagan and Christian Elements in the Religious Syncretism Among the Shoshone Indians of Wyoming, Stockholm: Scripta Instituti Donneriani Aboensis, 1969.

JILEK-AALL, LOUISE, Alcohol and the Indian-White Relationship: A Study of the Functions of Alcoholics Anonymous Among Coast Salish Indians, *Confinia Psychiatrica*, 21 #4 (1978) 193–233, esp. p. 224.

JOHNSTON, V. S., Effects of Mescaline Analogues on the Operant Behavior of Rats, Ph.D. diss., Department of Psychiatry, Edinburgh, 1967.

JONES, DAVID E., *Sanapia, A Comanche Medicine Woman*, New York: Holt, Rinehart, and Winston, 1975.

KEEN, SAM, Sorceror's Apprentice, *Psychology Today*, December 1972, 90, 96, 98–100.

KELLOGG, R., M. KNOLL, & J. KÜGLER, Form-Similarity Between Phosphenes of Adults and Pre-School Children's Scribblings, *Nature* (London), 208 (1965) 1129–30.

KENNEDY, JOSEPH, *Coca Exotica, The Illustrated Story of Cocaine*, Rutherford, Madison, and Teaneck, N.J.: Fairleigh Dickinson University Press, 1985; London: Cornwall Books, 1985.

———, Tesguino Complex: The Role of Beer in Tarahumara Culture, *American*

Anthropologist, 65 (1963) 620–24.

KING, M. E., & I. R. TRAYLOR, JR. (eds.), *Art and Environment in Native America*, Special Publications, Lubbock: Texas Tech University, 1974.

KING, WAYNE, University Press Books: University of California, *New York Times Book Review*, 19 October 1982.

KLEPS, ART, letter to the editor, *New York Times Book Review*, 4 February 1973, 24–25.

———, *Millbrook: The True Story of the Early Years of the Psychedelic Revolution*, North Troy, Vt.: Neo-American Church, Inc., 1975.

———, *The Neo-American Church Catechism*, Millbrook, N.Y.: Krija Press of Sri Ram Ashram, 1967.

KNOLL, MAX, Anregung geometrischer Figuren und anderen subjektiver Lichtmuster in elektrischen Feldern, *Zeitschrift für Psychologie*, 17 (1958) 110–26.

———, O. HOFER, D. LAWDER, & J. M. LAWDER, Reproductionsbarkeit von elektrisch angeregten Lichterscheinungen (Phosphene) bei zwei Versuchspersonen innerhalb von 6 Monaten, *Elektromedezin*, 7 #4 (1962) 235–42.

———, & J. KUGLER, Subjective Light Pattern Spectroscopy in the Electroencephalic Frequency Range, *Nature* (London), 184 (1959) 1823–24.

———, J. KUGLER, J. ECHMIER, & O. HOFER, Note on the Spectroscopy of Subjective Light Patterns, *Journal of Analytic Psychology*, 7 (1962) 55–69.

———, *The Religions of the American Indians*, Berkeley: University of California Press, 1975.

IVERSON, L. L., & S. H. SNYDER (eds.), on Huntinghorse, *see* Tsa Toke, Monroe.

———, S. D. IVERSON, & S. H. SNYDER (eds.), *Handbook of Psychopharmacology*, New York: Plenum Press, 1978.

JANNINGER, OTTO, & GERTRUDE PALTIN, *A Bibliography of LSD, Mescaline, from the Earliest Researches to the Beginnings of Suppression*, San Francisco: Fitz Hugh Memorial Library, 1971.

JELLINIK, ROGER, The Education of a Shaman, *New York Times*, 14 May 1971.

JILEK, W. G., review of Bergman, *Transcultural Psychiatric Research Review*, 9 (October 1972) 158–61.

———, J. KUGLER, O. HOFER, & D. LAWDER, Effects of Chemical Stimulation of Electrically-induced Phosphenes on their Bandwidth, Shape, Number, and Intensity, *Confinia Neurologica*, 23 (1963) 201–220.

KRIPPNER, STANLEY, review of DeMille, Don Juan Papers, *Phoenix: Journal of Transpersonal Anthropology*, 5 #2 (1981) 133–36.

KROEBER, ALFRED L., *Handbook of the Indians of California*, Bureau of American Ethnology Bulletin 68, Washington, 1925, pp. 502–504.

LA BARRE, WESTON, Amerindian Religions, pp. 51–57 in Faruqi & Sopher.

———, Anthropological Perspectives on Hallucination and Hallucinogens, pp. 9–52 in Siegel & West.

———, Anthropological Views of *Cannabis*, essay-review of Rubin, in Gretel H. & Pelto Pertti (eds.), *Reviews in Anthropology*, 4 #3 (May–June 1977) 237–49.

———, AUTOBIOGRAPHY OF A KIOWA INDIAN, Lincoln: University of Nebraska Press, 1987; also *Microcard Publications of Primary Records in Culture and Personality*, 2 #15 (December 1957) 40.

———, Comments on Marlene Dobkin de Rios, *Current Anthropology*, 15 #2 (1974) 157–58.

———, Confession as cathartic therapy in American Indian tribes, pp. 36–49 in Ari Kiẹv (ed.), *Magic, Faith, and Healing*, New York: Free Press, 1964.

———, *El Culto de Peyote*, Mexico, D.F.: Premia Editora, 1980.

———, *Culture in Context: Selected Writings*, Durham, N.C.: Duke University Press, 1980.

———, The Diabolic Root, *New York Times Magazine*, 1 November 1964; also pp. 193–97 in Wax & Buchanan.

———, *The Ghost Dance: Origins of Religion*, New York: Doubleday, 1970; Delta, 1972.

———, Hallucinogens and the Shamanic Origins of Religion, in Rossi, Buettner-Janusch, & Coppenhaver; reprinted from Ott.

———, History and Ethnography of *Cannabis*, pp. 93–107 in La Barre, *Culture in Context*.

———, letter to the editor, *Journal of Psychedelic Drugs*, 9 #4 (October–December 1977), 351.

———, A Major Center of Amerindian Hallucinogens, letter to the editor, *Journal of Psychedelic Drugs*, 9 #4 (October–December 1977) 351.

———, Les mouvements religieux nés de l'acculturation en Amérique du Nord, *Histoire des Religions*, Paris: Gallimard, Encyclopédie de la Pléiade, 1969, 2: 1–40.

———, Peyotegebrauch bei nordamerikanischen Indianern, in Völger & Welck, 2:476–78.

———, Peyotl and Mescaline, *Journal of Psychedelic Drugs*, 11 #1–2 (January–June 1979) 33–39.

———, Psychedelics Galore, *Duke University Letters*, 4 (13 December 1979) 1–3.

———, Religious Freedom of Indians Again Upheld, *American Anthropologist*, 67 (1965) 505.

———, A "Retort Courteous" to Omer C. Stewart, *American Anthropologist*, 81 (1979) 113–14.

———, review article on Wasson, in *American Anthropologist*, 72 (1970) 368–73; also in La Barre, *Culture in Context*, pp. 108–15.

———, review of Berrin, in *American Indian Arts Magazine*, 5 #1 (November 1977) 72.

———, review of Bourguignon, Cross-cultural Perspectives, in *Transcultural Psychiatric Research Review*, 10 (April 1973) 19–21.

———, review of DeMille, Castaneda's Journey, in *Journal of Psychological Anthropology*, 2 #3 (1979) 377–78.

———, review of Furst, *To Find Our Life: The Peyote Hunt of the Huichols of Mexico* (film), in *American Anthropologist*, 72 (1970) 1201.

———, review of Åke Hultkrantz, Religions of the American Indians, in *American Ethnologist*, 7 #4 (1980) 786–87.

———, review of Myerhoff, *Peyote Hunt*, in *Natural History*, 83 #8 (October 1974) 85–87.

———, review of Schultes & Hofmann, *Plants of the Gods*, in *American Ethnologist*, 9 #1 (Fall 1981) 195–96.

———, review of Schultes & Hofmann, *Plants of the Gods*, in *Journal of Psychoactive Drugs*, 13 #1 (January–March 1981) 105.

———, review of Wasson, The Wondrous Mushroom, in *American Ethnologist*, 8 #1 (Fall 1981) 195–96.

———, Shamanic Origins of Religion and Medicine, *Journal of Psychedelic Drugs*, 11 #1–2 (January–June 1979) 7–11.

———, A Step Backward, *American Anthropologist*, 66 (1964) 1172.

LAMB, F. BRUCE, Comment on Bock's review of DeMille, *The Don Juan Papers*, in *American Anthropologist*, 83 (1981) 641.

LANDES, RUTH, *The Prairie Potawatomi: Tradition and Ritual in the Twentieth Century*, Madison: University of Wisconsin Press, 1970.

LANGNESS, L. L. (ed.), *Other Fields, Other Grasshoppers: Readings in Cultural Anthropology*, New York: Harper and Row, 1937.

LEACH, EDMUND, High School, *New York Review of Books*, 5 June 1969, pp. 12–13.

LE CLAIR, THOMAS, review of Castaneda, *Second Ring*, in *Saturday Review*, 2 #4

(1978) 38.

LEE, G., Chumash Mythology in Paint and Stone, *Pacific Coast Archaeological Society Quarterly*, 13 (July 1957) 1–14.

LEMBERGER, LOUIS, & ALAN RUBIN, *Physiological Disposition of Drugs of Abuse*, New York: Spectrum Publications, 1976.

LEONARD, JOHN, review of Castaneda, *Second Ring*, in *New York Times*, 29 December 1977.

LEVI, A. W., review of Castaneda, *Separate Reality*, in *Saturday Review*, 21 August 1971.

LEWIS, THOMAS H., A Syndrome of Depression and Mutism in the Oglala Sioux, *American Journal of Psychiatry*, 132 #7 (July 1975) 753–55.

LIBRARY JOURNAL, 102 (1 November 1977) 2267.

LITWIN, G. H., & R. METZNER, Reactions to Psilocybin Administered in a Supportive Environment, *Journal of Nervous and Mental Diseases*, 137 (1963) 561–73.

LUHAN, MABEL DODGE, *Intimate Memoirs, 1933–1937*, Vol. 3, *Movers and Shakers*, Chap. 11, Peyote, and vol. 4, Edge of Taos Desert, New York: Harcourt, Brace & Co., 1936 and 1937.

LUNA, LOUIS EDUARDO, appointed Guggenheim Fellow, 1986, for "A Study of the Ethnobotany and Ethnomedicine of the Colombian and Peruvian Amazon."

LUNDSTRÖM, JAN, & STIG AGURELL, Thinlayer chromatography of the peyote alkaloids, *Journal of Chromatography*, 30 (1967) 271–72.

McCLELLAND, DAVID, The 60s in Perspective, *Harvard Crimson*, 177 #67 (25 April 1983) 3.

MacCORMACK, JOHN, In Hard-Hit South Texas; Dealing Peyote Can Still Turn a Profit, *Philadelphia Inquirer*, 21 May 1981, reprinted from *Dallas Times-Herald*.

McLEARY, J. A., P. S. SYPHERD, & D. L. WALKINGTON, Antibiotic activity of an extract of peyote (*Lophophora williamsii*

[Lewinii] Coulter, *Economic Botany*, Vol. 14.

MADSDEN, WILLIAM, Don Juan and Castaneda: Who's the Real Trickster?, review of DeMille, *Castaneda's Journey*, in *Los Angeles Times Book Review*, 14 January 1977, p. 28.

———, & CLAUDIA MADSDEN, review of Castaneda, in *Natural History*, 80 #6 (June 1971) 74–76, 78.

MANDELL, ARNOLD J., The Neurochemistry of Religious Insight and Ecstasy, in Berrin.

MAQUET, JACQUES, Castaneda: Warrior or Scholar?, *American Anthropologist*, 80 (1978) 362–63.

MARRIOTT, ALICE, & CAROL K. RACHLIN, *Peyote* (translated into French by Verena Ossent), L'Aurore, Canada: Bibliothèque d'Ethnobotanie, 1978.

MASTERS, R. E. L., & J. HOUSTON, *The Varieties of Psychedelic Experience*, New York: Holt, Rinehart, and Winston, 1955, pp. 7–12, 40–47, 67, 152, 159.

MAURER, D. W., Peyote Is Not a Drug of Addiction, *American Anthropologist*, 1960, 684–85.

MENNINGER, KARL, Reading Notes, *Psychiatric News*, 20 October 1978.

MERKUR, DANIEL, The Psychodynamics of the Navajo Coyoteway Ceremonial, *Journal of Mind and Behavior*, 2 #3 (Autumn 1981) 243–57.

MERRILL, WILLIAM, Indigenous Drug Use in Aboriginal America, Master's thesis, University of North Carolina, Chapel Hill, 1972, Chap. 6, "Peyote."

———, An Investigation of Ethnographic and Archeological Specimens of Mescal Beans, *Sophora secundiflora*, in American Museums, Technical Report No. 6, *Research in Ethnobotany*, Contributions (Ann Arbor: University of Michigan Museum of Anthropology), Vol. 1 (1977).

———, A Narcotic Complex in North America?, paper presented at the 13th Annual Meeting of the Northeastern

Anthropological Association, Burlington, Vt., 1973.

———, review of A. Marriott & Carol K. Rachlin, Peyote, in *Keystone Folklore*, 20 #3 (Summer 1975).

MICHAUX, HENRI, *Connaissance par les Gouffres*, Paris: Gallimard, 1961; translated by Haakon Chevalier as *Light Through Darkness*, New York: Orion Press, 1963.

———, *Les grandes épreuves de l'esprit, et les innombrables petites*, Paris: Gallimard, 1967.

———, *L'infini turbulent*, Paris: Mercure de France, 1957; translated by Michael Fineberg as *Infinite Turbulence*, Calder and Boyars, 1976.

———, *Miserable Miracle*, Monaco: Rocher, 1956; translated by Louise Varèse as *Miserable Miracle (Mescaline)*, San Francisco: City Lights, 1969.

———, *Paix dans les Brisements*, 1959.

MILLER, MICHAEL, Drug Gurus Come Back to Harvard, *Harvard Crimson*, 177 #56 (25 April 1983) 1–2 (issue also contains Leary/Alport Scrapbook).

MILLSPAUGH, C. F., *American Medical Plants: An Illustrated and Descriptive Guide to the American Plants Used in Homeopathic Remedies*, 2 vols., New York: Hoericke and Tafel, 1887.

MILTON, JOHN R. (ed.), *Conversations with Frank Waters*, Chicago: Swallow Press, Saga Books, 1971.

MITGANG, HERBERT, Behind the Best Sellers: Carlos Castaneda, *New York Times Book Review*, 5 March 1978.

MOONEY, JAMES, Mescaline and Lipan Apache Notes, 1897 MS No. 425, Bureau of American Ethnology, Smithsonian Institution, Washington, D.C.

MORGAN, GEORGE H., The Ethnobotany of Sweet Flag Among North American Indians, (Harvard) *Botanical Museum Leaflets*, 28 #3 (September 1980) 235–46.

———, Man, Plant, and Religion: Peyote Trade in the Mustang Plains of Texas, Ph.D. diss., Department of Geography, University of Colorado, 1976.

———, & OMER C. STEWART, Peyote Trade in South Texas, *Southwestern Historical Quarterly*, 87 #3 (1984) 269–96.

MULLER, KAL, Huichol Art and Acculturation, in Berrin.

MYERHOFF, BARBARA, The Deer-Maize-Peyote Symbol Complex Among Huichol Indians, *Anthropological Quarterly*, 43 (1970) 64–78.

———, Peyote and the Huichol World-View: The Structure of Mystic Vision, pp. 417–38 in Rubin.

———, Peyote and the Mystic Vision, in Berrin.

———, *The Peyote Hunt: The Sacred Journal of the Huichol Indians*, Ithaca: Cornell University Press, 1975; also in paperback.

NATIONAL INSTITUTE OF MENTAL HEALTH, National Clearinghouse for Drug Information, *Selective Reference Series*, 4 #1 (January 1972).

NEWCOMB, WILLIAM, The Peyote Cult of the Delaware Indians, *Texas Journal of Science*, 18 #2 (June 1956) 202–11.

———, *The Rock Art of Texas Indians*, Austin: University of Texas Press, 1967, pp. 37–80.

NIKLITZSCHEIK, ALEXANDER, *Water Lilies and Water Plants*, London: Chatto and Windus, 1932.

NOEL, DANIEL C. (ed.), *Seeing Castaneda: Reactions to the "Don Juan" Writings of Castaneda*, New York: G. P. Putnam's Sons, Capricorn Books, 1976.

NORMAN, JAMES, The Huichols: Mexico's People of Myth and Magic, *National Geographic*, 151 #6 (June 1977) 832–35.

OATES, JOYCE CAROL, Anthropology or Fiction?, *New York Times Book Review*, 26 (November 1972) 41.

———, Don Juan's Last Laugh, *Psychology Today*, 8 #4 (September 1974) 10–12, 30.

OFFICER, JAMES E. (ed.), *Symposium on Anthropology and the American Indian*, San Francisco: Indian Historian Press, 1973.

OLNEY, R. K., Mescaline, *Texas Medicine*, 68 #7 (1972) 80–82.

OPLER, MARVIN K., *Cross-Cultural Uses of Psychoactive Drugs (Ethnopharmacology)*, in Clark and del Giudice.

OTT, JONATHAN, *Hallucinogenic Plants of North America*, Berkeley: Wingbow Press, 1976.

——— (guest editor), *Journal of Psychedelic Drugs*, January–June 1975.

———, & JEREMY BIGWOOD (eds.), *Teonanacatl: Hallucinogenic Mushrooms of North America* (extracts from the Second International Conference on Hallucinogenic Mushrooms, near Port Townsend, Washington), Seattle: Madrona Publishers, 1978.

PARSONS, ELSIE CLEWS, Notes on the Caddo, *American Anthropological Association Memoirs*, 57 (1941) 50–53.

PELTO, GRETEL, & PERTTI PELTO (eds.), *Reviews in Anthropology*, 4 #3 (May–June 1977) 237–49.

PEREZ DE BARADOS, JOSÉ, Drogas alucinogenas de los indios Americanos, *Antropologia y Etnologia* (Madrid), 3 (1950) 9–107.

PEYOTE, report of U.S. Congress House Committee on Indian Affairs, Washington: Government Printing Office, 1918.

PEYOTE Y LOS HUICHOLES, Mexico: Secretario de Educacion Publica, 1972.

PISCITELLI, ELIZABETH F., MS on Peyotism in Process: A Study of Diffusion and Acculturation, 1941, Wellesley College.

PUBLISHERS WEEKLY, 210 #10 (6 September 1976) 60; 212 #22 (28 November 1977) 42.

RAM DASS, BABA, *The Huichol Cosmology*, Workshop Cassette, Hot Springs Lodge, Big Sur, Calif., 93920.

REICHEL-DOLMATOFF, G., *Beyond the Milky Way: Hallucinatory Images of the Tukano Indians*, Latin American Studies, No. 42, Los Angeles: University of California, Los Angeles, 1978.

———, *The Shaman and the Jaguar: A Study of the Narcotic Drugs Among the Indians of Colombia*, Philadelphia: Temple University Press, 1975.

RIESMAN, PAUL, The Collaboration of Two Men and a Plant, *New York Times Book Review*, 20 October 1972, 7, 10–12.

ROBINSON, SCOTT, *Huichol Peyote Hunt*, film, 1976.

ROSEMAN, BERNARD, *The Peyote Story*, Hollywood, Calif.: Wilshire Book Co., 1966.

ROSEN, LAWRENCE, response to Stewart, *American Anthropologist*, 79 (1981) 111–13.

ROSSI, JOHN, JOHN BUETTNER-JANUSCH, & BRIAN COPENHAVER (eds.), *Full Circle*, New York: Praeger, 1977.

RUBIN, VERA (ed.), *Cannabis and Culture*, The Hague: Mouton, 1975.

RUSSELL, FINDLEY, Marine Toxins and Venomous and Poisonous Marine Animals, *Advances in Marine Biology*, 3 (1967) 255–384.

SAN FRANCISCO CONFERENCE ON HALLUCINATIONS IN NATIVE AMERICAN SHAMANISM AND MODERN LIFE, 28 September–1 October 1978.

SCHAFFSMA, P., review of Newcomb, *Rock Art*, in *American Anthropologist*, 70 (1968).

SCHLEIFFER, HEDWIG (ed.), *Sacred Narcotic Plants of the New World Indians: An Anthology of Texts from the 16th Century to Date*, New York: Hafner Press, 1973.

SCHULTES, RICHARD EVANS, Antiquity of the Use of New World Hallucinogens, *Archeomateria*, 2 (1987) 59–72, 64–66.

———, *Atlas des plantes hallucinogènes du monde*, Montreal· Aurore, Bibliothèque d'Ethnobotanie, 1978; translated by Jocelyn Lapage from *Golden Guide, Hallucinogenic Plants*, 1976.

———, Avenues for Future Ethnobotanical Research into New World Hallucinogens, pp. 25–55 in Du Toit; also in *Journal of Psychedelic Drugs*, 9 #3 (July–September 1977) 247–63.

———, Botanical and Chemical Distribution of Hallucinogens, *Annual Review of Plant Physiology*, 21 (1970) 571–94.

———, Foreword, in Omer C. Stewart & David F. Aberle (eds.), *Peyotism in the West*, Salt Lake City: University of Utah Press, Anthropological Papers, No. 108, 1984.

———, *Hallucinogenic Plants*, New York: Golden Press; Racine, Wisc.: Western Publishing Co., 1976.

———, *Hallucinogenic Plants*, 50-minute lecture of New York Horticultural Society, 1973, available from Pacific Tape Library, 3516 Venice Blvd., Los Angeles, CA 90019.

———, Hallucinogens of Plant Origin, *Science*, 158 (1969) 246–54.

———, Iconography of New World Hallucinogens, *Arnoldia*, 41 #3 (May–June 1981) 80–128.

———, Man and Marihuana, *Natural History*, 82 (1975) 59–63, 80, 82.

———, Mexico and Colombia: Two Major Centers of Hallucinogens, *Journal of Psychedelic Drugs*, 9 #2 (April–June 1977).

———, The New World Indians and Their Hallucinogenic Plants, *Bulletin des Stupifiants*, 21 #3 (1969) 3–16; 21 #4 (1969) 17–30; and 22 #1 (1970) 25–53.

———, An Overview of Hallucinogens in the Western Hemisphere, pp. 3–54 in Furst, *Flesh of the Gods*.

———, Peyote and the American Indian, *Nature*, 30 (1937) 155–57.

———, Plants and Plant Constituents in Mind-Altering Agents Throughout History, pp. 219–41 in Iverson, Iverson, & Snyder, *Handbook*.

———, The Unfolding Panorama of the New World Hallucinogens, pp. 336–54 in Gunkel.

———, & A. HOFMANN, *The Botany and Chemistry of Hallucinogens*, Springfield, Ill.: Charles C. Thomas, 1973.

———, & A. HOFMANN, *Plants of the Gods*, New York: McGraw-Hill, 1979.

SHARON, DOUGLAS, *The Wizard of Four Winds: A Shaman's Story*, New York: Free Press, 1979.

SHEPARDSON, MARY, Navajo Factionalism and the Outside World, pp. 83–89 in Basso & Opler.

SIEGEL, RONALD W., Inside Castaneda's Pharmacy, *Journal of Psychoactive Drugs*, 13 #3 (October–December 1981) 325–32.

———, & JOLYON WEST (eds.), *Hallucinations: Behavior, Experience and Theory*, New York: John Wiley & Sons, 1975.

SILVERMAN, DAVID, *Reading Castaneda*, London: Routledge and Kegan Paul, 1976.

SISKIN, EDGAR E., *Washo Shamans and Peyotists: Religious Conflict in an American Indian Tribe*, Salt Lake City: University of Utah Press, 1983.

SMITH, HOUSTON, Do Drugs Have Religious Import?, *Journal of Religious Philosophy*, 61 #19 (17 September 1964).

———, Mescalin and Metaphysics: The Case of Huxley and His Critics, *New Perspectives in Faith and Freedom*, 8 (1955) 141–43.

SMITH, M. G., The Peyote Cult in Oklahoma, *El Palacio*, 29 (1930) 241–42.

SNODGRASS, JEANNE C., *American Indian Painters: A Biographical Directory*, 1968.

SONTAG, SUSAN (ed.), *Antonin Artaud: Selected Writing*, translated by Helen Weaver, New York: Farrar, Strauss, and Giroux, 1976.

SPICER, EDWARD W., review of Castaneda, *Don Juan*, in *American Anthropologist*, 71 (1969) 320–23.

SPINDLER, GEORGE, Joe Nepah, A "Schizophrenic" Menominee Peyotist, *Journal of Psychoanalytic Anthropology*, 10 #1 (Winter 1987) 1–16.

STAFFORD, BARRY (ed.), *Selected Writings of Edward S. Curtis: The Portable Curtis*, Berkeley, Calif.: Creative Arts Book Co., 1976.

STAFFORD, PETER, *Psychedelic Encyclopedia*, Berkeley, Calif.: And/Or Press, 1977, p. 16.

———, & BRUCE EISNER, The Great White

Shamans: Notes on the Hallucinogens in Native American Shamanism and Modern Life Conference in San Francisco, September 28–October 1, 1978.

STAMETS, PAUL, *Psilocybe Mushrooms and Their Allies*, Seattle: Homestead Book Co., 1978.

STASH [STUDENT ASSOCIATION FOR THE STUDY OF HALLUCINOGENS] staff, *Mescaline and Peyote: A STASH Literature Review*, Educational Offprint Series, No. 210, Madison, Wisc., 1974.

STASH, *Psilocybin and Psilicin, The Magic Mushroom*, Madison, Wisc.: STASH Press, 1975.

STENCHEVER, M. A., Chromosome Breakage in Users of Marihuana, *American Journal of Obstetrics*, 118 #1 (1974) 106–13.

STEWART, OMER C., Ethnohistorical Aspects of Peyotism and Mescalism, *Journal of Altered States of Consciousness*, 5 (1979–80) #4 277–96.

——, An Expert Witness Answers Rosen, *American Anthropologist*, 81 (1979) 108–11.

——, The Native American Church, pp. 188–96 in W. R. Wood & Margot Liberty (eds.), *Anthropology on the Great Plains*, Lincoln: University of Nebraska Press, 1980.

——, Origin of the Peyote Religion in the United States, *Plains Anthropologist*, 19 (65) (1974) 211–23.

——, Peyote, *Encyclopedia Americana*, New York: American Corporation, 1954, 21:700.

——, Peyote and the Law, in William C. Sturtevant (ed.), *Handbook of North American Indians*, Washington: Smithsonian Institution, forthcoming.

——, *Peyote Religion*, Norman: University of Oklahoma Press, 1987.

——, The Peyote Religion, pp. 673–81 in Warren L. D'Azevedo (ed.), Great Basin, vol. 11 of *Handbook of North American Indians*, ed. William C. Sturtevant, Washington: Smithsonian Institu-

tion Press, 1986.

——, Peyotism and Mescalism, *Plains Anthropologist*, 25 (90) (1980) 297–309.

——, A Reply to La Barre's "Retort Courteous," *American Anthropologist*, 81 (1978) 114–15.

——, review of Benitez, *Magic Land*, and Reichel-Dolmatoff, *Shaman and Jaguar*, in *Journal of Ethnic Studies* (Bellingham: Western Washington State College, 1976), 97–99.

——, review of David E. Jones, *Sanapia, Comanche Medicine Woman*, in *American Anthropologist*, 74 #4 (September 1975) 655–56.

——, review of La Barre, *Peyote Cult*, in *American Anthropologist*, 79 (1981) 930–32.

——, review of John Milton, Conversations with Frank Waters, in *Colorado Magazine*, 51 #3 (1974) 238–39.

——, Taos Factionalism, *American Indian Culture and Research Journal*, 8 #1 (1984) 37–57.

——, & DAVID ABERLE (eds.), *Peyotism in the West*, Anthropological Papers, No. 108, Salt Lake City: University of Utah Press, 1984.

——, & J. S. SLOTKIN, Peyotism, *Encyclopaedia Britannica*, 1966, 17:790–91.

STRACHAN, DON, Debunking Castaneda on the "Solid Basis of Hunches," *Los Angeles Times Book Review*, 6 February 1977, p. 3.

——, In Search of Don Juan, *New West*, 4 #3 (29 January 1979) 90–91.

STUMP, A., Peyote, *Saga*, 20 #3 (June 1963) 81–83.

TAYLOR, NORMAN, *Flight from Reality*, New York: Duell, Sloan & Pearce, 1944.

TAYLOR, ROBERT, review of Noel, *Seeing Castaneda*, in *Boston Globe*, 20 January 1976.

THURMAN, MELBURN D., Supplementary Material on the Life of John Wilson, *Ethnohistory* 20 #3 (Summer 1970) 279–87.

TILGHMAN, Z. A., *Quanah, the Eagle of the*

Comanche, Oklahoma City: Harlow, 1938.

Tsa Toke, Monroe [Huntinghorse], Peyote Painting, in F. H. Douglas and R. d'Harnoncourt (eds.), *Indian Art in the United States*, New York: Museum of Modern Art, 1941, p. 210.

——, Peyote Painting, in G. B. Jacobson and J. D'Ucel (eds.), *Les Peintres Indiens d'Amérique*, Nice: Sawedzicki, 1950, Vol. 2, pl. 77.

Underhill, Ruth, *Red Man's Religion*, Chicago: University of Chicago Press, 1965, pp. 2–3, 164, 265–69.

——, Religion Among American Indians, *Annals of the American Academy of Political and Social Sciences*, 311 (May 1957) 127–37.

United Nations Conference for the Adoption of a Protocol on Psychotropic Substances, Official Records, New York: United Nations, 1973.

Vogt, Evon Z. (ed.), *Handbook of Middle American Indians*, 2 vols., Austin: University of Texas, 1969, *Ethnology*, 1:498, 2:806–808, 811, 820, 864, 867.

Völger, Gisela, & Karen von Welck (eds.), *Rausch und Realität: Drogen im Kulturvergleich* (3 vols.), Cologne: Rautenstrauch-Joest Museum für Völkerkunde der Stadt Köln, 1982, 2:476–78.

Wagner, Roland W., Pattern and Process in Ritual Syncretism: The Case of Peyotism Among the Navajo, *Journal of Anthropological Research* (formerly *Southwestern Journal of Anthropology*), 31 #2 (1975) 162–81.

——, Some Pragmatic Aspects of Navajo Peyotism, *Plains Anthropologist*, 20 (69) (1975) 197–206.

Wall Street Journal, article on Castaneda, 196 #65 (1 October 1980) 1.

Walters, Ray, Paperbacks: New and Noteworthy, *New York Times Book Review*, 11 January 1981.

Wasson, Gordon, The Divine Mushroom: Primitive Religion and Hallucinatory Agents, *Proceedings of the American Philosophical Society*, 102 (1958) 221–23.

——, The hallucinatic fungi of Mexico: An inquiry into the origin of religious ideas, [Harvard] *Botanical Museum Leaflets*, 19 #9 (1961) 137–62; see also *Economic Botany*, 20 (1963) 25–73.

——, review of Castaneda, *Journey*, in *Economic Botany*, 27 #1 (January–March 1973) 151–52.

——, review of Castaneda, *Separate Reality*, in *Economic Botany*, 26 #1 (January–March 1972) 98–99.

——, review of Castaneda, *Tales of Power*, in *Economic Botany*, 28 #3 (July–September 1974) 245–46.

——, review of Castaneda, *Teachings*, in *Economic Botany*, 28 #2 (April–June 1969) 197.

——, The role of "flowers" in Nahuatl culture: A suggested interpretation, [Harvard] *Botanical Museum Leaflets*, 23 (1973) 305–24.

——, *The Wondrous Mushroom: Mycolatry in Mesoamerica*, New York: McGraw Hill, 1980.

——, Soma of the Aryans, An Ancient Hallucinogine, *Bulletin for Narcotics*, 22 #3 (1970) 25–30.

——, Albert Hofmann, & Carl A. P. Ruck, *The Road to Eleusis: Unveiling the Secret of the Mysteries*, New York: Harcourt Brace Jovanovich, 1978.

Waters, F., *Masked Gods*, Albuquerque: University of New Mexico Press, 1950, pp. 133–38, 258.

Wax, Murray L., & R. W. Buchanan (eds.), *Solving "The Indian Problem": The White Man's Burdensome Business*, New York: New Viewpoints, 1975.

Wellman, Klaus F., North American Indian Rock Art and Hallucinogenic Drugs, *Journal of the American Medical Association*, 239 #15 (14 April 1978) 1524–27.

——, *A Survey of North American Indian Rock Art*, Graz, Austria: Akademisch-Druck und Verlagsanstalt, 1978.

Wilk, Stan, Castaneda: Coming of Age in Sonora, review of *Tales of Power*, in *American Anthropologist*, 79 (December 1977) 84–91.

———, letter to the editor, *New York Times Book Review*, 7 May 1978.

———,, review of Castaneda, *Separate Reality*, in *American Anthropologist*, 74 #4 (August 1972) 921–22.

Young, Dudley, The Magic of Peyote, *New York Times Book Review*, 20 September 1968, p. 30.

Young, Lawrence, et al., *Recreational Drugs*, New York: Macmillan, 1977.

Zentner, J. L., review of Anderson, *Peyote the Divine Cactus*, in *Journal of Psychoactive Drugs*, 13 #4 (October–December 1980) 401–404.

INDEX TO FIFTH EDITION ENLARGED

"

Maricopa: 24, 55, 131
Marihuana (*Cannabis indica*): 20–22, 25, 26, 39, 91, 133–35, 141, 224, 268–70, 289, 305
Marriott, Alice: 203, 286
Massachusetts: 214, 231, 232
Matacuna: 134
Mátéfi, L.: 227
Maurer, D. W.: 222–23
May, George (Wichita): 1
Maya: 78, 99, 307
Mayo: 34, 38
Mazatec: xi, 194, 202
Meal, ritual: *see* Ritual meal (= Peyote-breakfast)
Medicine power: xiv, 200, 255, 305
Meetings: purpose of, 43, 58–59, 81; times of, 43, 53, 58–59, 73
Mellen, C., III: 235
Menninger, Karl: 261, 301
Menomini: 116, 194, 195, 197, 198, 199, 204–205, 217, 261–62, 298
Merriam, A. P.: 203, 205
Merrill, W. L.: 286, 300
Mescal (*Agave americana*): 15, 21, 105, 204, 308; *see also* Pulque; Tequila: Tesvino
"Mescal" (misnomer for *Lophophora williamsii* = peyote): 15, 204, 231
"Mescal bean" (*Sophora secundiflora*): 15, 26, 39, 45, 47 (Fig. 2), 54, 62, 105–109, 117, 126–27, 131, 135, 137, 151–53, 196, 205, 218–19, 263; *see also* Red Bean
"Mescal Bean Cult" (= "Mescalism"): 54, 105–109, 117, 196, 150–51, 204–205, 217–19, 302–304; *see also* Red Bean Cult
"Mescal Bean Eaters" (= peyotists): 217
"Mescal buttons" (misnomer for *Lophophora williamsii*): 15, 200, 218
Mescalero Apache: 2, 15, 18, 27, 38–43, 48, 52, 54–57, 59–61, 63, 66, 70, 73, 81, 82, 97–98, 110–12, 121, 162, 194, 198, 259–60, 299
Mescaline (chief psychotropic alkaloid in *Lophophora williamsii*, but absent in *L. diffusa*): xi, xiii, 139–48, 193, 195–96, 202–204, 219–23, 227–36, 252–56, 266, 269–70, 290, 291, 302, 303, 306
"Mescalito": 307
Mesquaki: 217
Mexican Government: 233
Mexican Indians: vii, 7, 11–40, 52, 54–57, 69, 71–73, 78, 90, 94, 109, 126, 143, 162, 193–98, 203, 214, 216, 218–21, 226, 227–31, 256–59, 267; *see also* Acaxee, Aztec; Cahuilla; Caxcane; Chichimeca; Coahuiltecan; Cora; Guachachile; Huichol; Jumano; Lacandone; Maratine;

Maya; Mayo; Mixtec; Nahuatl; Opata; Otomi; Seri; Tepecano; Tepehuane; Tamaulipecan; Tarahumari; Tlaxcaltican; Tubar; Yaqui; Yucatecan; Zacatecan
Meyerhoff, Barbara: 257
Michaux, H.: 203, 228
Michel, Concha: 202
Michelson, T.: 1, 101–102
Miller, Henry: xi
Minnesota: 121, 265
Mirel, Elizabeth: 234
Missionaries: 197, 202, 206; *see also* Christian elements
Missouri: 82, 95
Miwok: 134–35
Mixe: 304–305
Mixtec: 133
Modoc: 116
Mohave: 15, 134, 135
Mohawk: 153
Molina, A. de: 16
Momaday, M. Scott (Kiowa): 300
Mono: 134–136
Montana: 29, 203, 213, 214, 217, 218, 225, 235
Moon (= ground-altar): 44 (Fig. 1), 46–48, 53, 55, 56, 61, 63–65, 67, 69, 70, 73–80, 190, 192, 197, 216
Mooney, James: 1, 13–15, 19–21, 28, 46, 48, 51, 54, 64–66, 94, 111, 114, 124, 127, 131, 151, 152, 169, 197, 203, 217, 227, 260, 263, 292
Moore, H. C.: 199
Mopope, Stephen (Kiowa): 190, 192, 203
Morgan, F. F.: 147
Morning Star: 31, 35, 37, 45, 46, 51, 56, 57, 62, 67
Murdock, Cecil (Kickapoo): 1
Murdock, Henry (Kickapoo): 1
Murphy, D. F.: 1
Mushrooms, narcotic: 39, 133, 196, 220, 228–29; *see also* Psilocybin; Teonanácatl
Music, peyote: 195, 202–204, 216; *see also* Singing; Songs

Nahuatl: 15, 16; *see also* Aztec
Narcotic complex: 263–64
Narcotics: 202, 204, 219, 222–25; *see also* Drugs, psychotropic
Natchez: 78, 133
Native American Church: vii, xii, xiii, 1, 3, 25, 29, 56, 57, 63, 76, 77, 85, 89, 93, 102, 114, 115, 119, 122, 146, 149–50, 165, 167–74, 194, 195, 197, 203, 205, 213, 214, 216–18, 225, 235, 265–66, 270, 294, 295, 296, 300

Nativistic movements: 89, 207; *see also*
    Ghost Dance; Sons of the Sun
Navaho: 12, 24, 55, 69, 133–35, 194, 195,
    197–99, 202, 204, 215–16, 224, 260–61,
    298–99, 300
Nebraska: 29, 79, 101, 116, 164, 171, 195,
    217
Negroes: ix, x, 60, 118, 165, 172–74, 197,
    263
"Neo-American Church": vii, xii, 294, 300
Nettl, B.: 202, 216
Nevada: 29, 197, 223, 224, 301
Newcomb, W. W.: 199
New Mexico: 29, 113, 126, 151, 195, 224
New York: 233
Nicarao: 99
Nickels, Anna B.: 200
Niedhammer, M.: 195
Non-ritual uses of peyote: 23–29; *see also*
    Curing; Divination; Doctoring; Proph-
    ecy; War
Noon, John: 2
North Carolina: 133, 204, 269, 295, 296, 297
North Dakota: 29, 195, 216, 224

Oates, Joyce Carol: 273
Oglala Sioux: 99, 307
Ojibwa: 99; *see also* Chippewa
Oklahoma: 15, 29, 65, 67, 73, 77, 102, 114–
    16, 120, 127, 153, 157, 158, 166–72, 201,
    203, 213, 217, 223
Olcott, Deana: 204
Ololiuhqui (*Rivea corymbosa*): xi, 10, 26, 130,
    134, 202, 228–29, 233, 263
Omagua: 134
Omaha: 61, 68, 73, 75, 79, 106, 113, 116–17,
    120, 122, 127, 158, 159, 163, 164, 171,
    194, 196, 197, 199, 265
Opata: 14, 15, 28, 133, 134
Opler, M. E.: 2, 22, 40, 42, 63, 65, 66–67,
    86, 110, 113, 162, 194, 198, 200, 201, 259
Opler, M. K.: 193, 194, 200, 205
Origin legend: 13–14, 25, 29, 33, 60, 90,
    102, 197, 263
Orlovsky, Peter: xv
Orso, Camille: 215
Ortega, J.: 10
Osage: 1, 52, 59–65, 67, 70, 72, 77, 78, 82,
    85, 86, 89, 93, 96, 99, 108, 113, 117, 121,
    122, 156–61, 163, 165, 166, 171, 194–96,
    198
Osmond, H.: 222, 233
Oto: 1, 17, 22, 23, 26, 27, 50, 52, 53, 55,
    59–61, 63–65, 67, 68, 70, 71, 94, 97, 99,
    102, 106, 108, 113, 116–18, 120–22, 143,
    153, 159, 161–62, 165–71, 174, 190–91,
    192, 194, 196, 197, 292, 294

Otomi: 14
Ott, Jonathan: 286

Painting, body: 31, 33, 40, 45, 61–63, 73, 90,
    107
Paintings, peyotist: 203, 266–67; *see also* Art,
    peyotist
Paiute: 34, 38, 89, 120, 194, 195, 198–200,
    203, 262, 299
Paminky: 134
Pan-Indianism: 54, 60–61, 121, 203, 204,
    213, 215, 217
Panther, Collins (Shawnee): 1
Panther, Tom (Shawnee): 1, 18, 19, 71
Papago: 24, 25, 28, 194, 195
Parker, Quanah (Comanche): 20, 25, 47, 52,
    63, 73, 82, 85, 88, 96, 100, 113, 115, 116,
    118, 166, 223, 297
Parsons, Elsie Clews: 79, 87–88, 94, 110,
    111, 120, 213
Paviotso: 120
Pawnee: 1, 26, 59–61, 63, 64, 68, 71, 78, 79,
    81–85, 89, 91, 106, 107, 113, 118–20,
    157, 166, 172, 194, 196
Peace Corps: xvii
Peoria: 153
Peru: 256, 275, 302
Petrullo, V.: xii, 63, 145, 151, 152, 157–61,
    190, 195, 199, 200, 204, 262
Pettit, Jim (Oto): 1
Peyote:
    amount eaten, 65–67
    antiquity of use, 195, 291
    as medicine, 206; *see also* Curing;
        Doctoring
    botany of, 10–17
    chemistry of, 138, 221, 252–56; *see also*
        Peyote, physiology of; Pharmacology
    cost of in 1954, 195; in 1957, 268
    earliest reference to (1860), 306, 307
    etymology, 124
    journey to obtain, *see* Journey, ritual
    non-habit forming, 193
    non-ritual uses of, 17, 18, 22, 23–29, 106,
        107, 134, 195–97, 201–202, 204, 219,
        261
    origin legend, 197, 263
    physiology of, 139–50, 221, 252–55
    range of plant, 11, 251–52
    ritual journey to obtain, 55–57, 197; *see*
        also Journey, ritual
    ritual meal, *see* Ritual meal
    taxonomy, 287–88
Peyote Woman: 13–14, 22, 46, 47, 51, 52, 56,
    75, 85, 90, 198
Peyotism:
    aberrant cults in, 197–99, 216; *see also*

102, 106, 107, 113, 120, 131, 151, 156,
158, 194, 196
Wilcock, J.: 229
Wilson, Alfred (Cheyenne): 1, 65, 93–94,
114, 120, 167, 170, 171, 213
Wilson, B. R.: 262
Wilson, John (Caddo-Delaware): 15, 18, 20,
27, 43, 46, 55, 61, 63, 65, 72, 73, 76–78,
80–82, 85, 90, 100, 101, 113, 115,
117–19, 121, 122, 151–61, 190, 192, 199,
262
Winnebago: 1, 18, 27, 28, 56, 59–62, 64, 65,
67, 69, 70, 72, 73, 75, 77, 79, 80–87, 89,
91, 96–99, 101, 113, 116, 117, 120–22,
152, 158, 159, 163–66, 193, 194, 197,
198, 203, 262, 266
Wisconsin: 121, 203
Wissler, Clark: 2, 69, 89, 114, 213
Witchcraft: 18, 20, 22, 26–29, 35, 42, 54, 73,
86, 88, 94, 97–98, 131
Woman, Peyote: *see* Peyote Woman
Women: 22, 27, 34, 41, 45, 46, 48, 50–53, 55,
60, 62, 65, 81, 85, 119, 198, 204–205,
216–17

Wyandot: 59
Wyoming: 29, 214, 215, 224

Yahé, or yajé (*Haemadictyon Amazonicum*):
24, 39, 134
Yankton: 121, 301
Yaqui: 28, 40, 271–72, 275
Yavapai: 69, 133
Yellowknife: 99
Yippies: x, xvii
Yokuts: 134
Yucatecan: 99
Yuchi: 38, 50, 52, 60, 69, 78, 114, 119–21,
133, 190
Yuma: 15, 24, 25, 40, 131, 134, 135

Zacatecan: 19, 23, 28, 30, 37
Zaehner, R. C.: 228
Zen: 228, 272
Zinberg, N. E.: 234
Zingg, R. M.: 13, 24, 26, 34, 39, 84, 105, 110,
132
Zuñi: 24, 25, 134, 135, 194, 195